Teaching Students with Special Needs in Inclusive Settings

Second
Canadian
Edition

Teaching Students with Special Needs in Inclusive Settings

Second Canadian Edition

Tom E.C. Smith
University of Arkansas

Edward A. Polloway
Lynchburg College

James R. Patton
University of Texas

Carol A. Dowdy
University of Alabama at Birmingham

Nancy Heath
McGill University

Laureen J. McIntyre
University of Saskatchewan

Garnett C. Francis
University of Saskatchewan

PEARSON

A and B

Toronto

Library and Archives Canada Cataloguing in Publication

Teaching students with special needs in inclusive settings / Tom E.C. Smith ... [et al.]. — 2nd Canadian ed.

Includes bibliographical references and index.
ISBN 0-205-44547-0

1. Children with disabilities—Education. 2. Inclusive education.
I. Smith, Tom E. C

LC1203.C3T42 2005   371.9'046   C2005-904012-2

ISBN 0-205-44547-0

Vice-President, Editorial Director: Michael J. Young
Executive Acquisitions Editor: Christine Cozens
Marketing Manager: Leigh-Anne Graham
Signing Representative: Duncan Mackinnon
Associate Editor: Paula Drużga
Production Editor: Charlotte Morrison-Reed
Copy Editor: Tara Tovell
Proofreader: Susan Broadhurst
Production Coordinator: Janis Raisen
Composition: Joan M. Wilson
Permissions Research: Sandy Cooke
Art Director: Julia Hall
Cover and Interior Design: Anthony Leung
Cover Image: (ZF) Grace, Masterfile

2 3 4 5   10 09 08 07 06

Printed and bound in the United States of America.

For

Debi, Jake, Alex, Suni,

Carolyn and Lyndsay,

Joy and Kimi,

Jim, Cameron, and Meredith

T.E.C.S.
E.A.P.
J.R.P.
C.A.D.

In memory of Dr. Winnifred (Madge) Hall, a caring and insightful educator and researcher.

N.H.

For all of our former and present students who have inspired us to be lifelong learners.

L.J.M.
G.C.F.

Brief Contents

Contents

3

Teaching Students with Communication Disorders   45

4

Teaching Students with Learning Disabilities 77

5

Teaching Students with Attention Deficit/ Hyperactivity Disorder 112

Teaching Students with Emotional or Behavioural Disorders   142

Teaching Students with Intellectual Disabilities   170

Teaching Students with Sensory Impairments 190

Teaching Students with Autism, Traumatic Brain Injury, and Other Low-Incidence Disabilities 221

10

Teaching Students Who Are Gifted 247

11

Teaching Students Who Are at Risk 277

Classroom Organization and Management 300

Teaching Students with Special Needs in Elementary Schools 328

14

Teaching Students with Special Needs in Secondary Schools 358

15

Working with Families of Students with Exceptionalities 388

About the Authors

Tom E. C. Smith is currently Professor and Head, Department of Curriculum and Instruction, University of Arkansas. He has been on the faculties of the University of Arkansas at Little Rock, University of Alabama at Birmingham, and the University of Arkansas for Medical Sciences. Prior to receiving his EdD from Texas Tech University, he taught children with mental retardation, learning disabilities, and autism at the elementary and secondary levels. President Clinton appointed him to three terms on the President's Committee on Mental Retardation. He has served as the Executive Director of the Division on Developmental Disabilities of the Council for Exceptional Children since 1996. His current professional interests focus on legal issues and special education.

Edward A. Polloway is a Professor of Education and Human Development at Lynchburg College in Virginia, where he has taught since 1976. He also serves as Vice President for Graduate Studies and Community Advancement. He received his doctoral degree from the University of Virginia and his undergraduate degree from Dickinson College in Pennsylvania. He has served twice as president of the Division on Developmental Disabilities of the Council for Exceptional Children and on the board of directors of the Council for Learning Disabilities. He also served on the committee that developed the 1992 definition of mental retardation for the American Association on Mental Retardation. He is the author of 12 books and 100 articles in the field of special education with primary interests in the areas of learning disabilities and mental retardation.

James R. Patton is an Educational Consultant and Adjunct Associate Professor at the University of Texas at Austin. He received his EdD from the University of Virginia. He is a former high school biology teacher and elementary-level special education resource teacher. He has also taught students who were gifted and those who were gifted/learning disabled. His professional interests include transition, life skills instruction, adult issues related to individuals with special needs, behavioral intervention planning, and classroom accommodations. He has served on national boards of the Division on Developmental Disabilities, the Council for Learning Disabilities, and the National Joint Committee on Learning Disabilities.

Carol A. Dowdy is Professor of Special Education at the University of Alabama at Birmingham, where she has taught since receiving her EdD degree from the University of Alabama, Tuscaloosa. She was written eight books on special education and published 34 articles on learning disabilities. She has served on the national board of the Council for Learning Disabilities and the Professional Advisory Board for the Learning Disabilities Association of America, and she has worked closely with the federal department of Vocational Rehabilitation to assist in their efforts to better serve adults with learning disabilities.

Nancy Heath is Associate Professor of Integrated Education and School Psychology in the Department of Educational and Counselling Psychology at McGill University. She received her Ph.D. from the Ontario Institute of Studies in Education at the University of Toronto. She has taught and worked with students with special needs and consulted with teachers for more than 15 years. She has published 18 articles and presented at more than 30 national and international conferences in the area of social and emotional functioning of children and adolescents with special needs. She is on the editorial board of the *Canadian Journal of Special Education* and is a reviewer for the *Canadian Journal of School Psychology*. She takes pride in continuing to work in schools as a consultant to teachers and as a member on the governing board of Willingdon Elementary School.

Laureen J. McIntyre is Assistant Professor in the College of Education at the University of Saskatchewan, where she teaches undergraduate and graduate courses in speech and language development and acquisition, special education, educational psychology, and applied measurement and evaluation. As an American- and Canadian-certified speech-language pathologist, Laureen worked in both community and school settings prior to completing her Ph.D. in Educational Psychology (specifically Special Education) at the University of Alberta. Her research interests include the language basis of learning difficulties and disabilities (particularly reading difficulties), teachers' knowledge of language, early identification and intervention of speech and language difficulties and disabilities, the education of exceptional children, and applied measurement and evaluation in the domains of health and education.

Garnett C. Francis is a doctoral student in Educational Psychology at the University of Saskatchewan. With an M.A. in Special Education, she has worked as a classroom teacher, a behavioural consultant, an administrator of a Pupil Services Branch in an urban school division, and a Senior Program Manager in the Special Education Branch with Saskatchewan Learning. She has worked in the College of Education at the University of Saskatchewan as a Sessional Lecturer since 1992, and was Assistant Professor (term position) during the 2003–2004 academic year.

Preface

Since the original edition of *Teaching Students with Special Needs in Inclusive Settings* was published, the delivery of services and supports to students with disabilities and other special needs in general classroom settings has expanded significantly. Research indicates that more and more schools are implementing inclusive education models each year. While the success of inclusion is difficult to validate due to inherent research problems and variant terminology used, research does tend to indicate that including students with disabilities and other special needs in general education classrooms proves beneficial to both these students as well as students without disabilities. With teacher training programs addressing the need to better prepare general educators to deal effectively with students with diverse learning needs, it is likely that the inclusion movement will continue to move forward.

As with previous editions, we feel that we must indicate our position on inclusion. When the movement began several years ago, the general interpretation of inclusion was "all or none"—all students, regardless of the severity of disability, all of the time, in general education classrooms. As inclusion has been implemented, this all-or-none position has moderated significantly. It is our belief that inclusion means that all children with disabilities *belong* with their nondisabled, chronological-age peers in the same classes, in the same school they would be attending if they were not disabled. However, it is also our belief that these students must be provided with appropriate educational opportunities. This could include the provision of supports in the general education classroom, but it may also mean the education of some students, at specific times during the day, in specialized settings where they can receive interventions that could not be provided as effectively in the general classroom setting.

Chapter Objectives are a teaching and learning aid that outline the material to be covered in the chapter.

Each opening vignette is a case study relating to the topic of the chapter. After studying the chapter, students will be able to answer all of the questions at the end of the vignette with confidence.

It remains our strong belief that students with disabilities and other special needs must be provided educational services that are appropriate for them, as determined by professionals in consultation with parents and family members. The appropriateness of the services definitely includes the location where students will be provided their educational program. Serving students based on educational need rather than clinical label or service delivery model should be the purpose of all special programming; individual student needs must remain the critical element in designing appropriate programs.

Features of the SECOND Canadian Edition

Too often special education in Canada is taught without reference to or acknowledgement of the substantial differences between the Canadian system of special education and that of the United States. Although Canada has been strongly influenced by the progression of special education services in the U.S., its provincial and territorial educational jurisdictions make it unique. Canada has 12 different approaches to special education definitions and service delivery. With the emergence of a new territory, Nunavut, which currently uses the educational guidelines of the Northwest Territories, we may soon be looking at 13 different models. A pre-service teacher in Canada needs to be aware of the range of services that exist throughout the country. Throughout this Second Canadian Edition the differences and similarities across Canada are highlighted. However, unlike some Canadian editions, this one strives to make pre-service teachers aware of the situation in the United States as well; instead of being limited to a review of Canadian service, this edition frequently contrasts the Canadian situation to the more generally recognized U.S. system of special education. In this way students are best informed about current special education practices throughout North America.

For this edition a number of changes were made. The first chapter was adapted to focus on Canadian special education policies and definitions of exceptionalities by province/territory; it also includes a summary of the U.S. special education policy. References to Canadian research, statistics, and prevalence appear throughout the text. The perspective on multicultural education was updated with more current views on approaches to the multicultural classroom. The ethnic diversity represented in the text now reflects Canadian diversity as described by Census Canada. Personal Spotlights in every chapter feature Canadian teachers, parents, and individuals with disabilities. Each chapter now has a list of recommended topical resources that are appropriate for Canadian teachers, including Canadian and international associations, books, videos, and resource guides. Similarly, each chapter provides a short description of recommended relevant websites with information and resources that will be helpful to Canadian teachers.

Margin notes are centred around four themes: Teaching Tip, Further Reading, Cross-Reference, and Consider This.

Finally, this edition represents a more concise text appropriate for an undergraduate course on exceptionalities. The first three chapters of the U.S. edition were condensed into two, one introducing exceptionalities, service delivery, and the inclusive classroom, and the second exploring how to design inclusive classrooms. Information on classroom management and organization has been moved to a separate chapter in the Second Canadian Edition. This information, formerly included in the chapter on behaviour and/or emotional disorders, may potentially affect students with all types of exceptionalities. Therefore, it is important that this information be discussed in the context of all students with exceptionalities and not just students with behaviour and/or emotional disorders.

As in previous editions, the book contains pedagogical features, including chapter opening objectives, vignettes, and chapter summaries. Margin notes are organized around four themes. **Teaching Tip** provides brief, specific suggestions related to the corresponding content in the chapter. **Further Reading** gives the reader a reference to learn more about a particular topic. **Cross-Reference** provides additional information that is found in other chapters in the text. Finally, a margin note called **Consider This** presents issues that call for problem-solving or thinking through particular problems.

Each chapter includes specific boxed features that highlight **technology**, **cultural diversity**, and **inclusion strategies**. These features are intended to provide more depth to a specific topic than is found in the text. **Personal Spotlights** highlight Canadian teachers, parents of children with special needs, and individuals with special needs. These people bring reality to discussions in the text and provide insight into the most important participants pursuing the challenge of inclusion.

The topics presented in these four features are listed on the pages that follow.

Diversity Forum boxes provide in-depth information about how a teacher in an inclusive classroom can meet the needs of the culturally diverse students of today.

Diversity Forum

Inclusion Strategies

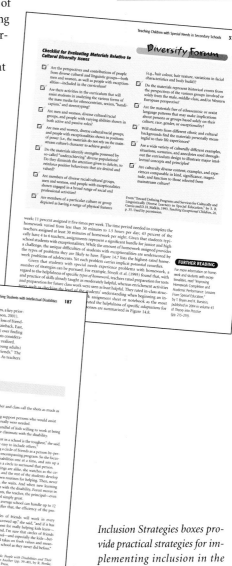

Inclusion Strategies boxes provide practical strategies for implementing inclusion in the classroom.

Personal Spotlight boxes highlight teachers, parents of students with special needs, and individuals with special needs, providing insight into the views of people who deal most closely with the challenge of inclusion.

Personal Spotlight

Technology Today

Technology Today boxes feature practical information and discuss the ever-changing technology available to the teachers and students in today's inclusive classrooms.

Instructor's Supplements

The Second Canadian Edition of *Teaching Students with Special Needs in Inclusive Settings* is accompanied by the following supplements that all instructors will find helpful:

The **Instructor's Manual** contains chapter overviews, discussion topics, Handouts, and Study Guides.

The **Test Item File** (in Word) consists of Multiple Choice, Matching, Short Answer/Short Essay, and Essay Questions.

Approximately 30 to 50 **PowerPoint Slides** per chapter.

Please note that all of these supplements are available online. They can be downloaded by instructors from a password-protected location on Pearson Education Canada's online catalogue (vig.pearsoned.ca). Simply search for the text, then click on "Instructor" under "Resources" in the left-hand menu. Contact your local sales representative for further information.

Acknowledgements

By the very nature of the Canadian special education situation, this book required the help and co-operation of every provincial and territorial Ministry of Education Special Education branch. We want to thank all those people who went out of their way to answer our questions and send us relevant materials. To all the individuals who shared their personal stories with us, we offer our most sincere appreciation and thanks.

We would like to thank all those who reviewed the Second Canadian Edition and offered valuable suggestions:

Anna Barrafato, Concordia University
Riva Bartell, University of Manitoba
Cheryll Duquette, University of Ottawa
Don Dworet, Brock University
Alan L. Edmunds, University of Western Ontario
Sonja C. Grover, Lakehead University
Elizabeth Jordan, University of British Columbia
Joan K. Scott, Red Deer College
Scott Anthony Thompson, University of Regina

We would also like to thank Pearson Education for all of the support provided to us during the completion of this project, particularly Duncan Mackinnon, Paula Druzga, and our copy editor Tara Tovell.

Inclusive Education: An Introduction

1

Chapter Objectives

After reading this chapter, you should be able to

- describe the evolution of services for students with exceptionalities in Canada
- describe some of the diversity evident in public schools as demonstrated by exceptionalities
- describe the process for obtaining services for students with exceptionalities
- discuss formal and informal assessment techniques
- describe the role of the classroom teacher in assessment and in developing and using individualized education programs (IEPs)

Amanda is 11 years old and has experienced many difficulties in school. As a beginning kindergarten student, she did not exhibit many of the readiness skills that most of her peers did. In Grade 1, she continued to fall behind and her teacher, Ms. Bell, referred her for an educational assessment. The assessment revealed that Amanda fell into the mild intellectual disability range, and is therefore eligible for special education support services. An Individualized Education Plan (IEP) was developed, and Amanda was placed in a special education classroom for half of the school day. Amanda immediately did better. Her academic skills improved and her social skills progressed. She remained in this type of placement—roughly half-time in a general classroom and half-time in the special education classroom—for the next two years. By the middle of Grade 3, however, Amanda was not progressing academically and her behaviour was deteriorating. For the first time, she indicated that she did not like school and frequently got sick in the mornings before school time. At her program review in May, the teachers described the inclusive service model that was being introduced to their school the next year. Amanda's parents were apprehensive. They were concerned that their daughter's behaviour problems would increase and that she would fall further behind her peers. However, with the urging of school personnel they agreed to try the new arrangement.

At the beginning of Grade 4, Amanda seemed out of sorts in the classroom. Although she was supported by special education personnel, she had difficulty adjusting to the new classroom and to her classmates. This situation was greatly improved by the middle of the year. Amanda's teacher implemented co-operative learning activities, and Amanda began to feel more comfortable in the classroom. She did better academically and her social skills improved. She came to enjoy playing with some of her classmates, who also valued her company. By the end of Grade 4, Amanda was successfully included in all aspects of her class—not only the academic activities.

Now in Grade 5, Amanda is blossoming. She is improving academically and has made many new friends. Her parents are amazed at her attitude toward school. Although program adaptations and modifications have been and continue to be made, Amanda knows she is a full-fledged member of the class.

Questions to Consider

1. Why did Amanda initially do better when she was placed in a special education classroom?

2. Why did Amanda begin to develop behaviour problems in the special education classroom?

3. What factors make inclusion successful for students with disabilities and for those without?

Introduction

As recently as the 1960s, many individuals with disabilities were separated from the general public, living and receiving their education in residential facilities. As people began to recognize the debilitating effects of institutionalization, the **normalization movement** emerged (Wolfensberger, 1972). Normalization proponents believed that all individuals, regardless of disability, should be provided with an education and a living arrangement as normal as possible. This conviction led to significant changes for individuals with special needs. People who had been institutionalized for years returned to their communities, and at the same time educational rights for individuals with special needs became a focus of the legal system.

In the United States, the American Rehabilitation Act, Section 504 (1973), "guaranteed the rights of persons with handicaps in... educational institutions that receive federal moneys" (Stainback, Stainback, & Bunch, 1989). The Education for All Handicapped Children Act (PL 94-142) was passed by Congress in 1975, requiring each state to educate children with disabilities. This Act was re-authorized in 1990 under the title of Individuals with Disabilities Education Act (IDEA), and states:

> To the maximum extent appropriate, children with disabilities... are educated with children who are not disabled, and that special classes, separate schooling, or other removal of children with disabilities from the regular environment occurs only when the nature or severity of the disability is such that education in regular classes with the use of supplementary aids and services cannot be attained satisfactorily.

In Canada, the movement toward inclusion was somewhat slower and different in nature. Each province or territory has its own Education Act or School Act governing education in schools within its jurisdiction, including special education services. However, with Canada's adoption, in 1982, of the *Constitution Act*, which included the **Canadian Charter of Rights and Freedoms** guaranteeing the rights of all individuals with disabilities, Canada became the first country in the world to enshrine the rights of people with disabilities in a constitution. The Charter of Rights and Freedoms, which came into effect in 1985, states in section 15.(1) that

> Every individual is equal before and under the law and has the right to equal protection of the law without discrimination based on race, national or ethnic origin, colour, religion, sex, age, or mental or physical disability.

Smith and Foster (1996) describe how all educational policy at every level (provincial/territorial and board/district) must abide by the Charter. Every province and territory has established its own policy documents, but all have moved steadily toward inclusion of students with special needs. Canadian proponents of inclusive education believe that students with disabilities, regardless of severity, should be included in the regular classroom (O'Brien, Snow, Forest, & Hasbury, 1989). They argue that educators are responsible for adapting the regular classroom to meet the students' needs. The provinces and territories adhere to the inclusive model to varying degrees, but all are committed to the principle of inclusion. As a teacher, you will need to learn the current special education guidelines and terminology for your own province or territory.

FURTHER READING

For a more detailed discussion of the history of special education in Canada, read Chapter 1 in *Including Exceptional Students: A Practical Guide for Classroom Teachers, Canadian Edition*, by M. Friend, W. Bursuck, and N. Hutchinson, published by Allyn & Bacon Canada in 1998.

CONSIDER THIS

In Canada, education falls under provincial/territorial jurisdiction. What are the advantages and disadvantages of having education under provincial/territorial jurisdiction?

Development of Special Services

Prior to the 1970s and the normalization movement, students with physical disabilities or intellectual disabilities were provided with services, albeit nearly always in self-contained, isolated classrooms. These students rarely interacted with nondisabled students, and their teachers did not routinely come into contact with other teachers in the school. In addition to isolating the students, the existing programs were small. Therefore, very few students were served. Beyond these public school programs, children received services in **residential programs**. Typically, children with intellectual disabilities and with sensory deficits were placed in these settings. These residential programs offered daily living supports as well as some education and training. In 1970, a report by Roberts and Lazure, entitled *One Million Children: A National Study of Canadian Children with Emotional and Learning Disorders*, called for integration and instruction based on learning characteristics, not categories. This landmark report, combined with Wolfensberger's work at the National Institute of Mental Retardation in Toronto (Wolfensberger, 1972) which emphasized the importance of a normal environment for all individuals, contributed to the changes in education in Canada in the 1970s.

Since the mid-1970s, services to students with disabilities have changed dramatically. Not only are more appropriate services provided by schools, but they also are frequently provided in both resource rooms and in general education classrooms by collaborating special education and classroom teachers. Services for students with disabilities evolved in three distinct phases: (1) **relative isolation**, (2) **integration** (or **mainstreaming**), and (3) **inclusion**. In the relative isolation phase, students were either denied access to public schools or were permitted to attend in isolated settings. In the integration phase, which began in the 1970s, students with disabilities were mainstreamed, or integrated, into general education programs when they were considered ready to handle the general education program. Finally, the inclusion phase, introduced in the early 1980s, emphasized that students with disabilities should be fully included in school programs and activities. This phase differed from the integration phase in a minor, but very significant way.

While both integration and inclusion resulted in students with disabilities joining general classrooms, inclusion assumes that these students belong in general classrooms—in the integration phase they were considered to be special education students who were placed in the general classroom part of the time. Recently, the importance of empowerment and self-determination for students with disabilities has been a focus of inclusion efforts, to better prepare students for the highest degree of independence possible (Polloway, Smith, Patton, & Smith, 1996). Figure 1.1 depicts the historical changes in the education of students with disabilities in public education.

FIGURE 1.1

Historical Changes in Education for Students with Disabilities

From "Historic Changes in Mental Retardation and Developmental Disabilities," by E. A. Polloway, J. D. Smith, J. R. Patton, and T. E. C. Smith, 1996, *Education and Training in Mental Retardation and Developmental Disabilities, 31*, p. 9. Used by permission.

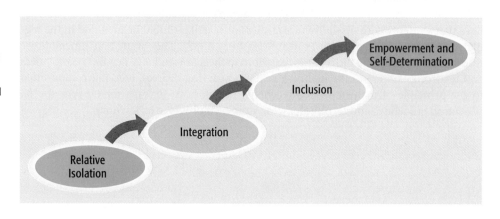

All children are eligible for public education in Canada; therefore, teachers in today's public schools must provide instruction and other educational services to meet the needs of a very diverse student population. They must develop ways to serve students with exceptionalities in general education environments (Smith & Smith, 1989). Traditionally, teacher education programs for classroom teachers have focused on teaching students who do not have learning or behaviour problems. However, today's teachers must be prepared to teach students with a variety of diverse needs. Providing an appropriate education for a diverse group of students, including students with exceptionalities, is definitely challenging; however, it can also be exciting and highly rewarding.

Using "People First" Language

One of the results of the inclusion movement has been a change in the way individuals with exceptionalities are labelled. "People first" language communicates that having exceptionality is only part of a person. It does not define them. The following list provides examples of using "people first" language:

Say	Do Not Say
Person with a disability	The disabled person
Children with autism	Autistic children
Classroom for students with mental retardation	The mentally retarded classroom
Students with visual impairments	Blind students
Bus for students with disabilities	Special education bus
Individuals with disabilities	Disabled individuals
Disability or disabled	Handicap or handicapped
The boy with cerebral palsy	The crippled boy
The girl with a hearing impairment	The deaf girl
The student with a learning disability	The learning disabled student

Students with Special Needs

Many students do not fit the mould of the "typical" student. Those with identified disabilities, those who are classified as gifted and talented, and those who are "at risk" of developing learning and behavioural problems are among them. It has been estimated that, in Canada, approximately 10 percent of school-age children have a recognized exceptionality. Another undetermined number experience learning and behaviour problems, but have not been classified as having a disability. Still another group of students who require special attention are those at risk of developing learning and behavioural problems. These students include potential dropouts, those from minority cultures, those who speak English as a second language, those from low-income homes, those who abuse drugs or alcohol, those who become pregnant, those from single-parent homes, and those considered "socially maladjusted" (Morgan, 1994a).

Adding all these students together, plus those who obviously need assistance but do not fit into any distinct group, results in a group that comprises about half of all students in public schools. Although many of these students do not fit into the specific classification as "disabled"—and are therefore ineligible for special education services—school personnel cannot afford to ignore their special problems (Cosden, 1990; Greer, 1991; Hill, 1991; Morgan, 1994b).

Diversity among students in public schools represents the "norm" rather than the exception (Johnson, Pugach, & Devlin, 1990). If our public schools are to be effective, school personnel must address the varying needs of students. They must be able to identify students with learning and behavioural needs and develop and implement appropriate educational programs for them. A first step for classroom teachers is to understand the types of student diversity they will encounter.

Students with Exceptionalities

One of the largest groups of students with diverse learning and behavioural needs in the public school system, and also the most visible, consists of students who have been formally classified as having **exceptionalities**.

Students with exceptionalities are defined differently in different provinces and territories. In New Brunswick, students with exceptionalities are defined as "individuals for whom a special education program is considered a necessity. [These] may be individuals having behavioural, communicational, intellectual, physical, perceptual or multiple exceptionalities." The British Columbia Ministry of Education defines students with special needs as those who "have difficulties of an intellectual, physical, sensory, emotional or behavioural nature, or have a learning disability or have exceptional gifts or talents" (British Columbia Ministry of Education, 2002). In Prince Edward Island, students needing special education services are described as "those students within the public school system whose educational needs require interventions different from, or in addition to, those which are needed by most students" (Prince Edward Island Education, 2001). In Saskatchewan, students are defined as having exceptional needs if they have been identified as having "physical, intellectual and learning disabilities, sensory impairments, social, emotional or behavioural challenges, and language delays and disorders" (Saskatchewan Learning, 2000). Similar definitions are found across the country, sharing the characteristic listing of exceptionalities and frequently the statement that the student needs special services.

One other approach to the defining of students with exceptionalities exists in some provincial and territorial education documents—namely, the absence of a definition! For example, in the *Education Act* (1995) of the Northwest Territories, no mention is made of what constitutes exceptionality. Instead, the Act focuses on the rights of all students to an inclusive education and support services to meet individual needs. However, even where provincial or territorial guidelines are not provided for identifying exceptionalities, practice at the school level often involves assessment for exceptionalities. Specific categories of exceptionality recognized by the different jurisdictions vary marginally, but the majority of jurisdictions include the following categories:

- Learning disabilities
- Speech or language impairments
- Intellectual disabilities
- Emotional/behavioural disorders
- Multiple disabilities
- Auditory impairments
- Orthopedic impairments
- Other health impairments
- Visual impairments
- Autism
- Fetal alcohol syndrome (FAS)
- Traumatic brain injury (TBI)

CONSIDER THIS

What similarities do students with disabilities share with students from racial minorities? Are educational services being offered to both groups of students in a similar fashion?

FURTHER READING

For detailed information about the legal rights of students with exceptionalities in the different provinces and territories, read W. J. Smith and W. F. Foster's *Equal Educational Opportunity for Students with Disabilities: A Source Book for Parents, Advocates and Professionals*, published in 1996 by McGill University's Office of Research on Educational Policy.

Many different types of students are found in these 12 categories. For example, the broad area of other health impairments includes students with cardiac problems, asthma, mental health disorders, and sickle cell anemia. Even the category of learning disabilities comprises an extremely heterogeneous group of students.

The fact that disability categories are composed of different types of students makes simple conclusions about them impossible. Students who need special assistance do not all fit neatly into disability categories. Many times it is hard to know into which category a child would best fit. Consider a child with an attention-deficit disorder who has poor academic skills despite high intelligence and who often behaves disruptively. A child such as this could be categorized by many provincial/territorial guidelines as having either a behavioural disorder or a learning disability—no jurisdiction has an attention-deficit disorder category.

The majority of students with disabilities experience mild disabilities and spend their school days in general education classrooms. A smaller number of students, with more severe disabilities, were more typically educated in segregated special education environments. However, today students with more severe disabilities are frequently included in general education classrooms part—or even all—of the time. The following section provides a brief overview of each of the major disability categories recognized in most schools.

CROSS-REFERENCE

For more information on specific disabilities, see Chapters 3–11.

Intellectual Disability   The disability category that has been recognized for the longest time in most school districts is **intellectual disability**. Students with intellectual disabilities are usually identified through intelligence tests and measures of adaptive behaviour, which look at a person's ability to perform functional activities expected of age and cultural norms. By definition, they score less than 70–75 on individual intelligence tests and have concurrent deficits in adaptive behaviour (American Association on Mental Retardation, 1992). Their general characteristics include problems in learning, memory, problem solving, adaptive behaviour, and social skills (Beirne-Smith, Patton, & Ittenbach, 1994).

Learning Disabilities   The disability category that accounts for more than 50 percent of all students served by special education is learning disabilities. This category is beset with problems of definition and programming, but continues to include more children than all other special education categories combined (Smith, Dowdy, Polloway, & Blalock, 1997). In general, students with learning disabilities do not achieve commensurate with their abilities. According to the Learning Disabilities Association of Canada (LDAC), "Learning Disabilities are due to genetic and/or neurological factors or injury that alters brain functioning in a manner which affects one or more process related to learning" (LDAC, 2002).

Emotional/Behavioural Disorders   Students with emotional and behavioural disorders cause disruptions for themselves or others in their environment through inappropriate behaviours or expressions of emotion. Professionals serving children with these problems differ on definitions of the problems and the types of services they provide (Kauffman & Wong, 1991). Partly due to the complexity of definition and the lack of agreement regarding appropriate intervention, students presenting behavioural challenges are frequently underserved.

Sensory Problems   Some students have problems with sensory skills—their visual or auditory abilities. The majority of information provided by teachers is presented orally or visually; therefore, deficits in these areas can result in significant problems. Visual impairment includes two subcategories: blindness and low vision. The category of auditory impairment covers both students who are deaf and students who are hard-of-hearing.

Orthopedic Impairments   Many students experience problems related to their physical abilities. Cerebral palsy, spina bifida, amputations, and muscular dystrophy are a few examples. For these students, physical access to educational facilities and accommodating problems with writing and manipulation are important concerns.

Other Health Impairments   This disability category includes a wide variety of problems—for example, cardiac problems, acquired immune deficiency syndrome (AIDS), diabetes, epilepsy, and asthma. In some provinces students with mental health conditions are also included in this category. For students with these disabilities, medical needs take precedence. School personnel must work closely with medical and other professionals to provide appropriate services.

FURTHER READING

Information about autism can be found in Chapter 9, which focuses on severe disabilities and health problems.

Autism   Autism is a lifelong disability that primarily affects communication and social interactions. Children with autism typically relate to people, objects, and events in abnormal ways; they insist on structured environments and display many self-stimulating behaviours. Autism is not recognized as a separate category by most provinces and territories.

Traumatic Brain Injury   Traumatic brain injury (TBI) was defined by Savage (1988) as an insult to the brain that often results in impaired cognitive, physical, or emotional functioning. Students with TBI are typically served under the disability category that relates to their functional limitations (e.g., intellectual disability for cognitive deficits and learning disabilities for erratic academic performance).

CONSIDER THIS

Why should students with severe disabilities not be served in institutional or in other segregated settings? Should some children be placed in such settings? Why or why not?

Fetal Alcohol Syndrome   Fetal alcohol syndrome is "a combination of physical and central nervous system abnormalities. People who have FAS are born with it and have the condition for their entire lives. Fetal alcohol syndrome is caused by drinking alcohol during pregnancy" (Saskatchewan Institute on Prevention of Handicaps, 2004). Students with fetal alcohol syndrome (FAS) are typically served under the disability category that relates to their functional limitations (e.g., intellectual disability for cognitive deficits and learning disabilities for erratic academic performance).

Speech and/or Language Impairments   For some children, speech difficulties form a serious problem. Children with speech impairments are considered eligible for services under most provincial and territorial jurisdictions. Teachers need to work closely with speech-language pathologists when dealing with this group of students. As language disorders are associated with many exceptionalities, including intellectual disabilities, emotional or behavioural disorders, learning disabilities, autism, TBI, and FAS, students with exceptionalities and their teachers frequently need support from a speech-language pathologist.

Students Classified as Gifted and/or Talented   Some students differ from their peers by having above-average intelligence and learning abilities. These students, classified as gifted and talented, were traditionally defined and identified using intelligence quotient test scores (IQ scores). An IQ score of 120, 130, 140, or higher was the primary criterion for identifying a gifted and talented student. Current criteria are much broader. Although definitions vary, most focus on students who are capable of making significant contributions to society in a variety of areas, spanning academic endeavours, creativity, mechanical skills, motor skills, and skills in the fine arts.

Students at Risk of School Problems

Some students, who neither fit into a specific disability category nor have an above-average capacity to achieve academically, also experience difficulty achieving success at school. These students, classified as being at risk, manifest characteristics that could easily lead to learning and behaviour problems (Barr & Parrett, 2001). Students considered at risk include the following:

- Students who are abused or neglected
- Students who abuse drugs and alcohol
- Students from minority cultures
- Students living in poverty
- Students who become pregnant
- Students who speak English as a second language
- Students who are in trouble with the justice system

These students may present unique problems for teachers who must meet their educational needs in general education classrooms. Educational programs will need to be modified to meet student needs. Students "at risk" need support to build **resiliency**. Schools can be a necessary protective factor for them.

Obtaining Services for Students with Special Needs

The majority of students who receive special education services are first identified by the regular classroom teacher. It is usually the classroom teacher at the elementary level who initiates the process that will result in a student receiving special education services. This process may involve a number of different school personnel depending on the situation and the specific school, as well as the province or territory. Typically, a school team becomes involved. This team, referred to by different names, generally includes the regular classroom teacher, special education personnel (resource teacher, special education board/district consultant, school psychologist or guidance counsellor), the principal, and specific medical or social service personnel depending on the nature of the student's difficulty. While all of these individuals will take part in a formal identification of a student, the process of obtaining services almost always begins with the teacher. Ideally, it should adhere to the steps outlined in Figure 1.2.

Throughout the process of obtaining special services for a student a variety of assessments are completed.

Assessment Practices

Assessment is the process of gathering relevant information to use in making decisions about students (Salvia & Ysseldyke, 2004). It is a dynamic, continuous process that guides and directs planning for students with suspected or known disabilities. Teachers play four major roles in regard to school-based assessment and, as a result, need to have skills in all four areas.

1. Teachers are *consumers* of assessment information. In this role, they must be able to understand assessment information.
2. Teachers are *producers* of assessment information. They must be able to generate assessment information by administering tests, conducting observations, and so on.

CONSIDER THIS

Should students who are considered at risk of developing learning and behaviour problems be provided with special services? Why or why not?

CONSIDER THIS

How can schools deal with the financial impact of special services for students with disabilities? Is there a limit as to how much should be spent on a single child? From province to province this varies. Should it be the same across the country?

FIGURE 1.2

Steps from Prereferral to IEP and Checklists of the Teacher's Responsibilities

From D. P. Hallahan, J. M. Kauffman & J. W. Lloyd. *Introduction to Learning Disabilities*, Second Edition, © 1999. Published by Allyn and Bacon, Boston, MA. Copyright © 1999 by Pearson Education. Reprinted by permission of the publisher.

STEPS LEADING TO THE IEP

1. A teacher notices that a student is having serious academic or behavioural difficulty.
2. The teacher consults the student's parents and tries the instructional or behaviour management strategies she or he believes will resolve the problem.
3. If the problem is not resolved the teacher asks for the help of the school team.
4. With the help of the team, the teacher implements and documents the results of strategies designed to resolve the problem.
5. If the problem is not resolved after reasonable implementation of the team's suggestions, the teacher makes a referral for evaluation by the school psychologist.
6. The school psychologist evaluates the student.
7. With the results of the evaluation components in hand, the school team determines whether the student is eligible for special education.
8. If the student is found eligible, then an IEP must be written.

WHAT SHOULD I DO BEFORE MAKING A REFERRAL?

☑ Hold at least one conference to discuss your concerns with the parents (or make extensive and documented efforts to communicate with the parents).

☑ Check all available school records, and interview other professionals involved with the student to make sure you understand the student's history and efforts to help that have already been made.

☑ Ask the school team—or the principal, the school psychologist, and at least one other teacher who knows the student—to help you devise strategies to solve the problem.

☑ Implement and document the results of the academic and behaviour management strategies you have tried.

WHAT INFORMATION SHOULD I BE ABLE TO PROVIDE AT THE TIME OF REFERRAL?

☑ A statement of exactly what you are concerned about

☑ An explanation of why you are concerned

☑ Detailed records from your observations of the problem, including samples of academic work

☑ Records documenting the strategies you have used to try to resolve the problem and the outcomes of those strategies

3. Teachers are *communicators* of assessment information, by virtue of the fact that much of what we do in schools today is team-based. Teachers must be able to share assessment information with others (professionals, parents, students).
4. Teachers are *developers* of assessment instruments. Most teachers will find that they have to create assessment techniques to accomplish some education-related tasks.

This information-gathering process should focus primarily on identifying the strengths of children considered "at risk"; appropriate adaptations can then be designed to facilitate student success in the inclusive environment of a general education classroom. Later, assessment will measure the success of instructional and behavioural interventions implemented in the general education classroom. Assessment can pinpoint problems that should be addressed in general education classes; it does not necessarily lead to special education placement.

Purpose of Assessment

Assessment is critical in each of the major phases of the planning process. During the **screening** phase, including the steps of prereferral and referral, the concerns expressed by teachers and parents are the result of their informal "assessment" of the student's lack of progress. Their concern comes from their observations and interactions with the student in the natural environment. When parents and teachers get concerned, they may consult others who have worked with the child and review previous records or current work. At this point these students are at risk for failure, and the first level of assessment for special education services has begun.

When a referral is made, the identification and **eligibility** phase of assessment begins. During this phase the child is formally evaluated to determine if he or she has a disability and which special education services would be most appropriate. The student's intellectual ability, strengths, and limitations are evaluated individually by trained professionals. These results are shared with the IEP team.

Assessment data are needed for **program planning**. Existing data are studied further, and new data may be collected to help the IEP team select goals and objectives or benchmarks, as well as to identify the most effective methods of instruction to include in the IEP. After the IEP has been implemented, assessment is conducted to **monitor** and **evaluate** the student's progress.

Approaches to Assessment

Salvia and Ysseldyke (2004) identified four approaches used to gather information on students: (1) observation, (2) recollection (by means of interview or rating scale), (3) record or portfolio review, and (4) testing. Data collected through naturalistic **observation** can be highly accurate and provide detailed, relevant information on how the student performs in the natural environment. The observer may be systematically looking for one or more specific behaviours, such as inattention or inappropriate comments. In this approach, the frequency, duration, and intensity of the behaviour(s) are usually recorded for study. The student's behaviour can then be compared to normal standards of his or her peers or to the individual's previous behaviour. Another method of collecting observational data is more anecdotal, in which case the observer records any behaviour that seems significant. This type of data may be more subjective than the systematic recordings and harder to validate. Observational data may also be collected using audiotape or videotape.

In data collection involving **recollection**, individuals familiar with the student are asked to recall events and interpret the behaviours. The most commonly used are interviews or ratings scales that can be obtained from the students through a self-report or from peers, family members, teachers, counsellors, or others. Through interviews, parents' concerns and preferences can be determined. Since interviews are generally held in person, reactions to questions can be observed and, when appropriate, questions can be explored more thoroughly. **Ratings scales** offer a structured method of data collection involving asking the rater to respond to a statement by indicating the degree to which an item describes an individual. When using rating-scale data, care should be taken to confirm the rater's ability to understand the scale and determine the possibility of bias in reporting.

Another important component of assessment is record or **portfolio review**. Existing information such as school cumulative records, databases, anecdotal records, non-school records, or student products (often found in a student's portfolio) should be reviewed carefully for insight into the student's needs and strengths. Usually a school will consider the same kinds of records for each child being considered, to maintain consistency.

The most common method of gathering information on students is through testing. **Testing**, formal or informal, is the process of presenting challenges or problems to students and measuring the student's competency, attitude, or behaviour by evaluating his or her responses (Ysseldyke & Olsen, 1999).

Formal Assessment

Formal assessment instruments are generally available commercially. They typically contain detailed guidelines for administration, scoring, and interpretation, as well as statistical data regarding **validity**, reliability, and **standardization procedures**. They are most often **norm-referenced**; that is, the tests provide quantitative information comparing the performance of an individual student to others in his or her norm group (determined, for example, by age, grade, or gender). Test results are usually reported in the form of test quotients, percentiles, and age or grade equivalents. These tools are most useful early in an assessment procedure, when relatively little is known of a student's strengths and weaknesses, and thus they may help identify areas in which informal assessment can begin. The ability to compare the student to his or her age and grade peers is also an advantage in making eligibility and placement decisions and fulfilling related administrative requirements. Table 1.1 (on page 13) is a useful assessment resource that shows the relationship across various types of scores obtained through standardized testing.

Professionals can make more informed decisions about the use of formal instruments if they study the instrument and become familiar with its features, benefits, and possible liabilities. One way to do so is to consult one or more of the excellent resources on tests.

Although formal testing provides quantitative and sometimes qualitative data based on student performance, tests can only obtain a measure of a student's best performance in a contrived situation; they cannot broadly represent a student's typical performance under natural conditions. When considered in isolation, the results of formal tests can also result in lost data that can lead to poor decisions in placement and instructional planning. Rigid administration and interpretation of test results can obscure, rather than reveal, a student's strengths and weaknesses. It has become increasingly apparent that traditional, formal approaches must be augmented with assessment techniques that more accurately represent a student's typical skills.

Informal Assessment

Informal tests and measurements are usually more loosely structured than formal instruments and are more closely tied to teaching. Such tools are typically devised by teachers to determine what skills or knowledge a child possesses. Their key advantage is the direct application of assessment data to instructional programs. By incorporating assessment results into the teaching program and by monitoring student responses each day, teachers can achieve a more accurate assessment of growth in learning or behavioural change.

Criterion-referenced testing (CRT) compares a student's performance with a criterion of mastery for a specific task, disregarding his or her relative standing in a group. This type of informal assessment can be especially useful when documentation of progress is needed for accountability because the acquisition of skills can be clearly demonstrated. As Taylor (2000) stresses, CRTs are quite popular because they focus attention on specific skills in the curriculum, provide measures of progress toward mastery, and assist teachers in designing instructional strategies. Traditionally, most criterion-referenced tests have been produced by teachers, but recently publishers have begun to produce assessment tools of this type.

TABLE 1.1   Relation of Various Standard Scores to Percentile Rank and to Each Other

| Percentile Rank | Standard Scores | | | | | |
	Quotients	NCE Scores	T-scores	Z-scores	Stanines	Deficit
99	150	99	83	+3.33	9	
99	145	99	80	+3.00	9	
99	140	99	77	+2.67	9	
99	135	99	73	+2.33	9	
98	130	92	70	+2.00	9	
95	125	85	67	+1.67	8	
91	120	78	63	+1.34	8	none
84	115	71	60	+1.00	7	
75	110	64	57	+0.67	6	
63	105	57	53	+0.33	6	
50	100	50	50	+0.00	5	
37	95	43	47	−0.33	4	
25	90	36	43	−0.67	4	
16	85	29	40	−1.00	3	mild
9	80	22	37	−1.34	2	
5	75	15	33	−1.67	2	moderate
2	70	8	30	−2.00	1	
1	65	1	27	−2.33	1	
1	60	1	23	−2.67	1	severe
1	55	1	20	−3.00	1	

From "The Role of Standardized Tests in Planning Academic Instruction," by D. D. Hammill and B. R. Bryant, 1991. *Handbook on the Assessment of Learning Disabilities*, edited by H. L. Swanson (p. 377). Austin, TX: Pro-Ed. Copyright 1991 by Pro-Ed, Inc. Used by permission.

One important and popular form of criterion-referenced assessment is **curriculum-based assessment**. Unlike norm-referenced tools, it uses the actual curriculum as the standard and thus provides a basis for evaluating and modifying the curriculum for an individual student (McLoughlin & Lewis, 2000). This type of assessment can have a role in many important tasks: identification, eligibility, instructional grouping, program planning, progress monitoring, and program evaluation. Curriculum-based assessment can focus attention on changes in academic behaviour within the context of the curriculum being used, thus enhancing the relationship between assessment and teaching (Deno & Fuchs, 1987).

Curriculum-based measures can be developed through systematic analysis of a given curriculum, selection of specific items, and construction of assessment formats (e.g., questions, cloze activities, worksheets). Although manuals and other resources for developing curriculum-based instruments exist, they serve primarily as guides. Instruments used in the classroom should reflect the curriculum being followed there.

TEACHING TIP

When entering a new school system, ask the principal or your teacher colleagues to describe the assessment instruments typically used. If curriculum-based assessment has not been developed, organize a grade-level team to begin this important process.

Personal Spotlight

Director of Special Education Sally Deck

Sally Deck is the director of special education for the Red Deer Catholic Regional Division (RDCRD) in Red Deer, Alberta. Before joining the administrative team at Central Office, Sally taught both in the regular classroom and in special education classrooms from elementary grades to high school. While a classroom teacher, Sally collaborated closely with educational assistants, counsellors, parents and other teachers to provide inclusive educational programming for students with special needs.

Sally has a bachelor of education degree from the University of Alberta with a major in special education and a master of education degree from the University of Calgary, specializing in educational leadership. Sally has presented her work at several provincial teachers' conferences on topics including teaching pro-social skills to children, and teaching gifted children in the regular classroom. She co-authored a teaching resource entitled *SKILLS: Strategies for teaching students listening, learning and social skills*, which was jointly funded by RDCRD and the Alberta Teachers' Association Educational Trust Fund. The focus of Sally's presentations and writing reflect her vision and belief in inclusive education.

In her current position as director of special education, Sally travels to all of the schools, both rural and urban, in the Red Deer Catholic Regional Division, to facilitate programming for students with special needs. In the case of students with special needs who are new to the school division, Sally will often organize a case conference at the school so the teaching team—including the parents and, if appropriate, the student—can develop a personal educational program. The team also considers any accommodations, modifications, equipment, occupational therapy, physical therapy, speech/language therapy and/or mental health services that may be appropriate.

The Individualized Program Plan (IPP) is the key document that drives the program for the student with special needs. The regular classroom teachers are typically responsible for the co-ordinating of the students' IPPs. Sally conducts workshops during the fall of each school year, for teachers who are new to the IPP process. The teachers learn the key components of the IPP, and they are given preparation to work on their students' IPP. Their understanding of the link from the assessment data to the areas of need, to the long-term goals and short-term objectives, to the review updates, and finally to the year-end review and the transition plan inform their planning and increase its effectiveness. Support from the school administrators, collaboration with the school counsellor, the parents, the special education teacher and leadership from Central Office all work together to have a positive impact on inclusive educational programs for students with special needs. Sally is proud to be a part of this team.

Curriculum-based assessment can focus attention on changes in a student's academic behaviour.

Alternative assessment procedures have emerged as dissatisfaction with group-administered standardized tests has increased. Two terms commonly used to describe these procedures are **authentic assessment** and portfolio assessment. These assessment methods use similar techniques such as requiring students to construct, produce, perform, or demonstrate a task. These types of student responses are considered alternatives to typical testing responses, such as selecting from multiple-choice items, a technique commonly used on standardized, formal tests. An example of an authentic assessment would be assigning a student the task of asking for help from an individual whom he or she does not know. The individual being asked would be trained to evaluate the quality of the interaction and recommend the supports or accommodations that a student might need to improve the interaction (Ysseldyke & Olsen, 1999). Portfolio assessment was described in the previous section on assessment approaches.

Ecological Assessment

Ecological assessment is another approach used with many types of informal assessment. As educational assessment has increasingly begun to reflect a trend toward appreciating the ecology of the student, data obtained are now more frequently analyzed in relation to the child's functioning in his or her various environments. Although a full discussion of ecological assessment is beyond the scope of this chapter, the following information highlights some basic considerations, and the nearby Inclusion Strategies feature provides an example of a classroom ecological inventory.

The focus of ecological assessment is to place the evaluation process within the context of the student's environment. Its central element is functionality—how well the student functions in the current environment or the one into which he or she will be moving. This focus shifts a program's emphasis toward determining how to build on strengths and interests.

An emphasis on ecological assessment necessarily broadens the assessment process. Additionally, it offers professionals a way of validating findings. The following questions can help teachers better understand the child and why he or she is having difficulty succeeding in school. Answers should help educators develop a positive learning environment and identify specific strategies to reduce negative impacts on learning.

- In what physical environment does the child learn best?
- What is useful, debilitating, or neutral about the way the child approaches the task?
- Can the student hold multiple pieces of information in memory and then act upon them?
- How does increasing or slowing the speed of instruction affect the accuracy of a child's work?
- What processing mechanisms are being taxed in any given task?
- How does this student interact with a certain teaching style?
- With which professional has the child been most successful? What characteristics of the person seem to contribute to the child's success?
- What is encouraging to the child? What is discouraging?
- How does manipulating the mode of teaching (e.g., visual or auditory presentation) affect the child's performance? (Waterman, 1994, pp. 9–10)

Issues of Bias in Assessment

The importance of ensuring fair and equitable assessment procedures cannot be underestimated. The number of K–12 students from diverse cultures is expected to increase. This trend will present one of the greatest challenges for special educators—accurately assessing culturally and linguistically diverse students for disabilities (Council for Exceptional Children, 1997).

As Wallace et al. (1992) stress, bias in the evaluation of students, particularly those from a minority background, "can and will significantly affect the educational opportunities afforded these youngsters. To minimize the effects of bias in the evaluation, it is absolutely essential that every [professional]... be aware of the various ways in which bias is exhibited and take steps to minimize its effects when making educational decisions." (p. 473)

Many sources of possible bias can be found in the assessment process, ranging from administrative practices, such as proximity to student and physical contact, to gender of tester and testee, cultural and ethnic prejudice, and linguistic variance. This kind of information should be used when assessing all individuals whose differences might lead to test bias.

Of special concern is the accurate assessment of individuals who experience sensory or motor disabilities. For example, individuals who have hearing impairments may require a nonverbal test, whereas persons who have visual impairments require measures that do not rely on object manipulation and do not include cards or pictures (Hoy & Gregg, 1994). An individual with a severe motor impairment may have limited voluntary responses and may need to respond via an eye scan or blink.

Students who have multiple disabilities compound the difficulties of administering the assessment task. Browder and Snell (1988) note that some individuals simply lack

Classroom Ecological Inventory

Special Education Teacher _____   Grade _____ Date _____

General Education Teacher _____   Number of Students in General Class _____

Student _____

PART 1: CLASSROOM OBSERVATION

Physical Environment

Directions: Please circle or provide the appropriate answer.

1. Is there an area for small groups?   Yes   No
2. Are partitions used in the room?   Yes   No
3. Is there a computer in the classroom?   Yes   No
4. Where is the student's desk located? (for example, front of room, back, middle, away from other students, etc.) _____
    _____

Teacher/Student Behaviour

Directions for #1–#4: Please circle the appropriate answer.

1. How much movement or activity is tolerated by the teacher?   Much   Average   Little   Unclear
2. How much talking among students is tolerated?   Much   Average   Little   Unclear
3. Does the teacher use praise?   Much   Average   Little   Unclear
4. Was subject taught to the entire group or to small groups?   Entire   Small

Directions for #5–#7: Please provide an appropriate answer.

5. During the observation, where did the teacher spend most of the time? (for example, at the board, at teacher's desk, at student's desk)

6. What teaching methods did you observe while in the classroom? (for example, teacher modelled the lesson, asked students to work at board, helped small groups, helped individual students) _____
    _____

7. How did the teacher interact with students who appeared to be low achieving or slower than their classmates? (for example, helped them individually, talked to them in the large group) _____

Posted Classroom Rules

If classroom rules are posted, what are they?

Special Education	**General Education**
_____	_____
_____	_____
_____	_____

Is there any other pertinent information you observed about this classroom that would be helpful in reintegrating the student? (for example, crowded classroom)

_____
_____
_____

▼

PART 2: TEACHER INTERVIEW

Classroom Rules	**Special Ed**	**General Ed**
1. During class are there important rules? (Yes or No)	_____	_____
2. If yes, how are they communicated? (for example, written or oral)	_____	_____
3. If class rules are *not* posted, what are they?	_____	_____
	_____	_____
	_____	_____
4. If a rule is broken, what happens? What is the typical consequence?	_____	_____
5. Who enforces the rules? (teacher, aide, students)	_____	_____

Teacher Behaviour

	Special Ed	**General Ed**
1. a. Is homework assigned? (Yes or No)	_____	_____
b. If so, indicate approximate amount (minutes) of homework, and	_____	_____
c. the frequency with which it is given.	_____	_____

Directions for #2–#4: Using a 3-point scale (1=Often, 2=Sometimes, 3=Never), rate each item according to frequency of occurrence in class. Place an asterisk (*) in the right-hand margin to indicate important differences between the special and regular education classrooms.

	Special Ed	General Ed
2. Assignments in Class		
a. Students are given assignments:		
• that are the same for all	_____	_____
• that differ in amount or type	_____	_____
• to complete in school at a specified time	_____	_____
• that, if unfinished in school, are assigned as homework	_____	_____
b. Evaluation of assignment:		
• teacher evaluation	_____	_____
• student self-evaluation	_____	_____
• peer evaluation	_____	_____
3. Tests		
a. Tests are		
• presented orally	_____	_____
• copied from board	_____	_____
• timed	_____	_____
• based on study guides given to students prior to test	_____	_____
• administered by resource teacher	_____	_____
b. Grades are:		
• precentages (example, 75%)	_____	_____
• letter grades (example, B+)	_____	_____
• both	_____	_____

	Special Ed	General Ed
4. Academic/Social Rewards		
a. Classroom rewards or reinforcement include:		
• material rewards (example, stars)	_____	_____
b. Classroom punishment includes:		
• time out	_____	_____
• loss of activity-related privileges (example, loss of free time)	_____	_____
• teacher ignoring	_____	_____
• reprimands	_____	_____
• poorer grade, loss of star, etc.	_____	_____
• extra work	_____	_____
• staying after school	_____	_____
• physical punishment (example paddling)	_____	_____

5. To what extent do each of the following contribute to an overall grade? Estimate the percentage for each so that the total sums to 100%.

	Special Ed	General Ed
• homework	_____	_____
• daily work	_____	_____
• tests	_____	_____
• class participation	_____	_____

6. Please list skills that have been taught since the beginning of the school year (general education teacher only):

Skill	Will Reteach Later? (Yes or No)

From "Classroom Ecological Inventory," by D. Fuchs, P. Fernstrom, S. Scott, L. Fuchs, and L. Vandermeer, 1994, *Teaching Exceptional Children*, 26, 14–15.

TABLE 1.2	Suggested Adaptations for Test Taking Checklist

Behavioural and Environmental Adaptations

Distracted/off task

- ❏ Provide both written and verbal instructions
- ❏ Provide additional space between work areas
- ❏ Place student near teacher and/or in the front of the class
- ❏ Develop a secret signal for on-task behaviour
- ❏ Keep work area free from unnecessary materials (e.g., books, pencils)
- ❏ Provide positive feedback
- ❏ Enforce behaviour management system
- ❏ Seat apart from others

Completion of Task-Related Adaptations

Getting started and completing tasks

- ❏ Reduce length of test (e.g., select questions to be answered)
- ❏ Allow additional time
- ❏ Break test into shorter tasks (e.g., break every 10 minutes)
- ❏ Establish a reward system
- ❏ Set timer for designated amount of work time and allow student to take a one-minute break after the timer is complete
- ❏ Provide checklist of appropriate behaviours

Processing difficulties

- ❏ Allow use of manipulatives (e.g., counting blocks)
- ❏ Provide both written and verbal instructions

- ❏ Take frequent breaks
- ❏ Break test into shorter tasks
- ❏ Provide list of things to do

Difficulty keeping place when reading

- ❏ Provide large-print version
- ❏ Allow use of place keeper (e.g., bookmark, paper)
- ❏ Create version of test with fewer questions per page

Academic Adaptations

Difficulty with reading comprehension

- ❏ Identify key vocabulary (e.g., highlight or underline)
- ❏ Review key vocabulary
- ❏ Read questions or passages to student

Difficulty with writing

- ❏ Allow oral response
- ❏ Have proctor or teacher write student response
- ❏ Allow the use of computer or word processor

Difficulty with mathematics

- ❏ Have calculation read to student
- ❏ Allow the use of a calculator
- ❏ Break task into smaller parts
- ❏ Reduce the number of questions to be answered (e.g., answer only even-numbered questions)

From *Step-by-Step Guide: For Including Students with Disabilities in State and District-wide Assessments* (p. 29) by D. P. Bryant, J. R. Patton, & S. Vaughn, 2000, Austin, TX: Pro-Ed.

"test behaviours." For example, they may refuse to stay seated for an assessment session or may exhibit interfering self-stimulatory behaviour, such as hand flapping or rocking.

Further, test results should not be unduly affected by disabilities in receptive or expressive language capabilities. Such disabilities may cause the test to measure the problem itself, rather than assess the level of functioning.

Considered collectively, these problem areas can make traditional testing procedures ineffective, resulting in discriminatory practices despite the best intentions of the tester (Browder & Snell, 1988; Luckasson et al., 1992). Implementation of accommodations appropriate for the needs of each student with a disability greatly reduces this type of test bias. Refer to Table 1.2 for a list of commonly used adaptations.

Hoy and Gregg (1994) note that **nondiscriminatory evaluation** requires that data be gathered by a school team in a nondiscriminatory fashion, with an awareness of how bias could enter the decision-making process and with the knowledge of how to control it. This general admonition serves as a backdrop to more specific cautions on assessment procedures.

- The assessment process should be initiated only when sufficient cause is documented.
- Parents must consent to the assessment, and they have the right to participate in and appeal any determinations made and any program decisions that follow from assessment.
- Assessments are to be undertaken only by fully qualified professionals.
- Assessment procedures must be adjusted to account for specific disabilities in hearing, vision, health, or motor impairment.

▷ Assessments should be adapted for individuals whose culture or language differs from the population upon whom the instruments were standardized.

▷ Conclusions and recommendations should be made on the basis of multiple sources of data, including input from people directly acquainted with the person (e.g., parents) and direct observations of the student.

▷ Periodic reassessments must be made (at least every three years) to re-evaluate previous judgments and to consider necessary programming changes.

As Polloway and Jones-Wilson (1992) note, the cautions that must be considered in assessment can generally be summarized in one key point: The express purpose of undertaking assessment is to provide information that will lead to effective programming. Thus, the utility of the results is measured by how closely they ultimately relate to effective instruction.

Role of the Classroom Teacher

The list that follows suggests ways in which the general education professional can take an active role in the assessment process.

1. Ask questions about the assessment process. Special education teachers, school psychologists, speech-language pathologists and other professionals should be committed to clarifying the nature of the assessments used and the interpretation of the results.

2. Seek help as needed in conveying information to parents. Special education teachers may offer you needed support during a conference.

3. Provide input. Formal test data should add to observations in the classroom about a student's ability, achievement, and learning patterns. When formal tests indicate higher abilities than observed in the classroom, re-evaluate your perceptions of the student's ability. A valid diagnostic picture should bring together multiple sources of data.

4. Observe assessment procedures. If time and facilities (e.g., a one-way mirror) permit, you will find that observing can be educational and can enhance your ability to take part in decision making.

5. Consider issues of possible bias. Formal assessments are often administered by an individual relatively unknown to the child (e.g., a psychologist); therefore, inadvertent bias factors between examiner and examinee may creep into the results. Conversely, classroom underachievement and behaviour can lead to bias as well. Work together with the psychologist and other professionals to ensure an unbiased process.

6. Avoid viewing assessment as a means of confirming a set of observations or conclusions about a student's difficulties. Assessment is exploratory and may not lead to expected results. Too often, after a student is judged ineligible for special services, various parties feel resentment toward the assessment process. Keep in mind that the purpose is to elicit useful information to help the student, not to arrive at a foregone decision about eligibility that may please the student, parent, or teacher.

Individualized Education Programs (IEPs)

The results of assessment should be translated into educational plans for instructional goals. The **individualized education program (IEP)**—sometimes referred to as the individualized program plan (IPP), the individual student support plan (ISSP), or the personal program plan (PPP)—is a description of services planned for students with exceptionalities. The IEP is a requirement under most provincial and territorial jurisdictions (Smith & Foster, 1996).

CONSIDER THIS

Do you feel that the role of the classroom teacher in the assessment process is realistic? In what areas do you feel comfortable participating? In what areas are you uncomfortable?

TEACHING TIP

When the results of standardized tests differ significantly from your observations of and experiences with a child, consult the examiner. Provide samples of the student's work or report your observations. Additional assessment may be necessary.

CONSIDER THIS

Should all students be required to have an individualized education program (IEP)? What would be the advantages, disadvantages, and general impact of such a requirement?

FURTHER READING

The development of the IEP should be a team process. For an example of how to do this at the middle school level, read "Middle School Teachers Planning for Students with Learning Disabilities" by S. Vaughn and J. S. Schumm, in *Remedial and Special Education*, published in 1994 in volume 15, pages 152–161.

The intent of this requirement was to place the focus of intervention on individual needs. The IEP itself is ideally developed by the school team. After analyzing relevant diagnostic data, the team writes an IEP reflecting the student's educational needs. In some provinces and territories the IEP is required independent of any identification process. The overriding concept behind the IEP is that all educational programming should be driven by the needs of the student. If academic, behavioural, or social needs are identified, then goals need to be written to address these needs. In other words, services are determined by individual need, not by availability.

The IEP Team

The educational program is developed by the IEP team. School districts should ensure that the IEP team assembled for each student with a disability includes the following:

1. The parents of the student
2. At least one general education teacher of the student (if the student is in general education classrooms)
3. A qualified special education teacher
4. A representative of the school district who is
   a. qualified to provide or supervise the provision of specially designed instruction to meet the unique need of students with disabilities
   b. knowledgeable about the general education curriculum
   c. knowledgeable about the availability of resources of the school district
   d. an individual who can interpret the instructional implications of evaluation results
5. Other individuals who have knowledge or special expertise regarding the student, including related service personnel as appropriate (at the discretion of the parent or the school district)
6. The student, if appropriate

Although IEPs may serve varied purposes, Polloway and Patton (1993) list the three most prominent ones. First, IEPs can provide instructional direction. Well-written goals can help remedy an approach to instruction that consists of pulling together isolated or marginally related exercises. Second, IEPs can function as the basis of evaluation; annual goals then serve as standards against which to judge student progress and teacher effec-

Parental involvement in the development of the individualized education program is both a requirement as well as an important aspect in the design of appropriate school programs.

tiveness and efficiency. Third, IEPs can improve communication among members of the team. IEPs should facilitate planning and program implementation among staff members, teachers, and parents, and, as appropriate, between teachers and students.

How then should teachers approach the task of formulating and using individualized education programs?

For the IEP process to function well, teachers must move beyond seeing IEPs as mere paperwork and view them as instruments that help tailor individual programs to address areas of instructional need. Teachers need to use the plan as a basis for teaching decisions. Only then can annual goals, which should serve as the basis for determining short-term objectives, be reflected in ongoing instructional planning. The discussion that follows illustrates the principles underlying the development of IEPs.

Three Key Components of an IEP

The major components in the IEP document that guide intervention are (1) present levels of educational performance, (2) measurable annual goals, and (3) short-term objectives, or benchmarks. These three elements provide the foundation that directs the services that will be implemented.

The first component, **present level of educational performance**, provides a summary of assessment data on a student's current functioning, which subsequently serves as the basis for establishing annual goals. Therefore, the information should include data for each priority area in which instructional support is needed. Depending on the individual student, consideration might be given to reading, math, and other academic skills, written and oral communication skills, vocational talents and needs, social skills, behavioural patterns, study skills, self-help skills and other life skills, and motor skills.

Performance levels can be provided in various forms, such as formal and informal assessment data, behavioural descriptions, and specific abilities delineated by checklists or skill sequences. Functional summary statements of an individual's strengths and areas of need draw on information from a variety of sources rather than relying on a single source. Test scores in math, for example, might be combined with a description of how the child performed on a curriculum-based measure such as a computational checklist. In general, the phrasing used to define levels of performance should be positive and describe things the child can do. For example, the same information is conveyed by the two following statements, but the first demonstrates a more positive approach: "The student can identify 50 percent of times table facts," versus "The student does not know half of the facts." Appropriately written performance levels provide a broad range of data in order to help generate relevant and appropriate annual goals. In addition, Gibb and Dyches (2000) recommend that present levels of educational performance include some sense of how the disability affects the student's involvement and progress in the general curriculum and logical cues for writing the accompanying goals.

The second, and central, IEP instructional component is **annual goals**. Each student's goals should be individually determined to address unique needs and abilities. Since it is obviously impossible to predict the precise amount of progress a student will make in a year, goals should be reasonable projections of what the student will accomplish. To develop realistic expectations, teachers can consider a number of variables, including the chronological age of the child, the expected rate of learning, and past and current learning profiles.

Annual goals should be measurable, positive, student-oriented, and relevant (Polloway, Patton, & Serna, 2001). *Measurable* goals provide a basis for evaluation. Statements should use terms that denote action and can therefore be operationally defined (e.g., *pronounce, write*), rather than vague, general language that confounds evaluation and observer agreement (e.g., *know, understand*). *Positive* goals provide an appropriate direction for

FURTHER READING

For further information on developing IEPs, order a resource guide entitled *Individual Education Planning for Students with Special Needs*, copyright © 2001, by writing to the Special Programs Branch of the British Columbia Ministry of Education, P.O. Box 9165 Stn Prov. Govt., Victoria, BC V8W 9H4, or emailing to ipp@mail.qp.gov.bc.ca.

CONSIDER THIS

Some individuals are negative about the use and value of IEPs. Do you see a purpose in their development? How would you improve the process?

FURTHER READING

The use of a computer-generated IEP is still controversial. To explore this issue further, read *Special Education Technology: Classroom Applications* by R. B. Lewis, published in 1993 by Brooks.

TEACHING TIP

As a general education teacher, you should be invited to participate in the IEP meeting of any child in your class. If you were not present, ask the special education teacher for a copy of the student's IEP, including the summary on the child's strengths, weaknesses, and goals, to incorporate into your daily planning.

instruction. Avoiding negative goals creates an atmosphere conducive to good home–school relationships and makes it easier to chart student progress. Goals should also be *oriented to the student*. Developing students' skills is the intent, and the only measure of effectiveness should be what is learned, rather than what is taught. Finally, goals must be *relevant* to the individual's actual needs in terms of remediation and other desirable skills.

Annual goals should subsequently be broken down into **short-term objectives**, given in a logical and sequential series to provide a general plan for instruction. Short-term objectives, the third major IEP component, can be derived only after annual goals are written. They should be based on a task analysis process; skill sequences and checklists can be used to divide an annual goal into components that can be shaped into precise objectives. Each broad goal will generate a cluster of objectives. The four criteria applied to annual goals are also appropriate to short-term objectives. Since objectives are narrower in focus, an objective's measurability should be enhanced with a criterion for mastery. For example, a math short-term objective might read, "Given 20 multiplication facts using numbers 1–5, John will give correct answers for 90 percent." These benchmarks should be obtained from the general education curriculum being used by the student's typically achieving peers. A portion of an IEP containing annual goals, short-term objectives, and method of evaluation is presented in Table 1.3. Teachers should familiarize themselves with the format for IEPs used by their boards.

Role of the Classroom Teacher

It is essential that the classroom teacher take part in the IEP meeting so that the document reflects the student's needs in the inclusive classroom. Furthermore, the IEP itself should be referenced throughout the year. In particular, the teacher should keep the goal and objective clusters at hand so that the IEP can influence instructional programs.

TABLE 1.3 Examples of Lark's IEP Goals and Objectives

Goal 2: Lark will follow school and team rules.

Objectives	Criteria	Evaluation Procedures
Lark will wear appropriate clothing to school	0 occurrences per week of being sent home for dress code violations	Teacher observation using school dress code requirements
Lark will use appropriate language on the bus and at school	0 occurrences per week of inappropriate language	Number of referrals to office or disciplinary actions for inappropriate language
Lark will talk respectfully to teachers and other school personnel	0 referrals for inappropriate language per week	Number of referrals to office or disciplinary actions for inappropriate language

Goal 4: Lark will develop effective organizational and study skills.

Objectives	Criteria	Evaluation Procedures
Lark will record all class assignments in a daily planner	90%	Daily checks by teacher and grandmother
Lark will complete and submit assignments	4 of 5 days (80%) with 80% accuracy	Daily records in teacher grade books
Lark will attend and participate in the student homework support group	6 of 8 times/month (75%)	Student self-evaluation and peer evaluations of participation

Adapted from *Collaboration for Inclusive Education: Developing Successful Programs* (p. 226) by C. Walther-Thomas, L. Korinek, V. McLaughlin, & B. T. Williams, 2000, Boston: Allyn and Bacon.

FIGURE 1.3

IEP for Student with Learning Disability in the General Education Classroom

From N. Dunavant, 1993, Homewood School System, Birmingham, AL.

Student Name _____   Year _____ Page _____

Area: General Classroom Placement

Annual Goal: _____ will maintain average or above-average

grades in all general _____ grade academic classes.

Objectives:

1. _____ will participate in general class activities 5 of 5 days per week.

2. _____ will complete general class assignments on time 5 of 5 days per week.

3. _____ will complete homework assignments 4 of 5 days per week.

4. _____ will average 70 percent or higher on tests taken in the general academic classes.

5. _____ will self-evaluate progress by meeting with a resource teacher a minimum of once per grading period.

Type of Evaluation:

Projected Check Date _____

Date/Degree of Mastery _____

_____

Progress will be monitored every nine weeks, and the report card will document the meeting of objectives.

Note: This student _____ does/ _____ does not require classroom modifications.

An IEP's annual goals and short-term objectives ultimately should be reflected in instructional plans in the classroom. But short-term objectives are not intended to be used as weekly, let alone daily, plans. Teachers should refer to the document periodically to ensure that instruction is consistent with the student's long-term needs. When significant variance is noted, it may become the basis for a correction in instruction or perhaps a rationale for a change in the goals or objectives of the IEP. Figure 1.3 shows a sample IEP.

In concluding their discussion on IEPs, Epstein et al. (1992) counsel teachers not to lose sight of the spirit of individualization that should guide the IEP process. Teachers need to view the documents as tools for meeting students' individual needs. Unless guided by the rationale and spirit that informed the original development of the IEP concept, the process can degenerate into a mere bookkeeping activity. Instead, well-thought-out IEPs should form the foundation for individually designed educational programs for students with disabilities.

CONSIDER THIS

Do you think the IEP in Figure 1.3 is adequate for a student in a totally inclusive setting? What safeguards does it provide to ensure success?

TEACHING TIP

The IEP is a plan, not a contract. If teachers make good faith efforts to implement IEPs, they cannot be held responsible for lack of progress. Ongoing communication with the IEP team is critical, and a revision of the IEP may be necessary.

Summary

- As recently as the 1960s, students with disabilities were not provided services in the regular schools.
- In Canada, the Charter of Rights and Freedoms, which is part of our Constitution, guarantees the rights of all people, including those with disabilities.
- Canada is the only country in the world that has the rights of individuals with disabilities included in the Constitution.
- Education is the responsibility of the provinces and territories.
- All provinces and territories must adhere to the Charter of Rights and Freedoms and not discriminate on the basis of mental or physical disability.
- All provinces and territories are committed in principle to inclusive education.

▶ Services for students with exceptionalities have evolved significantly over the past 20 years.

▶ Current services for students with disabilities focus on inclusion—including students in general education classrooms as much as possible.

▶ Today's student population is very diverse and students with a variety of exceptionalities are part of it.

▶ A sizeable percentage of students are at risk of developing problems, present learning or behaviour problems, or may be classified as having a disability.

▶ Although recognized categories of disabilities exist, many students do not fit neatly into a specific category.

▶ Students who are at risk of developing problems, and those considered gifted and talented, also require special attention from school personnel.

▶ Assessment goes beyond testing, encompassing a broader range of methods that help define a student's strengths and problems. It can lead to the development of educational interventions.

▶ Formal assessment is based on the administration of commercial instruments, typically for survey or diagnostic purposes.

▶ Informal assessment includes a variety of tools that can enhance a teacher's knowledge of students' learning needs.

▶ Curriculum-based measures are tied to the class curriculum and assess a student within this context.

▶ Ecological assessment places the evaluative data within the context of a student's environment.

▶ The control of bias in assessment is essential to accurate and fair evaluation.

▶ Classroom teachers may not administer formal assessments, but they contribute in important ways to any assessment process and should be informed about the process.

Resources

Alberta Education, Special Education Branch. (1995). *Awareness Series*. Edmonton, AB.

This series of 15 information brochures helps teachers understand, recognize, and plan for children with a variety of exceptionalities. Examples are Tourette syndrome, fetal alcohol syndrome, asthma, and visual impairments.

Weblinks

Council for Exceptional Children

www.cec.sped.org/

This website, which provides information about a variety of exceptionalities, is an excellent starting point for all teachers working with children with exceptionalities or in a diverse classroom.

The Disability Resource Monthly WebWatcher

www.disabilityresources.org/

This site, self-described as "a website for students that are studying in the field of disability, as well as professionals working within it," is a resource centre providing information on other links, news, books, contacts, associations, and forums related to disability. The WebWatcher is a subject guide to all the resources related to disabilities that are available on the internet. Accessed by alphabetical listing, it is updated monthly and provides relevant sites by disability.

The Special Education Yahoo Subdirectory

http://dir.yahoo.com/Education/Special_Education/

Many sites related to special education are listed in this directory. Although the majority of sites are American in origin, the material is highly relevant for all special education.

The Disabilities, Society and Culture, Yahoo Subdirectory

http://dir.yahoo.com/Society_and_Culture/Disabilities/

Recommended by Canada's *Ability Network* magazine, this directory of sites related to society and culture of disabilities covers a huge range of issues pertinent to disabilities. For example, some of the directories are relevant to independent living (44 websites), education (51 websites), children (31 websites), parent support, personal experiences, and specific disabilities (568 websites).

Instructor's Manual

http://news.yahoo.com/fc?tmpl=fc&cid=34&in=world& cat=disabilities_and_the_disabled

Instructor's Manual provides a summary of all recent news stories pertaining to individuals with disabilities. A quick browse on a regular basis will provide readers, especially professors, with the most current issues in the field and good material for discussion in class.

Designing Inclusive Classrooms

2

Chapter Objectives

After reading this chapter, you should be able to

- describe the different service delivery models used in meeting the needs of students with special needs
- describe the advantages and disadvantages of the different service delivery models
- describe the role of special education and regular classroom teachers in the different service delivery models
- describe methods that enhance the inclusion of students with exceptionalities
- delineate five critical dimensions of inclusive classrooms
- describe the role of classroom management, curricular options, and accommodative practices in inclusive classrooms
- discuss the range of personnel supports in inclusive classrooms
- explain how to create and maintain successful inclusive classrooms
- describe different methods of maintaining inclusive programs after they are initiated

ibby is a popular high-achieving student in Ms. Jordan's Grade 3 class. At the beginning of the school year Rhonda, a new student, was placed in Ms. Jordan's classroom. Rhonda has cerebral palsy and a mild intellectual impairment. Rhonda rarely talked, did not follow Ms. Jordan's directions very well, and had difficulty reading. Libby, and all the other students in the class, thought Rhonda was really dumb and did not want anything to do with her in the classroom, on the playground, or in the lunchroom.

Ms. Baker, the special education teacher, started working with Rhonda in the classroom to improve her reading skills. Libby and all her friends thought this proved that Rhonda was dumb and really did not belong in the class. About two weeks later, Ms. Baker asked if any of the students in Ms. Jordan's class wanted to be a peer tutor. None of the students knew what a peer tutor was, but thought that it sounded pretty important. Libby volunteered and was chosen to be a peer tutor. When Ms. Baker and Ms. Jordan met with Libby and talked to her about what it meant to be a peer tutor, they explained that Rhonda had some learning problems and needed some extra help in the classroom. Libby had not known she would have to work with Rhonda when she volunteered, but she decided to try it out for a little while.

When Libby began working with Rhonda, she discovered that she loved helping others. Libby also learned a very important fact that she quickly spread to all her classmates—Rhonda was okay. In fact, Rhonda was pretty cool. Getting to know Rhonda made Libby stop and think about people's differences. From then on, Rhonda was considered by all the students in Ms. Jordan's class as an equal. The big step in getting her to be accepted was to get one of the most popular students in the room to accept her as a fellow classmate.

Questions to Consider

1. Do you think that Ms. Jordan and Ms. Baker planned for this result?

2. Can events be planned to orchestrate social interactions among students with and without exceptionalities in the classroom?

3. Who is responsible for facilitating the acceptance of students with exceptionalities into general education classrooms?

4. What are some other ways that Ms. Jordan could have encouraged the students in the class to accept Rhonda?

Introduction

The idea of including students with special needs in general education classrooms continues to receive significant attention on a philosophical level. It is implemented for a variety of reasons; chief reasons are to improve educational opportunities and social development (Salend, 2000) and to give all students equal opportunities. However, too little discussion has focused on specific ways to implement inclusion successfully. Addressing the needs of a growing, diverse student population is a daunting challenge for today's schools. Adding students with exceptionalities to the mix only increases the challenges faced by general educators. This chapter discusses some of the key features of sound inclusive settings. It also addresses how to create and maintain these settings and the collaborative relationships that are critical to help them function well. It is important to note, however, that not all students' needs are best met in the regular classroom. Although the regular classroom is the starting place when considering the best environment in which to deliver a student's educational program, the continuum of placement options available to each student needs to be considered as part of team planning.

Terminology in special education can vary depending on the source. Some commonly used terms will be defined as follows:

Placement: The term *placement* can mean the physical setting of a student's educational program, or the educational program that has been created for the student. In this text, the term *placement* will be used to refer to the physical environment in which a student is being educated, while the term *program* will be used to refer the child's educational program.

Accommodation: The term *accommodation* will be used to refer to the "specialized support and services that are provided to enable students with diverse needs to achieve learning expectations. This may include technological equipment, support staff, and informal supports" (Saskatchewan Learning, 2000, p. 145).

Adaptation: The term *adaptation* will be used to refer to the "adjustments to curriculum content, instructional practices, materials or technology, assessment strategies, and the learning environment made in accordance with the strengths, needs, and interests of the learner" (Saskatchewan Learning, 2000, p. 145).

Modification: The term *modification* will be used to refer to changes in policy that will support students with exceptionalities in their learning (e.g., altering school curriculum or attendance policy).

Educating Students with Exceptionalities

The setting in which students with exceptionalities should receive educational and related services is a much-discussed, much-debated topic. In fact, as early as 1989, Jenkins and Heinen wrote that the issue has "received more attention, undergone more modifications, and generated even more controversy than have decisions about how or what these students are taught" (p. 516). The topic has continued to be much discussed and remains one of the key issues in the field of education for children with exceptionalities. Simply saying the word *inclusion* "is likely to engender fervent debate" (Kavale & Forness, 2000, p. 279).

Most students with exceptionalities experience mild disabilities and are included in general education classrooms for at least a portion of each school day. A smaller number of students, with more severe disabilities, are more typically educated in segregated special education environments (McLeskey, Henry, & Hodges, 1999). However, even some students with more severe disabilities are included in general education classrooms part of the time (Hobbs & Westling, 1998). Students who are gifted and/or talented, who are also classified as exceptional students, are also typically educated in the regular classroom.

CONSIDER THIS

Think about the services that students with exceptionalities had when you were in school. Did you make contact and interact much with students with exceptionalities? Why or why not?

FURTHER READING

For more information on beliefs regarding inclusion, read Stanovich and Jordan's article "Canadian Teachers' and Principals' Beliefs About Inclusive Education as Predictors of Effective Teaching in Heterogeneous Classrooms" in volume 98, issue 3 of *The Elementary School Journal*, 1998 (pp. 221–238).

While still raging, the debate about where students should be educated has shifted in favour of more inclusion, which can be implemented in many different ways. Students can be placed in general education classrooms for most of the school day and be "pulled out" periodically and provided instruction in resource settings by special education teachers. Or, they can be placed full time in general education classrooms. In the latter case, special education teachers may go into general education classrooms and work with students who are experiencing difficulties or collaborate directly with classroom teachers to develop and implement methods and materials that will meet the needs of many students. Schools use the model that best meets the individual's needs, developed through the IEP process.

Programs in Which Students Receive Intervention in Special Education Settings

CONSIDER THIS

What kinds of problems are created when students with exceptionalities enter and leave general education classrooms over the course of the day? How can teachers deal with these problems?

Traditionally, students with exceptionalities received their educational programs in specialized classrooms, typically called self-contained special classrooms. Serving students with exceptionalities in special programs was based on the presumption that general educators did not have the skills necessary to meet the needs of all students representing different learning needs (Shanker, 1994–1995). This placement option has been considered a "stage" in the movement from isolation for students with exceptionalities to inclusion (Safford & Safford, 1998). The result was the removal of students from the general education environment and an education provided by specialists.

The Special Education Classroom Approach

FURTHER READING

Read about fostering inclusive values in S. J. Salend's article "Fostering Inclusive Values in Children: What Families Can Do," in volume 37, issue 1 of *Teaching Exceptional Children*, 2004 (pp. 64–69).

In the special education classroom approach, students receive the majority of their educational program from a special education teacher specifically trained to serve the population of students with intellectual disabilities, learning disabilities, or some other specific disability.

Self-contained special education classes were the preferred and dominant service model between 1950 and 1970 (Idol, 1983; Podemski et al., 1995; Smith, 1990; Smith et al., 1986). Special education teachers were trained to teach students with exceptionalities—but usually only students with one kind of disability—in all subject areas. However, the primary focus was on a functional curriculum. Students placed in self-contained

Children with exceptionalities were often educated in isolated, self-contained classes between 1950 and 1970.

special education classrooms rarely interacted with their typically achieving peers, often even eating lunch alone. Likewise, the special education teacher interacted very little with typically achieving students or classroom teachers.

Many general education teachers liked the self-contained special class model because they did not have to deal with students who differed from their view of "typical" children. The role of classroom teachers in the self-contained model was extremely limited. Their primary role was to refer students to the special education program, but they rarely had to instruct them. Referrals primarily occurred in lower elementary grades, where the majority of students with exceptionalities are identified.

The movement away from special class programs has not been without dissent. Advocates for special classes have noted several problems with inclusion. Arguing against including all students with exceptionalities in general education classes, Fuchs and Fuchs (1994–1995) note that separate settings have several advantages:

- Education is provided by well-trained special educators.
- Education is selected from a variety of instructional methods, curricula, and motivational strategies.
- The system monitors student growth and progress.

Regardless of these advantages, the self-contained model has had many critics. The movement away from self-contained classrooms was sparked by several factors, including the following:

- Students served in special classes are isolated from their typically achieving peers.
- Students do not have "typical" role models.
- Students may be isolated from many of the activities that are engaged in by typically achieving students.
- Special education teachers in special class models have limited interaction with general education teachers.
- Special education students are considered to "belong" to the special education teacher and program.
- Typically achieving students do not have the opportunity to interact with students with exceptionalities.
- Teachers are required to teach all areas rather than relying on colleagues with specialized expertise in selected areas.

Special classes, which segregate students with exceptionalities from their typically achieving age peers, cannot be considered a "normal" school placement and were therefore criticized by adherents to the normalization philosophy of the 1970s. One way to implement the normalization philosophy was through inclusion, which resulted in the widespread reduction of special classes.

One final reason for the decline of the self-contained special class model was a growing awareness of the diversity of students with exceptionalities. Although the special class was the predominant model, the majority of students with exceptionalities served in special education were those with mild intellectual disabilities. As exceptional populations, such as students with learning disabilities or emotional problems, became recognized, the number of students needing special education grew significantly. The feasibility of serving all of these students in isolated special classes became less attractive. On the other hand, including these students in general classrooms would benefit all of them (Wang, Reynolds, & Walberg, 1994–1995).

The Resource Room Model

The primary service delivery option used for most students with exceptionalities (except for those with speech impairments) is the resource room model. The **resource room** is a

CONSIDER THIS

Often, parents of students with intellectual disabilities are more supportive of inclusion than parents of students with less severe disabilities. Why do you think this is the case?

CROSS-REFERENCE

Read Chapter 6 to see how modelling appropriate behaviours can have an impact on students with serious emotional disturbances.

FURTHER READING

Consider some of the issues arising in the training of preservice teachers to teach in inclusive classrooms in Stanovich and Jordan's article "Preparing General Educators to Teach in Inclusive Classrooms: Some Food for Thought," in *The Teacher Educator*, volume 37, issue 3, 2002 (pp. 173–185).

FURTHER READING

For an extensive discussion on **normalization**, read one of the early articles on European approaches and innovations in serving the handicapped, written by K. D. Juul and published in *Exceptional Children*, volume 44, 1978.

special education classroom. However, unlike the self-contained special class, students go to the resource room only for special instruction. Students who are served by the resource room model spend part of each school day with their typically achieving, chronological age peers and attend resource rooms for special assistance in addressing their areas of difficulty (Friend & Bursuck, 2002). Although all of Canada is committed to the inclusion of students with exceptionalities in the regular classroom, the use of the resource room is still prevalent across the country (Schwean, Saklofske, Shatz, & Falk, 1996).

Advantages of the Resource Room Model   Several obvious advantages make the resource room model preferable to the self-contained special class. Most important, students with exceptionalities have an opportunity to interact with their chronological age peers. Other advantages include the following:

▶ Students are more visible throughout the school and are more likely considered to be a part of the school.
▶ Students have the opportunity to receive instruction from more than one person.
▶ Students have the opportunity to receive instruction from "specialists" in specific academic areas.
▶ Special education teachers have the opportunity to interact with general education teachers and be an active part of the school staff.

Disadvantages of the Resource Room Model   Despite the numerous advantages of the resource room model, this approach does not offer the ultimate answer to the complex question of where students with exceptionalities should be educated. Identifying students as needing special education and requiring them to leave the general education classroom, even for only part of the day, can be detrimental. Guterman (1995) found this concern to be one "unifying element" among students interviewed about their special education placement.

Dunn's article in 1968 questioned the efficacy of serving students with exceptionalities in separate classes. His article, along with others, helped move the field from segregated to integrated services. Research currently being reported is similarly questioning the efficacy of resource room services. While there are many advantages to serving students with exceptionalities in resource rooms, there are some obvious disadvantages, including the following:

▶ Pull-out programs are disruptive to the routine of the general classroom.
▶ Students who exit the classroom to receive specialized services may be ostracized.
▶ Communication between the resource room teacher and general classroom teachers, which must be mandatory for programs to be successful, is often difficult.
▶ Students may become confused if teachers use different strategies to teach similar content.
▶ Students may miss some favourite activities when they are pulled out for resource room instruction.

Role of Special Education Personnel   In the resource room model, a key role of special education personnel is to collaborate with classroom teachers to deliver appropriate programs to students with exceptionalities. Special education teachers cannot simply focus on their students only when they are in the special education classroom. Close collaboration between the special education teacher and the classroom teacher must occur to ensure that students receiving instruction in the special education classroom and general education classroom are not becoming confused by contradictory methods, assignments, curricula, and so on. The special education teacher should take the lead in opening up lines of communication and in facilitating collaborative efforts.

Role of the Classroom Teacher   Unlike the special class model, the resource room model requires that classroom teachers play numerous roles related to students with exceptionalities. One primary role is referral. The majority of students with mild disabilities and other special needs are referred for services by classroom teachers. Students with mild intellectual disabilities, learning disabilities, and mild behaviour problems are usually in elementary classrooms before their problems become apparent enough to warrant a referral for special education. General education teachers are often the first to recognize that a student is experiencing problems that could require special education services.

Classroom teachers also play the important role of implementing interventions that can bring improvement in problem areas and thereby prevent unnecessary referrals. As a result, fewer students may be labelled with a disability and served in special education programs. Labelling students with exceptionalities has identified advantages (e.g., access to funding) and disadvantages (e.g., stigmatizing).

Inclusive Education Programs

Just as full-time special class placement of students with exceptionalities received criticism in the early 1970s, resource room programs began to be criticized in the 1980s. Since the mid-1980s there has been a call for dismantling the **dual education system** (general and special) in favour of a unified system dedicated to meeting the needs of all students. Rather than spend much time and effort identifying students with special problems and determining if they are eligible for special education services, proponents of a single education system call for providing appropriate services to all students.

Inclusion Model

The model for more fully including students with special needs in general education programs, referred to as the inclusion model, has been defined in many different ways. Unfortunately, the term **full inclusion** was originally used, suggesting that all students with exceptionalities, regardless of the severity of the disability, be included full time in general education classes (Kavale & Forness, 2000). This approach was advocated by several professional and advocacy groups, most notably the Canadian Association for Community Living (CACL), The Association for the Severely Handicapped (TASH), and Arc (formerly the Association for Retarded Citizens). Their encouragement of full-time general education classroom placement for all students provoked much criticism and skepticism. In advocating such an approach, proponents basically asserted that there was no need for a continuum of placement options for students, since the least restrictive environment was always the general education classroom for all students (Kavale & Forness, 2000).

Currently, the term **inclusion** is used to identify the movement to provide services to students with exceptionalities in general education settings (Smith & Dowdy, 1998). While acknowledging that some students with exceptionalities may need some services outside the general classroom, proponents suggest that all students with exceptionalities belong with their typically achieving peers. Smith (1995) states that inclusion means "(1) that every child should be included in a regular classroom to the optimum extent appropriate to the needs of that child while preserving the placements and services that special education can provide; (2) that the education of children with disabilities is viewed by all educators as a shared responsibility and privilege; (3) that there is a commitment to include students with disabilities in every facet of school; (4) that every child must have a place and be welcome in a regular classroom" (p. 1).

Although proponents of inclusion have articulated numerous reasons to support the model (e.g., Stainback & Stainback, 1984), many others oppose its implementation (e.g., Fuchs & Fuchs, 1994–1995). Several professional and advocacy groups support the continued use of a **continuum of services** model. These include the Council for Exceptional

FURTHER READING

Read about teachers' attitudes toward labelling in B. Norwich's "The Connotation of Special Education Labels for Professionals in the Field," in volume 26, issue 4 of the *British Journal of Special Education*, 1999 (pp. 179–183); and/or A. Weisel and H. Tur-Kaspa's "Effects of Labels and Personal Contact on Teachers' Attitudes toward Students with Special Needs," in volume 10, issue 1 of *Exceptionality*, 2002 (pp. 1–10).

FURTHER READING

Read several 1980s articles on the move to integration. Here are a few suggestions: "Effective Special Education in Regular Classes," by M. C. Wang and J. W. Birch, published in *Exceptional Children*, volume 52, 1984; and "Integration versus Cooperation: A Commentary," by Stainback and Stainback, published in *Exceptional Children*, volume 54, 1987.

CONSIDER THIS

How can terms such as *mainstreaming, inclusion,* and *full inclusion* complicate the planning of services for students with exceptionalities? What could be done to clarify terminology?

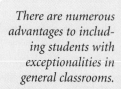

Children (CEC), the Canadian National Institute for the Blind (CNIB), the Family Network for Deaf Children, the Learning Disabilities Association of Canada (LDAC), and the Council for Children with Behaviour Disorders. The nearby Inclusion Strategies feature provides the CEC position statement on inclusion.

A continuum of services model, also termed cascade of services model, provides placement and programming options for students with exceptionalities along a continuum of least-to-most restrictiveness. "Students are given the opportunity to move sequentially between program alternatives as their needs change" (Saskatchewan Learning, 2000, p. 145). These options may range from regular classroom placement (less restrictive) to residential settings (most restrictive).

Advantages of Inclusion   There are many different advantages to inclusion, including opportunities for social interaction (Hunt et al., 2000), ease in accessing the general curriculum (King-Sears, 2001; Wehmeyer, Lattin, & Agram, 2001), academic improvement (Hunt et al., 2001), and positive outcomes for students with and without exceptionalities (Federico, Herrold, & Venn, 1999; Rieck & Wadsworth, 1999; Salend & Duhaney, 1999).

Although not mandatory, parental and teacher support for inclusion is very important. Hobbs and Westling (1998) note that many parents have mixed views. While they believe that inclusion has some obvious benefits for their children, they also worry about their children being in integrated placements. The concept has simply "not been embraced by all parents" (Palmer, Fuller, Arora, & Nelson, 2001, p. 481).

Teachers, for the most part, have expressed support for inclusion. After reviewing several studies, Scruggs and Mastropieri (1996) noted that most teachers support inclusion, are willing to teach students in their classrooms (although those who respond in this way are fewer than those who support the concept), and believe that inclusion results in positive benefits for students with exceptionalities and does not harm other students or the instructional process. In a recent study, it was determined that both teachers and parents of children with and without exceptionalities generally supported inclusion both at the beginning and at the end of a school year in which inclusive practices were utilized. However, there were some differences in the support of these two groups, and both groups had a variety of concerns related to inclusion (Seery, Davis, & Johnson, 2000).

CEC Policy on Inclusive Schools and Community Settings

The Council for Exceptional Children (CEC) believes all children, youth, and young adults with disabilities are entitled to a free and appropriate education and/or services that lead to an adult life characterized by satisfying relations with others, independent living, productive engagement in the community, and participation in society at large. To achieve such outcomes, there must exist for all children, youth, and young adults a rich variety of early intervention, educational, and vocational program options and experiences. Access to these programs and experiences should be based on individual educational need and desired outcomes. Furthermore, students and their families or guardians, as members of the planning team, may recommend the placement, curriculum option, and the exit document to be pursued.

CEC believes that a continuum of services must be available for all children, youth, and young adults. CEC also believes that the concept of inclusion is a meaningful goal to be pursued in our schools and communities. In addition, CEC believes children, youth, and young adults with disabilities should be served whenever possible in general education classrooms in inclusive neighbourhood schools and community settings. Such settings should be strengthened and supported by an infusion of specially trained personnel and other appropriate supportive practices according to the individual needs of the child.

POLICY IMPLICATIONS

Schools. In inclusive schools, the building administrator and staff, with assistance from the special education administration, should be primarily responsible for the education of children, youth, and young adults with disabilities. The administrator(s) and other school personnel must have available to them appropriate support and technical assistance to enable them to fulfill their responsibilities. Leaders in state/provincial and local governments must redefine rules and regulations as necessary, and grant school personnel greater authority to make decisions regarding curriculum, materials, instructional practice, and staffing patterns. In return for greater autonomy, the school administrator

and staff should establish high standards for each child, youth, and young adult, and should be held accountable for his or her progress toward outcomes.

Communities. Inclusive schools must be located in inclusive communities; therefore, CEC invites all educators, other professionals, and family members to work together to create early intervention, educational, and vocational programs and experiences that are collegial, inclusive, and responsive to the diversity of children, youth, and young adults. Policy makers at the highest levels of state/provincial and local government, as well as school administration, also must support inclusion in the educational reforms they espouse. Further, the policy makers should fund programs in nutrition, early intervention, health care, parent education, and other social support programs that prepare all children, youth, and young adults to do well in school. There can be no meaningful school reform, nor inclusive schools, without funding of these key prerequisites. As important, there must be interagency agreements and collaboration with local government and business to help prepare students to assume a constructive role in an inclusive community.

Professional Development. And finally, state/provincial departments of education, local educational districts, and colleges and universities must provide high-quality preservice and continuing professional development experiences that prepare all general educators to work effectively with children, youth, and young adults representing a wide range of abilities and disabilities, experiences, cultural and linguistic backgrounds, attitudes, and expectations. Moreover, special educators should be trained with an emphasis on their roles in inclusive schools and community settings. They also must learn the importance of establishing ambitious goals for their students and of using appropriate means of monitoring the progress of children, youth, and young adults.

Adopted by the CEC Delegate Assembly, 1993, San Antonio, Texas.

From the Council for Exceptional Children, 1920 Association Drive, Reston, VA 22091. Used by permission.

Disadvantages of Inclusion Just as there are many supporters of inclusion and reasons for its implementation, there are also professionals and parents who decry the movement. Among the reasons why they oppose inclusion are the following:

1. General educators have not been involved sufficiently and are therefore unlikely to support the model.

FURTHER READING

For more information on the disadvantages of inclusion, read the articles by Fuchs and Fuchs and by Shanker in *Educational Leadership*, December 1994/January 1995. The articles were part of a special issue on inclusion.

CONSIDER THIS

How can some of the problems caused by inclusion be addressed to facilitate success in school for all students?

2. General educators as well as special educators do not have the collaboration skills necessary to make inclusion successful.
3. Limited empirical data exist to support the model. Therefore, full implementation should be put on hold until sound research supports the effort.
4. Full inclusion of students with exceptionalities in general education classrooms may take away from students without exceptionalities and lessen their quality of education.
5. Current funding, teacher training, and teacher certification are based on separate education systems.
6. Some students with exceptionalities do better when served in special education classes by special education teachers.

Although some of these criticisms may have merit, others have been discounted. For example, research indicates that the education of typically achieving students is not negatively affected by inclusion (National Study on Inclusion, 1995). Therefore, though the movement has its critics, research provides support for the idea that inclusion works for most students with exceptionalities.

Role of Special Education Personnel   In the inclusion model, special education personnel become much more integral to the broad educational efforts of the school. In the dual system, special education teachers provide instructional programming only to students identified as disabled and determined eligible for special education programs under provincial or territorial guidelines. In inclusive schools these teachers work with a variety of students, including those having difficulties but not identified specifically as having a disability. The special education teacher works much more closely with classroom teachers in the inclusion model, resulting in increased opportunities for all students.

Role of the Classroom Teacher   The role of the classroom teacher also changes dramatically. Instead of focusing primarily on identification and referral, and possibly providing some instructional services to students with exceptionalities, teachers in the inclusive school become fully responsible for all students, including those with identified exceptionalities. Special education support personnel are available to collaborate on educational programs for all students, but the primary responsibility is assumed by the classroom teacher.

Classroom teachers play a vital role in the education of students with exceptionalities. As noted by Hobbs and Westling (1998), teachers possibly play the most important role in the success of inclusion. Classroom teachers must be able to perform many different functions, such as the following:

- Acting as a team member on assessment and IEP committees
- Advocating for children with exceptionalities when they are in general education classrooms and in special programs
- Counselling and interacting with parents of students with exceptionalities
- Individualizing instruction for students with exceptionalities
- Being innovative in providing equal educational opportunities for all students, including those with exceptionalities

Sharing responsibility among classroom teachers, special education teachers, and other specialists, such as reading teachers, is the key to providing effective educational programs for all students (Voltz, Brazil, & Ford, 2001).

In general, the classroom teacher controls the educational programs for all students in the classroom, including students with exceptionalities, students at risk for developing problems, and those classified as gifted and/or talented. The attitude of the teacher toward students and the general climate the teacher establishes in the classroom impacts the success of all students, particularly those with exceptionalities.

Methods That Enhance Inclusion of Students with Exceptionalities

The concept of inclusion purports that students with special needs can be active, valued, fully participating members of a school community in which diversity is viewed as the norm and high-quality education is provided through a combination of meaningful curriculum, effective teaching, and necessary supports (Halvorsen & Neary, 2001). Anything less is unacceptable. Inclusion is distinctly different from the notion of integration or mainstreaming, in which students with special needs are educated in physical proximity to their age peers, yet without significant attention paid to the qualitative features of this arrangement. Both integration and mainstreaming begin with the notion that students with exceptionalities belong in special classes and should be integrated as much as possible in general classrooms. Inclusion, on the other hand, assumes that all students *belong* in the general education classroom and should be pulled out only when appropriate services cannot be provided in the inclusive setting. While seemingly a simple difference, these two approaches vary significantly (Halvorsen & Neary, 2001). Many different factors are critical to the success of inclusion. Webber (1997) identified five essential features that characterize successful inclusion of students with special needs. These are: (1) a sense of community and social acceptance, (2) appreciation of student diversity, (3) attention to curricular needs, (4) effective management and instruction, and (5) personnel support and collaboration. Voltz, Brazil, and Ford (2001) list three critical elements—(1) active, meaningful participation in the mainstream, (2) sense of belonging, and (3) shared ownership among faculty. Finally, Mastropieri and Scruggs (2001) add administrative support to the list.

When in place, the features noted by Webber (1997), Voltz et al. (2001), and Mastropieri and Scruggs (2001) make the general education classroom the best possible placement option for many students with exceptionalities. If these features are not present, however, the likelihood of inclusion being successful is significantly limited. The five dimensions for successful inclusion are discussed in the following sections.

Sense of Community and Social Acceptance

In desirable inclusive settings, every student is valued and nurtured. Settings such as this promote an environment in which all members are seen as equal, all have the opportunity to contribute, and all contributions are respected. Deno, Foegen, Robinson, and Espin (1996) describe ideal school settings as "caring and nurturant places with a strong sense of community where all children and youth belong, where diversity is valued, and where the needs of all students are addressed" (p. 350).

Students with special needs are truly included in their classroom communities only when they are appreciated by their teachers and socially accepted by their classmates. An understanding teacher more effectively meets students' instructional and curricular needs, and social acceptance among classmates contributes to students' self-perception of value. Meeting both students' educational and social needs is critical to creating effective inclusive settings and responsible learning environments. It is imperative that we address the need for acceptance, belonging, and friendship (Voltz et al., 2001); Lang and Berberich (1995) suggest that inclusive classrooms should be characterized as settings where basic human needs are met. Figure 2.1 highlights critical needs that should be prominent in an inclusive classroom community.

FURTHER READING

For more information on the ideal school setting, read "Facing the Realities of Inclusion for Students with Mild Disabilities," by S. L. Deno and colleagues, published in volume 30 of the *Journal of Special Education* in 1996 (pp. 345–357).

FURTHER READING

For more practical suggestions about how to include students with mild disabilities, read *Exceptions: A Handbook of Inclusion Activities for Teachers of Students at Grade 6–12* by Deborah Murphy et al. You can order this publication from the Learning Resources Distributing Centre in Edmonton, AB. (Phone: (403) 427-5775; Fax: (403) 422-9750; Website: **www.lrdc.edc.gov.ab.ca/**)

FIGURE 2.1

The Basic Needs of Children in a Learning Environment

From *All Children Are Special: Creating an Inclusive Classroom* (p. 73), by G. Lang and C. Berberich, 1995, York, ME: Stenhouse Publishers. Used by permission.

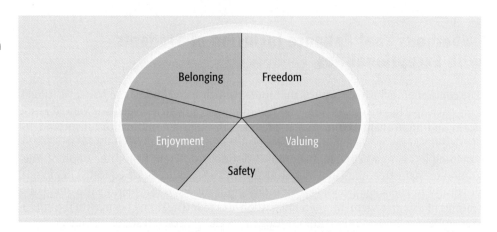

Teachers play a very critical role in creating a positive classroom environment (Favazza, Phillipsen, & Kumar, 2000). Several factors controlled by teachers are essential to establishing a successful inclusive setting. These factors include teacher attitude, teacher expectations, teacher competence, teacher collaborative skills, and teacher support (Mastropieri & Scruggs, 2001; Salend, 1999).

Teachers must have a positive attitude about students with special needs being in their classrooms. Students are aware of the support given by their teachers to students with exceptionalities, and they have a tendency to model these attitudes and behaviours. As a result, teachers "need to examine their own attitudes and behaviours as they relate to interactions with students and the acceptance of individual differences" (Salend, 1999, p. 10). If they are not supportive of the inclusion of these students, other students will detect this attitude and be less likely to accept the students (Salend, 1999).

Teachers also have to expect students with special needs to perform at a high level. Students often achieve at a level expected of them; if teachers expect less, they get less. A great deal of research has shown that teachers actually treat students whom they consider underachievers differently than they treat other students (Jones & Jones, 2001).

Teachers also need to have the skills necessary to meet the instructional needs of students with special needs (Mastropieri & Scruggs, 2001). Teaching all students the same way will not be effective for many students.

Teachers also must prepare students to interact with others whose physical characteristics, behaviours, or learning-related needs require special consideration. (Specific techniques for doing this will be presented later in the chapter.) Sometimes students need to be educated about diversity and disabilities to reduce the fear of differences. While teachers can serve as excellent role models for acceptance of diversity, they can also facilitate interactions and acceptance by orchestrating situations where students with and without exceptionalities interact.

When determining if the school promotes a sense of community and social acceptance, school personnel can ask the following questions (Voltz et al., 2001):

▶ Are students with exceptionalities disproportionately teased by other students?
▶ Do students with exceptionalities seem to enjoy being in the general education classroom?
▶ Do typically achieving students voluntarily include students with exceptionalities in various activities?
▶ Do typically achieving students seem to value the ideas and opinions of students with exceptionalities? Do students with exceptionalities seem to value the ideas and opinions of typically achieving students?
▶ Do students with exceptionalities consider the general education classroom to be their "real class"? Do they consider the general education teacher to be one of their "real teachers"? (p. 25)

In addition to teachers, students also play a critical role in the success of inclusion. Both students with exceptionalities and typically achieving students need to understand and accept diversity. Attitudes begin to develop in young children (Favazza et al., 2000); therefore, it is critical that teachers of young children create a positive, accepting attitude and model acceptance to their young students.

Students must also achieve a level of interaction that leads to classroom communities where peer understanding and support are the norm. "The more consistently students receive the message that school is a place where everyone belongs and is cared for, will get needed support, and has something to contribute, the more likely it is that classroom programs will be effective" (Korinek et al., 1999, p. 5). Though 100 percent success cannot be guaranteed in making inclusion work in every classroom, well-prepared students and capable, optimistic, caring teachers can set the stage for a positive educational experience for each person in the class.

While students may develop friendships and a classroom community naturally, teachers can do some things to facilitate the process. Friendship facilitation should be an integral part of both special education and general education teachers' roles in inclusive settings (Turnbull, Pereira, & Blue-Banning, 2000). Facilitation can occur through organized group activities, pairing students for various tasks, seating arrangements, buddy systems, and other methods.

CONSIDER THIS

How likely is it that students with special needs will be successfully included if teachers leave peer acceptance of these students to chance? Why?

TEACHING TIP

When preparing a class for the inclusion of students with special needs, use a variety of techniques. Do not rely on only one method, such as a discussion or the showing of one film (e.g., use simulations, guest speakers, etc.).

Appreciation of Student Diversity

School personnel involved in the education of students with exceptionalities must have a positive attitude about serving this group of students. If teachers feel that they are being asked to do things that are unnecessary, the entire classroom climate may be affected. Teachers set the example for students in their classrooms by either accepting and supporting students with exceptionalities or rejecting them. Therefore, the philosophy of educators regarding special education is critical to the success of these students.

All educational personnel need to be able to articulate their philosophy of education in general, as well as the way in which it relates to children with special needs. A philosophy should include the purposes of general education, the purposes of special education, characteristics of educational programs that meet the needs of all children, and a personal vision translated into practical applications (Bates, 2000). In order to incorporate these ideas into a philosophy of education, Bates (2000) suggests teachers answer the following questions:

1. Who am I?
2. What do I value?
3. How do I define myself as an educator?
4. What is my vision of education?
5. How does education serve individuals and society?
6. How might my vision of education be implemented?

These questions can be answered as they relate to education in general and to serving children with special needs in particular.

In addition to having a personal philosophy of education that forms the basis for meeting the needs of all children, including those with special needs, educators must be aware of the code of ethics that is used to govern meeting the needs of students with special needs. The Council for Exceptional Children (CEC), the primary professional group of special education personnel, has a code of ethics that could be adopted by all educators serving this group of students. All educators should adhere to professional ethics in meeting the needs of the diverse group of students in our schools.

FURTHER READING

Visit the CEC website to review the Code of Ethics for Educators of Persons with Exceptionalities: **www.cec.sped.org/ps/code.html**.

FURTHER READING

For more information on the different types of diversity found in classrooms, read S. E. Schwartz and B. D. Karge's book, *Human Diversity: A Guide for Understanding* (2nd ed.), published by McGraw-Hill in 1996.

In order to maximize learning, a teacher needs to understand each individual in the classroom as well as possible. The increasing diversity of today's classrooms makes teaching a very complex activity that will likely only get more complex in the future as our culture becomes more diverse (Maheady, Harper, & Mallette, 2001). In addition to recognizing and responding to each student's educational needs, teachers must be sensitive to the cultural, community, and family values that can have an impact on a student's educational experience. For instance, the nature of teacher–student interactions may be affected directly by certain cultural factors, or the type of home–school contact will be dictated by how the family wants to interact with the school.

Different types of diversity exist within classroom settings. It is important to recognize and celebrate each one. Schwartz and Karge (1996) have identified the following types of differences: racial and ethnic diversity; gender and sexual orientation; religious diversity; physical, learning, and intellectual differences; linguistic differences; and behaviour and personality diversity. Although the following chapters focus on areas of exceptionality, and to a lesser extent cultural diversity, teachers should consider the much broader range of individual variance.

Diversity is enriching. All students can flourish in an atmosphere in which diversity is recognized, opportunities exist to better understand its various forms, and differences are appreciated. Clearly, a classroom setting that champions differences provides a welcoming environment for students whose learning, physical, emotional, and social needs vary from those of their classmates. All students benefit from being in an inclusive classroom (Voltz et al., 2001). Students learn tolerance and the ability to accept differences in each other, as well as having opportunities to benefit from co-operative learning and other alternative instructional strategies.

Attention to Curricular Needs

Many discussions of inclusion lose track of an important consideration: what the student needs to learn. Teachers must seriously look at the curriculum and ask what students are learning and how students with exceptionalities can access the curriculum (Pugach & Warger, 2001). If the individual curricular needs of a student are not being met, the curriculum must be adapted or the educational placement must be re-examined. Not meeting the curricular needs of students will definitely make it difficult for the student to learn, but it will also likely lead to behaviour problems (Jones & Jones, 2001). A student's learning and life needs should always be the driving force in programmatic efforts and decisions (Smith & Hilton, 1994). Good teachers vary their curricula to meet the needs of the students (Walther-Thomas, Korinek, McLaughlin, & Williams, 2000). While some students with exceptionalities included in general classrooms may be able to deal effectively with the curricula, many need substantial modifications (Van Laarhoven, Coutinho, Van Laarhoven-Myers, & Repp, 1999). Fortunately, most curricular needs can usually be addressed within the context of the general educational classroom.

Curricular concerns include two issues: (1) content that is meaningful to students in a current and future sense, and (2) approaches and materials that work best for them. Dealing with the first issue helps ensure that what students need to learn (i.e., knowledge and skills acquisition) is provided within the inclusive setting. The second issue involves choosing how to teach relevant content. Scruggs and Mastropieri (1994) found that the provision of appropriate curriculum appeared to be meaningfully associated with success in general education classes. Teachers can modify the academic level of the content and focus more on functional objectives, reduce the content to a manageable amount, and change how students are asked to demonstrate mastery of the content.

Effective Management and Instruction

Another essential component of successful inclusive settings is the effective management of the classroom and effective instruction provided by the teacher to meet the wide range of needs of students (Voltz et al., 2001). These practices include four elements: (1) successful classroom management, (2) effective instructional techniques, (3) appropriate adaptive and/or accommodative practices, and (4) instructional flexibility. Successful inclusion is improbable without effective practices in these areas.

Successful Classroom Management   Classrooms that encourage learning are characterized by sound organizational and management systems. Classroom management—including physical, procedural, instructional, and behaviour management—sets the stage for the smooth delivery of instruction. Effective classroom management is required if students are to benefit from any form of instruction, especially in inclusive classrooms where students display a wide range of diversity (Jones & Jones, 2001). Learning will not be optimal for any student without effective classroom organization and management. (Refer to Chapter 12 for more information on classroom management.)

Effective Instructional Techniques   Teachers must feel comfortable using a wide variety of instructional techniques to meet the diverse needs of individuals in their classrooms (Voltz et al., 2001). An impressive body of literature validates the effectiveness of certain instructional practices (Brody & Good, 1986; Rosenshine & Stevens, 1986). Obviously, when instructional techniques are ineffective, successful inclusion will not occur. Students with exceptionalities, especially those eligible for special education services, by definition, have learning problems. As a result, effective instructional techniques must be used for these students to be successful. Mastropieri and Scruggs (1993) have summarized key elements of effective instructional practice: daily review, specific techniques for presenting new information, guided practice, independent practice, and formative evaluation. These concepts are addressed throughout the chapters of this book as they apply to children with various special needs. Chapters 13 and 14 specifically address instructional concerns in elementary and secondary classes, respectively.

Appropriate Adaptive and/or Accommodative Practices   Some students will require special adaptations to the physical environment, the curriculum, the way instruction is provided, or the assignments given to them. Scruggs and Mastropieri (1994) note that instructional supports are a key variable in classrooms where inclusion is successful. Chapters 3 to 11 provide examples of disability-specific adaptations and/or accommodations that might be needed.

  The concept of supports within classrooms, a particularly critical one, refashions inclusion as "**supported education**" (Snell & Drake, 1994). Supports include adaptations, accommodations, and modifications to enhance learning and acceptance in the general education curriculum. As previously outlined, adaptations consist of changes in the manner in which students are taught. They include changes in instruction, assignments and homework, and testing. Accommodations refer to the specialized support and services provided to students to meet their educational needs. Modifications, on the other hand, generally refer to changes in policies that may affect students with exceptionalities. One example is altering the school curriculum or attendance policy. Whenever possible, adaptive and/or accommodative supports should be designed so that they benefit not only students with special needs, but other students in the class as well (Stainback, Stainback, & Wehman, 1997). The idea has merit for three primary reasons. First, it

CONSIDER THIS

If examples of good inclusive classrooms are unavailable in a school board/district, how can teachers find such examples to observe?

CROSS-REFERENCE

For more information on appropriate classroom management techniques for inclusive settings, see Chapter 12.

CONSIDER THIS

How can appropriate adaptive and/or accommodative practices benefit all students, including those with special needs?

provides support to other students who will find the adaptations helpful. Second, this approach can minimize overt attention to the fact that a certain student needs special adaptations. Third, it enhances the likelihood that teachers will see the specific strategy as feasible, desirable, and helpful. The issue of equality or "fairness" often arises when teachers are considering the implementation of adaptations and/or accommodations for students with exceptionalities. It is important to remember that equity refers to an individual receiving what he or she needs to succeed, and equality refers to everyone receiving the same thing (Lavoie, 1989). Teachers making adaptations and/or accommodations for students with exceptionalities is an equity issue, and therefore teachers should not feel guilty about giving students what they need to succeed.

One support that can have a significant impact on the success of inclusion efforts is the use of **assistive technology**. Ranging from low-tech (e.g., optical devices) to high-tech (e.g., computer-based augmentative communication systems) applications, assistive technology can allow students with specific exceptionalities to participate fully, or even partially, in ongoing classroom activities. Moreover, as Woronov (1996) acknowledges, typically achieving students can benefit from assistive technology as well. The nearby Technology Today feature presents internet resources that can support inclusion.

Instructional Flexibility The ability to respond to unexpected and changing situations to support students with special needs is a key characteristic of responsible inclusive settings. As Schaffner and Buswell (1996) note, classroom teachers need to develop the capabilities that families have acquired to react successfully and spontaneously to challenges that arise on a day-to-day basis. Teachers must be flexible; they must be able to handle behaviour problems, provide extra support during instruction, modify assessment techniques, and orchestrate social interactions (Jones & Jones, 2001).

Personnel Support and Collaboration

Students with special needs will require personnel supports to allow them to benefit from placement in inclusive settings, in addition to the instructional supports noted earlier (adaptive practices and assistive technology). Special education teachers, **paraeducators**

Web Resources on Inclusion and Disability

Inclusion	Disability Resources	
http://education.umn.edu/ICI.html	www.iser.com	www.ldonline.org
http://interwork.sdsu.edu	www.ed.gov/about/offices/list/osers/osep/index.html	www.downsyndrome.com
www.nyise.org/college.htm	www.tash.org	www.iltech.org
www.ldonline.org	www.schwablearning.org	www.hsdc.org
	www.mnsu.edu/comdis/depthp/links.html	www.ncld.org

From *Quick Guide to the Internet for Special Education 2000 Edition* (p. 13) by M. Male and D. Gotthoffer, 2000, Boston: Allyn and Bacon.

(teacher aides), and other related service professionals, such as speech-language pathologists, occupational and physical therapists, psychologists, counsellors, and audiologists, are typically involved in providing supports to students with exceptionalities. They also assist general education teachers in inclusive settings through a variety of collaborative models, including collaboration-consultation, peer support systems, teacher assistance teams, and co-teaching. Table 2.1 summarizes these approaches. Equally important is administrative support for inclusion, as reflected by attitudes, policies, and practices at the district and individual school level (Podemski et al., 1995; Mastropieri & Scruggs, 2001).

The use of teams to provide services to students with exceptionalities, especially students included in general education classrooms, has grown significantly over the past several years. A primary reason for this growth is the realization that it takes a creative use of human resources to effectively implement an inclusion teaching model. As one study found, "Working as a team enables teachers to plan more effectively, to problem-solve more efficiently, and to intervene with a student throughout the school day" (Allsop, Santos, & Linn, 2000, p. 142).

The use of teacher aides to provide direct support to students with significant learning problems is occurring more commonly (Giangreco et al., 2001). If their knowledge of working with students with exceptionalities is minimal, these paraeducators must be trained and supervised carefully if they are to provide critical assistance to students in inclusive classrooms. The practice could have great potential as long as proper safeguards ensure that paraeducators implement support services effectively. However, it is important to note when working with a teacher aide that it is the classroom teacher who remains primarily responsible for a student's educational program.

Establishing a **circle of friends** for students can assist the development of a peer support network. Such a network is particularly important for students who are different and new to a classroom situation. As Pearpoint, Forest, and O'Brien (1996) assert:

> In the absence of a natural circle of friends, educators can facilitate a circle process, which can be used to enlist the involvement and commitment of peers around an individual student. For a student who is not well connected or does not have an extensive network of friends, a circle of friends process can be useful. (p. 74)

FURTHER READING

For more information on critical variables that must be in place for co-operative teams to be successful, refer to the article "Process Variables Critical for Team Effectiveness," by J. L. Fleming and L. E. Monda-Amaya, in volume 22 of *Remedial and Special Education*, 2001 (pp. 158–171).

CONSIDER THIS

How could the use of paraeducators or teacher aides be a detriment to the successful inclusion of students with special needs in a general education classroom?

TEACHING TIP

Plan to orchestrate opportunities for students with exceptionalities to act as full members of the classroom. Use methods such as peer support systems.

TABLE 2.1	Types of Collaborative Efforts	
Approach	Nature of Contact with Student	Description
Collaboration–Consultation	Indirect	General education teacher requests the services of the special education teacher (i.e., consultant) to help generate ideas for addressing an ongoing situation. The approach is interactive.
Peer Support Systems	Indirect	Two general education teachers work together to identify effective solutions to classroom situations. The approach emphasizes the balance of the relationship.
Teacher Assistance Teams	Indirect	Teams provide support to general education teachers. Made up of core members plus the teacher seeking assistance, it emphasizes analyzing the problem situation and developing potential solutions.
Co-Teaching	Direct	General and special education teachers work together in providing direct service to students. Employing joint planning and teaching, the approach emphasizes the joint responsibilities of instruction.

From *Cooperative Teaching: Rebuilding the Schoolhouse for All Students* (p. 74), by J. Bauwens and J. J. Hourcade, 1995, Austin, TX: Pro-Ed. Used by permission.

The use of a circle of friends is further discussed in Chapter 7.

The five critical dimensions we have discussed—(1) a sense of community and social acceptance, (2) an appreciation of student diversity, (3) attention to curricular needs, (4) effective management and instruction, and (5) personnel support and collaboration—are essential to making inclusive settings effective. Appropriate programming for students with exceptionalities should always be based on an "individual student's needs as determined by an interdisciplinary team and represented by the student's IEP" (Smith & Hilton, 1994, p. 8). Just as important, however, is the need to evaluate those instructional settings on the basis of the five critical dimensions. Successful inclusion hinges on them.

Maintaining Effective Inclusive Classrooms

Setting up a responsible inclusive classroom does not guarantee that it will remain effective over time. Constant vigilance concerning the critical dimensions of inclusive settings and ongoing re-evaluation of standard operating procedures can ensure continued success. Blenk (1995) describes an effective process of ongoing evaluation:

> On a daily basis, teaching colleagues should be observing inclusive procedures and educational techniques. These observations need to be shared among the teacher group to decide whether the practice achieved its intended outcomes, and if not, what changes could occur. Individual staff conferences and meetings, even if they are only two minutes long, need to happen on an ongoing basis to maintain communication in the teaching staff and to share experiences and impressions, sometimes at that moment! (p. 71)

A related method of dealing with ongoing issues is the use of problem-solving sessions (Roach, 1995). This strategy involves teachers meeting and working together to find ways to handle specific inclusion-related situations that have become problematic. In addition to identifying resources that might be helpful, the teachers also generate new strategies to try out. For problem solving to be useful, teachers must have sufficient time to meet and implement the proposed solution. Support from administrators can be very helpful in this area. Principals who are supportive of inclusion and team problem solving often find ways to alter schedules in a way that allows more teaming opportunities.

Final Thought

The concept of inclusion and its practical applications will keep evolving as just one of the changing dynamics in the schools today. According to Ferguson (1995), "The new challenge of inclusion is to create schools in which our day-to-day efforts no longer assume that a particular text, activity, or teaching mode will 'work' to support any particular student's learning" (p. 287). The inclusive classroom contains many students with diverse needs; therefore, teachers must be equipped to address an array of challenges. In order to do so effectively, teachers need to create classroom communities that embrace diversity and that are responsive to individual needs. This includes teachers actively collaborating with professionals (colleagues, support personnel), and engaging in continuing education opportunities to expand their knowledge base in the area of special education.

Personal Spotlight

Classroom Teacher Florence Eastwood

Florence Eastwood has been a classroom teacher in Manitoba for 28 years, during which time she has taught Grades 1 to 6. For the last 18 years she has worked half-time and has job shared a regular classroom with a variety of teaching partners. Over the course of her career, Florence has worked with hundreds of students, many of whom demonstrated exceptional learning needs.

Florence has a bachelor of arts, a bachelor of education, and a post-baccalaureate degree. She feels that beginning teachers are often not well enough equipped for the demands of inclusion. New teachers benefit from mentors who can support and advise them as they encounter the challenges that exceptional students bring to the classroom.

In Florence's school, support for students with exceptionalities is provided through teamwork. Regular meetings between a student's classroom teacher, the resource teacher, and paraprofessional support staff keep everyone on track. Frequent consultation with other team members, including parents, administrators, and division support staff, keeps everyone on the same page and working toward the same goals.

Florence believes that a high level of support for students and teachers is the key to successful inclusion. Sufficient support at the primary (K–3) level is especially important. It is often during this time that exceptional learning needs are being identified and exceptionalities are being diagnosed. Given the importance of early intervention, it is crucial that support be provided during this critical time and not be dependent on diagnoses that may not come until later.

The wise use of human resources is of great importance to student success. We must guard our paraprofessional support to maximize support for student learning. Florence believes that teaching *all* of the kids who come into our classroom is our job. She believes that we need to do all that we can to meet their learning needs so that they can achieve success and thrive at school.

Summary

- Although current services for students with exceptionalities focus on inclusion, a range of services still exists in most Canadian schools.
- Key service delivery models are the self-contained classroom, the resource room, and the inclusive classroom.
- There are advantages and disadvantages for each model of service delivery.
- In the self-contained model, special education teachers were trained to teach specific types of students, primarily based on clinical labels.
- Classroom teachers had a very limited role in special education in the self-contained classroom model.
- The role of the regular classroom teacher increases as you move from the self-contained to an inclusive model.
- Inclusion of students with special needs in general education classes has received more attention on a philosophical level than on a practical level.
- Five essential features must be in place to ensure maximum success of inclusion: a sense of community and social acceptance, appreciation of student diversity, attention to curricular needs, effective management and instruction of students, and access to adequate personnel supports.
- The concept of inclusion affirms that students with special needs can be active, valued, and fully participating members of the school community.
- Students with special needs will be truly included in their classrooms only when they are appreciated by their teachers and socially accepted by their classmates.
- Teachers play a critical role in the success of inclusion.
- The curricular needs of students cannot be lost in the philosophical and political debate on inclusion.
- Effective classroom management is an important component in a successful inclusive classroom.
- Adaptive and/or accommodative practices that are good for students with special needs are usually good for all students.

❱ Appropriately trained personnel, in adequate numbers, form a major factor in successful inclusion programs.

❱ Both staff and students must be prepared for inclusion.

❱ Once inclusion is initiated, it is important to monitor how well its five essential features are working together to ensure ongoing success.

 esources

Pierangelo, Roger. (1998). *Special educator's complete guide to 109 diagnostic tests.* Englewood, NJ: Centre for Applied Research in Education.

The author provides information on how to review evaluation measures, interpret test scores, incorporate results in individualized education programs, and remediate specific disabilities.

Bauer, A. M., & Shea, T. M. (1999). *Inclusion 101: How to teach all learners.* Baltimore, MD: Paul H. Brookes Publishing.

Here is a practical hands-on guide that gives teachers the skills to meet the needs of students in the inclusive classroom. Recommended by the Council for Exceptional Children.

Weblinks

Alberta Education, Learning Resources Distributing Centre
www.lrc.education.gov.ab.ca/pro/default.html
For more resources on inclusion strategies for students with exceptionalities, visit the Centre's site. All of the resources have been reviewed and approved by Alberta's ministry of education.

Alberta Education, Special Education Branch
http://ednet.edc.gov.ab.ca/
Visit this website to gain more information on resources (videos, books, resource guides, and handbooks) on all aspects of students with special needs.

Renaissance Group
www.uni.edu/coe/inclusion/
For an excellent list of teacher strategies, needed teacher competencies, and ways to prepare for inclusion as well

as resources, visit the Inclusive Education website produced by the Renaissance Group, a consortium of universities noted for their teacher preparation in inclusive education.

Circle of Inclusion
http://circleofinclusion.org/
For information on inclusion in early childhood (birth through age eight), visit the Circle of Inclusion website, a co-operative venture between some U.S. in-service training services, the University of Kansas Department of Special Education, and other associations. The site is funded by the U.S. Department of Education, Office of Special Education. It provides strategies and staffing models, allows you to meet people who are involved in inclusive programs online, enables you to visit inclusive programs online, shares print materials and articles important for inclusive settings, and suggests other helpful links.

Teaching Students with Communication Disorders 3

With Contributions from Kathleen Fad

Chapter Objectives

After reading this chapter, you should be able to

- define the concept of communication and describe its major components, language and speech
- discuss communication disorders, including the different types of disorders and some of their characteristics
- describe various classroom adaptations and/or accommodations appropriate for students with speech and language disorders
- describe typical language development in children
- discuss language differences that are due to culture and examine ways that teachers can deal with these differences

eclan, an active five-year-old, is the youngest of three children. When Declan started kindergarten, his parents reported to his teacher Ms. Dunne that he had some problems saying all of his sounds correctly in words, and that he used shorter sentences when speaking than either of his older brothers had at his age. However, they were not concerned because they had been told by their family doctor that Declan would "grow out" of these difficulties. As the school year has progressed, Ms. Dunne has not noticed any change in Declan's use of sounds, and he seems to also have difficulty following multi-step directions, initiating and maintaining interactions with his peers during free play activities, and learning new vocabulary words that are introduced during class activities. Ms. Dunne wants to refer Declan for a speech and language evaluation with the speech-language pathologist who provides services to the school. However, Declan's parents are reluctant to consent to the referral since they are sure he will "grow out" of these difficulties.

Questions to Consider

1. Do children typically "grow out" of their speech and/or language difficulties?

2. How can Ms. Dunne revisit the subject of making a speech and language referral with Declan's parents?

3. Why would early intervention be important for a child like Declan? How might his speech and language difficulties impact his learning in the classroom?

Introduction

For most of us, the ability to communicate is a skill we take for granted. Our communication is effortless and frequent. In one day, we might share a story with family members, discuss problems with our co-workers, ask directions from a stranger on the street, and telephone an old friend. When we are able to communicate easily and effectively, it is natural to participate in both the commonplace activities of daily living and the more enjoyable experiences that enrich our lives.

However, when communication is impaired, absent, or qualitatively different, the simplest interactions may become difficult or even impossible. Moreover, because the communication skills that most of us use so fluently and easily almost always involve personal interactions with others, disorders in speech or language may also result in social problems. For children, these social problems are most likely to occur in school. School is a place not only for academic learning, but also for building positive relationships with teachers and enduring friendships with peers. When a student's communication disorder, however mild, limits these experiences, makes him or her feel different and inadequate, or undermines confidence and self-esteem, the overall impact can be devastating.

Communication problems are often complex. There are many types of communication disorders, related to both speech and language. This chapter describes strategies that teachers can use with students who have such disorders. Suggestions will address specific communication disorders as well as associated problems in socialization and adjustment.

Basic Concepts about Communication Disorders

CONSIDER THIS

How would your life be different if you could not talk, or if you could not write, or if you could not hear?

Communication and Communication Disorders Defined

Speech and **language** are interrelated skills, tools that we use for communication. Heward (2003) defines the related terms this way:

> *Communication* is the interactive exchange of information, ideas, feelings, needs, and desires. It involves encoding, transmitting, and decoding messages. Each communication interaction includes three elements: (1) a message, (2) a sender who expresses the message, and (3) a receiver who responds to the message.... *Language* is a formalized code used by a group of people to communicate with one another. All languages consist of a set of abstract symbols—sounds, letters, numbers, elements of sign language—and a system of rules for combining those symbols into larger units... *Speech* is the oral production of language. Although it is not the only possible vehicle for expressing language (e.g., gestures, manual signing, pictures, and written symbols can also be used), speech is the fastest, most efficient method of communication by language.... Speech is also one of the most complex and difficult human endeavors. (pp. 326–328)

Various cultures develop and use language differently, and the study of language is a complex topic. The **American Speech-Language-Hearing Association (ASHA)** (1982) includes the following important considerations in its discussion of language: (1) language evolves within specific historical, social, and cultural contexts; (2) language is rule-governed behaviour; (3) language learning and use are determined by the interaction of biological, cognitive, psychosocial, and environmental factors; and (4) effective use of language for communication requires a broad understanding of human interactions, including associated factors such as nonverbal cues, motivation, and sociocultural roles (p. 949).

Language development and use are very complicated topics; therefore, determining what is *normal* and what is *disordered* communication is also difficult. According to Haynes and Pindzola (1998), a communication difference is considered a disability in any of the following situations:

▶ The transmission and/or perception of messages is faulty.
▶ The person is placed at an economic disadvantage.
▶ The person is placed at a learning disadvantage.
▶ The person is placed at a social disadvantage.
▶ There is a negative impact upon the emotional growth of the person.
▶ The problem causes physical damage or endangers the health of the person. (p. 6)

In order to better understand communication disorders, it is helpful to be familiar with the dimensions of language and the terms used to describe related disorders.

Types of Communication Disorders

In its definition of communicative disorders, ASHA (1993) describes both speech disorders and language disorders. **Speech disorders** include impairments of *voice, articulation,* and *fluency.* **Language disorders** are impairments of *comprehension* or *use of language,* regardless of the symbol system used. A language disorder may involve the *form* of language, the *content* of language, or the *function* of language. Specific disorders of language form include **phonologic**, syntactic, and **morphologic impairments**. **Semantics** refers to the content of language, and **pragmatics** is the system controlling language function. Figure 3.1 contains the definitions of communication disorders as described by ASHA. The terms in this figure will be discussed in more detail later in the chapter. The category of communication disorders is broad in scope and includes a wide variety of problems, some of which may overlap. It is not surprising that this group of disorders includes a large proportion of all students with disabilities.

Prevalence and Causes of Communication Disorders

After learning disabilities, speech and language impairments are the most common disability seen in the schools. It is estimated that 8 to 10 percent of school-age children have some type of speech or language impairment (Winzer, 1999). These students have impairments in their ability to send or receive a message, to articulate clearly or fluently, or to comprehend the pragmatics of social interactions. The majority of them also have other disabilities, such as learning disabilities, autism, or traumatic brain injury, so they are served under a variety of categories. In Canada, students with communication disorders constitute about 17 percent of all students with disabilities (Nessner, 1990). Almost all students with speech or language impairments are 6 to 12 years of age (Winzer, 1999). For this reason, most of the suggestions in this chapter focus on that age group, although many of the language development activities would also be useful for older students.

Identification and Assessment

Students with speech or language impairments receive services under a variety of categories depending on the appropriate provincial or territorial guidelines. The categories used in the Yukon, Saskatchewan, and Alberta indicate the range. In the Yukon, learning disabilities and speech and language impairments are combined under the heading of "communication exceptionality" (Yukon Education, Special Programs Services, 1995). In

---

CONSIDER THIS

Can you think of instances in which you have been involved wherein communication between two or more persons was so poor that problems resulted?

CROSS-REFERENCE

See Chapter 4 on learning disabilities, and consider the integral link between language disorders and learning disabilities. Also see Table 3.4: Linguistic, Social, Emotional, and Academic Problems Related to Language Disorders, presented later in this chapter.

TEACHING TIP

If a student in your class is experiencing speech and/or language difficulties, refer the student to your school's speech-language pathologist for an evaluation **as soon as possible**.

CONSIDER THIS

What are the advantages of serving most of the students with communication disorders in general education classrooms? When would pullout services be appropriate?

COMMUNICATION DISORDERS

A. A *speech disorder* is an impairment of the articulation of speech sounds, fluency and/or voice.

1. An articulation disorder is the atypical production of speech sounds characterized by substitutions, omissions, additions or distortions that may interfere with intelligibility.

2. A fluency disorder is an interruption in the flow of speaking characterized by atypical rate, rhythm, and repetitions in sounds, syllables, words, and phrases. This may be accompanied by excessive tension, struggle behaviour, and secondary mannerisms.

3. A voice disorder is characterized by the abnormal production and/or absences of vocal quality, pitch, loudness, resonance, and/or duration, which is inappropriate for an individual's age and sex.

B. A *language disorder* is impaired comprehension and/or use of a spoken, written, and/or other symbol systems. The disorder may involve (1) the form of language (phonology, morphology, and syntax), (2) the content of language (semantics), and/or (3) the function of language in communication (pragmatics) in any combination.

1. Form of Language
   a. *Phonology* is the sound system of a language and the rules that govern the sound combinations.
   b. *Morphology* is the system that governs the structure of words and the construction of word forms.
   c. *Syntax* is the system governing the order and combination of words to form sentences, and the relationships among the elements within a sentence.

2. Content of language
   a. *Semantics* is the system that governs the meanings of words and sentences.

3. Function of Language
   a. *Pragmatics* is the system that combines the above language components in functionally and socially appropriate communication.

C. A *hearing disorder* is the result of impaired auditory sensitivity of the physiological auditory system. A hearing disorder may limit the development, comprehension, production, and/or maintenance of speech and/or language. Hearing disorders are classified according to difficulties in detection, recognition, discrimination, comprehension, and perception of auditory information. Individuals with hearing impairment may be described as deaf or hard of hearing.

1. *Deaf* is defined as a hearing disorder that limits an individual's aural/oral communication performance to the extent that the primary sensory input for communication may be other than the auditory channel.

2. *Hard of Hearing* is defined as a hearing disorder, whether fluctuating or permanent, which adversely affects an individual's ability to communicate. The hard-of-hearing individual relies on the auditory channel as the primary sensory input for communication.

D. *Central auditory processing disorders* are deficits in the information processing of audible signals not attributed to impaired peripheral hearing sensitivity or intellectual impairment. This information processing involves perceptual, cognitive, and linguistic functions that, with appropriate interaction, result in effective receptive communication of auditorily presented stimuli. Specifically, CAPD refers to limitations in the ongoing transmission, analysis, organization, transformation, elaboration, storage, retrieval, and use of information contained in audible signals. CAPD may involve the listener's active and passive (e.g., conscious and unconscious, mediated and unmediated, controlled and automatic) ability to do the following:

- attend, discriminate, and identify acoustic signals;
- transform and continuously transmit information through both the peripheral and central nervous systems;
- filter, sort, and combine information at appropriate perceptual and conceptual levels;
- store and retrieve information efficiently; restore, organize, and use retrieved information;
- segment and decode acoustic stimuli using phonological, semantic, syntactic, and pragmatic knowledge; and attach meaning to a stream of acoustic signals through use of linguistic and nonlinguistic contexts.

COMMUNICATION VARIATIONS

A. Communicative difference/dialect is a variation of a symbol system used by a group of individuals that reflects and is determined by shared regional, social, or cultural/ethnic factors. A regional, social, or cultural/ethnic variation of a symbol system should not be considered a disorder of speech or language.

B. *Augmentative/alternative communication* systems attempt to compensate and facilitate, temporarily or permanently, for the impairment and disability patterns of individuals with severe expressive and/or language comprehension disorders. Augmentative/alternative communication may be required for individuals demonstrating impairments in gestural, spoken, and/or written modalities.

FIGURE 3.1

Definitions of Communication Disorders from ASHA

From "Definitions of Communication Disorders and Variations," by the American Speech-Language-Hearing Association Ad Hoc Committee on Service Delivery in Schools, 1993, *ASHA, 35 (Suppl. 10),* pp. 40–41. Reprinted by permission of the American Speech-Language-Hearing Association.

CROSS-REFERENCE

Refer to Chapter 8 for more information on auditory processing disorders, also termed central auditory processing disorders.

Saskatchewan, school divisions receive diversity funding on a per student basis based on their total enrolment. School divisions are expected to use this funding to support diverse student needs including speech and language (Saskatchewan Learning Special Education Funding, 2003). And in Alberta, a specific communication exceptionality category specifies the severity of a student's communication disorder (Alberta Learning, 2004). Regardless of the category, the focus across the country remains on providing services to these children in the regular classroom wherever possible. The traditional model of pull-out services for speech therapy occurs only in cases where intensive specific intervention is required.

Speech Disorders

This section of the chapter discusses speech disorders that include problems in *articulation, voice,* and *fluency.* The discussion includes (1) a description and definition, (2) a brief explanation of causes, and (3) information related to identifying problems serious enough to require a referral for possible assessment or remediation. Next, suggestions for classroom teachers will be presented.

Articulation, Phonological, and Motor Speech Disorders

On their website, the Canadian Association of Speech-Language Pathologists and Audiologists (CASLPA) differentiates between the speech sound disorders of articulation, phonology, and motor speech. Articulation disorders are described to "occur when a person cannot correctly pronounce one or more sounds" (CASLPA, May 2004). For example, an individual who only has difficulty pronouncing the *r* sound at the beginning of words may be described as having an articulation disorder. Phonological disorders involve more than the inability to correctly pronounce one or more sounds. Phonological disorders are "errors of many sounds that form patterns" (CASLPA, May 2004). The patterns of sound errors differ in type and severity for each individual, while **motor speech disorders** are "articulation disorders caused as a result of neurological damage such as stroke or head injury" (CASLPA, May 2004). **Articulation** and phonological **disorders** are the most common speech disorders, affecting about 10 percent of preschool and school-age children (ASHA, 2002). The ability to articulate clearly and use the phonological code correctly is a function of many variables, including a student's age, developmental history, oral-motor skills, and culture. Although some articulation and phonological errors are normal and acceptable at young ages, when students are older these same errors may be viewed as developmentally inappropriate and problematic. The most common types of articulation errors include: **distortions**, **substitutions**, **omissions**, and **additions** (McReynolds, 1990; Van Riper & Erickson, 1996). (See Table 3.1.)

CONSIDER THIS

Think of all the young children you have encountered who have had articulation or phonological problems. Have most of the problems improved over time without intervention, or has intervention been required?

Causes of Problems in the Phonological System   Articulation and phonological impairments can be either *organic* (i.e., having an identifiable physical cause) or *functional* (i.e., having no identifiable organic cause). When you encounter a child with articulation or phonological disorders, consider the child's environment. Some functional disorders may be related to the student's opportunities to learn appropriate and inappropriate speech patterns, including opportunities to practise appropriate speech, fluctuating hearing loss due to otitis media during early development, and the absence or presence of good speech models. Some functional articulation and phonological problems have causes that may be related to complex neurological or neuromuscular activities and might never be understood. Differences in speech can also be related to cultural and linguistic factors. These differences often do not constitute a speech disorder and will be discussed later in the chapter.

TABLE 3.1	The Four Kinds of Articulation Errors	
Error Type	Definition	Example
Distortion	A sound is produced in an unfamiliar manner.	Standard: Give the pencil to Sally. Distortion: Give the pencil to Sally. (the /p/ is nasalized)
Substitution	Replace one sound with another sound.	Standard: The ball is red. Substitution: The ball is wed.
Omission	A sound is omitted in a word.	Standard: Play the piano. Omission: P_ay the piano.
Addition	An extra sound is inserted within a word.	Standard: I have a black horse. Addition: I have a balack horse.

Reprinted with the permission of Macmillan Publishing Company from *Human Communication Disorders, Third Edition*, by George H. Shames and Elisabeth H. Wiig. Copyright © 1990 by Macmillan Publishing Company.

Organic articulation and phonological disorders are related to the neurological and physical abilities required in the process of producing speech sounds, which is a highly complex activity involving intricate, precise, and rapid co-ordination of neurological and muscular interactions. According to the American Psychiatric Association (2000), organic causes of speech impairments may include hearing loss, cleft palate, dental malformations, or tumours. Brain damage and related neurological problems may also result in motor speech disorders such as verbal apraxia and dysarthria. The severity of articulation and phonological disorders can vary widely, depending in part on the causes of the disorders.

CROSS-REFERENCE

Refer to Chapter 8 for a detailed definition of otitis media, and to learn more about the impact of otitis media on speech and language development.

When Articulation and Phonological Errors Are a Serious Problem We know the developmental patterns for normal sound production, and therefore can recognize those children who are significantly different from the norm. According to Sander (1972), the normal pattern of consonant sound production falls within relatively well-defined age limits. For example, children usually master the consonant *p* sound by age three, but may not produce a correct *s* sound consistently until age eight. Although young children between ages two and six often make articulation or phonological errors as their speech develops, similar errors in older students would indicate a problem. At age three it might be normal for a child to say *wabbit* instead of *rabbit*. If a 12-year-old made the same error, it would be considered a problem, and the teacher should refer the student to a **speech-language pathologist** for an evaluation. Figure 3.2 presents this pattern of normal development.

For a general education teacher, evaluating a student's articulation or phonological errors requires looking at the big picture—that is, how well the student is doing in class and whether the articulation or phonological disorder is interfering with either overall academic performance or social adjustment. A few common-sense considerations may give some insight into whether the student has a serious problem and what, if anything, should be done about it:

CONSIDER THIS

How could cultural differences have an impact on a child's development of the specific sounds listed in Figure 3.2?

▶ *Take note of how understandable the student's speech is*

This factor may vary over time and across individuals. Sometimes, the context of the student's speech will make it easier for listeners to understand her or him. Also, some errors

FIGURE 3.2

Ages at Which 90 Percent of All Children Typically Produce a Specific Sound Correctly

Note: Average estimates and upper age limits of customary consonant production. The solid bar corresponding to each sound starts at the median age of customary articulation; it stops at an age level at which 90 percent of all children are customarily producing the sound. The θ symbol stands for the breathed "th" sound, as in *bathroom,* and the δ symbol stands for the voiced "th" sound, as in feather (Smith and Luckasson, 1992, p. 168).

From "When Are Speech Sounds Learned?" by E. K. Sander, 1972, *Journal of Speech and Hearing Disorders, 37,* p. 62. Reprinted by permission of the American Speech-Language-Hearing Association.

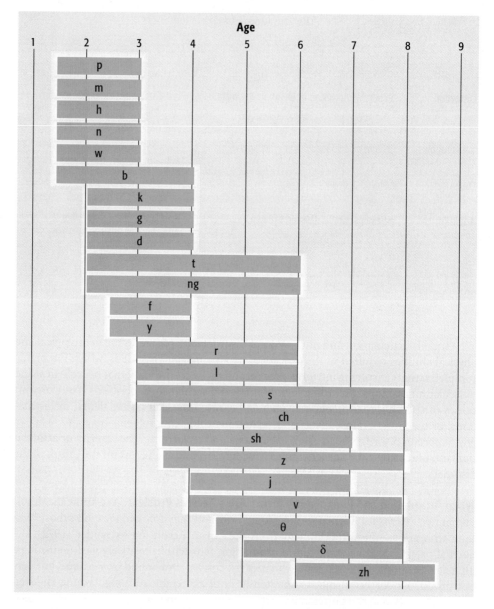

are easier to understand than others. For example, omissions are usually more difficult to understand than distortions or substitutions. Individuals who spend more time around the student, and who are more familiar with his or her patterns of error, will likely find the individual easier to understand. Therefore, it is important to judge how understandable the student's speech would be if you were a stranger to whom he or she was speaking.

▶ *Consider how many different errors the student makes.*

If the errors are consistent—that is, if the student repeats the same error rather than numerous different errors—he or she will be easier to understand. Peers and teachers will become familiar with these speech problems, and the student will have less of a problem relating to others. However, the problem should still be addressed so that the student's speech is understandable to strangers.

▶ *Observe whether the articulation errors cause the student problems in socialization or adjustment.*

If a student with articulation problems is ridiculed, excluded, or singled out because of a speech problem, then the teacher may want to refer the student for a speech-language evaluation. Likewise, if a student is reluctant to speak in class, or seems self-conscious or embarrassed by articulation or phonological errors, the general education teacher should seek an evaluation.

▶ *Consider whether the problems are due to physical problems.*

If they are, be sure that the student is referred to a physician. Some articulation problems are due to malformations of the mouth, jaw, or teeth. When the problems are structural, such as cleft lip or palate, they can often be corrected surgically. Likewise, dental malocclusions (abnormal closures and fit of the teeth) can be corrected with orthodontic treatment.

The early identification and intervention of speech and/or language disorders is extremely important in making effective gains. Do not wait to see if an individual will "grow out" of his or her difficulties. Refer the individual to a certified speech-language pathologist for an evaluation if parents or teachers have any concerns with his or her speech or language skills.

Voice Disorders

Voice disorders are abnormalities of speech related to volume, quality, or pitch. Voice problems are not very common in children, and it is difficult to distinguish an unpleasant voice from one that would be considered disordered. People generally tolerate a wide range of voices. Our voices are related to our identities and are an integral part of who we are and how we are recognized; therefore, we usually allow for individual differences in voice.

According to Heward (2003), there are two basic types of voice disorders: **phonation** and **resonance**. Phonation refers to the production of sounds by the vocal folds. Humans have two vocal folds, which are located in the larynx and lie side by side. When we speak, healthy vocal folds vibrate, coming together smoothly along the length of their surfaces, separating, and then coming together again. These movements are usually very rapid and are controlled by the air pressure coming from the lungs. The rate of vibration controls the pitch of our voices (slow movements result in a low pitch, and a faster rate results in a high pitch). If the vocal folds do not meet and close together smoothly, the voice is likely to sound breathy, hoarse, husky, or strained.

Disorders of resonance involve either too many sounds coming out through the air passages of the nose (hypernasality) or the opposite, too little resonance of the nasal passages (hyponasality). Hypernasality sounds like talking through one's nose or with a "twang," and hyponasality sounds like one has a cold or a stuffy nose. Resonance is related to what happens to air that travels from the vocal folds into the throat, mouth, and nasal cavity; therefore, when there are abnormalities in any of these structures or in the associated musculature, resonance problems can result.

Causes of Voice Disorders   Voice disorders can result from vocal abuse and misuse, trauma to the larynx from accidents or medical procedures, or congenital malformations of the larynx, nodules, or tumours. Disorders caused by abuse or misuse are the most common and most easily prevented voice disorders in school-age children. Sometimes, voice disorders are related to other medical conditions, so that when students evidence a voice disorder, the speech-language pathologist will often refer them to an otolaryngologist (ear, nose, and throat doctor) for an examination. Some examples of

TEACHING TIP

General classroom teachers should screen all students in their classes, especially during the early elementary grades, to determine which students have speech sound problems that might require intervention.

Articulation or phonological problems can result in problems in socialization or adjustment.

organic problems related to voice disorders include congenital anomalies of the larynx, Reye's syndrome, juvenile arthritis, psychiatric problems, Tourette syndrome, physical trauma to the larynx, and cancer. Most of these conditions are relatively rare; therefore, it may be more likely that the student's voice disorder is a functional problem, perhaps resulting from learned speech patterns (Hall, Oyer, & Haas, 2001).

When Voice Disorders Are a Serious Problem Classroom teachers can help prevent voice disorders among their students by modelling and promoting healthy vocal habits in the classroom, on the playground, and at home. A student who has a voice disorder should be observed over the course of several weeks, since many symptoms of voice disorders are similar to other temporary conditions such as colds, seasonal allergies, or minor respiratory infections (Hall, Oyer, & Haas, 2001). One way to get a meaningful measure of the student's speech during this time is to tape-record him or her several times during the observation period. The tape recordings will be helpful to the speech-language pathologist and will provide a basis for comparison. Again, our voices are part of our identity, and, quite often, differences in voice quality, volume, or pitch may be considered to be part of who we are, rather than a problem that requires correction. Teachers might ask themselves the following questions before referring a student for evaluation of a voice disorder:

- Is the student's voice having such an unpleasant effect on others that the student is excluded from activities?
- Is there a possibility that the voice disorder is related to another medical condition?
- Might the voice quality be related to a hearing loss?

Teachers should also monitor the quality of their own voices throughout the school year, since individuals in the teaching profession are more likely to develop voice problems than individuals in any other profession (Fritzell, 1996).

Fluency Disorders

Fluency refers to the pattern of the rate and flow of a person's speech. Normal speech has a rhythm and timing that is regular and steady; however, normal speech patterns also include some interruptions in speech flow. We all sometimes stumble over sounds, repeat syllables or words, mix up speech sounds in words, speak too fast, or fill in pauses with "uh" or "you know." Often dysfluencies of speech are related to stressful or demanding situations. When the interruptions in speech flow are so frequent or pervasive that a speaker cannot be understood, when efforts at speech are so intense that they are uncomfortable, or when they draw undue attention, then the dysfluencies are considered a problem (Hallahan & Kauffman, 1995).

Many young children, especially those between the ages of two and five, demonstrate dysfluencies in the course of normal speech development. Parents and teachers may become concerned about young children's fluency problems, but most of these dysfluencies of early childhood begin to disappear by age five. The most frequent type of fluency disorder is **stuttering**, which affects about 2 percent of school-age children, more often boys than girls (Smith & Luckasson, 1992).

Fluency problems usually consist of blocking, repeating (e.g., M-m-m-m-mommy), or prolonging sounds, syllables, words, or phrases (e.g., Mmmmmmommy). In *stuttering*, these interruptions are frequently obvious to both the speaker and the listener. Often, they are very disruptive to the act of speaking, much more so than disorders of articulation or voice. When the speech dysfluencies occur, listeners may become uncomfortable and try to finish the speaker's words, phrases, or sentences. This discomfort is exacerbated when a speaker's stuttering is accompanied by gestures, facial contortions, or physical movements. Because stuttering is such a pronounced interruption of normal speech and also has a profound impact on listeners, the disorder receives a lot of attention, even though it is not as prevalent as other communication disorders.

Causes of Stuttering Although many causes of stuttering have been suggested over the years, the current thinking among professionals in the field of communication disorders is that there may be many different causes of the disorder. According to Van Riper and Emerick (1984), these theories include (1) the view that stuttering is related to emotional problems, (2) the idea that stuttering is the result of a person's biological makeup or of some neurological problem, and (3) the view that stuttering is a learned behaviour. The most persistent theory is that stuttering is a learned behaviour resulting from normal dysfluencies evident in early speech development. Also, the role that heredity plays in the development of stuttering remains interesting, in light of the fact that male stutterers typically outnumber females.

There seems to be no doubt that the children who stutter are very vulnerable to the attitudes, responses, and comments of their teachers and peers. When considerable attention is focused on normal dysfluencies or when students begin to have negative feelings about themselves because of their stuttering, they may become even more anxious and their stuttering may get worse. Most students who stutter beyond the age of five years will require therapy by a speech-language clinician.

When Fluency Disorders Are a Serious Problem We know speech dysfluencies are a normal developmental occurrence for many children. However, some children will continue to experience these dysfluencies beyond their preschool and early school years. It would be difficult for a parent or teacher to determine whether the dysfluencies a child is demonstrating are normal nonfluencies. Therefore, parents and/or classroom teachers should refer any children experiencing dysfluencies to a speech-language pathologist for a speech and language evaluation. Teachers may wish to consider the following questions when monitoring a student's speech dysfluencies:

▶ *Are the dysfluencies beginning to occur more often in the student's speech or beginning to sound more effortful or strained?*
  Keep track of the quality of the student's speech and his or her periods of fluency and dysfluency on a calendar. This will provide concrete information as to whether dysfluencies are occurring more often, as well as whether the quality of the student's speech is changing (e.g., strained, effortful, etc.).

▶ *Is there a pattern to situations in which the student is dysfluent?*
  Collect information about the student related to his dysfluencies. With careful observation, teachers may be able to determine if a student's dysfluencies occur under specific conditions—that is, with certain individuals, in particular settings, or when in stressful situations.

▶ *Is the student experiencing social problems?*
  Carefully monitor unstructured situations to determine the level of the student's acceptance by peers. Much of the socialization that occurs in school takes place in the cafeteria, on the playground, in the halls, on the bus, and in other nonacademic settings. When a student is not successfully relating to peers in these environments because of his or her dysfluencies, then the problem is likely to grow worse.

▶ *Is the student confident?*
  Talk to the student to ascertain his or her level of confidence and self-esteem. One of the biggest problems facing children who stutter is the interactive effect of the disorder. The more they are dysfluent, the more anxious, fearful, or nervous they become when they speak, thereby increasing the likelihood of stuttering. Children caught in this cycle of behaviour may be so self-conscious that they avoid situations in which they are required to speak and thus become isolated from friends and teachers.

TEACHING TIP

When deciding whether to refer a child for a speech and language evaluation, teachers should keep a log to record instances of dysfluency and the activities occurring with the student and rest of the class when dysfluencies occur. They should also note circumstances in which dysfluencies do not occur.

Classroom Accommodations for Students with Speech Disorders

Build a Positive Classroom Climate   Regardless of the type of speech disorder that students in general education classes demonstrate, it is crucial that teachers make every effort to create a positive, accepting, and safe climate. The following points are helpful to remember when dealing with children who have articulation/phonological, fluency, or voice disorders:

- Talk with the student privately about his or her speech difficulties. Acknowledge your awareness of the difficulties he or she is experiencing, and stress your belief that his or her speech will improve with practice.
- Encourage the student's family to actively support the student's educational and communication goals. Teachers and speech-language pathologists should ensure that a child's parents are an integral part of their child's educational and communication intervention program.
- Don't think of or refer to students with speech disorders in terms of their behaviours (i.e., they are "students," not "stutterers").
- Work closely with the speech-language pathologist, following suggestions and trying to reinforce specific skills.
- Encourage the student.
- Be positive.
- Accept the child just as you would any other student in the class.
- Model good speech and language skills for your students. Children can improve their speech and language skills by listening to good speech and language models
- Provide lots of opportunities for students to participate in oral group activities.
- Give students lots of chances to model and practise appropriate speech.
- Maintain eye contact when the student speaks.
- Be a good listener.
- Don't interrupt or finish the student's sentence for him or her.
- When appropriate, educate other students in the class about speech disorders and about acceptance and understanding.

FURTHER READING

For more information on working with speech-language pathologists, read the article "Collaboration: Working with the Speech-Language Pathologist" by R. G. Kerrin, published in volume 21 of *Intervention in School and Clinic*, 1996 (pp. 56–59).

TEACHING TIP

Self-monitoring strategies, such as record keeping, can facilitate a student's attempts to monitor his or her own speech.

Help Students Learn to Monitor Their Own Speech   Students who have been working with a speech-language pathologist to improve their speech skills may be at a point in their intervention when they are ready to work on their speech skills at the conversational level. By using simple contract formats, teachers can help students focus on using the skills they learn in speech therapy. When students are aware of how to make sounds correctly, they can then practise, monitor their own performance, and earn reinforcement from the teacher or parents whenever specific criteria are met.

Work with Peers or Parents   If students are to master speech skills, they will need to practise the skills taught by the speech-language pathologist on a regular basis in many different settings. One way for students to practise specific sounds is to use practice exercises like those in Loehr's *Read the Picture Stories for Articulation* (Loehr, 2002; see Figure 3.3.) With a partner, students can use short periods of downtime such as those between or before classes to work on their articulation. Students can also use these types of activities to work at home with their parents. First, the student is trained in the speech therapy setting on a specific phoneme in a key word, for example, the initial *s* sound in *seal*. After the student has reached 90 percent mastery of producing the *s* sound at the beginning of words, she or he then reads a story that contains words beginning with the *s* sound to a classmate or to his or her parents. Each practice session should take no more than five minutes and will provide students with practice that is simple and fun. In the classroom, both partners should be reinforced for their participation. However, it is important to note that each student who experiences articulation or phonological

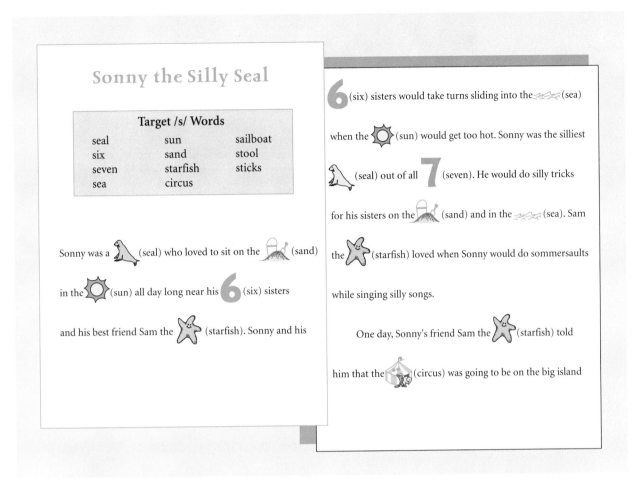

Sonny the Silly Seal

Target /s/ Words

seal	sun	sailboat
six	sand	stool
seven	starfish	sticks
sea	circus	

Sonny was a (seal) who loved to sit on the (sand) in the (sun) all day long near his 6 (six) sisters and his best friend Sam the (starfish). Sonny and his

6 (six) sisters would take turns sliding into the (sea) when the (sun) would get too hot. Sonny was the silliest (seal) out of all 7 (seven). He would do silly tricks for his sisters on the (sand) and in the (sea). Sam the (starfish) loved when Sonny would do sommersaults while singing silly songs.

One day, Sonny's friend Sam the (starfish) told him that the (circus) was going to be on the big island

FIGURE 3.3

Sample Form for Articulation Practice

From *Read the Picture Stories for Articulation* (2nd ed., pp. 19–20) by J. Loehr, 2002, Austin, TX: Pro-Ed. Used by permission.

difficulties demonstrates individual strengths and needs. Parents and teachers should consult with a student's speech-language pathologist prior to implementing **any** type of speech practice activity in the classroom or at home.

Modify Instruction and Materials   *The Pre-Referral Intervention Manual (PRIM)* (McCarney & Wunderlich, 1988) presents numerous ways of intervening with students who demonstrate speech errors. Some of the suggestions include the following:

- Set up a system of motivators to encourage students' efforts.
- Highlight material to identify key syllables and words in a passage.
- Give students practice listening so that they can learn to discriminate among sounds, fluent speech patterns, and good vocal habits.
- Reduce the emphasis on competition. Competitive activities may increase students' stress and result in even more speech errors.

Teach Students Their Own Strategies   Many of the speech problems that students demonstrate while young can be corrected and modified with therapy. While the therapy is going on, the teacher and speech-language pathologist should focus on giving students strategies for successful learning. Students can use these strategies to maximize their academic and social strengths. Some of these strategies also require accommodations on the part of the teacher in structuring situations and requirements.

Students with speech disorders can learn strategies that will help them to maximize their social strengths.

- Encourage students to participate in groups in which responses do not have to be individually generated.
- Teach students to reinforce themselves by recognizing when they are doing well and by appreciating themselves.
- Let students practise skills with a friend in real situations so that they are not afraid or nervous when it's the "real thing."
- Let students tape-record their own speech and listen carefully for errors so that they can discriminate between correct and incorrect sounds.
- Help students come up with strategies for dealing with specific people or situations that make them nervous (walking away, counting to 10 before they speak, deep breathing, etc.).

Language Disorders

Language is the system we use to communicate our thoughts and ideas to others. According to Lahey (1988), language is a code "whereby ideas about the world are expressed through a conventional system of arbitrary signals for communication" (p. 2). The interrelationships of what we hear, speak, read, and write become our format for sharing information.

For most of us, spoken language is the tool we use to communicate our ideas, but even the most articulate, fluent, pleasant speech would be useless without a language system that enables us to understand and be understood. Language is an integral component of students' abilities in reading, writing, and listening. Disorders of language may have a serious impact on academic performance. In recent years, the emphasis in the field of communication disorders has shifted away from remediation of speech problems to an increased focus on language disorders. Estimates today are that 50 to 80 percent of the children seen by speech-language pathologists have language disorders (Wiig, 1986).

CONSIDER THIS

Try to go through a social situation without using oral language. Did you become frustrated when attempting to make your needs or ideas known to other people? How did you deal with the frustrations?

More important for classroom teachers, however, is the fact that remediation of language disorders will often be as much their responsibility as it is the speech-language pathologist's. Although remediation of speech problems is provided primarily in a therapeutic setting and then supported and reinforced by the classroom teacher, teachers will often direct and manage overall language development.

We know that humans can communicate in several ways. We generally describe modes of communication as either **receptive language**, which involves receiving and decoding or interpreting language, or **expressive language**, which is the encoding or production of a message. Reading and listening are examples of receptive language; writing and speaking are forms of expressive language.

As with speech disorders, knowing the normal sequence of language development is important in working with students with language disorders. Some children may be delayed in their development of language but still acquire skills in the same sequence as other children. Other children may acquire some age-appropriate language skills but have deficits in other specific areas. Table 3.2 shows the normal patterns of language development for children with language disorders and children without language disorders. Although they may refer to these general patterns of language development to judge students' overall progress, teachers should not expect every child to follow this precise sequence on these exact timelines.

Dimensions of Language

Earlier in the chapter, some terminology related to language disorders was introduced. In addition, we refer to the dimensions of language and their related impairments in terms of form, content, and function (or use). Students can demonstrate impairments in any or all of these areas.

Form **Form** describes the rule systems used in oral language. Three different rule systems are included when we discuss form: **phonology**, **morphology**, and **syntax**.

Phonology is the rule system that governs the individual and combined sounds of a language. Phonological rules vary from one language to another. For example, some of the guttural sounds heard in German are not used in English, and some of the vowel combinations of English are not found in Spanish. The ability to process and manipulate the phonological components of language has been shown to be a critical component in the development of early reading skills.

Morphology refers to the rule system controlling the structure of words. Free morphemes can stand alone in word formation (e.g., *stop*), while bound morphemes cannot stand alone (e.g., *un-*, *-ed*, *-ing*). The structures of words govern their meanings, therefore, comparative suffixes such as *-er* or *-est* and plural forms such as the *s* that changes *book* to *books* are important. Hall, Oyer, and Haas (2001) provide an example of how morphemes (units of meaning) can change a basic word into similar words with many different meanings:

> The word "friend" is composed of one free morpheme that has meaning. One or more bound morphemes may be added, making "friend*ly*," "*un*friendly," "friend*less*," "friend*liness*," "friend*ship*," and "friend*lier*." There are rules for combining morphemes into words that must be followed (e.g., "*dis*friend" is not an allowable word and thus has no meaning). (p. 61)

Syntax is the ordering of words in such a way that they can be understood. Syntax rules determine where words are placed in a sentence. Just like phonology, syntax rules

CONSIDER THIS

Remember when some children with whom you are familiar began to talk. What were some of their first words? What factors influence a child's early oral language development?

CROSS-REFERENCE

Language disorders and behavioural disorders frequently co-exist. Refer to Chapter 6 to learn more about emotional and behavioural disorders.

TABLE 3.2	Language Development for Children with Language Disorders and without Language Disorders				
Language-Disordered Child			Normally Developing Child		
Age	Attainment	Example	Age	Attainment	Example
27 months	First words	*this, mama, bye bye, doggie*	13 months	First words	*here, mama, bye bye, kitty*
38 months	50-word vocabulary		17 months	50-word vocabulary	
40 months	First two-word combinations	*this doggie more apple this mama more play*	18 months	First two-word combinations	*more juice here ball more TV here kitty*
48 months	Later two-word combinations	*Mimi purse Daddy coat block chair dolly table*	22 months	Later two-word combinations	*Andy shoe Mommy ring cup floor keys chair*
52 months	Mean sentence length of 2.00 words		24 months	Mean sentence length of 2.00 words	
55 months	First appearance of -ing	*Mommy eating*	24 months	First appearance of -ing	*Andy sleeping*
63 months	Mean sentence length of 3.10 words		30 months	Mean sentence length of 3.10 words	
66 months	First appearance of is	*The doggie's mad*	30 months	First appearance of is	*My car's gone!*
73 months	Mean sentence length of 4.10 words		37 months	Mean sentence length of 4.10 words	
79 months	Mean sentence length of 4.50 words		37 months	First appearance of indirect requests	*Can I have some cookies?*
79 months	First appearance of indirect requests	*Can I get the ball?*	40 months	Mean sentence length of 4.50 words	

From "Language Disorders in Preschool Children" by L. Leonard, in *Human Communications Disorders: An Introduction* (4th ed., p. 179), edited by G. H. Shames, E. H. Wiig, and W. A. Second, 1994, New York: Macmillan. Copyright © 1994. Reprinted with permission of Merrill, an imprint of Macmillan Publishing Company.

vary from one language to another. Rules governing negatives, questions, tenses, and compound or simple sentences determine the meanings of word combinations. For example, the same words used in different combinations can mean very different things: *The boy hit the ball* is not the same as *The ball hit the boy.*

All of these rule systems affect how we use and understand language. Children's abilities to understand and correctly use all of these rules related to form develop sequentially as their language skill develops. Language form is important not only in spoken language, but in written language and in sign language systems, as well as in augmentative and alternative communication (AAC), discussed later in this chapter.

Content *Content* refers to the intent and meaning of language and its rule system; *semantics* deals with the meaning of words and word combinations. Without specific words to label and describe objects or ideas, our language would have no meaning. When students fail to comprehend concrete and abstract meanings of words, inferences, or figurative expressions, it is difficult for them to understand more subtle uses of language such as jokes, puns, similes, proverbs, or sarcasm. As children mature, they are better able to differentiate meanings of similar words, classify them according to similarities, understand abstract meanings of words, and comprehend figurative language.

Use When we use language in various social contexts, we follow another set of rules, *pragmatics.* The purpose and setting of our communication as well as the people with whom we are communicating determine the language we use. If children are to build and maintain successful relationships with others, it is important that they understand and effectively use skills appropriate to the context. For example, when children speak to adults, it is helpful if they use polite, respectful language; when they speak to their friends, they will most likely use less formal spoken language, demonstrate more relaxed body language, and take turns while talking (Owens, 1996).

Types and Causes of Language Disorders

Hallahan and Kauffman (1991) have described four basic categories of language disorders: absence of verbal language, qualitatively different language, delayed language development, and interrupted language development. Table 3.3 from Naremore (1980) summarizes these four categories and includes some suspected causes of each. For children who are not deaf, a complete absence of language would likely indicate severe emotional disturbance or a severe developmental disorder. Qualitatively different language is also associated with developmental disorders and emotional disturbance. A good example of this type of problem is the echolalic speech of children with autism, who may repeat speech they hear in a singsong voice and fail to use their spoken language in a meaningful way. Delayed language occurs when a child develops language in the same sequence as other children, but at a slower rate. Causes of delayed language include intellectual disability, hearing loss, or lack of stimulation or appropriate experiences. Sometimes language development is interrupted by illness or physical trauma. This type of language problem is increasingly common among children as a result of traumatic brain injury (TBI). In general education classrooms, teachers may encounter any or all of these types of language disorders ranging from very mild to severe.

Indicators of Language Impairments

Some teachers may have an overall sense that a student is demonstrating language problems; others may not notice anything amiss. Wiig and Semel (1984) have identified some indicators of language problems by grade levels:

▷ Primary grades:
  Problems in following verbal directions
  Difficulty with preacademic skills (recognizing sound differences)
  Phonics problems
  Poor word-attack skills
  Difficulties with structural analysis
  Problems learning new material

TEACHING TIP

Teaching students appropriate social skills helps them understand how to modify their language in different social situations and when interacting with different speakers (i.e., friends versus unfamiliar others).

CROSS-REFERENCE

Language disorders are integrally linked to autism spectrum disorders. Refer to Chapter 9 to learn more about disorders that are considered to be part of the autism spectrum.

TEACHING TIP

If you suspect a child of having language problems, keep a record of the problems to better determine if a referral for services is warranted. Always consult a speech-language pathologist if you are unsure if the difficulties observed necessitate a referral.

TABLE 3.3	Types of Language Disorders and Their Causes

Type	Commonly Suspected Causative Factors or Related Conditions
No Verbal Language Child does not show indications of understanding or spontaneously using language by age 3.	▶ Congenital or early acquired deafness ▶ Gross brain damage or severe mental retardation/developmental disabilities ▶ Severe emotional disturbance
Quantitatively Different Language Child's language is different from that of nondisabled children at any stage of development—meaning and usefulness for communication are greatly lessened or lost.	▶ Inability to understand auditory stimuli ▶ Severe emotional disturbance ▶ Learning disability ▶ Mental retardation/developmental disabilities ▶ Hearing loss
Delayed Language Development Language follows normal course of development, but lags seriously behind that of most children who are the same chronological age.	▶ Mental retardation ▶ Experiential deprivation ▶ Lack of language stimulation ▶ Hearing loss
Interrupted Language Development Normal language development begins but is interrupted by illness, accident, or other trauma; language disorder is acquired.	▶ Acquired hearing loss ▶ Brain injury due to oxygen deprivation, physical trauma, or infection

Adapted from "Language Disorders in Children," by R. C. Naremore. In *Introduction to Communication Disorders*, edited by T. J. Hixon, L. D. Shriberg, and J. H. Saxman, 1980, p. 224. Englewood Cliffs, NJ: Prentice-Hall. Used by permission.

▶ Intermediate grades:
Word substitutions

Inadequate language processing and production that affects reading comprehension and academic achievement

▶ Middle and high school:
Inability to understand abstract concepts

Problems understanding multiple word meanings

Difficulties connecting previously learned information to new material that must be learned independently

Widening gap in achievement when compared to peers

FURTHER READING

For more information on language disorders and learning disabilities, refer to the information sheet entitled *Language-Based Learning Disabilities* found on the ASHA website at **www.asha.org**.

Teachers can also check for linguistic, social, emotional, and academic problems that are related to language disorders (Ratner & Harris, 1994). These problems are shown in Table 3.4. In addition, Figure 3.4 presents a checklist of behaviours that may indicate either speech or language problems. Children who have language disorders sometimes develop patterns of interaction with peers, teachers, and family members that may result in behaviour problems. The behaviour problems might seem to have nothing to do with language problems but may in fact have developed in response to inabilities to read, spell, talk, or write effectively.

TABLE 3.4		Linguistic, Social, Emotional, and Academic Problems Related to Language Disorders
Linguistic Problems	Language structure	Omissions and distortions of speech sounds Omissions of parts of words or word endings Sounds or syllables of words out of sequence Immature sentence structure
	Language meaning	Difficulty understanding directions and questions Confusion of basic concepts and ideas Limited vocabulary Literal interpretation of figurative language and jokes Poor word classification and association skills
	Language use	Difficulty beginning, maintaining, and ending conversations Difficulty taking turns in conversations and other classroom activities Difficulty understanding the listener's point of view Overuse of pauses, fillers, and repetitions in conversation
	Metalinguistics	Difficulty expressing ideas about language Poor phonemic awareness skills (rhyming, syllabification, phonics)
Social Problems	Conversational deficits	Poor eye contact Inappropriate comments and responses to questions Providing insufficient information when describing, relaying information, or giving directions Poor social language use (please, thank you)
	Social interaction issues	Poor sense of fair play Unable to set limits or boundaries Difficulty with new situations Difficulty expressing wants, needs, and ideas
Emotional Problems	Personal issues	Poor self-concept Low frustration level Perseverative and repetitious
	Emotional-interaction issues	Inability to accept responsibility Gullible Sensitive to criticism Poor coping strategies
Academic Problems	Classroom issues	Poor retention of learning Problems with organizing and planning Difficulty problem solving Left/right confusion Symbol reversals Difficulty expressing known information Poor generalization of knowledge to new situations Difficulty with higher-level thinking skills (deduction, inference) Poor judgment and understanding of cause and effect Inability to monitor and self-correct Poor memory
	Metacognition	Inability to talk about academic tasks Inability to self-regulate behaviours

Adapted from *Understanding Language Disorders: The Impact on Learning* (pp. 171–174) by V. L. Ratner and L. R. Harris, 1994, Eau Claire, WI: Thinking Publications. Reprinted with permission.

FIGURE 3.4

Teacher's Checklist of
Behaviours That May
Indicate Communication
Disorders

SPEECH

☑ Poor articulation

☑ Different voice quality

☑ Dysfluencies

☑ Slurred conversational speech

LANGUAGE

☑ Has problems following oral directions

☑ Speech rambles; isn't able to express ideas concisely

☑ Appears shy, withdrawn, never seems to talk or interact with others

☑ Asks questions that are off-topic

☑ Has a poor sense of humour

☑ Has poor comprehension of material read

☑ Doesn't plan ahead in pencil/paper activities

☑ Takes things literally

☑ Is not organized; appears messy

☑ Doesn't manage time well; has to be prodded to complete assignments

Classroom Accommodations for Students with Language Disorders

Numerous strategies can be used in general education classrooms to improve students' language skills and remedy language deficits. Consult with a speech-language pathologist and other special education personnel, such as the resource room teacher, to individualize classroom suggestions for students with language disorders. The following section presents some ways of structuring learning situations and presenting information to enhance communication.

Improve Students' Comprehension in the Classroom   Clary and Edwards (1992) suggest some specific activities to improve students' receptive language skills:

▶ *Give students practice in following directions.*

Begin with one simple direction, and then increase the length of the list of directions. Have the student perform a simple task in the classroom such as closing the door, turning around, and so on.

▶ *Have students pair up and practise descriptions.*

Place two students at a table separated by a screen. Place groups of identical objects in front of both students. Have one describe one of the objects; the other must determine which object is being described. Reverse roles with new sets of objects.

▶ *Let students work on categorizing.*

Orally present a list of three words. Two should be related in some way. Ask a student to tell which two are related and why (e.g., horse, tree, dog). For younger students, start by having students compare and organize physical objects (e.g., plastic animals, plastic food) and pictorial representations of the objects (i.e., pictures cut out of magazines) before moving to orally presented words.

The nearby Inclusion Strategies feature provides some additional suggestions for teaching listening skills.

Give Students Opportunities for Facilitative Play   This type of interaction provides modelling for the students so that they can imitate and expand their own use of language. For example:

▶ The teacher models self-talk in a play activity. ("I'm making the cars go.")
▶ The teacher elicits comments from the student and then expands on them. ("Yes, the cars are going *fast*.")
▶ The teacher uses "buildups" and "breakdowns" by expanding on a student's ideas, breaking them down, and then repeating them. ("Red car go? Yes, look at the red car. It's going fast on the road. It's going to win the race.") (Nowacek & McShane, 1993)

Use Naturalistic Techniques and Simulated Real-Life Activities to Increase Language Use
Often, the most effective techniques to instill language acquisition and use are those that will be easy for teachers to use and easy for students to generalize to everyday situations. Teachers can encourage generalization by using naturalistic and situational strategies and real-life activities.

CROSS-REFERENCE

When reading Chapters 13 and 14, consider specific activities that could be used to teach listening skills to elementary students and secondary students.

INCLUSION Strategies

Strategies to Improve Listening Skills in the Classroom

▶ Allow for clarification and repetition of questions during oral tests
▶ Limit the use of figurative language, complex, or passive sentences. When figurative language expressions are used (e.g., "He let the cat out of the bag"), provide explanations of the expressions' literal and figurative meanings.
▶ Be an interesting speaker—use gestures, facial expressions, movement, and variety in your voice.
▶ Encourage students to ask questions.
▶ Identify students who are having difficulty listening in class and pair them with "study buddies."

▶ Keep sentence structures simple and direct.
▶ Limit concentrated listening time to short intervals.
▶ Make simple adaptations in your classroom to improve acoustics (e.g., place felt pads on the bottoms of chair/desk legs to dampen their sound when they are moved)
▶ Reduce noise levels in the classroom during listening tasks.
▶ Refer students experiencing listening difficulties to an audiologist for a hearing assessment.
▶ Repeat and rephrase information for students.

▶ Strategically seat students with listening difficulties (e.g., away from classroom door, at front of classroom).
▶ Speak slowly and pause between thoughts.
▶ Use advanced organizers and preview questions to help focus listening.
▶ Use the blackboard and other visual aids (e.g., overhead projector, videos).

Adapted from *It's Time to Listen: Metacognitive Activities for Improving Auditory Processing in the Classroom* (2nd ed., pp. 9–15) by P. A. Hamaguchi, 2002, Austin, TX: Pro-Ed.

CONSIDER THIS

What can you do as a classroom teacher to ensure the
speech and language skills
students develop through the
use of these strategies continue
to improve in the classroom
environment?

▶ Naturalistic Techniques

Try cloze activities. ("What do you need? Oh, you need paint and a _____. That's right, you need paint and a brush.")

Emphasize problem solving. ("You can't find your backpack? What should you do? Let's look on the hook. Is your coat there? What did we do to find your coat? That's right, we looked on the hook.")

Use questioning techniques. ("Where are you going? That's right, you are going to lunch.")

▶ Simulated Real-Life Activities

Let students simulate a newscast or commercial.

Have students write and follow their own written directions to locations in and around the school.

Play "social charades" by having students act out social situations and decide on appropriate responses.

Have one student teach an everyday skill to another (e.g., how to shoot a basket).

Using real telephones, give students opportunities to call each other, and to give, receive, and record messages.

Develop Students' Conversational Skills through Story Reading   McNeill and Fowler (1996) give some excellent suggestions for helping students with delayed language development. Since students with language development problems often do not get the results they want through their ordinary conversations, they need more practice. What better way to practise effective language skills than through story reading?! Students of all ages enjoy being read to, whether individually or in small groups while students are young, or in larger classes when they are in intermediate or secondary grades.

These authors suggest four specific strategies for teachers to use when reading stories aloud:

▶ Praise the students' talk.
▶ Expand on their words.
▶ Ask open-ended questions.
▶ Pause long enough to allow students to initiate speaking.

In addition, they emphasize taking turns, so that students have an opportunity to clarify their messages, hear appropriate language models, and practise the unspoken rules of communication. McNeill and Fowler (1996) also recommend coaching parents in how to give their children opportunities to talk and how to respond when their children *do* talk. When parents pause, expand on answers, and ask open-ended questions that require more than just "yes" or "no" responses, they can become their children's best teachers.

Use Music and Play Games to Improve Language   Teachers should always try to have some fun with students. Using music and playing games are two ways language can be incorporated into enjoyable activities.

▶ Music

Use songs that require students to request items (e.g., rhythm sticks or tambourines passed around a circle).

Have picture symbols for common songs so that students can request the ones they like.

Use props to raise interest and allow students to act out the story (e.g., during "Humpty Dumpty" the student falls off a large ball).

Use common chants such as "When You're Happy and You Know It," and let students choose the action (e.g., clap your hands).

TEACHING TIP

In order to improve students'
conversational skills, teachers
can encourage their students to
(1) use greetings or lead-ins
when initiating a conversation
(e.g., "Hi, how are you this
morning?" or "How was... ?"; or
(2) ask open-ended questions
to maintain a conversational
topic (e.g., "Oh you went to the
mall. Then what happened?").

FURTHER READING

For more information on this
technique, read the article
"Using Story Reading to Encourage Children's Conversations,"
by J. H. McNeill and S. A.
Fowler, published in 1996 in
volume 28 of *Teaching Exceptional Children* (pp. 43–47).

▶ Games That Require Language Comprehension and Expression Skills

Play "Simon Says."

Play "Musical Chairs" using words rather than music. (Pass a ball around a circle. When the teacher says a magic word, the student with the ball is out.)

Use key words to identify and organize students. ("All of the boys with red hair stand up. Everyone who has a sister sit down.")

Play "Twenty Questions." ("I'm thinking of a person." Students ask yes-or-no questions.)

Arrange Your Classroom for Effective Interactions   For students who have either speech or language difficulties, the physical arrangement of the classroom can contribute to their success. The following guidelines may improve students' language development:

▶ Give instructions and important information when distractions are at their lowest.
▶ Use consistent attention-getting devices, either verbal, visual, or physical cues (e.g., switching off the classroom light, raising your hand in the air).
▶ Be specific when giving directions (e.g., "Please finish page 12 in your math book.").
▶ Write directions on the chalkboard, flipchart, or overhead so that students can refer to them. For younger students, post picture cues in the room to remind students of the directions you have given them (e.g., picture of paintbrush to remind students they are to complete their painting project).
▶ Use students' names frequently when talking to them.
▶ Emphasize what you're saying by using gestures and facial expressions.
▶ Pair students up with buddies for modelling and support.
▶ Allow for conversation time in the classroom so that students can share information and ideas.
▶ Encourage students to use calendars to organize themselves and manage their time. (Breeding, Stone, & Riley, n.d.)

Use Challenging Games with Older Students   Older students may require continued intervention to improve their language skills. However, the activities chosen must be appropriate and not seem like "baby" games. Thomas and Carmack (1993) have collected ideas to involve older students in enjoyable, interactive tasks:

▶ Read fables or stories with morals. Discuss outcomes, and focus on the endings.
▶ Do "Explain That." Discuss common idiomatic phrases, and help students discover the connection between the literal and figurative meanings (e.g., *She was on pins and needles*).
▶ "Riddlemania" presents riddles to students and has them explain what makes them humorous.
▶ Have "Sense-Able Lessons." Bring objects to see, taste, hear, and smell, and compile a list of students' verbal comments. (p. 155)

Modify Strategies to Develop Students' Learning Tools   When facilitating language development for older students, help them develop their own strategies to use in challenging situations (Thomas & Carmack, 1993). Requiring them to use higher-order thinking skills will both require and stimulate higher-level language.

▶ Pair students to find word meanings. Use partners when working on categories such as synonyms or antonyms. Let students work together to master using a thesaurus.
▶ Teach students to categorize. Begin with concrete objects that they relate to easily, such as types of cars or names of foods, and then move to more abstract concepts such as feelings or ideas.
▶ Play reverse quiz games like "Jeopardy!" in which students have to work backward to think of questions for answers. (pp. 155–163)

FURTHER READING

For more information on fun activities that can facilitate the use of language, read *The Developmentally Appropriate Inclusive Classroom in Early Education,* written by R. Miller and published in 1996 by Delmar.

TEACHING TIP

Ask your students questions that encourage them to use their language skills. For example, "Tell me about your picture" instead of asking "Is that a house?" or "What did you do yesterday in gym class?" instead of asking "Did you play volleyball in gym yesterday?"

Work Collaboratively with the Speech-Language Pathologist LINC (Language IN the Classroom) is a program adapted for use in schools (Breeding et al., n.d.). The program philosophy holds that language learning should occur in the child's most natural environment and in conjunction with other content being learned. The development of students' language should relate to their world and should be a learning experience, not a teaching experience.

The purpose of the program is to strengthen the language system of those students in general education classrooms who need to develop coping and compensatory skills to survive academically. Another goal is to transfer language learned from the therapy setting to the classroom, thereby allowing children to learn to *communicate,* rather than merely *talk.* The teacher and the speech-language pathologist must both be present for the approach to be successful. The two professionals work together to plan unit lessons that develop language skills in students.

Hiller (1990) presents an example of how LINC works. His elementary school implemented classroom-based language instruction. At the beginning of the program, the speech-language pathologist visited each classroom for a specified amount of time each week (90 minutes) during the language arts period. The first 45 minutes were used for an oral language activity, often a cooking activity from the *Blooming Recipes* workbook (Tavzel, 1987). During the second 45 minutes, students did paragraph writing. For example, after preparing peanut butter on celery ("Bumps on a Log"), students responded to these questions:

What was the name of the recipe we made?

Where did we do our preparing?

Who brought the peanut butter, celery, and raisins?

How did we make "Bumps on a Log"?

When did we eat "Bumps on a Log"?

Why do you think this recipe was called "Bumps on a Log"?

Responses were written on the board or on an overhead transparency. Students copied the responses in paragraph format.

Teachers and speech-language pathologists later extended the activities to teaching language lessons on current topics, team-teaching critical thinking activities during science experiments, and team planning and teaching social studies units. Reports from Hiller's and other schools using LINC programs described better collaboration among professionals, more accurate language referrals, and increased interest in speech-language activities among the entire staff.

Use Storytelling and Process Writing When children listen to and retell a story, they incorporate it into their oral language repertoire. McKamey (1991) has described a structure for allowing students to retell stories they had heard, to tell stories from their own experience, and to write down and illustrate their oral presentations. In process writing, students are instructed based on what they can already do. This and other balanced literacy approaches often allow students who have had negative language experiences to begin to succeed, to link written and spoken language, and to grow as communicators.

Language Differences

Children's patterns of speech and use of language reflect their culture and may be different from that of some of their peers. It is important not to mistake a language *difference* for a language *disorder,* but also a disorder must not be overlooked in a student with language differences. Variations in family structure, child-rearing practices, family perceptions and attitudes, and language and communication styles can all influence students' communication (Wayman, Lynch, & Hanson, 1990).

Acquiring English as a Second Language

Students who are learning English as a second language often exhibit error patterns that can look like language disorders, when they are, in fact, part of the normal process of second-language acquisition (Roseberry-McKibbin & Brice, 2002). It is crucial that teachers of students who are English-language learners recognize these patterns as language differences rather than communication disorders in order to avoid unnecessary referrals:

▶ Interference or transfer: Students may make errors in English form because of the influence of structures or patterns in their native language.
▶ Silent period: Children who are learning a new language focus on listening to and attempting to understand the new language before trying out what they have learned. This silent period may last as long as a year in very young children and as briefly as a few weeks or months in older children.
▶ Code switching: Languages are blended in phrases or sentences such that students alternate between the two.
▶ Subtractive bilingualism: As students learn English, they can begin to lose skill and proficiency in their native language if it is not also supported and valued.

Relationship between Communication Style and Culture

Culture has a strong influence on the *style* of communication. Many areas of communication style can be affected by factors such as gender, status, and age roles; rules governing interruptions and turn taking; use of humour; and how to greet or leave someone (Erickson, 1992). Teachers must be aware of the many manifestations of culture in nonverbal communication, as well. Differences in rules governing eye contact, the physical space between speakers, use of gestures and facial expression, and use of silence can cause dissonance between teachers and students of differing cultures. Walker (1993) has described how differences such as directness of a conversation, volume of voices, and reliance on verbal (low-context) versus nonverbal (high-context) parts of communication affect attitudes toward the speaker. Teachers can respond to cultural differences in several ways. These suggestions are adapted from Walker (1993) and should be helpful for teachers who want to enhance both overall achievement and communication skills with students who are culturally or linguistically different:

▶ Try to involve community resources, including churches and neighbourhood organizations, in school activities.
▶ Invite parents to visit your classroom in order to learn more about students' families and to encourage parent participation in classroom and school activities.
▶ Allow flexible hours for conferences.
▶ Question your own assumptions about human behaviour, values, biases, personal limitations, and so on.
▶ Try to understand the world from the student's perspective.
▶ Ask yourself questions about an individual student's behaviour in light of cultural values, motivation, and world views, and how these relate to his or her learning experiences.
▶ Remind yourself and your students to celebrate and value cultural and linguistic differences among individuals in their school and community
▶ Consult with a speech-language pathologist to understand how to differentiate between students who have language differences and students who have language disorders.

FURTHER READING

For a detailed discussion of bilingual education and special education, see a book written by Margaret Winzer and Kasper Mazurek of the University of Lethbridge: *Special Education in Multicultural Contexts*, published in 1998 by Prentice-Hall.

TEACHING TIP

Remember the basic tenets of nondiscriminatory assessment when evaluating students with diverse cultural backgrounds or when reviewing assessment data that have already been collected (refer to the section discussing assessment considerations).

Considerations in Assessment

Assessment in the area of communication disorders is often complicated, just as it is for students with other disabilities. Linguistic differences are a contributing factor. For example, one Canadian secondary school enrolled students with 54 languages other than English (Housego, 1990). The number of students in our classrooms who are linguistically different and who require services in ESL (English as a second language) or who are limited English proficient (LEP) are increasing. Language differences may affect a student's oral and written communication. Therefore, teachers should consult with personnel in special education, ESL, speech and language services, and bilingual education to obtain appropriate evaluation and programming services for these students. Observation is an important form of assessment, particularly when assessing students who are linguistically different. The nearby Diversity Forum feature provides some suggestions for observing these children.

There are many considerations for assessment personnel who work with students having cultural and linguistic differences. The following suggestions have been adapted from Toliver-Weddington and Erickson (1992) and may be useful for classroom teachers who suspect that students may have communication disorders.

- When screening with tests, always select tests that have the most valid items for the skills to be assessed.
- Consider procedural modifications such as lengthening the time limit.
- Try to assess whether the minority child has had access to the information.
- Consider scoring the test in two ways, first as the manual indicates, then allowing credit for items that may be considered correct in the child's language system and/or experiences. (Record and report both ways and indicate the adjustments.)
- Focus on what the child does well rather than what he or she cannot do.

Because of the increasing number of students in public schools from cultural and/or linguistic minority groups, teachers are recognizing the need for information related to learning and communication styles as well as modifications to curriculum and instruction. Although many of these children will never be identified as having a communication disorder, teachers in general education must be aware that differences in language and culture may often affect a student's apparent proficiency in both oral and written communication.

Diversity Forum

Considerations for Observing Linguistically Different Students

1. Identify exactly what is to be observed. Be specific and know what you are watching as a part of the ongoing behaviour stream in classroom settings.
2. Record the time, date, and duration of your observation.
3. Number your observations of the same children across days. Important here is a systematic context and an easy, readily available reminder that this is, for example, the third observation of Juan, Tom, Hector, and Zoraida.
4. Make notes of what you are observing in a descriptive, specific form that tells exactly what occurred. Also, jot down any unexpected events that happened during your observation. However, when taking notes of these occurrences, it is helpful to note that they were "unexpected."
5. Keep notes of your interpretations of what happened.

From V. Gonzalez, R. Bruce-Vega, & T. Yawkey. *Assessment and Instruction of Culturally and Linguistically Diverse Students with or At-Risk of Learning Problems* © 1997. Published by Allyn and Bacon, Boston, MA. Copyright © 1997 by Pearson Education. Reprinted by permission of the publisher.

The cultural background of a child will influence many aspects of the style of communication that is used.

Augmentative and Alternative Communication (AAC)

According to ASHA (2004c), "Augmentative and alternative communication (AAC) refers to ways (other than speech) that are used to send a message from one person to another." The term **augmentative communication** denotes techniques that supplement or enhance communication by complementing whatever vocal skills the individual already has such as gestures, facial expressions, and writing (ASHA, 2004c). Other individuals (e.g., those who are severely neurologically impaired and cannot speak) must employ techniques that serve in place of speech—in other words, **alternative communication** (e.g., communication boards).

AAC is a multimodal system consisting of four components (symbols, aids, techniques, and strategies) that can be utilized in various combinations to enhance communication. Communication techniques used in AAC are usually divided into either *aided* or *unaided forms.* Unaided techniques include nonverbal methods used in typical communication and do not require any physical object or entity in order to express information (e.g., speech, manual signs or gestures, facial communication). Aided communication techniques require a physical object or device to enable the individual to communicate (e.g., communication boards, charts, and mechanical or electrical devices). There are substantial numbers of individuals who lack speech because of intellectual disabilities, traumatic brain injury, deafness, neurological disorders, or other causes. Therefore, in recent years there has been an increased demand for augmentative and alternative communication. A student's communication skills and needs will change over time, as will the types of technology and methods available to support communication. Thus, the educational team should continually monitor and regularly re-evaluate the usefulness of each AAC approach used by their students. The nearby Technology Today feature lists the types of computer applications suitable for students with speech and language disorders.

Speech and Language Disorders and Types of Computer Applications

Disorder	Types of Applications
ARTICULATION	Phonologic analysis, intelligibility analysis, drill and practice, and games
VOICE	Biofeedback programs and client information
FLUENCY	Biofeedback and relaxation programs
SYNTACTIC	Language sample analysis, drill and practice, games, and tutorials
SEMANTIC	Language sample analysis and cognitive rehabilitation
PRAGMATIC	Problem solving and simulations
HEARING IMPAIRMENT	Visual feedback, sign language instruction with CAI, and telecommunication applications

From "Computers and Individuals with Speech and Language Disorders," by P. S. Cochran and G. L. Bull. In *Computers and Exceptional Individuals*, edited by J. D. Lindsey, 1993, p. 146. Austin, TX: Pro-Ed. Used by permission.

Students who are unable to use spoken language to communicate may use a basic nonautomated **communication** device with no electronic parts. For example, a communication board or a communication book containing symbols, words, and/or letters. Typically, this kind of device will contain common words, phrases, or numbers that can be arranged in either an alphabetic or nonalphabetic format. Nonautomated communication devices are easy to construct and can be modified to fit the student's vocabulary. Therefore, these devices are very useful in communicating with teachers, family members, and peers. There are several commercially available sets of symbols, including *The Picture Communication Symbols* (Mayer-Johnson, 2004), *The Oakland Picture Dictionary* (Kirsten, 1981), and the graphic database *Boardmaker* (Mayer-Johnson, 2004).

Electronic communication aids encompass a wide variety of capabilities, from simple to complex. Aids that produce voice are known as voice output communication aids or VOCAS. There are a large number of different voice output communication aids available that vary greatly in their level of sophistication and complexity (e.g., aids that speak on message, aids with keyboards). The voice output may be amplified, digitized, or utilize synthetic speech. Often, a voice synthesizer is used to produce speech output, and written output is produced on printers or displays. Software, which is becoming increasingly sophisticated, can accommodate the many different needs of individuals who cannot produce spoken and/or written language. Some examples of electronic communication aids and their key features are shown in Table 3.5.

Facilitated Communication

Facilitated communication is a process that has recently been used with individuals who have developmental disabilities, including autism. First introduced by Rosemary Crossley in Australia, facilitated communication usually involves having someone support the arm or wrist of the person with autism, who then points to pictures, objects, printed letters, and words, or types letters on a keyboard. The keyboard is often connected to a computer so that the individual's words can be displayed or printed (Kirk, Gallagher, & Anastasiow, 1993). Supposedly the facilitator's support enables the individual to point or to type out words and phrases.

TEACHING TIP

The speech-language pathologist should always be consulted when selecting any type of technology for use with students with speech and language difficulties.

CROSS-REFERENCE

Refer to Chapter 9 to read more about the use of facilitated communication with autism spectrum disorders.

TABLE 3.5	Electronic Communication Aids and Their Key Features

BigMack

A large, colourful, single message digitizer.

Record and re-record a message, song, sound, story line, or choice of up to 20 seconds.

A picture or label can easily be stuck to the large button.

Can be accessed by pressing anywhere on the large button or by a separate switch.

Can be used as a switch to control other devices, toys, or appliances.

Lightwriter SL35

A compact, portable keyboard will speak what is typed into it.

Text messages are displayed on the two-way screen, and synthesized speech is used.

Can be customized for people with more complex needs.

Add-ons such as key guards can be purchased, and a range of models are available.

Reduces keystrokes by using memory and word prediction.

ChatPC

Based on a palmtop Windows CE computer.

Housed in a durable case to give additional protection and additional amplification.

Has a colour touch screen, and over a hundred pages of messages can be programmed.

An onscreen keyboard is available, and this speaks out what is typed into it.

3000+ symbols are supplied and can be supplemented with scanned or digital images.

Speech output can be digital or synthetic.

Changes can be made on the device or on a computer and then downloaded.

Dynavox 3100

Touchscreen device offers word layouts, symbol layouts, or a combination of both.

Many preprogrammed page sets, suitable for users with a wide range of ability levels.

Flexible layout can be thoroughly customized.

Symbol-supported word prediction encourages literacy.

DecTalk speech synthesis offers nine different voices.

Can be accessed via touchscreen, mouse, joystick, or switches.

Auditory and visual scanning modes are possible.

Built-in infrared for environmental controls and computer access.

Biklen (1990) has conducted much of the work done in facilitated communication and has reported success with the procedure. However, results of objective research on the effectiveness of facilitated communication have found no conclusive evidence supporting the method. The ASHA position paper on facilitated communication (1995, March) cautions that the scientific validity and reliability of this method have yet to be proven.

Enhancing Inclusive Classrooms for Students with Communication Disorders

The traditional service delivery model for speech and language intervention used to involve regular pullout sessions in which speech-language pathologists worked with students in a setting outside of the regular classroom. However, a combination of intervention approaches can be effective when providing speech and language services to students in public schools. Just as academic services to students with disabilities have become more and more integrated into general education programs, speech-language services are following a more inclusive model. This collaboration between the classroom teacher and special education staff might involve having the speech-language pathologist in the classroom to work with individual students, small groups, or the entire class. This could include having the teacher and speech-language pathologist teach alternate lessons or portions of a lesson, or co-teaching the same lesson at the same time.

FURTHER READING

In order to learn more about the use of facilitated communication, refer to the article "Assessing 'Alternative' Therapies for Communication Disorders in Children with Autism Spectrum Disorders: Facilitated Communication and Auditory Integration Training," by B. Siegel and B. Zimnitzky, in volume 22, issue 2 of *Journal of Speech-Language Pathology and Audiology*, 1998 (pp. 61–73).

Personal Spotlight

Speech-Language Pathologist Sharon Bond

Sharon Bond has been a speech-language pathologist (SLP) for the past 32 years, working with preschool children, their families, and a variety of other professionals committed to community-based services. She received her bachelor of science and master of science degrees in speech-language pathology at Lamar University in Beaumont, Texas. Sharon is currently completing her doctoral studies in the Faculty of Rehabilitation Medicine at the University of Alberta. She has a particular interest in the area of listening; specifically her doctoral research focuses on the impact of listening behaviours on the expressive language of young children.

Sharon's professional career has involved working as both an urban SLP in the province of Alberta and a rural SLP in Southern Saskatchewan. In her current position, Sharon is part of an interdisciplinary team providing services to children from birth to five years of age and their families. In addition to a speech-language pathologist, this team includes an audiologist, a pediatrician, a nurse practitioner, and community health nurses. Sharon is also a clinical supervisor for student SLP practicums in the Speech-Language Pathology and Audiology program at the University of Alberta.

Sharon's work with children who are experiencing communication delays and/or disorders is guided by a strong belief in family-centred practice. She believes children's communication concerns must be viewed in the context of their families and the interactions that take place with each member. The family must be considered an integral part of any assessment and/or treatment program. Family needs, timelines, concerns, beliefs, and culture must be taken into account. During treatment, family members should be provided with the information and skills that they need to facilitate the improvement of their child's communication skills. Sharon also believes that family involvement should continue to be emphasized when children with communication difficulties enter the school system.

CONSIDER THIS

What are some of the advantages and disadvantages, to both the child and general classroom teacher, for pullout speech-language intervention?

As schools try to maximize the positive impact of professional collaboration, it is important to recognize and overcome the barriers inherent in the process. According to Kerrin (1996), the barriers to greater collaboration among speech-language professionals and teachers can include the following:

▶ Territorial obstacles (*"This is my job; that is your job."*)
▶ Time concerns (*"When are general education teachers supposed to find the time to meet, plan, and modify?"*)
▶ Terror (*"I'm afraid this new way won't work."*)

Fortunately, Kerrin has also offered some good ideas for overcoming these obstacles. She suggests that team members act on the following tips:

▶ Try to be flexible and creative when scheduling conferences.
▶ Encourage everyone involved to ask questions.
▶ Invite speech-language professionals into the classroom.
▶ Ask for assistance in planning.
▶ Maintain open, regular communication.
▶ Keep an open mind, a co-operative spirit, and a sense of humour.

Future Trends

Several forces are changing the field of communication disorders in today's schools. First, general education teachers are likely to see more students with moderate to severe disabilities in their classrooms. The movement toward more inclusive environments for students will require classroom teachers to provide more classroom-based interventions for these students. Second, the caseloads of speech-language pathologists are continuing to grow, and there is an ever-increasing demand for services, especially in the area of language disorders. Although pullout speech-language intervention is typically still being offered, many of the services are delivered in an increasingly collaborative framework, with teachers and speech-language pathologists co-operating and sharing resources.

Another area of change is the expected continuation of technological advances. Some of the improved technology has already been described here; however, it is virtually impossible to keep up with the rapid improvements in this area. With continued improvements in technology, students with more severe communication disorders will have opportunities to interact with family members, teachers, and peers, perhaps participating in activities that would have seemed impossible 10 years ago.

Author's note: The author would like to express her appreciation to Janice Maxwell, B.A., M.S. (SLP), for her contributions to the practical information that was presented in this chapter. Janice is an exemplary speech-language pathologist and a wonderful friend to teachers in general education.

Summary

- Most people take the ability to communicate for granted.
- It is estimated that 8 to 10 percent of school-age children have some type of speech or language impairment.
- Communication problems result in difficulties in even simple interactions.
- Speech and language are interrelated skills that we use for communication.
- Speech disorders include impairments of fluency, voice, articulation and/or phonology. Articulation and/or phonological disorders are the most common speech disorders
- Voice disorders are related to volume, quality, or pitch.
- Language disorders are impairments of the comprehension (receptive language) or use of language (expressive language); disorders may be related to the form (phonology, morphology, syntax), content (semantics), or use (pragmatics) of language.
- Language difficulties are integrally linked to a variety of disorders (i.e., autism spectrum disorders, learning disabilities, emotional and/or behavioural disorders)
- Building a positive classroom environment is an important accommodation for students with speech and language problems.
- Teachers can make numerous accommodations and modifications for students with language disorders.
- Some language difficulties may be due to the cultural or linguistic diversity of students.
- Technology, through augmentative and alternative communication, can greatly facilitate the language use of persons with speech and language problems.

Resources

Ontario Ministry of Education, Ministry of Training. (1992). *Hearing and communication resource guide*. Toronto: Queens Printer of Ontario.

This resource guide covers hearing loss and communication with a detailed section on language development and ways to foster language. The 56-page document is also available on the internet to download at www.edu.gov.on.ca/eng/document/resource/resource.html.

Alberta Education, Special Education Branch. (1996). *Teaching students with learning disabilities*. Edmonton: Author.

A whole section on the communication and language domain appears within this resource. There are specific classroom strategies for dealing with articulation difficulties, fluency difficulties, word retrieval difficulties, and other problems.

 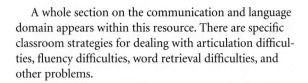

Weblinks

American Speech-Language-Hearing Association
www.asha.org
This site provides parents and educators valuable information and resources on communication disorders.

Canadian Association of Speech-Language Pathologists and Audiologists
www.caslpa.ca
This site gives the public information on the practice of speech-language pathology and audiology in Canada, and provides useful links to other websites (e.g., to provincial speech-language and hearing associations).

Ontario Association for Families of Children with Communication Disorders (OAFCCD)
www.oafccd.com/
The Association's website has a wonderful array of resources, related links, personal stories, supports, and information on children with communication disorders as well as children's activities.

Ontario Association for Families of Children with Communication Disorders, Lanark, Leeds, & Grenville Chapter
www.oafccd.com/lanark/
Here is a particularly effective website with resources, information, chat rooms, inspirational poems, stories, quotes, excellent related links for education and families, and superb kid links. The site has won numerous awards and is a must visit.

Net Connections for Communication Disorders and Sciences: An Internet Guide by Judith Maginnis Kuster
www.mnsu.edu/comdis/kuster2/welcome.html
This website has an excellent list of Internet sources related to all different types of communication disorders. A teacher will be able to find information and strategies on all communication disorders from stuttering or fluency disorders to ESL or voice disorders.

Teaching Students with Learning Disabilities

4

Chapter Objectives

After reading this chapter, you should be able to

- identify the characteristics of learning disabilities
- discuss the impact of cultural diversity on identification and intervention for students with learning disabilities
- describe the criteria for eligibility for learning disability services
- discuss and compare the traditional approaches to intervention for individuals with learning disabilities at the preschool, elementary, and secondary levels
- describe the challenges faced by adults with learning disabilities
- make modifications in teaching methods and classroom management to address academic, social and emotional, and cognitive differences

Alan was six years old when he eagerly started kindergarten. Problems began to emerge as the reading program expanded from picture books with lots of repetition to books frequently containing unknown words. Alan had difficulty using context clues, and he had limited phonemic awareness in decoding a new word. His first report card showed "needs improvement" in reading, listening, and following directions. The bright spot in Alan's Grade 1 achievement was his above-average functioning in math, his ability to attend, and good social skills. Alan was promoted to Grade 2. Over the summer, his family moved to another province.

Alan adjusted to the new school and worked well for the first nine weeks of review. He then began to have trouble finishing his work. He became frustrated with written assignments and often complained of stomach aches, asking to stay home from school. His teachers felt that he was still adjusting to a new school.

By the middle of the year, his parents and teacher agreed that accommodations were needed, as did the school team. The special education teacher put together material to review skills and phonemic elements he had not mastered. Alan's parents agreed to work on this material at home. He also worked with a Grade 5 peer helper who read with him one-on-one three days a week. The classroom teacher agreed to restate oral instructions, to continue working on phonics, and to encourage Alan to predict unknown words based on meaning and evaluate whether the word he guessed fit with the rest of the words in the sentence.

After six weeks the school team still felt that Alan was struggling too much, so they recommended a special education referral. His tests showed average intelligence and deficits in reading skills, writing, and listening. It was determined that Alan had a learning disability, making him eligible for special education services. Although signs of learning disabilities were present, the school proceeded slowly in identifying him as a child with a learning disability, aware that labelling can be detrimental to children.

Alan attended a resource class in Grade 3. Through these services, his reading of multisyllabic words greatly improved, as did his writing and listening skills. By Grade 4, he remained in the general education classroom full time, needing only periodic work with the resource teacher.

Questions to Consider

1. What alerted Alan's teacher to suspect a learning disability?

2. How might his move have been a factor in his school performance?

3. What would have happened to Alan if he had not had special education services in Grade 3?

78

Introduction

Just as it is difficult to distinguish children with **learning disabilities (LD)** from their peers by looks, you cannot distinguish adults with learning disabilities from other adults. You may be surprised to find that many important and famous people have achieved significant accomplishments in spite of experiencing a severe learning disability. Adults with learning disabilities can be found in all professions. They may be teachers, lawyers, doctors, factory workers, or politicians! Read the vignette that follows, and see if you can identify the name of the individual with a learning disability.

During his childhood, this young man was an outstanding athlete, achieving great success and satisfaction from sports. Unfortunately, he struggled in the classroom. He tried very hard, but he always seemed to fail academically. His biggest fear was being asked to stand up and read in front of his classmates. He was frequently teased about his class performance, and he described his school days as sheer torture. His only feelings of success were experienced on the playing field.

When he graduated from high school, he didn't consider going to university because he "wasn't a terrific student, and never got into books all that much." Even though he was an outstanding high-school pole vaulter, he did not get a single scholarship during his senior year. He had already gone to work with his father when he was offered a $500 football scholarship from Graceland College. He didn't accept that offer; instead he trained in track and field. Several years later, he won a gold medal in the Olympics in the gruelling decathlon event! In case you haven't guessed, this story is about Bruce Jenner.

Other famous people with learning disabilities include Leonardo da Vinci, Tom Cruise, Winston Churchill, Woodrow Wilson, F. W. Woolworth, Walt Disney, Ernest Hemingway, Albert Einstein, George Bernard Shaw, and Thomas Edison (Harwell, 1989; Silver, 1995). Individuals with learning disabilities are often misunderstood and teased early in life for their inadequacies in the classroom. In order to succeed in life, they had to be creative and persistent. Adults with learning disabilities rely on sheer determination to overcome their limitations and focus on their talents.

Perhaps the most difficult aspect of understanding and teaching students with learning disabilities is the fact that the disability is hidden. When students with obviously normal intelligence fail to finish their work, interrupt inappropriately, never seem to follow directions, and turn in sloppy, poorly organized assignments, it is natural to blame poor motivation, lack of effort—even an undesirable family life.

However, the lack of accomplishment and success in the classroom does have a cause; the students are not demonstrating these behaviours to upset or irritate their teachers. A **learning disability** is a cognitive disability; it is a disorder of thinking and reasoning. The dysfunction is presumed to be in the central nervous system; therefore, the presence of the disability is not visible.

The individuals with learning disabilities named earlier have experienced the frustration of living with a disability that is not easily identified. Children with learning disabilities look like the other students in their grade. They can perform like the other students in some areas, but not in others. As seen with Alan in the first vignette, a child with a learning disability may have good social skills and make good grades in math, but fail in reading. Another child with a learning disability may be able to read and write at grade level, but fail in math and get in trouble for misconduct. Students with learning disabilities also may perform inconsistently. They may know spelling words on Thursday and fail the test on Friday. Each individual identified with a learning disability will have unique strengths and areas of need.

In this chapter you will study the strengths and needs of children, youth, and adults who experience unexplained underachievement. Professionals from many fields have joined the search for a definition and causes of these disabilities, as well as methods to identify affected

CONSIDER THIS

Reflect on the students who were your classmates during elementary and secondary school. Do you remember any peers who had good academic abilities in some areas and low achievement in others? Were they ever accused of not trying or being lazy? They may have been misunderstood children with learning disabilities.

children and to successfully accommodate or remediate aspects of their exceptionality. The answers are still evolving, but much progress has been made in this exciting field.

Basic Concepts about Learning Disabilities

Learning Disabilities Defined

The initial studies of children later described as having learning disabilities were done by physicians interested in brain injury in children. Over the years, more than 90 terms were introduced into the literature to describe these children (Deiner, 1993). The most common terms included *minimal brain dysfunction (MBD)*, *brain damaged*, *central process dysfunction*, and *language delayed*. Separate definitions were also offered to explain each term, which only added to the confusion. The term *specific learning disabilities* was first adopted publicly in 1963 at a meeting of parents and professionals. Kirk (1962) developed the generic term *learning disabilities* in an effort to unite the field, which was torn between individuals promoting different theories on underachievement. The term was received favourably because it did not have the negative connotations of the other terms and did describe the primary characteristic of the children.

In the United States the most widely used definition of learning disabilities is the one featured in the *Individuals with Disabilities Education Act* (IDEA) (Mercer, Jordan, Allsopp, & Mercer, 1996). This definition was used in the 1990 and 1997 versions of the Act and has two parts. The first part was taken from a 1968 report by a committee appointed by the United States Office of Education (USOE); the second was developed in 1977 to provide guidelines on how to apply the definition. The two parts together comprise the present definition used federally in the United States, which is, as follows:

> "Specific learning disability" means a disorder in one or more of the basic psychological processes involved in understanding or in using language, spoken or written, which may manifest itself in an imperfect ability to listen, think, speak, read, write, spell or to do mathematical calculations. The term includes such conditions as perceptual handicaps, brain injury, minimal brain dysfunction, dyslexia, and developmental aphasia. The term does not include children who have learning problems which are primarily the result of visual, hearing, or motor handicaps, of mental retardation, or emotional disturbance, or of environmental, cultural, or economic disadvantage. (USOE, 1977, p. 65083)
>
> A specific learning disability occurs in a student if (1) s/he does not achieve commensurate with his/her age and ability in one or more of several specific areas when s/he has been given suitable instructional experiences, and (2) the student shows a severe discrepancy between achievement and intellectual ability in one or more of seven areas: (a) oral expression, (b) listening comprehension, (c) written expression, (d) basic reading skill, (e) reading comprehension, (f) mathematics calculation and (g) mathematics reasoning. (Lerner, 1993)

Although this two-part definition is commonly used in the United States, there has been criticism about its use of nonspecific terms (e.g., "perceptual handicaps") and the omission of the acknowledgment that learning disabilities can coexist with other handicaps (Wong, 1996). Therefore, a joint committee of representatives from parent and professional organizations worked together to develop an improved definition of learning disabilities that first emerged in 1981 and was updated in 1997 to read, as follows:

> Learning disabilities is a general term that refers to a heterogeneous group of disorders manifested by significant difficulties in the acquisition and use of listening, speaking, reading, writing, reasoning, or mathematical abilities. These disorders

are intrinsic to the individual, presumed to be due to central nervous system dysfunction and may occur across the life span. Problems in self-regulatory behaviours, social perception, and social interaction may exist with learning disabilities but do not by themselves constitute a learning disability. Although learning disabilities may occur concomitantly with other handicapping conditions (for example, sensory impairment, mental retardation, serious emotional disturbance) or with extrinsic influences such as cultural differences, insufficient or inappropriate instruction, they are not the result of these conditions or influences. (National Joint Committee on Learning Disabilities, NJCLD, Hammill, 1993, p. 4)

These definitions are the two most frequently used from among many definitions that have been suggested by a variety of organizations (see Hammill, 1990, for review). In Canada, Bernice Wong, a leading author and researcher in the field of learning disabilities, notes that the Canadian definition is closely aligned with the NJCLD definition; however, it emphasizes social and emotional problems to a greater extent (Wong, 1996).

In 2002, the Learning Disabilities Association of Canada (LDAC) defined learning disabilities as follows:

Learning disabilities refer to a number of disorders which may affect the acquisition, organization, retention, understanding or use of verbal or nonverbal information. These disorders affect learning in individuals who otherwise demonstrate at least average abilities essential for thinking and/or reasoning. As such, learning disabilities are distinct from global intellectual deficiency.

Learning disabilities result from impairments in one or more processes related to perceiving, thinking, remembering or learning. These include, but are not limited to: language processing; phonological processing; visual spatial processing; processing speed; memory and attention; and executive functions (e.g., planning and decision-making).

Learning disabilities range in severity and may interfere with the acquisition and use of one or more of the following:

- oral language (e.g., listening, speaking, understanding);
- reading (e.g., decoding, phonetic knowledge, word recognition, comprehension);
- written language (e.g., spelling, written expression); and
- mathematics (e.g., computation, problem solving).

Learning disabilities may also involve difficulties with organizational skills, social perception, social interaction and perspective taking.

Learning disabilities are lifelong. The way in which they are expressed may vary over an individual's lifetime, depending on the interaction between the demands of the environment and the individual's strengths and needs. Learning disabilities are suggested by unexpected academic under-achievement or achievement which is maintained only by unusually high levels of effort and support.

Learning disabilities are due to genetic and/or neurobiological factors or injury that alters brain functioning in a manner which affects one or more processes related to learning. These disorders are not due primarily to hearing and/or vision problems, socio-economic factors, cultural or linguistic differences, lack of motivation or ineffective teaching, although these factors may further complicate the challenges faced by individuals with learning disabilities. Learning disabilities may co-exist with various conditions including attentional, behavioural and emotional disorders, sensory impairments or other medical conditions. (Learning Disabilities Association of Canada Definition, 2002)

Although the above definition has been accepted by LDAC and has influenced the definitions adopted by the individual provinces or territories, the actual identification of children with learning disabilities varies across the country (Wiener & Siegel, 1992).

Prevalence and Causes of Learning Disabilities

In today's schools, there are by far more students with learning disabilities than with any other disability. In both Canada and the United States, it is estimated that approximately half of all exceptional students have learning disabilities (U.S. Department of Education, 1995; Wong, 1996).

Experts generally agree that learning is hindered in children with learning disabilities because of neurobiological abnormalities, or atypical brain development and/or function causing a problem in how the brain processes information (Fedorowicz, Benezra, MacDonald, McElgunn, Wilson, & Kaplan, 2001). This causes an unexpected discrepancy between intelligence and achievement. Why this happens generally remains unknown. The literature suggests several causes, primarily hereditary factors and trauma experienced before birth, during birth, and after birth.

1. *Genetic and hereditary influences:* Some studies have cited the large number of relatives with learning problems in children identified with learning disabilities. Chromosomal abnormalities and structural brain differences have also been linked to learning disabilities. Raskind (2001) describes the progress that has been made identifying the gene location for a learning disability in reading. Research in this area continues to show promise.
2. *Causes occurring before birth:* Learning problems have been linked to injuries to the embryo or fetus caused by the birth mother's use of alcohol, cigarettes, or other drugs, such as cocaine and prescription and nonprescription drugs. Through the mother, the fetus is exposed to the toxins, causing malformations of the developing brain and central nervous system. Although significant amounts of overexposure to these drugs may cause serious problems, such as intellectual disabilities, no safe levels have been identified. For more information, refer to the section on Fetal Alcohol Spectrum Disorders (FASD) presented in Chapter 9.
3. *Causes occurring during birth process:* Traumas during birth may include prolonged labour, anoxia, prematurity, and injury from medical instruments such as forceps. Although not all children with a traumatic birth are found to have learning problems later, a significant number of children with learning problems do have a history of complications during this period.
4. *Causes occurring after birth:* High fever, encephalitis, meningitis, stroke, diabetes, head trauma, and pediatric acquired immune deficiency syndrome (AIDS) have been linked to learning disabilities. Malnutrition, poor postnatal health care, and lead ingestion can also lead to neurological dysfunction (Hallahan, Kauffman, & Lloyd, 1999; Fedorowicz et al., 2001).

Advances in neurological research and use of computerized neurological techniques such as computerized axial tomography (CAT) scan and positron emission tomography (PET) scan have made professionals more inclined to believe in a neurological explanation of learning disabilities. Widespread use of these tests to identify a learning disability has not been forthcoming for several reasons: such procedures are expensive and invasive, and the documented presence of a neurological dysfunction does not affect how the child is taught (Hallahan et al., 1999). However, this research is important to advance knowledge of this type of disability and in the future may help determine the effectiveness of various treatment techniques. Studies are currently under way to monitor the impact of various reading interventions on the results of neuroimaging (Pugh et al., 2001). A neurophysicist recently recommended using neuroimaging to identify young children with reading problems for treatment purposes, noting that learning to read can

CONSIDER THIS

Often parents will ask teachers what causes a learning disability. You might discuss some of the possible causes and suggest that the single cause is seldom identifiable for individual children. Reassure them that pinpointing the cause is not a factor in planning and implementing effective intervention strategies.

cause the brain to change and become like the brain of good readers (Richards, 2001). It is interesting to think about the possibility that one day brain imaging could be used to determine the best methods for teaching.

Characteristics of Students with Learning Disabilities

Learning disabilities are primarily described as a deficit in academic achievement (reading, writing, and mathematics) and/or language (listening and/or speaking). However, children with learning disabilities may have significant problems in other areas, such as social interactions and emotional maturity, attention and hyperactivity, memory, cognition, metacognition, motor skills, and perceptual abilities. It is also important to understand that students with learning disabilities tend to be overly optimistic regarding some of their abilities, masking strategy and skill deficits. They may need more support in these areas than they report that they need (Klassen, 2002). Learning disabilities are presumed to be a central nervous system dysfunction; therefore, characteristics may be manifested throughout the lifespan (preschool to adulthood) (Bender, 2001).

The most common characteristics of students with learning disabilities are described briefly in the following sections, concentrating on the challenges they may create in a classroom. Students with learning disabilities are a heterogeneous group. A single student will not have difficulties in all of these areas. In addition, any area could be a strength for a student with learning disabilities, and the student might exceed the abilities of his or her peers in that area. For example, a student with strong abilities in math, metacognition, and social skills may experience limitations in reading, writing, and attention. Another student might have strengths in attention, writing, and reading, and be challenged in math, social skills, and metacognition. An understanding of these characteristics will be important in developing prereferral interventions, in making appropriate referrals, and in identifying effective accommodations and intervention strategies. Figure 4.1 displays the possible strengths and areas of need of children with learning disabilities.

Academic Difficulties   During the elementary years, a discrepancy between ability and achievement begins to emerge in students with learning disabilities. Often puzzling to

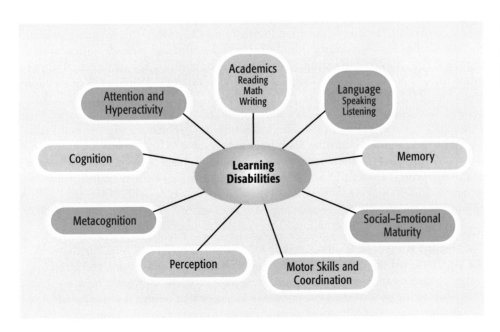

FIGURE 4.1

Areas of Possible Strengths and Needs of Students with Learning Disabilities

During Grades 2 through 6, academic problems begin to become obvious.

TEACHING TIP

Just as students who demonstrate reading difficulties may have difficulties understanding and using language, students with receptive and expressive language difficulties may have difficulties reading. Consult with the speech-language pathologist and reading consultant in your school division to determine whether students demonstrating reading and/or language difficulties require further assessments in either area.

teachers, they seem to have strengths similar to their peers in several areas, but their rate of learning in other areas is unexpectedly slower. In the vignette that began this chapter, Alan provides a typical profile of a child with learning disabilities: above-average ability in math; average ability in language, attention, and social skills; and severe difficulties in reading, written expression, and listening.

The academic problems that serve to identify a learning disability fall into the areas of reading, math, and written expression. The most prevalent academic difficulty for students with learning disabilities is reading. However, this does not mean that a learning disability is the same thing as a reading disability. Although people equate learning disabilities with reading disabilities, reading problems form only one type of academic learning disabilities (Weber, 1994; Wong, 1996). There are also spelling, writing, and mathematics disabilities, as well as nonacademic learning disabilities such as perceptual, memory, and visual-motor. Lyon et al. (2001) reported that approximately 80 percent of the children identified with a learning disability have primary difficulties in the area of reading and related language functions. Problems may be noted in *basic reading skills* and *reading comprehension*. Children with learning disabilities may struggle with oral reading tasks. They may read in a strained voice with poor phrasing, ignore punctuation, and grope for words like a much younger child. Oral reading problems cause tremendous embarrassment to these children. Polloway, Patton, and Serna (2001) confirm that a student's self-image and feelings of confidence are greatly affected by reading experience. Difficulties in reading skills can also lead to acting-out behaviour and poor motivation.

Some children with learning disabilities may be able to say the words correctly but not remember what they have read. Comprehension problems may include one or more of the following: (1) identifying the main idea, (2) recalling basic facts and events in a sequence, and (3) making inferences or evaluating what has been read (Mercer, 1997). A child with a specific difficulty in reading may be described as having **dyslexia**. Dyslexia has been defined by the International Dyslexia Association (IDA) as follows:

> Dyslexia is a specific learning disability that is neurological in origin. It is characterized by difficulties with accurate and/or fluent word recognition and by poor spelling and decoding abilities. These difficulties typically result from a deficit in the phonological component of language that is often unexpected in relation to other cognitive abilities and the provision of effective classroom

instruction. Secondary consequences may include problems in reading comprehension and reduced reading experience that can impede growth of vocabulary and background knowledge. (IDA, 2002)

Another major academic problem area is mathematics. Students with learning disabilities may have problems in *math calculations* or *math reasoning* (LDAC, 1987). These conceptual and skill areas include difficulties in the four operations, the concept of zero, regrouping, place value, basic math concepts (e.g., one-to-one correspondence, sets), and solving math problems. Children may have *abilities* in calculation but have *disabilities* in math reasoning; they may make many errors in calculations but be able to perform calculations to solve a math word problem. Often, the rate of response interferes with success in math; for example, a child may be able to perform the skill, but be unable to complete the number of problems required during the time allowed. Robinson, Manchetti, and Torgesen (2002) proposed that for some children this math difficulty may be due to either problems in the phonological processing of the features of spoken numbers or failure to grasp meaningful aspects of numbers. They note that 43 percent of the students with a math disability also have reading problems. It is hoped that math disabilities will soon be studied as intensely as reading disabilities. A disability in math may be referred to as **dyscalculia**.

Learning disabilities in the area of *writing* are beginning to receive more recognition as a potentially serious problem. The three main areas of concern are handwriting, spelling, and written expression, including mechanics and creativity. The impact of written language problems increases with a student's age because so many school assignments require a written product. A learning disability in writing may be referred to as **dysgraphia**.

Language Difficulties   Individuals may demonstrate *oral expression* (speaking) and/or *listening comprehension* difficulties. These two areas control our ability to communicate with others; therefore, any areas of weakness can have a major impact on quality of life—including life in a general education classroom! Studies have found that more than 60 percent of students with learning disabilities have some type of language disorder (Bryan, Bay, Lopez-Reyna, & Donahue, 1991). Common oral language problems include difficulty in retrieving words; children often use a less appropriate word because the right word will not come to them. The response rate of children with learning disabilities may be slower than that of their nondisabled peers, and they may speak more slowly. If ample time is not allowed for a response, the student's behaviour may be misinterpreted as failure to understand or refusal to participate. Children with learning disabilities tend to use simpler, less mature language and confuse sequences in retelling a story. These areas of weakness in expressive language suggest possible difficulties in receptive language or listening, as well (Smith, 1994). Listening problems also can be easily misinterpreted. A child with a disability in listening demonstrates his or her difficulties in a negative way, for example, by failing to follow directions or by appearing oppositional or unmotivated. A teacher's careful observation and assessment of a student's language ability is important for ensuring the student's success.

An area of concern, and a subject of current research pertaining to children with language-learning disabilities, is the use of language in social communication situations or **pragmatics**. Children with these disabilities are sometimes unsuccessful in fully participating in conversation. They may need extra time to process incoming information, or they may not understand the meaning of the words or word sequences. They may miss nonverbal language cues. They may not understand jokes; they may laugh inappropriately or at the wrong times. Group work is often difficult, as is giving or following directions. Language disabilities can contribute significantly to difficulties in other social situations as well.

CROSS-REFERENCE

Refer to Chapter 3 to review other language areas in which students with learning disabilities may demonstrate difficulties.

CROSS-REFERENCE

Often students with learning disabilities have social-emotional problems and will present challenges in behaviour management in the classroom. Refer to Chapter 6 for more information in this area.

TEACHING TIP

Encourage students who have listening difficulties to ask questions when listening to a speaker (e.g., "You said to finish Chapter 3. Does this mean we're supposed to answer the chapter questions?"). This can help students to clarify the message a speaker is conveying.

Social-Emotional Problems   The social and emotional functioning of individuals with learning disabilities has become a focus of investigation only fairly recently. For many years the majority of research on learning disabilities was in the academic or processing areas (Bender, 1998). However, in recognition of the importance of examining the noncognitive functioning of children with learning disabilities, a 1994 issue of a major journal in the field was devoted to the study of the social-emotional development of students with learning disabilities (Bender, 1994).

In a review of the literature, Judith Wiener (1987) concluded that students with learning disabilities tend to be rated by their peers as less likeable. Furthermore, in work that Dr. Wiener and colleagues at the University of Toronto completed (Wiener & Harris, 1993; Wiener, Harris, & Shirer, 1990), it was found that labelling a child as having a learning disability affected peer ratings. Children who were not school-identified as having a learning disability received higher peer ratings than those who were identified even when they otherwise met the same criteria. Therefore, children identified by the school as having a learning disability are at risk of poor social acceptance. Research by Kavale and Forness (1996) demonstrated that 75 percent of students identified as having a learning disability were significantly different from their nondisabled peers on most measures of social competence.

Emotionally, children and adolescents with learning disabilities appear to be at greater risk of depression and negative self-perceptions of academic performance (Bender, 1998). Students with learning disabilities report more depressive symptoms, more severe depression, and more negative self-perceptions than students without learning disabilities (Heath, 1996). Specifically, students with learning disabilities report negative self-perceptions of academic performance, but may report adequate or even high self-perceptions in other areas, such as athletics, physical appearance, and social acceptance (Heath & Wiener, 1996). Nancy Heath, in her self-perception and mood laboratory at McGill University, has studied the self-perceptions and mood of children and adolescents with learning disabilities longitudinally. She has found that frequently students with learning disabilities report inaccurately positive self-perceptions of academic performance, but that these self-perceptions serve to buffer the students from depressive symptoms that often occur in the face of ongoing failure (Heath, 1995). Thus, students with learning disabilities who had a more realistic understanding of their academic difficulties reported higher levels of depression than those who denied having academic difficulties. Dr. Heath's research team is investigating the possible role of teacher feedback in these students' self-perceptions and mood.

In summary, Gorman (1999) proposes that learning disabilities may result in or increase emotional distress. Emotional issues may mask or exacerbate a child's learning difficulties. However, she notes that positive emotional health can enhance the performance of students with learning disabilities. By being sensitive to these issues, you can take care to include students with learning disabilities in supportive situations and provide reinforcement for specific successes. General praise statements such as "Good work!" or "You are really smart!" will not have much impact because they are not believable to the students. Commenting on or rewarding specific accomplishments will be more effective. Additional examples of appropriate interventions in this area for inclusive classrooms will be discussed later in this chapter and in future chapters.

Attention Difficulties and Hyperactivity   Attention is a critical skill in learning. Conte (1991) suggests that to be effective learners, children must be able to initiate attention, direct their attention in the appropriate direction, sustain their attention according to the task demands, and shift attention when appropriate. Difficulties in these areas can have an impact on all aspects of success in school. When children are "not paying attention," they cannot respond appropriately to questions, follow directions, or take notes during a lecture. The excess movement of a hyperactive student can draw sharp criticism when it negatively affects the learning environment. Social problems occur when the student interrupts others and does not listen to his or her peers. Students with attention problems often have trouble finishing assignments or rush through their work with little regard for detail. Estimates of the number of students with learning disabilities who have attention problems vary widely based on the stringency of the criteria used to define the attention deficit (DeLong, 1995; Semrud-Clikeman et al., 1992). However, the majority of individuals with learning disabilities do not have attention-deficit disorders (Weber & Bennett, 1999). Attention deficits are covered more thoroughly in Chapter 5.

Memory Difficulties   Several studies have suggested that students with learning disabilities have more difficulties in memory than students without learning disabilities (Beale & Tippett, 1992). Students with memory problems have trouble retaining learned information. They may have difficulty in repeating information recently read or heard, following multiple step directions, or performing tasks in the correct sequence. Teachers and parents may also report that the memory skills are inconsistent—for example, such a student may know the multiplication facts on Thursday and fail the test on Friday! O'Shaughnessy and Swanson (1998) suggest that the problem is mainly with an inability to code new information for memory storage. The good news is that when children with learning disabilities are taught a memory strategy, they tend to perform memory tasks as well as their typically achieving peers.

Cognition Difficulties   Cognition refers to the ability to reason or think (Hallahan et al., 1996). Students with problems in this area may make poor decisions or frequent errors. They may have trouble getting started on a task, have delayed verbal responses, require more supervision, or have trouble adjusting to change. Understanding social expectations may be difficult. They may require concrete demonstrations. They often have trouble using previously learned information in a new situation.

Metacognition Difficulties   Hallahan et al. (1999) refer to **metacognition** as "thinking about thinking." Metacognitive deficits include the inability to control and direct one's own attention and mental processes (Wong, 1991). Students with problems in this area might have difficulty focusing on listening, purposefully remembering important information, connecting that information to prior knowledge, making sense out of the new information, and using what they know to solve a problem. They often lack strategies for planning and organizing, setting priorities, and predicting and solving problems. An important component of metacognition is the ability to evaluate one's own behaviour and behave differently when identifying inappropriate behaviours or mistakes.

Perceptual Differences   Perceptual disorders affect the ability to recognize stimuli being received through sight, hearing, or touch and to discriminate between and interpret the sensations appropriately. A child with a learning disability might not have any problems in these areas, or he or she might have deficits in any or all of them. Research has shown that visual perception is more important at very young ages, but is not a major requirement for higher-level academics (Smith, 1994). Identification of deficits and training in the perceptual processes was emphasized in the early 1970s; however, it is no longer a prominent consideration in the education of children with learning disabilities.

Motor Skills and Co-ordination Problems   This area has also been de-emphasized in the identification of an intervention for children with learning disabilities because it is not

CROSS-REFERENCE

Students with learning disabilities may also have attention deficit/hyperactivity disorders. This topic is covered more extensively in Chapter 5.

TEACHING TIP

Help students with memory difficulties remember and follow oral directions by breaking up longer directions into multiple steps (e.g., "Turn to page 12 in your math book; complete questions 1, 3, and 5; hand in your work.").

FURTHER READING

To learn more about metacognition and learning disabilities, read the chapter "Metacognition and Learning Disabilities" in B. Wong's book *Learning about Learning Disabilities* (2nd ed.), 1998 (pp. 277–307).

directly related to academics. However, it is common for children with learning disabilities to display problems in gross motor areas; they often cannot throw and catch a ball or may have a clumsy gait. Common fine motor deficits include difficulties with cutting with scissors, buttoning clothing, and handwriting. Occupational therapists refer to this profile as a developmental co-ordination disorder (DCD) and have acknowledged the overlap between this disorder and learning disabilities for more than a decade (Martini, Heath, & Missiunia, 1999). Consideration of motor skills and co-ordination is important in the selection of a vocational program and ultimately in the identification of a career.

Identification, Assessment, and Eligibility

In the United States, as mentioned earlier, the federal Office of Education specified criteria for identifying a learning disability (USOE, 1977), stating that there must be a "severe discrepancy" between achievement and intellectual ability. Similarly, the Learning Disabilities Association of Canada definition (LDAC, 1987, 2002) indicates that individuals with learning disabilities will have potentially average, average, or above-average intelligence with delays in specific areas (e.g., reading, writing, or arithmetic). In general, definitions of learning disability all suggest a discrepancy between intelligence and achievement; however, the assessment of the discrepancy remains controversial (Bender, 1998), as does the validity of intelligence measures in individuals with learning disabilities (Siegel, 1989). For example, IQ scores may underestimate an individual's competence since most individuals with a learning disability "have deficiencies in one or more of the component skills that are part of these IQ tests" (Siegel, 1999, p. 311). A discrepancy between IQ and achievement may also discriminate against individuals from lower socio-economic backgrounds, since "IQ scores are significantly correlated with socioeconomic status" (Siegel, 1999, p. 313). The debate as to which is the best method for identifying learning disabilities continues in the literature (e.g., D'Angiulli & Siegel, 2003; Siegel, 1999; Vellutino, Scanlon, & Lyon, 2000). Despite these criticisms, in practice, most school psychologists try to establish that a significant difference, or discrepancy, exists between a student's achievement and intelligence, thereby identifying a learning disability (Weber, 1994).

In a Canadian Council for Exceptional Children survey, it was found that percentages of children identified as having a learning disability varied widely across the country. Quebec identified 10.2 percent of its child population as having a learning disability, Nova Scotia 7.0 percent, Ontario 3.1 percent, Saskatchewan 1.7 percent, and British Columbia 1.3 percent (Wiener & Siegel, 1992). Furthermore, school board to school board the percentage of children identified as having a learning disability can vary.

As Weber (1994) notes in his book, *Special Education in Canadian Schools*, these variations can be explained only by the fact that there must be significant differences in identification procedures from province to province. For example, in Quebec the "learning difficulty" definition stipulates only that the student be one or two years below grade level in any achievement area. In contrast, in Ontario the learning disabilities definition requires the results of an IQ test and a significant discrepancy between intellectual functioning and achievement; it also requires the exclusion of all other exceptionalities as causes of the low achievement. The Quebec definition uses much less stringent criteria than the Ontario definition does; as a result, a higher number of children are identified as having a learning disability in Quebec. Ultimately, as a teacher in a Canadian school, you need to familiarize yourself with the criteria used in your province and school division. Be aware of characteristics of students with learning disabilities to know when you might want to further document a student's strengths and areas of need for a possible referral to the school psychologist or school team.

Difficulty of Identifying Preschool Students with Learning Disabilities The criteria for determining a learning disability (USOE, 1977) mainly involve academic and language deficits that emerge in the elementary years; therefore, the identification of disabilities and delivery of special education services for preschool children are very controversial (Jenkins & O'Connor, 2001). The National Joint Committee on Learning Disabilities (NJCLD) issued a paper in 1988 describing this issue. They noted that the greatest complication in identifying preschool children with learning disabilities is the tremendous differences in growth and maturation that children manifest, which are normal and may not represent a learning disability. Hallahan et al. (1999) present two arguments against early identification of learning disabilities. The first concerns the difficulty in diagnosis that results from the inadequacy of assessment tools and procedures for this age group. Young children may have language and other skills that are lower than expected based on IQ, but it is difficult to determine whether these are the result of a learning disability, a maturational lag, or the effect of diverse educational experiences, language, and/or culture. The second argument takes into account the risk of diagnosing a learning disability where none exists, thus labelling and burdening the child unnecessarily. However, this argument does not address the fact that an equal risk is taken when a student who needs special educational services is not diagnosed and appropriately assisted; this student may be burdened by difficulties and failure that could have been avoided.

Critics call current practice for learning disabilities identification the "wait and fail" effect as the gap or discrepancy between ability and achievement becomes large enough to be labelled as a severe discrepancy that warrants services (MacMillan & Siperstein, 2001). Lyon et al. (2001) concluded that a child must be 9 years old before discrepancy from IQ can be measured reliably. Thus, under the discrepancy model, potentially life-changing failure occurs for several years. They suggest that early intervention can be so critical for disabilities in the area of reading that children with a strong family history of attention difficulties or reading failure should be labelled at risk and placed in a preventive intervention program to strengthen their areas of weakness. The American Academy of Pediatrics (1988) recommends the following benchmarks for ascertaining risk of learning disabilities:

1. *Language delay:* Children should be putting sentences together by age 2 1/2.
2. *Difficulty with speech:* By the age of 3, a child's language should be understandable by adults more than 50 percent of the time.
3. *Co-ordination problems:* By the age of 5, children should be tying shoes, buttoning clothes, hopping, and cutting with scissors.
4. *Short attention span:* Although attention span increases with age, between ages 3 and 5, children should be sitting and attending while a short story is read to them. (p. 35)

Cultural and Linguistic Diversity

Learning disabilities are found in approximately 5 percent of the school-age population and the number of school-age children with cultural and language diversity is growing steadily; therefore, many children will inevitably fall into both groups (Gerstein & Woodward, 1994). Although the issues related to educating all culturally diverse children apply to the population of children with learning disabilities as well, the existence of a learning disability does bring additional challenges in assessment for identification, program planning, instructional implementation, and personnel preparation.

FURTHER READING

The text *Children and Adults with Learning Disabilities* by T. E. C. Smith, C. Dowdy, E. Polloway, and G. Blalock, published by Allyn & Bacon in 1997, devotes a chapter to the important topic of diversity and learning disabilities.

CONSIDER THIS

Understanding and speaking a language other than English may have a significant impact on the assessment process. Inappropriate referrals, identification of a disability, and/or inappropriate programming might result.

Accurately identifying a learning disability in the presence of cultural diversity is no small challenge. School personnel must carefully determine that the differences related to diversity are not the primary cause of a student's learning difficulties. Teachers sometimes expect less from students from diverse cultural backgrounds and view special education as the most viable placement option for them (Gerstein, Brengleman, & Jimenez, 1994). As a result, a disproportionate number are referred for assessment and ultimately funnelled into special education settings. Moecker (1992) found that too often a diagnosis of learning disability was based on intelligence and achievement tests administered in English without considering cultural and language difference. Thus, a child's failure to make progress may not be the result of a learning disability but the failure of the education system to respect and adequately respond to cultural and language differences. However, it is certainly possible that a child with a low socioeconomic level or one who speaks English as a second language could have a central nervous system dysfunction that results in a learning disability.

In Canada, we have a large multicultural community as well as a policy of official bilingualism and second language immersion programs (Wiener & Siegel, 1992). Beyond that, 1.3 percent of children in Canada are from First Nations communities and have specific language, learning, and cultural requirements. Differentiating learning disabilities from problems with English or French as a second language is a major diagnostic issue (Wiener & Siegel, 1992). Furthermore, second language instruction is often problematic for students with learning disabilities (Trites, 1981). In situations where the second language instruction is limited, the problems may be minimal; however, in situations where children are instructed in a second language for most or all of their schooling, the child with a learning disability will encounter significant difficulties (Carey, 1987). New Brunswick francophones and Quebec anglophones, as well as francophones across Canada, are especially subject to these problems.

McGill researcher Maggie Bruck (1982) has argued that, as children with learning disabilities experience difficulty in both their first and second language programs, removing them from an immersion program is not beneficial; what matters is that they can obtain appropriate remedial assistance. Nevertheless, in practice, a common recommendation for students with learning disabilities in an immersion program is to transfer them to a first language instruction program. Also, most students with learning disabilities prefer to be instructed in their first language.

In summary, multicultural and second language components make the identification and instruction of Canadian students with learning disabilities quite complex.

When a student is determined eligible for special education services, the process of designing and implementing an appropriate educational plan is critical. Teachers may be uninformed about the short- and long-term goals held by families from different cultures. Therefore, family participation and ongoing communication about progress are essential. Consulting with the student's family, members of the community (e.g., community leaders from different cultural backgrounds), and professionals in your own school (e.g., colleagues, principal) can assist the classroom teacher in developing and implementing appropriate educational programming for culturally and/or linguistically diverse students.

TEACHING TIP

Teachers can utilize holistic approaches to literacy development to address the varied linguistic needs of students (e.g., utilize thematic literature units to integrate language teaching across the curriculum; use daily journal entries to encourage daily writing practice).

Strategies for Curriculum and Instruction

Over the years, treatment procedures for individuals with learning disabilities have been a source of controversy. In the 1970s, advocates for perceptual training of auditory and visual processes debated those who advocated direct instruction in the deficit academic area(s) (Engelmann & Carnine, 1982). A convincing article by Hammill and Larsen (1974) analyzed research showing that perceptual training did little to improve basic academic skills. This triggered a move toward a skills approach in which direct instruction was implemented in the areas of academic deficit. More recently, language, social-emotional, and cognitive-metacognitive areas have received positive attention. Many approaches have gained acceptance as research-based methods for improving the skills and developing the abilities of children and adults with learning disabilities. Other nontraditional approaches have been proposed and some even have a large following, though they may not be supported by research. Teachers need to be well informed on all approaches so that they can provide objective information to parents who seek to understand and address their child's difficulties. The following section discusses the accepted traditional approaches for each age level and provides a brief overview of some of the nontraditional approaches.

Traditional Approaches

In a review of various treatment approaches, Elksnin et al. (2001) conclude that no single approach to learning disabilities can be cited as the best. They suggest that each model has a "partial view of the truth," and "each individually is too narrow to be useful for all students" (Elksnin et al., 2001, p. 189). Lloyd (1988) suggests that the most effective treatment approaches are structured and goal oriented, provide multiple opportunities for practice, include a strategy, foster independence, and are comprehensive and detailed. Many of the following approaches adhere to these time-tested principles. They all can be implemented in a general education classroom and may benefit many typically achieving students as well. The strategies are discussed according to age levels—preschool, elementary, secondary, and adult. The largest section concerns the elementary school student; however, many elementary-level techniques are equally effective at the secondary level.

Preschool Services   In addition to the controversy surrounding assessment and identification of learning disabilities in preschool children, much has been written for and against the educational effectiveness and cost-effectiveness of early intervention programs for these children. Bender (2001) summarizes research in this area by stating that early intervention for some preschool children with learning disabilities—particularly those from low socioeconomic minority groups—is effective.

Mercer (1997) provides an overview of the curriculum models primarily used in preschool programs for children with learning disabilities. These include developmental, cognitive, and behavioural models. The **developmental model** stresses provision of an enriched environment. The child is provided numerous experiences and opportunities for learning. Development is stimulated through language and storytelling, field trips, and creative opportunities. These activities are particularly effective with diverse learners (Craig, Hull, Haggart, & Crowder, 2001).

The **cognitive model** (or constructionist model) is based on Piaget's work. Stimulating the child's cognitive or thinking abilities is the primary focus. Activities are designed to improve memory, discrimination, language, concept formation, self-evaluation, problem solving, and comprehension. This new area of research is experiencing great success.

Concepts learned by direct instruction and the theory of reinforcement form the basis for the **behavioural model**. Measurable goals are set for each student, behaviours are observed, and desirable behaviour is reinforced. Direct instruction is provided to accomplish goals, and progress is charted to provide data that determine the next instructional task. For example, Abbott, Walton, and Greenwood (2002) used research on phonemic awareness to identify skills appropriate for K, 1, and 2. Students showing low

CONSIDER THIS

According to Lyon's study, intervention in reading skills in Grades 1 to 3 is critical. Should all students who are behind their peers in reading ability be helped during these years? What are possible positive and negative outcomes of providing a "special education" program for all of these children at risk for later failure?

FURTHER READING

Learn more about risk and resilience by reading Morrison and Cosden's (1997) article, "Risk, Resilience, and Adjustment of Individuals with Learning Disabilities," in volume 20 of *Learning Disability Quarterly*, 1997 (pp. 43–60).

performance during the regular shared book activities were given lessons several times a week depending on their level of weakness. Performance was closely monitored and intervention intensified as needed.

Mercer (1997) recommends a program that combines features from each approach. He suggests some structure, availability of free-choice activities, direct instruction in targeted areas, daily charting and feedback, developmental activities, and spontaneous learning experiences. McCardle, Cooper, Houle, Kart, and Paul-Brown (2001) speak to the importance of the birth-to-five period as the foundation for learning as children acquire knowledge and develop abilities—particularly in the area of reading. They, like others, speak against the "wait to fail" approach where children are not identified as struggling readers until Grade 3 or 4. These researchers recommend a focus on book reading, writing, and fine-motor activities like colouring and drawing, as well as on developmental experiences that enhance vocabulary and increase language and communication skills.

TEACHING TIP

In order to build social interaction skills, encourage preschool children to interact with peers in a variety of community settings (e.g., library story hour, swimming lessons).

These methods allow individual needs to be met in an inclusive setting without stigmatizing the children. Children at this age are more likely to be falsely identified as learning disabled because of a maturational lag or lack of educational opportunities; therefore, it is particularly important to teach them in inclusive settings if at all possible. Lyon et al. (2001) agree that the most efficient way to intervene early in reading is through general education. They and others recommend that resources be allocated for intervention instead of the expensive process of determining eligibility. Lyon et al. (2001) summarized several studies stating that when intervention is used with the bottom 18 percent of the student population and works on 70 percent, the number of at-risk children requiring services drops from 18 to 5.4 percent.

CROSS-REFERENCE

Read more about curricular content and instructional adaptations for elementary level students in Chapter 13.

Elementary Services   By Grade 5, 76 percent of the children with learning disabilities have been identified; more children are identified during Grades 1 and 2 than at any other time (McLesky, 1992). The importance of intervention during the early elementary years is validated by Lyon et al. (2001), suggesting that over 70 percent of the children with a reading disability in Grade 3 remained disabled in grade 12. Similarly, Cunningham and Stanovich (1997) found that reading ability in Grade 1 was a strong predictor of reading ability in Grade 11. As discussed in the section on characteristics,

Most children with learning disabilities are identified during early elementary grades.

many of these areas of difficulty remain a problem throughout an individual's life. The intervention begun during elementary years may be equally important at the secondary level and for some adults. Intervention is important in academic and language difficulties, social-emotional problems, and cognitive and metacognitive deficits.

Children with learning disabilities may have academic and language deficits in any or all of the following areas:

- Basic reading skills
- Reading comprehension
- Math calculation
- Math reasoning
- Written expression
- Oral expression
- Listening

These areas are usually the focus of an elementary curriculum, and therefore, they can very often be addressed in the general education classroom. Both general and special education teachers have been trained to provide instruction in these areas, so collaborative teaching is possible. Due to the uneven skill development and unique areas of strength and need in children with learning disabilities, individualized assessment is required to identify areas that specifically need to be addressed. Informal methods, such as the curriculum-based assessment discussed in Chapter 1, are usually effective for planning instruction. This assessment should include an evaluation of the student's strengths, which may indicate the most effective method for instruction.

Student strengths and areas of need are very diverse; therefore, a single method of teaching may not meet the needs of all students with learning disabilities. For example, in the area of reading instruction, the general education teacher may use a reading approach based on reading literature for meaning; development in areas such as phonics is assumed to occur naturally as the reader becomes more efficient. In this method, often referred to as the **whole language method**, the teacher might note difficulty with a phonetic principle during oral reading and subsequently develop a mini-lesson using text to teach the skill. Resources are available on using this method to teach students with learning disabilities (Rhodes & Dudley-Marling, 1996). Unfortunately, many children with learning disabilities do not readily acquire the alphabet code because of limitations in processing the sounds of letters. Research has shown a dramatic reduction in reading failure when comprehensive, explicit instructions are provided in **phonemic awareness**, as seen when a **structured sequential phonics program** is used that focuses on decoding and fluent word recognition, processing text to construct meaning, vocabulary, spelling, and writing. A small number of children will need an intense small-group or one-on-one format (Foorman & Torgesen, 2001). A survey of teaching practices used by special education teachers nominated as effective literacy teachers showed that they used the best of whole language and direct instruction. See Table 4.1 to review the practices and philosophies of these outstanding teachers.

One strength of the whole language method is its focus on the comprehension of authentic reading material; the teacher using the phonics method must purposely develop those important comprehension skills. These two reading methods are discussed further in Chapter 13.

Another way to facilitate success for students with learning disabilities in inclusive settings is teaching a **strategy** to apply during the process of learning new information or skills. A strategy is defined by Deshler and Lenz (1989) as an individual's approach to a task. It includes how "a person thinks and acts when planning, executing, and evaluating performance on a task and its subsequent outcomes" (p. 203). Students with learning

TABLE 4.1

General Philosophies and Learning Environments

Identify with a Whole Language Philosophy

Use of the language experience approach

Create a literate environment in the classroom, including in-class library, chart stories, signs and labels, and word lists

Use of themes to organize reading and writing instruction, with these themes extending into other curricular areas

Attempt to motivate literacy encouraging positive attitudes, providing positive feedback, reducing risks for attempting literacy activities, accepting where students are and working from that point, creating an exciting mood, encouraging personal interpretations, and conveying the importance of reading and writing in daily life

Encourage ownership and personal decision making

General Teaching Processes

Ability grouping for half of instruction, however, not in the form of traditional reading groups

Small group and individualized instruction is predominant

Direct instruction of attending behaviours

Direct instruction of listening skills

Assess learning styles and adjustment of instruction accordingly

Parent communication and involvement—specific reading and writing activities occurring with parents at home

Monitor progress several times a week by both formal and informal methods

Teaching of Reading

Types of Reading and Materials

Total class and individual silent reading

Individual oral reading, including round-robin reading

Different types of materials used—materials with controlled reading level, outstanding children's literature, materials that provide practice in specific phonetic elements and patterns (about half as often as the others)

What Is Taught

Concepts of print, including punctuation, sounds associated with print, concept of words and letters, parts of a book, directionality of print; taught both in context and isolation

Alphabetic principle and alphabet recognition; taught in context, isolation, with games and puzzles

Letter–sound associations, auditory discrimination, and visual discrimination; taught in context, isolation, with games and puzzles

Decoding skills taught several times a day in both context and isolation, most frequently teaching sounding out words and use of context cues

Explicit teaching of phonics based on individual student needs

Explicit teaching of sight words

Develop new vocabulary, using words from stories, other reading and writing, and student-selected words

Direct teaching of comprehension strategies, most frequently teaching prediction of upcoming events, finding the main idea, and activation of prior knowledge

Explicit attempts to develop background knowledge

Teach text elements, including character analysis, sequence of events, theme, details, and plot

Teach about various illustrators

Instructional Practice—Both Traditional and Whole Language

Use of worksheets and workbooks for specific instructional purposes

Use of frequent drill and repetition (for learning such things as sight words, phonic elements, spelling words, letter recognition), occurring both in the context of reading and writing and in more traditional practice methods

Tracing and copying of letters and words

Daily reading, both independent and in groups

Read stories to students with students "reading along"

Overt modelling of reading and writing

Comprehension questions asked for nearly all stories read

Weekly use of literature discussions

Use of story mapping or webbing to teach text elements

Publish students' work

Teaching Writing

Frequent writing (several times a week to several times a day)

Model the writing process

Students write stories, journals, and books

Guided writing

Write in response to reading

Teach planning, drafting, and revising as part of writing

Teach punctuation, both in context of real writing and in isolation

Teach spelling, including high-frequency words, words from spelling and reading curriculum, and words from students' writing

Acceptance and encouragement of invented spelling

From "Literacy in Special Education" (p. 221), by J. L. Rankin-Erickson and M. Pressley, 2000, *Learning Disabilities Research and Practice, 15*(4), 206–225.

disabilities may not automatically develop strategies for learning, or the one they develop may be inefficient. For example, using mnemonic strategies can help students with learning disabilities who are demonstrating memory problems. In order to remember 4 x 8 = 32 the student might associate "door" for "4," "gate" for "8," and a "dirty shoe" for "32." Therefore, the association to visualize would be a door on a gate by a dirty shoe (Wood & Frank, 2000). The phases of one effective strategy to increase reading comprehension are highlighted in the nearby Inclusion Strategies feature. Additional strategies are discussed in Chapter 13.

An example of a simple strategy is a *personal spelling dictionary.* Students can enter words that they frequently miss or that are important in the environment, and weekly spelling tests can be generated from the entries (Scheuermann, Jacobs, McCall, & Knies, 1994). Lists from a spelling book are often too long for students with learning disabilities; also, the words are taken out of context and may not be transferred to the student's writing. In order to create a personal spelling dictionary, use a small loose-leaf binder that is tabbed every few pages to designate each letter of the alphabet. When a student encounters a word he or she does not know how to spell, the correct spelling is obtained from the teacher, the dictionary, or a spelling buddy. The word is then entered into the correct section of the dictionary. The dictionary is always available to jog the memory about words learned in the past. This idea can be expanded to create a writing mechanics dictionary or a math dictionary.

TEACHING TIP

Many students with learning disabilities will resist the challenge to write because of prior negative feedback. Try giving them multiple opportunities without grading, and then grade only one or two skills at a time. For example, one week you might grade punctuation and the next, spelling. You can also give one grade for content and another for mechanics, and then average the two scores for the final grade.

CROSS-REFERENCE

Reading intervention and strategy instruction are discussed further in Chapters 13 and 14.

Reading Comprehension Strategies for the General Education Classroom

Brainstorming: Have students think about what they already know on the topic from prior lessons, reading, movies, and so forth.

Preview: Have students work in small groups to preview assigned text. Give them two minutes to search for clues about key ideas, characters, settings, etc. Give students six minutes to discuss their predictions and develop their "preview."

Click: After reading a designated portion of text, have students write down words they "click" on. These are words or information that they know about and that can extend information in text.

Clunk: When students "clunk," they come to words or information they don't recognize or understand and need to know to learn new information. These words/ideas are written down to explore for them through a "declunking" strategy. Strategies for solving "clunks" are as follows:

Strategies for Solving Clunks

Clunk card #1:   Reread the sentence with the clunk and the sentences before or after the clunk, looking for clues.

Clunk card #2:   Reread the sentence without the word. Think about what would make sense.

Clunk card #3:   Look for a prefix or suffix in the word that might help.

Clunk card #4:   Break the word apart and look for smaller words.

From "Teaching Reading Comprehension Skills to Students with Learning Disabilities in the General Education Classroom (Part II)" by S. Vaughn and J. Kingner, 1999, *Learning Disabilities, 9*(2), pp. 8–9. Used by permission.

Students with learning disabilities in the area of mathematics have been described by Gersten and Chard (1999) as lacking in "number sense." They propose that the traditional method of math instruction for students in special education that focuses on teaching algorithms and being drilled on number facts has led to a lack of general understanding. They described these students as being able to "do" math without "knowing" how to reason and communicate math meaning. Cawley and Foley (2001) describe methods of enhancing the quality of mathematics for students with learning disabilities by teaching the big ideas in math and using instructional techniques that promote students as problem solvers rather than routine followers. These methods in turn develop the "number sense" that encourages students to think about what they "know" and are "doing."

Written language is often difficult to master for children and adults with learning disabilities. Unfortunately, making too many adaptations in this area may result in underdeveloped skills. For example, if a student is always allowed to use another student's notes or allowed to take tests orally in place of written exams, the short-term benefits may be helpful, but instruction and experience in note taking and writing essay answers must be continued if growth is to occur in these areas. A study by Palinscar and Klenk (1992) suggests that special education teachers frequently limit students' writing tasks to copying words and filling out worksheets, so it is important in inclusive classrooms that students be exposed to a variety of writing opportunities. Students with learning disabilities must be given specific instruction in the fundamental aspects of writing if they are to be competent in this area (Graham & Harris, 1997).

Improvement in oral language may be stimulated by promoting a better self-concept and enriching the language environment. These techniques are discussed by Candler and Hildreth (1990). They suggest that poor self-concept can be addressed through encouraging more successful communication experiences and having the student self-evaluate the successes. The classroom can be designed with areas where students are encouraged to talk. Co-operative learning activities also promote increased verbal interactions. Providing opportunities for students to share their experiences and expertise is another nonthreatening way to promote use of oral language. Opportunities to engage in conversation, listening, and praise encourage individuals to share their thoughts and ideas.

Poor listening skills also limit individuals with learning disabilities, influencing success both in the classroom and in social interactions. In Heaton and O'Shea's (1995) effective strategy, which can be modified for use with all age groups, students follow these steps:

L   **L**ook at the teacher.
I   **I**gnore the student next to you.
S   **S**tay in your place.
T   **T**ry to visualize and understand the story.
E   **E**njoy the story.
N   **N**ice job! You're a good listener.

Computers and other technology can assist in teaching individuals with learning disabilities in inclusive classrooms. Olsen and Platt (1996) describe the following advantages of technology:

- It is self-pacing and individualized.
- It provides immediate feedback.
- It has consistent correction procedures.
- It provides repetition without pressure.
- It confirms correct responses immediately.
- It maintains a high frequency of student response.
- It builds in repeated validation of academic success.
- It is an activity respected by peers.
- It is motivating.

TEACHING TIP

In order to promote successful verbal interactions with peers, encourage students to take conversational turns (e.g., Student 1: "I really liked that movie we saw yesterday." Student 2: "It was pretty good. What did you like about it?")

▶ It encourages increased time on task.
▶ It minimizes the effects of the disability.

Writing is an area in which technology can be most helpful. The computer can also be used effectively for curriculum support in math, language arts, social studies, science, and other areas. Various types of software provide instructional alternatives such as tutoring, drill and practice, simulation, and games. Teachers should carefully evaluate each program for ease of use and appropriateness for exceptional students since there are so many choices available.

Intervention related to social interactions and emotional maturity is critical for many students with learning disabilities. The inclusion movement provides opportunities for interactions; the question is how to best prepare both the children with exceptionalities and their typically developing peers for positive interactions. Changing a student's self-image, social ability, and social standing is difficult. Until recently, the research and literature on learning disabilities focused primarily on the efficacy of treatments for the most obvious characteristic—academic difficulties. The importance of social skills is just now being recognized and given the attention it deserves.

Intervention in the area of social standing and interaction can take two courses: changing the child or changing the environment. Optimally, both receive attention. Good teaching techniques can lead to academic achievement and eventually to higher self-esteem. Teachers can create a positive learning environment by incorporating praise and encouragement for specific accomplishments (e.g., make positive comments about themselves and others). Teachers should also set goals and be very explicit about expectations for academic work and behaviour in the class. Teachers should monitor progress closely, and provide frequent feedback (Polloway et al., 2001).

The overall goal of social programs is to teach socially appropriate behaviour and social skills that are self-generated and self-monitored. The cognitive problems of students with learning disabilities often make this type of decision making very difficult. FAST is an example of a strategy that can be effectively applied to the social skills training curriculum. It aids in interpersonal problem solving by developing skills in questioning and monitoring, brainstorming solutions, and developing and implementing a plan to solve the problem. The steps are displayed in Figure 4.2.

Intervention in cognitive and metacognitive skills has only recently received support from learning disabilities professionals. Powerful techniques are being studied to improve learning. Some of the ideas are relatively simple and require only common sense. First, and most important, is being sure a child is paying attention to the stimulus being presented. Students' attention might be gained by dimming the lights, calling for attention, or establishing eye contact. Students' attention might be maintained by having students work for short periods of time and/or breaking up instruction with activities. Learning will not take place without attention.

Lerner (2000) suggests that teachers present new information in well-organized, meaningful chunks. As new information is presented to be memorized, it should be linked to previously learned, meaningful information. For example, to teach subtraction, the teacher would demonstrate the relationship to addition. Students should also be encouraged to rehearse new information and be given many opportunities for practice. These and other effective learning strategies are presented in Figure 4.3 and throughout the text.

Secondary Services Academic and language difficulties, social and emotional problems, and differences in cognitive and metacognitive functioning continue to plague many adolescents with learning disabilities. The focus in junior and high school is on content classes; therefore, **remediation** of basic skills often is minimal. Students who continue to benefit from remediation should be provided these opportunities.

TEACHING TIP

The amount of software available for supporting instruction can be overwhelming, and costly mistakes can be made when ordering a program based on a catalogue description alone. Organize a plan for the teachers in your school to share the names of effective software. Preview a copy before ordering, whenever possible.

CONSIDER THIS

Describe some situations you have observed in which a child displayed inappropriate social skills or responses in the classroom. How could the FAST strategy have been used to prevent recurring problems?

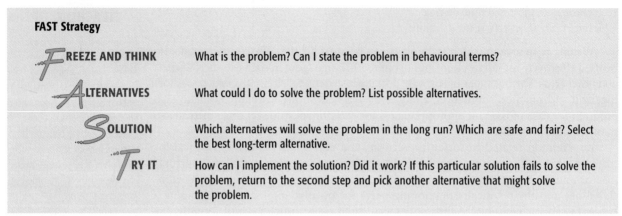

FAST Strategy

FREEZE AND THINK   What is the problem? Can I state the problem in behavioural terms?

ALTERNATIVES   What could I do to solve the problem? List possible alternatives.

SOLUTION   Which alternatives will solve the problem in the long run? Which are safe and fair? Select the best long-term alternative.

TRY IT   How can I implement the solution? Did it work? If this particular solution fails to solve the problem, return to the second step and pick another alternative that might solve the problem.

FIGURE 4.2

Strategies for Developing Interpersonal Problem Solving

From "FAST Social Skills with a SLAM and a Rap," by R. McIntosh, S. Vaughn, and D. Bennerson (1995), *Teaching Exceptional Children*, 28(1), 37–41. Used by permission.

CONSIDER THIS

Review the strategies described in Figure 4.3. Discuss situations in which each one would be helpful for students.

CROSS-REFERENCE

Read more about facilitating student success at the secondary level in Chapter 14.

However, the adaptations described in the next section and the learning strategies described in the previous section can also be used with secondary students to facilitate basic skill acquisition and to make learning and performance more effective and efficient (Deshler, Ellis, & Lenz, 1996). For example, instead of trying to bring basic skills to a level high enough to read a chapter in a content area textbook written on grade level, a teacher might assist students in comprehension by reading the heading and one or two sentences in each paragraph in a chapter. Figure 4.4 shows how the PASS method can be used as a reading comprehension strategy.

The teacher can also make an impact on student learning and performance by accounting for individual differences when developing lesson plans. Many students fail, not because of an inability to perform but because they do not understand directions, cannot remember all the information, or cannot process verbal information fast enough. Most adults and older children automatically lower the language they use when speaking to younger children or individuals with obvious disabilities. Unfortunately they do not typically do so when speaking to school-age children and adults with LD—even though the latter may have language-based learning disabilities. Johnson (1999) suggests the following strategies to meet the needs of students with language difficulties in an inclusive classroom setting:

▶ Be conscious of the level of language used, including rate of presentation, complexity of vocabulary, and sentence structure.
▶ Prepare a list of relevant terms prior to instruction; pretest students to determine their level of understanding.
▶ Adjust the level of language until students have basic concepts.
▶ Use demonstrations as needed.
▶ Repeat instructions individually to students if necessary.
▶ Select a method of testing knowledge to match the student's best method of communication. For example, a student may be able to select the correct answer from options given but not be able to answer open-ended questions. (p. 6)

As noted earlier in the chapter, a major problem for secondary students with learning disabilities is low self-concept and social and emotional problems that often stem from years of school failure. In order to help ameliorate unhappiness, school environments must be structured to create successful experiences. One method involves **self-determination**, or making students more active participants in designing their educational experiences and monitoring their own success; this can be done by teaching self-awareness and self-advocacy skills. Students should use these skills as active participants in their IEP meetings. Participation in IEP meetings is particularly important when

Self-Questioning

Students quietly ask themselves questions about the material. This process is also referred to as verbal mediation. The internal language, or covert speech, helps organize material and behaviour. Camp and Bash (1981) suggest the following types of questions:

What is the problem? (or) What am I supposed to do?

What is my plan? (or) How can I do it?

Am I using my plan?

How did I do?

Verbal Rehearsal and Review

Students practise and review what they have learned. This self-rehearsal helps students remember. People forget when the brain trace, which is a physical record of memory, fades away. Recitation and review of material to be learned help the student remember.

Students observe the instructor's modelling of verbalization of a problem.

Students instruct themselves by verbalizing aloud or in a whisper.

Students verbalize silently.

Organization

To aid in recall, students figure out the main idea of the lesson and the supporting facts. The organization of the material has a great deal to do with how fast we can learn it and how well we can remember it. Already-existing memory units are called chunks, and through chunking, new material is reorganized into already-existing memory units. The more students can relate to what they already know, the better they will remember the new material.

Using Prior Knowledge

New material is linked to already-existing memory units. The more students can relate what they are learning to what they already know, the better they will remember.

Memory Strategies

If new material is anchored to old knowledge, students are more likely to remember it. For example, one student remem-bered the word *look* because it had two eyes in the middle. Some pupils can alphabetize only if they sing the "ABC" song. Some adults can remember people's names by using a mnemonic device that associates the name with a particular attribute of that individual, for example "blond Bill" or "green-sweater Gertrude."

Predicting and Monitoring

Students guess about what they will learn in the lesson and then check on whether their guesses were correct.

Advance Organizers

This technique establishes a mindset for the learner, relating new material to previously learned material. Students are told in advance about what they are going to learn. This sets the stage for learning and improves comprehension and the ability to recall what has been learned.

Cognitive Behaviour Modification

This behavioural approach teaches students self-instruction, self-monitoring, and self-evaluation techniques (Meichenbaum, 1977). There are several steps:

The teacher models a behaviour while giving an explanation.

The student performs the task while the teacher describes it.

The student talks the task through out loud.

The student whispers it to himself or herself.

The student performs the task with nonverbal self-cues.

Modelling

The teacher provides an example of appropriate cognitive behaviour and problem-solving strategies. The teacher can talk through the cognitive processes being used.

Self-Monitoring

Students learn to monitor their own mistakes. They learn to check their own responses and become conscious of errors or answers that do not make sense. To reach this stage requires active involvement in the learning process to recognize incongruities.

FIGURE 4.3

Learning Strategies

From *Learning Disabilities: Theories, Diagnosis, and Teaching Strategies* (6th ed.) (pp. 207–208), by J. W. Lerner, 1993, Houghton Mifflin Company. Used by permission.

a student is deciding whether to continue postsecondary education or to obtain employment after high school (Pocock et al., 2002).

Giving students more power and responsibility for determining their life outcome is very important at the secondary level; however, it is also important to maintain communication with parents and involve them in this process. Parents can promote responsibility in their children by setting clear expectations and consequences in regard to school achievement. Teachers can help by:

▶ Giving parents and students information on course assignments for the semester, available adaptations, and policies.

▶ Providing progress reports, including descriptive comments on the quality of homework.

FIGURE 4.4

PASS Reading
Comprehension Strategy

From *Teaching Strategies and Methods* (2nd ed.) (p. 29), by D. Deshler, E. S. Ellis, and B. K. Lenz, 1996, Denver, CO: Love Publishing. Reprinted by permission.

 REVIEW, REVIEW, AND PREDICT

Preview by reading the heading and one or two sentences.

Review what you know already about this topic.

Predict what you think the text will be about.

 SK AND ANSWER QUESTIONS

Content-Focused Questions

Who? What? When? Where? Why? How?

How does this relate to what I already know?

Monitoring Questions

Is my prediction correct?

How is this different from what I thought it was going to be about?

Does this make sense?

Problem-Solving Questions

Is it important that it make sense?

Do I need to reread part of it?

Can I visualize the information?

Do I need to read it more slowly?

Does it have too many unknown words?

Do I need to pay more attention?

Should I get help?

 UMMARIZE

Say what the short passage was about.

 YNTHESIZE

Say how the short passage fits in with the whole passage.

Say how what you learned fits with what you knew.

> Putting assignment calendars on brightly coloured paper to prevent misplacement.
> Collaborating with other teachers to prevent homework overloads.
> Communicating with parents regarding the amount of time students spend completing homework and adjusting workload correspondingly.
> Understanding that homework may be a low priority in some families where other stressors such as family illness or school attendance may be a priority.

Motivation is also a key ingredient to successful high school programming. It is important to note, however, that "motivation only enables us to do the best of what we're already capable of doing" (Lavoie, 1989). That is, as teachers we can motivate students to do the best they can but cannot expect increased motivation to "solve" students' learning difficulties. Fulk and Montgomery-Grymes (1994) suggest the following techniques for increasing motivation:

> Involve students in decision making.

1. Provide a menu from which students can select assignments to demonstrate knowledge.
2. Allow flexible due dates.
3. Involve students in scoring and evaluating their own work.

Adolescents should be active participants in meetings concerning them.

4. Vary the length of assignments for differing student abilities.

5. Set goals with the students.

▶ Create and maintain interest.

1. Challenge each student at the optimal level.

2. Show your enthusiasm as you introduce lessons.

3. Give clear, simple directions.

4. Set specific expectations.

5. Explain the relevance of each lesson.

6. Vary your teaching style.

▶ Address affective variables.

1. Maintain a positive classroom environment.

2. Give frequent feedback on performance.

3. Acknowledge all levels of achievement.

High school students with learning disabilities especially need to acquire transition skills (e.g., abilities that will help students be successful after high school in employment and independent living). For students in inclusive settings, teachers can find ways to integrate transition topics into the regular curriculum. For example, when an English teacher assigns letter writing or term papers, students might focus their work on exploring different career opportunities. Math teachers can bring in income tax and budget forms to connect them to a variety of math skills. When planning any lesson, ask yourself, "Is there any way I can make this meaningful to my students' lives after high school?" (See Table 4.2.)

Adults   The instruction provided in high school classes can have a powerful impact on the outcome for adults with learning disabilities. The life skills applications of various school activities and lessons are described in Chapter 14. Relevant lessons in the general education curriculum can help adults be more successful in many aspects of independent living. Individuals with learning disabilities are deficient in choosing and carrying out strategies and they do not automatically generalize previously learned information to new challenges. Other cognitive difficulties include organizing thoughts and ideas,

CROSS-REFERENCE

Read more about transition planning at the secondary level in Chapter 14.

TABLE 4.2	Examples of Study Skill Functions in and out of the Classroom	
Study Skill	*School Examples*	*Life Skills Applications*
Reading Rate	Reviewing an assigned reading for a test Looking for an explanation of a concept discussed in class	Reviewing an automobile insurance policy Reading the newspaper
Listening	Understanding instructions about a field trip Attending to morning announcements	Understanding how a newly purchased appliance works Comprehending a radio traffic report
Note Taking/ Outlining	Capturing information given by a teacher on how to dissect a frog Framing the structure of a paper	Writing directions to a party Planning a summer vacation
Report Writing	Developing a book report Completing a science project on a specific marine organism	Completing the personal goals section on a job application Writing a complaint letter
Oral Presentations	Delivering a personal opinion on a current issue for a social studies class Describing the results of a lab experiment	Describing car problems to a mechanic Asking a supervisor/boss for time off work
Graphic Aids	Setting up the equipment of a chemistry experiment based on a diagram Locating the most densely populated regions of the world on a map	Utilizing the weather map in the newspaper Deciphering the store map in a mall
Test Taking	Developing tactics for retrieving information for a closed-book test Comparing notes with textbook content	Preparing for a driver's licence renewal test Participating in television self-tests
Library Usage	Using picture files Searching a computerized catalogue	Obtaining travel resources (books, videos) Viewing current periodicals
Reference Materials	Accessing CD-ROM encyclopedias Using a thesaurus to write a paper	Using the yellow pages to locate a repair service Ordering from a mail-order catalogue
Time Management	Allocating a set time for homework Organizing a file system for writing a paper	Maintaining a daily "to do" list Keeping organized records for tax purposes
Self-Management	Ensuring that homework is signed by parents Rewarding oneself for controlling temper	Regulating a daily exercise program Evaluating the quality of a home repair

From *Teaching Students with Learning Problems to Use Study Skills: A Teacher's Guide* (p. 7), by J. J. Hoover & J. R. Patton, 1995, Austin, TX: Pro-Ed. Reprinted by permission.

integrating and remembering information from a variety of sources, and solving problems (Ryan & Price, 1992). Intervention in these areas must often be implemented for adults if the high school curriculum is not based on future needs and challenges (Dowdy & Smith, 1991).

An important study by Raskind, Goldberg, Higgins, and Herman (2002) identified characteristics of highly successful adults with learning disabilities. Development of many of these factors can be encouraged by teachers and other individuals; however, some factors seem to be innate personality traits of the individuals themselves (e.g., emotional stability). One of the strongest predictors for success was the desire and willingness to persist and work extremely hard. Understanding one's strengths and areas of need, identifying appropriate goals, and working proactively to meet them were also important. The successful adults developed a plan and then worked hard to accomplish their goals. They also developed and used support groups. These characteristics were more powerful predictors of success than academic achievement, IQ, life stressors, social-economic status, or race.

Unfortunately, many adults leave high school without the skills and confidence necessary to find employment to help them realize their maximum potential and to live independently. According to Michaels (1994), problems in work settings can include the following:

- Following instructions
- Getting started on tasks
- Maintaining attention to task
- Organizing and budgeting time
- Completing tasks
- Checking for errors
- Requesting support when appropriate
- Using self-advocacy skills to obtain resources
- Having difficulty with interpersonal skills

These skills can be taught and should be addressed in a secondary curriculum. For adults with learning disabilities, the Learning Disabilities Association of Canada (LDAC) offers a number of resources as well as access to a specific group of adults with learning disabilities that advises the Association. (See Resources at the end of the chapter.)

Controversial Approaches

Some interventions, often presented to the public through television or newsstand magazines, are controversial and have not been validated as effective for students with learning disabilities. Educators may be asked for an opinion on these therapies by parents who are attempting to find solutions to their children's frustrating problems. A brief overview of these nontraditional approaches follows. More extensive reviews are provided by Rooney (1991) and Silver (1995).

One recent controversial therapy involves the prescription of **tinted glasses** as a cure for dyslexia. In this approach, light sensitivity, proposed to interfere with learning, is treated by identifying a coloured lens to reduce sensitivity. Rooney (1991) notes that the studies that support this treatment do not meet acceptable scientific standards and should be viewed with caution.

An older treatment theory is **orthomolecular therapy**, involving vitamins, minerals, and diet. Proponents of this treatment claim that large doses of vitamins and minerals straighten out the biochemistry of the brain to reduce hyperactivity and to increase learning. Hair analysis and blood studies are used to determine the doses needed.

Feingold's Diet is another dietary treatment frequently cited. Feingold (1975) proposes that negative behaviours such as hyperactivity and limited learning are due to the body's reaction to unnatural substances such as food colourings, preservatives, and artificial dyes. His patients are asked to keep a comprehensive diary of their diet and to avoid harmful chemical substances. Other diets have focused on avoiding sugar and caffeine.

Another proponent of orthomolecular therapy suggests that negative behaviours result from allergies to food and environmental substances (Silver, 1995). The research on the efficacy of these diet-related interventions usually consists of clinical studies without control groups. The inclusion of control groups in experimental research "enables the researcher to determine whether the treatment has had an effect or whether one treatment is more effective than another" (Fraenkel & Wallen, 2000, p. 284). When control groups are used, the diets do not substantiate the claims made for them. Only a small percentage of children benefit from them.

Vision therapy or training is another controversial treatment for individuals with a learning disability. It is based on the theory that learning disabilities are the result of visual defects that occur when the eyes do not work together and that these deficits can be cured by visual training. This widespread practice has been supported primarily by groups of optometrists. The American Academy of Ophthalmology (1984) has issued a statement clearly stating that "no credible evidence exists to show that visual training, muscle exercises, perceptual, or hand/eye co-ordination exercises significantly affect a child's Specific Learning Disabilities" (p. 3).

Silver (1995) reviewed another controversial therapy involving the use of **vestibular dysfunction** medication to cure dyslexia. He notes that the relationship between dyslexia, the vestibular system, and the medication was not supported by research. Silver also warns that physicians often do not diagnose dyslexia consistently and are prescribing doses of medication that are not recommended by pharmaceutical companies.

Silver is also concerned about the widespread use of other medications such as Ritalin for learning and attention problems. He warns that prescriptions are often given based on the recommendations of parents or teachers alone, without a comprehensive evaluation. Rooney (1991) states that the actual effectiveness of the medication is less an issue than the concerns that (1) the medication is prescribed without a thorough evaluation, (2) educational and behavioural treatments are not implemented in conjunction with the medication, and (3) there is insufficient monitoring of the effects of the medication. Monitoring these effects is a very important part of the role of classroom teachers. Use of medication is discussed further in Chapter 5.

Classroom Adaptations for Students with Learning Disabilities

One important consideration for individuals of all ages with disabilities, including learning disabilities, is the appropriate use of adaptations during testing. Use of these adaptations helps ensure that common characteristics of learning disabilities, such as poor reading, distractibility, or slow work rate, do not lower the results of an assessment of the child's learning. Care must be taken when implementing these adaptations because, while disallowing fair adaptations prevents a student from demonstrating his or her knowledge, overly permissive adaptations will inflate scores. Inflated scores may give students an overestimate of their abilities and may lead to unrealistic postsecondary goals. They also may reduce pressure on schools to maintain high expectations and offer students a challenging program with intense instruction (Fuchs & Fuchs, 2001). These researchers note, however, that when students can be penalized for low test scores, as is the case for "high stakes" assessment, which is the gateway to promotion or graduation, a more liberal allowance of adaptations should be made.

When you are developing classroom adaptations, remember the wide range of behaviours identified earlier that might characterize individuals with learning disabilities. The heterogeneity in this population is sometimes baffling. No child with a learning disability is going to be exactly like any other, so teachers must provide a wide range of adaptations to meet individual needs. In the following sections, adaptations are discussed for each of the areas described earlier: academic and language deficits, social-emotional problems, and other differences such as attention, memory, cognition, metacognition, perception, and motor skills.

Academic and Language Problems

Students with learning disabilities may manifest problems in the academic areas of reading skill, reading comprehension, math calculation, math applications, listening, speaking, and written language. Chapters 13 and 14 provide extensive adaptations and modifications for students with learning disabilities at the elementary and secondary levels. Some general guidelines proposed by Chalmers (1991) include these:

▶ Preteach vocabulary, and assess the prior knowledge of students before you introduce new concepts.
▶ Establish a purpose for reading that gives students a specific goal for comprehension.
▶ Provide multiple opportunities to learn content: co-operative learning activities, study guides, choral responses, and hands-on participation.
▶ Provide oral and written directions that are clear and simple.
▶ Have students rephrase directions to make sure they understand them.
▶ Reduce time pressure by adjusting requirements: give more time to complete a challenging project, or shorten the assignment. Ask students to work every other problem or every third problem so they will not be overwhelmed.
▶ Provide frequent feedback, and gradually allow students to evaluate their own work.
▶ Have students use an assignment notebook to record important information and daily assignments.
▶ Provide options for students to demonstrate their knowledge or skill (e.g., videotape presentation, artwork, oral or written report).
▶ Use demonstrations and manipulatives frequently to make learning more concrete.
▶ Modify textbooks, as shown in Figure 4.5.
▶ When using worksheets, avoid crowding too much material on a single page.
▶ Provide a listening guide or a partial outline to assist students in note taking.
▶ Use a buddy system for studying or for note taking. Allow a good note taker to work with the student with the learning disability, sharing duplicated notes.
▶ Allow students to tape-record lectures.
▶ Reduce the homework load, or allow the parent to write the student's dictated answers.

FURTHER READING

Read Busch, Pederson, Espin, and Weissenburger's article investigating a first-year teacher's perceptions of teaching students with learning disabilities, in volume 35, issue 2 of the *Journal of Special Education*, 2001 (pp. 92–99).

TEACHING TIP

Each word-processing program has unique features. Try to have several programs available so students can experiment and find the one that works best for them.

FIGURE 4.5

Guidelines for Adapting Content Area Textbooks

Adapted from "Guidelines for Adapting Content Area Textbooks: Keeping Teachers and Students Content," by J. S. Schumm and K. Strickler, 1991, *Intervention in School and Clinic, 27*(2), pp. 79–84.

Determine "goodness of fit" by comparing the readability level of the text and the student's reading ability. If accommodations are needed, consider the following:

1. Substitute textbook reading by
▶ supplying an audiotape of the text.
▶ pairing students to learn text material together.
▶ substituting the text with direct experiences or videos.
▶ holding tutorial sessions to teach content to a small group.

2. Simplify text by
▶ developing abridged versions (volunteers may be helpful).
▶ developing chapter outlines or summaries.
▶ finding a text with similar content written at a lower level.

3. Highlight key concepts by
▶ establishing the purpose for reading.
▶ overviewing the assignment before reading.
▶ reviewing charts, graphs, vocabulary, and key concepts before reading.
▶ reducing amount of work by targeting the most important information or slowing down pace of assignments.

For students with learning difficulties in writing, a word processor can be invaluable. It allows students to see their work in a more legible format and simplifies proofreading and revising.

A variety of software programs meet the needs of students with learning disabilities. In addition to those that help students to work around or to accommodate their difficulties, there are programs that provide fun and interesting drill and skill-building activities for younger children. The programs that provide accommodations for students with learning disabilities include the common spell-checkers, grammar checkers, thesaurus options, and the less common voice word processors. The voice word processors allow students with learning disabilities to dictate their written work and then listen to the computer read it back to them. As a student dictates, the words appear on the screen where they can be read. The drill and skill-building programs consist of a variety of game-format drills in areas such as basic math facts, word attack, other reading skills, and spelling. Other skill-building programs that are appropriate for both younger and older students teach geography, history, science, and problem solving. A few of the best-established, award-winning programs are listed below; however, because new innovations occur constantly in the field, contact your local computer software outlet to obtain information on the newest software to fit your needs.

- Magic School Bus series by Microsoft: Software programs explore a variety of science activities in an interactive manner. Ages 6 to 10.
- Early Learning House series by Edmark Corporation: The series teaches a variety of math, reading, and science concepts. It includes Sammy's Science House, Millie's Math House, and Bailey's Book House. Ages 3 to 6.
- Reader Rabbits by the Learning Company: This program builds basic reading skills. Ages 3 to 8.
- Blaster series by Knowledge Adventure: Reading Blaster, Math Blaster, and Spelling Blaster software programs build basic skills through fun drills. Ages 5 and up.
- Carmen Sandiego series by the Learning Company: Where in the world is Carmen Sandiego? and Where in time is Carmen Sandiego? teach geography and history, respectively, using an interactive game format. Ages 8 and up.

In summary, software distributors that have consistently earned high ratings by educators are Knowledge Adventure (310-533-3400), the Learning Company (1-800-671-7831), and Edmark/Riverdeep (1-888-242-6747). Children and adolescents with learning disabilities benefit enormously from computer software where they can control their own learning.

Social-Emotional Problems

As discussed earlier, the social and emotional problems of individuals with learning disabilities may be closely tied to academic failure. Many of the academic adaptations and/or accommodations already described will encourage success in the classroom, which ultimately leads to a better self-concept, increased emotional stability, and greater confidence in approaching new academic tasks. A student who has weak or limited social skills may need previously described training. However, some adaptations and/or accommodations may still be needed even as the training begins to show results. Students may need to work in an isolated setting in the classroom during particularly challenging times. Distractions caused by peers may interfere with meeting academic challenges successfully. However, if teachers make the student with learning disabilities sit in a segregated portion of the room all the time, it sends a bad message to others. Including students with disabilities in group activities such as co-operative learning provides them with models of appropriate interactions and social skills. Identify the students in the classroom who seem to work best with individuals with a learning disability, and give them opportunities to interact. When conflicts arise, provide good modelling for the student by verbalizing the bad choices that were made and the good choices that could have been made.

Students with learning disabilities may have difficulty responding appropriately to verbal and nonverbal cues. Therefore, teachers should avoid sarcasm and use simple concrete language when giving directions and when teaching. If a student has difficulty accepting new tasks without complaint, consider providing a written assignment that the student can refer to for direction. When a student frequently upsets or irritates others in the classroom, you might agree on a contract to reduce the inappropriate behaviour and reinforce positive peer interaction. Periodically review the rules for the classroom, and keep them posted as a quick reference. In order to assist students who have difficulty making and keeping friends, you can subtly point out the strengths of the individual with the learning disability to encourage the other students to want to be his or her friend. Allowing a student to demonstrate his or her expertise in an area or to share a hobby may stimulate conversations that can eventually lead to friendships.

Many students with learning disabilities cannot predict the consequences of negative behaviour. Therefore, teachers need to explain the consequences of rule breaking and other inappropriate actions. Though you can implement many behaviour management techniques to reinforce positive behaviour, it is important to train the student in methods of **self-monitoring** and **self-regulation**. The ultimate goal is for the student to be able to identify socially inappropriate behaviour and get back on track.

Cognitive Differences

Cognitive problems described earlier include deficits in attention, perception, motor abilities, problem solving, and metacognition. Adaptations and accommodations for individuals exhibiting problems in attention will be described more fully in Chapter 5. Adaptations and/or accommodations can also help individuals with difficulties or preferences in the area of perception. For some students, presenting information visually through the overhead projector, reading material, videos, and graphics will be most effective. Other individuals will respond better by hearing the information. Teachers can accommodate these individual differences by identifying the preferred style of learning and ensuring that instruction and directions are provided in the preferred style by teaching in a multisensory fashion that stimulates both auditory and visual perception. Combining seeing, saying, writing, and doing provides multiple opportunities for presenting new information. It also helps children remember important information.

Difficulties in the area of motor abilities might be manifested as poor handwriting skills or difficulty with other fine motor activities. Accommodations might include overlooking the difficulties in handwriting and providing a grade based not on the appearance of the handwriting but on the content of the material. You might allow students with such difficulties to provide other evidence of their learning, such as oral reports or special projects, or allow students to use a word processor or speech activated software when completing assignments. Let them select physical fitness activities that focus on their areas of strength, rather than their areas of need.

Students with difficulties in problem solving require careful direction and programming. Their difficulties in reasoning skills make them especially prone to academic failures. The instructional strategies described earlier will remedy problems in this area; also frequent practice and modelling of problem-solving strategies will strengthen developing skills.

Students with problems in the area of metacognition need to keep an assignment notebook or a monthly calendar to project the time needed to complete tasks or to prepare for tests. Students should be taught to organize their notebooks and their desks so that materials can be retrieved efficiently. If students have difficulty following or developing a plan, assist them in setting long-range goals and breaking down those goals

FURTHER READING

Read about teachers' perceptions of learning disabilities in Ferri, Keefe, and Gregg's article "Teachers with Learning Disabilities: A View from Both Sides of the Desk," in volume 34, issue 1 of *Journal of Learning Disabilities*, 2001 (pp. 22–32).

FURTHER READING

Tips for accommodating a variety of behaviours associated with learning disabilities and attention deficit can be found in a text by C. A. Dowdy, J. R. Patton, E. A. Polloway, and T. E. C. Smith, *Attention-Deficit/Hyperactivity Disorder in the Classroom: A Practical Guide for Teachers*, published in 1997 by Pro-Ed.

TEACHING TIP

When giving students a series of directions (e.g., when giving an assignment), pair oral directions with written directions. This will give students a visual representation of your directions to reference.

into realistic steps. Prompt them with questions such as "What do you need to be able to do this?" Help students set clear time frames in which to accomplish each step. Assist them in prioritizing activities and assignments, and provide them with models that they can refer to often.

Encourage students to ask for help when needed and to use self-checking methods to evaluate their work on an ongoing basis. Reinforce all signs of appropriate self-monitoring and self-regulation in the classroom. These behaviours will facilitate success after high school.

Adaptations and/or accommodations for attention deficits and hyperactivity are addressed in Chapter 5.

Promoting a Sense of Community and Social Acceptance

CONSIDER THIS

What are your personal strengths and challenges? How are you alike and different from your family members and your peers? We are all different—can we learn to celebrate our differences?

After identifying an appropriate educational plan for individuals with learning disabilities and determining the adaptations and/or accommodations that should lead to a successful educational program, the next challenge is to ensure that the children in the general education classroom and the child with the learning disability understand the disability and the need for special education. Primarily, children should be made aware that all people are different.

Teaching tips for general educators are offered in Chapters 13 and 14, which focus on behaviour management and adaptations and/or accommodations for elementary and secondary classrooms. The following list of recommended guidelines for teaching children and adolescents with learning disabilities has been compiled from work by Mercer (1997), Deiner (1993), and Bender (2001):

1. Be consistent in class rules and daily schedule of activities.
2. State rules and expectations clearly. Tell children what to do—not what *not* to do. For example, instead of saying, "Don't run in the halls," say, "Walk in the halls."
3. Give advance organizers to prepare children for any changes in the day's events and to highlight the important points to be covered during instructional time.
4. Eliminate or reduce visual and auditory distractions when children need to concentrate. Help children focus on the important aspects of the task.
5. Give directions in clear, simple words. A long series of directions may need to be broken down and given one at time. Reinforcement may be needed as each step is completed.
6. Begin with simple activities focused on a single concept and build to more abstract ideas as the child appears ready. If problems occur, check for the presence of the prerequisite skills or knowledge of the vocabulary being used.
7. Use concrete objects or demonstrations when teaching a new concept. Relate new information to previously known concepts.
8. Teach the children strategies for remembering.
9. Present information visually, auditorially, and through demonstration to address each child's preferred learning style.
10. Use a variety of activities and experiences to teach or reinforce the same concept. Repetition can be provided without inducing boredom.
11. Use activities that are short or that encourage movement. Some children may need to work standing up!
12. Incorporate problem-solving activities or other projects that involve the children. Use both higher-level and lower-level questions.
13. Always gain the student's attention before presenting important information.
14. Use co-operative instructional groupings and peer tutoring to vary modes of instruction.
15. Plan for success!

Personal Spotlight

Provincial Department of Education Specialist Daniel Demers

Daniel Demers comes to special education and learning disabilities with a passion and from a multiperspective approach, as a parent of two exceptional children who went through French immersion in a minority setting, as a teacher and school principal in dual-track schools, and as a specialist and consultant in the field of learning disabilities.

Daniel has 16 years of experience in French immersion and special education. He holds a bachelor's degree in education with minors in psychology, learning disabilities, and French, as well as a master of arts in curriculum design and learning disabilities. He has lectured extensively across Canada and has spoken in Finland and in the U.S. on learning disabilities, differentiated curriculum/teaching, and effective collaborative school-based teams. Daniel also taught theory and laboratory courses at Simon Fraser University as a sessional instructor in the field of learning disabilities and teacher training.

Currently, Daniel is a special education consultant with the Student Services Division of the Department of Education in Nova Scotia. Responding to the minister and deputy minister of education through the director of student services, the Student Services Division develops policies and resources to support students in the public school system of Nova Scotia and in their transitions into and out of the system. Daniel works in French and in English for the French and English populations of the province's public school system. He is one of three special education consultants.

Special education in Nova Scotia is mandated and framed by the policies and guidelines of the *Special Education Policy Manual* and other documents and handbooks. The policy manual contains the policies and guidelines and procedures that provide a framework for student services and the programming needs of all Nova Scotia public school learners, but specifically for the education of students with special needs. Principally, the manual describes the Program Planning Process and the Program Planning Team, as well as the Individualized Program Plan development. The *Special Education Policy Manual* furthers the rights and regulations found in the *Education Act*.

Each school board has at least one student services co-ordinator who co-ordinates the support services of professionals and paraprofessionals. In close collaboration with the program and services directors of each board, and with various divisions of the Department of Education, policies, guidelines, and resources are developed and professional development is implemented in each board. The Department of Education supports inclusive schooling. Inclusion is defined as "an attitude and a value system that promotes the basic rights of all students to receive appropriate and quality educational programming and services in the company of their peers" (Nova Scotia Department of Education, 2005).

Daniel says, "Every time I interact with a learner, a book, a colleague or an article, or when I participate in a collaboration, I find myself in the strange world of teaching and learning at the same time; this is the way I often describe metacognition, this ongoing executive scaffolding is guided and regulated by the mentorship of research & knowledge and the actualization of learning. The mentorship and the knowledge come from people who have played an important role in my construction of knowledge and provided me with a repertoire of strategies. These 'people' are sometimes research papers, books, etc. Sometimes these are actual mentors, professors, friends; students who imparted knowledge or made you acquire this knowledge. I was lucky enough to have several mentors who played and still play critical roles in my life. The actualization of learning is a more practical and hands on way of using successes to shape your decisions. Critically analysing interventions can provide a starting point that will avoid reinventing the wheel if you wish or even ending up with square wheels. It often provides you with a way to differentiate instruction or learning in a respectful way and in a least restrictive environment. My experience has taught me that you need to place the student in the driver's seat to achieve learning. Many students seem happy enough to be passengers in the process. Many don't even want to be in the car. Therefore, it does not really matter how good the curriculum is or how important, if you are not first able to change the passive participant into an active, metacognitive constructor of knowledge. If not, it seems that only the teachers learn."

Summary

- A learning disability is frequently misunderstood because it is not visible. It may be mistaken for purposely uncooperative behaviour.
- The study of learning disabilities is a relatively young field, and basic definitions, etiology, and criteria for special education eligibility remain controversial.
- The most widely used criterion for identifying a learning disability is a severe discrepancy between ability and achievement that cannot be explained by another disabling condition or lack of learning opportunity.
- School personnel must determine that the primary cause of a student's learning difficulties is not cultural or linguistic diversity.
- Cultural and linguistic differences need to be taken into account when any assessment of a student's skills occurs so that the student is not mistakenly referred to a special education setting.
- Characteristics of learning disabilities are manifested across the lifespan.
- Learning disabilities are manifested in seven areas of academics and language: reading skills, reading comprehension, mathematical calculations, mathematical reasoning, written expression, oral expression, and listening comprehension.
- Other common characteristics of learning disabilities include social-emotional problems and difficulties with attention and hyperactivity, memory, cognition, metacognition, motor skills, and perceptual abilities.

- Teaching strategies for preschool children with LD include developmental, cognitive, and behavioural models.
- Interventions for elementary children with learning disabilities address academic and language deficits, social-emotional problems, and cognitive and metacognitive problems.
- Secondary students with learning disabilities continue to need remediation of basic skills, but they also benefit from strategies that will make them more efficient learners.
- A secondary curriculum that includes application of life skills can produce successful outcomes for adults with learning disabilities.
- Successful adults with learning disabilities are goal directed, work hard to accomplish their goals, understand and accept their strengths and limitations, and advocate for themselves.
- Adaptations and/or accommodations in the general education classroom can address the academic, social-emotional, and cognitive, metacognition, and attentional differences of students with learning disabilities.
- The role of the classroom teacher includes using effective teaching strategies and accommodations to address the challenges of students with LD, as well as helping a child with a learning disability and other children in the general class understand and accept a learning disability.
- Students need to be aware that all people are different; this awareness will promote a positive, accepting atmosphere in the general education classroom.

Resources

Books

Learning Disabilities Association of Canada. (1999). *The Learning Disabilities Association of Canada (LDAC) resource directory*. Ottawa: Author.

The LDAC Directory is the only comprehensive up-to-date listing of services throughout Canada for children, youth, and adults with learning disabilities. It, like the title below, is available from the Association (see National Association below).

Learning Disabilities Association of Canada. (1998). *Advocating for your child with learning disabilities: A guide developed for parents by the Learning Disabilities Association of Canada*. Ottawa: Author.

This practical guide for parents provides straightforward information on how to advocate for your child with LD as he or she moves through the school system.

Winebrenner, Susan. (1996). *Teaching kids with learning difficulties in the regular classroom: Strategies and techniques every teacher can use to challenge and motivate struggling students*. Minneapolis, MN: Free Spirit Publishing.

A valuable collection of easy-to-use strategies is backed up by scenarios that illustrate each technique. Winebrenner, a skilled classroom teacher, presents techniques for dealing with diverse learning styles, language literacy, science, math, social studies, behaviour problems, and more. Special "Question and Answer" sections address specific issues and concerns. There are more than 50 reproducible pages to use with students.

Videos

A Mind of Your Own. National Film Board.

This 37-minute video, excellent viewing for students in elementary and secondary classes, will heighten awareness about the experience of having a learning disability. Students with learning disabilities tell about their experiences in school.

How Difficult Can This Be? Understanding Learning Disabilities: The F.A.T. City Workshop by Richard Lavoie. (1989). Etobicoke, ON: PBS and Visual Educational Centre.

This video provides a simulation of h... disability while teaching the viewer abou... disabilities. Teachers remember it for yea... view it again and again. Many school boa... local chapters of learning disabilities associations have a copy of the video for loan.

National Association

Learning Disabilities Association of Canada
323 Chapel Street, Suite 200, Ottawa, ON K1N 7Z2
Phone: (613) 238-5721; Fax: (613) 235-5391
Email: ldactaac@fox.nstn.ca
Website: **www.ldac-taac.ca**

 **eblinks**

Learning Disabilities Association of Ontario (LDAO)
www.ldao.ca/
LDAO's site, one of the few specifically Canadian sites on learning disabilities, provides a number of resources and suggested books and videos, as well as other related links.

Learning Disabilities Online
www.ldonline.org/index.html
This site provides information on research, links, articles, and more. It is recommended by the Learning Disabilities Association of Canada.

Division for Learning Disabilities (DLD)
www.dldcec.org/
One of 17 divisions of the Council for Exceptional Children, DLD provides mainly American links, but there is information that is applicable to all individuals with LD.

Council for Learning Disabilities (CLD)
www.cldinternational.org/
The CLD site provides services to professionals who work with individuals with learning disabilities. Information

focuses on interventions for teachers working with individuals with LD. Journal and conference information are available.

National Centre for Learning Disabilities (NCLD)
www.ncld.org
As this site reflects, the NCLD develops training and educational materials for parents and practitioners.

Learning Disabilities Association of America (LDA)
www.ldanatl.org
Visit this website to see the range of resources available through the Association. The LDA national office has a resource centre of more than 500 publications for sale; it also operates a film rental service.

Provincial/Territory Websites
www.edu.gov.on.ca/eng/relsites/oth_prov.html
In order to explore the learning resources produced by the departments of education in each of Canada's provinces and territories, use the link above to explore their websites.

5 Teaching Students with Attention Deficit/ Hyperactivity Disorder

Chapter Objectives

After reading this chapter you should be able to

- discuss the basis for providing services to students with attention deficit/hyperactivity disorder (AD/HD)
- describe the characteristics and identification process for students with AD/HD, including the impact of cultural diversity
- discuss educational, technological, and medical intervention
- discuss strategies to enhance instruction and classroom accommodations
- discuss methods for promoting a sense of community and social acceptance

Jake was always described as a "handful." He was the second son, so his mom was used to lots of noise and activity, but nothing prepared her for Jake. He was always into something, he climbed everything, he pulled all the toys out at once, and he was fussy and seldom slept. As he entered school, his mom hoped that the scheduled day would help, but his teachers complained and called her often to discuss how difficult Jake was to manage. He was held back in kindergarten to allow him an extra year to mature, but he didn't make the progress that was hoped for. He was still disruptive and frequently in trouble with teachers.

At the same time, everyone else seemed to love Jake. He talked all the time and could really entertain a group. From the beginning, he was an excellent athlete. Baseball, swimming, football, wrestling, and basketball kept him busy but didn't really leave enough time for homework to be completed properly. He was described as "all boy!" Because he was so intelligent, he was able to make passing grades without much effort, but he never excelled in school. Teachers always called him an underachiever and told his parents frequently that he just wasn't trying. He tried medication for one year for his hyperactivity, but that was dropped over the summer and never started again.

During high school Jake was a skilled wrestler, achieving medals in local and provincial competitions. He made the regional all-star football team, but his teachers still complained about his attitude and commitment to his studies; he had a short attention span and was easily distracted. Jake became frustrated as more effort was needed to pass all his subjects. He wanted to go to a good university and expected a scholarship, but he had to graduate with a grade point average that met the university's standards. With this goal in mind, he agreed to begin taking medication, and he and his mom met with his teachers to develop a plan to improve his grades and behaviour. Jake also met with a psychologist several times to discuss strategies that would make him more independent. The plan worked, and Jake got his scholarship. Without the adaptations, strategy training, and medication, Jake and his parents wonder how different his life would be.

Questions to Consider

1. How could Jake's early school years have been made more successful?

2. How successful do you think Jake will be in university?

Introduction

Attention deficit/hyperactivity disorder (AD/HD) is a complex condition that has been a major concern in public education for several years. It is a complicated but intriguing topic and a real challenge for classroom teachers. This condition remains controversial because professional perspectives and personal opinions vary regarding the nature of AD/HD and effective intervention techniques. In the past few years awareness of this disability has significantly increased, along with successful intervention plans for students who struggle with it.

In the United States, students with attention-deficit disorder who need special education or related services can qualify for those services under existing special education categories. However, in a school-based study of students with AD/HD, Reid et al. (1994) found that only 50 percent of these students were receiving special services under the legal and educational provisions noted above. Nearly 52 percent of students with AD/HD were identified as behaviourally disordered, 29 percent were identified as learning disabled, and 9 percent were identified as "mentally retarded." These findings serve to illustrate the difficulty in identifying and serving students with AD/HD.

In Canada, provincial educational jurisdictions do not list AD/HD as a distinct category of exceptionality (Friend, Bursuck, & Hutchinson, 1998). In general, the policy in most Canadian provinces is that children with AD/HD may qualify for services under other categories such as behavioural disorders and learning disabilities. The identification of a student with an AD/HD requires a physician's input; and although it has significant impact in the school setting, it is not primarily an educational diagnosis.

Teachers must understand AD/HD in order to recognize the characteristics of AD/HD and, most important, to implement effective intervention strategies and accommodations to facilitate success for these students in their classrooms.

CONSIDER THIS

Do the results of the study by Reid and his colleagues surprise you? Although you have not yet studied behavioural disorders or intellectual disabilities, can you predict how they differ from learning disabilities? How would AD/HD overlap with these other disabilities?

Basic Concepts about Attention Deficit/ Hyperactivity Disorder

Attention deficit/hyperactivity disorder is an invisible, hidden disability in that no unique physical characteristics differentiate these children from others. However, AD/HD is not hard to spot in the classroom.

> Just look with your eyes and listen with your ears as you walk through the places where children are—particularly those places where children are expected to behave in a quiet, orderly, productive fashion. In such places, children with AD/HD will identify themselves quite readily. They will be doing or not doing something which frequently results in their receiving a barrage of comments and criticisms such as, "Why don't you ever listen?" "Think before you act." "Pay attention." (Fowler, 1992, p. 3)

Unfortunately, the disabling behaviours associated with AD/HD may be misunderstood and misinterpreted as a sign of being lazy, disorganized, and even disrespectful. The condition can be recognized only through specific behavioural manifestations that may occur during the learning process. As a **developmental disability**, AD/HD becomes apparent before the age of seven; however, in as many as 70 to 80 percent of the cases, it continues to cause problems in adulthood (Heiligenstein, Conyers, Berns, & Miller,

1998). During the school years, AD/HD may have an impact on success in both academic and nonacademic areas. It occurs across all cultural, racial, and socioeconomic groups. It can also affect children and adults with all levels of intelligence (Weyandt, 2001).

Attention Deficit/Hyperactivity Disorder Defined

Although a variety of terms have been used over the years to describe this disorder, currently the term used in the *Diagnostic and Statistical Manual of Mental Disorders,* Fourth Edition, Text Revision (*DSM-IV-TR*), *attention deficit/hyperactivity disorder* is most common. On a global level, the *International Classification of Diseases* (10th ed.; *ICD-10,* 1992) is used to describe this disorder. This classification system uses the term **hyperkinetic disorders** to describe conditions related to problems in attention and hyperactivity.

AD/HD primarily refers to deficits in attention and behaviours characterized by impulsivity and hyperactivity. The *DSM-IV-TR* (American Psychiatric Association, 2000) classifies AD/HD as a disruptive disorder expressed in persistent patterns of inappropriate degrees of attention or hyperactivity-impulsivity. A distinction must be made between AD/HD and other disorders such as conduct disorder (e.g., physical fighting) and oppositional defiant disorder (e.g., recurrent patterns of disobedience). The *DSM-IV-TR* has been widely adopted as a guide to the diagnosis of AD/HD. According to this document, AD/HD encompasses four types of disabilities. The identification of the specific type of AD/HD depends on the number and type of symptoms that can be ascribed to the child. The four types of diagnoses include: attention deficit/hyperactivity disorder, predominantly inattentive type; attention deficit/hyperactivity disorder, predominantly hyperactive-impulsive type; attention deficit/hyperactivity disorder, combined type; and attention deficit/hyperactivity disorder not otherwise specified.

The teacher is often the first to bring the AD/HD-like behaviours to the attention of the parents. When parents initiate contact with the school to find help, they will be served best by teachers who are already well informed about this condition and the special education assessment process.

Prevalence and Causes of Attention Deficit/Hyperactivity Disorder

AD/HD is more common than any other child psychiatric disorder (Nolan, Volpe, Gadow, & Sprafkin, 1999). Estimates of the prevalence of attention deficit/hyperactivity disorder in school-age children range from a conservative figure of less than 2 percent to a more liberal figure of 30 percent; however, 3 to 7 percent is most probable (American Psychiatric Association, 2000). The extreme differences found in prevalence figures reflect the lack of agreement on a definition and the difficulty and variance in identification procedures. Regardless of the exact prevalence figure, most students with this condition attend general education classrooms. Hyperactivity and impulsivity are most likely to be observed in preschool and elementary children; inattention is more common in adolescents. While boys are overrepresented in each subtype (Nolan et al., 1999), there is some concern that girls and children from minority families are at risk for not being identified (Bussing, Zima, Perwien, Belin, & Widawski, 1998). Several individuals have noted that the prevalence of AD/HD is increasing; however, it is generally felt that this perception is due to the increased media attention that alerts parents and teachers and to better training of clinicians and physicians (Weyandt, 2001). According to the Canadian Pediatric Society, the prevalence of attention deficit/hyperactivity disorder in school-age children ranges from 3 to 5 percent.

FURTHER READING

The *DSM-IV-TR* is a diagnostic guide and classification system for mental disorders. Survey a copy to see the range of disorders included. Select a disorder, such as conduct disorder or oppositional defiant disorder, and compare the criteria for identification to that of AD/HD.

There are many different theories regarding the cause of AD/HD.

Although the exact cause of AD/HD is unknown, several theories have been proposed, and rigorous research is ongoing. Most professionals agree that AD/HD is a neurobiologically based condition. Following is a summary of the research on possible causes, as summarized by Weyandt (2001):

◗ Neuroanatomical—related to brain structure. Unexplained differences such as smaller right frontal regions, smaller brain size in boys with AD/HD, and a smaller cerebellum have been found. It is not known whether these differences are due to genetics or the environment, or if they are even related to or responsible for the symptoms of AD/HD.

◗ Neurochemical—related to a chemical imbalance in the brain or a deficiency in chemicals that regulate behaviour. This research usually focuses on neurotransmitters, chemicals in the brain responsible for communication between brain cells and necessary for behaviour and thought to occur. Stimulant medication is proposed to stimulate or regulate production of the neurotransmitters and increase brain activity. As a result of conflicting findings, this research is currently inconclusive.

◗ Neurophysiological—related to brain function. Various medical tests such as the EEG and brain scans have suggested that individuals with AD/HD have reduced brain activity (were found to be in a low state of arousal) and reduced blood flow in the right frontal region, an area that produces important neurotransmitters and helps regulate impulse control, attention, and planning. To be considered conclusive, these tests need to be validated on many more individuals at various ages and on both females and males.

◗ Neuropsychological—dysfunction of the frontal lobes resulting in deficits in attention, self-regulation, impulsivity, and planning, collectively called executive function. Renowned researcher Dr. Russell Barkley (1997) proposed a unifying theory that individuals with AD/HD have deficits in behavioural inhibition that is caused by physiological differences in the brain. These differences result in the executive function deficits listed previously in addition to impairments in working memory, problem solving, motor control, and using internal speech (i.e., self-talk) to guide behaviour. Other studies support this model, but again, more research is needed.

Some data suggest that genetics plays a significant role in AD/HD, evidenced by a higher prevalence rate in some families. Studies have shown that biological parents, and siblings, and other family members of individuals with this disorder have higher rates of AD/HD than expected in the general population. For example, one study found that if one biological parent has AD/HD, there is a 57 percent chance that a child will have the condition (Biederman et al., 1995).

Barkley (1999–2000) also noted that pre- and postnatal events may cause AD/HD. Premature birth is associated with AD/HD; other events include complications during pregnancy, fetal exposure to tobacco or alcohol, head trauma, lead poisoning in preschool years, and strep infection. While many factors are still being seriously considered as a potential cause of AD/HD, others have little or no evidence to support them. These include aspects of the physical environment such as fluorescent lighting, soaps, disinfectants, yeast, preservatives, food colouring, aspartame, certain fruits and vegetables, sugar, social factors, and poor parental management (Barkley, 1998; Weyandt, 2001).

For most students, the precise cause of the problem may never be understood. Although many parents want to understand why their children have a developmental disability such as AD/HD, its cause is really not relevant to educational strategies or medical treatment. These can succeed without pinpointing the root of the problem.

Characteristics of Students with Attention Deficit/ Hyperactivity Disorder

The characteristics of AD/HD manifest themselves in many different ways in the classroom. Recognizing them and identifying accommodations or strategies to lessen the impact in the classroom constitute a significant challenge for teachers. The characteristics listed in the *DSM-IV-TR* criteria highlight the observable behaviours. Barkley (1998) groups these characteristics into the following three most common areas of difficulty:

1. *Limited sustained attention or persistence of attention to tasks:* Particularly during tedious, long-term tasks, the students become rapidly bored and frequently shift from one uncompleted activity to another. They may lose concentration during long work periods and fail to complete routine work unless closely supervised. The problem is not due to inability to comprehend the instructions, memory impairment, or defiance. The instructions simply do not regulate behaviour or stimulate the desired response.

2. *Reduced impulse control or limited delay of gratification:* This feature is often observed in an individual's difficulty in waiting for his or her turn while talking to others or playing. Students may not stop and think before acting or speaking. They may have difficulty working toward long-term goals and long-term rewards, preferring to work on shorter tasks that promise immediate reinforcement.

3. *Excessive task-irrelevant activity or activity poorly regulated to match situational demands:* Individuals with AD/HD are often extremely fidgety and restless. Their movement seems excessive and often not directly related to the task—for example, tapping pencils, rocking, or shifting positions frequently. They also have trouble sitting still and inhibiting their movements when the situation demands it.

CROSS-REFERENCE

Refer to the opening vignette in this chapter. Identify which of Jake's characteristics would lead a teacher or parent to suspect AD/HD.

Other areas of difficulty in psychological functioning include working memory or remembering to do things, sensing time or using time as efficiently as their peers, and using their internal language to talk to themselves in order to think about events and purposefully direct their own behaviour. They have problems inhibiting their reaction to events, often appearing more emotional or hotheaded and less emotionally mature. They are easily frustrated and seem to lack willpower or self-discipline. They may have difficulty following instructions or rules, even following their own "to-do" lists. They demonstrate considerable variation in the quantity, quality, and speed with which they perform their assigned tasks. Their relatively high performance on some occasions, coupled with low levels of accuracy on other occasions, can be baffling. Low levels of performance often occur with repetitive or tedious tasks.

The symptoms are likely to change from one situation to another. More AD/HD symptoms may be shown in group settings, during boring work, when students are without supervision, and when work has to be done later in the day. Individuals behave better when there is immediate payoff for doing the right thing, when they enjoy what they are doing or find it interesting, when they are in one-on-one situations, and when they can work earlier during the day (Barkley, 1998).

The characteristics of AD/HD may also be present in adulthood; only an estimated 20 percent to 35 percent of children with the disorder will not be impaired as adults. For some individuals the condition continues to cause problems and limitations in the world of work, as well as in other life activities. Figure 5.1 provides a summary of common characteristics for varying age groups including adults. Barkley (1999–2000) reports that adults with AD/HD are more likely to be fired, typically change jobs three times more often than adults without the disorder in a 10-year period, are more likely to divorce, and typically have more traffic citations and accidents. On the positive side, the outcome is much brighter for individuals with AD/HD who receive treatment such as medication, behaviour management, and social skills training. Research is currently investigating the best jobs for individuals with AD/HD; highly intense jobs and those requiring brainstorming have been suggested. Up to 35 percent may be self-employed by the age of 30. In any case, AD/HD and the treatment of AD/HD can have significant effects on adult outcomes. Teachers who can identify and plan meaningful interventions for students with AD/HD can have a powerful impact on their success during the school years as well as their quality of life as adults.

TEACHING TIP

As another technique for recording a student's behaviour, observe a child for 3 to 5 minutes every hour during a school day, and document whether the child is on or off task. Record what the child is supposed to be doing, what he or she is actually doing, and the consequences of that behaviour (e.g., praise, ignoring). Figure the percentage of on- and off-task behaviour.

FIGURE 5.1

Common Characteristics of Individuals with AD/HD

From *An AD/HD Primer* (p. 17) by L. L. Weyandt, 2001, Boston: Allyn and Bacon.

Early Childhood
Excessive activity level
Talking incessantly
Difficulty paying attention
Difficulty playing quietly
Impulsive and easily distracted
Academic underachievement

Middle Childhood
Excessive fidgeting
Difficulty remaining seated
Messy and careless work
Failing to follow instructions
Failing to follow through on tasks
Academic underachievement

Adolescence
Feelings of restlessness
Difficulty engaging in quiet sedentary activities

Forgetful and inattentive
Impatience
Engaging in potentially dangerous activities
Academic underachievement

Adulthood
Feelings of restlessness
Difficulty engaging in quiet sedentary activities
Frequent shifts from one uncompleted activity to another
Frequent interrupting or intruding on others
Avoidance of tasks that allow for little spontaneous movement
Relationship difficulties
Anger management difficulties
Frequent changes in employment

Identification, Assessment, and Eligibility

Although in the United States the assessment of an AD/HD is the responsibility of public education personnel (Cantu, 1993), in Canada the identification of an AD/HD ultimately requires the involvement of a physician or psychiatrist. As Weber and Bennett (1999) indicate in their book, *Special Education in Ontario*, while educational jurisdictions acknowledge AD/HD, similar to how they acknowledge conditions like Tourette syndrome, AD/HD is not an exceptionality category in the education systems across Canada. However, the identification of an AD/HD in a student frequently begins in the school through a teacher or parent referral to the school psychologist or school team. Because of the large overlap between attention deficits and other recognized exceptionalities, such as learning disabilities and behavioural disorders, the school assessment of the student with suspected AD/HD is essential. Therefore, teachers should be familiar with the specific behaviours and the commonly used assessment techniques associated with attention-deficit disorders. Formal assessment for AD/HD should require the teacher to complete measures assessing the student's behaviour at school, documenting behaviour over a period of time and in different settings, and to conduct ongoing monitoring of the child's behaviour in response to medication (Schwean, Parkinson, Francis, & Lee, 1993).

Weyandt (2001) supports the participation of teachers as an important source of information in AD/HD assessment. She notes that teachers spend a significant amount of time with students in a variety of academic and social situations and have a better sense of normal behaviours for the comparison group. Burnley (1993) proposes a four-part plan that could be implemented to structure the assessment process for schools. A modified version of Burnley's process is depicted in Figure 5.2 and described in the following sections.

Steps in the Assessment Process

Step 1: Preliminary Assessment and Initial School Team Meeting   Initially, a teacher who has been trained in identifying the symptoms of attention deficit/hyperactivity disorder may begin to observe that a particular student manifests these behaviours in the class-

FURTHER READING

Vicki Schwean and colleagues at the University of Saskatchewan write about the key role that teachers can and should play in the identification of and intervention for children who have AD/HD. For more information, read the 1993 article, "Educating the AD/HD Child: Debunking the Myths," by Schwean, Parkinson, Francis, and Lee, volume 9, issue 1, of the *Canadian Journal of School Psychology* (pp. 37–52).

FIGURE 5.2

AD/HD Process for
Identification and
Intervention

Modified from "A Team Approach
for Identification of an Attention
Deficit/Hyperactivity Disorder
Child," by C. D. Burnley, 1993,
The School Counselor, 40, pp.
228–230. Adapted by permission.
No further reproduction
authorized without written
permission from the American
Counseling Association.

STEP 1

Preliminary Assessment: Initial School Team Meeting

STEP 2

Formal Assessment: Follow-up Meeting of School Team

STEP 3

Collaborative Meeting for Strategy Development

STEP 4

Follow-up and Progress Review

room to a greater degree than peers do. At this point, the teacher should begin to keep a log to document the child's AD/HD-like behaviours, noting the times at which behaviours appear to be more intense, more frequent, or of a longer duration. Figure 5.3 provides a simple format for this observational log. For example, a teacher might document behaviour such as constantly interrupting, excessive talking, not following directions, leaving a designated area, not finishing assignments, or not turning in homework.

If the teacher's anecdotal records confirm the continuing presence of these behaviours, the referral process should be initiated and the observational log turned in as documentation. At that point a less biased observer should come into the classroom to provide comparative information (Schaughency & Rothlind, 1991). Schaughency and Rothlind (1991) caution that this form of data collection is costly in terms of professional time; however, if the observation period is not long enough, behaviour that occurs infrequently may be missed. The assessment team should realize that direct observation is just one source of information to be considered in the identification process.

As soon as the school suspects that a child is experiencing attention problems, the parents should be notified and invited to meet with the school team. Often, the parents, the teacher, the principal, and the school special education teacher will come together for the initial meeting. During this meeting, parents should be asked to respond to the

FIGURE 5.3

Sample Form for
Documenting Classroom
Manifestations of AD/HD-
like Behaviours

Teacher: _____ School: _____

Child: _____ Grade: _____ Age: _____

Class Activity	Child's Behaviour	Date/Time

observations of the school personnel and describe their own experiences with attention problems outside of the school setting. If the team agrees that additional testing is needed, a referral is made to the school psychologist, who will direct the assessment process. The psychologist must understand the impact of AD/HD on the family; the bias that might occur during the assessment process because of cultural, socioeconomic, language, and ethnic factors; and other conditions that may present like AD/HD and prevent an accurate diagnosis.

Step 2: Formal Assessment Process: Follow-up Meeting of the School Team   Although schools are not required to use a specific set of criteria to identify attention deficit/hyperactivity disorder, the *DSM-IV-TR* criteria described earlier are highly recommended (Weyandt, 2001). The following questions, recommended by Schaughency and Rothlind (1991), need to be addressed during the formal assessment process:

1. Is there an alternative educational diagnosis or medical condition that accounts for the attention difficulties?
2. Are the behaviours demonstrated by the child developmentally appropriate? (For example, children with intellectual disabilities may be diagnosed correctly as having AD/HD, but only if their attention problems are significantly different from those of the children at comparable developmental levels.)
3. Does the child meet the *DSM-IV-TR* criteria?
4. Do the AD/HD-like behaviours affect the child's functioning in several settings, such as home, school, and other social situations?

A variety of methods and assessment procedures will be needed to answer these questions. The school system will most likely interview the child, parents, and teachers; obtain a developmental and medical history; review school records; review and/or evaluate intellectual and academic performance; administer rating scales to the child, parents, teachers, and possible peers; and document the impact of the behaviour through direct observation.

After the necessary observations have been made, the interview process can begin. According to Weyandt (2001), an interview with parents might include the following topics:

- The student's medical, social-emotional, and developmental history
- Family history
- Parental concerns and perception of the problem
- The student's behaviour at home
- Academic history and previous testing

Woodrich (1994) recommends that the following areas be addressed during the teacher interview:

- Class work habits and productivity
- Skill levels in academic subjects
- Length of time attention can be sustained for novel tasks and for monotonous tasks
- Degree of activity during class and on the playground
- Class structure and standards for self-control
- Degree of compliance with class rules
- Manifestation of more serious conduct problems
- Onset, frequency, and duration of inappropriate behaviour in the antecedent events
- Peer acceptance and social skills
- Previous intervention techniques and special services now considered appropriate

An interview with the child is appropriate in many cases, to determine the child's perception of the reports by the teacher, attitude toward school and family, and perception of relationships with peers. Although the child's responses will be slanted by personal feelings, it still is an important source of information.

The assessment of achievement and intelligence can document the effect the condition is having on the individual's success at school and is essential to determine if the child can qualify for services in categories of learning disabilities or intellectual disabilities. Also, knowing the levels of intelligence and achievement will help eventually in developing an intervention plan.

Rating scales that measure the presence of AD/HD symptoms are widely used to quantify the severity of the behaviours. They offer a way to measure the extent of the problem objectively. Several informants who know the child in a variety of settings should complete rating scales. The results should be compared to responses from interviews and the results of observations. Some rating scales are limited to an assessment of the primary symptoms contained in the *DSM-IV-TR* criteria; other assessment instruments are multidimensional and might address emotional-social status, communication, memory, reasoning and problem solving, and cognitive skills such as planning and self-evaluation. Figure 5.4 contains an excerpt from the "Strengths and Limitations Inventory: School Version" (Dowdy, Patton, Smith, & Polloway, 1998).

When the school team reconvenes to review all of the data, the *DSM-IV-TR* (2000) criteria should be considered.

The school team should look for consistency across reports from the assessment instruments and the informants to validate the existence of AD/HD. If it is confirmed, the team must determine if it has caused an adverse effect on school performance and if a special educational plan is needed. Montague, McKinney, and Hocutt (1994) cite the following questions developed by the Professional Group on Attention and Related Disorders (PGARD) to guide the team in determining educational needs:

1. Do the AD/HD symptoms negatively affect learning to the extent that there is a discrepancy between the child's productivity with respect to listening, following directions, planning, organizing, or completing academic tasks requiring reading, math, writing, or spelling skills?
2. Are inattentive behaviours the result of cultural or language differences, socioeconomic disadvantage, or lack of exposure to education?
3. Are the inattentive behaviours evidence of stressful family functioning (e.g., death or divorce), frustration related to having unattainable educational goals, abuse, or physical or emotional disorders (e.g., epilepsy or depression)?

If question 1 is answered positively and questions 2 and 3 are answered negatively, the team can conclude that there is an educational need that requires special services. At that point, a planning meeting should address the educational program.

Step 3: Collaborative Meeting for Strategy Development   This meeting might be very emotional and overwhelming for parents, or it might generate relief and hope that the services can truly assist the child. The team must be sensitive to the feelings of the parents and take adequate time to describe the results of the testing. If the parents are emotionally upset, it may help to wait a week before developing the intervention plan for school services.

Step 4: Follow-up and Progress Review   After the educational plan has been developed, the parents and school personnel should monitor the child's progress closely to ensure

TEACHING TIP

Begin a parent conference by relating the strengths of the student! Give parents time to respond to the limitations observed in the school setting by reporting examples of behaviour from home and other environments.

	Never Observed	Sometimes Observed	Often Observed	Very Often Observed
ATTENTION/IMPULSIVITY/HYPERACTIVITY				
Exhibits excessive nonpurposeful movement (can't sit still, stay in seat).				
Does not stay on task for appropriate periods of time.				
Verbally or physically interrupts conversations or activities.				
Does not pay attention to most important stimuli.				
REASONING/PROCESSING				
Makes poor decisions.				
Makes frequent errors.				
Has difficulty getting started.				
MEMORY				
Has difficulty repeating information recently heard.				
Has difficulty following multiple directions.				
Memory deficits impact daily activities.				
EXECUTIVE FUNCTION				
Has difficulty planning/organizing activities.				
Has difficulty attending to several stimuli at once.				
Has difficulty monitoring own performance throughout activity (self-monitoring).				
Has difficulty independently adjusting behaviour (self-regulation).				
INTERPERSONAL SKILLS				
Has difficulty accepting constructive criticism.				
Exhibits signs of poor self-confidence.				
EMOTIONAL MATURITY				
Inappropriate emotion for situation.				
Displays temper outbursts.				
Does not follow classroom or workplace "rules."				

FIGURE 5.4

Sample Test Items from "Strength and Limitations Inventory: School Version"

From *Attention Deficit/Hyperactivity Disorder in the Classroom: A Practical Guide for Teachers* (pp. 112–113), by C. A. Dowdy, J. R. Patton, T. E. C. Smith, and E. A. Polloway, 1998, Austin, TX: Pro-Ed. Reprinted by permission.

success. Adjustments may be needed occasionally to maintain progress. For example, reinforcement for good behaviour may eventually lose its novelty and need to be changed. The ultimate goal is to remove accommodations and support as the child becomes capable of regulating his or her behaviour. As the setting and school personnel change each year, re-evaluating the type of special services needed will yield benefits. As the student becomes more efficient in learning and demonstrates better social skills, new less restrictive plans must be designed to complement this growth.

Cultural and Linguistic Diversity

When AD/HD coexists with cultural and linguistic diversity, it presents a special set of challenges to the educator. Failure to address the special needs of these children can be detrimental to their academic success. Issues related to assessment and cultural diversity have been discussed previously; the same concerns exist in the identification and treatment of students with AD/HD. To address the needs of multicultural students with AD/HD, teachers must become familiar with their unique values, views, customs, interests, and behaviours and their relation to instructional strategies (Wright, 1995). More research is needed to explore the multicultural issues related to AD/HD.

Teachers must learn to recognize the cultural differences of each child in the classroom. The majority of teachers (both in special and general education) in Canada are Caucasian; generally, they lack training related to meeting the individual needs of culturally diverse children. During the identification process, the team must recognize cultural differences and influences for what they are, rather than labelling them as a symptom of attention deficit/hyperactivity disorder.

Barkley (1998) raises the issue that a chaotic home environment exacerbates the problems of children with AD/HD. Although the homes of many children with AD/HD may seem disorganized and the parenting characterized by inconsistencies or lack of structure, teachers and schools should seriously question such judgments. The Canadian Pediatric Society (1998) emphasizes the importance of understanding the "transactional approach" when dealing with children with school problems, particularly with children with AD/HD. The **transactional approach** acknowledges that over time the child's difficulty will affect all aspects of his or her environment which, in turn, will affect the child. In other words, to understand the parenting or home environment we must recognize the cumulative effect of the child's difficulties on the parenting. We are left with a "chicken or the egg" question about poor parenting and children with AD/HD. When teachers use carefully organized and structured instruction, students with AD/HD benefit. Wright (1995) suggests that, first and foremost, teachers should treat students with respect, attempt to establish good rapport with them, and only then impose instructional demands. When teachers use carefully organized and structured instruction, these students benefit.

Sleeter and Grant (1993) encourage teachers to make educational experiences more meaningful to students by developing activities and homework that acknowledge cultural differences and build on the specific experiences of the student. Teachers can integrate personal and community experiences into teaching an academic concept to help make it relevant to students.

The Role of Medication

Since many students with AD/HD will be prescribed medication by their physicians, teachers need to understand the types of medications often used, their side effects, and

Most children with AD/HD are in general education classrooms.

the way they work. Medication therapy can be defined as treatment by chemical substances that prevent or reduce inappropriate behaviours, thus promoting academic and social gains for children with learning and behaviour problems (Dowdy et al., 1998). Studies have shown that different outcomes occur for different children. In 70 to 80 percent of the cases, children with AD/HD (ages six and older) respond in a positive manner to psychostimulant medication (Baren, 2000; Barkley, 1999–2000). The desired outcomes include increased attention, more on-task behaviour, completion of assigned tasks, improved social relations with peers and teachers, increased appropriate behaviours, and reduction of inappropriate, disruptive behaviours such as talking out, getting out of seat, and breaking rules. These changes frequently lead to improved academic and social achievement as well as increased self-esteem. Virginia Douglas at McGill University has been one of the central researchers in the field of AD/HD in children. She and her colleagues at the Montreal Children's Hospital have documented an improvement in flexible thinking as a result of psychostimulant medication in children with AD/HD (Douglas, Barr, Desilets, & Sherman, 1995). In addition, at Dalhousie University in Halifax, Bawden and colleagues examined the effects of stimulants on preschoolers with attention-deficit disorders and found significant improvements on a variety of attentional tasks (Byrne, Bawden, DeWolfe, & Beattie, 1998).

For some children, the desired effects do not occur. In these situations the medication has no negative effect, but simply does not lead to the hoped-for results. However, parents and teachers often give up too soon, prematurely concluding that the medication did not help. It is important to contact the physician when no effect is noticed, because the dosage may need to be adjusted or a different type of medication may be called for. Barkley (1999–2000) reports that when individuals continue to try different stimulants when one fails, the success rate rises to 90 percent.

Another possible response to medication is to experience side effects. Side effects are changes that are not desired. The most common side effect, loss of appetite, occurs more than 50 percent of the time; however, it has not been found to affect adult stature (Barkley, 1999–2000). Figure 5.5 lists the most common side effects of the medications used for AD/HD. This checklist may be used by parents and teachers when communicating with physicians. Teachers should constantly be on the lookout for signs of side effects and report any concerns to parents or the child's physician.

FIGURE 5.5

Stimulant Side Effects
Checklist

From *AD/HD Project Facilitate: An In-Service Education Program for Educators and Parents* (p. 55), by R. Elliott, L. A. Worthington, and D. Patterson, Tuscaloosa, AL: University of Alabama. Used by permission.

Side Effects Checklist: Stimulants

Child _____ Date Checked _____
Person Completing Form _____ Relationship to Child _____

I. SIDE EFFECTS

Directions: Please check any of the behaviours which this child exhibits while receiving his or her stimulant medication. If a child exhibits one or more of the behaviours below, please rate the extent to which you perceive the behaviour to be a problem using the scale below (1 = Mild to 7 = Severe).

	Mild						Severe
1. Loss of appetite	1	2	3	4	5	6	7
2. Stomachaches	1	2	3	4	5	6	7
3. Headaches	1	2	3	4	5	6	7
4. Tics (vocal or motor)	1	2	3	4	5	6	7
5. Extreme mood changes	1	2	3	4	5	6	7
6. Cognitively sluggish/disoriented	1	2	3	4	5	6	7
7. Excessive irritability	1	2	3	4	5	6	7
8. Excessive nervousness	1	2	3	4	5	6	7
9. Decreased social interactions	1	2	3	4	5	6	7
10. Unusual or bizarre behaviour	1	2	3	4	5	6	7
11. Excessive activity level	1	2	3	4	5	6	7
12. Light picking of fingertips	1	2	3	4	5	6	7
13. Lip licking	1	2	3	4	5	6	7

II. PSYCHOSOCIAL CONCERNS

Please address any concerns you have about this child's adjustment to medication (e.g., physical, social, emotional changes; attitudes toward the medication, etc.).

III. OTHER CONCERNS

If you have any other concerns about this child's medication (e.g., administration problems, dosage concerns), please comment below.

IV. PARENT CONCERNS (FOR PARENTS ONLY)

Using the same scale above, please check any behaviours which this child exhibits while at home.

	Mild						Severe
1. Insomnia; sleeplessness	1	2	3	4	5	6	7
2. Possible rebound effects (excessive hyperactivity, impulsivity, inattention)	1	2	3	4	5	6	7

The most commonly prescribed medications for AD/HD are **psychostimulants** such as Dexedrine (dextroamphetamine), Ritalin (methylphenidate), and Adderall (amphetamine salts). Studies have shown that Ritalin accounts for 90 percent of the market in stimulants prescribed (Weyandt, 2001). This medication is considered a "mild central nervous system stimulant, available as tablets of 5, 10, and 20 mg for oral administration" (*Physician's Desk Reference*, 1994, p. 835). A typical dosage of Ritalin for an initial trial is 5 mg, two to three times daily. The dosage will be increased until the optimal response is obtained with the fewest side effects. The medication is thought to stimulate the underaroused central nervous system of individuals with AD/HD, increasing the amount or efficiency of the neurotransmitters needed for attention, concentration, and planning (Weyandt, 2001). Students who are described as anxious or tense, have tics, or have a family history or diagnosis of **Tourette syndrome** are generally not given Ritalin

(*Physician's Desk Reference*, 1999). Adderall is gaining in usage partly because it is effective for up to 15 hours and a second dose does not have to be taken at school. The specific dose of medicine must be determined individually for each child. Generally, greater side effects come from higher dosages, but some students may need a high dosage to experience the positive effects of the medication. No clear guidelines exist as to how long a child should take medication; both adolescents and adults respond positively to these stimulants. Constant monitoring, preferably through behavioural rating scales completed by parents and teachers, is essential.

Antidepressants are also used to manage AD/HD. They are prescribed less frequently than psychostimulants and might include Tofranil (imipramine), Norpramin (desipramine), and Elavil (amytriptyline). These medications are generally used when negative side effects have occurred with stimulants or when the stimulants have not been effective, or when an individual is also depressed. The long-term use of antidepressants has not been well studied. Again, frequent monitoring is necessary for responsible management. Other medications that are used much less frequently include antipsychotics such as Mellaril (thioridazine), Thorazine (chlorpromazine), Catapres (clonidine), Eskalith (lithium), and Tegretol (carbamazepine). Whatever medication is prescribed by the child's physician, teachers should ask the physician for a thorough description of the possible positive and negative outcomes for that medication. Table 5.1 contains a list of common myths associated with medication treatment for AD/HD.

TABLE 5.1   Common Myths Associated with AD/HD Medications

Myth	Fact
Medication should be stopped when a child reaches teen years.	Research clearly shows there is continued benefit to medication for those teens who meet criteria for diagnosis of AD/HD.
Children tend to build up tolerance for medication.	Although the dose of medication may need adjusting from time to time due to weight gain or increased attention demands there is no evidence that children build up a tolerance to medication.
Taking medicine for AD/HD leads to greater likelihood of later drug dependency or addiction.	A study by the National Institutes of Health (2000) suggested that Children and adolescents with AD/HD who had used medication were less likely to engage in deviant behaviour or substance abuse.
Positive response to medication is confirmation of a diagnosis of AD/HD.	The fact that a child shows improvement of attention span or a reduction of activity while taking AD/HD medication does not substantiate the diagnosis of AD/HD. Even some normal children will show a marked improvement in attentiveness when they take AD/HD medication.
Medication stunts growth.	AD/HD medications may cause an initial and mild slowing of growth, but over time the growth suppression effect is minimal if not nonexistent in most cases.
Ritalin dulls a child's personality and can cause depression.	If a child's personality seems depressed or less spontaneous, the dosage should probably be lowered.
AD/HD children who take medication attribute their success only to medication.	When self-esteem is encouraged, children taking medication attribute their success not only to the medication but to themselves as well.

Adapted from "What Teachers and Parents Should Know About Ritalin" (pp. 20–26) by C. Pancheri and M. A. Prater, 1999, *Teaching Exceptional Children* (March/April).

The following are considerations for teachers of students taking medication (Fowler, 1992; Howell, Evans, & Gardiner, 1997):

▶ Handle the dispensing of medication discreetly. Don't make announcements in front of the class that it's time for a child to take his or her pill. Students, especially teens, are often very embarrassed by the necessity to "take a pill" during school. If it is not given in private, they may refuse the medication.

▶ Make sure the medication is given as prescribed. Although the child should not be pulled away from an important event, the dosage should be given as close as possible to the designated time.

▶ Avoid placing too much blame or credit for the child's behaviour on the medication. *All* children will have good and bad days. When problems arise, teachers should avoid comments such as "Did you take your pill this morning?"

▶ Monitor the behaviour of the child, looking for any side effects.

▶ Communicate with the school nurse, the parents, and the physician.

Remember, not all children diagnosed with attention deficit/hyperactivity disorder need medication. The decision to intervene medically should come only after a great deal of thought about the possibility of a variety of interventions. Children whose impairments are minimal are certainly less likely to need medication than those whose severe impairments result in major disruptions.

Although teachers and other school personnel are important members of a therapeutic team engaged in exploring, implementing, and evaluating diverse treatment methods, the decision to try medication is primarily the responsibility of the parents and the physician. Teachers are generally cautioned by their school systems not to specifically recommend medication because the school may be held responsible for the charges incurred. Educators, therefore, find themselves in a dilemma when they feel strongly that medication is needed to address the symptoms of the AD/HD. However, teachers must also realize that medication alone is insufficient. Students with AD/HD need a multimodal approach, including the cognitive and behavioural strategies addressed in the following section.

Strategies for Instruction and Classroom Adaptations and Accommodations

Since no two children with attention deficit/hyperactivity disorder are exactly alike, a wide variety of interventions and service options must be used to meet their needs. Success for these students depends on the qualifications of the teacher, effective strategies for instruction, and classroom adaptations and accommodations.

Classroom Adaptations and Accommodations

Since attention deficit/hyperactivity disorder describes a set of characteristics that affect learning, most interventions take place in the school setting. Any approach to addressing the needs of students with AD/HD must be comprehensive. Figure 5.6 depicts a model of educational intervention built on four intervention areas: environmental management, instructional accommodations, student-regulated strategies, and medical management (Dowdy et al., 1998). Medical management was described previously. This section identifies specific strategies for addressing the challenges of AD/HD in the classroom.

FIGURE 5.6

Model for AD/HD
Intervention

From *Attention-
Deficit/Hyperactivity Disorder in
the Classroom: A Practical Guide
for Teachers,* by C. A. Dowdy, J. R.
Patton, E. A. Polloway, & T. E. C.
Smith, 1997, Austin, TX: Pro-Ed.

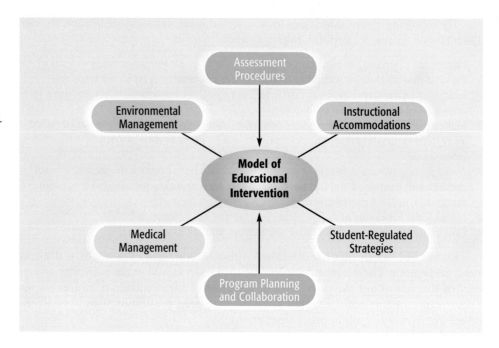

CROSS-REFERENCE

Teachers should develop a list of
procedures to make the classroom run smoothly. For example, how should students
request help? How should they
respond during a fire drill? For
more tips in this area, refer to
Chapter 12, on classroom
management.

Managing the Classroom Environment   A classroom with even one or two students with
AD/HD can be difficult to manage. Teachers need to be skilled in classroom management.
Rather than reacting spontaneously—and often inconsistently—to disruptive situations,
teachers should have a management system to help avoid crises. Dowdy et al. (1998)
define *classroom management* as a combination of techniques that results in an orderly
classroom environment where social growth and learning can occur. Good classroom
management is beneficial for all students, including those with AD/HD. Techniques
include group management, physical management, and behaviour management.

Group Management   Though they benefit all members of a class, group management techniques are critical in managing the behaviour of individual students with AD/HD. One of
the most basic and effective techniques is to establish classroom rules and consequences for
breaking those rules. Children with AD/HD need to understand the classroom rules and
school procedures in order to be successful. Jones and Jones (1995) suggest that students
feel more committed to following rules when they have contributed to developing them.
The rules should be displayed prominently in the room and reviewed periodically, if students with AD/HD are to retain and follow them. It is important for teachers to apply
the rules consistently, even though students can sometimes frustrate teachers and make
them want to "give in." Teachers may start the process of rule development by offering
one or two rules of their own and then letting the children pick up with their own ideas.
The following is a list of recommendations for developing rules (Dowdy et al., 1998).

▌ State rules positively and clearly. A rule should tell students what to do instead of what
not to do!
▌ Rules should be stated in simple terms so students can easily understand them. For young
students, rules can be depicted with drawings and figures.
▌ The number of rules should be no more than five or six.
▌ Rules should be displayed conspicuously in the room.
▌ Rules should be practised and discussed at the beginning of the year and periodically
throughout the year.

Personal Spotlight

Teacher with an Attention Deficit/Hyperactivity Disorder, Elementary Teacher, Katie Boisvert

Katie teaches in an elementary French immersion program in an English language school in Montreal, Quebec. Katie has students with different abilities and challenges in her class, and she is known for her empathy and warmth for all of them. Katie also has an attention-deficit disorder.

Katie describes how school was for her and how she came to be a teacher.

"A teacher once told me that my work was too disorganized and since she could not make sense of it, no one ever would. That was three years ago and I was just about to finish my teaching degree! When I was a child, my grades were never exceptional and I could not focus in class no matter how interesting it was. But worst of all, I was always getting in trouble. I was very agitated and could never get along with the other children. I had no friends and basically no self-esteem. My work was messy, often late, half done or not done at all. It seemed like I could never get the instructions right. I desperately wanted to belong, but somehow knew I was different.

"I made my way through high school and college having the impression that no matter how long I studied, I was set for failure. Still I kept going and somehow found myself in university trying to pursue a degree in education. Maybe I was drawn to education because my own school experience was so bad. It was when I was studying to be a teacher that I discovered that I had AD/HD. To me, in light of my past experiences, the diagnosis made a lot of sense. The "label" was a relief: it made me understand what had been going on all those years. What didn't make sense to me is, why didn't anyone ever realize there was something wrong and that I needed help? I didn't get help so I had to help myself. All these years I have worked to develop my own strategies to deal with my disability. I am still working to find my own way and continuing to develop more strategies, but now I have support and understanding.

"I have now been teaching for two years and I have a great class. Every day is an amazing experience. I enter the class in the morning with the belief that all of the children can learn and progress. We work together to achieve this goal. They help me be more organized and they challenge my creativity. In return, I help them find ways and strategies to facilitate their learning. We try to respect everyone's differences!"

- For students with AD/HD, role-playing how to carry out the rules is an effective technique.
- Adopt rules and consequences that you are willing to enforce.
- Positively reinforce students who abide by the rules. It is more effective to reinforce the students who abide by the rules than to punish those who break them.
- To avoid misunderstandings, communicate rules and consequences to parents. It is helpful to have parents and students sign a contract documenting their understanding of the rules.

Time management is also important in effective classroom management. Students with AD/HD thrive in an organized, structured classroom. Many of the acting-out and inappropriate behaviours occur during unscheduled, unstructured free time, when the number of choices of activities may become overwhelming. If free time is scheduled, limit the choices and provide positive reinforcement for appropriate behaviour during free time. Encourage students to investigate topics that interest them and to complete projects that bring their strengths into play.

Polloway and Patton (1993) suggest that teachers begin each day with a similar routine. The particular activity is not as important as the consistency. For example, some teachers like to start the day with quiet reading, whereas others might begin with singing, recognizing birthdays, or talking about special events that are coming up. This routine will set the stage for a calm orderly day, and students will know what to expect from the teacher. Secondary teachers need to advise students of scheduling changes (e.g., assembly,

CONSIDER THIS

What are some appropriate activities to begin and end the day or class period for elementary and secondary students?

pep rally) and provide a brief overview of the topics and activities to be expected during the class period.

Like the beginning of the day, closure on the day's or the class period's activities is important for secondary students. Reviewing the important events of the day and describing the next day's activities help students with AD/HD. Take the time to provide rewards for students who have maintained appropriate behaviour during the day. If parents are involved in a contract, discuss the transmitted notes and review homework that might have been assigned during the day.

To work successfully with students with AD/HD, group students to create the most effective learning environment. They may be taught more effectively in small groups of four to seven students and may complete work more successfully as a team. Perhaps two or three students may need to receive more individualized instruction. The teacher should plan the makeup of the groups to combine students with AD/HD with other students who will be supportive, positive role models. The resulting peer modelling of abiding by the rules is often more effective than teacher-directed behaviour management. Also, students with AD/HD may become friends with students without AD/HD if they work together in co-operative learning groups (Landau, Milich, & Diener, 1998).

Teachers may want to offer incentives to individual students and groups to reward outstanding work. You might place a marble in a jar each time students are "caught being good." When the jar is filled the class receives an award such as a picnic or a skating party. Another technique involves adding a piece to a puzzle whenever the teacher recognizes that the class is working especially hard. When the puzzle is complete, the class is rewarded. These group incentives can be very effective; however, some students will need an individual behaviour management plan to aid in directing their behaviour.

Physical Management   The physical environment of a classroom can also have an impact on the behaviours of students with AD/HD. The arrangement of the room is most important. The classroom needs to be large enough for students to have space between themselves and others, so they will be less likely to impose themselves on one another. Each student needs some personal space.

Desk arrangement is also important. Research has shown that distractions may be reduced by using standard rows or a semicircle; placing a child with AD/HD with five or six students around a table can be very distracting (Flick, 1998). The student with AD/HD should be near the teacher in order to focus attention on the information being presented in the classroom. But students should never be placed near the teacher as a punitive measure. A seat near the front may help the student who is distracted by someone's new hairstyle or flashy jewellery. There should also be various places in the room where quiet activities can take place, where small groups can work together, where sustained attention for difficult tasks can be maintained, and where a relaxed and comfortable environment can be enjoyed for a change of pace. At one time, classrooms with lots of visual stimulation were considered inappropriate for students with AD/HD, leading to the creation of sterile environments with colourless walls and no bulletin boards. This is no longer considered necessary; however, order is needed in the classroom; materials should be located consistently in the same place, and bulletin boards should be well organized. Set aside places where students can work in a carrel or other private space with minimal visual and auditory stimuli, and have a place for a child who seems underaroused to be able to move around and get rejuvenated (Carbone, 2001).

Behavioural Support   Behavioural support techniques can enhance the education of students with AD/HD, especially those that reward desired behaviour. For example, when students with AD/HD are attending to their tasks, following classroom rules, or participating appropriately in a co-operative learning activity, their behaviours should be positively reinforced. Unfortunately, teachers often ignore appropriate behaviour and call attention only to what is inappropriate. When students receive attention for actions that are disruptive or inconsiderate, the negative behaviours can be reinforced and may thus increase in frequency.

Positive reinforcement tends to increase appropriate behaviour (Reid, 1999). Teachers should consider which rewards appeal most to the individuals who will receive them. Common ones include small toys, free time, time to listen to music, time in the gym, opportunities to do things for the teacher, having lunch with the teacher, and praise. Because a reward that acts as a reinforcer for one student may not work for another, teachers might generate a menu of rewards and allow students to select their own. Rewards do not have to be expensive; in fact, simply allowing students to take a break, get a drink of water, or sharpen a pencil may be just as effective as providing expensive toys and games.

Another helpful idea in working with children with AD/HD is called the Premack principle. Also known as "grandma's law," it is based on the traditional comment "If you eat your vegetables, then you can have your dessert" (Polloway, Patton, & Serna, 2001, p. 74). The teacher announces that a reward or highly desired activity will be awarded to students after they complete a required or desired activity. For example, students might be required to sit in their seats and complete work for 15 minutes; then a snack or free time will follow. This simple technique can be very effective for students with AD/HD.

Negative reinforcement (removing an aversive stimulus) is also effective in increasing desired behaviour. For example, students might be told that those who complete 15 of the assigned 25 math questions in the remaining 20 minutes of class time will not have to complete the task as homework. Removal of homework (the aversive stimulus) will motivate "on-task" behaviour. This technique is also often effective for students with AD/HD.

Often students will need an individual plan that focuses on their particular needs. Sometimes this plan involves the creation of a "contract." Together, student and teacher develop goals to improve behaviour and then put these goals in writing. They also stipulate consequences for not following the contract and reinforcement for completing the contract (Westling & Koorland, 1988). This instrument provides structure and forms an explicit way to communicate with children with AD/HD and their parents. Downing (2002) offers the following guidelines for making and using such contracts:

- Determine the most critical area(s) of concern.
- Consider when the behaviour usually occurs, the events that trigger it, and why you think the behaviour is occurring.
- Specify the desired behaviour in measurable terms, using clear, simple words.
- Specify the reinforcers that will be used and the consequences that will follow if the contract is not fulfilled.
- See that both teacher and student sign the contract (and the parents, when appropriate).
- Keep a record of the student's behaviour.
- Provide the agreed-upon consequences or reinforcements in a timely fashion.
- When the goal is reached, celebrate, and write a new contract!

A sample contract is provided in Figure 5.7.

Be cautious with the use of contracts. As an agreement between the student and the teacher, and sometimes the parents, it must not be coercive. It is also essential that the student be able to do those things listed in the contract. In other words, the student must be able to achieve success.

Another behaviour management technique is cueing or signalling students with AD/HD when they are on the verge of inappropriate behaviour. First, student and teacher sit down privately and discuss the inappropriate behaviour that has been creating problems in the classroom. The teacher offers to provide a cue when the behaviour begins to be noticed. Teachers and students can have fun working together on the signal, which

CONSIDER THIS

These ideas are effective with elementary-age students. Generate some reinforcers that would be more effective in secondary settings.

CONSIDER THIS

What is an example of how the Premack principle can be applied for elementary, junior, and high school students?

FIGURE 5.7

An Example of a
Contingency Contract

From "Individualized Behavior
Contracts" (p. 170) by J. A.
Downing, 2002, *Intervention in
School and Clinic*, 37(3).

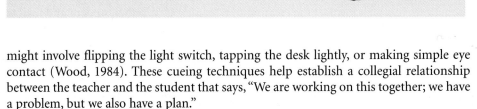

I, Bobby, agree to:

▷ Follow the classroom rules and teacher's directions.

▷ Handle conflict situations appropriately, using the strategies I have learned
rather than running away.

▷ Express my negative feelings in a calm, quiet voice without making threats
and/or refusing to do what I am told.

For this effort, I will earn:

▷ Fifteen minutes of free time at the end of each successful day to play *The
Magic School Bus Explores the Rainforest* computer game.

▷ A visit from Billy the Boa Constrictor at the end of every week if I am successful
for at least 4 out of 5 days.

Date:

Student Signature:

Teacher Signature:

Cueing or signalling students is one method that teachers can use to help get their attention.

might involve flipping the light switch, tapping the desk lightly, or making simple eye contact (Wood, 1984). These cueing techniques help establish a collegial relationship between the teacher and the student that says, "We are working on this together; we have a problem, but we also have a plan."

Making Instructional Accommodations

Barkley (1999–2000) says, "Knowing what to do is a strategy problem. Doing what you know is a motivational problem." His research suggests that AD/HD may be caused by neurological differences in the motivational centre of the brain; however, children with AD/HD are often misunderstood and labelled lazy or unmotivated, as if they are choosing not to perform at their maximum potential. Teacher comments such as "I know you can do this work, because you did it yesterday" or "You can do better; you just aren't trying" probably suggest a lack of understanding of the inconsistent performance characteristic of this disability (Flick, 1998). Instead, teachers need to find ways to cope with the frustration and stress that are sometimes involved in working with the students, while modifying their teaching style, their curriculum, and possibly their expectations in order to engineer academic success for the students.

Modifying Teacher Behaviour Since students with AD/HD are not easily stimulated, they need novelty and excitement in their learning environment. Although structure and consistency are extremely important, students need challenging, novel activities to keep them focused and learning. The Web offers endless ideas for "jazzing up" lesson plans or developing new ones. See the nearby Technology Today feature to explore some options.

Web Tools for Lesson Plans

Use tools available on the Web like the following to enhance lesson plans and shorten preparation time:

- www.classbuilder.com/
- www.edhelper.com/ Generates worksheets and puzzles for any content area.

- http://teachers.teach-nology.com/web_tools/ Generates planners, bingo cards, learning contracts, and more.
- www.educationalpress.org/educationalpress/ Focuses on flashcards and game boards for beginning reading skills.

- www.theeducatorsnetwork.com Provides comprehensive links to lessons.
- www.schoolexpress.com/ Emails a free thematic unit each week.
- www.kimskorner4teachertalk.com Provides bulletin board ideas, ice-breakers, and more.

For more ideas visit www.Teaching K-8.com and click on "Classroom Activities."

Weyandt (2001) reports that the incidence of inappropriate behaviour increases during nonstimulating, repetitive activities. She suggests that teachers vary activities, allow and encourage movement that is purposeful and not disruptive, give frequent breaks, and even let students stand as they listen, take notes, or perform other academic tasks. "Legal movement" such as pencil sharpening or a hall pass for walking to the restroom or getting water might be pre-approved for a student's restless times (Guyer, 2000). Here are some recommendations from Yehle and Wambold (1998) for enhancing large group instruction:

- Begin with an attention grabber (e.g., joke, question of the day).
- Distribute an outline of your lecture to assist with note taking; use the overhead projector and provide copies of overheads.
- Pace the lesson, giving more time for difficult concepts.
- Use visual aids such as a graphic organizer as often as possible.
- Clap, alter your tone of voice, or use different coloured chalk to draw attention to important material.
- Repeat important information several times during the lecture; ask students to repeat in unison.
- Ask frequent questions of individual students by name throughout the presentation.
- Walk around the room monitoring and checking work frequently.
- Try to turn a lesson into a game format (e.g., the "Jeopardy!" game show) for a fun review.

Templeton (1995) suggests that teachers speak clearly and loudly enough for students to hear, but not too fast. She points out that enthusiasm and humour will help engage students and excite those who might become easily bored and distracted. She also recommends helping students see the value in what they learn and the importance of the material. During a long lecture period, teachers might list main ideas or important questions on the chalkboard or by using the overhead projector, to help students focus on the most important information. When a student's attention does wander, a small, unobtrusive signal such as a gentle pat on his or her shoulder can cue the student to return to the task. To perk up tiring students, try a quick game of Simon Says or purposeful physical activities such as taking a note to the office, feeding the animals in the classroom, or returning books to the library. Prater (1992) provides a self-assessment for teachers to determine if they are doing everything they can to increase each student's attention to task during instructional time. This strategy for improving instruction for all students is included in the nearby Inclusion Strategies feature.

CONSIDER THIS

If you are currently teaching, complete the Time-on-Task Self-Assessment; if not, rewrite the questions and use them as an observation tool to evaluate a teacher who is willing to be observed. Analyze the results, and identify changes that could be made to improve learning in the classroom.

Time-on-Task Self-Assessment for Teachers

Read the following statements and rate yourself according to the following scale:

N	R	S	U	A
Never	**Rarely**	**Sometimes**	**Usually**	**Always**

DURING GROUP INSTRUCTION:

1. Students are attending to me before I start the lesson.
2. Students use choral group responses to answer questions.
3. Individual students answer questions or orally read when called in a random order.
4. I ask a question, then call on a student to answer.
5. Students answer correctly most of the questions I ask.
6. I have all my materials and supplies ready before class begins.
7. If possible, I write all the necessary material on the board, an overhead, or poster before instructing.
8. I use some type of signal with group responses.
9. Students are involved in reading directions, practice items, or the answers.
10. Students are involved in housekeeping procedures such as passing out papers.

DURING SEATWORK:

11. I move around the classroom checking students' work.
12. I can make eye contact with all of my students.
13. I allow students to work together and to talk about their seatwork.

14. Immediately after instruction my students can work on their seatwork without any questions.
15. Students need not wait for my assistance if they have questions about their seatwork.
16. I spend little time answering questions about what the students are to do next.
17. Most of my students finish their work about the same time.

DURING INSTRUCTION OR SEATWORK:

18. I spend little time reprimanding students for misbehaviour.
19. My students are not restless.
20. My students follow a routine for transition times (i.e., getting materials ready, collecting papers, lining up for lunch).
21. My students respond quickly during transition times.
22. I have well-defined rules for appropriate behaviour in my classroom.
23. I consistently provide appropriate consequences for students who are and remain on-task.
24. I teach my students self-management procedures (e.g., self-monitoring, self-instruction).

From "Increasing Time-on-Task in the Classroom," by M. A. Prater, 1992, *Intervention in School and Clinic, 28*(1), pp. 22–27.

Modifying the Curriculum Although students with AD/HD are typically taught in the general education classroom, using the regular curriculum, they need a curriculum adapted to focusing on "doing" and one that avoids long periods of sitting and listening. These adaptations can benefit all students. For example, experience-based learning, in which students might develop their own projects, perform experiments, or take field trips, can help all students grow as active learners. Cronin (1993) suggests that teachers modify curricula by using activities that closely resemble challenges and experiences in the real world. They can use story problems within traditional textbooks, curriculum-based experiments and projects, or lesson extensions such as writing letters to environmental groups to obtain more information than is offered in a textbook.

Describing a related curriculum model, Stephien and Gallagher (1993) suggest that problem-based learning provides authentic experiences in the classroom. In this model, students are asked to solve an "ill-structured problem" before they receive any instruction. Teachers act as coaches and tutors, questioning the student's hypotheses and conclusions and sharing their own thoughts when needed during "time out" discussions. Students act as doctors, historians, or scientists, or assume other roles of individuals who have a real stake in solving the proposed problem. When students "take ownership" of the problem, motivation soars. Teachers can model problem-solving strategies by thinking out loud and questioning their own conclusions and recommendations. This model increases self-directed learning and improves motivation.

Developing Student-Regulated Strategies

The previous sections on classroom environment and instructional accommodations focused on activities that the teacher directs and implements to increase the success of children with AD/HD. This section will describe student-regulated strategies. Dowdy et al. (1998) define student-regulated strategies as interventions, initially taught by the teacher, that the student will eventually implement independently.

Fiore, Becker, and Nerro (1993) note that these cognitive approaches directly address core problems of children with AD/HD, including impulse control, higher-order problem solving, and self-regulation. Because student-regulated strategies are new, teachers are encouraged to validate their effectiveness in their classrooms (DuPaul & Eckert, 1998).

The benefits of implementing self-regulation strategies for children with AD/HD include the following:

- Modifying impulsive responses
- Increasing selective attention and focus
- Providing verbal mediators to facilitate academic and social problem-solving challenges (e.g., self-talk to calm down during an argument)
- Teaching self-instructional statements to assist students in "talking through" problems and tasks
- Providing strategies that may develop prosocial behaviours and lead to improved peer relations (Rooney, 1993)

The following discussion addresses four types of student-regulated strategies: study and organizational tactics, self-management, learning strategies, and social skills.

Study and Organizational Tactics   Children with AD/HD have difficulty organizing their work and implementing effective study skills in general education classrooms. To help them with organization, teachers may designate space for students to keep materials, establish the routine of students writing down their assignments daily in an assignment notebook, and provide notebooks in different colours for each subject (Yehle & Wambold, 1998).

Hoover and Patton (1995) suggest teaching 11 study skills: increasing and/or adjusting reading rate according to the purpose for reading, listening, note taking, writing reports, giving oral presentations, using graphic aids, taking tests, using the library, using reference material, time management, and self-management. Students should practise planning as an organizational strategy. For an assignment such as a term paper, deciding how to break the task into small parts and how to complete each part should be practised before such an assignment is made. Students should also practise estimating how much time will be needed for various activities so they can establish appropriate and realistic goals. Outlining skills can also help with organization and planning. Students may want to use a word processor to order their ideas and to help organize their work.

TEACHING TIP

Practise what you teach! Identify an activity or task that you need to accomplish by a date in the future (e.g., develop a unit on ecology). Break down the steps to completion, including target dates. Model your planning skills by "thinking out loud" for your students. Doing this will make the concept of planning and organizing more concrete for them.

Self-Management   The primary goal of programs that teach self-management or self-control is to "make children more consciously aware of their own thinking processes and task approach strategies, and to give them responsibility for their own reinforcement" (Reeve, 1990, p. 76). Here are some advantages of teaching self-control:

▶ It saves the teacher's time by decreasing the demand for direct instruction.
▶ It increases the effectiveness of an intervention.
▶ It increases the maintenance of skills over time.
▶ It increases students' ability to use the skill in a variety of settings. (Lloyd, Landrum, & Hallahan, 1991, p. 201)

Polloway and Patton (1993) cite four types of self-regulation. In self-assessment, the individual determines the need for change and also monitors personal behaviour. In self-monitoring, the student attends to specific aspects of his or her own behaviour. While learning to self-monitor, a student can be given a periodic beep or other cue to signal that it is time for him or her to evaluate "on-" or "off-" task behaviour. In self-instruction, the student cues himself or herself to inhibit inappropriate behaviours or to express appropriate ones. In self-reinforcement, the student administers self-selected reinforcement for an appropriate behaviour that has been previously specified. Figure 5.8 demonstrates a self-management planning form that was completed to help a high school student control his talking out in class. Figure 5.9 provides a self-monitoring sheet for the student to use to reflect on his or her use of the strategy. Eventually the student will begin to automatically self-monitor and will begin to use the appropriate response to situations that previously triggered an inappropriate display of anger. Other behaviours commonly targeted for self-regulation include completing assignments (productivity), appropriate classroom behaviour (such as staying in one's seat), accuracy of work (such as percent correct), and staying on task.

Learning Strategies   Deshler and Lenz (1989) define a learning strategy as an individual approach to a task. It includes how an individual thinks and acts when planning, executing, or evaluating performance. The learning strategies approach combines what is going on in an individual's head (cognition) with what a person actually does

FIGURE 5.8

A Self-Management Strategy for Dealing with Anger

From "Collaborating to Teach Prosocial Skills" (p. 145) by D. H. Allsopp, K. E. Santos, & R. Linn, 2000, *Intervention in School and Clinic, 35*(3).

1. **W**ATCH for the "trigger."
   ▶ Count to 10.
   ▶ Use relaxation techniques.

2. **A**NSWER, "Why am I angry?"

3. **I**DENTIFY my options.
   ▶ Ignore the other person.
   ▶ Move away.
   ▶ Resolve the problem.
   ▶ "I feel this way when you . . ."
   ▶ Listen to the other person.
   ▶ Talk to the teacher.

4. **T**RY an appropriate option for dealing with my anger.

What was the trigger?	Why was I angry?	Did I identify my options?	What option did I choose and was it successful?
1.			
2.			
3.			
4.			
5.			

FIGURE 5.9

A Self-Monitoring Sheet for Dealing with Anger

From "Collaborating to Teach Prosocial Skills" (p. 146) by D. H. Allsopp, K. E. Santos, & R. Linn, 2000, *Intervention in School and Clinic, 35*(3).

(behaviour) to guide the performance and evaluation of a specific task. All individuals use strategies; however, not all strategies are effective. This type of intervention is particularly beneficial for students with AD/HD (DuPaul & Eckert, 1998). Babkie and Provost (2002) encourage teachers and students to create their own strategies or cues to teach a difficult concept or behaviour. A key word is identified that specifies the targeted area. A short phrase or sentence that tells the student what to do is written for each letter in the key word. Figure 5.10 shows a strategy developed to cue students to organize homework.

Social Skills   Students with attention deficit/hyperactivity disorder often do not exhibit good problem-solving skills and are unable to predict the consequences of their inappropriate behaviour; therefore, specific and direct instruction in social skills may be necessary. In order for students to be able to assess their own inappropriate behaviour and adjust it to acceptable standards, many may need social skills training first. Landau, Milich, and Diener (1998) recommended that training be done throughout the year in groups of four to eight, with classmates in groups of the same gender. The sessions should include practice, modelling, and reinforcement of appropriate behaviour during real-life peer problem situations. Including appropriate, well-liked children in each group can promote desirable modelling and encourage important new friendships.

Organization: **HOMEWORK**
Have a place to work
Organize assignments according to difficulty
Make sure to follow directions
Examine the examples
Weave my way through the assignments
Observe work for errors and omissions
Return work to school
Keep up the effort!

FIGURE 5.10

A Learning Strategy for Homework

From "Select, Write, and Use Metacognitive Strategies in the Classroom" (p. 174) by A. M. Babkie and M. C. Provost, 2002, *Intervention in School and Clinic, 37*(3).

Promoting Inclusive Practices for Attention Deficit/Hyperactivity Disorder

The Professional Group for Attention and Related Disorders (PGARD) proposes that most children with AD/HD can be served in the general education program by trained teachers providing appropriate instruction and modifications. In addition to activities that teachers can use to promote a supportive classroom environment, Korinek, Walther-Thomas, McLaughlin, and Williams (1999) suggest that school wide support be promoted through disability-awareness activities, the use of positive discipline, and the use of adult volunteers. They add that the entire community can become involved through the establishment of business partnerships and the provision of organized activities like scouting and other forms of sports and recreation. Of course school administrators have to make a commitment to dedicate resources for training and to facilitate change.

The two critical features for successful inclusion of students with AD/HD are the skills and behaviours of the teachers and the understanding and acceptance of the general education peers.

Community-Building Skills for Teachers

One of the most important aspects of promoting success for children with AD/HD is the teacher. Fowler (1992) suggests that success for children with AD/HD might vary from year to year, class to class, teacher to teacher. She reports that the most commonly cited reason for a positive or negative school experience is the teacher. She cites the following 17 characteristics of teachers as likely indicators of positive learning outcomes for students with AD/HD:

1. Positive academic expectations
2. Frequent review of student work
3. Clarity of teaching (e.g., explicit directions, rules)
4. Flexibility
5. Fairness
6. Active interaction with the students
7. Responsiveness
8. Warmth
9. Patience
10. Humour
11. Structured and predictable approach
12. Consistency
13. Firmness
14. Positive attitude toward inclusion
15. Knowledge of and willingness to work with students with exceptional needs
16. Knowledge of different types of effective interventions
17. Willingness to work collaboratively with other teachers (e.g., sharing information, requesting assistance as needed, participating in conferences involving students)

> **CONSIDER THIS**
>
> Use these characteristics of an effective teacher as a tool for self-assessment. Identify your strengths, and determine goals for improving your teaching skills.

Resources for Developing Awareness in Peers

Teachers with the traits listed in the previous section will provide a positive role model for students in how to understand and accept children with AD/HD. Teachers should confer with parents and the child with AD/HD to obtain advice on explaining AD/HD to other children in the classroom. The child with AD/HD may wish to be present during the explanation or even to participate in informing his or her classmates.

The following books may help introduce this topic to children.

Jumping Johnny Get Back to Work—A Child's Guide to AD/HD/Hyperactivity
  Michael Gordon, Ph.D., Author
  Connecticut Association for Children with LD
  18 Marshall Street
  South Norwalk, CT 06854
  (203) 838–5010

Shelley, the Hyperactive Turtle
  Deborah Moss, Author
  Woodbine House
  5616 Fishers Lane
  Rockville, MD 20852
  (800) 843-7323

Sometimes I Drive My Mom Crazy, but I Know She's Crazy about Me!
  Childworks
  Center for Applied Psychology, Inc.
  P.O. 61586
  King of Prussia, PA 19406
  (800) 962-1141

You Mean I'm Not Lazy, Stupid, or Crazy?
  Peggy Ramundo and Kate Kelly, Authors
  Tyrell & Jerem Press
  P.O. Box 20089
  Cincinnati, OH 45220
  (800) 622–6611

Otto Learns about His Medicine
  Michael Gaivin, M.D., Author
  Childworks
  Center for Applied Psychology, Inc.
  P.O. Box 61586
  King of Prussia, PA 19406
  (800) 962–1141

Eagle Eyes: A Child's View of Attention Deficit Disorder
  Jeanne Gehret, M.A., Author
  Childworks
  Center for Applied Psychology, Inc.
  P.O. Box 61586
  King of Prussia, PA 19406
  (800) 962–1141

Feelings about Friends
  Linda Schwartz, Author
  The Learning Works
  P.O. Box 6187
  Santa Barbara, CA 93160
  (800) 235–5767

Brakes: The Interactive Newsletter for Kids with AD/HD
  Magination Press
  19 Union Square West
  New York, NY 10003
  (800) 825–3089

Collaborating with Parents of Students with Attention Deficit/Hyperactivity Disorder

Teachers can often promote success for students with AD/HD by working closely with parents to practise and reinforce desirable academic and social behaviour. Flick (1998) suggests the following parent-centred activities:

▶ Practise and reinforce school behaviours such as following directions, completing homework, getting along with siblings and friends, and obeying rules.
▶ Post and review home and school rules frequently.
▶ Use the same signal used by the teacher to cue the child when inappropriate behaviours are observed; examples include the commonly used finger placed over lips or a more personal or "secret cue" developed in collaboration among the child, parents, and the teacher.
▶ Develop a home-school reporting system that communicates positive behaviours and problem areas between parents and teachers

Summary

- AD/HD is a complex condition that offers a real challenge to classroom teachers.
- In Canada AD/HD is not a separate category of exceptionality in provincial educational jurisdictions.
- AD/HD is a hidden disability with no unique physical characteristics to differentiate children who have it from others in the classroom.
- The diagnosis of AD/HD is primarily based on the criteria in the *Diagnostic and Statistical Manual of Mental Disorders (DSM-IV-TR)*.
- Many theories explain the cause of AD/HD; however, AD/HD is considered primarily a neurologically based condition.
- AD/HD manifests itself across the lifespan; characteristics include limited sustained attention, reduced impulse control, excessive task-irrelevant activity, deficient rule following, and greater than normal variability during task performance.
- The process of identifying AD/HD must be done in collaboration with a psychiatrist or a physician and at the school level. It includes a preliminary assessment, an initial meeting of the school team, a formal assessment and follow-up meeting of the school team, a collaborative meeting to develop an intervention plan, and follow-up and progress reviews.
- Cultural and linguistic diversity complicates issues related to assessment and treatment for children with AD/HD.
- The majority of students with AD/HD spend all or most of the school day in general education classes.
- An individual accommodation plan is written collaboratively with parents, professionals, and when possible, the student, to identify interventions that will create success in the general education classroom.
- Medication is frequently used to enhance the educational experience of students with AD/HD.
- The most commonly prescribed medication is a psychostimulant such as Dexedrine, Ritalin, or Adderall.
- Both positive outcomes and negative side effects should be monitored for individual children taking medication for AD/HD.
- Classroom adaptations include environmental management techniques, instructional adaptations, and student-regulated strategies.
- Techniques used to manage the classroom environment include strategies for group management, physical arrangement of the room, and individual behaviour management techniques.
- Through instructional accommodations, teachers modify their behaviour to include novel and stimulating activity, to provide structure and consistency, to allow physical movement as frequently as possible, to include cooperative learning activities, and to give both spoken and written direction.
- The curriculum for students with AD/HD should be stimulating and should include experience-based learning and problem-solving activities.
- Student-regulated strategies include study and organizational tactics, self-management techniques, learning strategies, and social skills training.
- Effective teachers for students with AD/HD provide positive classroom environments, review student work frequently, and are flexible, fair, responsive, warm, patient, consistent, firm, and humorous. They develop a knowledge of the strengths and needs of their students with AD/HD and know about different intervention strategies. They are also willing to work collaboratively with other teachers, parents, and professionals.

Resources

Books and Articles

Barkley, R. A. (1998). *Attention-deficit/hyperactivity disorder: A handbook for diagnosis and treatment* (2nd ed.). New York: Guilford Press.

This second edition incorporates the latest findings on the nature, diagnosis, assessment, and treatment of AD/HD. Clinicians, researchers, and students will find practical and richly referenced information on nearly every aspect of the disorder. As in the previous edition, Barkley is assisted with selected chapters by seasoned colleagues covering their respective areas of expertise and providing clear guidelines for practice in clinical, school, and community settings. In-depth assessment and treatment guidelines for adolescents and adults as well as

children are supported by updated outcomes documentation, and three new chapters focus specifically on working with adults. The second edition also explicates Barkley's groundbreaking theory of AD/HD as a developmental problem of self-control, evaluates *DSM-IV* diagnostic criteria, and surveys established and emerging pharmacological approaches.

DuPaul, G. J., & Stoner, G. (2004) *ADHD in the schools (2nd Edition): Assessment and intervention strategies.* New York: Guilford Press.

This reference and text provides guidance for school-based professionals meeting the challenges of AD/HD at any grade level. Comprehensive and practical, the book includes several reproducible assessment tools and handouts.

Janover, C. (1997). *Zipper: The kid with AD/HD.* Bethesda, MD: Woodbine House.

Zipper is a bright, well-intentioned Grade 5 student, but his impulsive behaviour gets him into trouble.

Munden, A. C., & Archelus, J. (2001). *The AD/HD handbook: A guide for parents and professionals.* New York: Jessica Kingsley.

It is a concise introductory handbook and provides essential information on the nature of AD/HD.

Pentecost, D. (1999). *Parenting the ADD child: Can't do? Won't do? Practical strategies for managing behaviour problems in children with ADD and AD/HD.* New York: Jessica Kingsley.

Robin, A. L. (2000). *ADHD in adolescents: Diagnosis and treatment.* New York: Guilford Press

This practical guide presents an empirically based "nuts-and-bolts" approach to understanding, diagnosing, and treating AD/HD in adolescents. Practitioners learn to conduct effective assessments and formulate goals that teenagers can comprehend, accept, and achieve. Educational, medical, and family components of treatment are described in depth and illustrated with detailed case material. Included are numerous reproducible handouts and forms.

Silver, L. B. (1999). *Attention deficit hyperactivity disorder: A clinical guide to diagnosis and treatment for health and mental health.* Washington, DC: American Psychiatric Press.

Providing a broad overview of the continuum of neurobiologically based conditions, this book thoroughly reviews disorders often found to be comorbid with AD/HD, including specific learning disorders, anxiety disorders, depression, anger-regulation problems, obsessive-compulsive disorder, and tic disorders.

Associations

Children and Adults with Attention Deficit/ Hyperactivity Disorder, Canadian Office

P.O. Box 43021, Edmonton, Alberta
T5J 4M8
Phone: (866) 434-9004; Local: (613) 731-1209
Website: **www.chaddcanada.org/**

Canadian CHADD will provide you with a variety of resources and can direct you to the CHADD chapter closest to you.

Children and Adults with Attention Deficit/ Hyperactivity Disorder, U.S. Office

8181 Professional Place, Suite 150, Landover, MD 20785
Phone: 1 (800) 233-4050/(301) 306-7070
Website: **www.chadd.org**

American CHADD has a wealth of resources and materials that pertain to individuals with AD/HD. It also has a very detailed and helpful website that is constantly updated.

 # Weblinks

Children and Adults with Attention-Deficit Hyperactivity Disorder (CHADD)

www.chadd.org/
This comprehensive website provides basic facts about AD/HD, current research, helpful strategies, up-to-date resources, and related links. The focus is on education, advocacy, and support for people with AD/HD, their parents, and educators.

CHADD Canada

www.chaddcanada.org/
This website describes the mission of CHADD in Canada and provides links to local chapters across the country.

The National Attention Deficit Disorder Association (ADDA)

www.add.org/
The Association's website is especially focused on the needs of adults and young adults with ADD, but is also relevant

for parents of children with ADD. It provides specific sites focused on family issues, school, and ADD, as well as a kids' area. An excellent aspect of this website is a bookstore for which the Association has selected and reviewed books and categorized them by topic (e.g., for parents, for children, for educators).

About.com

http://add.miningco.com/health/add/
Fascinating to browse, this website provides a guide to a huge array of information related to AD/HD. It covers parenting, educating, medication, comorbid disorders, career issues, and more, and offers book lists, video lists, and chat rooms.

6 Teaching Students with Emotional or Behavioural Disorders

Chapter Objectives

After reading this chapter you should be able to

- define emotional or behavioural disorders
- understand the complexity of defining emotional or behavioural disorders and how this complexity affects estimates of prevalence and service delivery
- describe the characteristics of children and youth with emotional or behavioural disorders (E/BD)
- discuss ways to identify and assess students with EBD
- identify effective interventions for students with EBD
- discuss the roles of teachers, families, and other support personnel in working together to meet the needs of students with EBD

Justin is a seven-year-old Grade 1 student who often seems to be in trouble. On the first day of school, he stole some crayons from one of his new classmates. When confronted with the fact that the crayons in his desk belonged to another student, Justin adamantly denied stealing them. Justin's behaviour became more difficult over the first six months of the school year. Ms. Tastad, Justin's teacher, uses a classroom management system that rewards students with check marks for appropriate behaviours. Students can redeem their check marks at the end of the week for various toys. Justin has never earned enough check marks to get a toy. Now he openly states that he doesn't care if he ever receives any check marks.

Justin's primary behavioural difficulty is his inability to leave his classmates alone. He is constantly pinching, pulling hair, or taking things from other students. Ms. Tastad has separated Justin's chair from those of the other students in an attempt to prevent him from bothering them. Still, he gets out of his chair and manages to create disturbances regularly. Ms. Tastad has sent Justin to the principal's office on numerous occasions. Each time he returns, his behaviour improves, but only for several hours. Then he returns to his previous behavioural patterns. Justin's schoolwork has suffered as a result of his behaviour problems. While many of his classmates are reading and writing their names, Justin still has difficulties associating sounds with letters and can print his name only in a rudimentary fashion.

Ms. Tastad has had four parent conferences about Justin. His mother indicates to Ms. Tastad that she does not know what to do with Justin. There is no father figure in the home, and Justin has already progressed to the point where her discipline does not work. Ms. Tastad and Justin's mother are both concerned that Justin's behaviour will continue to get worse unless some solution is found. They are currently discussing whether to retain him in Grade 1 for the next school year.

Questions to Consider

1. Why did the behaviour management system used by Ms. Tastad not work with Justin?

2. What positive behaviour support strategies can Ms. Tastad use that might result in an improvement in Justin's behaviour?

3. Would retention be likely to benefit Justin? Why or why not?

4. How would it potentially help or hurt Justin if he were labelled as EBD?

Introduction

Although most children and youth are disruptive from time to time, the majority do not display negative behaviours sufficient to create serious problems in school. Most comply with classroom and school rules without needing extensive interventions. However, some students' behaviours and emotions result in significant problems for themselves, their peers, and their teachers. This may be exacerbated by the way school personnel deal with various student behaviours. The student may not respond as expected to typical interventions. Students whose behaviours and emotions result in significant school problems, such as Justin in the preceding vignette, may require identification and intervention. At a minimum, they require that classroom teachers try different methods in an effort to enhance their school success, reduce their problem behaviour, and increase their prosocial behaviours.

Although emotional and behaviour problems are correlated with anxiety and mood disorders, and may result in serious actions such as suicides, they have primarily been associated with acting out and disruptive behaviours in classrooms—in general, discipline problems. The primary problem identified by most teachers when dealing with students with emotional and behaviour problems is classroom discipline.

Behaviour problems are a major concern for professional educators (Elam, Rose, & Gallup, 1996). In a survey of general education classroom teachers, the behaviour of students was cited as a primary reason for deciding to leave the teaching profession (Smith, 1990). Teachers noted that they spent too much time on student behaviour problems and not enough on instruction. An American study by Knitzer, Steinberg, and Fleisch (1990) found that 80 percent of all students identified as having emotional or behaviour problems are educated in regular schools. Nearly 50 percent of these students spend some or all of their school day in general education classrooms with general education classroom teachers, not special education teachers. Similarly, all of Canada is committed to the inclusion of children with emotional and behavioural disorders in the regular classroom. Sometimes there are pullout services available for these students too. In 1990 Dworet and Rathgeber, in a review of existing services across Canada, reported that services available in each of the provinces generally conformed to a range of educational services model. Schwean and colleagues also note that from province to province the services vary somewhat but generally range from full inclusion to a hospital setting (Schwean, Saklofske, Shatz, & Falk, 1996).

Students who experience emotional or behavioural disorders receive a variety of labels. The Council for Children with Behaviour Disorders (CCBD) of the Council for Exceptional Children refers to the group as emotionally disturbed or behaviourally disordered (EBD) because it believes the term better describes the students served in special education programs (October, 2000). EBD is the term that will be used throughout this chapter.

CONSIDER THIS

What kinds of children do you think of when you hear the term *emotionally disturbed*? What kinds of children do you think of when you hear the term *emotionally or behaviourally disordered*? Can these terms have an impact on teachers' expectations of children?

Providing positive and effective services to students with emotional or behaviour problems is a complex and difficult task. Complexities include difficulties in defining **emotional or behavioural disorders (EBDs)**, difficulties in measuring behaviour and emotions, diversity of behaviours among typical individuals, diversity of individuals with behaviour and emotional problems, and difficulties identifying children with behavioural or emotional disorders (Wicks-Nelson & Israel, 1991). Despite the problems, these children must be identified and provided with appropriate interventions or they will not meet their own academic potential, have difficulty building positive peer relationships, and their behaviour will continually disrupt the classroom environment.

Basic Concepts about Emotional or Behavioural Disorders

This section provides basic information about emotional or behavioural disorders. Understanding children with these problems will aid teachers and other educators in developing appropriate intervention programs. Figure 6.1 illustrates a parent's perspective on intervention programs.

Emotional or Behavioural Disorders Defined

In Canada no single definition of emotional or behavioural disorders is in use in schools, but practitioners have established certain commonalities in their understanding of what constitutes an emotional or behavioural disorder (Hallahan & Kauffman, 1997; Weber, 1994). These commonalities include the following:

- behaviour that goes to an extreme, that is significantly different from what is normally expected
- a behaviour problem that is chronic and does not quickly disappear
- behaviour that is unacceptable because of social or cultural expectations
- behaviour that affects the student's academic performance
- behaviour that cannot be explained by health, sensory, or social difficulties

In most cases, in identifying a student as having an emotional or behavioural disorder, the school assessment team will use criteria aimed at establishing these general assumptions. However, exactly how to apply the definition remains vague: when the definition is interpreted broadly, many more children are served than when it is interpreted narrowly. Provincial education funding protocols may not require identification, but expect service to be provided as part of supporting student diversity. For example, in Saskatchewan, Diversity Funding is provided to school divisions based on their total enrolment. School divisions are expected to use this funding to support students with a variety of diverse learning and behavioural needs, including those with emotional or behavioural disorders. These facts may explain the variability in prevalence estimates from province to province (Weber, 1994). In addition, Dworet and Rathgeber (1998) have noted that in the 10 jurisdictions across Canada that use definitions of EBD, 8 different definitions are in use. They found significant variability across Canada—and even within provinces—in exact definitions of EBD.

In Canada's National Longitudinal Survey of Children and Youth (NLSCY), 28.6 percent of Canadian children were determined to be vulnerable (Willms, 2002, p. 66). "These children are vulnerable in the sense that unless there is a serious effort to intervene on their behalf, they are prone to experiencing problems throughout their childhood and are more likely to experience unemployment and poor physical and mental health as young adults."(p. 3) The NLSCY also estimates the prevalence of vulnerable children in Canada, who are vulnerable due to behaviour problems, to be 19.1 percent (p. 67). Comparing this information with numbers of students identified and served throughout school divisions across Canada suggests that this population of students may well be underserved.

CONSIDER THIS

How would you, as a teacher, decide which behaviours are "significantly different" from behaviour normally expected? How would teachers' evaluation differ as a function of experience, tolerance levels, and school climate?

From: pchildress [mailto: patti@inmind.com]

Sent: Tuesday, June 6, 2000 11:42 PM

TO: Polloway, Edward 'Ed'

Subject: Re: Concerns

Dr. Polloway:

Thanks for trying to help and please keep thinking about resources that can assist me as both a teacher and a parent.

It bothers me tremendously when I see children with E/BD often getting a "raw deal." People seem to think that it is fine for these children to have a disorder and maybe/maybe not receive special services, but heaven forbid if they can't control themselves or if they do something that appears to be a bit irrational. At times I feel like I am jumping in front of a firing squad to protect that [child whom some seem to see as that] "bad kid that shouldn't be in school anyway." I would like to work with a group that supports parents, provides understanding and advocacy regarding disorders, and seeks support and additional resources for help, etc. What is available in this field? Much is needed.

I have always had a huge heart for "the kid who is a little bit or a long way out there" even before I became a parent of a child with a mood disorder.

From an educational perspective, I know that these children can be very difficult in a group; however, they seem to function much better when they feel in control, are able to make choices, and are spoken to in a calm tone.

From a parent's perspective, I am an educated individual with a traditional home makeup: dad, mom, daughter, and son. . .and I know the difficulties of saying, "Yeah, we've got a very bright child with mood problems." We've been through every medication from ritalin to cylert and clonodone. The next stop would be lithium, weekly counselling, and psychiatric treatment to regulate the medications. I want teachers to understand that getting "meds" is not an easy task or a quick fix. It has taken us over a year of trying various medications until we have, hopefully, found the right combination for now. It requires the constant efforts of counsellor, doctor, parents, and teachers working together and exchanging information.

Children without support have got to have advocates to help them get help. These children are very fragile and need to be treated as such. My heart goes out to such a child and the family that simply does not understand why their child is not like everybody else's. In the school environment, even when I listen to special education teachers, I do not find the same level of empathy and understanding for children with E/BD as for those with LD.

FIGURE 6.1

A Parent's Perspective on EBD: Patti Childress (Lynchburg, VA)

Classification of Emotional or Behavioural Disorders

Children who experience emotional or behavioural disorders make up an extremely heterogeneous population. Professionals typically have subcategorized the group into smaller, more homogeneous subgroups so that these students can be studied, understood, and served better (Wicks-Nelson & Israel, 1991). Several different classification systems are used to group individuals with emotional and behavioural disorders.

One classification system focuses on the clinical elements found in the field of emotional or behaviour problems. This system is detailed in the *DSM-IV-TR* (American Psychiatric Association, 2000), a manual widely used by medical and psychological professionals in both Canada and the United States, though infrequently used by educators. It categorizes emotional and behaviour problems according to several different clinical subtypes, such as developmental disorders, organic mental disorders, and schizophrenia. Educators need to be aware of the *DSM-IV-TR* classification system, because of the importance of working together with professionals from the field of mental health.

A second classification system was developed by Quay and Peterson (1987). They described six major subgroups of children with emotional and behavioural disorders:

1. Individuals are classified as having a **conduct disorder** if they seek attention, are disruptive, and act out. This category includes behaving aggressively toward others.
2. Students who exhibit **socialized aggression** are likely to join a "subcultural group," a group of peers who are openly disrespectful to their peers, teachers, and parents. Delinquency, truancy, and other "gang" behaviours are common among this group.
3. Individuals with **attention problems–immaturity** can be characterized as having attention deficits, being easily distractible, and having poor concentration. Many students in this group are impulsive and may act without thinking about the consequences.
4. Students classified in the **anxiety/withdrawal** group are self-conscious, reticent, and unsure of themselves. Their self-concepts are generally very low, causing them to simply "retreat" from immediate activities. They are also anxious and frequently depressed.
5. The subgroup of students who display **psychotic behaviour** may hallucinate, deal in a fantasy world, talk in gibberish, and display other bizarre behaviour.
6. Students with **motor excess** are hyperactive. They have difficulties sitting still, listening to another individual, and keeping their attention focused. Often these students are also hypertalkative. (See Chapter 5 for more information on hyperactivity.)

It is important for the teacher to know that students can demonstrate behaviour from a number of different dimensions or categories; in other words, the categories are not mutually exclusive. For example, Ryan, a Grade 8 student who is constantly disruptive and threatens both his peers and his teachers (conduct disorder), may also suffer from depression (anxiety/withdrawal).

More recently, R. Algozzine (2001) presented a definition to guide educational practices. While not adopted by any American or Canadian governmental agencies, it does illustrate a useful, alternative approach to defining this population:

> Students with behaviour problems are ones who, after receiving supportive educational services and counselling assistance available to all students, still exhibit consistent and severe behavioural disabilities that consequently interfere with their productive learning processes as well as those of others. The inability of these students to achieve adequate academic progress and satisfactory interpersonal relationships cannot be attributed to physical, sensory, or intellectual deficits. (p. 37)

Classification becomes less important when school personnel utilize a functional assessment/intervention model. This approach, which will be described in more detail later, emphasizes finding out which environmental stimuli result in inappropriate behaviours. Once these stimuli are identified and altered, the inappropriate behaviours may decrease or disappear (Foster-Johnson & Dunlap, 1993). In such instances, the process of classifying a student's behaviour problem becomes less relevant to the design of educational programs.

FURTHER READING

For more information on the American Psychiatric Association's classification of students with EBD, review the *Diagnostic and Statistical Manual (DSM-IV-TR)*, published in 2000.

CONSIDER THIS

Do students without disabilities ever exhibit these characteristics? What differentiates typical students from those classified as EBD?

Prevalence and Causes of Emotional or Behavioural Disorders

Compared to children classified as having learning disabilities and intellectual disabilities, the category of EBD has been thought to represent a smaller number of children.

Although prevalence rates vary by province or territory in Canada, most estimates place prevalence of EBD well below prevalence of learning disabilities. Estimates range from 0.0002 percent in Saskatchewan to 1.0 percent in Alberta, New Brunswick, and Newfoundland, with the Northwest Territories, Prince Edward Island, Ontario, and British Columbia falling somewhere between. Nova Scotia, Quebec, and the Yukon failed to provide prevalence rates, while Manitoba had a highly variable within-province prevalence of 0.5 percent to 2.0 percent depending on the specific definition used within regions (Dworet & Rathgeber, 1998). Thus, Dworet and Rathgeber report an average across-Canada prevalence of 0.49 percent based on their survey. Weber (1994) reports marginally different prevalence rates in *Special Education in Canadian Schools*. Using 1980s data he concludes that 0.78 percent of the school population in Canada was identified as having an EBD (Canada Council of Ministers of Education, 1983, as cited in Weber, 1994) with a range by province from 0.26 percent in Saskatchewan to 1.45 percent in Quebec. In summary, the differences between these two frequently cited Canadian sources are small—and notably less than the 6–10 percent prevalence estimates of EBD in school-age children (Kauffman, 1997; Kazdin, 1989).

However, recent information provided by NLSCY suggests that up to 19.1 percent of Canadian children are vulnerable to poor outcomes due to behavioural problems. According to the Organization for Economic Co-operation and Development (as cited in Willms, 2002, p. 67) 29.2 percent of Canadian youth failed to graduate from secondary schools at the typical age. Although not all of this percentage of students failed to graduate at a typical age due to behavioural disorders, certainly this is one example of a "poor outcome" that Canadian children with behavioural problems are vulnerable to. Statistics like these suggest that prevalence estimates of emotional or behavioural disorders may indeed be low. The specific number arrived at depends on the definition used, and the interpretation of the definition by individuals who classify students. It also depends on whether or not these students are even identified, served and "counted," or whether a number of these students are just "disciplined." However, the suggestion is that EBD may indeed be a dramatically underserved category of disability with far more students in need of supports than the less than 1 percent currently identified.

It is a safe assumption that students with emotional or behavioural disorders are typically the most underidentified in the school setting. In an American study, Lambros, Ward, Bocian, MacMillan, and Gresham (1998) indicated that the reasons for this condition include the following: the ambiguity of definitions used by the states, the limited training of school psychologists in conducting assessments for these students, the financial limitations of districts, and the general hesitation to apply labels such as behavioural disorder or seriously emotionally disturbed.

The discrepancy between identified and actual rates of children with EBD may also be due to students with EBD being identified as having other exceptionalities such as a learning disability. Or, if the students are showing more anxious or withdrawn behaviours, they may be overlooked altogether. Heath, a researcher at McGill University, has observed that teachers have difficulty identifying a student with depression if the student is simultaneously acting out.

Depression is a characteristic of students with emotional or behavioural disorders.

Among students classified as having emotional or behavioural disorders, the majority are males. Some studies have revealed that as many as 10 times more boys than girls are found in special classes for students with behavioural disorders (Rosenberg, Wilson, Maheady, & Sindelar, 1992).

Furthermore, prevalence of EBD is low in the early elementary grades and highest in late elementary and early high school; it then decreases in later high school years (Hallahan & Kauffman, 1997).

Many different factors can cause students to display emotional or behavioural disorders. These can be found in five different theoretical frameworks, including biological, psychoanalytical, behavioural, phenomenological, and sociological/ecological. Within each framework are numerous specific causal factors. Table 6.1 summarizes some of these variables by theoretical framework.

It is critical to note that many students experience emotional or behavioural disorders because of environmental factors that affect their lives. In Canadian society, potential causative elements may include variables related to family, school, and community factors. In Figure 6.2, a model designed in reference to antisocial youth outlines this interaction of factors. Thus, it is essential that a broad view of the problems experienced by students be considered.

Characteristics of Students with Emotional or Behavioural Disorders

Students with emotional or behaviour problems exhibit a wide range of characteristics that differ in type as well as intensity. The wide range of behaviours and emotions experienced by all individuals reflects the broad variety of characteristics associated with individuals with emotional or behaviour problems.

TABLE 6.1 — Causes of Serious Emotional and Behavioural Disorders

Theoretical Framework	Etiologies/Causal Factors
Biological	Genetic inheritance Biochemical abnormalities Neurological abnormalities Injury to the central nervous system
Psychoanalytical	Psychological processes Functioning of the mind: id, ego, and superego Inherited predispositions (instinctual process) Traumatic early-childhood experiences
Behavioural	Environmental events 1. Failure to learn adaptive behaviours 2. Learning of maladaptive behaviours 3. Developing maladaptive behaviours as a result of stressful environmental circumstances
Phenomenological	Faulty learning about oneself Misuse of defense mechanisms Feelings, thoughts, and events emanating from the self
Sociological/Ecological	Role assignment (labelling) Cultural transmission Social disorganization Distorted communication Differential association Negative interactions and transactions with others

From *Human Exceptionality* (p. 148), by M. L. Hardman, C. J. Drew, M. W. Egan, and B. Wolf, 1993, Boston: Allyn & Bacon. Used by permission.

FIGURE 6.2

The Development of
Antisocial Behaviour

From "Antisocial Behaviour,
Academic Failure, and School
Climate: A Critical Review" (p.
133) by A. McEvoy & R. Welker,
2000, *Journal of Emotional and
Behavioural Disorders, 8.*

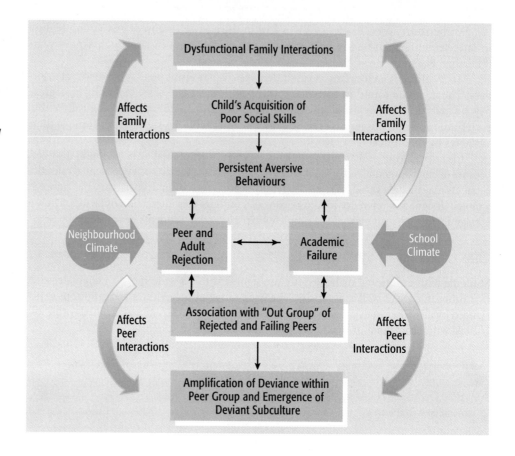

Problems typically associated with children with emotional and behavioural disorders include the following:

- Aggressive/acting-out behaviours (Grosenick, George, George, & Lewis, 1991; Kauffman, Lloyd, Baker, & Riedel, 1995)
- Social deficits (Smith & Luckasson, 1995)
- Inadequate peer relationships (Searcy & Meadows, 1994)
- Hyperactivity/distractibility
- Lying, cheating, and stealing (Rosenberg et al., 1992)
- Academic deficits (Bullock, 1992)
- Language disorders (Benner, Nelson, & Epstein, 2002)
- Depression (Kauffman et al., 1995; Wicks-Nelson & Israel, 1991)
- Anxiety (Kauffman et al., 1995; Wicks-Nelson & Israel, 1991)

CONSIDER THIS

Do students without disabilities ever exhibit these characteristics? What differentiates typical students from those classified as EBD?

Children classified as having emotional or behavioural disorders do not exhibit all of these characteristics. The ones exhibited by a particular child will depend on the nature of their emotional or behaviour problem.

A common, and helpful, way to conceptualize emotional or behavioural disorders is to categorize them as externalizing or internalizing behaviours. The list in Table 6.2 provides such an illustration.

One problem associated with emotional or behavioural disorders that is often overlooked is depression. According to American estimates, approximately 2 to 4 percent of elementary school children and 4 to 8 percent of adolescents suffer from depression (CEC, 1999). Further, Forness (cited by CEC, 1999) has estimated that between 30 and 40 percent of students in classes for EBD suffer from depression.

TABLE 6.2	Categorizing Emotional and Behavioural Disorders
Externalizing Behaviours	**Internalizing Behaviours**
Aggressive toward people and objects	Withdrawn
Temper tantrums	Apathetic, restricted activity levels
Defiant	Fixated on certain thoughts
Jealous	Avoids social situations
Disobedient	Fearful, anxious
Distrustful, blames others	Inferiority
Noncompliant	Sad, moody, depressed
Pattern of lying and stealing	Self-conscious, overly sensitive
Argumentative	Irritable
Lack of self-control	Inappropriate crying
Destructive	

From *Childhood Behavioural Disorders: Applied Research and Educational Practices* (2nd ed., p. 69) by R. Algozzine, L. Serna, & J. R. Patton, 2001, Austin, TX: Pro-Ed.

Teachers should be alert to signs of depression in order to assist students in the classroom where depression may be associated with an inability to concentrate or achieve. More dramatically, depression can be associated with suicide, estimated to be the third leading cause of death for adolescents and young adults.

Because of the high comorbidity rate between EBD and language deficits, speech language pathologists should be involved in assessment and intervention planning for students with EBD (Benner, Nelson, & Epstein, 2002)

While the focus of research on the characteristics of students with EBD is often on social and behavioural concerns, nevertheless it should not be overlooked that academic problems are also a key concern. As Anderson, Kutash, and Duchnowski (2001, p. 6) note, students with EBD and LD are often both frequently observed to exhibit "below-average achievement in content area courses, deficits in basic academics, a general lack of motivation toward school, and deficiencies in school-related skills such as note-taking and test-taking." Further, Anderson et al. (2001), in a five-year study of elementary school students, noted that students with EBD made limited progress in academic achievement when compared to their peers identified as LD.

The relationship between academic achievement and behavioural disorders may be most pronounced in instances of more significant antisocial behaviour. McEvoy and Welker (2000) summarized these issues as follows:

> Antisocial behaviour and academic failure reinforce one another within the context of ineffective school practices and ineffective parenting strategies. . . A pattern of academic failure provides few opportunities for the student to receive positive reinforcement. From the failing student's perspective, school then takes on aversive properties that increase the likelihood of escape, rebellion, uncooperativeness, and other negative behaviours. This cycle often results in school failure, dropping out, and involvement in delinquent groups. Conversely, ineffective school responses to antisocial conduct have negative implications and influence the academic performance of students in general. (p. 131)

Outcomes and Postschool Adjustment A critical concern for students with emotional and behavioural disorders is the determination of postschool outcomes. In a comprehensive, longitudinal study of such students, Greenbaum and colleagues (1998) reported on American students who were identified as having a serious emotional disturbance (SED) and were served in either a publicly funded residential mental health facility or a community-based special education program. While the severity of the disorders that these students experienced is likely to be greater than those of students in general education classrooms, this information should alert educators to the potential challenges that these students face. The researchers found that approximately two-thirds (66.5 percent) of the individuals had at least one contact with police in which the person was believed to be the perpetrator of a crime, and 43.3 percent had been arrested at least once. The most commonly reported crimes were property related.

For this same sample of students, educational outcomes were generally poor. For those who were young adults (over 18 years of age) at the time of the follow-up, 75.4 percent were assessed to be below their appropriate reading levels, and 96.9 percent were below appropriate levels in math achievement. Only one in four had obtained a regular high school diploma; an additional 17.4 percent had completed a GED. Approximately 43 percent had dropped out of school programs.

These data are consistent with the challenging picture that emerges from the American annual federal reports on IDEA, which indicate that students with EBD are the most likely to drop out of school (50.6 percent of students exiting school in 1998–99). In addition to students with mental retardation and autism, these students are also among the least likely to receive a high school diploma or certificate (41.9 percent) (U.S. Department of Education, 2002).

One somewhat encouraging finding is that students with EBD had greater success in adult education programs. Scanlon and Melland (2002) hypothesized that the context of adult programs may contribute to this success because such programs may be "less antagonizing and more accepting of any emotional or behavioural problems" (p. 253).

Students with emotional or behavioural disorders often have significant challenges in adjustment within the community. Maag and Katisyannis (1998) noted that successful adjustment is affected by the high dropout rate, which makes it difficult to establish and address transition goals within the student's IEP and individual transition plan. In addition, successful transition is affected by the high rates of unemployment, the increased likelihood of incarceration, and the persistence of mental health problems in adulthood.

A study reported by McConaughy and Wadsworth (2000) provided some guidance in predicting which individuals would fare better as adults. Based on life histories of these individuals, they concluded that young adults with good outcomes tended to have more stable and quality living situations, better family relationships, more positive relationships with friends, were more goal-oriented, and experienced more successes and fewer stresses than did young adults with poor outcomes. In addition, more young adults with good outcomes held full-time jobs in the community, and fewer associated with friends who used drugs or who were in trouble with the law or violent. (pp. 213–214)

Also, following up (after three years) on a group of American adolescents who participated in a statewide system of care, Pandiani, Schacht, and Banks (2001) reported that these individuals, when compared to other young people, were eight times more likely to be hospitalized for behavioural health care and the young men in the sample were five times as likely to be incarcerated. For young women, the rate of maternity was generally similar to the general population.

In the area of employment, critical to successful transition, Rylance (1998) reported that the key variables that increase an individual's chances of employment included basic academic skills, higher functional competence levels in school-related areas, and high school graduation. Successful school programs for these students tended to be ones that included effective vocational education and counselling programs and that motivated students to persist in school and obtain a diploma.

In conclusion, Burns, Hoagwood, and Maultsby (1999) noted, "Consensus about the critical outcomes for children with serious emotional and behavioural disorders at home, in school, and out of trouble is not difficult to obtain. Achieving such outcomes and more is the challenge!" (p. 685).

Identification, Assessment, and Programming

Students with emotional or behavioural disorders are evaluated for several purposes, including identification, assessment to determine appropriate intervention strategies, and determination of appropriate special education services. The first step is for students to be identified as potentially having emotional or behavioural problems. Teachers' awareness of the characteristics of students with these problems is critical in the identification process. Behavioural checklists can be used to identify students for possible referral.

Once students are identified as possibly having emotional or behavioural problems, they are referred for formal assessment to ascertain appropriate intervention strategies and to determine their eligibility for special education supports. Kaplan (1996) lists clinical interviews, observations, rating scales, personality tests, and neurological examinations as methods for obtaining information for assessment. Table 6.3 summarizes each of these procedures.

One encouraging new approach to the assessment of students with emotional and behavioural disorders is through the use of strength-based assessment. Unlike widely used deficit-oriented assessment models, strength-based assessment focuses on the student and his or her family "as individuals with unique talents, skills, and life events as well as with specific unmet needs. Strength-based assessment recognizes that even the most challenged children in stressed families have strengths, competencies, and resources that can be built on in developing a treatment approach" (Epstein, 1999, p. 258).

Epstein and Charma (1998) have developed a scale that complements assessment instruments that focus on difficulties experienced by the student in the school or home

TEACHING TIP

When you suspect a student of having an emotional or behavioural disorder, use systematic methods to collect observations of the student's behaviour (e.g., document the frequency, intensity, and duration of the behaviour(s)). This information will be useful when designing interventions and determining student progress or the success of interventions.

TABLE 6.3 — Assessment Procedures Used for Students with Emotional and Behavioural Disorders

Clinical Interview	• The clinical interview is the most common tool for assessment. • Questions are directed to the child and others regarding behaviours and any relevant relationships. • Some questions are planned; some are developed as the interview progresses. • The interview can be highly structured, using questions generated from the DSM-IV criteria.
Observation	• The observation can be structured with time limitations, or unstructured. • Observations should occur in a variety of different settings and at different times.
Rating Scales	• A rating scale contains a listing of behaviours to note. • It provides for much more structure than simple observation. • It ensures that certain behaviours are observed or asked about.
Personality Tests	• The two kinds of personality tests include self-completed inventories and projective tests. • Both kinds of personality tests can provide insightful information. • Interpretation of personality tests is subjective and needs to be done by a trained professional.

From *Pathways for Exceptional Children: School, Home, and Culture*, by P. Kaplan, 1996, St. Paul, MN: West Publishing.

FURTHER READING

To learn more about risk factors and protective factors, read "Preventing Antisocial Behaviour in Disabled and At-Risk Students" from Appalachia Educational Laboratory, available online from LD OnLine at http://www.ldonline.org/ld_indepth/add_adhd/ael_behavior.html

setting. As they noted (p. 3): "Strength-based assessment is defined as the measurement of those emotional/behavioural skills and characteristics that create a sense of personal accomplishment; contribute to satisfying relationships with family members, peers, and adults; enhance one's ability to deal with adversity and stress; and promote one's personal, social, and academic development."

A current focus in intervention planning is a study of Risk and Resiliency. Risk factors are those that increase a child's likelihood to experience negative life outcomes. A combination of risk factors present in a child's life increases overall risk. Resiliency is the ability to thrive despite risk. Protective factors are those that increase the likelihood that a child will be resilient and avoid negative life outcomes. There are a number of things that schools can do to increase resilience in their students with emotional or behavioural disorders. When schools have high expectations of their students and provide the supports necessary for the students to achieve the expectations, resiliency is evident. When schools focus on recognizing and using students' strengths and avoid the use of punitive disciplinary practices, students with emotional or behavioural disorders are able to be more resilient.

Functional Behavioural Assessment   One important approach to assessment warrants separate consideration because of its clear implications for intervention efforts. **Functional Behavioural Assessment (FBA)** provides a consideration of specific behaviours and behavioural patterns set within an environmental context. It has been defined as "an analysis of the contingencies responsible for behavioural problems" (Mallott, Whaley, & Mallott, 1997, p. 433). A sample FBA is presented in Figure 6.3

CONSIDER THIS

How can using functional behavioural assessment help teachers focus on specific issues related to inappropriate behaviours?

When determining appropriate intervention strategies, functional behavioural assessment provides extensive information for teachers. A functional assessment helps teachers better understand disruptive behaviours, which can lead to an insightful intervention approach. Foster-Johnson and Dunlap (1993) list the following variables that influence behaviours:

1. Physiological factors
   - Sickness or allergies
   - Side effects of medication
   - Fatigue
   - Hunger or thirst
   - Increased arousal due to a fight, missing the bus, a disrupted routine

2. Classroom environment
   - High noise level
   - Uncomfortable temperature
   - Over- or under-stimulation
   - Poor seating arrangement
   - Frequent disruptions

3. Curriculum and instruction
   - Few opportunities for making choices
   - Lack of predictability in the schedule
   - Inadequate level of assistance provided to the student
   - Unclear directions provided for activity completion
   - Few opportunities for the student to communicate
   - Activities that are too difficult
   - Activities that take a long time to complete
   - Activities that the student dislikes
   - Activities for which the completion criterion is unclear
   - Activities that might not be perceived as being relevant or useful by the student

TEACHING TIP

Whenever possible, teach appropriate social skills in the context in which they will be used. If they must be taught in a different context, plan for their transfer to more typical settings.

The Functional Behavioural Assessment (FBA) addresses the relationship among precipitating conditions, the behaviour, its consequences, and the function of the behaviour. The FBA also reflects a consideration of all relevant data gathered, both as background information and by using specific assessment techniques. Refer to the Functional Behavioural Assessment Discussion Guide (found on page 16 of the manual) for assistance in completing this form.

Behaviour # _3_ _Physical aggression/fighting_

Precipitating Conditions (Setting, time, or other situations typically occurring *before* the behaviour)	**Specific Behaviour** (*Exactly* what the student does or does not do)	**Consequences** (Events that typically *follow* the behaviour)	**Function of the Behaviour** (*Hypothesized purpose[s]* the behaviour serves)
☒ unstructured time in hallways/on the bus	Casey pushes, hits, trips other students, often students who are smaller; Casey's aggression occurs more often when no adults are watching her (on bus; in halls).	☒ teacher attention	☐ escape/avoidance
☐ academic instruction in		☒ peer attention	☒ gaining attention
☐ when given a directive to		☒ verbal warning/reprimand	☒ expression of anger
		☐ loss of privilege (what kind?)	☐ frustration
☒ when close to smaller students		☐ time out (where/how long?)	☒ vengeance
☐ when provoked by			☒ seeking of power/control
☐ when unable to		☒ detention (how long?) after school	☒ intimidation
☒ other when unsupervised		☐ removal from class	☐ sensory stimulation
☐ none observed		☒ in-school suspension (how long?) 3 days	☐ relief of fear/anxiety
		☐ other	☐ other

Specific Assessment Techniques Used to Analyze This Behaviour

☒ Observation   ☐ Student Interview   ☒ Administrative Interview   ☒ Parent Interview
☒ Behaviour Checklist/Rating Scale   ☐ Video/Audio Taping   ☒ Teacher Interview   ☐ Other _____

Relating Information/Considerations

Academic: _Low grades—homework not turned in_   Family: _Casey's behaviour has disrupted family life. Mother reports she is afraid of Casey._

Social/Peer: _Few friends_   Other: _____

FIGURE 6.3

An Example of a Functional Behavioural Assessment (FBA)

After reviewing these variables with a particular child in mind, teachers can devise interventions that target a specific variable to alter a particular behaviour (Foster-Johnson & Dunlap, 1993). McConnell, Hilvitz, and Cox (1998) present a 10-step procedure for conducting a functional behavioural assessment. Their approach shows how writing an intervention plan is a direct outgrowth of the assessment process. McConnell et al. (1998) stress that while an evaluation of the environmental context is necessary for developing hypotheses regarding the causes of a problem behaviour, the only valid way to reach a conclusion about behavioural influence is to change the environmental setting and/or the events associated with the behaviour, and to observe whether or not a change in behaviour results.

Strategies for Curriculum and Instruction for Students with Emotional or Behavioural Disorders

Students with emotional or behavioural disorders often present significant problems for teachers, especially in general education settings. Their behaviour may affect not only their own learning, but often the learning of others. The challenges of appropriately serving students with emotional or behavioural disorders are emphasized by the realities of how schools respond to these students.

Canadian provinces and territories are committed to the inclusion of children with EBD in the regular classroom. Although placement options for these students range from the regular classroom to a hospital setting, the majority of students with EBD will remain in the regular classroom for most of the time (Schwean, Saklofske, Shatz, & Falk, 1996). Dworet and Rathgeber (1998) argue that, since the services for students with EBD across Canada are so variable largely because of the lack of a clear definition, eligibility for services is hard to determine.

Emotional or Behavioural Disorders and Inclusion

The challenge of inclusion of students with emotional or behavioural disorders has given rise to a number of perspectives on the relative advantages of inclusive versus restrictive settings, which can prove helpful to teachers as they plan inclusive programs. McConnell's (2001) perspectives are presented in Table 6.4.

Because most students with emotional or behaviour problems are included in general education classrooms, teachers and special education teachers need to collaborate in developing and implementing intervention programs. Without this collaboration, appropriate interventions will be much less effective. Consistency in approach and in specific strategies among all teachers who work with the student is critical. If students receive feedback from the special education teacher that significantly differs from the feedback received from the classroom teacher, confusion often results, and success is compromised.

As more students with disabilities are included in general education classrooms, including students with emotional or behavioural disorders, the ability of students and teachers to effectively deal with behaviour problems is critical for success (Carpenter & McKee-Higgins, 1996). Rock, Rosenberg, and Carran (1995) studied the variables that affected this reintegration. Their findings indicate that success can be predicted when reintegration orientation, demographic characteristics of restrictive programs, and particular experiences and training of special educators are features of the reintegration process. Programs that were more likely to have better success at reintegration include

CONSIDER THIS

What role should mental health professionals play in serving students with EBD? How can educators work more cooperatively and effectively with mental health professionals?

	Advantages and Disadvantages of More Restrictive and Less Restrictive Placements for Students with Serious Emotional Disturbance	
TABLE 6.4		

Placements	Advantages	Disadvantages
Less Restrictive Regular classrooms (with and without support) Resource rooms	Prevents the regular educator from giving up on the student and turning to "experts" Permits students to model appropriate behaviour of their peers; increased interaction Possibly less expensive May be able to serve more students Students do not experience problems with reintegration Students follow general curriculum more easily	Expense and time required to train general educators to work with students and special educators to work collaboratively with general educators Problems with classroom management and discipline Lack of consistent expectations for the students Time and materials required for individualization Fear and frustration of general education
More Restrictive Separate classes Separate campuses Residential facilities Hospitals	Flexibility to provide different curricula and different goals Progress can be more closely monitored Accountability of program is more clearly defined Intervention can be more consistent Student follows only one set of guidelines and expectations One team for consistent discipline	Student's opportunities for peer interactions are limited, especially when student is not at neighbourhood school with peers from neighbourhood Travel time for students can be excessive No possible modelling of appropriate peers; no opportunities for socialization with nondisabled peers Difficulties with reintegration back into regular school or class

From "Placements" (p. 324) by K. McConnell, 2001, in R. Algozzine, L. Serna, & J. R. Patton (Eds.), *Childhood Behaviour Disorders: Applied Research and Educational Practices* (2nd ed), Austin, TX: Pro-Ed.

those with a more positive reintegration orientation; those with certain demographic characteristics, such as being located in a wing of the general classroom building; and particular training experiences of teachers, such as having reintegration training in several sites. Administrators might want to take these variables into consideration when planning the reintegration of students with emotional or behavioural disorders into general education programs.

Effective Instruction

Teaching students with emotional and behavioural disorders is clearly challenging. Research, however, does offer promising directions for effective instructional practices. As adapted from Wehby, Symons, Canale, and Go (1998), these practices should include the following:

- providing appropriate structure and predictable routines
- establishing a structured and consistent classroom environment
- establishing a consistent schedule with set rules and consequences and clear expectations
- fostering positive teacher–student interaction with adequate praise and systematic responses to problem behaviours

Personal Spotlight

Teacher Pamela J. Beatty

*P*am Beatty is a teacher in the Saskatoon Public School Division (SPSD) in Saskatoon, Saskatchewan. Since Pam began her teaching career in 1975 she has taught at elementary, secondary, and post-secondary levels. In her early career, Pam worked in northern rural communities in both Saskatchewan and Alberta, teaching students in regular elementary and secondary classrooms.

Pam has a master of education degree from the University of Saskatchewan (U of S), with a focus on behaviour. She has taught in the College of Education at the U of S as a sessional lecturer. She was also recently seconded by Saskatchewan Learning to work with a reference team and write the document, *Planning for Students with Fetal Alcohol Spectrum Disorders, A Guide for Educators* (available at http://www.sasked.gov.sk.ca/branches/children_services/special_ed/sepub.shtml).

Most of Pam's career has been with the SPSD, where she has taught primarily at the secondary level, including regular classes for typical learners, congregated special classrooms, and as a secondary resource teacher. Pam has also worked as a consultant for students with behaviour disorders and students with other exceptional learning needs, and has provided support for homebound students.

Currently, Pam is the teacher in a satellite, or storefront, program serving students aged 14 to 16 years whose behaviour makes it unlikely for them to be successful in typical educational settings. Behaviours of concern range from failure to attend school to violent and aggressive behaviour. Many of the students are involved with the Department of Justice. Many are drug involved.

Pam believes that her students are good kids who either have not had the same opportunities as other kids or who have not learned the strategies they need to be successful in conventional ways. She says that they often lack the support systems necessary to help them make good choices, so they fall back on what they know. Most of Pam's students also experience challenges to their learning. Several students demonstrate learning disabilities, while others experience mental health issues. Unfortunately, all too frequently these students have not received the intense educational support and/or the mental health support they needed and continue to need.

Pam believes that, as educators, we focus primarily on academics. She says that when there are skill deficits and/or emotional/social barriers to learning, we need to focus our energies and efforts on removing or at least ameliorating those barriers. "As teachers we often see these kids only as the problem or the perpetrator of negative behaviour when we should recognize that they are also the victims of circumstance, of manipulation, or of abuse."

- frequently implementing instructional sequences that promote high rates of academic engagement
- creating a classroom environment in which independent seat work is limited and sufficient time is allotted for establishing positive social interaction. (p. 52)

An important, emerging emphasis in effective instruction for students with EBD is to use functional assessment procedures as a basis for making effective classroom adaptations. For example, Kerr, Delaney, Clarke, Dunlap, and Childs (2001) demonstrated that adaptations based on assessment data, which identified activities associated with problem behaviour and also activities not associated with such behaviour, resulted in increased task employment, decreases in challenging behaviour, and increased academic productivity—all without significant difficulties in implementation by the teacher. Further, Reid and Nelson (2002) reported that FBA provides a promising approach with research validation for planning positive behavioural interventions, which can have a significant effect on improving student behaviour. They note that there remains a need for closer attention to the practicality of such interventions within the school setting to confirm that these methods will be acceptable to teachers. FBA-based approaches offer exciting opportunities to enhance instruction and influence successful inclusion practices. They will be discussed further later in the chapter.

Social Skills Instruction

Students with emotional and behavioural disorders frequently display deficits in social skills (Knitzer, 1990; Rosenberg et al., 1992). Elksnin and Elksnin (1998) stress the complexity of social skills, indicating that they include both overt, observable behaviours and covert actions that may relate more to problem solving. A list of typical social skills is presented in Table 6.5.

Social skills are typically learned from observing others who display appropriate skills, but when this doesn't happen, a more formal instructional effort must be made. When using a formal instructional process to teach social skills, the first step is to determine the student's level of social competence.

Assessing social skills requires eliciting informed judgments from persons who interact regularly with the student (Smith et al., 1993). Many different checklists are available to assist in assessing social competence. In addition, self-monitoring charts and sociometric measures may be used (Smith et al., 1993).

Following the assessment process, an instructional approach to teaching social skills must be developed. Numerous methods may be used to teach social skills and promote good social relations, including modelling, direct instruction, prompting, and positive practice (Searcy & Meadows, 1994). Teachers must determine the method that will work best with a particular student.

Quinn, Kavale, Mathur, Rutherford, and Forness (1999) reported a comprehensive research analysis of the use of social skills training with students with EBD. In general, they caution that only about half of students with EBD have been demonstrated to benefit from social skills training, particularly when the focus was on the broader dimensions of the social domain. Greater success was obtained when the focus was on specific social skills (e.g., social problem solving, social interaction, co-operation). Forness (1999) and Kavale (2001) hypothesized that the reason more substantive positive effects have not been obtained from social skills training may be that the training programs within the research studies were too limited in duration and intensity.

TABLE 6.5	Types of Social Skills
Interpersonal Behaviours	"Friendship-making skills," such as introducing yourself, joining in, asking a favour, offering to help, giving and accepting compliments, and apologizing.
Peer-Related Social Skills	Skills valued by classmates and associated with peer acceptance. Examples include working cooperatively, asking for and receiving information, and correctly assessing another's emotional state.
Teacher-Pleasing Social Skills	School success behaviours, including following directions, doing your best work, and listening to the teacher.
Self-Related Behaviours	Skills that allow a child to assess a social situation, select an appropriate skill, and determine the skill's effectiveness. Other self-related behaviours include following through, dealing with stress, understanding feelings, and controlling anger.
Assertiveness Skills	Behaviours that allow children to express their needs without resorting to aggression.
Communication Skills	Listener responsiveness, turn taking, maintaining conversational attention, and giving the speaker feedback.

From "Teaching Social Skills to Students with Learning and Behavioural Problems" (p. 132) by L. K. Elksnin and N. Elksnin, 1998, *Intervention in School and Clinic, 33.*

One reason social skills instruction may be problematic is that its effectiveness is challenged by the difficulty of achieving generalization across settings. Scott and Nelson (1998) cautioned teachers to realize that educational practices for achieving generalization in academic instruction are often insufficient for achieving similar outcomes in social skills instruction. They stress that any such instruction in artificial contexts will create difficulty in generalization, and therefore school-wide instruction, modelling, and the reinforcement of appropriate social behaviours taught within the context of the classroom are likely to be most effective. This instruction may be more effective when students who are not disabled are also involved in the training. While they stress the complexity of teaching social skills, Scott and Nelson (1998) also similarly stress the critical nature of learning within this area. Teachers are advised to consider social skills programs cautiously, implement them experimentally, and confirm that positive outcomes are obtained.

Classroom Adaptations for Emotional and Behavioural Disorders

Effective classroom management is critical for teachers with students with emotional and behavioural disorders because of the interference of their behaviour with their own learning and their impact on the learning of other students.

Standard Operating Procedures

Classroom rules and procedures are a critical management tool for students with EBD. Rules should be developed with the input of students and should be posted in the room. Remember that "the process of determining rules is as important as the rules themselves" (Zabel & Zabel, 1996, p. 169). Walker and Shea (1995) give the following examples of classroom rules:

- Be polite and helpful.
- Keep your space and materials in order.
- Take care of classroom and school property.
- Raise your hand before speaking.
- Leave your seat only with permission.
- Only one person in the rest room at a time. (p. 252)

Teachers should establish classroom procedures to ensure an orderly environment. These include procedures for the beginning of a period or the school day, use of classroom equipment, social interaction, the completion of work, group and individual activities, and the conclusion of instructional periods and the school day (Walker & Shea, 1995).

Physical Accommodations

The accessibility of the classroom warrants special attention. The concept of **accessibility** extends beyond physical accessibility, touching on overall program accessibility for students with special needs. This means that students with disabilities must be able to utilize the classroom like other students and that the room must be free of potential hazards. For students with EBD, accessibility is an issue when social isolation or time out is used for substantial periods of time. This type of treatment limits the student's access to the classroom and is therefore problematic.

The physical arrangement of the classroom has an impact on the behaviours of students with emotional and behavioural disorders. Attention to the classroom arrangement can both facilitate learning and minimize disruptions (Zabel & Zabel, 1996). The following considerations can help maintain an orderly classroom:

- Arranging traffic patterns to lessen contact and disruptions
- Arranging student desks to facilitate monitoring of all students at all times
- Physically locating students with tendencies toward disruptive behaviours near the teacher's primary location
- Locating students away from stored materials that they may find tempting
- Creating spaces where students can do quiet work, such as a quiet reading area

Preventive Discipline

Probably the most effective means of working with students who display emotional and behaviour problems is preventive in nature. If inappropriate behaviours can be prevented, then disruptions will be minimal, and the student can attend to the learning task at hand. **Preventive discipline** can be described as "the teacher's realization that discipline begins with a positive attitude that nurtures students' learning of personal, social, and academic skills" (Sabatino, 1987, p. 8). Rather than wait to respond to inappropriate behaviours, preventive measures remove the need for inappropriate behaviours.

Sabatino (1987) describes 10 components of a preventive discipline program:

1. Inform pupils of what is expected of them.
2. Establish a positive learning climate.
3. Provide a meaningful learning experience.
4. Avoid threats.
5. Demonstrate fairness.
6. Build and exhibit self-confidence.
7. Recognize positive student attributes.
8. Recognize student attributes at optimal times.
9. Use positive modelling.
10. Structure the curriculum and classroom environment.

The behaviours of teachers can have great impact on effective behaviour management.

Teacher behaviour can greatly facilitate preventive discipline. Teachers have to be consistent in discipline; they must not treat inappropriate behaviours from one student differently than they treat misbehaviour from other students. Teachers must also apply consequences systematically. Disciplining a student for an inappropriate behaviour one time and ignoring the same behaviour another time will only cause the student to be confused over expectations. This discussion on preventative discipline is consistent with the trend toward positive behavioural supports discussed in the next section.

General Behaviour Support Strategies

The development of **positive behaviour supports (PBS)** has been a significant achievement in the education of students with special needs and has particular relevance for students with EBD. Carr et al. (2002) describe PBS in this way:

> *Positive behaviour* includes all those skills that increase the likelihood of success and personal satisfaction in... academic, work, social, recreational, community, and family settings. *Support* encompasses all those educational methods that can be used to teach, strengthen, and expand positive behaviour and... increase opportunities for the display of positive behaviour. The primary goal of PBS is to help an individual change his or her lifestyle in a direction that gives... teachers, employers, parents, friends, and the target person him- or herself the opportunity to perceive and to enjoy an improved quality of life. An important but secondary goal of PBS is to render problem behaviour irrelevant, inefficient, and ineffective by helping an individual achieve his or her goals in a socially acceptable manner. (pp. 4–5)

Functional behavioural assessment is an important basis for the development of positive behavioural supports. PBS interventions provide an alternative to an emphasis on punitive disciplinary strategies and provide guidance to students with behavioural problems to make appropriate changes in their behavioural patterns. PBS emphasizes proactive, preventive strategies and early intervention with students deemed to be at risk.

As described by Lewis and Sugai (1999), an effective positive behavioural support program for a school should include the following components:

▶ specialized individual behaviour support for students with chronic behaviour problems
▶ specialized group behaviour support for students with at-risk problem behaviour
▶ universal group behaviour support for most students. (p. 4)

The system that Lewis and Sugai have developed emphasizes school wide programs that put in place a preventive, proactive system and provide a foundation for the appropriate design of programs for individuals experiencing significant behaviour problems.

Numerous positive behavioural support strategies have been developed for use with students experiencing emotional and behavioural problems. Along with additional strategies for classroom management, they will be discussed in detail in Chapter 12.

Particular behavioural strategies that have merit for use with students with EBD include the good behaviour game, contingency contracting, and individual behaviour management plans. In addition, Webber and Scheuermann (1991) outlined several reinforcement programs that can be used to eliminate inappropriate behaviours. These examples utilize *differential reinforcement of zero rates of undesirable behaviours (DRO)*, *differential reinforcement of incompatible behaviours (DRI)*, *differential reinforcement of lower rates of behaviours (DRL)*, and *differential rates of communicative behaviours (DRC)*.

Cognitive approaches are of particular importance to students with EBD. For students with EBD, a particular focus should be on the development of behavioural self-control in which students are taught to use self-management strategies throughout the day.

Another technique, the use of peer mediation, has also been used effectively with students with emotional and behavioural disorders. As Gable, Arllen, and Hendrickson (1994) noted, while most behavioural programs rely on adults to monitor and provide reinforcement for desirable behaviours, this technique instead relies on peers. After reviewing peer interaction studies, they concluded that peer behaviour modifiers could be effective among students with emotional and behavioural problems: "The generally positive results surfacing from the modest number of investigations in which EBD students have served as behaviour modifiers underscore the relevance of this procedure for those facing the daunting task of better serving students with emotional/behavioural disorders" (p. 275).

Table 6.6 provides some sample hypothesis statements and possible interventions related to functional behavioural assessment-based interventions. Such an approach does not lock teachers into specific strategies, thus allowing them to tailor interventions to specific behaviours and causes (Kauffman et al., 1995).

Behaviour Management

An important component of classroom management involves the management of those specific behaviours that disrupt the learning environment. Yet the ability to control inappropriate behaviours represents only a part of a comprehensive behaviour management program. Such a plan should also include techniques for creating new behaviours or

| | Intervention | |
| TABLE 6.6 — Sample Hypothesis Statements and Possible Interventions | | |
Hypothesis Statements	Modify Antecedents	Teach Alternative Behaviour
Suzy pinches herself and others around 11:00 A.M. every day because she gets hungry.	Make sure Suzy gets breakfast. Provide a snack at about 9:30 A.M.	Teach Suzy to ask for something to eat.
Jack gets into arguments with the teacher every day during reading class when she asks him to correct his mistakes on the daily reading worksheet.	Get Jack to correct his own paper. Give Jack an easier assignment.	Teach Jack strategies to manage his frustration in a more appropriate manner. Teach Jack to ask for teacher assistance with the incorrect problems.
Tara starts pouting and refuses to work when she has to sort a box of washers because she doesn't want to do the activity.	Give Tara half of the box of washers to sort. Give Tara clear directions about how much she has to do or how long she must work.	
Frank kicks other children in morning circle time and usually gets to sit right by the teacher.	Give each child a clearly designated section of the floor that is his or hers.	Teach Frank how to ask the children to move over. Teach Frank how to ask the teacher to intervene with his classmates.
Harry is off task for most of math class when he is supposed to be adding two-digit numbers.	Ask Harry to add the prices of actual food items. Intersperse an easy activity with the more difficult math addition so Harry can experience some success.	Teach Harry how to ask for help. Teach Harry how to monitor his rate of problem completion, and provide reinforcement for a certain number of problems.

From "Using Functional Assessment to Develop Effective, Individualized Interventions for Challenging Behaviors" (p. 49) by L. Foster-Johnson and G. Dunlap, 1993, *Teaching Exceptional Children, 25.* Used by permission.

Components of a Behaviour Management Plan

Conduct a Functional Assessment

1. Collect information.
   - ▶ Identify and define the target behaviour.
   - ▶ Identify events/circumstances associated with the problem behaviour.
   - ▶ Determine potential function(s) of the problem behaviour.

2. Develop hypothesis statements about the behaviour.
   - ▶ Events/circumstances associated with the problem behaviour.
   - ▶ Function/purpose of the behaviour.

Develop an Intervention (Based on Hypothesis Statements)

1. Teach alternative behaviour.
2. Modify events/circumstances associated with the problem behaviour.

From "Using Functional Assessment to Develop Effective, Individualized Interventions for Challenging Behaviors," by L. F. Johnson and G. Dunlap, 1993, *Teaching Exceptional Children, 25*, p. 46. Used by permission.

---

increasing desirable behaviours that are minimally existent. Moreover, a sound program must ensure that behaviours learned or changed will be maintained over time and demonstrated in different contexts; it must also teach self-control mechanisms. The Inclusion Strategies feature above describes the components of a behaviour management plan.

Multicultural Considerations

Educators must always remember the multicultural issues related to classroom management. Different cultural groups expect different behaviours from their children. Methods used for disciplining children vary significantly from group to group. Expectations of the school, regarding discipline and management principles, also vary from culture to culture.

As schools become increasingly more diverse, teachers and other school personnel must take the time to learn about the different cultures represented in the school district. Having a better understanding of parents' expectations of the school as well as of their children can facilitate communication between parents and school personnel and lead to more effective behaviour management programs.

Medication

Many students with emotional and behavioural problems experience difficulties in maintaining attention and controlling behaviour. For students experiencing these problems, "medication is the most frequently used (and perhaps overused) intervention" (Ellenwood & Felt, 1989, p. 16). Many different kinds of medication have been found to be effective with students' behaviour problems (Forness & Kavale, 1988) including stimulants, tranquilizers, anticonvulsants, antidepressants, and mood-altering drugs.

The use of medication to help manage students with emotional and behaviour problems is controversial and has been investigated extensively. Findings include the following:

1. Medication can result in increased attention of students.
2. Medication can result in reduced aggressive behaviours.
3. Various side effects can result from medical interventions.
4. The use of medication for children experiencing emotional and behavioural problems should be carefully monitored. (Smith et al., 1993, p. 214)

Numerous side effects may accompany medications taken by children for emotional and behavioural problems. Ritalin is commonly prescribed to help students with attention and hyperactivity problems. Several potential side effects of Ritalin include nervousness, insomnia, anorexia, dizziness, blood pressure and pulse changes, abdominal pain, and weight loss. Teachers can monitor side effects by keeping a daily log of student behaviours that could be attributed to the medication (Dowdy, Patton, Smith, & Polloway, 1997).

Enhancing Inclusive Classrooms for Students with Emotional or Behavioural Disorders

Classroom teachers usually make the initial referral for students with emotional or behavioural problems (Polloway & Smith, 1992). Unless the problem exhibited by the student is severe, it may have gone unrecognized until the school years. In addition to referring students, classroom teachers must be directly involved in implementing the student's individualized education program (IEP) because the majority of students in this category receive at least a portion of their educational program in general education classrooms. General education classroom teachers must deal with behaviour problems much of the time because there are a large number of students who occasionally display inappropriate behaviours, although they have not been identified as having emotional or behavioural disorders.

Kauffman and Wong (1991) point out that "effective teaching of behaviourally disordered students may require skills, attitudes, and beliefs different from those of teachers who work effectively with more ordinary students" (p. 226). However, no single characteristic will guarantee success for teachers dealing with students who are experiencing emotional and behavioural problems.

Supports for General Education Teachers

Since most students with emotional or behavioural disorders are educated in general classrooms, classroom teachers are the key to the success of these students. Too often, if these students do not achieve success, the entire classroom will be disrupted. Therefore, appropriate supports must be available to teachers. They include special education personnel, psychologists and counsellors, and mental health service providers.

The level of collaboration among professionals who provide services to this group of students is critical. The involvement of mental health professionals, and in some cases, personnel from the juvenile justice system, child welfare system, and social work agencies will be of benefit to students with EBD and to their families, as well as to school personnel. Without a close working relationship among the many groups who serve children and adolescents with EBD, services will be fragmented and disorganized. Refer to

CONSIDER THIS

Can general classroom teachers effectively deal with students who have emotional or behavioural disorders in their classrooms? What factors will enhance the likelihood of success?

Collaboration: Ways to Involve Other Personnel

1. The school principal or administrator can
   - ❯ Advocate for and support the student with emotional or behavioural disorder and his/her family
   - ❯ Supply any necessary equipment or materials
   - ❯ Provide flexibility in staffing patterns
   - ❯ Show support for the teachers involved

2. The school guidance counsellor can
   - ❯ Advocate for and support the student and his/her family
   - ❯ Provide individual counselling sessions
   - ❯ Work with other students who may be reinforcing the inappropriate behaviour of the disruptive student
   - ❯ Offer the teacher information about the student's needs

3. The school psychologist can
   - ❯ Review the teacher's behaviour management plan and make recommendations for changes
   - ❯ Observe the student in the classroom and in other settings to collect behavioural data and note possible environmental instigators

   - ❯ Collect and provide any useful data on the student's learning and behavioural needs that may be useful in planning appropriate interventions and support strategies.

4. The social worker can
   - ❯ Provide additional information about the home environment
   - ❯ Schedule regular visits to the home
   - ❯ Collaborate with other public agencies that may be of assistance

5. Other teachers can
   - ❯ Provide curricular and behaviour management suggestions that work for them
   - ❯ Offer material resources
   - ❯ Provide carryover and consistency for the tactics used

Adapted from *The Special Educator's Handbook* (p. 119), by D. L. Westling and M. A. Koorland, 1989, Boston: Allyn & Bacon. Used with permission.

---

the nearby Inclusion Strategies for suggestions on how to involve other professionals in meeting the needs of students with EBD.

Special educators should be available to collaborate with teachers regarding the development of behavioural as well as instructional supports. A particularly helpful way to assist classroom teachers involves modelling methods of dealing with behaviour problems. Dr. Ingrid Sladeczek of McGill University continues to study various methods of school psychologist and parent/teacher conjoint consultation to manage behavioural disorders in the regular classroom. She is the first in Canada to study empirically the effectiveness of conjoint behavioural consultation (Sladeczek & Heath, 1997; Wayland & Sladeczek, 1999).

At times, it is best for students with emotional or behavioural problems to leave the general education setting and receive instruction from special educators. School psychologists and counsellors are other critical team members in providing a comprehensive program for students with EBD. They can provide intensive counselling to students with emotional or behavioural disorders; they may also consult with teachers about implementation of specific programs, such as a student's individual behaviour management plan.

Finally, mental health personnel can provide helpful supports for teachers. Too often, mental health services are not available to schools; however, some schools are beginning to develop school-based mental health programs that serve students with emotional or behavioural disorders. These programs, jointly staffed by school personnel and mental health staff, provide supports for teachers as well as direct interventions for students. If mental health services are not available in a particular school, teachers should work with school administrators to involve mental health specialists with students who display emotional and behavioural problems.

Currently, in Montreal, an innovative program that works to include students with moderate to severe EBD in the regular classroom is under way. At the heart of the program is a partnership between hospital personnel, school personnel, and community agencies. The Family School Support and Treatment Team aims to bring the needed expertise and support into the classroom, rather than removing the student. Although still under examination this model has been very efficient in increasing teachers' willingness to have students with EBD in their classes (Heath & McLean-Heywood, 1999).

In Saskatoon, Saskatchewan, the Early Skills Program is a mental health program that provides services to kindergarten students with EBD within the school setting.

Summary

- Most children and youths are disruptive from time to time, but most do not require interventions. Some students' emotional or behavioural problems are severe enough to warrant interventions.
- Many problems complicate serving students with emotional and behavioural disorders, including inconsistent definitions of the disorder, the large number of agencies involved in defining and treating it, and limited ways to objectively measure the extent and precise parameters of the problem.
- Definitions for emotional disturbance and behavioural disorders are typically subject to alternative explanations.
- There is limited consistency in classifying persons with emotional and behavioural problems.
- Determining the eligibility of students with EBD is difficult because of problems with identification and assessment.
- The estimated prevalence of students with emotional and behavioural problems ranges from a low of 1 percent to a high of 30 percent.
- Students with emotional and behavioural problems are significantly underserved in schools.
- Students with EBD are commonly included in general education classes. General education teachers and special

education teachers must collaborate so that there is consistency in the development and implementation of intervention methods.
- A variety of curricular, classroom, and behavioural management strategies are available to enhance the educational programs for students with EBD.
- Social skills development is important for students with EBD.
- Interventions based on functional behavioural assessment, preventive discipline, and positive behavioural supports are important methods for reducing the impact of problems or for keeping problems from occurring.
- General education teachers must realize that the skills, attitudes, and beliefs needed to work effectively with students with EBD may vary from those that are effective for nondisabled students.
- Positive reinforcement and peer tutoring are possible tactics for preventing students with EBD from feeling isolated in the general education classroom.
- Special education teachers and mental health personnel need to be available to provide guidance for general education teachers who are implementing a student's behaviour management plan.

Resources

Handbooks/Documents

Algozzine, R., Serna, L., & Patton, J. R. (2001). *Childhood behavior disorders: Applied research and educational practices* (2nd ed.). Austin, TX: Pro-Ed.

This book addresses foundations, theoretical perspectives, intervention practices, and programmatic consider-ations derived from professional competencies. It provides the balance of theory, research, and practical relevance needed by students, practising teachers, and other professionals.

American Psychiatric Association. (2000). *Diagnostic and statistical manual of mental disorders* (DSM IV-TR). Washington, DC: Author.

British Columbia Ministry of Education, Special Education Branch. (1996). *Teaching students with learning and behavioural differences: A resource guide for teachers.* Victoria: Author.

This resource guide provides an array of strategies for classroom management as well as suggested resources related to behavioural and learning difficulties.

DeBruyn, R., & Larson, J. (1984). *You can handle them all.* Manhattan, KS: The Master Teacher Inc.

This practical manual for managing even the most difficult student comes recommended by the B.C. Ministry of Education, Special Education Branch.

Fad, K., Patton, J. R., & Polloway, E. A. (2000). *Behavioral intervention planning: Completing a functional behavioral assessment and developing a behavioral intervention plan* (2nd ed.). Austin, TX: Pro-Ed.

This book provides school personnel with the most up-to-date tools necessary to complete a functional behavioural assessment (FBA), determine whether a behaviour is related to the disability of the student (manifestation determination), and develop a behavioural intervention plan (BIP).

Kauffman, J. M. (1993). *Characteristics of emotional and behavioral disorders of children and youth.* Columbus, OH: Merrill.

This text combines descriptions of emotional and behavioural disorders with discussion and interpretation of current research on their development. Material is organized around five basic concepts: the nature of disorders and conceptual approaches to them; methods and rationale for assessment; major casual factors; characteristics of disordered emotion and behaviour; and a personal statement about teaching students who exhibit such disorders.

Rockwell, Sylvia (1995). *Back off, cool down, try again: Teaching students how to control aggressive behavior.* Reston, VA: Council for Exceptional Children.

Rockwell, Sylvia. (1993). *Tough to reach, tough to teach: Students with behavior problems.* Reston, VA: Council for Exceptional Children.

Sylvia Rockwell's two guides that provide a practical approach to dealing with students with behaviour problems are very successful with teachers and have been recommended by the Council for Exceptional Children.

Videos

Lavoie, R. (1994). Last one picked, first one picked on: Learning disabilities and social skills. Available at http://ldonline.learningstore.org/products/LD1002.html

Every child has experienced embarrassment or rejection in social situations. Host Richard Lavoie explains why kids with learning disabilities are often isolated and rejected, and sometimes have a particularly hard time making and keeping friends. Practical suggestions for improving children's social skills are also provided.

Lavoie, R. (1997). When the chips are down: Learning disabilities and discipline. Available at http://ldonline.learningstore.org/products/LD1002.html

Host Richard Lavoie, well-known expert on learning disabilities, offers practical advice on dealing with behavioural problems quickly and effectively. He shows how preventative discipline can anticipate many problems before they start. He also explains how teachers and parents can create a stable, predictable environment in which children with learning disabilities can flourish.

Webster-Stratton, C. (1998). The teacher video tape series. Eugene, OR: Castalia.

Webster-Stratton, C. (1987). The parent and children video tape series. Eugene, OR: Castalia.

These videotape series, which come with a handbook, provide suggestions for managing a variety of behaviour problems of children ages 3 to 10 and show actual demonstrations. The use of these videotapes to improve parent and teacher ability to better manage behaviour is being studied by Dr. Webster-Stratton and by McGill University's Dr. Sladeczek.

Laser Disk

ACCESS, The Education Station. (1992). Improving classroom behaviour: A preventive approach. Edmonton, AB: ACCESS, The Education Station, Media Resource Centre.

This laser disk, which comes with a workbook, helps teachers develop strategies to prevent behaviour problems from occurring or escalating for children in elementary and early childhood programs.

Association

Council for Children with Behaviour Disorders (CCBD)

As a division of the Council for Exceptional Children, CCBD is an international professional organization committed to promoting and facilitating the education and general welfare of children and youth with behavioural or emotional disorders. CCBD, whose members include educators, parents, and a variety of professionals, actively pursues quality educational services and program alternatives for persons with behavioural disorders; advocates for the needs of such children and youth; emphasizes research and professional growth as vehicles for better understanding behavioural disorders; and provides professional support for persons who are involved with and serve children and youth with behavioural disorders. CCBD currently includes 37 active subdivisions throughout the United States and Canada. For information about the Canadian CCBD, contact Joyce Mountsteven in Toronto at 416-397-3590 or by email joyce.mountsteven@tdsb.on.ca, or Christine Boyczuk at 306-587-2811.

Weblinks

Council for Children with Behaviour Disorders (CCBD)
www.ccbd.net
The Council for Children with Behaviour Disorders (CCBD) is a division of the Council for Exceptional Children. This site has a number of recent relevant publications, suggested resources, and a list of upcoming relevant events/conferences. (See Association for more information.)

B.C. Ministry of Education
www.bced.gov.bc.ca/specialed/landbdif/toc.htm
The ministry's resource guide on learning and behavioural difficulties appears online. In addition to providing specific classroom strategies, this website also lists related resources.

Depression and Bipolar Support Alliance (DBSA)
www.dbsalliance.org/
The Association's website provides information about adolescent depression, including a screening list of symptoms specifically for adolescents, a list of symptoms for the use of others in the student's life, and a suicide prevention plan.

7 Teaching Students with Intellectual Disabilities

Chapter Objectives

After reading this chapter, you should be able to

- discuss the concept of intellectual disability
- summarize key definitional and classification considerations
- identify the instructional implications of common characteristics of students with intellectual disabilities
- highlight the transitional needs of students with intellectual disabilities
- apply considerations of the needs of students with intellectual disabilities to curriculum design
- present ways of enhancing the inclusion of students with intellectual disabilities

cott is currently a junior at Centennial High School. He has been receiving special education supports throughout his school career. Prior to kindergarten, he had been identified as "at risk" in part because of language delays and also in part because of the difficult home situation in which he was raised (his grandmother has been his guardian since his mother was incarcerated when Scott was four years old; his father has not been part of his life since he was an infant).

When Scott began elementary school, he was identified as developmentally delayed. However, when assessments were completed on Scott at age eight, he was formally identified as intellectually disabled.

Scott has progressed well in part because of his continued involvement in general education classrooms through elementary school and into high school. With in-class support and periodic remedial instruction, he has developed his reading skills to the equivalent of Grade 4 level with comparable achievement in mathematics and other academic areas. Currently, the focus of his program is on building his academic skills in the inclusive environment and complementing these with a functional curriculum to prepare him for success in the community.

Scott has become an active participant in the development of his individualized educational program and, more recently, his individual transition plan. His short-term objective is to obtain his driver's licence, for which he is currently eligible based on chronological age. He is currently enrolled in both an instructional program to complete the written portion of the test and the behind-the-wheel component. A longer-term focus of his program is to prepare him for competitive employment in the community. Through a series of community-based instructional programs, he has become aware of the options that are available to him, and an apprenticeship program in maintenance at the local Wal-Mart will be available next year. Scott's success is a combination of his motivation to succeed, detailed planning by key individuals in his life, and ongoing support provided by teachers, his grandmother, his football coach, and several significant peers who are more academically able.

Questions to Consider

1. How can Scott's curriculum include peers who are not disabled and use the functional curriculum designed by special educators?

2. How can the curriculum balance short-term objectives and preparation for competitive employment and independent living?

3. What strategies can enhance a positive influence from peers?

4. What available community resources will aid his transition to independent living?

Introduction

The Canadian Association for Community Living (CACL) is an association that works to promote the full participation of people with intellectual disabilities in all aspects of community life. The membership includes both individuals with intellectual disabilities and advocates for them.

The CACL defines an intellectual disability as an impaired ability to learn which sometimes causes difficulty in coping with the demands of daily life, noting that the disability is usually present from birth and differs from mental or psychiatric illness. An intellectual disability is sometimes referred to as "mental retardation," although the CACL (2004) states, "We have been informed by people who have an intellectual disability that they resent being labelled by this term. For this reason, we always refer to people for who they are, rather then by what they are (i.e., the "disabled"). Preferred terms are: people who have an intellectual disability, people who have a mental handicap, and people who have a developmental disability."

However, the largest North American organization in the field continues to use the term *mental retardation*. The American Association of Mental Retardation (AAMR) is an international multidisciplinary association of professionals responsible for defining mental retardation. In the schools, even more variation is seen in terminology and may occasionally lead to confusion about the "correct" descriptor.

For the purposes of our discussion we will respect the CACL position and use the term "intellectual disability," although in the formal definition specified by the AAMR, the less preferred term mental retardation is used. Bear in mind that the actual terminology is less important than respecting the preferences of students and parents regarding terminology.

In the field of intellectual disabilities, the past decade or so has seen momentous changes. Shifts in public attitudes toward persons with intellectual disabilities and the resulting development and provision of services and supports for them have been truly phenomenal. Consequently, the first decade of the new millennium is an exciting time to be participating in the changing perspectives on intellectual disabilities (Polloway, Smith, Patton, & Smith, 1996).

Basic Concepts about Intellectual Disabilities

The concept of intellectual disability is a broad one. It includes a wide range of functioning levels, from mild disabilities to more severe limitations. The discussion in this chapter initially will address the global concept of intellectual disability. Then the remainder of the chapter will focus on the educational implications of intellectual disabilities.

Intellectual Disabilities Defined

It has been difficult for professionals to formulate definitions of intellectual disabilities that could then be used to govern practices such as assessment and placement. Intellectual disability has been most often characterized by two dimensions: limited intellectual ability and difficulty in coping with the social demands of the environment. Thus, all individuals with intellectual disabilities must, by definition, demonstrate some degree of impaired mental abilities, most often reflected in an intelligence quotient (IQ) significantly below average, which relates to a **mental age (MA)** appreciably lower than the individual's chronological age (CA). In addition, these individuals would necessarily demonstrate less mature adaptive skills, such as social behaviour or functional academic skills, when compared to their same-age peers. For individuals with mild disabilities, this discrepancy can be relatively subtle and may not be readily apparent in a casual interaction outside of school. These individuals may be challenged most dramatically by the school setting, and thus between the ages of 6 and 21 their inability to cope may be most evident—for example, in problems with peer relationships, difficulty in compliance with adult-initiated directions, or academic challenges. Although discussed as a comprehensive disability, intellectual disability has been typically defined, and diagnosed, as reflecting limitations in two dimensions: intellectual functioning and adaptive skills.

In 1992, the American Association on Mental Retardation revised its definition in order to bring it into line with recent developments and thus reflect changes in current thinking about persons with intellectual disabilities. According to Luckasson et al. (1992), and as shown in Table 7.1.

> Mental retardation refers to substantial limitations in present functioning. It is manifested by significantly sub-average intellectual functioning, existing concurrently with related limitations in two or more of the following applicable adaptive skill areas: communication, self-care, home living, social skills, community use, self-direction, health and safety, functional academics, leisure, and work. Mental retardation begins before age 18. (p. 8)

The 1992 definition retains the focus of earlier AAMR definitions on the two key dimensions of intelligence and adaptation as well as the modifier of age of onset. However, the conceptual basis varies from those earlier efforts. The 1992 definition reflects a more *functional approach,* thus shifting focus to the individual's functioning within the community rather than giving weight mainly to the psychometric and clinical aspects of the person (e.g., IQ scores, limited adaptive behaviour evaluations).

A number of responses were made to the Luckasson et al. (1992) definitional system (e.g., Schalock et al., 1994; MacMillan, Gresham, & Siperstein, 1993; Polloway, 1997; Luckasson, Schalock, Snell, & Spitalnik, 1996; and Smith, 1994). These responses and others provided the basis for further work, which led to the 2002 revision.

CONSIDER THIS

What are some dangers of relating the concept of intellectual disability to a numerical index, such as IQ?

TABLE 7.1	Examples of Conceptual, Social, and Practical Adaptive Skills

Conceptual
▶ Language (receptive and expressive)
▶ Reading and writing
▶ Money concepts
▶ Self-direction
 	
Social
▶ Interpersonal
▶ Responsibility
▶ Self-esteem
▶ Gullibility (likelihood of being tricked or manipulated)
▶ Naiveté
▶ Follows rules
▶ Obeys laws
▶ Avoids victimization
	Practical
	▶ Activities of daily living
	    Eating
	    Transfer/mobility
	    Toileting
	    Dressing
	▶ Instrumental activities of daily living
	    Meal preparation
	    Housekeeping
	    Transportation
	    Taking medication
	    Money management
	    Telephone use
	▶ Occupational skills
	▶ Maintains safe environments

From *Mental Retardation: Definition, Classification, and Systems of Supports* (p. 42) by R. Luckasson 2002, Washington, DC: American Association on Mental Retardation.

The 2002 revised definition, accessed from the AAMR website (www.aamr.org), reads as follows:

> Mental retardation is a disability characterized by significant limitations both in intellectual functioning and in adaptive behaviour as expressed in conceptual, social, and practical adaptive skills. This disability originates before age 18. The following five assumptions are essential to the application of the stated definition of mental retardation.
>
> 1. Limitations in present functioning must be considered within the context of community environments typical of the individual's age peers and culture.
> 2. Valid assessment considers cultural and linguistic diversity as well as differences in communication, sensory, motor, and behavioural factors.
> 3. Within an individual, limitations often coexist with strengths.
> 4. An important purpose of describing limitations is to develop a profile of needed supports.
> 5. With appropriate personalized supports over a sustained period, the life functioning of the person with mental retardation generally will improve.

This definition reflects some similarities to the Luckasson et al. (1992) definition (e.g., set of assumptions used to clarify intent) and some modifications in presentation (e.g., description of adaptive skills). It represents a next logical step in the continued efforts by professionals to define the concept of mental retardation.

Classification of Intellectual Disabilities

Historically, classification in this field has been done by both etiology (i.e., causes) and level of severity. Whereas the former has limited application to nonmedical practice, the latter has been used by a range of disciplines, including education and psychology. The classification system cited most often in the professional literature is one reported by Grossman (1983). This system uses the terms **mild**, **moderate**, **severe**, and **profound mental retardation**, which are summative judgments based on both intelligence and adaptive behaviour assessment. Often, however, the emphasis has been on the former only, so IQ scores have unfortunately been equated with level of functioning.

Terms such as **educable** and **trainable** reflect an alternative system that has been used in some school environments. These terms remain in use today in some places and some students with intellectual disability are referred to as EMR (educable mentally retarded) and TMR (trainable mentally retarded). However, they are inherently stereotypical and prejudicial terms; consequently (and appropriately) they have often been criticized, and should no longer be used.

One alternative has been to classify intellectual disabilities according to only two levels of functioning (i.e., mild and severe) and to avoid reliance on IQ scores in considerations of level of severity. Consideration of level of adaptive skills would thus be used as a yardstick for determining level of intellectual disability, resulting in a more meaningful, broad-based system of classification.

Finally, an emerging alternative is the classification system of Luckasson et al. (1992), which has particular merit for use in inclusive settings. According to this system, classification is not derived from levels of disability, but rather from needed **levels of support**. Thus, this system would classify the *needs*, rather than the *deficits*, of the individual. Individuals would be designated as needing limited, extensive, or pervasive levels of support as related to each of the adaptive skills areas (see Table 7.2). Of course, in a given area,

	Intermittent	Limited	Extensive	Pervasive
TABLE 7.2	*Levels of Support X Intensity Grid*			
Time Duration	As needed	Time limited, occasionally ongoing	Usually ongoing	Possibly lifelong
Time Frequency	Infrequent, low occurrence		Regular, anticipated, could be high frequency	High rate, continuous, constant
Settings Living, Work, Recreation, Leisure, Health, Community, etc.	Few settings, typically one or two settings		Across several settings, typically not all settings	All or nearly all settings
Resources Professional/ Technological Assistance	Occasional consultation or discussion, ordinary appointment schedule, occasional monitoring	Occasional contact or time limited but frequent regular contact	Regular, ongoing contact or monitoring by professionals typically at least weekly	Constant contact and monitoring by professionals
Intrusiveness	Predominantly all natural supports, high degree of choice and autonomy		Mixture of natural and service-based supports, lesser degree of choice and autonomy	Predominantly service-based supports, controlled by others

From "The 1992 AAMR Definition and Preschool Children: Response from the Committee on Terminology and Classification," by R. Luckasson, R. Schalock, M. Snell, and D. Spitalnik, 1996, *Mental Retardation, 34*, p. 250.

an individual may also not need any support to function successfully. These levels of support are defined as follows:

Intermittent: Supports on an "as needed" basis, episodic in nature. Short-term supports may be needed during lifespan transitions (e.g., job loss or an acute medical crisis).

Limited: Supports are consistent over time, are time-limited but not intermittent, and may require fewer staff and less cost than more intense levels of support (e.g., employment training or transitional supports during the school-to-adult period).

Extensive: Supports characterized by regular involvement (e.g., daily) in at least some environments (e.g., long-term support and long-term home living support).

Pervasive: Supports characterized by their constancy and high intensity; provided across environments, potentially life-sustaining in nature. Pervasive supports typically involve more staff and intrusiveness than extensive or limited supports. (Adapted from Luckasson et al., 1992, p. 26)

CONSIDER THIS

What are some advantages to using a classification system based on levels of support rather than levels of severity?

The supports classification system of the AAMR manual (Luckasson et al., 1992) has been further explicated in another publication by Luckasson, Schalock, Snell, and Spitalnik (1996). Table 7.2 presents a grid showing different levels of intensity of supports to illustrate the way that this classification system can be put into practice.

The Luckasson et al. (1992) classification received general support in the field, particularly in the area of programs for adults with mental retardation, although it did not have a significant impact on research and school practices after its development. Polloway,

Terms such as educable and trainable have often been used to categorize students with intellectual disabilities, but are no longer acceptable.

Smith, Chamberlain, Denning, and Smith (1999) found that 99 percent of research papers that were published in three mental retardation journals (1993–1997) and that relied on a system to describe research participants continued to use the levels-of-deficit model from the Grossman (1983) manual rather than relying on the levels-of-support system.

Prevalence, Causes, and Characteristics of Intellectual Disabilities

CROSS-REFERENCE

Review the causes of other disabilities (see Chapters 3–11) to determine the overlap of etiological factors.

CONSIDER THIS

Why do you think the prevalence of students identified as having an intellectual disability has declined so much over the past 20 years?

There are hundreds of known causes of intellectual disabilities, and at the same time, numerous cases exist for which the cause is unknown. Table 7.3 outlines some causes to show the complexity of this area of concern. When all of these different causes of intellectual disability are considered, it is estimated that about 1 million Canadians, or 3 percent of the population, have an intellectual disability (CACL, 2005).

Intellectual disabilities are associated with a number of challenges to learning. Table 7.4 identifies the most significant learning domains, lists representative problem areas, and notes certain instructional implications. In addition, the table focuses on related concerns for cognitive, language, and sociobehavioural development.

Identification, Assessment, and Eligibility

Procedures for the identification of intellectual disability differ from province to province. However, common requirements include evidence of significantly below average intellectual functioning combined with impairments in adaptive functioning. Eligibility for special education services depends on the degree of intellectual impairment and its effect on the adaptive functioning of the student. The degree of intellectual impairment is determined through psychological assessment carried out by registered psychologists using an individually administered test of intellectual functioning and other measures as appropriate. The *Diagnostic and Statistical Manual of Mental Disorders – Fourth Edition* (*DSM-IV*) specifies four degrees of severity of mental retardation. They are:

- Mild mental retardation: IQ level 50–55 to approximately 70
- Moderate mental retardation: IQ level 35–40 to 50–55
- Severe mental retardation: IQ level 20–25 to 35–40
- Profound mental retardation: IQ level below 20 or 25. (p. 42)

TABLE 7.3	Selected Causes of Intellectual Disabilities	
Cause	**Nature of Problem**	**Considerations**
Down Syndrome	Trisomy 21 (3 chromosomes on this pair) IQ range from severe retardation to nonretarded	Wide variance in learning characteristics Classic physical signs Most common chromosomal anomaly
Environmental Disadvantage	Elements of poverty environment (e.g., family constellation, resources, educational role models)	Can be related to mild retardation Commonly associated with school failure
Fetal Alcohol Syndrome	Caused by drinking during pregnancy Related to toxic effects of alcohol	Associated with varying degrees of disability May be accompanied by facial and other malformations and behavioural disturbances Among the three most common biologically based causes of retardation
Fragile X Syndrome	Genetic disorder related to the gene or X chromosome	Most often transmitted from mother to son Frequently associated with retardation in males and learning disabilities in females (in some instances) May be accompanied by variant patterns of behaviour (e.g., self-stimulation), social skills difficulties, language impairment
Hydrocephalus	Multiple causes (e.g., genetic, environmental) Disruption in appropriate flow of cerebrospinal fluid on the brain	Previously associated with enlarged head and brain damage Controlled by the implantation of a shunt
Phenylketonuria	Autosomal recessive genetic disorder	Associated with metabolic problems in processing high-protein foods Can be controlled via restrictive diets implemented at birth
Prader-Willi Syndrome	Chromosomal error of the autosomal type	Associated with biological compulsion to excessive eating Obesity as a common secondary trait to retardation
Tay-Sachs Disease	Autosomal recessive genetic disorder	Highest risk for Ashkenazic Jewish persons Associated with severe disabilities and early mortality No known cure Prevention by means of genetic screening

The degree of impairment in adaptive functioning informs the educational planning. The individual education plan reflects the student's individual needs and builds on individual strengths.

Transition Considerations

Occupational success and community living skills are among the critical life adjustment variables that ensure successful transition into adulthood. At the Centre for Research and Education in Human Services in Ontario, Lord (1991) identified another crucial aspect: the empowerment of individuals with disabilities through their involvement in the community. However, the research on these variables does not inspire overconfidence.

TABLE 7.4   Characteristics and Implications of Intellectual Disabilities

Domain	Representative Problem Areas	Instructional Implications
Attention	Attention span (length of time on task) Focus (inhibition of distracting stimuli) Selective attention (discrimination of important stimulus characteristics)	Teach students how to actively monitor their attention (i.e., self-monitoring). Highlight salient cues.
Use of Mediational Strategies	Production of strategies to assist learning Organizing new information	Teach specific strategies (rehearsal, labelling, chunking). Involve students in active learning process (practise, apply, review). Stress meaningful content.
Memory	Short-term memory (i.e., over seconds, minutes)—common deficit area Long-term memory—usually more similar to that of persons who are nondisabled (once information has been learned)	Because strategy production is difficult, students need to be shown how to use specific strategies in order to proceed in an organized, well-planned manner. Stress meaningful content.
Generalized learning	Applying knowledge or skills to new tasks, problems, or situations Using previous experience to formulate rules that will help solve problems of a similar nature	Teach in multiple contexts. Reinforce generalization. Remind students to apply what they have learned.
Motivational considerations	External locus of control Outerdirectedness Lack of encouragement to achieve Failure set (expectancy of failure)	Create environment focused on success opportunities. Emphasize self-reliance. Promote self-management strategies. Encourage problem-solving strategies (vs. only correct responses).
Cognitive Development	Ability to engage in abstract thinking Symbolic thought, as exemplified by introspection and hypothesizing	Provide concrete examples in instruction. Encourage interaction between students and the environment, being responsive to their needs so that they may learn about themselves as they relate to the people and objects around them.
Language Development	Delayed acquisition of vocabulary and language rules Possible interaction with cultural variance and language dialects Speech disorders (more common than in general population)	Create environment that facilitates development and encourages verbal communication. Provide opportunities for students to interact with language. Provide opportunities for students to use language for a variety of purposes and with different audiences. Encourage student speech and active participation.
Sociobehavioural considerations	Social adjustment Problems in "everyday intelligence" (Greenspan, 1996) Self-concept Social acceptance Classroom behavioural difficulties (e.g., disruptions) Teach students to be aware of the importance of attention.	Promote social competence through direct instruction in social skills. Reinforce appropriate behaviours. Seek an understanding of reasons for inappropriate behaviour. Involve peers as classroom role models. Program for social acceptance. Use peers in reinforcing.

In *Disability Community and Society*, the Roeher Institute of Canada (1996, p. 42) notes that people with intellectual disabilities are generally poor: that is because of the difficulties encountered in finding paid employment outside the sheltered workshop setting. The Institute cites that "only 31% of people with intellectual disabilities have jobs; 61% of people with intellectual disabilities with jobs work in sheltered settings." According to CACL (2004), "People with intellectual disabilities face major barriers to decent jobs with living wages. When people lack access to education, volunteer and community opportunities in their childhood and youth, labour force exclusion is often the result in their adulthood. It is estimated that 65% of adults with intellectual disabilities are either unemployed or outside of the labour force."

More recent outcomes have been more optimistic when effective transition programs are in place: "There are many innovative adult literacy, training, and employment initiatives that are helping to build the capacity of community colleges, literacy programs, employers, and community services to ensure the adult education and workplace inclusion of people with intellectual disabilities" (CACL, 2004). Examples of the challenges of adulthood in terms of life demands are summarized in Table 7.5.

> **TEACHING TIP**
>
> Students with intellectual disabilities should be taught functional skills that will prepare them for success as adults.

TABLE 7.5   Major Life Demands

Domain	Subdomain	Sample Life Demands
Employment/ Education	General job skills	Seeking and securing a job Learning job skills Maintaining one's job
	General education/ training considerations	Gaining entry to postsecondary education/training settings (higher education, adult education, community education, trade/technical schools, military service) Finding financial support Utilizing academic and system survival skills (e.g., study skills, organizational skills, and time management)
	Employment setting	Recognizing job duties and responsibilities Exhibiting appropriate work habits/behaviour Getting along with employer and co-workers
Home and Family	Home management	Setting up household operations (e.g., initiating utilities) Cleaning dwelling Laundering and maintaining clothes and household items
	Financial management	Creating a general financial plan (e.g., savings, investments, retirement) Paying bills Obtaining government assistance when needed (e.g., medicare, food stamps, student loans)
	Family life	Preparing for marriage, family Maintaining physical/emotional health of family members Planning and preparing meals (menu, buying food, ordering take-out food, dining out)
Leisure Pursuits	Indoor activities	Performing individual physical activities (e.g., weight training, aerobics, dance, swimming, martial arts) Participating in group physical activities (e.g., racquetball, basketball)
	Outdoor activities	Engaging in general recreating activities (e.g., camping, sightseeing, picnicking)

FURTHER READING

For more information on students with intellectual disabilities and educational demands at the secondary level, read T. E. C. Smith and I. K. Puccini's article "Secondary Programming Issues," published in 1996 in volume 31 of *Education and Training in Mental Retardation and Developmental Disabilities* (pp. 320–327).

In general, the vast majority of adults with intellectual disabilities can obtain and maintain gainful employment. However, a number of critical factors influence their success. First, postschool adjustment hinges on their ability to demonstrate personal and social behaviours appropriate to the workplace. Second, the quality of the transition programming provided will predict subsequent success. Such programs recognize that programming must reflect a top-down perspective (i.e., from community considerations to school curriculum) that bases curriculum on the demands of the next environment in which the individual will live, work, socialize, and recreate.

Third, the workplace of the future poses special challenges. The more complex demands of the workplace will become increasingly problematic for this group. Many of the jobs that traditionally have been available to individuals with mental retardation (e.g., in the service industry) may be in shorter supply. Finally, individuals with mental retardation are likely to have increased leisure time. Thus an important component of transition planning should be preparing students to use their leisure time in rewarding and useful ways (Patton, Polloway, & Smith, 2000).

While general education teachers would be quite unlikely to have full responsibility for meeting the transitional needs of students with mental retardation, nevertheless this focus is one of the most critical curricular and instructional aspects of their needs. Patton and Dunn (1998) summarized the essential features of transition, highlighting the following:

▶ Transition efforts must start early and planning must be comprehensive.
▶ Decisions must balance what is ideal with what is possible.
▶ Active and meaningful student participation and family involvement are essential.
▶ Supports are beneficial and used by everyone.
▶ Community-based instructional experiences have a major impact on learning.
▶ The transition planning process should be viewed as a capacity-building activity.
▶ Transition planning is needed by all students.

Transition planning is critical to success for students with intellectual disabilities, and therefore school districts can profit significantly from analyzing the life outcomes of their graduates. Sitlington and Frank (1998) developed a practitioner's handbook for conducting follow-up studies that provides an appropriate approach to collecting such data.

Strategies for Curriculum and Instruction

The education of students with intellectual disabilities in inclusive settings is a challenge. Without question, however, educators must deliver quality programs, or else the prognosis for young adults with intellectual disabilities will not be positive.

Challenges for General Education

FURTHER READING

For more information on practices for successful inclusion of a student with intellectual disabilities in the regular classroom, read R. Freeze, Z. M. Lutfiyya, J. Van Walleghem, and M. C. Cozzual's article "The roles of non-disabled peers in promoting the social competence of students with intellectual disabilities in inclusive classrooms," published in 2004 in volume 14, issue 1 of *Exceptionality Education Canada.*

The data on postschool outcomes point out areas that teachers who work with students with intellectual disabilities in inclusive settings must address. These concerns should be kept in mind as curricula and instructional plans are developed and implemented in conjunction with special education teachers. Patton et al. (1996) identify four primary goals for individuals who have mild intellectual disabilities: productive employment, independence and self-sufficiency, life skills competence, and opportunity to participate successfully within the schools and the community. These goals should guide the educational program for these students.

Personal Spotlight

Graduates of Integrated Classrooms Hannah Lusthaus and Tina Lemieux

When asked what the best thing was about school, Hannah quips, "Graduation!"

At 22 Hannah and Tina, best friends for 19 years, are enjoying the freedom of having their own apartments. "I like being able to see my boyfriend whenever I want," says Hannah. "Yeah, all the time, all the time!" adds Tina, laughing. "No, no, I always make time for my best friend Tina!" "Not so much as for Tim," insists Tina. "I do, I do!" "Okay, Hahn... we both like to be with each other and our boyfriends."

Hannah and Tina both have an intellectual disability.

Dorothy, Tina's mother, tells how, as Tina grew up and they moved into different school board districts, the family's desire to have Tina included in the local community school and regular classroom was received with varying degrees of acceptance. "It was so different place to place. In high school, it was difficult but finally they tried something creative— they had Tina in the high achieving class and that worked very well. The kids were very accepting and Tina modelled her behaviour on theirs. It was great." Tina tells what she liked about school: "Being with other people I like, that is the best to me—a good reason for school."

Hannah's mother, Evy, tells about the struggle to have Hannah accepted into the regular class at the neighbourhood school during a time when other children with Hannah's disability were being sent to segregated schools. "It was difficult to achieve but once Hannah was allowed to attend, I found that most teachers were very successful by making down-to-earth common-sense adaptations that enabled Hannah to be a part of the class and to learn at her own level."

Both Tina and Hannah have moved on from being integrated in their neighbourhood schools for the majority of their schooling. They attended the John Abbott College work-study program after high school, and now both have jobs and live in their own apartments within a supportive apartment building. Tina works at a large pet store looking after the animals which she loves (even the iguanas!), and Hannah works at Concordia University, cataloguing CDs at the radio station and assisting with the Concordia basketball team. Hannah tells how, after her older sister and brother moved away from home, it was her turn to do it. Now that her brother is getting married, she and Tim are talking about it too. It is clear that she has every expectation that she will follow in the footsteps of her siblings—and she has!

However, it has not always been easy for Tina and Hannah. They are reluctant to talk about the difficulties they have had. Instead, they move on to what they liked. Hannah tells of one inclusion experience that meant a lot to her: "I had a bad experience. A bad time— one's enough. Usually, I liked the teachers and the classes and especially when I got good grades. But I remember this one guy, he was big and... uh... big and, not really a bully ("He was bossy," says Tina.) No! Not bossy, but mean. Tough and mean, mean, mean. ("That's a bully," says Tina.) No, no, not a bully, just big and tough and mean. Anyway, uh... my teacher uh she was being mean, really mean to me," Hannah says, "and this big tough guy he did something about it. The big tough guy he went and told her off! It was the one person... I can't believe this big tough guy and he did that... stuck up for me!" (Says Tina, "Yeah, yeah, that's good.")

Tina adds, "I had wonderful teachers. They gave me a lot of good skills. Remember with Linda, we learned to read and you know, Hannah, what was it?" "Reading," says Hannah. "No, no, with Linda the other... you know, not read..." "Count?" asks Hannah. "Yes, yes, thank you, Miss Hannah!" replies Tina. "Numbers. That was good. But some bad was... kids criticizing me, like 'What is *she* doing here?!' You know people being mean, calling me names... I had a lot of good experiences."

If you were to talk to Tina and Hannah, you would be amazed at their resilience, their focus on the positive. You would also be filled with a good feeling about what is possible for students with an intellectual disability.

In terms of *employment,* teachers should build students' career awareness and help them see how academic content relates to applied situations; at the secondary level, this thrust should include training in specific job skills. This concern should be the primary focus of vocational educators who work with these students.

In terms of *independence* and *self-sufficiency,* young adults with mild intellectual disabilities need to become as responsible for themselves as possible. As Miller (1995)

TEACHING TIP

Instructional activities for students with intellectual disabilities should focus on development of self-determination skills.

states, the educational goal "is to develop self-directed learners who can address their own wants and concerns and can advocate for their goals and aspirations" (p. 12). Thus, successful inclusion of students who have intellectual disabilities depends on the ability of teachers, peers, and the curriculum to create a climate of empowerment. One essential element of empowerment is self-determination (Wehmeyer, 1993, 1994). As Wehmeyer (1993, p. 16) noted:

> Self-determination refers to the attitudes and abilities necessary to act as the primary causal agent in one's life, and to make choices and decisions regarding one's quality of life free from undue external influence or interference.

A series of specific behaviours constitute self-determination. For example, Zhang (2001) included the following: "making choices, making decisions, solving problems, setting and attaining goals, being independent, evaluating our performance, self-studying, speaking up for self, having internal motivations, believing in one's own abilities, being aware of personal strengths and weaknesses, and applying strengths to overcome weaknesses" (p. 339).

A third key consideration is the inclusion of *life skills* in the curriculum, focusing on the importance of competence in everyday activities. This area includes, but is not limited to, use of community resources, home and family activities, social and interpersonal skills, health and safety skills, use of leisure time, and participation in the community as a citizen (e.g., compliance with legal and cultural standards). With the increased commitment to inclusion, a particularly challenging consideration for both general and special educators will be ways to include a life skills and transitional focus within the general education curriculum beginning at the elementary school level and reflected throughout formal schooling.

A critical concern relative to school and community inclusion and to life adjustment is the acquisition of social skills. A useful model has been developed by Sargent (1998). Skill areas include classroom-related skills; school-building–related skills; personal skills; interaction initiative skills; interaction response skills; community-related skills and work-related skills.

A fourth consideration, successful *community involvement* requires that students experience inclusive environments. Students with intellectual disabilities can learn to participate in school and community by being included in general education classrooms. Although school inclusion is viewed by some as an end in itself, it is better viewed as a condition that can provide instruction and training for success in subsequent inclusive community activities. As a necessary step toward this goal, individuals with intellectual disabilities should be included in general education programs to the maximum extent possible.

Finally, consideration must be given to the perspectives of the individuals themselves about educational programs and their outcomes. To provide a picture of the views of the outcomes of interventions with persons with mental retardation, Fox and Emerson (2001) solicited input from persons with mental retardation, parents, clinical psychologists, nurses, program managers, and direct support workers. The focus was on two groups of individuals with mental retardation who also had challenging behaviours: children and young adults living at home and young adults in group homes. The most salient outcomes for these two groups identified by stakeholders present an interesting contrast. While program managers, nurses, and psychiatrists, for example, stressed reductions in the severity of challenging behaviours for both groups of individuals, persons with mental retardation from both groups identified increased friendships and relationships as their priority outcome goals.

FURTHER READING

For more information on best practices for promoting and supporting self-determination, read the *Self-Determination Sourcebook* and the *Self-Determination Handbook* by R. Freeze and M. Updyke, published in 2000 by the Canadian Council for Exceptional Children (CCEC), available at http://canadian.cec.sped.org/publication_traits.htm.

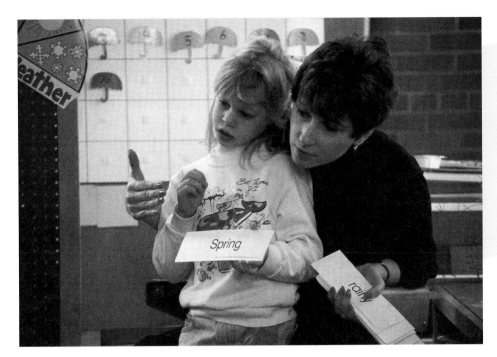

A key to successful inclusion for students with intellectual disabilities is provision of appropriate supports.

General Considerations for Inclusion

The key to including students with intellectual disabilities in the general education classroom is providing necessary and appropriate supports, such as personal supports, natural supports (e.g., parents, friends), support services, and technical supports. This model, **supported education**, assumes that individuals should be maintained in inclusive classroom settings to the maximum degree possible and supported in those locations in order to ensure successful learning.

Strains have occurred during the transition to the supports model, because a too frequent tendency has been simply to physically place the student in the classroom, rather than achieve the more appropriate goal of supported education. Inclusion should involve supported education and focus on welcoming and involving persons with intellectual disabilities in the general education classroom. Merely placing students in general education without social integration and active classroom participation is not the intent of inclusion and will be far less likely to result in positive gains for students. Likewise, adults with intellectual disabilities who live in the community but do not participate in community activities do not fulfill the true spirit of inclusion.

Wehmeyer, Lattin, and Agram (2001) developed a model related to access to the general curriculum for individuals with mental retardation. Presented in Figure 7.1, the model reflects the fact that a series of key decisions needs to be made in curriculum development in order for students to succeed in the general education classroom. Particular emphases include the use of assistive technology, the development of curricular adaptations (see the next section), the augmentation of the curriculum (to include emphases on strategy training, self-determination), and the availability of curricular alternatives (which stress a more functional emphasis often not present in the general curriculum).

TEACHING TIP

The supports model emphasizes providing whatever supports are necessary to enable a student with intellectual disabilities to succeed in a general education setting.

CROSS-REFERENCE

See Chapters 1 and 2 to review the purposes of including students with disabilities in general education settings.

FIGURE 7.1

A Model to Gain Access to
the General Curriculum

From "Achieving Access to the
General Curriculum for Students
with Mental Retardation: A
Curriculum Decision-Making
Model" (pp. 327–342) by M. L.
Wehmeyer, D. Lattin, & M. Agram,
2001, *Education and Training in
Mental Retardation and
Developmental Disabilities, 36.*

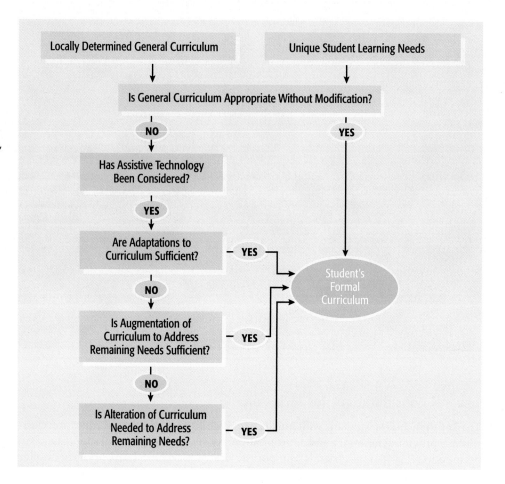

Classroom Accommodations for Students with Intellectual Disabilities

As inclusion becomes a more common alternative for students with disabilities in general, and individuals with intellectual disabilities in particular, the regular curriculum has become the "program of choice" for more students with mental retardation. Review of data on the preferences of general education teachers concerning modifications and adaptations for such students indicates that preferred adaptations typically revolve more around changes in instructional delivery systems and response modes (e.g., testing adaptations such as extended time) than in changes in the actual curriculum or the standards associated with the curricular content (e.g., Polloway, Epstein, & Bursuck, 2002; Polloway, Bursuck, Jayanthi, Epstein, & Nelson, 1996; see also Chapter 13). Therefore, to the extent that these observations are verified, it is likely that a specialized curriculum may less commonly be available for students with mild mental retardation (Patton et al., 2000). Nevertheless, given the preceding discussion, teachers need to be aware of the importance of a functional focus within the curriculum in order to enhance learning and adult outcomes for students with intellectual disability.

Table 7.4 (see page 178) presented an outline of the common characteristics associated with intellectual disabilities, along with their implications for instruction. When they are considered collectively, certain instructional themes emerge. Teachers should focus on accommodations that

> ensure attention to relevant task demands.
> teach ways to learn content while teaching content itself.
> focus on content that is meaningful to the students, to promote learning as well as to facilitate application.
> provide training that crosses multiple contexts.
> offer opportunities for active involvement in the learning process.

One promising approach that has merit for all students and can particularly benefit students with intellectual disabilities is the use of cognitively oriented instructional methods. Based on the premise that learning problems experienced by low-achieving students are due more to a lack of knowledge regarding the processes involved in independent learning than of any underlying deficits, these approaches incorporate learning strategies, metacognition, and cognitive behaviour modification (e.g., self-monitoring) as exciting alternatives to traditional instructional practices. Their potential for students with mild intellectual disabilities is clear (see Polloway, Patton, Smith, & Buck, 1997).

Curricular adaptations are likewise important to consider. In general, the key focus should be on relevant and meaningful curricular content that students can master and apply to their current and future lives. Teachers should focus on the subsequent environments for which students will prepare (in terms of learning, working, residing) as a basis for curriculum design. The subsequent-environments rationale has applicability across the school levels as individuals prepare for successful transitions and life challenges. Most important is the assurance that the secondary school curriculum prepares students with intellectual disabilities (as well as all students) for adulthood, whether that means further education, job placement, or independent living.

To make the curriculum appropriate for students with intellectual disabilities, specific adaptations can enhance learning and increase relevance. One useful format, developed by Wehman (1997) (see Table 7.6), offers useful ideas for curriculum modification.

TEACHING TIP

The use of peer supports can greatly enhance the success of students with intellectual disabilities in general education settings.

Technological Considerations

Assistive technology can further enhance classroom adaptations. Although students with intellectual disabilities can benefit from a variety of technological applications, the

TABLE 7.6   Typical and Modified Curriculum Outcomes for Students with Intellectual Disabilities

Grade Level	Typical Outcomes	Modified Outcomes
Grade 2: Language Arts	Learn 10 spelling words per week and be able to use them correctly in sentences.	Identify 15 safety words (e.g., stop, poison) and functional words (e.g., men, women).
Grade 4: Language Arts	Read a book and write a two-page report, using correct grammar, punctuation, and spelling.	Listen to a taped book, tape a personal reaction to the story, and illustrate the story.
Grade 6: Social Studies	Locate all 10 provinces and 3 territories on a map, and name their capitals.	Locate own province/territory and those immediately adjacent to it, and name the capitals.
Grade 8: Social Studies	Name and explain the functions of the government in power, the Opposition, and the Senate.	Describe the jobs of the prime minister, the leader of the Opposition, and a member of the Senate.
Grade 10: Science	Describe the body systems of three different mammals, and identify the major components and functions of each system.	Label diagrams of the human body, identifying each body system and its purpose and naming major body organs.

key concern is that technology be used in a way that effectively enhances learning. Hasselbring and Goin (1993) note that technology can be used to facilitate the acquisition of new skills, the development of fluency and proficiency, maintenance of skills over time, and generalization to new situations. Conscious attention to the use of technology for each of these four respective stages of learning will greatly enhance the effectiveness of technological approaches in supporting classroom adaptations. The nearby Technology Today feature describes how assistive technology devices can affect the learning environment.

Promoting Inclusive Practices for Students with Intellectual Disabilities

Beyond the curricular and instructional considerations summarized previously, several other considerations are central to the successful inclusion of students with intellectual disabilities. The first concern is the creation of a sense of community in the school in general and the classroom in particular. As noted earlier, successful inclusion represents supported education—an environment where students succeed because they are welcomed, encouraged, and involved (i.e., supported) in their learning.

The challenge for teachers seeking to successfully include students with intellectual disabilities thus reaches beyond the students' acquisition of, for example, specific academic skills. Rather, it requires finding ways to provide a "belonging place" for them in the

---

Assistive Technology

Assistive technology can be low- or high-tech devices designed to remove barriers or provide practical solutions to common everyday problems.... [Such] devices can be applied in the classroom to assist a student with learning curriculum content or in a community setting to promote skill development and participation.

Assistive technology can include such complex devices as (1) an environmental control unit to allow an individual with little or no mobility to control his or her environment (e.g., turn on the lights), (2) a voice-activated computer to allow an individual with mobility or sensory impairments to input data on a computer and receive output information, (3) augmentative communication systems to allow an individual with poor speech to be able to communicate with others (e.g., electronic communication aids), and (4) microswitches to allow an individual to perform a more complex task by reducing the number of steps to

complete it to one press on the switch or to allow someone with poor motor skills to access something by touching a very large switch pad as opposed to a small button or lever. In addition, switches can be activated by a number of means, such as sound, air, light, or movement, and are very versatile as to the functions they can perform.

Assistive technology can also include low-tech devices or modifications that can be very inexpensive and easy to apply, such as (1) a reach device to assist an individual with picking things off the floor or taking something off a high shelf, (2) a precoded push button phone to allow an individual with poor memory to complete a call to an important or frequently used number by lightly touching a large colour-coded button, (3) audiotape instruction to allow an individual with cognitive or

sensory impairments to have access to the instructions, directions, or classroom materials in a format that can be repeated as often as necessary to either learn or perform a task, and (4) a holder made out of wood with suction cups on the bottom that will keep a bowl or pan in place to allow an individual to mix ingredients using only one hand.

The range of high- and low-tech devices to assist with completing an activity or just to make the task easier is virtually endless. Many of these devices are commercially available while others can oftentimes be developed by any interested persons. The major ingredients for developing useful assistive technology devices are creativity, open-mindedness, and resourcefulness.

Adapted from "Severe Mental Retardation," by P. Wehman and W. Parent. In *Exceptional Individuals in School, Community, and Work*, edited by P. Wehman, 1997, pp. 170–171. Austin, TX: Pro-Ed. Used by permission.

general education classroom. Such a place can be created through friendships, a key priority outcome as expressed by persons with mental retardation (Fox & Emerson, 2001).

Despite the broad support for inclusion, it does bring with it the potential loss of friendships present in traditional, self-contained classes. For example, Stainback, Stainback, East, and Sapon-Shevin (1994) note the concern of adolescents (and their parents) over finding dating partners in general education classes. Teachers should be sensitive to this consideration and promote an environment in which the benefits of friendships can be realized.

A helpful strategy for promoting social acceptance for students (and young adults) with intellectual disabilities involves "circles of support," or "circles of friends." The nearby Inclusion Strategies feature discusses an example of such a program. As teachers

Circles of Friends in Schools

Marsha Forest came away from her Joshua Committee experiences as if she had put on a better pair of glasses. Her position as a professor of special education suddenly seemed less important to her. She spent long hours on the road helping school boards, principals, and teachers to see how everybody can experience richness when someone with a disability is placed in a regular classroom and the so-called regular students are encouraged to form a circle of friends around that person.

Forest always believed in getting teachers down to meticulous detail when it came to educating persons with disabilities. Now, however, she saw that some of the most valuable educational steps can come *naturally* from regular classmates, if the right conditions exist in the classroom.

She also knew that parents and teachers fear peer group pressure. After all, when kids get together these days, they can give themselves quite an education—one that often shapes lives more powerfully than adults can shape them. But peer group education doesn't always lead to belligerence and destruction and drugs. It can lead to caring and nurturing and helping others do healthy things they had never done before.

This twist, however, generated fears in some teachers when it dawned on them that a circle of friends might foster better growth and development in a student than they were capable of teaching.

And so Forest moved into regular schools and worked hard at

1. helping boards and principals understand the circles-of-friends process.
2. finding a teacher and class willing to include a person with a disability.
3. helping the regular teacher handle any initial fears about the venture.
4. letting the teacher and class call the shots as much as possible.
5. providing strong support persons who would assist only when they really were needed.
6. then finding a handful of kids willing to work at being friends with their classmate with the disability.

"The first placement in a school is the toughest," she said. "After that, it's usually easy to include others."

Forest sees building a circle of friends as a person-by-person process, not an all-encompassing program. So she focuses on students with disabilities one at a time, and sets up a framework that enables a circle to surround that person.

Because no two settings are alike, she watches as the circle, the regular teacher, and the rest of the students develop and co-ordinate their own routines for helping. Then, never predicting an outcome, she waits. And when new learning takes place in the person with the disability, Forest moves in and makes all the students, the teacher, the principal—even the board members—feel simply great.

According to her, the average school can handle up to 12 of these arrangements. After that, the efficiency of the process may diminish.

She doubts that circles of friends will work in every school. "If a school is all screwed up," she said, "and if it has lost its zest and commitment for really helping kids learn—forget it. On the other hand, I'm sure that circles of friends can help make a good school—and especially the kids—better. Then coming to school takes on fresh values and meaning. Some enjoy coming to school as they never did before."

Adapted from *Circles of Friends: People with Disabilities and Their Friends Enrich the Lives of One Another* (pp. 39–40), by R. Perske, 1988, Nashville, TN: Abingdon Press.

consider developing such systems, they should not overlook the benefits to students who are not disabled, which may include enhanced attitudes, personal growth, and a sense of civic responsibility in addition to the benefits of friendship (Hughes et al., 2001).

Final Thoughts

TEACHING TIP

Curricular decisions for students with intellectual disabilities should always be made with the student's future needs in mind.

As special and general education teachers jointly develop and implement educational programs for students with intellectual disabilities, they should keep in mind that these students require a comprehensive, broad-based curriculum to meet their needs. The most effective programs will provide appropriate academic instruction, adapted to facilitate learning. However, the curriculum cannot solely be academic in orientation, but rather should focus on developing social skills and transition skills to facilitate the students' success in general education classrooms and subsequent integration into the community.

In making curricular choices, teachers will have to consider how responsive the general education classroom can be to the needs of students with intellectual disabilities. The ultimate goal is not simply school inclusion but rather community or "life" inclusion; the curriculum that achieves that purpose most effectively is the most appropriate one. As Cassidy and Stanton (1959) suggested nearly four decades ago, the key question in evaluating the effectiveness of programs for students with intellectual disabilities is *effective for what?* What is it the schools are to impart to the students? The challenge of inclusion for students with intellectual disabilities is to ensure that the curriculum they pursue prepares them for their future.

Summary

- The concept of intellectual disability has variant meanings to professionals and the lay public.
- The three central dimensions of the definition are lower intellectual functioning, deficits or limitations in adaptive skills, and an onset prior to age 18.
- The 1992 AAMR definition retains the three dimensions but also stresses the importance of four assumptions: cultural and linguistic diversity, an environmental context for adaptive skills, the strengths of individuals as well as their limitations, and the promise of improvement over time. A revised definition (2002) has further updated work in this area.
- Common practice in the field has been to speak of three general levels of intellectual disability—mild, moderate and severe—but emerging efforts in classification stress levels of needed supports rather than levels of disability.
- Social competence is a critical component of instructional programs for students with mental retardation. Teaching social skills can have a positive effect on successful inclusion both in school and in the community.
- Educational programs must be outcomes-oriented and attend to transitional concerns so that students receive the appropriate training to prepare them for subsequent environments. The curriculum should thus have a top-down orientation.

- Attention difficulties can be addressed by modifying instruction to highlight relevant stimuli and by teaching students to monitor their own attention.
- Teachers should teach not only content but also mediation strategies that facilitate learning. Examples include rehearsal, classification, and visual imagery.
- Memory problems respond to mediation strategies (as above) and to an emphasis on content that is meaningful and relevant.
- Cognitive development for students with intellectual disabilities can be enhanced by emphasizing active interaction with the environment and concrete experiences.
- Many students with a history of failure have an external locus of control, which can be enhanced by an emphasis on successful experiences and by reinforcement for independent work.
- To enhance language development, teachers should provide a facilitative environment, structure opportunities for communication, and encourage speech.
- Opportunities for inclusion are essential and should focus on social benefits such as friendship while not neglecting curricular needs.

Resources

Hileman, Camilla. (1997). *Point! click! & learn!!!* Arlington, TX: Future Horizons Publishers.

Here is a user-friendly guide to educational software programs for individuals with developmental disabilities.

British Columbia Ministry of Education, Special Programs Branch. (1996). *Students with intellectual disabilities: A resource guide for teachers.* Victoria: Author.

Saskatchewan Learning, Special Education Branch. (2001). *Creating opportunities for students with intellectual or multiple disabilities.* Regina, SK: Author.

Teachers will find these very practical resources for supporting their work with students with intellectual disabilities.

Weblinks

Canadian Association for Community Living (CACL)
www.cacl.ca/
The CACL advocates the full inclusion of individuals with intellectual disabilities in the community. The Association's website provides information, supports, and leads on other websites focused on inclusion. Checking it out is essential if you have questions regarding Canadian law about inclusion of individuals with disabilities and transition to the workplace or want to reach a provincial or territorial association.

Roeher Institute
www.roeher.ca
As Canada's leading organization to promote the equality, participation, and self-determination of people with intellectual and other disabilities, the Institute examines the causes of marginalization and provides research, information, and social development opportunities. It states, "If you are looking for a contact person, an organization, articles or books on a particular topic in the disability field, lists of resources, examples of innovative inclusionary practices, annotated bibliographies—in other words, information of any kind to support the inclusion of people with disabilities—we have it, or we can help locate it." The website is a must visit for all individuals working with people with disabilities.

TASH: Disability Advocacy Worldwide
www.tash.org/
Here is an excellent site for learning about the disability rights movement and finding links to other Web sites relevant to a variety of exceptionalities. "TASH" used to stand for The Association for the Severely Handicapped. Although the Association no longer uses the title, it has retained the acronym. TASH is an international association of people with disabilities, their family members, other advocates, and professionals. TASH's mission and commitment is to achieving full inclusion and participation of persons with disabilities in all aspects of life. Its website provides a wealth of information relevant to achieving that goal.

American Association of Mental Retardation
www.aamr.org/
The website of this Association, which has chapters in both Canada and the United States, provides information, resources, related links, and a bookstore of current books in the area of intellectual disability.

Canadian Council for Exceptional Children (CCEC)
http://canadian.cec.sped.org/
CCEC has been an active member of the International Council for Exceptional Children since it was founded in 1922. CCEC advocates for exceptional students, including those with intellectual disabilities.

8 Teaching Students with Sensory Impairments

Chapter Objectives

After reading this chapter, you should be able to

- explain the nature of low-incidence disabilities
- define hearing impairment and visual impairment
- describe educationally relevant characteristics of students with hearing impairments and visual impairments
- describe adaptations, accommodations, and modifications for students with hearing impairments and visual impairments

*I*t was only the end of September, but Ana was already beginning to fall behind most of her peers in Grade 2. Although she was promoted at the end of Grade 1, she did not acquire most of the skills necessary for success in Grade 2.

For the first half of Grade 1, Ana had tried very hard. She wanted to learn to read like her classmates, but seemed always to miss out on sounding letters and words correctly. According to her teacher, Ms. Pryor, Ana also appeared to daydream a lot. The teacher frequently had to go to Ana's desk to get her attention when giving directions and assignments. By the middle of Grade 1, Ana seemed to be giving up. Her efforts always fell short. Her spelling was poor, and her reading skills were not improving. She began having behaviour problems, which Ms. Pryor attributed to the influence of her older brother, who was always getting into trouble. Ana's parents were interested but did not have any answers. They said that Ana was in her own world at home and often did not respond to what was happening around her. In addition to Ana's poor academic skills and behaviour problems, she also had difficulties with her peers. She was not very popular, and some of the other students made fun of her poor articulation of certain words.

Ms. James, Ana's new Grade 2 teacher, decided to refer Ana for vision and hearing screening. Sure enough, Ana was found to have a hearing loss in both ears. Although the loss was not significant enough to warrant specialized placement, it did suggest that a hearing aid might be useful.

Thanks to the awareness of Ms. James, Ana's hearing loss was detected before she experienced more failure. Unfortunately, she had missed much of what she should have learned during Grade 1 and kindergarten, probably because of the hearing impairment.

Questions to Consider

1. Should schools routinely screen kindergarten and Grade 1 students for hearing and vision problems? Why or why not?

2. What can Ana's Grade 2 teacher do to help her overcome the problems created by the late identification of her hearing impairment?

Introduction

As with other students with exceptionalities, there remains some debate regarding the best setting in which to provide services to students with **sensory impairments** (e.g., visual and hearing impairments). Historically, many students with sensory impairments were served in residential settings. However, today most students with sensory impairments are placed in general education settings. Most are capable of handling the academic and social demands of these settings. However, for these students to receive an appropriate education, a variety of accommodations may be needed, including the use of sophisticated equipment for communicating or listening. Students with sensory impairments may also need the support of additional personnel (e.g., an *interpreter* or *Braille instructor*).

In order to provide appropriate adaptations and/or accommodations, teachers must have accurate information about how to modify their classrooms and adapt instruction to meet student needs. In addition, they need to understand the psychosocial aspects of these types of disabilities. For some students with sensory problems, special consultants may also be needed to assist general education teachers. Ultimately, teachers must feel comfortable and confident that they can address the range of needs these students present.

Sensory impairments are considered *low-incidence* disabilities, since there are not large numbers of these students in the school population. Weber (1994) cites data suggesting that 0.06 percent of the school population are identified as having a visual impairment and 0.14 percent as having a hearing impairment. These groups represent a very small percentage of all students who have a disability.

However, having only one student with a sensory impairment in a classroom may seem overwhelming, as this student may require a variety of modifications in classroom management and adaptations and/or accommodations in certain instructional practices. Students with both vision and hearing losses present significant challenges for educators; *multisensory impairments* will be covered in Chapter 9.

CONSIDER THIS

Should students whose only disability is hearing or visual impairment be segregated in residential schools, often many miles away from their families?

Hearing Impairment

Hearing impairment is a hidden disability—an observer cannot typically tell from looking at physical features alone that a person's hearing is impaired. However, in any context where communicative skills are needed, hearing limitations become evident.

Students with a hearing loss pose a variety of challenges to the general classroom teacher. When students with profound hearing losses are placed in general education classes, they may need major accommodations (e.g., an interpreter).

The number of students who have some degree of hearing loss (i.e., mild to severe) is more noteworthy, because these students can function in general education settings more easily when certain accommodations are provided. In order to achieve this purpose, it is critical for teachers to understand the nature of hearing impairments and to know how to address the needs associated with these conditions. In addition to these students, other students may have a minimal hearing loss. These students have hearing losses that are not severe enough to be eligible for special education services; however, they are at a distinct disadvantage in the general education classroom if the teacher does not recognize their problem (Kaderavek & Pukulski, 2002). Students who have received cochlear implants may also be included in the regular classroom.

The importance of language acquisition and usage to the development of cognitive abilities and achievement in academic subject areas is unassailable (Polloway, Miller, & Smith, 2003). While the greatest effect of a hearing impairment is on a student's ability to hear someone speak, "its impact on communication development dramatically alters social and academic skill acquisition" (Brackett, 1997, p. 355). Language is a dominant consideration when discussing appropriate education for students with hearing losses (Mayer, Akamatsu, & Stewart, 2002).

Basic Concepts about Hearing Impairment

The following sections provide basic information on hearing impairments. Teachers who build a solid working knowledge in this area can teach more effectively and communicate more clearly with other professionals and with families.

Hearing Impairment Defined The fact that a number of different terms are associated with hearing loss often causes confusion. Three terms frequently encountered in print and in professional conversation are *hearing impairment, deafness,* and *hard of hearing.*

1. *Hearing impairment* is the generic term that has frequently been used to cover the entire range of hearing loss.
2. *Deafness* describes a hearing loss that is so severe that speech cannot be understood through the ear alone, with or without aids.
3. *Hard of hearing* describes individuals who have a hearing loss that makes it difficult, but not impossible, to understand speech through the ear alone, with or without a hearing aid. (Moores, 2001)

More detailed definitions of the terms *deaf* and *hard of hearing* are provided by the American Speech-Language and Hearing Association (ASHA). ASHA defines the term *deaf* as "a hearing disorder that limits an individual's aural/oral communication performance to the extent that the primary sensory input for communication may be other than the auditory channel," whereas the term *hard of hearing* is defined as "a hearing disorder, whether fluctuating or permanent, which adversely affects an individual's ability to communicate. The hard-of-hearing individual relies on the auditory channel as the primary sensory input for communication" (ASHA, 1993). ASHA's (1993) definition of the term *deaf* is supported by the Canadian Association of the Deaf (CAD), whose position is that "deafness is medically defined by the extent of loss of functional hearing and by dependence upon visual communication" (CAD, 2002).

Hearing loss is often measured in decibel loss (dB). Individuals with losses from 26 to 90 dB are considered hard of hearing, whereas those with losses greater than 90 dB are classified as profoundly hearing impaired. Minimal hearing loss, which can also cause problems for students, is defined as a loss of between 16 and 25 decibels (Kaderavek & Pakulski, 2002).

Classification of Hearing Impairment Hearing loss can be categorized in several ways. Typically, a hearing loss is described by three attributes: the type of hearing loss, the degree of the hearing loss (e.g., minimal to profound), and the configuration of the hearing loss (e.g., flat, sloping, reverse, bilateral or unilateral, fluctuating or stable) (ASHA, 2004d). When describing hearing loss in terms of the part of the auditory system that is damaged, there are three types of hearing loss: conductive hearing loss, sensorineural hearing loss, and mixed hearing loss (Northern & Downs, 2002). Table 8.1 summarizes the audiological, communicational, and educational implications for each type of loss. A **conductive hearing loss**

Occurs when sound is not conducted efficiently through the outer and middle ears, including the ear canal, eardrum, and the tiny bones, or ossicles, of the middle ear. Conductive hearing loss usually involves a reduction in sound level, or the ability to hear faint sounds. This type of hearing loss can often be corrected through medicine or surgery. (ASHA, 2004d)

For example, a conductive loss may be the result of impacted ear wax (**cerumen**), a build up of fluid in the middle ear, or ear infections. The most common type of hearing loss in children is **otitis media** (ASHA, 2004d). "Otitis media is an inflammation of the middle ear (the area behind the ear drum) that is usually associated with the build up of fluid. The fluid may or may not be infected. Symptoms, severity, frequency, and length of the condition vary" (ASHA, 2004d). A build up of fluid in the middle ear, whether infected or not, typically results in a **fluctuating** hearing loss. This type of loss may adversely impact speech and language development in young children, since children would be missing out on speech and language models and experiences (e.g., missing fragments of what was said by a speaker). A fluctuating hearing loss may also severely impact academic achievement in school-age children. For example, students may not always hear verbal exchanges taking place during teacher and peer interactions. Students may, therefore, only receive part of the information that was presented or discussed in the classroom.

A second type of hearing loss is a **sensorineural hearing loss**. A sensorineural hearing loss

> Occurs when there is damage to the inner ear (**cochlea**).... Sensorineural hearing loss involves a reduction in sound level, or ability to hear faint sounds, but also affects speech understanding or ability to hear clearly.... Sensorineural hearing loss cannot be corrected medically or surgically. It is a permanent loss. (ASHA, 2004d)

For example, a sensorineural hearing loss may be the result of an injury sustained at birth, genetic syndromes, viruses, head trauma, aging, exposure to noise, or tumours (ASHA, 2004d). As with a conductive hearing loss, a sensorineural hearing loss can adversely impact a child's speech and language development and academic achievement. A third type of hearing loss is a **mixed hearing loss**. A mixed hearing loss occurs when both a conductive and sensorineural hearing loss are present (Northern & Downs, 2002).

A disorder that is associated with hearing loss, but typically present in individuals without a hearing impairment, is an **auditory processing disorder** (APD). An auditory processing disorder (APD)

> May be broadly defined as a deficit in the processing of information that is specific to the auditory modality. The problem may be exacerbated in unfavourable acoustic environments. It may be associated with difficulties in listening, speech understanding, language development, and learning. In its pure form, however, it is conceptualized as a deficit in the processing of auditory input. (Abel, S., cited in Jerger & Musiek, 2000, p. 468)

For example, an auditory processing disorder may be the result of head trauma, stroke, or congenital brain damage "that can cause problems understanding what is being said, even though sensorineural and conductive hearing is normal" (Flexer, 1999, p. 69). A child with an auditory processing disorder may have difficulty understanding speech or directions (especially in environments in which there is excessive activity and/or noise), decoding letters, sound blending or spelling, or may seem to "mishear" and substitute similar sounding words (Minnesota Department of Education, 2003). Although auditory processing disorders and attention deficit/hyperactivity disorders are two separate disorders, they possess similar characteristics (e.g., inattentive, distracted). It is important to note, however, that these disorders can occur independently or they can coexist (Keller & Tillery, 2002).

Prevalence and Causes of Hearing Impairment   Only about 0.14 percent of school-age children are served in special education programs for students with hearing

---

FURTHER READING

To learn more about the similarities between auditory processing disorders and attention-deficit disorders (ADD and AD/HD), refer to the document "Introduction to Auditory Processing Disorders" on the Minnesota Department of Education's website: http://education.state.mn.us/content/059872.pdf.

CONSIDER THIS

Is it important for teachers to know the type of hearing loss experienced by a student? Why or why not?

TABLE 8.1 Symptoms Associated with Conductive Hearing Loss; Unilateral Hearing Loss; Mild, Bilateral Sensorineural Hearing Loss; and Moderate-to-Severe Bilateral Sensorineural Hearing Loss

	Audiological	Communicative	Educational
Conductive Hearing Loss	Hearing loss 30 dB (range 10–50 dB); Poor auditory reception; Degraded and inconsistent speech signal; Difficulty understanding under adverse listening conditions; Impaired speech discrimination; Hearing loss overlays developmental requirement for greater stimulus intensity before infants can respond to and discriminate between speech; Inability to organize auditory information consistently	Difficulty forming linguistic categories (plurals, tense); Difficulty in differentiating word boundaries, phoneme boundaries; Receptive language delay; Expressive language delay; Cognitive delay	Lower achievement test scores; Lower verbal IQ; Poorer reading and spelling performance; Higher frequency of enrolment in special support classes in school; Lower measures of social maturity
Unilateral Hearing Loss	Hearing loss moderate to profound; Impaired auditory localization; Difficulty understanding speech in presence of competing noise; Loss of binaural advantage: binaural summation, binaural release from masking	Tasks involving language concepts may be depressed	Lags in academic achievement: reading, spelling, arithmetic; Verbally based learning difficulties; High rate of grade repetition; Self-described: embarrassment, annoyance, confusion, helplessness; Less independence in the classroom
Mild Bilateral Sensorineural Hearing Loss	Hearing loss 15–20 dB; Speech recognition depressed; Auditory discrimination depressed; Amplification considered: FM systems, classroom amplification	Potential problems in articulation; Problems in auditory attention; Problems in auditory memory; Problems in auditory comprehension; Possible delays in expressive oral language; Impact on syntax and semantics	Impact on vocabulary development; Lowered academic achievement: arithmetic problem solving, math concepts, vocabulary, reading comprehension; Educational delays progress systematically with age
Moderate-to-Severe Bilateral Sensorineural Hearing Loss	Hearing loss 41 dB–90 dB; Noise and reverberation significantly affect listening and understanding; Audiologic management: essentials, amplification recommendations, monitor hearing for: –otitis media –sudden changes in hearing –progressive hearing loss	Deficits in speech perception; Deficits in speech production (mild-to-moderate articulation problems); Language deficits from slight to significant: syntax, morphology, semantics, pragmatics; Vocabulary deficits	Slight to significant deficits in literacy (reading and writing); Deficits in academic achievement; High rate of academic failure; Immaturity; Feelings of isolation and exclusion; Special education supports needed

From "Hearing Loss and Its Effect," by A. O. Diefendorf. In *Hearing Care for Children*, edited by F. N. Martin and J. G. Clark, 1996, p. 5. Boston: Allyn & Bacon. Used by permission.

CROSS-REFERENCE

Review the etiological sections of Chapters 3 through 9, and compare the causes of hearing impairments and other disabilities. There are many common factors.

impairments in Canada. Hearing impairments become more prevalent as individuals get older; therefore, the number of people experiencing hearing loss in the total population is higher than the number found in schools. It is estimated that between 2 and 5 percent of the total population has some degree of hearing loss.

Many different factors can lead to hearing impairments. These include genetic causes (Moores, 2001); developmental anomalies (Clark & Jaindl, 1996); toxic reaction to drugs, infections, prematurity, and Rh incompatibility (Moores, 2001); birth trauma (Chase, Hall, & Werkhaven, 1996); and allergies (Lang, 1998). Knowing the specific cause of a hearing impairment is usually less important for school personnel, since the cause rarely affects interventions needed by students.

Characteristics of Students with Hearing Impairment   The characteristics of students with hearing impairment vary greatly. Four categories of characteristics are especially meaningful to the classroom setting: (1) psychological, (2) communicational, (3) academic, and (4) social-emotional. Specific characteristics that fall into each of these general categories are listed in Table 8.2. (Table 8.1 listed characteristics associated with types and degrees of hearing losses.)

Identification, Assessment, and Eligibility   The ease of identifying students with hearing impairment is related to the degree of hearing loss. Students with severe losses are more easily recognized, while those with mild losses may go unrecognized for many years or even their entire school career (Kaderavek & Pakulski, 2002). Teachers should be aware of certain indicators of possible hearing loss and refer students who show these signs for a comprehensive assessment (Stewart & Kluwin, 2001). Teachers should consider referring a student for a comprehensive audiological evaluation if some of the following behaviours are present (Kaderavek & Pakulski, 2002; Moores, 2001; Stewart & Kluwin, 2001):

▶ Turns head to position an ear in the direction of the speaker
▶ Asks for information to be repeated frequently

Some children may require an audiological evaluation to investigate their hearing skills.

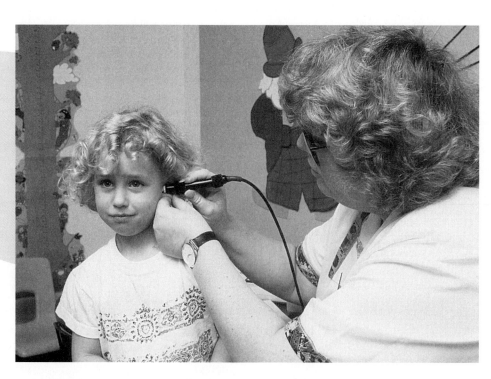

TABLE 8.2	Possible Characteristics of Students with Hearing Impairments
Area of Functioning	**Possible Effects**
Psychological	▶ Intellectual ability range similar to hearing peers ▶ Problems with certain conceptualizations
Communicational	▶ Poor speech production (e.g., unintelligibility) ▶ Tested vocabulary limited ▶ Problems with language usage and comprehension, particularly abstract topics ▶ Voice quality problems
Social–Emotional	▶ Less socially mature ▶ Difficulty making friends ▶ Withdrawn behaviour—feelings of being an outsider ▶ Possible maladjustment problems ▶ May resent having to wear a hearing aid or use other amplification devices ▶ May be dependent on teacher assistance
Academic	▶ Achievement levels significantly below those of their hearing peers ▶ Reading ability most significantly affected ▶ Spelling problems ▶ Limited written language production ▶ Discrepancy between capabilities and performance in many academic areas

▶ Uses a loud voice when speaking
▶ Does not respond when spoken to
▶ Gives incorrect answers to questions
▶ Has frequent colds, earaches, or infections
▶ Appears inattentive and daydreams
▶ Has difficulty following directions
▶ Is distracted easily by visual or auditory stimuli
▶ Misarticulates certain speech sounds or omits certain consonant sounds
▶ Withdraws from classroom activities that involve listening
▶ Has a confused expression on face
▶ Has a restricted vocabulary
▶ Fidgets or moves about in seat

A teacher's careful observations and referral can spare a student months or years of struggle and frustration. While all students referred will not be found to have a significant hearing loss, they should be referred so that an assessment can be made to determine which students need additional supports.

Formal Assessment The assessment of hearing ability requires an **audiologist** to use various audiological techniques. An audiologist is a professional who assesses hearing difficulties, selects and fits hearing aids, designs and implements (re)habilitation strategies for hearing impaired clients, and consults regarding hearing conservation and noise exposure (CASLPA, 2004). The most common method of evaluating hearing is behavioural audiometry which includes pure tone air/bone conduction testing and speech audiometry. In **pure-tone audiometry**, sounds of different frequencies are presented at increasing levels of intensity through the use of an audiometer. The audiometer is a device that tests

TEACHING TIP

Teachers should keep records of students who display these types of behaviours to determine if there is a pattern that might call for a referral.

hearing sensitivity by air conduction (ear phones) and bone conduction (bone conduction vibrator). Bone conduction testing is often used to determine if there are problems in the sensorineural portion of the hearing mechanism (occurring in the inner ear).

The role of pediatric audiology has grown significantly in the past years. Audiologists are more involved in assessment with the advent of new technology (Herer & Reilly, 1999). For example, in Canada there are established Universal Newborn Hearing Screening (UNHS) programs (e.g., Alberta, Ontario). Health Canada is currently in the process of developing guidelines for hearing detection and intervention in Canada. For more information on newborn hearing screening, visit the Hearing Foundation of Canada's website (www.thfc.ca/screening.html).

Informal Assessment In addition to the formal assessment conducted by audiologists, teachers and other school personnel should engage in informal assessment of students, especially those suspected of having a hearing impairment. Informal assessment focuses on observing students for signs that might indicate a hearing loss. Tables 8.1 and 8.2 list indicators that, if recorded over a period of time, show that a student may need formal assessment.

Eligibility The eligibility of students for special education and related services is determined by provincial and territorial guidelines, which are based on certain levels of decibel loss. Teachers should not be concerned about specific eligibility criteria, but should refer students who display characteristics suggesting the presence of a hearing loss to an audiologist for a hearing evaluation.

Strategies for Curriculum and Instruction for Students with Hearing Impairments

Students with hearing impairment may present a significant challenge for general education teachers. Language is such an important component of instruction that students who have problems processing language because of hearing losses make it difficult for teachers to use standard instructional methods effectively. Teachers have to rely on the supports provided by special education staff and specialists in hearing impairments to assist them in meeting the needs of these students.

Realities of the General Education Classroom Students with hearing impairments vary greatly in their need for supports in the general education classroom. Students with mild losses, generally classified as hard of hearing, typically need minimal supports. In fact, these students resemble their typically achieving peers in most ways. If amplification assistance can enable these students to hear clearly, they will need little specialized instruction (Dagenais, Critz-Crosby, Fletcher, & McCutcheon, 1994).

Students with severe hearing impairments, those classified as deaf, present unique challenges to teachers. Specialized instructional techniques usually involve alternative communication methods; the use of interpreters may be a necessity for these students. (See Figure 8.1.) Therefore, general education teachers may need to know how to utilize the services of an interpreter to facilitate the success of students with significant hearing losses.

Continuum of Placement Options Students with hearing impairments are educated in the complete continuum of placement options, depending on their individual needs. These range from general education classrooms to residential schools for the deaf. "The topic of educational placement has generated more controversy in the education of chil-

TEACHING TIP

Children will have limited benefit from language-learning experiences if they are experiencing hearing difficulties. Refer any child you suspect of having hearing problems to an audiologist for a complete assessment.

FURTHER READING

Refer to the ASHA website (www.asha.org) and/or the Canadian Association of Speech-Language Pathology and Audiology (CASLPA) website (www.caslpa.ca) for more information on hearing loss and its impact on speech and language development.

CONSIDER THIS

How do educational needs differ for these two students: a student with a mild hearing loss who can effectively use a hearing aid and a typically achieving student?

CROSS-REFERENCE

Review the continuum of placement options for students with all exceptionalities, including those with hearing impairments, listed in Chapter 1.

FIGURE 8.1

Interpreters in Educational Settings

GENERAL GUIDELINES	

GENERAL GUIDELINES
- Include the interpreter as a member of the IEP team to help determine the communication needs of the student.
- Request an interpreter (i.e., do not let parents interpret for their children) for certain important situations (e.g., transition planning meetings).
- Supervise the interpreter if this person has additional classroom tasks.
- Meet with the interpreter regularly to discuss the needs of the student and to review ongoing communication patterns.
- Evaluate the effectiveness of interpreters.

SPECIFIC SUGGESTIONS
- Allow the interpreter to be positioned so that the student can easily see both the teacher (or media) and the interpreter.
- Prepare the interpreter for the topic(s) that will be covered and the class format that will be followed.
- Provide copies of all visual materials (e.g., overhead transparencies) before class begins.
- Be sensitive to the "time-lag" factor associated with interpreting—the few-word delay that the interpreter lags behind the spoken message.
- Program breaks in lecturing if at all possible.
- Limit movement so that the student can see the interpreter and teacher without difficulty.
- Check student understanding regularly—ensure that the student does not fake understanding.

dren who are hard of hearing and deaf than any issue in curriculum" (Edwards, 1996, p. 403). As with all students with exceptionalities, there is no single educational setting that is best for all students with hearing impairments. Often the choice of where the deaf student is placed is a result of the parents' feelings rather than educational reasons. One view holds that deaf students should be integrated in the hearing school and learn oral language; the other view states that deaf students should be placed in a school for the deaf and learn sign language to maximize their development. Still, the trend continues toward educating more students with hearing impairments in the general education classroom. Figure 8.2 describes the types of supports that students with hearing impairments will need in inclusive settings. They resemble those needed by students with other exceptionalities except for a few services specific to students with hearing problems.

Classroom Adaptations and/or Accommodations for Students with Hearing Impairments

As mentioned earlier, the general education setting is appropriate for most students who are hard of hearing and for many students who are deaf. However, this statement is true only if the specific needs of these students are taken into consideration.

The following sections provide recommendations for meeting the needs of students with hearing difficulties in general education classrooms. Specific suggestions are also given. Both general recommendations and specific suggestions are clustered under four major areas: management considerations, curricular and instructional adaptations and/or accommodations, social-emotional interventions, and technology.

CONSIDER THIS

What are some obvious advantages and disadvantages to the different placement options for students with hearing impairments?

FURTHER READING

Read more about the oral and sign language education debate in James MacDougall's article, "Irreconcilable Differences: The Education of Deaf Children in Canada", in volume 44, issue 1 of *Education Canada*, 2004.

IN-SCHOOL SUPPORT
- Classroom teacher
- Teacher's aide
- Resource teacher
- Principal

CLASSROOM SERVICES
- Educational interpreter
- Note taker

CONSULTING SERVICES
- Teacher of the hearing impaired
- Educational audiologist
- Speech–language pathologist

SCHOOL COLLABORATIVE TEAM
- Special education consultant
- Psychologist
- Social worker
- Other professionals on request (e.g., occupational therapist, pediatrician, psychiatrist, neuropsychologist)

FIGURE 8.2

Types of Supports for Students with Hearing Impairments in Inclusive Settings

From "Educational Management of Children with Hearing Loss," by C. Edwards. In *Hearing Care for Childen*, edited by F. N. Martin and J. G. Clark, 1996, p. 306. Boston: Allyn & Bacon. Used by permission.

CROSS-REFERENCE

Review Chapter 12 for information on rules and procedures appropriate for *all* students with disabilities–and even students without disabilities.

Management Considerations

The effective management of a classroom is critical to maximizing the potential for learning. This important topic is covered in detail in Chapter 12. Attention to classroom management can help include students with various degrees of hearing impairment in general education settings.

Standard Operating Procedures   The dimension of standard operating procedures refers to the rules, regulations, and procedures that operate in a classroom. Students who have hearing impairments must be subject to the same requirements as other students. Some procedures may have to be modified to accommodate special needs. For instance, students may be allowed to leave their seats to get the attention of a student who cannot hear a spoken communication.

Teachers should always confirm that students understand the rules and procedures developed for the classroom. Teachers may also want to establish a buddy system (i.e., a peer support system). In this type of system, a student with normal hearing is assigned to assist the student with a hearing impairment in, for example, following procedures for a fire drill or helping the student take notes during a class lecture.

Physical Considerations   Seating is the major consideration related to the physical setup of the classroom. Teachers need to ensure that students are seated to maximize the use of their **residual hearing** or to have an unobstructed view of an interpreter. Information presented visually is extremely helpful to these students; therefore, they need to be positioned to take advantage of all visual cues (Berry, 1995). The following are some specific suggestions (Luckner & Denzin, 1998):

- Seat students in the best place to facilitate attending and participating.
- Seat students in a semicircular arrangement to increase sight lines for the students and the teacher.
- Position the teacher so students can read his or her facial cues (e.g., lips, facial expressions).
- Position the teacher so he or she faces students when speaking.

In addition, make sure that you seat students who use interpreters so that they can easily see the interpreter, the teacher, and any visuals that are used. It is important to note

Personal Spotlight

Orientation and Mobility Specialist Bonnie Lawrence

Bonnie Lawrence is currently an orientation and mobility specialist working with children with visual impairments who live in their communities and receive educational services in local public schools. Her current caseload includes children who are classified as totally blind as well as other students who have varying degrees of vision loss. Bonnie's primary responsibility is to train students in developing independent travel skills by using a long cane and in using technological aids, such as a monocular. She works with children in all grades, kindergarten through high school. Although most of her time is spent with children in school settings, she also works with them in the community to help them develop independent travel skills outside the school setting. Bonnie says that she likes many different things about her job, but the thing she likes best is that the students she works with live with their families and go to school with their typically achieving peers rather than receiving educational services in a residential school program. She likes the independence associated with her job and the fact that she can make a real difference with the students she serves. "It is so gratifying to be able to see students with visual problems be able to go from one point to another without having to depend on someone else to help them. They truly become more independent in all aspects of their life as a result of being able to travel independently."

The only negative aspect Bonnie experiences in her job is the amount of time she has to spend travelling from one student to another. She works with children who live in a large geographical area and often has to drive several hours to work with only one student. However, despite this inconvenience, she knows that itinerant services are the only effective method of serving students with visual impairments in rural areas in their home and school settings. In Bonnie's words, "I can't imagine doing anything else; I love what I do."

that seating a student with a hearing loss near the front of the class is rarely the only accommodation that needs to be made. In contrast to teaching methods of the past, today very little may happen at the front of the classroom (Crawford, 1998).

Creating a Favourable Environment for Students   As noted in the preceding section, more than preferential seating is necessary for students with a hearing loss. Attention must be given to creating a supportive acoustical environment throughout the classroom. Changes that can be made to dampen excess noise in the classroom, in order to provide an accommodating acoustical environment (Scott, 1997), include:

- Acoustical ceiling tiles
- Carpeting
- Thick curtains
- Rubber tips on chair and table legs
- Proper maintenance of ventilation systems, lighting, doors, and windows

Preinstructional Considerations   Teachers must also carefully plan ahead to deliver instruction in a way that will benefit students with hearing impairments. The following list gives many practical suggestions:

- Allow students to move about the classroom to position themselves for participation in ongoing events.
- Let students use swivel chairs to facilitate positioning for participation in classroom discussions and activities.
- Reduce distracting and competing noise by changing the classroom environment (e.g., carpeting on floor, corkboard on walls).

▶ Ensure that adequate lighting is available to maximize students' view of facial and body cues (e.g., peers, teacher, interpreter).

▶ Provide visual reminders indicating the amount of time left for an activity or until the end of class (e.g., write time left on the board).

▶ Use co-operative learning arrangements to facilitate student involvement with hearing peers.

▶ Include a section of the lesson plan for special provisions for students with hearing impairments.

▶ Acquire or develop visually oriented materials to augment orally presented topics—use overhead projection systems when appropriate.

▶ Use homework assignment books, and make sure that students understand their assignments.

▶ Specific suggestions related to grouping, lesson planning, materials acquisition and adaptation, and homework systems can be found in Chapter 13.

Curricular and Instructional Considerations

All basic elements of effective instructional practice will benefit students with hearing impairments. However, certain specific ideas will enhance their learning experiences.

Communication   Perhaps the most challenging aspect of teaching students whose hearing is impaired is making sure that (1) they participate in the communicational activities (i.e., teacher to student, student to teacher, student to student) that are occurring in the classroom and (2) they are able to handle the reading and writing demands of the class. Language and communication tend to dominate the teaching of students with hearing losses (Mayer et al., 2002). Students who have profound hearing losses must rely on alternative methods of communication such as sign language or speech reading. Students with profound hearing losses typically do not become facile with standard forms of English; therefore, they can have significant problems in the areas of reading and writing. Sign language does not follow the grammatical conventions of English.

When students using some form of manual communication—usually **American Sign Language (ASL)**—are in general education classrooms, teachers are not required to learn this language. However, teachers should make an effort to know some of the more common signs and to be able to finger-spell the letters of the alphabet as well as the numbers 1 to 10.

If students can communicate only by using sign language, an interpreter will most likely need to be present. Teachers should know basic information about the role and functions of an interpreter.

Teachers should be conscious of how well they are communicating with their students. The teacher's speech, location, and movement in the classroom can affect the facility with which a student with a hearing impairment can follow a discussion or lecture. The proper use of assistive equipment (e.g., amplification devices) can also make a difference. This topic is covered in a subsequent section.

Delivery of Instruction   Teachers need to utilize a host of practices that allow students to learn more effectively and efficiently. One suggestion already mentioned, the use of visually oriented material, is especially valuable for students with hearing problems. The following are additional suggestions:

▶ Make sure students are attending.

▶ Provide short, clear instructions.

▶ Speak clearly and normally—do not exaggerate the pronunciation of words.

▶ Keep your face visible to students.

- Avoid frequent movement around the classroom, turning your back on students while talking, and standing in front of a bright light source.
- Use gestures and facial expressions.
- If the student reads speech and you have a moustache and beard, make sure that your facial hair is trimmed to maximize visibility.
- Maintain eye contact with the student, not the interpreter.
- Check with students to confirm that they are understanding what is being discussed or presented.
- Encourage students to request clarification and to ask questions.
- Identify other speakers by name so that students can more easily follow a discussion among more than one speaker.
- Repeat the comments of other students who speak.
- Paraphrase or summarize discussions at the end of a class session.
- Write information when necessary.
- Have students take responsibility for making themselves understood.
- Provide students with advance organizers such as outlines of lectures and copies of overhead transparencies.
- Preview new vocabulary and concepts prior to their presentation during a lecture.
- Use the demonstration-guided practice–independent practice paradigm as often as possible (see Polloway & Patton, 1993, for more information).
- Utilize a variety of instructional formats, including demonstrations, experiments, and other visually oriented activities.
- Emphasize the main points covered in a lecture both verbally and visually.
- Use lots of visual aids (e.g., overhead transparencies, slides, diagrams, charts, multimedia) to explain material.
- Provide summaries, outlines, or scripts of videotapes, videodiscs, or films.
- Let students use microcomputers for word processing and for checking their spelling and grammar.

Teaching secondary-level content classes to students with hearing impairments is uniquely challenging. The nearby Inclusion Strategies feature provides suggestions for teaching science to students who are hearing impaired.

Co-teaching has been shown to be one effective method for teaching students with hearing losses in general education classrooms. This model encourages general classroom teachers, special education teachers, speech-language pathologists, and/or hearing consultants to combine their skills in an inclusive setting. "Co-teaching allows teachers to respond to the diverse needs of all students, provides another set of hands and eyes, lowers the teacher-student ratio, and expands the amount of professional expertise that can be directed to student needs" (Luckner, 1999, p. 150).

Social-Emotional Considerations

Classrooms constitute complex social systems. In addition to development of scholastic abilities and academic support skills, personal development is also occurring. Students need to learn how to get along with their peers and authority figures while they learn how to deal with their beliefs and emotions. While the available research suggests that students with hearing impairments develop similarly, socially and emotionally, to their hearing peers (Moores, 2001), teachers still need to be able to help students develop a realistic sense of their abilities (i.e., strengths and weaknesses), become more responsible and independent, interact appropriately with their peers, and enhance their self-concept and sense of belonging (Luckner, 1994). The following are some specific suggestions:

- Create a positive, supportive, and nurturing classroom environment.
- Encourage class involvement through active participation in classroom activities and interaction in small groups.

Teaching Science to Students Who Are Hearing Impaired

The following are several suggestions on how to give better individual attention in teaching science to students who are hearing impaired:

1. Individualize assignments so that students progress at their own rate and at the end of the period hand in what they have accomplished. This may be a laboratory or written assignment.

2. Extend special recognition to a student who goes beyond minimum acceptance level for doing and formulating laboratory investigation.

3. Use multiple resources, including texts in class. If a student has difficulty reading one text, endeavour to find another or attempt to help him or her learn the material in ways other than through books.

4. Offer special activities for the academically talented. Let them assist you in preparing solutions and materi-als for laboratory work. They should gain experiences that are educationally desirable.

5. Encourage students to do research. They should consult with a scientist or engineer in the community on their research problem. Local industries, museums, zoos, botanical gardens, and hospitals have resource people who will often help.

6. Have students from the upper grades go to some of the lower grades and demonstrate a scientific principle or explain a science project. This approach has the advantage of giving recognition to the younger students and motivating them to greater achievement.

7. Encourage parents to obtain books and to take trips advantageous to science students. Parents often welcome a suggestion from the teacher about books and type of trips to help enrich their children's science education.

▶ Let students know that you are available if they are experiencing problems and need to talk.
▶ Help the students with normal hearing understand the nature of hearing impairment and the ways in which they can assist.
▶ Practise appropriate interactive skills.
▶ Encourage and assist students to get involved in extracurricular activities.
▶ Help students develop problem-solving abilities.
▶ Help students develop realistic expectations.
▶ Prepare students for dealing with the demands of life and adulthood.

Technology

Technology has been beneficial for individuals with hearing impairments (Stewart & Kluwin, 2001). Students with hearing impairments placed in general education classrooms often use devices to help them to maximize their communicational abilities (Easterbrooks, 1999), and they need a supportive environment in which to use these devices (McAnally, Rose, & Quigley, 1999). Teachers need a working knowledge of these devices so that they can ensure that the student benefits from the equipment.

Assistive Listening Devices   *Assistive listening devices (ALDs)* include hearing aids and other devices that amplify voices and sounds, communicate messages visually, or alert users to environmental sounds (Marschark, Lang, & Albertini, 2002).

Children with even small losses, those in the 16 to 25 dB range, may have problems hearing faint or distant speech without some amplification (Iskowitz, 1998). Hearing aids are the predominant ALDs found in schools. These devices pick up sound with a microphone, amplify and filter it, and then convey that sound into the ear canal through a loudspeaker, also called a receiver (Marschark et al., 2002). They work very well with students who experience mild-to-severe hearing losses (Iskowitz, 1998). The nearby Technology Today feature describes hearing aids and other ALDs that can be used in school programs. It is also important to note that an increasing number of profoundly hearing impaired students are receiving cochlear implants. "Cochlear implants are electronic devices that contain a current source and an electrode array that is implanted into the cochlea; [an] electrical current is then used to stimulate the surviving auditory nerve fibres" (ASHA, 2004e, p.1).

To assist students in maximizing the use of their ALDs, teachers should

- know what type of ALD a student uses;
- understand how the device works: on/off switch, battery function (e.g., selection, lifespan, insertion), volume controls;
- be able to determine whether a hearing aid is working properly;
- help students keep their hearing aids functioning properly (e.g., daily cleaning, appropriate storage);
- make sure students avoid getting their aids wet, dropping or jarring them, spraying hairspray on them, and exposing them to extreme heat (Shimon, 1992);
- keep spare batteries on hand;
- ensure that the system is functioning properly;
- perform daily troubleshooting of all components of the system (Brackett, 1990);
- make sure background noises are minimized.

This information should provide teachers with a beginning understanding of how to meet the needs of students with a hearing loss. We strongly recommend that teachers consult with hearing specialists (e.g., an audiologist, hearing consultant, and/or teacher of the deaf) to determine the best possible adaptations and/or accommodations to provide an appropriate educational environment for students with hearing problems.

Promoting Inclusive Practices for Students with Hearing Impairments

Being an integral part of the inclusive school community is important for students with hearing impairments who receive their educational programs in public schools, especially for those placed in general education classrooms. Physically situating students in classrooms does not automatically result in their being included members of the class. Therefore, teachers must ensure that students become part of the community of the school and class and are socially accepted by their peers.

Teachers may have to orchestrate opportunities for interaction between students with hearing impairments and their typically achieving peers. These opportunities could include grouping, pairing students for specific tasks, assigning buddies, and establishing a circle of friends. Kluwin (1996) suggests using dialogue journals to facilitate this interaction. Students are paired (one student with a hearing impairment and one without) to make journal entries and then exchange them. Rather than assign deadlines, allow students to exchange journal entries whenever they desire. You may need to give them ideas appropriate for sharing, to get them started. Reinforce students for making and exchanging journal entries. This approach encourages interactions between students with hearing impairments and their typically achieving peers without using a rigidly structured activity or assignment.

FURTHER READING

In order to learn more about cochlear implants refer to Moore & Teagle's article, "An Introduction to Cochlear Implant Technology, Activation, and Programming," in volume 33 of *Language, Speech, And Hearing Services in Schools*, 2002 (pp. 153–161).

TEACHING TIP

When students in your classroom use assistive listening devices, learn as much about the devices as possible so that you will be able to maximize their use (e.g., how to find and replace batteries).

CROSS-REFERENCE

Review Chapter 2 for additional considerations to help teachers enhance the student's acceptance in the general education setting.

CONSIDER THIS

Do you think that students with hearing impairments can be included and accepted in the classroom by their peers? Should students with hearing impairments be isolated in institutions with other students who have hearing losses? Why or why not?

ALDs at a Glance

Assistive devices, whether used as stand-alone systems or in conjunction with hearing aids, amplify voices and sounds, communicate messages visually, or alert users to environmental sounds. Subcategories within the major classifications address a variety of hearing needs in different situations.

The ability of a device to perform in a specific setting can be determined by studying the specifications of the individual product in conjunction with a patient's case history.

In general, dispensers interested in expanding their scope of practice to include assistive technology, or those who want to broaden their involvement in this area, can use the following overview as a guide to the kinds of technology available in the field:

Amplification

In some settings, hearing aids alone are less effective than ALDs in discerning voices in the presence of background noise or picking up speech clearly from a distance. Large-area amplification systems as well as portable personal devices improve the signal-to-noise ratio at the listener's ear, making it easier for users to hear and understand speech, whether watching television at home or listening to a lecture in a public auditorium.

Amplification devices can be further divided into hard-wired or wireless systems.

▶ In hard-wire devices, the user is connected to the sound source by a wire and, consequently, limited in movement by the length of the cord connected to an earphone headset, hearing aid, or neck loop. Hard-wired systems are more appropriate for television watching and small-group business or social settings than for listening in large public areas.

▶ Wireless systems, in which sound is transmitted from the source to the listener's ear by means of electromagnetic energy, invisible light waves, or on radio bands, are more practical in large public areas, like theatres and lecture halls. Typically, users access the system from a telecoil circuit built into their hearing aids or from a receiver attached to a headset.

1. An induction loop wireless system transmits sound in the form of electromagnetic energy. A loop of wire that encircles a room receives the signal from an amplifier connected to a lecturer's microphone or, in small settings, to a tape recorder or television.
2. An infrared wireless system transmits sound via light waves. A photo detector diode picks up infrared light and changes the information into sound, which users hear with a hearing aid, telecoil feature, or earphones.
3. In an FM wireless system, sound is transmitted and received via radio waves.

Communications

Assistive technology facilitates communication by telephone for deaf and hard-of-hearing people. Cost and the degree of hearing loss determine appropriateness of products, which are available in a number of forms. Consult manufacturers for advantages and limitations of individual products.

▶ *Amplified replacement handsets* are available for most telephone models, for use at home and at work.

▶ *In-line telephone amplifiers* splice an existing handset and telephone base to a device that amplifies a voice. Portable, strap-on amplifiers can be attached directly to the handset.

▶ *TDD (telecommunications devices for the deaf)*, also known as *TTs (text telephones)*, supply a visual medium for communication. A TDD user types a message that is translated into electrical pulses and sent over a telephone line to the receiving TDD or to an intercept operator. Some TDDs can be used in conjunction with personal computers.

▶ *Decoders* provide closed captioning subtitles for television and VCR viewing.

Alerting

Alerting devices signal users to sound by means of visual, auditory, or vibrotactile stimuli. In general, alerting devices detect sound (e.g., a telephone, doorbell, or smoke alarm) and either amplify the sound or convert it to another signal, such as a flashing light, to make the person aware of the sound.

▶ *Visual* alerting devices connected to lamps flash different patterns to differentiate among sounds. One pattern can be programmed to signal that the telephone is ringing, while another indicates the doorbell.

▶ *Auditory* alerting devices amplify the sound or convert it to a lower pitch, which is more easily audible than high-frequency sound.

▶ *Vibrotactile* devices respond to sound with a gentle shaking motion. The ringing of an alarm clock or smoke detector, for instance, makes the mattress vibrate. Body-worn vibrotactile devices are available also.

From "ALDs at a Glance," 1996, *The Hearing Journal, 49*, p. 21. Used by permission.

Supports for the General Education Teacher

Students with hearing impairments often create major challenges for general classroom teachers, primarily because of the language barrier that hearing loss often creates. Therefore, teachers must rely on support personnel such as educational consultants who specialize in the area of hearing impairment, interpreters, audiologists, and medical personnel to assist them in their efforts to provide appropriate educational programs.

Visual Impairments

Students with visual impairments also pose unique challenges to teachers in general education classrooms. Although the number of students whose vision creates learning-related problems is not large, having one such student in a classroom may require a host of adaptations and/or accommodations.

Vision plays a critical role in the development of concepts, the understanding of spatial relations, and the use of printed material. Thus children with visual problems have unique educational needs. "Learning the necessary compensatory skills and adaptive techniques—such as using Braille or *optical devices* for written communication—requires specialized instruction from teachers and parents who have expertise in addressing disability-specific needs" (Corn et al., 1995, p. 1). See Technology Today (on page 216) for examples of optical devices and technology available for students with visual impairments. Teachers may be able to use their usual instructional techniques with some modifications with students who have some functional vision. However, for students who have very little or no vision, teachers will need to implement alternative techniques to provide effective educational programs.

General education classes are appropriate settings for many students with visual impairments. However, teachers working with these students need to understand the nature of a particular student's vision problem to be able to choose appropriate adaptive and/or accommodative tactics. They need basic information related to four categories: (1) fundamental concepts of vision and visual impairment, (2) signs of possible visual problems, (3) typical characteristics of students with visual problems, and (4) specific adaptive and/or accommodative techniques for meeting student needs.

Basic Concepts about Visual Impairments

Visual Impairments Defined A number of different terms are associated with this concept; therefore, confusion regarding the exact meaning of visual terminology is often a problem. These are the most frequently used terms and their definitions:

▶ *Visual impairment* is a generic term that includes a wide range of visual problems.
▶ *Blindness* has different meanings depending upon context, resulting in some confusion. *Legal blindness* refers to a person's visual acuity and field of vision. It is defined as a visual acuity of 20/200 or less in the person's better eye after correction, or a field of vision of 20° or less. Visual acuity of 20/200 or less means that a person who is legally blind can see at 20 feet what a person with good vision can see at 200 feet. An educational definition of *blindness* implies that a student must use Braille (a system of raised dots that the student reads tactilely) or aural methods in order to receive instruction (Heward, 2000).
▶ *Low vision* indicates that some functional vision exists to be used for gaining information through written means with or without the assistance of optical, nonoptical, or electronic devices (Kirk, Gallagher, & Anastasiow, 2000).

TEACHING TIP

Try using an idea from a children's game to work with children with visual impairments. Just as you would ask a blindfolded child what information he or she needs to make progress in the game, ask the children what assistance or information they need in order to benefit from your teaching.

CONSIDER THIS

Some students who are classified as blind are actually able to read print and do not need to use Braille. Are there descriptors other than *blind* and *low vision* that would better describe students with visual impairments for educational purposes?

Students with **low vision** are capable of handling the demands of most classroom settings. However, they will need some modifications to perform successfully. Students who are blind (i.e., have very little or no vision) will need major adaptations and/or accommodations to be successful in general education settings.

Classification of Visual Impairments   Visual problems can be categorized in a number of ways. One typical method organizes visual problems as refractive errors (e.g., farsightedness, nearsightedness, and astigmatism); retinal disorders; disorders of the cornea, iris, and lens; and optic nerve problems. In addition to common refractive problems, which usually can be improved with corrective lenses, other visual problems include the following:

- *Strabismus*—improper alignment of the eyes
- *Nystagmus*—rapid involuntary movements of the eye
- *Glaucoma*—fluid pressure buildup in the eye
- *Cataract*—cloudy film over the lens of the eye
- *Diabetic retinopathy*—changes in the blood vessels of the eye caused by diabetes
- *Macular degeneration*—damage to the central portion of the retina, causing central vision loss
- *Retinitis pigmentosa*—genetic eye disease leading to total blindness (Smith & Luckasson, 1998)

Tunnel vision denotes a condition caused by deterioration of parts of the retina, which leaves the person with central vision only. Individuals who have tunnel vision can see as if they are looking through a long tube; they have little or no peripheral vision.

Regardless of the cause of the visual problem, educators primarily have to deal with its functional result. Whether or not the student has usable residual vision is an important issue, as is the time at which the vision problem developed. Students who are born with significant visual loss have a much more difficult time understanding some concepts and developing basic skills than students who lose their vision after they have established certain concepts (Warren, 1994).

Prevalence and Causes of Visual Impairments   Vision problems are common in our society. Fortunately, corrective lenses allow most individuals to see very efficiently. However, many individuals have vision problems that cannot be corrected in this way. As with persons with hearing impairments, the number of individuals who have visual impairments increases with age as a result of the aging process. In the school-age population, approximately 0.06 percent of students are classified as visually impaired. However, according to the Canadian National Institute for the Blind (1999), the prevalence rates vary by region. The Institute notes that First Nations peoples are at increased risk of visual impairments both in youth and with age due to premature birth, trauma, and diabetes. Dr. Farrell, a member of the board of directors of the Canadian National Institute of the Blind (CNIB), states, "The risk of vision loss is three to four times greater in First Nations Peoples than it is in the general population."

Etiological factors associated with visual impairments include genetic causes, physical trauma, infections, premature birth, anoxia, and retinal degeneration. *Retrolental fibroplasia (RLF)* was a common cause of blindness in the early 1950s, when premature infants were exposed to too much oxygen in incubators. Once the cause of this problem was understood, it became nearly nonexistent. However, this cause of blindness is reasserting itself as medical science faces the challenge of providing care to infants born more and more prematurely. Blindness sometimes accompanies very early premature birth.

Characteristics of Students with Visual Impairments   The most educationally relevant characteristic of students who have visual impairments is the extent of their visual efficiency. More specific characteristics can be categorized as psychological, communicational, academic, and social-emotional. These areas are listed in Table 8.3.

FURTHER READING

Refer to the CNIB's website for more information on visual impairments, and the products and services that are available for individuals who are visually impaired (www.cnib.ca).

TABLE 8.3	Possible Characteristics of Students with Visual Impairments
Area of Functioning	*Possible Effects*
Psychological	▶ Intellectual abilities similar to those of sighted peers ▶ Concept development can depend on tactile experiences (i.e., synthetic and analytic touch) ▶ Unable to use sight to assist in the development of integrated concepts ▶ Unable to use visual imagery
Communicational	▶ Relatively unimpaired in language abilities
Social/Emotional/ Behavioural	▶ May display repetitive, stereotyped movements (e.g., rocking or rubbing eyes) ▶ Socially immature ▶ Withdrawn ▶ Dependent ▶ Unable to use nonverbal cues
Mobility	▶ Distinct disadvantage in using spatial information ▶ Visual imagery and memory problems with functional implications
Academic	▶ Generally behind sighted peers

Identification, Assessment, and Eligibility   Students with visual impairments can be easily identified if their visual loss is severe. However, many students have milder losses that are much more difficult to identify and may go several years without being recognized. Teachers must be aware of behaviours that could indicate a vision problem. Figure 8.3 summarizes possible symptoms of vision problems.

Formal Assessment   Students are screened for vision problems in schools, and when problems are suspected, a more in-depth evaluation is conducted. The typical eye examination assesses two dimensions: visual acuity and field of vision. Visual acuity is most often evaluated by the use of a **Snellen chart**.

As Smith (2001) notes, two versions of this chart are available: the traditional version using alphabetic letters of different sizes, and the other version using the letter *E* presented in different spatial arrangements and sizes. Regardless of the assessment used, the person conducting it should have expertise in the area of visual impairment (Corn et al., 1995).

Once students are identified as having possible vision problems, they should be referred for more extensive evaluations. **Ophthalmologists**, medical doctors, and **optometrists** (who specialize in evaluating vision and prescribing glasses) are typically involved in this more extensive evaluation. These specialists determine the specific nature and extent of any vision problem.

Informal Assessment   A great deal of informal assessment should be completed by school personnel. As with students with hearing impairments, the informal assessment of students with visual impairments focuses on observation. Teachers and other school personnel note behaviours that might indicate a vision loss or change in the vision of the child. Once students are identified as having a problem, school personnel must be alert to any changes in the student's visual abilities.

Eligibility   In Canada, students with a 20/200 acuity or worse in the better eye with best correction are identified as blind, whereas those with a visual acuity of 20/70 to 20/200 are considered as having low vision.

TEACHING TIP

For students who are not doing well in their academic work and who display some of these symptoms, conduct a functional visual screening to determine if the child should be referred for more formal screening (see Figure 8.3).

FIGURE 8.3

Symptoms of Possible
Vision Problems

From *Exceptional Learners:
Introduction to Special Education*
(7th ed.) (p. 358), by D. P.
Hallahan and J. M. Kauffman,
1997, Boston: Allyn & Bacon. Used
by permission.

Behaviour	
	Rubs eyes excessively
	Shuts or covers one eye, tilts head, or thrusts head forward
	Has difficulty in reading or in other work requiring close use of the eyes
	Blinks more than usual or is irritable when doing close work
	Holds books close to eyes
	Is unable to see distant things clearly
	Squints eyelids together or frowns
Appearance	
	Crossed eyes
	Red-rimmed, encrusted, or swollen eyelids
	Inflamed or watery eyes
	Recurring styes
Complaints	
	Eyes that itch, burn, or feel scratchy
	Cannot see well
	Dizziness, headaches, or nausea following close eye work
	Blurred or double vision

Strategies for Curriculum and Instruction for Students with Visual Impairments

Students with visual impairments need specific curricular and instructional modifications, adaptations, and/or accommodations. For students with low vision, these changes may simply mean enlarging printed materials to sufficient size so that the student can see them. For students with little or no vision, modifications, adaptations, and/or accommodations must be more extensive.

Realities of the General Education Classroom

Students with visual impairments present a range of needs. Those who are capable of reading print, with provided support, often require minimal curricular changes; those who must read using Braille require significant changes. Teachers should remember that even students who are capable of reading print may need adaptations and/or accommodations in many day-to-day activities. These may be as simple as ensuring appropriate contrast in printed materials and having students sit in a place that will optimize their vision.

Continuum of Placement Options

As with students with hearing impairments, students with visual problems may be placed anywhere on the full continuum of placement options, ranging from general education classrooms to residential schools for students with visual impairments. Students must be evaluated individually to determine the appropriate educational placement. Although some blind students function very well in general education settings, many are placed in residential schools where they receive more extensive services.

Classroom Adaptations and/or Accommodations for Students with Visual Impairments

Certain classroom adaptations and/or accommodations will enhance the quality of programs for students with visual problems. This section recommends ways to address the needs of these students, organized according to four categories: general considerations, management considerations, curricular and instructional adaptations and/or accommodations, and social-emotional interventions.

General Considerations

When educating students with visual impairments, the unique needs of each student must be considered (Desrochers, 1999). However, some general practices apply for most, if not all, students with these problems. These practices include the following:

- Ask the student if assistance is needed.
- Do not assume that certain tasks and activities cannot be accomplished without adaptations, accommodations, or modifications.
- Include students with visual impairments in all activities that occur in the class.
- Use seating arrangements to take advantage of any vision the child can use.
- Encourage the use of residual vision.

Remember that many characteristics of students with visual impairment (e.g., intelligence, health) may not be negatively affected by the vision problem.

Management Considerations

A variety of classroom management tactics can be helpful to students who have vision problems. Classroom management is discussed in detail in Chapter 12. When students with vision problems are present, attention needs to be given to standard operating procedures, physical considerations, and preinstructional considerations.

Standard Operating Procedures   The same standards of expected behaviour should be applied to all students, including those who have visual problems. However, students with visual limitations may need special freedom to move around the classroom, to find the place where they can best see demonstrations or participate in activities.

Physical Considerations   Students with visual problems need to know the physical layout of the classroom so that they can navigate through it without harming themselves. Teachers have to orient students with visual problems to the classroom by taking them around the classroom and noting certain features, such as the location of desks, tables, and materials. A clock orientation approach is useful—for example, the front of the class is 12 o'clock, at 3 o'clock is the teacher's desk, at 6 o'clock is the reading table, and at 9 o'clock is the area for students' coats and backpacks. Appropriate seating is extremely important for students who are able to use their existing vision. Placement of the student's desk, lighting, glare, and distractions should be considered when situating such students in the classroom. Guarantee that the classroom is free of hazards (e.g., low-hanging mobiles or plants) that could injure students who have a visual impairment. Label storage areas and other parts of the classroom for students with visual impairment by using raised lettering or Braille.

Some students with exceptionalities require the use of *specialized equipment,* such as wheelchairs, hearing aids, and other types of amplification systems, communication devices, adaptive desks and trays, prone standers (i.e., stand-up desks), and medical equipment. Teachers need to understand how the equipment works, how it should be used, and what adaptations will need to be made to the classroom environment to accommodate the student using it. The other students in the classroom should be introduced to the special equipment as well. Instructional lessons on specific pieces of equipment will not only be helpful in creating an inclusive environment, but may also provide a basis for science and health curricular tie-ins. Suggestions include the following:

▶ Identify what special equipment will be needed in the classroom well ahead of the arrival of the student who needs it.
▶ Learn how special equipment and devices work and how they can be repaired—this task usually can be accomplished by talking with parents.
▶ Learn how to identify problems or malfunctions in medical equipment.
▶ Find out how long students need to use time-specified equipment or devices.
▶ Let students with hearing impairments sit on swivel chairs with casters so they can move about to follow a discussion involving many participants. (Salend, 1994)

Preinstructional Considerations   Teachers should plan ahead to adapt instruction to the needs of students with visual impairments. Class schedules must allow extra time for students who use large-print or Braille materials, as it takes longer to use these materials.

Test-taking procedures may need to be adapted, for example, by preparing an enlarged version of the test, allowing extra time, or arranging for someone to read the test to the student.

Some students may need special instruction in study skills such as note taking, organizational skills, time management, and keyboarding. These become increasingly important as students move to middle school and high school.

The following are some specific adaptation and/or accommodation suggestions:

▶ Assign a classmate to assist students who may need help with mobility in emergency situations.
▶ Teach all students in the class the proper techniques of being a sighted guide.
▶ In advance, inform staff members at field-trip sites that a student with a visual problem will be part of the visiting group.
▶ Tell students with visual problems that you are entering or leaving a room so that they are aware of your presence or absence.
▶ Have all students practise movement patterns that you expect of them, to maintain an orderly classroom.
▶ Orient students to the physical layout and other distinguishing features of the classroom.
▶ Maintain consistency in the placement of furniture, equipment, and instructional materials—remove all dangerous obstacles.
▶ Keep doors to cabinets, carts, and closets closed.
▶ Assist students in getting into unfamiliar desks, chairs, or other furniture.
▶ Eliminate auditory distractions.
▶ Seat students to maximize their usable vision and listening skills—often a position in the front and centre part of the room is advantageous.
▶ Seat students so that they are not looking into a source of light or bothered by glare from reflected surfaces.
▶ Ensure that proper lighting is available.
▶ Create extra space for students who must use and store a piece of equipment (e.g., Brailler, notebook computer).
▶ As a special section of the lesson plan, include notes for meeting the needs of students with visual problems.

TEACHING TIP

Have vision specialists, such as an orientation and mobility specialist, come into your class and demonstrate sighted guide techniques and other strategies that provide supports for students with visual impairments.

FURTHER READING

Learn more about making literacy instruction more accessible to students who are blind or visually impaired in P. Ann MacCuspie's (2002) article, "Access to Literacy Instruction for Students Who Are Blind or Visually Impaired," available on the CNIB's website (www.cnib.ca/eng/publications/access_to_literacy.htm).

Classmates can assist students with visual problems in areas such as mobility.

Curricular and Instructional Considerations

Teacher-Related Activities As the principal agents in delivering instruction, teachers should use techniques that will ensure success for students who have visual problems. A special challenge involves conveying primarily visual material to those who cannot see well. For example, it will require some creativity on the part of the teacher to make a graphic depiction of the circulatory system in a life science book (a two-dimensional illustration) accessible to a student who can see little or not at all. Three-dimensional models or illustrations with raised features might address this need. Teachers have to decide what should be emphasized in the curriculum when students with visual impairments are in their classes. As a result of the wide array of curricular options for students with visual impairments, teachers must "(a) address the multifaceted educational requisites of their students, (b) ensure that instruction occurs in all areas of greatest need and (c) ensure that sufficient instructional time is allocated for identified educational priorities" (Lueck, 1999, p. 54).

TEACHING TIP

Make sure that students with visual impairments have ample storage area near their desks for materials such as large-print or Braille books and other equipment.

Materials and Equipment Special materials and equipment can enhance the education of students who have visual impairments. Some materials (e.g., large-print materials) are not appropriate for all and must be considered in light of individual needs. Vision specialists can help teachers select appropriate materials and equipment.

Many materials found in general education classrooms may pose problems for students who have problems with their vision. The *size* and *contrast* of print materials have a real effect on students with visual problems. For instance, low-contrast materials (in which information does not stand out well on a page) and books that are printed on glossy paper can be difficult for some students to use. Print size can generally be taken care of with magnification devices; however, little can be done to enhance the poor contrast often found on photocopies. Consider these points when using photocopies:

- Avoid using both sides of the paper (ink often bleeds through, making it difficult to see either side).
- Avoid old or light worksheet masters.
- Avoid worksheet masters with missing parts or creases.

FURTHER READING

For additional information on existing concerns in literacy education for students who are blind or visually impaired, review the CNIB's position statement entitled, "The Freedom To Read, The Right To Read," available on the CNIB website (www.cnib.ca/eng/fps/right-to-read.htm).

TEACHING TIP

Have a student who uses a Braille writer demonstrate the Braille code and methods of writing Braille to members of the class so they can understand the learning medium used by students with visual impairments.

▷ Give the darkest copies of handouts to students with visual problems.
▷ Do not give a student with a visual impairment a poor copy and say, "Do the best you can with this."
▷ Copy over lines that are light with a dark marker.
▷ Make new originals when photocopies become difficult to read.
▷ Avoid the use of coloured inks that may produce limited contrast.
▷ Do not use coloured paper—it limits contrast.

Although large-print materials seem like a good idea, they may be used inappropriately. Barraga and Erin (1992) recommend that these materials be used only as a last resort, since they may not be readily available. They believe that large-print materials should be utilized only after other techniques (e.g., optical devices or reduction of the reading distance) have been tried.

Teachers also may want to use concrete materials (i.e., realia—realistic representations of actual items). However, concrete representations of large real-life objects may not be helpful for young students, who may not understand the abstract notion of one thing representing another. Teachers must carefully ensure that all instructional materials for students with visual impairments are presented in the appropriate medium for the particular student (Corn et al., 1995).

Various optical, nonoptical, and electronic devices are also available for classroom use. These devices help students by enlarging existing printed images. If these devices are recommended for certain students, teachers will need to learn about them to ensure that they are used properly and to recognize when there is a problem. Teachers should practise the use of optical and electronic devices with students after consultation with a vision specialist.

Some students with more severe visual limitations may use Braille as the primary means of working with written material. They may use instructional materials that are printed in Braille and may also take notes using it. Through the use of computers, a student can write in Braille and have the text converted to standard print. The reverse process is available as well. If a student uses this system of communication, the teacher should consult with a vision specialist to understand how it works.

The following are some specific adaptation and/or accommodation suggestions:

▷ Call students by name, and speak directly to them.
▷ Take breaks at regular intervals to minimize fatigue in listening or using a Brailler or optic device.
▷ Ensure that students are seated properly so that they can see you (if they have vision) and hear you clearly.
▷ Vary the type of instruction used, and include lessons that incorporate hands-on activities, co-operative learning, or the use of real-life materials.
▷ Use high-contrast materials, whether on paper or on the chalkboard—dry-erase boards may be preferable.
▷ Avoid using materials with glossy surfaces and, if possible, copied material.
▷ Use large-print materials only after other methods have been attempted and proved unsuccessful.
▷ Use environmental connectors (e.g., ropes or railing) and other adaptations for students with visual problems for physical education or recreational activities (Barraga & Erin, 1992).
▷ Avoid using written materials with pages that are too crowded.

Social-Emotional Considerations

Although the literature is mixed on whether students with visual impairments are less well adjusted than their sighted peers (Hallahan & Kauffman, 2000), there is evidence that some students with visual problems experience social isolation (Huurre,

Komulainen, & Aro, 1999). As a result, many students with visual problems will benefit from attention to their social and emotional development. Social skill instruction may be particularly useful (Sacks, Wolffe, & Tierney, 1998). However, because social skills are typically learned through observing others and imitating their behaviours, it is difficult to teach these skills to students who are not able to see.

Concern about emotional development is warranted for all students, including students with visual problems. Teachers should make sure that students know that they are available to talk about a student's concerns. A system can be developed whereby a student who has a visual impairment can signal the need to chat with the teacher. It is extremely important that teachers are accessible and let students know that someone is concerned about their social and emotional needs.

The following are some specific adaptation and/or accommodation suggestions:

- Encourage students with visual problems to become independent learners and to manage their own behaviours.
- Create opportunities for students to manipulate their own environment (Mangold & Roessing, 1982).
- Reinforce students for their efforts.
- Help students develop a healthy self-concept.
- Provide special instruction to help students acquire social skills needed to perform appropriately in classroom and social situations.
- Teach students how to communicate nonverbally (e.g., use of hands, etc.).
- Work with students to eliminate inappropriate mannerisms that some students with visual impairments display (e.g., "I notice the other kids do not...").

Technology

As with students with hearing impairments, students with visual problems often use technological devices to assist them in their academic work and daily living skills. Low-vision aids include magnifiers, closed-circuit televisions, and **monoculars**. These devices enlarge print and other materials for individuals with visual impairments.

Many other technological devices are used by students with visual impairments. Refer to the nearby Technology Today feature for samples of some of these technological devices.

While access to the internet is relatively easy for students without visual problems, many students with visual impairments may have difficulty. Certain technological devices can make access to the internet available. Braille printers and speech input/output devices can help achieve access. Access and computer training can give students with visual impairments a vast resource that can have a profound positive impact on their education (Heinrich, 1999).

Promoting Inclusive Practices for Students with Visual Impairments

Students with visual impairments, like students with hearing impairments, need to be part of the school community. Many students can be included without special supports. However, for others, teachers may need to consider the following (Amerson, 1999; Desrochers; 1999; Torres & Corn, 1990):

1. Remember that the student with a visual impairment is but one of many students in the classroom with individual needs and characteristics.
2. Use words such as *see*, *look*, and *watch* naturally.

Assistive Technology for Visual Impairments

AI Squared, ZoomText Xtra Level 2

This software-based screen magnifier enlarges all text and graphics on the Windows display. It also features contrast and colour enhancements that make it easy for the visually impaired user to locate key items such as pointers and highlight bars. Although this is primarily a screen magnifier, the product can also deliver some spoken output, reducing eye fatigue during prolonged reading.

Alva Access Group, OutSpoken for Macintosh

This screen reader for the Macintosh represents the only commercially available solution for blindness access to the Macintosh. It uses the built-in speech system of the Macintosh to read important elements of the screen as the user navigates around the display.

Alva Access Group, InLarge for Macintosh

This software-based screen magnifier enlarges all text and graphics on the Macintosh screen. It also features contrast and colour enhancements that make it easy for the visually impaired

user to locate key items such as pointers and highlight bars.

Arkenstone, An Open Book

This customized Optical Character Recognition system enables students with visual impairments or learning disabilities to read typewritten materials without human intervention. The system uses a computer and scanner to take a digital picture of a printed page. The software then converts the digital picture into the equivalent of typewritten text. The text is then either displayed on the computer screen in enhanced print, displayed in Braille on a refreshable Braille display, or read aloud via a speech synthesizer.

Artic Technologies, TransType

This portable electronic note-taking device is designed specifically for blind individuals requiring a mobile method for taking, storing, and retrieving notes. The device is no larger than a notebook-computer-style keyboard. Since it has no display, the device is light, rugged, and quite portable. The built-in speech synthesizer allows the user to easily review the contents of many different files stored in the unit's memory. The note taker includes several applications including alarms, stopwatch, terminal program, and a talking five-function calculator. When connected to a computer via a

serial connection, the device can serve as a speech synthesizer on nearly any computer. The TransType also connects easily to a printer for hard copy production.

Blazie Engineering, Braille n' Speak/Type n' Speak

This family of portable electronic note takers allow blind students to independently take written notes in class or on the go. As the note takers use a built-in speech synthesizer to review created files, no display is required or included. In addition to being highly portable note takers, these units also contain a number of built-in options including a talking scientific calculator. The Braille n' Speak (BNS) requires the user to enter all information via its seven-key Braille keyboard, while the Type n' Speak (TNS) has a QWERTY style keyboard. Both units can be connected to either a Braille embosser or ink printer for hard-copy printouts.

Duxbury Systems, Duxbury Braille Translator

This Braille translation software allows the user to transform a common word processor file from ASCII characters to Grade II Braille. Once translated, the file can be sent to one of several Braille embossers on campus.

Enabling Technologies, Juliet Braille Embosser

This device is the Braille equivalent to an ink printer. It allows the computer to

3. Introduce students with visual impairments the same way you would introduce any other student.
4. Include students with visual impairments in all classroom activities, including physical education, home economics, and so on.
5. Encourage students with visual problems to seek leadership and high-profile roles in the classroom.
6. Use the same disciplinary procedures for all students.
7. Encourage students with visual problems to move about the room just like other students.
8. Use verbal cues as often as necessary to cue the student with a visual impairment about something that is happening.
9. Provide additional space for students with visual impairments to store materials.

produce the Braille system of characters on heavy card-stock paper. Unlike many Braille embossers, the Juliet is capable of embossing on both sides of a page, thus dramatically reducing paper use and the bulk of documents printed on a single-sided embosser. This device must be used in conjunction with a Braille translator such as the Duxbury Braille Translator to produce properly formatted Grade II Braille.

Franklin Electronic Publishing, Language Master

These handheld devices allow students to quickly search for definitions and spellings of difficult or troublesome words. The systems also allow the user to locate synonyms and antonyms for particular words. Finally, the units include a speech synthesizer allowing them to read definitions and spellings aloud.

Henter-Joyce, JAWS for Windows (JFW)

This powerful screen-reading package affords speech output and Braille access to the newest operating systems (Windows 95, Windows 98, Windows NT, Windows 2000, and Windows XP). Its high configurability makes it a good choice for the most demanding screen reading tasks. With JFW, blind or visually impaired computer users can independently use most Windows-based software including email, web browsers, word processing, spreadsheets, and databases. The software uses a standard sound card to produce a clear synthesized voice in any of several languages. For users who prefer Braille output over speech, JFW supports full access to the computer via a refreshable Braille display such as the Braille Window.

HumanWare, Braille Window

This 45-cell refreshable Braille display allows blind and deaf-blind users to access a variety of Windows-based software through tactile Braille output. The display is used in conjunction with a PC and either a screen-reading software package like JAWS for Windows or other Braille ready software such as An Open Book. The display supports both the common six-dot Braille or eight-dot computer Braille.

HumanWare, Keynote Companion

This palm-top-sized note taker is equipped with both speech synthesis and a small LCD display. The intuitive word processor software allows the user to create a variety of documents that can be easily modified, stored, and reviewed with speech. The device easily connects to a printer for a hard-copy printout of important information. The device also features a talking scientific calculator and a telecommunications program.

Kurzweil Educational Systems, Kurzweil 1000

This powerful Optical Character Recognition software allows the computer to scan printed materials and render them in a spoken and large-print output. The system features voice recognition allowing control over scanning and read-ing operations by voice in addition to traditional keyboard control. Finally, the built-in definitions dictionary provides full definitions and synonyms for hundreds of thousands of words.

Optalec, SVGA Closed-Circuit Television (CCTV)

This device assists students with visual impairments or learning disabilities by allowing them to enlarge and embolden the contents of printed materials. As with a traditional CCTV, the user places the printed material on an X-Y table. The image is then captured by a video camera, allowing the user to adjust magnification level, focus, brightness, contrast, and coloration. This unit differs from a traditional CCTV in that it shares a single display/monitor with an existing PC. The user can thus (with the press of a button or foot pedal) select a full-screen view of the computer, CCTV, or a split screen containing both. This system allows the user to easily read printed materials while working simultaneously with a computer.

Telesensory, Versapoint Braille Embosser

This Braille embosser allows a PC running a Braille translation software package to emboss Braille on heavy tractor-fed paper. A Braille embosser is the Braille equivalent of an ink printer.

Adapted from Assistive Technology Center, MSU Resource Center for Persons with Disabilities (RCPD), East Lansing, MI 48824-1033. Used with permission.

10. Allow students with visual impairments to learn about and discuss with other classmates special topics related to visual loss.
11. Model acceptance of visually impaired students as an example to other students.
12. Encourage students with visual impairments to use their specialized equipment, such as a Braille writer.
13. Discuss special needs of the child with a visual impairment with specialists, as necessary.
14. Always tell a person with a visual impairment who you are as you approach.
15. Help students avoid inappropriate mannerisms associated with visual impairments.
16. Expect the same level of work from students with visual impairments as you do from other students.
17. Encourage students with visual impairments to be as independent as possible.

18. Treat children with visual impairments as you treat other students in the classroom.
19. Provide physical supports for students with concomitant motor problems.
20. Include students with visual impairments in outdoor activities and team sports.

In your efforts to promote a sense of community, consider that some students with visual impairments may have different cultural backgrounds than the majority of students in the school. School personnel must be sensitive to different cultural patterns. Bau (1999) noted seven different cultural values that could have an impact on the provision of services to students with visual impairments. These include communication, health beliefs, family structure, attitude toward authority, etiquette, expectations of helping, and time orientation. In order to communicate clearly with a family that speaks a different language, you may need to use a language interpreter. Being sensitive to the culture and family background of students with visual impairments facilitates the delivery of appropriate services.

Supports for the General Education Teacher

As noted earlier, general education teachers can effectively instruct most students with visual impairments, with appropriate supports. A vision specialist may need to work with students on specific skills, such as Braille; an orientation and mobility instructor can teach students how to travel independently; an adaptive physical education instructor can help modify physical activities for the student with visual impairment. Counsellors, school health personnel, and vocational specialists may also provide support services for general education teachers. School personnel should never forget to include parents in helping develop and implement educational supports for students with visual impairments. In a recent study, McConnell (1999) found that a model program that included family involvement and support greatly assisted adolescents with visual impairments to develop career choices and values. Other ways to enhance the education of students with visual impairments are the following:

- Get help from others. Teach other students to assist in social as well as academic settings. Call parents and ask questions when you do not understand terminology, equipment, or reasons for prescribed practices.
- Learn how to adapt and modify materials and instruction.
- Learn as much as you can, and encourage the professionals you work with to do the same. Find out about training that may be available and ask to go.
- Suggest that others, especially students, become informed. Use your local library and bookstores to find print material that you can read and share.

Summary

- Many students with sensory deficits are educated in general education classrooms.
- For students with sensory impairments to receive an appropriate education, various adaptations and/or accommodations must be made.
- Students with hearing and visual problems represent a very heterogeneous group.
- Most students with hearing problems have some residual hearing ability.
- The term *hearing impairment* includes individuals with deafness and those who are hard of hearing.

- The effect of a hearing loss on a student's ability to understand speech is a primary concern for teachers.
- An audiometric evaluation determines the type and severity of a hearing disorder.
- Several factors should alert teachers to a possible hearing loss in a particular student.
- Teachers in general education classrooms must implement a variety of adaptations and/or accommodations for students with hearing impairments.
- The seating location of a student with hearing loss is critical for effective instruction.

- The most challenging aspect of teaching students with hearing problems is making sure that they participate in the communicational activities that occur in the classroom.
- Specialized equipment, such as hearing aids and other assistive listening devices (e.g., FM systems), may be necessary to ensure the success of students with hearing losses.
- Vision plays a critical role in the development of concepts such as understanding the spatial relations of the environment.
- Teachers must use a variety of adaptations and/or accommodations for students with visual impairments.
- Most students with visual impairments have residual or low vision.
- Refractive errors are the most common form of visual impairment.
- Visual problems may be congenital or occur later in life.

- The most educationally relevant characteristic of students who have visual impairments is the extent of their visual efficiency.
- It is critical that students with visual impairments be socially accepted in their general education classrooms.
- Academic tests may need to be adapted when evaluating students with visual impairments.
- Special materials may be needed when working with students with visual problems.
- Using large-print and non-glare materials may be sufficient adaptations for many students with visual impairments.
- A very small number of students require instruction in Braille.
- Specialists to teach Braille and develop Braille materials may be needed in order to successfully place students with visual impairments in general education classrooms.

Resources

Resource Guides and Other Print Materials

Alberta Education, Special Education Branch. (1995). *Teaching students who are deaf or hard of hearing.* Edmonton: Author.

Alberta Education, Special Education Branch. (1996). *Teaching students with visual impairments.* Edmonton: Author.

These resource guides from Alberta Education, Special Education Branch, are excellent sources of information about teaching students with visual and hearing impairments in the classroom. Teachers new to teaching such students in their classrooms will find the books invaluable. Additional teaching resources are suggested.

British Columbia Ministry of Education, Special Programs Branch. (1995). *Students with visual impairments: A resource guide to support classroom teachers.* Victoria: Author.

British Columbia Ministry of Education, Special Programs Branch. (1995). *Hard of hearing and deaf students: A resource guide to support classroom teachers.* Victoria: Author.

Teachers will find these very practical teacher resource guides good for working with students with visual or hearing impairments. A number of simple tips and suggestions are included.

Quigley, Stephen, and King, Cynthia. (1989). *Reading milestones.* Bellevue, WA: Dormac Inc.

These readers and workbooks are linguistically controlled and specifically designed for children who are hearing impaired.

Rikhe, C. H., et al. (1989). "A classroom environment checklist for students with dual sensory impairments." *Teaching Exceptional Children, 22*(1), 44–46.

A good summative check of the classroom for teachers of students with dual sensory impairments, this checklist helps teachers be aware of what aspects of their classroom need to be adapted.

Metropolitan Toronto School Board. (1993). *Vision video: Integrating the visually impaired student in the 90s.* Toronto: Author.

This video demonstrates specific teaching methods and adaptations necessary for the integration of students with visual impairments (K–12) as well as current technology which can assist students with such impairments.

Associations

The following national organizations offer a variety of positions on the education of students with hearing impairments. Many have provincial/territorial offices.

The Canadian Hearing Society
271 Spadina Road, Toronto, ON M5R 2V3
Voice: (416) 964-9595
TTY: (416) 964-0023
Fax: (416) 928-2525
Website: **www.chs.ca/**

Canadian Association of the Deaf
Suite 203, 251 Bank Street, Ottawa, ON K2P 1X3
Phone/TTY: (613) 565-2882
Fax: (613) 565-1207
Email: cad@cad.ca
Website: **www.cad.ca/**

Canadian Hard of Hearing Association (CHHA)
2435 Holly Lane, Suite 205, Ottawa, ON K1V 7P2
Voice: 1 (800) 263-8068; (613) 526-1584
TTY: (613) 526-2692
Fax: (613) 526-4718
Email: chhanational@chha.ca
Website: **www.cyberus.ca/~chhanational/**

Canadian Association of Educators of the Deaf and Hard of Hearing
Kiki Papaconstantinou, National Director
Mackay Center, 3500 Decarie Blvd.,
Montreal, PQ H4A 3J5
Phone: (514) 482-0500 ext. 278
Fax: (514) 482-4536
Email: kiki@mackayctr.org

CAEDHH Journal
c/o Department of Educational Psychology
6-102 Education North, University of Alberta,
Edmonton, AB T6G 2G5
Website: **www.education.ualberta.ca/educ/ journals/caedhh.html**

Canadian National Institute for the Blind (CNIB)
1929 Bayview Avenue, Toronto, ON M4G 3E8
Phone: (416) 486-2500
Website: **www.cnib.ca/**

The Institute provides a variety of resources, services, and related websites. Its library is a huge resource of books, magazines, newspapers, and information, all of which are available to anyone who is blind or print disabled (including individuals with learning disabilities). The Institute has a website specifically for children (CNIB Library: For Kids) which includes a newsletter on audiocassette, summer reading clubs, creative writing and Braille accuracy competitions, pen pals, and lists of good websites for children who are blind, visually impaired, or print disabled. Finally, the CNIB Library: VISUNET: CANADA provides materials to individuals and school libraries through mail or over the internet.

eblinks

The Canadian Hearing Society
www.chs.ca/
An excellent website to first learn about individuals who are hard of hearing or deaf, this site provides information, resources, and links related to both manual/sign approaches to education, oral approaches, and deaf culture. A must visit for anyone working with students who are deaf or hard of hearing.

The Canadian Association of the Deaf
www.cad.ca/
A variety of information relevant to people interested in learning about the deaf community and deaf education appears here. There is a fair and good introduction to the area of the deaf and hard of hearing.

DeafCanadaOnline
www.deafcanada.com/
An online site maintained by individuals who are part of the deaf community in Canada, this site lists Canadian, American, and international websites related to education of the deaf, social and political issues, business, religion, resources, sports, recreation, social services, and interpreters. In addi-

tion, contributors provide current events and news as well as humour and resources on their own site. Content is constantly updated and expanding.

Canadian Hard of Hearing Association (CHHA)
www.chha.ca/
Here is a good site for those who are interested in learning more about the integration of people who are hard of hearing into the mainstream. The site provides resources and links committed to the goal of integration.

Canadian Association for the Education of the Deaf and Hard of Hearing (CAEDHH)
www.education.ualberta.ca/educ/journals/caedhh.html
The CAEDHH Journal site serves teachers of students who are deaf or hard of hearing.

Canadian National Institute for the Blind
www.cnib.ca/
This excellent website provides a huge source of information, resources, and activities relevant to individuals with varying degrees of visual impairment.

Teaching Students with Autism, Traumatic Brain Injury, and Other Low-Incidence Disabilities

9

After reading this chapter, you should be able to

- define and describe students with autism spectrum disorders
- define and describe students with traumatic brain injury
- define and describe students with health problems and physical disabilities
- describe various intervention strategies for students with autism, traumatic brain injury, health problems, and physical disabilities

Curtis's parents noted something different about their child when he was about two years old. Up until that time he had developed perfectly. He walked at 13 months, started babbling at about 15 months, and loved to play with adults and other children. Then things began to change. His babbling stopped, he developed sort of a blank stare, his early success at toilet training seemed to be reversed, and he stopped paying any attention to other children and adults. When he was about three years old, his parents took him to the provincial children's hospital, and the diagnosis was autism. What a shock! Curtis was placed in a preschool program and has been receiving special education services ever since. Now at the age of seven, he is enjoying being in a regular Grade 2 classroom. In both kindergarten and Grade 1 he was placed in a self-contained special education classroom. During these two years, Curtis seemed to regress. He actually started picking up some of the other children's stereotypical, self-stimulating behaviours. His parents convinced the school to give Curtis a try in the regular classroom for Grade 2, with some special education support. Now, in December, Curtis seems to be doing very well. While he has very little oral language, he seems to enjoy being with his typically achieving peers and is able to do most of the academic work with the assistance of a paraprofessional.

Questions to Consider

1. Is there a preferred placement for children with autism?

2. What kinds of supports should be available for Curtis to facilitate his success in the regular classroom?

3. Is a child ever *ready* for inclusion, or does the school have to make the placement decision and provide the necessary supports to make it work?

Introduction

The previous chapter dealt with students with sensory impairments, typically considered low-incidence disabilities because they do not occur in many children. In addition to these two categories of disabilities, many other conditions that occur relatively rarely in children can result in significant challenges for these students, their families, school personnel, and other professionals. These conditions include autism spectrum disorders (ASD), traumatic brain injury (TBI), fetal alcohol spectrum disorders (FASD), and a host of physical and health problems that may be present in school-age children, such as cerebral palsy, spina bifida, AIDS, cystic fibrosis, epilepsy, and diabetes.

Many general education classroom teachers will teach their entire careers without encountering children with these problems. However, because children with these kinds of conditions may be included in their future classrooms, teachers need to generally understand the conditions and how to support these students in the classroom. This chapter will provide substantial information on autism spectrum disorders and traumatic brain injury; other conditions will be presented more briefly. Often, schools provide support personnel for teachers and students with these types of problems. Therefore, teachers should not have to "go it alone" when working with students with these disabilities. Behavioural specialists, psychologists, physical therapists, occupational therapists, and other health personnel are often available to provide services to students and supports to their teachers (Wadsworth & Knight, 1999). The fact that many different professionals provide services for some of these children may have repercussions for students of certain cultural backgrounds. Individuals from some cultures, for example, prefer to interact with only one person at a time, rather than a team of individuals. Professionals providing services must be sensitive to the cultural traits that characterize different families. They should consider the unique characteristics of each student's cultural background.

It is impossible to describe every single condition experienced by children with autism, TBI, and other low-incidence disabilities. Though this chapter will discuss the more well-known conditions and some that are unique and interesting, the conditions described here do not form an exhaustive list. Rather, they cover only a small range of the problems experienced within these groups.

CONSIDER THIS

What are some problems that may be encountered by general classroom teachers with which specialists could provide assistance?

Basic Concepts about Autism

Autism is a pervasive developmental disorder that primarily affects social interactions, language, and behaviour. Although autism has been glamorized by several movies, such as *Rain Man* (1988), many students with this condition do not have the incredible abilities reflected in the movie. Also, even for students with extraordinary skills, the presence of autism still has a significant impact on individuals and their families. The characteristics displayed by individuals with autism vary significantly; some individuals are able to assimilate into community settings and activities, whereas others have major difficulties achieving such normality (Scheuermann & Webber, 2002). Needless to say, "children and youth with autism spectrum disorders are a particularly unique group, even when compared with other children with disabilities" (Simpson, 2001, p. 68).

The Geneva Centre for Autism in Toronto, Ontario, explains what is meant by autism spectrum disorders, stating that

> Autism is often referred to as a "spectrum disorder," meaning that its symptoms and characteristics can present themselves in a variety of combinations, ranging from mild to quite severe. The phrase "autism spectrum disorders (ASD)" refers to a broad definition of autism including the classical form of the disorder [Autistic

Disorder] as well as Pervasive Developmental Disorder (PDD), Rett's syndrome, Asperger syndrome, and Childhood Disintegrative Disorder. (Geneva Centre, 2004)

The study of autism has had a confusing and controversial history since the condition was first described less than 50 years ago by Dr. Leo Kanner (Scheuermann & Webber, 2002). Some of the early controversy centred on attempts to relate the cause of autism to poor mother–child bonding. Eventually this hypothesis was disproved, but it caused a great deal of guilt, confusion, and misunderstanding. Many professionals once thought that children with autism made a conscious decision to withdraw from their environment because of its hostile nature. During the 1980s, autism was found to be an organic disorder, eliminating much of this speculation (Eaves, 1992).

In most jurisdictions in Canada, autism is not a separate category of exceptionality. Instead, students with autism are served under such categories as intellectual disability, communication disorder, or learning disability, depending on the severity of the condition.

Autism is a relatively rare condition, occurring in only about 1 per 2000 children. In the United States during the 1993–94 school year, 18 903 children were classified as having autism, which accounted for only 0.3 percent of children in special education programs, making it one of the smallest disability categories recognized in the schools (U.S. Department of Education, 1995). No figures are available for Canada, largely due to the lack of a separate category. Eaves (1992) notes that the prevalence rate is 6 to 10 per 10 000 individuals. Compared to the 300 per 10 000 prevalence rate of intellectual disabilities (Beirne-Smith, Patton, & Ittenbach, 1994), autism represents a very low-incidence disability. Some children have a higher risk for autism than others. For example, children who are born with rubella and those classified as having fragile X syndrome are more likely to develop autism than other children (Blackman, 1990). In general, however, autism strikes randomly in all segments of society.

Defining Autism

Although many definitions of autism have been developed, no single definition has been universally accepted. However, it is important to be familiar with two definitions: the one in the U.S. Individuals with Disabilities Act (IDEA), used primarily by educators, and the one found in the ***Diagnostic and Statistical Manual of Mental Disorders (DSM-IV-TR)***, used by psychologists and medical professionals. IDEA defines autism as "a developmental disability that primarily results in significant deficits in verbal and non-verbal communication and social interactions, generally evidenced before the age of 3 years and adversely affects the child's educational performance" (34 CFR 300.7(b) (1))."

There are other definitions of autism that are popular among some groups. For example, on the website for the Autism Society of Canada (ASC) a link to the definition established by the Autism Society of America is provided. The Autism Society of America, the primary parent advocacy group associated with autism, defines autism using the following definition (Autism Society of America, 2000a):

Autism is a complex developmental disability that typically appears during the first three years of life. The result of a neurological disorder that affects the functioning of the brain, autism and its associated behaviors have been estimated to occur in as many as 1 in 500 individuals. Autism is four times more prevalent in boys than girls and knows no racial, ethnic, or social boundaries. Family income, life-style, and educational levels do not affect the chance of autism's occurrence.

Autism interferes with the normal development of the brain in the areas of social interaction and communication skills. Children and adults with autism typically have difficulties in verbal and non-verbal communication, social interactions, and leisure or play activities. The disorder makes it hard for them to

CONSIDER THIS

How can movies that depict persons with disabilities help, as well as hurt, the cause of providing appropriate educational opportunities to students with disabilities?

FURTHER READING

In order to learn more about the disorders that fall under the umbrella of autism spectrum disorders, read sections in the *Diagnostic and Statistical Manual* (2000) *(DSM-IV-TR)* of the American Psychiatric Association that deal with autism and pervasive developmental disorder (PDD).

Personal Spotlight

Provincial Learning Consultant Anita Nargang

Anita Nargang is currently working with Saskatchewan Learning as a consultant in the area of autism and with the University of Regina as a sessional instructor in educational psychology. Anita's experience as a classroom teacher has been at the elementary and middle-school level (K–9). She has also worked as a school division special education co-ordinator. Anita has a master of education degree from the University of Regina.

Anita is also a parent of a son who has autism. Having sat on both sides of the table, she believes strongly in the collaborative process. Communication is very important when working with individuals with exceptionalities. Parents and educators have to come together to work out a plan that best meets the needs of the student.

Anita believes that as educators we must endeavour to get to know these unique individuals; we must build rapport with

them in order to create a comfort level that is conducive to learning. One of the greatest obstacles, she believes, that autistic students face is being able to "show what they know." If they feel comfortable and the teacher knows the students' strengths and areas of weakness, this obstacle is reduced greatly.

Anita believes that parents and educators have to communicate clear expectations to their students and children. We must keep raising the bar and challenging our students. We must keep moving forward slowly, steadily, taking small steps until our students reach their goals. Our jobs are to prepare students for what lies beyond the school/home doors. We must try to make their education meaningful and functional so that they can be happy, contributing members of our society.

communicate with others and relate to the outside world. They may exhibit repeated body movements (hand flapping, rocking), unusual responses to people or attachments to objects, and they may resist changes in routines. (p. 3)

Identification of Children with Autism

Just as autism is hard to define, children with autism are difficult to identify. Problems related to the identification of these children include the following:

▷ Children with autism display many characteristics exhibited by individuals with other disabilities, such as speech and language disorders.
▷ Many children with autism, because they exhibit disorders across multiple domains, are mistakenly classified as having multiple disabilities.
▷ No stable classification system is used among educators and other professionals who encounter children with autism. (Eaves, 1992)

Still another problem in identifying children with autism is the large, diverse group of professionals responsible for the evaluation and diagnosis. In diagnosing some disabilities, educators function as the lead professionals; in the area of autism, pediatricians, speech-language pathologists, psychologists, audiologists, and social workers are typically involved as well. Working with such a large group of individuals can cause difficult logistical problems. Diverse definitions and eligibility criteria, different funding agencies, and varying services complicate the process of identifying and serving these children and adults.

Causes of Autism

There is no single specific cause of autism, but a variety of factors can result in this disability. Organic factors such as brain damage, genetic links, and complications during pregnancy may cause this condition, though in most cases, no cause can be confirmed (Kaplan, 1996).

FURTHER READING

For more information on identifying children with autism, read the chapter on autism by R. C. Eaves in P. J. McLaughlin & P. Wehman's book, *Developmental Disabilities,* published in 1997 by Andover Press in Boston.

Characteristics of Individuals with Autism

The Autism Treatment Services of Canada (ATSC) notes that children with autism have difficulty relating to other people, avoid eye contact, and have significant impairments in communication, although ATSC adds, "If a person were to walk into a room full of people with autism, they would likely be struck more by the differences than the similarities." Nevertheless, autism carries numerous distinct characteristics. Some of the more pervasive include verbal and nonverbal communication impairments (Dyches, 1998), auditory-based sensory impairments (Orr, Myles, & Carlson, 1998), and problems relating to other individuals (Autism Society of America, 2000b). Scheuermann and Webber (2002) describe the characteristics of autism using two major groups: behavioural deficits and behavioural excesses.

1. Behavioural deficits
   ▶ Inability to relate to others
   ▶ Lack of functional language
   ▶ Sensory processing deficits
   ▶ Cognitive deficits

2. Behavioural excesses
   ▶ Self-stimulation
   ▶ Resistance to change
   ▶ Bizarre and challenging behaviours
   ▶ Self-injurious behaviours

Although most of these characteristics are negative, some children with autism present some positive, as well as unexpected, characteristics. For example, Tirosh and Canby (1993) describe children with autism who also have hyperlexia, which is defined as "an advance of at least one standard deviation (SD) in the reading over the verbal IQ level" (p. 86). For these children, spelling and contextual reading also appeared to be advanced.

In some cases, children with autism display unique **splinter skills**, or islands of precocity where they display areas of giftedness. "Common splinter skills include (1) calendar abilities, such as being able to give the day of the week for any date you might provide (e.g., May 12, 1896); (2) the ability to count visual things quickly, such as telling how many toothpicks are on the floor when a box is dropped; (3) artistic ability, such as the ability to design machinery; and (4) musical ability, such as playing a piano" (Scheuermann & Webber, 2002, p. 9). These types of skills are found in only a small number of children with autism, but they do add interest to studying children with this disability.

Classroom Adaptations for Students with Autism

Formerly, the prognosis for individuals with autism was pessimistic; most children with autism would grow into adulthood with severe impairments. However, intensive intervention programs have been somewhat effective with this group. No single method is effective with all children with autism, partly because these children display widely variable characteristics (Heflin & Simpson, 1998). However, several different techniques have shown positive results (Kaplan, 1996). Table 9.1 summarizes some of these techniques.

Growing evidence shows that placing children with autism with their typically achieving peers in general education settings, with appropriate supports, can make a significant difference in their behaviours. Appropriate role models appear to be very important. Recent research also indicates that behavioural treatment of children with autism, especially young children, may result in significant long-term gains in intellectual and adaptive behaviour areas (McEachlin et al., 1993). Also, social skills training has been shown to be effective for this group of children (Kamps et al., 1992).

CROSS-REFERENCE

Review the section in Chapter 6 on children with serious emotional disturbance (SED). Compare the characteristics of children with autism and those with SED. How are these children similar and different?

CONSIDER THIS

How might splinter skills confuse family members about the abilities and capabilities of a child with autism?

TEACHING TIP

Peer buddies can be very useful to a student with autism in a general education classroom. Peers can serve as excellent role models and provide supports for these students.

TEACHING TIP

Always remember that students with autism present a wide range of characteristics, strengths, and weaknesses. Treat each child as a unique individual, and do not expect them all to need the same kinds of services.

TABLE 9.1	Classroom Tips for Teaching Children with Autism

Tip	Reason
1. Teaching a child with autism should be seen as a team approach with many professionals helping the classroom teacher.	The child with autism being educated in a regular class has probably been treated by many professionals who have extensive experience with the child. Their experiences and suggestions are of great help to the teacher. Regular consultations should be scheduled.
2. Learn everything possible about the child's development, behaviour, and what services the child has received.	Understanding the nature of the child's difficulties and what has been accomplished previously can serve as a beginning for designing a program that will enable the child to learn.
3. Try to foster an atmosphere of shared decision making with other professionals responsible for the child's progress.	Successful models for integration of children with autism into regular classes show that shared decision making among all professionals leads to superior results.
4. Do not assume that children with autism have mental retardation.	The serious behavioural and linguistic difficulties of these children may lead to the assumption that they have mental retardation. The meaning of intelligence tests for children with autism is subject to question.
5. Beware of even suggesting that parents have caused their children's difficulties.	Blaming parents is counterproductive since parental help is so often required. However, in the case of autism, old discredited theories did suggest such a connection. Even though these ideas have been proven false, parental guilt may be present.
6. Prepare the class for the child with autism.	Discussing the nature of autism and some behaviours, such as rocking, may help allay the concerns of other children in the class.

From *Pathways for Exceptional Children* (p. 595), by P. S. Kaplan, 1996, St. Paul, MN: West Publishing. Used by permission.

Regardless of the specific intervention used, professionals developing programs for children with autism should ask these questions (Heflin & Simpson, 1998):

1. What are the anticipated outcomes of the programming option?
2. What are the potential risks?
3. How will the option be evaluated?
4. What proof is available that the option is effective?
5. What other options would be excluded if this option is chosen?

Since there is no single, best method for teaching students with autism, school personnel must have available a variety of intervention strategies. Ruble and Dalrymple (2002) suggest a variety of environmental supports that can facilitate the success of students with autism. These are listed in Table 9.2.

In addition, Egel (1989) has emphasized two important principles that should inform educational programs for children with autism: the use of functional activities and an effort to make programs appropriate for the student's developmental level and chronological age. Children with autism grow up to be adults with autism; the condition cannot be cured. As a result, educational programs should help them deal with the daily needs that will extend throughout their lives. To help educators focus more on the functionality of curriculum choices, they should ask themselves the following questions:

1. Does the program teach skills that are immediately useful?
2. Will the materials used be available in the student's daily environment?
3. Will learning certain skills make it less likely that someone will not have to do the task for the student in the future?

CONSIDER THIS

How should the curriculum for students with autism be balanced between academic skills and functional life skills?

CROSS-REFERENCE

Review in Chapter 7 program recommendations for students with intellectual disabilities. How are programs for these two groups of students similar and different?

If the answer to any of these questions is no, then the instructional program should be changed.

Programs for students with autism should also be age appropriate and **developmentally appropriate**. That is, the level of instruction should meet the developmental

TABLE 9.2	Environmental Supports for Children with Autism

Communicating to the Person (Receptive Language Supports)
Slow down the pace
State positively what to do (e.g., "Let's walk" instead of "Stop running")
Provide more information in visual format

Encouraging Communication from the Person (Expressive Language Supports)
Pause, listen, and wait
Encourage input and choice when possible
Provide alternative means, such as written words or pictures, to aid communication
Encourage and respond to words and appropriate attempts, rather than to behaviour

Social Supports
Build in time to watch, encourage watching and proximity
Practise on specific skills through natural activities with one peer
Structure activities with set interaction patterns and roles
Provide cooperative learning activities with facilitation
Facilitate recruitment of sociable peers to be buddies and advocates
Provide opportunity for shared experiences using interests and strengths

Expanding Repertoires of Interests and Activities
Capitalize on strengths and individual learning styles
Over time, minimize specific fears and frustrations
Use rehearsal with visuals

From "COMPASS: A Parent-Teacher Collaborative Model for Students with Autism" (p. 76) by L. A. Ruble & N. J. Dalrymple, 2002, *Focus on Autism and Other Developmental Disabilities, 17.* Used with permission.

Self-management is a promising intervention strategy for children with autism.

level of the individual. The individual's chronological age and developmental status must be considered together. These two realms are sometimes incongruent, making program planning a challenge (McDonnell, Hardman, McDonnell, & Kiefer-O'Donnell, 1995). In this case, developmentally appropriate materials must be modified to make them as age appropriate as possible. Remember to keep chronological and developmental status in mind when developing and implementing individualized education programs. These developmental levels should also be taken into consideration when implementing classroom adaptations.

A promising intervention strategy for children and adults with autism is **self-management**—implementing a variety of techniques that assist in self-control. Although total self-management is not possible for many students with autism, most students can be taught to improve their skills in this area (Alberto & Troutman, 1995). Koegel et al. (1992) studied four children with autism who displayed a variety of inappropriate behaviours, including **self-injurious behaviours** (or self-abusive behaviours), running away from school personnel, delayed echolalic speech (repeating what is said to them), hitting objects, and stereotypical twirling of hair. After several sessions in which the children were taught how to use self-management strategies, such as **self-recording** (documenting their own behaviour) and **self-reinforcement** (giving themselves reinforcers), marked improvement occurred. The results indicate that "the lack of social responsivity that is so characteristic in autism can be successfully treated with self-management procedures, requiring minimal presence of a treatment provider in the children's natural environments" (p. 350). This particular study focused on self-management related to social skills, yet hints at the possibility that such interventions could be successful in other areas.

Over the past several years, a major controversy has erupted in the education of children with autism over the use of **facilitated communication**, a process in which a *facilitator* helps the person with autism (or some other disability related to expressive language) type or use a keyboard for communication purposes. The process is described by Biklen, Morton, Gold, Berrigan, and Swaminathan (1992) as follows:

> Facilitated communication involves a series of steps. The communicator types with one index finger, first with hand over hand or hand-at-the-wrist support and then later independently or with just a touch to the elbow or shoulder. Over time, the communicator progresses from structured work such as fill-in-the-blanks/cloze exercises and multiple-choice activities to open-ended, typed, conversational text. (p. 5)

Although this method was once touted as the key to establishing communication with children with autism, recent studies have cast doubt on its authenticity. The heart of the controversy concerns how to validate the technique. Advocates of the method offer numerous qualitative research studies as proof of success, yet recent quantitative research raises significant questions about the program. After reviewing much of the empirical research related to facilitated communication, Kaplan (1996) reported that evidence often shows that the facilitator influences the person with autism, though the facilitator may be unaware of it. Yet despite the growing evidence questioning the efficacy of facilitated communication, Kaplan says that "it would be incorrect to suggest that because excesses sometimes creep into the way the method is used, it should completely be abandoned" (p. 585). In other words, although little empirical evidence supports facilitated communication, it could still be an effective means of communication for some individuals and should not be abandoned totally until more study is done. It is unlikely, however, that facilitated communication is the miracle many people had hoped it would be.

FURTHER READING

For more information on teaching self-management skills to students with autism, read *Applied Behavior Analysis for Teachers,* by P. A. Alberto and A. C. Troutman, published by Merrill in 1995; and "Improving Social Skills and Disruptive Behavior in Children with Autism through Self-management" in volume 25 of the *Journal of Applied Behavior Analysis* by L. K. Koegel, R. L. Koegel, C. Hurley, and W. D. Frea.

Asperger Syndrome

During the past few years, a condition associated with autism has received a great deal of attention. This condition, called **Asperger syndrome**, was first described in 1944 by Hans Asperger (Griswold et al., 2002) but largely ignored until it was first included in *DSM-IV* (Safran, 2002). In general, students classified as having Asperger syndrome share many of the same characteristics of children with autism, but also display some unique features. "Clinical features of Asperger syndrome include social interaction impairments, speech and communication characteristics, cognitive and academic characteristics, sensory characteristics, and physical and motor-skill anomalies" (Myles & Simpson, 1998, p. 3). These characteristics, for the most part, are the same as those found in children with autism (McLaughlin-Cheng, 1998). Children with Asperger syndrome differ from those with autism in having higher cognitive development and more typical communication skills. Table 9.3 shows the similarities and differences of the behavioural characteristics of children with Asperger syndrome and children with autism.

Autism is a very significant disability. Characterized by language and social deficiencies, the condition results in lifelong problems for the person with autism and the person's family. As more research into autism is completed, better methods of managing and teaching children with autism will be developed.

CONSIDER THIS

How can the use of invalidated procedures harm students? Why do some ideas become popular with some educators and family members before they are proved effective?

Basic Concepts about Traumatic Brain Injury

Traumatic brain injury (TBI) is defined by the American Speech-Language and Hearing Association as "an injury to the head [that] may cause interference with normal brain functions" (ASHA, 2004f). These types of injuries could be the result of a foreign object, such as a bullet, entering the brain and causing damage to specific areas (a penetrating injury), or the result of a blow to the head, such as an injury sustained in a car accident (a closed head injury) (ASHA, 2004f). Traumatic brain injuries can affect psychological and cognitive abilities, speech and language, physical functioning, and personal and social behaviours.

Traumatic brain injury can result from a wide variety of causes, including falls, vehicle accidents, and even abuse. It can also be caused by lack of oxygen to the brain, infections, tumours, and strokes (Garcia, Krankowski, & Jones, 1998). Information about the severity of a traumatic brain injury is important for teachers to know, as it can provide a sense of the expected long-term outcomes for a student. Although no standardized system has been developed to describe levels of severity, Mira et al. (1992) offer the following one, which is derived from a variety of sources:

FURTHER READING

Traumatic brain injuries are largely preventable (e.g., preventing injuries in motor vehicle accidents by wearing appropriate safety restraints). For more information on the prevention of traumatic brain injuries, and classroom resources to address this issue, refer to the Safe Kids Canada website (www.safekidscanada.ca).

Mild: Signs of concussion or a blow resulting in some after-effects, such as dizziness or loss of consciousness, for less than an hour; no skull fracture; majority of brain injuries are mild.

Moderate: Loss of consciousness for 1 to 24 hours or evidence of a skull fracture; may develop secondary neurological problems such as swelling within the brain and subsequent complications; neurosurgery may be required.

Severe: Loss of consciousness for more than 24 hours, or evidence of contusion (actual bruising of brain tissue) or intracranial hematoma (bleeding within the brain); long-term medical care is likely; typical sequelae (consequences) include motor, language, and cognitive problems.

The social-emotional and cognitive deficits caused by the injury may persist long after physical capabilities recover. Students with TBI can experience a host of confus-

TABLE 9.3	Behavioural Comparison of Asperger Syndrome and Autism	
	Asperger Syndrome	**Autistic Syndrome**
1. Intelligence measures		
Standardized scores	Average to high average range	Borderline through average range
2. Language		
Development	Normal development	Delayed onset, deficits
Pragmatic language		
a. Verbal	Deficits can be observed	Delayed and disordered
b. Nonverbal	Deficits (e.g., odd eye gaze)	Deficits can be severe
3. Communication		
Expressive	Within normal limits	Deficits can be observed
Receptive	Within normal limits	Deficits can be observed
4. Social responsiveness		
Attachment		
a. Parents	Observed responsiveness	Lack responsiveness
b. Caregivers	Observed responsiveness	Lack responsiveness
c. Peers	Observed responsiveness	Lack responsiveness
Interactions		
a. Initiations to peers	Frequent, poor quality	Minimal frequency
b. Positive responses to peers	Frequent, awkward, and pertains to self-interests	Minimal frequency
c. Symbolic play	No impaired symbolic play	Absence of symbolic play
d. Reciprocal play	Observed but awkward	Minimal frequency
e. Coping	Deficits observed in quality	
f. Friendships	Minimal frequency	Minimal frequency
g. Requests for assistance	Observed but awkward	Minimal frequency
Emotional self-regulation		
a. Emotional empathy	Observed but awkward	Deficits can be observed
b. Emotional responsiveness	Observed but could be extreme	Aloof, indifferent
5. Physical/motor		
a. Gross motor	Observed deficits–controversial	No observed deficits
b. Repetitive behaviour	Observed	Observed

From "Asperger Syndrome and Autism: A Literature Review and Meta-analysis" (p. 237) by E. McLaughlin-Cheng, 1998, *Focus on Autism and Other Developmental Disabilities, 13.* Used by permission.

ing and frustrating symptoms. "There is an inability to concentrate; short-term memory is affected; one's self-confidence is undermined; self-esteem is diminished; the personality changes;... the family and friends are affected" (Infusini, 1994, pp. 4–5). Teachers must guard against minimizing an injury because it presents no visible evidence and many children exhibit typical behaviours. Some students with TBI will experience academic success, while others will have long-term lingering effects of their injury (Table 9.4).

The prognosis for recovery depends on many variables. Initially, it is "influenced by the type of injury and the rapidity and quality of medical and surgical care" (Bigge, 1991, p. 197). Later, it will be influenced by the nature of rehabilitative and educational intervention.

TABLE 9.4	Persisting Features of Traumatic Brain Injury

Area of Functioning	Possible Effects
Physical/Medical	▶ Fatigue and reduced stamina ▶ Seizures (5%) ▶ Headaches ▶ Problems with regulation of various functions (e.g., growth, eating, body temperature)
Sensory	▶ Hearing problems (e.g., conductive and/or sensorineural loss) ▶ Vision problems (e.g., blurred vision, visual field defects)
Cognitive	▶ Memory problems (e.g., storage and retrieval) ▶ Attentional difficulties ▶ Intellectual deficits ▶ Reasoning and problem-solving difficulties
Language-Related	▶ Word retrieval difficulties ▶ Motor-speech problems (e.g., dysarthria) ▶ Language comprehension deficits (e.g., difficulty listening) ▶ Difficulty acquiring new vocabulary and learning new concepts ▶ Socially inappropriate verbal behaviour
Behavioural/Emotional	▶ Problems in planning, organizing, and problem solving ▶ Disinhibition ▶ Overactivity ▶ Impulsivity ▶ Lack of self-direction ▶ Helplessness or apathy ▶ Inability to recognize one's injury

From *Traumatic Brain Injury in Children and Adolescents: A Sourcebook for Teachers and Other School Personnel* (pp. 71–72), by M. P. Mira, B. F. Tucker, and J. S. Tyler, 1992, Austin, TX: Pro-Ed. Used by permission.

Classroom Adaptations for Students with Traumatic Brain Injury

The transition of students with TBI from rehabilitation facilities to school settings needs to be co-ordinated among a number of people. Intervention involves the efforts of professionals from many different disciplines, including teachers (Bergland & Hoffbauer, 1996). In addition to the injury itself and its implications for functioning and potential learning, students probably will have missed a significant amount of schooling. All of these factors can have a significant impact on educational performance. An effective educational program creates a positive attitude about the student's prognosis that reaches beyond just speaking positively. Teachers communicate a positive attitude by the type of programming they present and by the level of expectations they establish. Remember to "keep expectations for students' performance high. Often, this means providing students with mild TBI with multiple opportunities for practice that do not carry penalties for inaccuracy" (Hux & Hackley, 1996). This will show the students that programs and instruction are designed to support them and not just to give them a grade. They will respond better when programs do not seem punitive.

Students identified with a traumatic brain injury will likely have an individualized education plan put in place to address their educational needs. Teachers will need to address the specific areas that have been identified as problematic for the individual. Table 9.5 gives ideas for helping students with problems that may result from TBI.

CONSIDER THIS

What can school personnel do to facilitate the transition of children with TBI from hospital and residential settings to the public school? What kind of relationship should school personnel and hospital personnel maintain with each other after the transition is completed?

| **Table 9.5** | Recommended Instructional Strategies for Children with TBI |

Use a multimodal approach (overheads, videos, hands-on activities) when presenting material and instructions for assignments.	Encourage questions.
	Break down large assignments into smaller components.
Teach compensatory strategies to students and structure choices.	Use task analyses to determine skill acquisition and maintenance.
Begin class with review and overview of topics to be covered.	Ask the student how he or she could improve learning.
Provide the student with an outline of the material to be presented, to assist in comprehension.	Use a variety of open-ended and multiple-choice questions to encourage independent thinking.
Emphasize main points and key ideas frequently.	Present difficult material in a simplified fashion, using illustrations or diagrams if possible.
Incorporate repetition into instruction.	Provide the student with cues when appropriate.
Provide specific, frequent feedback on student performance and behaviour.	

From "Enhancing the Schooling of Students with Traumatic Brain Injury" (p. 65) by L. Keyser-Marcus, L. Briel, P. Sherron-Targett, S. Yasuda, S. Johnson, & P. Wehman, 2002, *Teaching Exceptional Children, 34.* Used with permission.

A well-planned program of instruction should focus on "retaining impaired cognitive processes, developing new skills or procedures to compensate for residual deficits, creating an environment that permits effective performance, identifying effective instructional procedures, and improving metacognitive awareness" (Ylvisaker, Szekeres, Hartwick, & Tworek, 1994, p. 17). The impact of the injury may require that the student learn compensatory strategies to make up for deficits. Such strategies can address problems with attending, language comprehension, memory, sequencing, and thought organization.

The following suggestions will help provide a positive learning program and environment for students with TBI:

- Prepare classmates for the re-entry of a fellow student who has sustained a traumatic brain injury—it is important to discuss any changes in physical functioning and personality.
- Modify the classroom to ensure safety and to address any specific needs of the student.
- Minimize visual and auditory distractions that may interfere with attention to task.
- Be familiar with any special equipment that might be needed (e.g., augmentative communication devices).
- Be familiar with the effects and administration procedures of prescribed medications.
- Consider special seating, depending on needs.
- Ensure that students are attending to instructional activities—teach students to monitor their own attention behaviour.
- Help students with memory problems by teaching them mnemonic strategies.
- Assist students who are having difficulty with organization.
- Break down learning tasks into substeps.
- Create many opportunities for the student to use problem-solving skills.
- Allow extra time for students to respond to questions, take tests, complete assignments, and move from one setting to another.
- Teach students social skills appropriate for their age and needs.
- Implement behaviour reduction techniques to eliminate inappropriate and undesirable behaviours.

TEACHING TIP

Develop and implement intervention programs based on the student's specific needs. TBI results in a wide variety of deficits, producing a great diversity of needs.

▶ Help students to understand the nature of their injury.
▶ Provide information about academic, social, and psychomotor progress to families on a regular basis. Describe the nature of the educational program to them.

Fetal Alcohol Spectrum Disorders

Maternal consumption of alcohol during pregnancy can result in damage to a woman's unborn child. Fetal alcohol spectrum disorder (FASD) is

> an umbrella term [not a diagnostic term] used to refer to the damage or range of disabilities caused by alcohol consumption during pregnancy. These disabilities are lifelong conditions that affect not only the individual, but also the family and the community. The disabilities caused by prenatal alcohol exposure are often described as hidden or invisible because the physical characteristics can be subtle and may go unrecognized. (Saskatchewan Learning, 2004, p. 1.3)

Disorders that may be included under the umbrella term of FASD include: fetal alcohol syndrome (FAS), partial fetal alcohol syndrome (pFAS), alcohol-related birth defects (ARBD), and alcohol-related neurodevelopmental disorder (ARND) (Saskatchewan Learning, 2004). Although a team of professionals may be involved in the assessment of an individual suspected of presenting with a disorder related to prenatal alcohol exposure, the diagnosis of these disorders must be made by a medical doctor (Saskatchewan Learning, 2004). It is also important to note that students with FASD will demonstrate diverse physical, health, academic, and learning characteristics.

FURTHER READING

For more information on definitions and effective practices with fetal alcohol spectrum disorders, read the document "Planning for Students with Fetal Alcohol Spectrum Disorders: A Guide for Educators" (2004), found on the Saskatchewan Learning website (www.sasked.gov.sk.ca).

Basic Concepts about Low-Incidence Health Problems and Physical Disabilities

As noted in the beginning of this chapter, many health and **physical disabilities** may be present in children that result in a need for special education and related services. The remainder of this chapter will provide a quick guide to some of these disabilities and some considerations for educators. Teachers who work with children with one of these conditions should refer to a more thorough reference work to learn more about it. Margin notes in this text suggest such sources of information.

Asthma

FURTHER READING

For more information on asthma, read *Understanding Physical, Sensory, and Health Impairments*, by K. W. Heller, P. A. Alberto, P. E. Forney, and M. N. Schwartzman, published in 1996 by Brooks/Cole.

In Canada, 5 to 10 percent of Canadians, and as many as 20 percent of children, have asthma. According to the Asthma Society of Canada, asthma is the most common chronic childhood disease, the number-one cause of emergency room visits in pediatric centres, and the number-one cause of school absenteeism.

It is characterized by repetitive episodes of coughing, shortness of breath, and wheezing. These characteristics result from the narrowing of small air passages, caused by irritation of the bronchial tubes by allergic reactions to various substances, such as animal dander, air pollutants, and pollens. Asthma attacks can be very dangerous and should be taken seriously by school personnel. Specific suggestions for teachers include the following:

▶ Know the signs and symptoms of respiratory distress (Getch & Neuhart-Pritchett, 1999).
▶ Ensure that students have proper medications and that they are taken at the appropriate times.

▶ Allow students to rest when needed, as they often tire easily.
▶ Eliminate any known **allergens** from the classroom.
▶ Determine what types of physical limitations might have to be set (e.g., restriction of a certain physical activity that can induce attacks), but otherwise encourage students to play games and participate in activities.
▶ Recognize the side effects of prescribed medication.
▶ Remain calm if an attack occurs.
▶ Allow the student to participate in nonstressful activity until an episode subsides.
▶ Introduce a vaporizer or dehumidifier to the classroom when recommended by the student's physician.
▶ Work on building up the student's self-image.
▶ Sensitize other students in the class to the nature of allergic reactions.
▶ Develop an effective system for helping the student keep up with schoolwork, as frequent absences may occur.

Educators can ask the following questions to determine whether a school is prepared to deal with students with asthma (National Heart, Lung, and Blood Institute, 1998):

1. Is the school free of tobacco smoke all of the time, including during school-sponsored events?
2. Does the school maintain good indoor air quality?
3. Is a school nurse in the school all day, every day?
4. Can children take medicines at school as recommended by their doctor and parents?
5. Does the school have an emergency plan for taking care of a child with a severe asthma attack?
6. Does someone teach school staff about asthma, asthma management plans, and asthma medicines?
7. Do students with asthma have good options for fully and safely participating in physical education class and recess? (p. 168)

Childhood Cancer

Childhood cancer can take several different forms, including **leukemia**, lymphoma, tumours of the central nervous system, bone tumours, tumours affecting the eyes, and tumours affecting various organs (Heller, Alberto, Forney, & Schwartzman, 1996). Treatment of cancer includes chemotherapy, radiation, surgery, and bone marrow transplantation. Suggestions for teachers who have children with cancer include the following:

▶ Express your concern about a student's condition to the parents and family.
▶ Learn about a student's illness from hospital personnel and parents.
▶ Inquire about the type of treatment and anticipated side effects.
▶ Refer the student for any needed special education services.
▶ Prepare for a student's terminal illness and possible death.
▶ Encourage discussion and consideration of future events.
▶ Allow for exceptions to classroom rules and procedures when indicated (e.g., wearing a baseball cap to disguise hair loss from chemotherapy).
▶ Be available to talk with a student when the need arises.
▶ Share information about the student's condition and ongoing status with teachers of the student's siblings.
▶ Be prepared to deal with issues concerning death and dying with students.
▶ Provide information to school staff and parents, as needed (Hoida & McDougal, 1998). See the nearby Inclusion Strategies feature for ideas.
▶ Facilitate the student's re-entry into school after an extended absence.

CONSIDER THIS

What are some ways that teachers can maintain contact with students with cancer during their extended absences from the classroom? How can the teacher facilitate contact between other students and the student with cancer?

INCLUSION Strategies

How to Handle the Issue of Death

Almost all students will want to know, but be afraid to ask, whether their classmate can die from the cancer. If a classmate asks, respond honestly with something like "Nobody knows. Some children as sick as _____ have died, some other children have gotten better and are just fine. We don't know what will happen to _____, but [she/he] and [her/his] doctors are working very hard to make [her/him] well." If the class does not raise the issue of death, you *should* bring it up. Ask a question such as "Have any of you known anyone who has died from cancer?" (You will get nods.) Once you have raised the question, you can address it. "Cancer is a very serious disease and people do die from it." Then proceed with, "Nobody knows..."

Remember that elementary school children do not have the philosophical understanding of death that teenagers and adults do. Until children are capable of formal operational thought, they cannot truly conceptualize the finality of death. As educators we know that it is futile to try to teach history with concepts of past and future generations until children are 11 or 12 years old. Most elementary school students have had some experience with a pet or older relative who has died. They do understand that it means that the person does not come back. Be careful of the language you use. One child thought he was going to die when he was told

he would be "put to sleep" for his operation. He knew his dog had been "put to sleep" and never came back. By having a discussion, you may be able to clarify such misconceptions. Generally, children are much more concerned with the concrete and immediate consequences to themselves and their friend. The classmates and friends of the ill student will understand that their friend is worried about physical pain, needles, and bodily harm. Some children will view their friend as a hero for having conquered forces they all fear. Children of this age are able to feel for another's pain. Most children have had flu, viruses, mouth sores, nausea, and even hospital experiences from which they are able to relate personal pain to that of another. The more you emphasize things children understand, the more you will tap into their altruism in helping their ill classmate.

Older children (and sometimes teachers) may be worried that their friend might die suddenly while they are together. The basic fear is that they would not know what to do or how to handle the situation. Assure them that children do not die suddenly. They get much sicker first. Their doctors and parents would be taking care of them, and they would not be in school.

From "Children with Cancer in the Classroom," by V. C. Peckham, 1993, *Teaching Exceptional Children, 26,* p. 31. Used by permission.

Teachers who have students with cancer should learn about the child's illness from medical personnel.

Cerebral Palsy

Cerebral palsy (CP) is a disorder of movement or posture that is caused by brain damage. It affects the voluntary muscles and often leads to major problems in communication and mobility. Cerebral palsy is neither progressive nor communicable (Gersh, 1991; Schleichkorn, 1993). It is also not "curable" in the usual sense of the word although education, therapy, and applied technology can help persons with cerebral palsy lead productive lives.

Between 6 and 10 individuals for every 10 000 in the population have cerebral palsy (Eaves, 1992). There are three primary methods for classifying individuals with cerebral palsy: by type (physiological), by distribution (topological) (Inge, 1992), and by degree of severity (Bigge, 1991). Table 9.6 describes the different types of cerebral palsy according to two classification systems. The primary intervention approach for children with cerebral palsy focuses on their physical needs. Physical therapy, occupational therapy, and even surgery often play a part. Specific suggestions for teachers include the following:

- Create a supportive classroom environment that encourages participation in every facet of the school day.
- Allow extra time for students to move from one location to another.
- Ask students to repeat verbalizations that may be hard to understand because of their speech patterns.
- Provide many real-life activities.
- Learn the correct way for the student to sit upright in a chair or wheelchair and the methods of using adaptive equipment (e.g., prone standers).
- Understand the functions and components of a wheelchair and any special adaptive pieces that may accompany it.
- Consider the use of various augmentative communication techniques with students who have severe cerebral palsy (Musselwhite, 1987).
- Encourage students to use computers that are equipped with expanded keyboards if necessary or other portable writing aids for taking notes or generating written products.
- Consult physical and occupational therapists to understand correct positioning, posture, and other motor function areas.

TEACHING TIP

Develop some simulation activities for typically achieving students that will help them understand mobility problems. Trying out wheelchairs and restricting the use of arms or hands will help them understand the problems experienced by some students with cerebral palsy.

TABLE 9.6 Classification of Cerebral Palsy

Topographical Classification System	Classification System by Motor Symptoms (Physiological)
A. *Monoplegia:* one limb	A. Spastic
B. *Paraplegia:* legs only	B. Athetoid
C. *Hemiplegia:* one-half of body	1. Tension
D. *Triplegia:* three limbs (usually two legs and one arm)	2. Nontension
	3. Dystonic
E. *Quadriplegia:* all four limbs	4. Tremor
F. *Diplegia:* more affected in the legs than the arms	C. Rigidity
	D. Ataxia
G. *Double hemiplegia:* arms more involved than the legs	E. Tremor
	F. Atonic (rare)
	G. Mixed
	H. Unclassified

From *Understanding Physical, Sensory, and Health Impairments* (p. 95), by K. W. Heller, P. A. Alberto, P. E. Forney, and M. N. Schwartzman, 1996, Pacific Grove, CA: Brooks/Cole. Used by permission.

Cystic Fibrosis

Cystic fibrosis is an inherited, fatal disease that results in an abnormal amount of mucus throughout the body, most often affecting the lungs and digestive tract. On the average, children will live to their mid-teens. Teachers must make sure that children with cystic fibrosis take special medication before they eat. As the disease progresses, it greatly affects stamina and the student's physical condition. Here are some specific suggestions for dealing with students with this disease.

▶ Prepare students in class for the realities of this disease (e.g., coughing, noncontagious sputum, gas).
▶ Learn how to clear a student's lungs and air passages, as such assistance may be needed after certain activities.
▶ Know the medications a student must take and be able to administer them (e.g., enzymes, vitamins).
▶ Consider restricting certain physical activities.
▶ Inquire about the therapies being used with the student.
▶ Support the implementation of special diets if needed.
▶ Provide opportunities for students to talk about their concerns, fears, and feelings.
▶ Ensure that the student is included in all class activities to whatever extent is possible.
▶ Prepare students for the eventual outcome of the disease by discussing death and dying.

FURTHER READING

For more information on cystic fibrosis, read *Understanding Physical, Sensory, and Health Impairments,* by K. W. Heller, P. A. Alberto, P. E. Forney, and M. N. Schwartzman, published in 1996 by Brooks/Cole.

Multisensory Impairments

Students who have visual impairments or auditory impairments create unique problems for educators. When students present deficits in both sensory areas, their needs become extremely complex.

Students who have multisensory impairments may be blind or deaf, or they may have degrees of visual and auditory impairments that do not classify as blindness or deafness. "The Helen Keller National Center estimates that about 94% of such individuals have residual hearing or residual sight that can facilitate their educational programs" (Marchant, 1992, p. 114). Obviously, individuals identified with multisensory impairments present a variety of characteristics. While these characteristics represent those exhibited by students who only have visual and hearing impairments, the overlap of the two exceptionalities results in significant educational needs.

Wolfe (1997) suggests the following educational techniques for teachers to use when working with students with multisensory impairments:

▶ Use an ecological approach to assessment and skill selection to emphasize functional needs of students.
▶ Use a variety of prompts, cues, and reinforcement strategies in a systematic instructional pattern.
▶ Use time delay prompting, where time between prompts is increased.
▶ Use groups and co-operative learning strategies.
▶ Implement environmental adaptations, such as enlarging materials, using contrasting materials, altering seating arrangements, and reducing extraneous noises to maximize residual hearing and vision of the student.

TABLE 9.7

Indicators of Diabetes
(Juvenile Diabetes)

Increased thirst

Increased appetite

Weight loss

Fatigue

Irritability

Increased urination

Diabetes (Juvenile Diabetes)

Diabetes is a metabolic disorder in which the pancreas cannot produce sufficient insulin to process food (Holcomb et al., 1998). Teachers should be alert to possible symptoms of diabetes, including increased thirst, appetite, and urination; weight loss; fatigue; and irritability. (See Table 9.7.) Children with type I (insulin-dependent) diabetes must take daily injections of insulin. School personnel must have knowledge of the special dietary

TABLE 9.8	Hyperglycemia and Hypoglycemia		
Category	*Possible Symptoms*	*Cause*	*Treatment*
Ketoacidosis; hyperglycemia (too much sugar)	Symptoms occur gradually (over hours or days): polyuria; polyphagia; polydipsia; fatigue; abdominal pain; nausea; vomiting; fruity odour on breath; rapid, deep breathing; unconsciousness	Did not take insulin; did not comply with diet	Give insulin; follow plan of action
Insulin reaction; hypoglycemia (too little sugar)	Symptoms occur quickly (in minutes): headache; dullness; irritability; shaking; sweating; lightheadedness; behaviour change; paleness; weakness; moist skin; slurred speech; confusion; shallow breathing; unconsciousness	Delayed eating; participated in strenuous exercise; took too much insulin	Give sugar; follow plan of action

From *Understanding Physical, Sensory, and Health Impairments* (p. 302), by K. W. Heller, P. A. Alberto, P. E. Forney, and M. N. Schwartzman, 1996, Pacific Grove, CA: Brooks/Cole. Used by permission.

needs of these children and understand their need for a daily activity regimen. Some specific suggestions on dealing with diabetic students include:

- Communicating regularly with the family to determine any special needs the student may have.
- Scheduling snacks and lunch at the same time every day.
- Being prepared for hypoglycemia—a situation in which the student needs to have sugar.
- Helping the student deal with the disease.
- Understanding the distinction between having too much insulin in the body and not having enough. Table 9.8 above describes both of these conditions and actions to address them.

TEACHING TIP

Before an emergency develops, be prepared to deal with students with diabetes in your classroom. Keep a list of symptoms to watch for and things to do if a student has too much or too little insulin.

Epilepsy

Epilepsy is a series of recurrent convulsions, or seizures, that are caused by abnormal electrical discharges in the brain (Smith, 1998). There are several different types of epilepsy, determined by the impact of abnormal brain activity. Table 9.9 details four types. In Canada, up to 2 percent of the population have been diagnosed with epilepsy. The Epilepsy Foundation of America (1992) notes the following significant signs of the disorder: (1) staring spells, (2) tic-like movements, (3) rhythmic movements of the head, (4) purposeless sounds and body movements, (5) head drooping, (6) lack of response, (7) eyes rolling upward, and (8) chewing and swallowing movements. Medical intervention is the primary recourse for individuals with epilepsy. Most people with epilepsy are able to control their seizures with the proper regimen of medical therapy (Agnew, Nystul, & Conner, 1998).

Even persons who respond very well to medication have occasional seizures. Therefore teachers and other school personnel must know what actions to take should a person experience a generalized seizure. Figure 9.1 summarizes the steps that should be taken when a child has a seizure. Teachers, parents, or others need to record behaviours that occur before, during, and after the seizure because they may be important to treatment of the disorder.

TEACHING TIP

Turn a student's seizure into an educational opportunity for other students. Ensure that students know that they cannot "catch" epilepsy from someone.

TABLE 9.9	Four Types of Seizures
Generalized (grand mal)	▷ Sudden cry, fall, rigidity, followed by muscle jerks ▷ Shallow breathing, or temporarily suspended breathing, bluish skin ▷ Possible loss of bladder or bowel control ▷ Usually lasts 2–3 minutes
Absence (petit mal)	▷ Blank stare, beginning and ending abruptly ▷ Lasting only a few seconds ▷ Most common in children ▷ May be accompanied by blinking, chewing movement ▷ Individual is unaware of the seizure
Simple Partial	▷ Jerking may begin in one area of body, arm, leg, or face ▷ Cannot be stopped but individual is aware ▷ Jerking may proceed from one area to another area
Complex Partial	▷ Starts with blank stares, followed by chewing and random activity ▷ Individual may seem unaware or dazed ▷ Unresponsiveness ▷ Clumsy actions ▷ May run, pick up objects, take clothes off, or other activity ▷ Lasts a few minutes ▷ No memory of what occurred

From *Understanding Physical, Sensory, and Health Impairments* (p. 78) by K. W. Heller, P. A. Alberto, P. E. Forney, and M. N. Schwartzman, 1996, Pacific Grove, CA: Brooks/Cole. Used by permission.

FIGURE 9.1

Steps to Take When Dealing with a Seizure

From *Seizure Recognition and Observation: A Guide for Allied Health Professionals* (p. 2), Epilepsy Foundation of America, 1992, Landover, MD: Author. Used by permission.

In a generalized tonic–clonic seizure, the person suddenly falls to the ground and has a convulsive seizure. It is essential to protect him or her from injury. Cradle the head or place something soft under it—a towel or your hand, for example. Remove all dangerous objects. A bystander can do nothing to prevent or terminate an attack. At the end of the episode, make sure the mouth is cleared of food and saliva by turning the person on his or her side to provide the best airway and allow secretions to drain. The person may be incontinent during a seizure. If the assisting person remains calm, the person will be reassured when he or she regains consciousness.

Breathing almost always resumes spontaneously after a convulsive seizure. Failure to resume breathing signals a complication of the seizure such as an aspiration of food, heart attack, or severe head or neck injury. In these unusual circumstances, cardiopulmonary resuscitation must start immediately. If repeated seizures occur, or if a single seizure lasts longer than five minutes, the person should be taken to a medical facility immediately. Prolonged or repeated seizures may suggest *status epilepticus* (nonstop seizures), which requires emergency medical treatment. In summary, *first aid for generalized tonic–clonic seizures is similar to that for other convulsive seizures.*

▷ Prevent further injury. Place something soft under the head, loosen tight clothing, and clear the area of sharp or hard objects.

▷ Force no objects into the person's mouth.

▷ Do not restrain the person's movements unless they place him or her in danger.

▷ At the end of the episode, turn the person on his or her side to open the airway and allow secretions to drain.

▷ Stay with the person until the seizure ends.

▷ Do not pour any liquids into the person's mouth or offer any food, drink, or medication until he or she is fully awake.

▷ Start cardiopulmonary resuscitation if the person does not resume breathing after the seizure.

▷ Let the person rest until he or she is fully awake.

▷ Be reassuring and supportive when consciousness returns.

▷ A convulsive seizure is not a medical emergency unless it lasts longer than five minutes or a second seizure occurs soon after the first. In this situation, the person should be taken to an emergency medical facility.

The U.S. Centers for Disease Control and the Food and Drug Administration (1988) published guidelines designed to protect health care workers and to ensure the confidentiality of patients with HIV infection. These guidelines include the following information that is useful for classroom teachers.

▷ Blood should always be handled with latex or nonpermeable disposable gloves. The use of gloves is not necessary for feces, nasal secretions, sputum, sweat, saliva, tears, urine, and vomitus unless they are visibly tinged with blood. Handwashing is sufficient after handling material not containing blood.

▷ In all settings in which blood or bloody material is handled, gloves and a suitable receptacle that closes tightly and is child-proof should be available. Although HIV does not survive well outside the body, all spillage of secretions should be cleaned up immediately with disinfectants. This is particularly important for cleaning up after a bloody nose or a large cut. Household bleach at a dilution of 1:10 should be used. Only objects that have come into contact with blood need to be cleaned with bleach.

▷ When intact skin is exposed to contaminated fluids, particularly blood, it should be washed with soap and water. Handwashing is sufficient for such activities as diaper change; toilet training; and clean-up of nasal secretions, stool, saliva, tears, or vomitus. If an open lesion or a mucous membrane appears to have been contaminated, AZT therapy should be considered.

FIGURE 9.2

Universal Precautions for Prevention of HIV, Hepatitis B, and Other Blood-Borne Pathogens

From *AIDS Surveillance Report* (p. 7), Centers for Disease Control, 1988, Atlanta, GA: Author. Used by permission.

HIV and AIDS

Human immunodeficiency virus (HIV) infection occurs when the virus attacks the body's immune system, leaving an individual vulnerable to infections or cancers. In its later stages, HIV infection becomes **acquired immunodeficiency syndrome (AIDS)**. Two of the fastest-growing groups contracting HIV are infants and teenagers (Johnson, Johnson, & Jefferson-Aker, 2001). HIV/AIDS is transmitted only through the exchange of blood or semen. Students with HIV/AIDS may display a variety of academic, behavioural, and social-emotional problems. Teachers need to take precautions when dealing with children with HIV/AIDS, hepatitis B, or any other blood-borne pathogen. See Figure 9.2 for specific precautions. Some specific suggestions for teachers include the following:

▷ Follow the guidelines (universal precautions) developed by the U.S. Centers for Disease Control and the U.S. Food and Drug Administration for working with HIV-infected individuals (see Figure 9.2).
▷ Ask the student's parents or physician if there are any special procedures that must be followed.
▷ Discuss HIV/AIDS with the entire class, providing accurate information, dispelling myths, and answering questions.
▷ Discuss with students in the class that a student's skills and abilities will change over time if he or she is infected with HIV/AIDS.
▷ Prepare for the fact that the student will die, especially if AIDS is present.
▷ Ensure that the student with HIV/AIDS is included in all aspects of classroom activities.
▷ Be sensitive to the stress that the student's family is undergoing.

CONSIDER THIS

Students with HIV and AIDS should not be allowed to attend school because of their potential ability to infect other students. Do you agree or disagree with this statement? Why or why not?

FURTHER READING

For more information about HIV and AIDS, read "Special Educators' Knowledge of HIV Transmission: Implications for Teacher Education Programs," by R. M. Foley and M. J. Kittleson, published in 1993 in volume 16 of *Teacher Education and Special Education*.

Muscular Dystrophy

Muscular dystrophy is an umbrella term used to describe several different inherited disorders that result in progressive muscular weakness (Tver & Tver, 1991). The most common and most serious form of muscular dystrophy is **Duchenne dystrophy**. In this

Children in wheelchairs need opportunities for social interactions.

CONSIDER THIS

Should students who require extensive physical accommodations be placed in the same school, so that all schools and classrooms do not have to be accessible? Defend your response.

TEACHING TIP

Get in a wheelchair and try to move about your classroom to see if it is fully accessible; often, areas look accessible but are not.

CROSS-REFERENCE

Review intervention approaches for students with intellectual disabilities, found in Chapter 7, and determine which ones would be appropriate for a student with intellectual disability and Prader-Willi syndrome.

type of muscular dystrophy, fat cells and connective tissue replace muscle tissue. Individuals with Duchenne dystrophy ultimately lose their ability to walk, typically by age 12. Functional use of arms and hands will also be affected. Muscle weakness will also result in respiratory complications. Teachers must adapt their classrooms to accommodate the physical needs of students. Most individuals with this form of muscular dystrophy die during young adulthood. Specific suggestions for teachers include the following:

⏵ Be prepared to help the student deal with the loss of various functions.
⏵ Involve the student in as many classroom activities as possible.
⏵ Using assistive techniques that do not hurt the individual, help the student as needed in climbing stairs or in getting up from the floor.
⏵ Understand the functions and components of wheelchairs.
⏵ Monitor the administration of required medications.
⏵ Monitor the amount of time the student is allowed to stand during the day.
⏵ Be familiar with different types of braces (short leg, moulded ankle-foot) students might use.
⏵ Prepare other students in class for the realities of the disease.

Prader-Willi Syndrome

Prader-Willi syndrome is a condition characterized by compulsive eating, obesity, and intellectual disability (Silverthorn & Hornak, 1993). Other characteristics include hypotonia (deficient muscle tone), slow metabolic rate, small or underdeveloped testes and penis, excessive sleeping, round face with almond-shaped eyes, nervous picking of skin, and stubbornness (Davies & Joughin, 1993; Silverthorn & Hornak, 1993; Smith & Hendricks, 1995). The only effective treatment for persons with Prader-Willi syndrome is weight management through diet and exercise.

Spina Bifida

Spina bifida is a "congenital condition characterized by a malformation of the vertebrae and spinal cord" (Gearheart, Weishahn, & Gearheart, 1996). It affects about 1 in 2000 births (Bigge, 1991). There are three different types of spina bifida: spina bifida occulta, meningocele, and myelomeningocele (Gearheart et al., 1996; Robertson et al., 1992).

The least serious form of spina bifida is spina bifida occulta. In this type, the vertebral column fails to close properly, leaving a hole in the bony vertebrae that protect the delicate spinal column. Generally, all that is required to treat this form of spina bifida is to surgically close the opening to protect the spinal column. This does not result in any problems. **Meningocele** is similar to spina bifida occulta in that the vertebral column fails to close properly, leaving a hole in the bony vertebrae. Skin pouches out in the area where the vertebral column is not closed. In meningocele, the outpouching does not contain any nerve tissue. Surgically removing the outpouching and closing the opening usually result in a positive prognosis without any problems. **Myelomeningocele** is the most common and most severe form of spina bifida. Similar to meningocele, it has one major difference: nerve tissue is present in the outpouching. Due to the presence of nerve tissue, this form of spina bifida generally results in permanent paralysis and loss of sensation. Incontinence is also a possible result of this condition (Bigge, 1991; Robertson et al., 1992). School personnel must ensure appropriate use of wheelchairs (see the nearby Technology Today feature) and accommodations for limited use of arms and hands. Teachers should do the following when working with a child with spina bifida:

▶ Inquire about any acute medical needs the student may have.
▶ Learn about the various adaptive equipment a student may be using (see Baker & Rogosky-Grassi, 1993).
▶ Maintain an environment that assists the student who is using crutches by keeping floors from getting wet and removing loose floor coverings.
▶ Understand the use of a wheelchair as well as its major parts.
▶ Learn how to position these students to develop strength and to avoid sores from developing in parts of their bodies that bear their weight, or that receive pressure from orthotic devices they are using. Individuals with spina bifida do not have sensation, therefore, they may not notice the sores themselves. Healing is complicated by poor circulation.
▶ Understand the process of **clean intermittent bladder catheterization (CIC)**, as some students will be performing this process to become continent and avoid urinary tract infections—the process involves insertion of a clean catheter through the urethra and into the bladder four times a day and can be done independently by most children by age six.
▶ Be ready to deal with the occasional incontinence of students. Assure the student with spina bifida that this is not a problem and discuss this situation with other class members.
▶ Learn how to deal with the special circumstances associated with students who use wheelchairs and have seizures.
▶ Ensure the full participation of the student in all classroom activities.
▶ Help the student with spina bifida develop a healthy, positive self-concept.
▶ Notify parents if there are unusual changes in the student's behaviour or personality or if the student has various physical complaints such as headaches or double vision—this may indicate a problem with increased pressure on the brain (Deiner, 1993).

Tourette Syndrome

Tourette syndrome is a neuropsychiatric disorder that occurs in males three times as often as in females, resulting in a prevalence rate for males as high as 1 in 1000 individuals (Hansen, 1992). The syndrome is "characterized by multiple motor and one or more vocal tics, which occur many times a day, nearly every day or intermittently, throughout a period of more than one year" (Crews et al., 1993, p. 25). Characteristics include various motor tics; inappropriate laughing; rapid eye movements; winks and grimaces; aggressive behaviours; in infrequent cases, intellectual disabilities; mild to moderate incoordination; and peculiar verbalizations. Most important, school personnel should be understanding with children who have Tourette syndrome. Monitoring medication and participating as a member of the interdisciplinary team are important roles for teachers and other school personnel.

FURTHER READING

For more information on spina bifida, read *Understanding Physical, Sensory, and Health Impairments,* by K. W. Heller, P. A. Alberto, P. E. Forney, and M. N. Schwartzman, published in 1996 by Brooks/Cole.

CONSIDER THIS

How should students with Tourette syndrome be dealt with when they shout obscenities and display other inappropriate behaviours that disrupt the classroom?

Pushing a Wheelchair

TECHNOLOGY TODAY

1. Over rough terrain or a raised area:

   a. Tilt the wheelchair by stepping down on tipping lever with foot as you pull down and back on hand grips.
   b. Continue to tilt chair back until it requires little or no effort to stabilize it.
   c. When the wheelchair is at the balance point, it can then be pushed over obstacles or terrain.
   d. Reverse the procedure and lower slowly. Make sure the wheelchair does not slam down or drop the last few inches.

2. Over curbs and steps:

   a. As you approach the curb or step, pause and tilt the wheelchair back to the balance point.
   b. When the wheelchair is stabilized, move toward curb until casters are on curb, and rear wheels come in contact with the curb.

   c. Move in close to the chair and lift the chair up by the handles. Roll the wheelchair up over the curb and push it forward.
   d. To go down, reverse the steps—back the wheelchair down off the curb without allowing it to drop down. Once rear wheels are down, step down on tipping lever and slowly lower casters.

3. Down a steep incline:

   a. Take the wheelchair down backward.
   b. The wheelchair can pick up speed too easily, and you can lose control if the wheelchair goes down first.
   c. Turn the chair around until your back is in the direction you plan to go.
   d. Walk backward, and move slowly down the ramp.
   e. Look backward occasionally to make sure you are staying on track and to avoid collisions.

Summary

- Children with physical and health needs are entitled to an appropriate educational program according to the Canadian Charter of Rights and Freedoms.
- Physical and health impairments constitute low-incidence disabilities.
- The severity, visibility, and age of acquisition affect the needs of children with physical and health impairments.
- Students with physical and health problems display a wide array of characteristics and needs.
- Autism is a pervasive developmental disability that primarily affects social interactions, language, and behaviour.
- Although originally thought to be caused by environmental factors, autism is now considered to be caused by organic factors, including brain damage and complications during pregnancy.
- Growing evidence suggests that placing students with autism in general education classrooms with their typically achieving peers results in positive gains for them.
- A condition associated with autism, Asperger syndrome was first included in the fourth edition of the *Diagnostic and Statistical Manual of Mental Disorders (DSM-IV-TR)*.
- Although many of the behavioural characteristics displayed by children with Asperger syndrome are similar to those displayed by children with autism, the former generally have higher cognitive development and more typical communication skills.
- Children with traumatic brain injury (TBI) exhibit a wide variety of characteristics, including emotional, learning, and behaviour problems.
- Asthma affects many children; teachers primarily need to be aware of medications to control asthma, side effects of medication, and the limitations of students with asthma.
- The survival rates for children with cancer have increased dramatically over the past 20 years. Teachers need to be prepared to deal with the emotional issues surrounding childhood cancer, including death issues. Children with cancer may miss a good deal of school; the school should make appropriate arrangements in these situations.
- Cerebral palsy is a condition that affects muscles and posture; it can be described by the way it affects movement or which limb is involved.
- Physical therapy is a critical component of treatment for children with cerebral palsy. Accessibility, communication, and social-emotional concerns are the primary areas that general educators must attend to.
- Cystic fibrosis is a terminal condition that affects the mucous membranes of the lungs.

- Juvenile diabetes results in children having to take insulin injections daily. Diet and exercise can help children manage their diabetes.
- Epilepsy is caused by abnormal activity in the brain that is the result of some brain damage or insult. Teachers must know specific steps to take in case children have a generalized tonic-clonic seizure in their classrooms.
- Infants and teenagers are two of the fastest-growing groups to contract HIV. Teachers need to keep up to date with developments in HIV/AIDS prevention and treatment approaches.
- Muscular dystrophy is a term used to describe several different inherited disorders that result in progressive muscular weakness and may cause death.

- Prader-Willi syndrome, a condition caused by a defect in the number 15 chromosome pair, is characterized by excessive overeating and mild intellectual disabilities.
- Spina bifida is caused by a failure of the spinal column to close properly; this condition may result in paralysis of the lower extremities.
- Tourette syndrome is a neuropsychiatric disorder that is characterized by multiple motor tics, inappropriate laughter, rapid eye movements, winks and grimaces, and aggressive behaviours.

Resources

British Columbia Ministry of Education, Special Programs Branch. (1995). *Awareness of chronic health problems: What the teacher needs to know.* Victoria: Author.

This practical information guide with specific classroom strategies for teachers covers 14 different health problems, including allergies, asthma, autism, cerebral palsy, Crohn's disease, diabetes, epilepsy, fetal alcohol syndrome, muscular dystrophy, and spina bifida.

Parent/Family resource: A resource package developed based on a parent survey and parent focus groups conducted by Alberta Health, the Alberta Community Health Nurses Association and the AIDS Network of Edmonton Society.

Parents indicated a need for more strategies and skills on how to discuss sexual issues, age-appropriate materials and background information on sexual development,

HIV/AIDs, and sexually transmitted diseases (STDs). The resource contains directories, brochures, posters, and contact information on videos. Age-appropriate materials are included, with consideration given to literacy and language challenges. Topics include sex, maturation, pregnancy, STDs, and HIV/AIDS prevention.

Jones, Melissa M. (1998). *Within our reach: Behavior prevention and intervention strategies for learners with mental retardation and autism.* (Available through the Council for Exceptional Children.)

This book is designed for teachers, parents, teacher trainees, and other service providers. It provides practical ways to resolve behavioural concerns about students with intellectual disabilities, autism, and other developmental disabilities. It focuses on responding to the communicative intent of various behaviour problems.

Weblinks

Autism Treatment Services of Canada
www.autism.ca/
Autism Treatment Services of Canada, a national affiliation of organizations, provides treatment, educational, management, and consultative services to people with autism and related disorders across Canada. Their website provides excellent information about all aspects of autism as well as related resources.

Asthma Society of Canada
www.asthma.ca
This website will help teachers work with students with asthma. It has a whole section on managing asthma at school for teachers, who often misunderstand the problem. In a class of 30 students, an average of 4 will have asthma. Thus, asthma is one of the most common health impairments in the classroom. The Asthma Society of Canada, a national organization, is devoted to enhancing the quality of life of people living with asthma.

Epilepsy International

www.epilepsy-international.com/

At this website there are forums where teachers can pose questions about epilepsy and receive informed answers. Any teacher of a student with epilepsy should find this site a useful resource.

Spina Bifida and Hydrocephalus Association of Canada

www.sbhac.ca/

This website is an excellent starting point for any parent or teacher of a child with spina bifida (SB). In addition to providing a fact sheet, it provides links to related sites and educational information on students with SB, especially about common learning disabilities associated with the problem.

The National Resource Centre for Traumatic Brain Injury

www.neuro.pmr.vcu.edu/

This American website provides practical information on traumatic brain injury for professionals, persons with brain injury, and family members.

Muscular Dystrophy Canada

www.mdac.ca/

This website provides information on all types of muscular dystrophy and related resources as well as a forum where you can pose questions to a qualified expert. This site is very useful for teachers who may be working with a student with muscular dystrophy.

Teaching Students Who Are Gifted

After reading this chapter you should be able to

- define giftedness
- describe the characteristics of students who are gifted
- describe ways to identify and evaluate students who are gifted
- describe appropriate instructional methods for students who are gifted
- identify ways to enhance curriculum and instruction within the general education setting

Adam is a lively, talkative young boy. His vocabulary and the way he lectures on his main interests, science and ecology, have resulted in the teachers laughingly referring to him as the "little professor." Despite his excellent verbal abilities, though, he does not excel in language arts—his spelling is poor and his handwriting messy. Adam loves math and science, and enjoys all sports.

Adam's Grade 3 teacher, Mr. Garner, has recommended Adam for the enrichment program at their school. Adam will attend a resource room with two or three other children to work on a special enrichment project which will be related to the classroom curriculum. The students will then present their project to their classmates.

However, Adam's Grade 2 teacher, Mrs. Petrakos, argues with Mr. Garner that the boy's time would be better spent improving his spelling and handwriting skills. A heated discussion in the staff room ensues. Mr. Garner is convinced that Adam is gifted and should be provided with opportunities to excel in his areas of strength. Mrs. Petrakos insists that, while Adam has good verbal skills, his average to below-average written work would suggest that he needs remediation more than enrichment. Although the two teachers finish by agreeing to disagree, Mr. Garner is happy when he learns that Adam's parents have made the decision to have him independently tested by a psychologist. They are considering a small private school that requires academic tests for entrance, and they want to know if Adam would be successful. Mr. Garner is sure the results of the psychologist's tests will prove him right.

When the results are finally shared with Mr. Garner, he realizes they don't tell him anything he did not know. Adam does exceptionally well on the verbal subtests of the intelligence testing and overall scores in the "Superior" range. In the achievement tests he is above average in reading and arithmetic, but slightly below average in spelling and written language.

Mr. Garner is still convinced that Adam is gifted, but he knows that even if he could share these results with Mrs. Petrakos, it wouldn't change her mind; she would remain convinced that Adam is not gifted.

Questions to Consider

1. Is Adam gifted? Why or why not?

2. What kind of programming would you put in place for Adam?

3. In Adam's school, formal identification as gifted is not available and is not required for enrichment activities. What are the advantages and disadvantages of this system?

Introduction

Children and youth such as Adam, who perform or have the potential to perform at levels significantly above those of other students, have special needs as great as those of students whose areas of need demonstrably limit their performance. These needs are notable because most of these students are likely to spend much of their school day in general education settings. As a result, teaching students who are gifted provides challenges to general education teachers that are equal to, if not greater than, those associated with meeting the needs of students with other special needs (McGrail, 1998). In order for classroom teachers to feel confident working with students who are gifted, classroom teachers should have basic information about giftedness and be able to implement some useful techniques for maximizing the students' educational experiences.

Although there is no general agreement on the best way to educate students who are gifted, many professionals argue that such students benefit from a curricular focus different from that provided in general education. Yet the vast majority of students who are gifted spend a considerable amount of time in the general education classroom, offering teachers the challenges and rewards of working with them.

The purpose of this chapter is twofold: (1) to provide basic information about giftedness in children and youth and (2) to suggest practices for working with these students in inclusive settings. This chapter is a primer only; confidence and competence in teaching students who are gifted come with study and experience. More in-depth information about teaching students who are gifted can be found by referencing additional sources (Clark, 2002; Colangelo & Davis, 2003; Coleman & Cross, 2001; Davis & Rimm, 1998; Heller et al., 2000).

Basic Concepts about Students Who Are Gifted

Students with exceptional abilities continue to be an underidentified, underserved, and often inappropriately served group. In some provinces/territories special services are available, but others do not identify or provide services for students who are gifted. Moreover, local school boards vary greatly in the type and quality of services provided—if indeed they are provided at all.

Students who could benefit from special programming are often not identified because of several factors. Teachers in general education may not be aware of the characteristics that suggest giftedness, particularly those associated with students who differ from the general student populations because of culture, gender, or exceptionality. Historically, ineffective assessment practices have not identified students who are gifted who come from diverse backgrounds.

For students who are identified as gifted, a common problem is a mismatch between their academic, social, and emotional needs and the programming they receive. In many schools, a limited amount of instructional time is devoted to special activities. Furthermore, some of the gifted programming that exists today is geared for students who are gifted in the linguistic and mathematical areas. In too many instances, students who are gifted do not receive the type of education they need in the general education classroom.

Services to students who are gifted remain controversial, partly because the general public and many school personnel hold misconceptions about these students. Hallahan and Kauffman (2003) highlight some of these misguided beliefs:

> People with special intellectual gifts are physically weak, socially inept, narrow in interests, and prone to emotional instability or early decline. *Fact:* There are wide individual

CONSIDER THIS

Should there be provincial/territorial legislation to provide appropriate educational programs for students who are gifted and talented?

variations, and most gifted individuals are healthy, well adjusted, socially attractive, and
morally responsible.

▶ Children with special gifts or talents are usually bored with school and antagonistic
toward those who are responsible for their education. *Fact:* Most gifted children like
school and adjust well to their peers and teachers, although some do not like school and
have social or emotional problems.

▶ Students who have a true gift or talent will excel without special education. They need
only the incentives and instruction that are appropriate for all students. *Fact:* Some gifted
children will perform at a remarkably high level without special education of any kind,
and some will make outstanding contributions even in the face of great obstacles to their
achievement. But most will not come close to achieving at a level commensurate with their
potential unless their talents are deliberately fostered by instruction that is appropriate for
their advanced abilities. (p. 455)

The portrayal of individuals who are gifted in movies is noteworthy. As Coleman and
Cross (2001) note, too often the portrayal has negative connotations. They described the
features of key characters in a number of recent movies. For example, in the movie *Little
Man Tate* (1991) the main character—a gifted boy—was portrayed to be dysfunctional.
The problem with negative portrayals of individuals who are gifted is that they lead to
inaccurate perceptions and attitudes, ultimately resulting in unfair, and often discriminatory, practices.

Many professionals in the field of gifted education find current services unacceptable and are frustrated by the lack of specialized programming for these students
(Feldhusen, 1998). Undoubtedly, the programming provided in inclusive settings to
students who are gifted should be improved. VanTassel-Baska (1998), highlighting key
beliefs regarding curriculum theory, remarks that students who are gifted should be
provided with curriculum opportunities that allow them to attain optimum levels of
learning. In addition, these curriculum experiences need to be carefully planned, implemented, and evaluated.

"Gifted" Defined

Our understanding of giftedness has changed over time, and the terminology used to
describe it has also varied. The term **gifted** is often used to refer to the heterogeneous
spectrum of students with exceptional abilities, although in Canada the term *developmentally advanced* is also recognized (Keating, 1990). Other terms, such as **talented** and
creative, are used to differentiate subgroups of people who are gifted.

Across Canada, definitions of giftedness vary. In British Columbia, the definition is
as follows:

> A student is considered gifted when she/he possesses demonstrated or potential
> abilities that give evidence of exceptionally high capability with respect to intel-
> lect, creativity, or the skills associated with specific disciplines. Students who are
> gifted often demonstrate outstanding abilities in more than one area. They may
> demonstrate extraordinary intensity of focus in their particular areas of talent or
> interest. However, they may also have accompanying disabilities and should not
> be expected to have strengths in all areas of intellectual functioning. (B.C.
> Ministry of Education, 2002)

In contrast, the Yukon defines intellectual exceptionality in this way: "intellectual
abilities are two or more standard deviations above the mean on a standardized, individually administered test of cognitive abilities in conjunction with superior performance
in one or more academic subjects as measured by standardized achievement tests or
classroom performance."

These two definitions illustrate two different approaches. While the Yukon's emphasis on standardized test scores significantly above the mean is the more traditional approach to giftedness, the broader definition offered by British Columbia is more illustrative of current thought in the field of giftedness. Of special interest in this type of definition is the reference to "potential abilities"—students do not have to have already produced significant accomplishments to be considered gifted. Also, the statement that the students should not be expected to have strengths in all areas should be noted, since many teachers believe that a student who is gifted must perform extremely well in all aspects of school. The majority of definitions used by provinces and territories adhere more to the model alluded to by British Columbia, which is based on Gardner's Theory of Multiple Intelligences, and Renzulli's three-ring conception of giftedness (British Columbia, 1995).

Gardner and Hatch (Gardner, 1983; Gardner & Hatch, 1989) have developed a very popular model that proposes the idea of **multiple intelligences**. It comprises seven areas of ability, which are presented in Table 10.1, along with examples of roles that might be characteristic of a person with a high degree of a given intelligence. The table also briefly describes the features of each type of intelligence.

If Gardner's ideas were followed closely, students would be assessed in all areas of intelligence. If found to have strengths in an area, students would be provided opportunities to expand their interests, skills, and abilities accordingly. The attractiveness of this conceptualization is that (1) it acknowledges some ability areas that are frequently overlooked and (2) it recognizes the importance of different types of intelligences and gives them all equal footing.

FURTHER READING

For more information on multiple intelligences, read Chapter 5 in the *Handbook of Gifted Education,* edited by N. Colangelo and G. A. Davis, published in 1997 by Allyn & Bacon.

TABLE 10.1   Multiple Intelligences

Intelligence	End States	Core Components
Logical–Mathematical	Scientist Mathematician	Sensitivity to, and capacity to discern, logical or numerical patterns; ability to handle long chains of reasoning
Linguistic	Poet Journalist	Sensitivity to the sounds, rhythms, and meanings of words; sensitivity to the different functions of language
Musical	Composer Violinist	Abilities to produce and appreciate rhythm, pitch, and timbre; appreciation of the forms of musical expressiveness
Spatial	Navigator Sculptor	Capacities to perceive the visual–spatial world accurately and to transform one's initial perceptions
Bodily–Kinesthetic	Dancer Athlete	Abilities to control one's body movements and to handle objects skillfully
Interpersonal	Therapist Salesperson	Capacities to discern and respond appropriately to the moods, temperaments, motivations, and desires of other people
Intrapersonal	Person with detailed, accurate self-knowledge	Access to one's own feelings and the ability to discriminate among them and draw upon them to guide behaviour; knowledge of one's own strengths, weaknesses, desires, and intelligences
Naturalistic	Naturalist Park Ranger	Affinity and appreciation for the wonders of nature

From "Multiple Intelligences Go to School: Educational Implications of the Theory of Multiple Intelligences," by H. Gardner and T. Hatch, 1989, *Educational Researcher, 18*(8), p. 6. Copyright © 1989 by the American Educational Research Association. Reprinted by permission of the publisher.

Concept of Creativity

Creativity is a major part of Renzulli's three-ring model. The concept is difficult to pinpoint, yet its importance as it relates to individuals who are gifted makes it a current topic for debate and discussion. As Coleman and Cross (2001) note, this topic has been part of the ongoing discussion of individuals who are gifted ever since the publication in 1959 of Guilford's seminal work on this topic.

As indicated previously, the concept is somewhat elusive, and no one definition explaining it has become popular. The concept can be characterized by the phrase "You know it when you see it." Coleman and Cross (2001) aptly describe the state of affairs:

> A single accepted definition of creativity does not exist. In fact, neither is there universal agreement about what relevant attributes are needed to define an act as creative. The difficulty of selecting relevant attributes illustrates the problem of defining creativity. The terms originality and novelty pervade the literature on creativity. They express a quantitative and a qualitative standard, but they fail to say to what criterion a person is being compared. (p. 240)

The concept of creativity continues to receive wide attention, and efforts to better understand it and be able to apply it in meaningful ways within the context of education are warranted.

Prevalence and Origins of Giftedness

The number of students who display exceptional abilities is uncertain. It is, of course, influenced by how giftedness is defined and how it is measured. A figure of 2 percent is cited to reflect the extent of giftedness in the school population (B.C. Ministry of Education, 1995). The critical reader should also note the distinction between the number of students served and the number of students who might be gifted. Only certain types of students who are

FIGURE 10.1

Renzulli's Three-Ring Conception of Giftedness

From *What Makes Giftedness?* (Brief #6, p. 10), by J. Renzulli, 1979, Los Angeles: National/State Leadership Training Institute. Reprinted by permission.

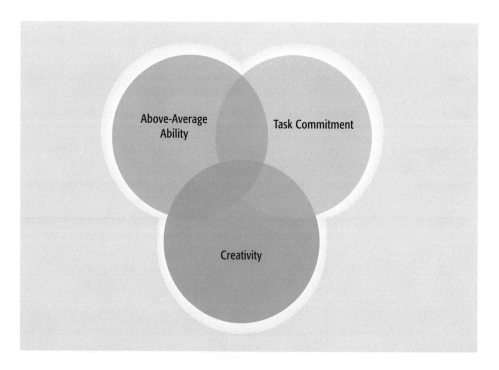

gifted may be served because of the methods used for identification. Another cautionary note is that such figures generally underestimate the number of students who are gifted who are ethnically or culturally different, disabled, or female. These subgroups are underrepresented in programs for students with exceptional abilities.

Much professional discussion has focused on what contributes to giftedness in a person. Most researchers suggest that giftedness results from the interaction between biology and environment. Research has shown that behaviour is greatly affected by genetics. Although this notion is sometimes overemphasized, genetic factors do play a role in giftedness. Other biological factors, such as nutrition, also have an impact on an individual's development.

The environment in which a child is raised also affects later performance and intellectual abilities. Homes in which significant amounts of stimulation and opportunity to explore and interact with the environment exist, accompanied by high expectations, tend to produce children more likely to be successful scholastically and socially.

CONSIDER THIS

How can the way in which "gifted" and "talented" are defined influence the prevalence of children classified?

Characteristics of Students Who Are Gifted

Students who are gifted demonstrate a wide range of specific aptitudes, abilities, and skills. Though they should not be overgeneralized or considered stereotypical, certain characteristics distinguish students who are gifted or talented. A comprehensive list, depicting the characteristics of students who are gifted, has been developed by Clark (2002); a summary is presented in Table 10.2.

An interesting phenomenon is the paradoxical negative effect of certain positive behaviours displayed by students who are gifted. For instance, students' sincere, excited curiosity about a topic being covered in class can sometimes be interpreted as annoying or disruptive by a teacher or fellow students. Their quick answers or certainty that they are right may be misconstrued as well, in that such desirable behaviour can be misperceived as problem behaviour.

Some characteristics can outright be problematic for students who are gifted. For instance, characteristics such as uneven precocity, interpersonal difficulties (possibly due to cognitive differences), underachievement, nonconformity, perfectionism, and frustration and anger may indeed be negative features (Davis & Rimm, 1998).

Clark (2002) also points out that different levels of ability and performance exist within the ranks of those who are gifted. She distinguishes among students who would be considered typical or moderately gifted, those who are highly gifted, and those who are exceptionally gifted. According to Clark, students who are highly gifted "tend to evidence more energy than gifted individuals; they think faster and are more intent and focused on their interests and they exhibit a higher degree of ability in most of the traits... identified with giftedness" (p. 63). Clark describes individuals who are exceptionally gifted as those who "seem to have different value structures... tend to be more isolated by choice and more invested in concerns of a meta-nature (e.g., universal problems)... seldom seek popularity or social acclaim" (p. 63). Both students who are highly gifted and students who are exceptionally gifted pose significant challenges to educators in meeting their needs within the general education classroom. Most of the discussion in this chapter is directed toward the typical student who is gifted.

An interesting characteristic that has important classroom implications is the gifted student's expenditure of minimum effort while still earning high grades (Reis & Schack, 1993). Many students who are gifted are able to handle the general education curriculum with ease. However, the long-term effect of being able to excel without working hard may be a lack of the work habits needed for challenging programs at a later point in time (i.e., advanced placement classes in high school or university).

TABLE 10.2	Differentiating Characteristics of the Gifted
Domain	*Characteristic*
The Cognitive Function	▸ Extraordinary quantity of information; unusual retentiveness ▸ Advanced comprehension ▸ Unusual varied interests and curiosity ▸ High level of language development ▸ High level of verbal ability ▸ Unusual capacity for processing information ▸ Accelerated pace of thought processes ▸ Flexible thought processes ▸ Comprehensive synthesis ▸ Early ability to delay closure ▸ Heightened capacity for seeing unusual and diverse relationships, integration of ideas, and disciplines ▸ Ability to generate original ideas and solutions ▸ Early differential patterns for thought processing (e.g., thinking in alternatives; abstract terms; sensing consequences; making generalizations; visual thinking; use of metaphors and analogies) ▸ Early ability to use and form conceptual frameworks ▸ An evaluative approach toward oneself and others ▸ Unusual intensity; persistent goal-directed behaviour
The Affective Function	▸ Large accumulation of information about emotions that have not been brought to awareness ▸ Unusual sensitivity to the expectations and feelings of others ▸ Keen sense of humour—may be gentle or hostile ▸ Heightened self-awareness, accompanied by feelings of being different ▸ Idealism and a sense of justice, which appear at an early age ▸ Earlier development of an inner locus of control and satisfaction ▸ Unusual emotional depth and intensity ▸ High expectations of self and others, often leading to high levels of frustration with self, others, and situations; perfectionism ▸ Strong need for consistency between abstract values and personal actions ▸ Advanced levels of moral judgment ▸ Strongly motivated by self-actualization needs ▸ Advanced cognitive and affective capacity for conceptualizing and solving societal problems ▸ Leadership ability ▸ Solutions to social and environmental problems ▸ Involvement with the metaneeds of society (e.g., injustice, beauty, truth)
The Physical/Sensing Function	▸ Unusual quantity of input from the environment through a heightened sensory awareness ▸ Unusual discrepancy between physical and intellectual development ▸ Low tolerance for the lag between their standards and their athletic skills ▸ Cartesian split—can include neglect of physical well-being and avoidance of physical activity
The Intuitive Function	▸ Early involvement and concern for intuitive knowing and metaphysical ideas and phenomena ▸ Open to experiences in this area; will experiment with psychic and metaphysical phenomena ▸ Creative approach in all areas of endeavour ▸ Ability to predict; interest in future

From *Growing Up Gifted* (6th Ed.) by Barbara Clark. Copyright 2002 by Merrill/Prentice Hall. Reprinted by permission.

Identification, Assessment, and Eligibility

General education teachers need to know about the assessment process used to confirm the existence of exceptional abilities. Teachers play a crucial role in the initial stages of the process, for they are typically the first to recognize that a student might be gifted.

The assessment process includes a sequence of steps, beginning with an initial referral (i.e., nomination) and culminating with the validation of the decision. General education teachers are largely responsible for identifying students who are gifted. Although many children displaying exceptional abilities may be spotted very early (i.e., preschool years), many are not recognized until they are in school. For this reason, teachers need to be aware of classroom behaviours that students who are gifted typically display. A listing of such behaviours is provided in Table 10.3.

Teachers who recognize such behaviours should determine whether a student should be evaluated more comprehensively. This usually involves nominating the student for gifted services. Teachers can take part in the next step in the assessment process as well. After a student has been nominated or referred, teachers can assemble information to help determine whether the student should receive special services. The following sources of information can contribute to understanding a student's demonstrated or potential

---

TABLE 10.3   Classroom Behaviours of Gifted Students

Does the child
- Ask a lot of questions?
- Show a lot of interest in progress?
- Have lots of information on many things?
- Want to know why or how something is so?
- Become unusually upset at injustices?
- Seem interested and concerned about social or political problems?
- Often have a better reason than you do for not doing what you want done?
- Refuse to drill on spelling, math, facts, flash cards, or handwriting?
- Criticize others for dumb ideas?
- Become impatient if work is not "perfect"?
- Seem to be a loner?
- Seem bored and often have nothing to do?
- Complete only part of an assignment or project and then take off in a new direction?
- Stick to a subject long after the class has gone on to other things?
- Seem restless, out of seat often?
- Daydream?
- Seem to understand easily?
- Like solving puzzles and problems?
- Have his or her own idea about how something should be done? And stay with it?
- Talk a lot?
- Love metaphors and abstract ideas?
- Love debating issues?

This child may be showing giftedness cognitively.

Does the child
- Show unusual ability in some area? Maybe reading or math?
- Show fascination with one field of interest? And manage to include this interest in all discussion topics?

Does the child
- Enjoy meeting or talking with experts in this field?
- Get math answers correct, but find it difficult to tell you how?
- Enjoy graphing everything? Seem obsessed with probabilities?
- Invent new obscure systems and codes?

This child may be showing giftedness academically.

Does the child
- Try to do things in different, unusual, imaginative ways?
- Have a really zany sense of humour?
- Enjoy new routines or spontaneous activities?
- Love variety and novelty?
- Create problems with no apparent solutions? And enjoy asking you to solve them?
- Love controversial and unusual questions?
- Have a vivid imagination?
- Seem never to proceed sequentially?

This child may be showing giftedness creatively.

Does the child
- Organize and lead group activities? Sometimes take over?
- Enjoy taking risks?
- Seem cocky, self-assured?
- Enjoy decision-making? Stay with that decision?
- Synthesize ideas and information from a lot of different sources?

This child may be showing giftedness through leadership ability.

Does the child
- Seem to pick up skills in the arts—music, dance, drama, painting, etc.—without instruction?
- Invent new techniques? Experiment?
- See minute detail in products or performances?
- Have high sensory sensitivity?

This child may be showing giftedness through visual or performing arts ability.

Too few students from minority cultural groups are identified as gifted and talented.

ability: formal tests; informal assessments; interviews with teachers, parents, and peers; and actual student products.

A helpful technique used in many school systems to determine the performance capabilities of students is **portfolio assessment**. Portfolios contain a collection of student-generated products, reflecting the quality of a student's work. They may also contain permanent products such as artwork, poetry, or videotapes of student performance (e.g., theatrical production, music recital).

As VanTassel-Baska, Patton, and Prillaman (1989) point out, students who are culturally different and those who come from socially and economically disadvantaged backgrounds are typically overlooked in the process of identifying students for gifted programs. For the most part, this problem results from entry requirements that stress performance on standardized tests. When students obtain low test scores on standardized instruments that may be biased against them, exclusion results.

It has also been difficult to identify and serve students who are gifted and also have disabilities. For instance, the problems that characterize a learning disability (e.g., problems in language-related areas) often mask high levels of accomplishment in other areas such as drama, art, or music. Special services or activities are warranted for these students.

After the student has been identified as gifted and begins to participate in special activities, ongoing assessment should become part of the student's educational program. Practical and personal needs should be monitored regularly (Del Prete, 1996). Practical concerns, such as progress in academic areas and realization of potential, can be evaluated. On the other hand, the personal needs of students who are gifted (e.g., feeling accepted and developing confidence) need to be addressed as well.

Multicultural Issues

As pointed out earlier, cultural diversity remains an area of concern in the education of students who are gifted. Too few students who are culturally different from the majority of their peers are identified and served through programs for students who are gifted. "Culturally diverse children have much talent, creativity, and intelligence. Manifestations of these characteristics may be different and thus require not only different tools for measuring these strengths, but also different eyes from which to see them" (Plummer, 1995, p. 290).

VanTassel et al. (1989), in summarizing the literature related to culturally different students who are gifted, note four major needs:

- Nontraditional measures for identification
- Recognition of cultural attributes and factors in deciding on identification procedures
- A focus on strengths in nonacademic areas
- Programs that capitalize on noncognitive skills that enhance motivation

Teachers should look for certain behaviours associated with giftedness in children who are culturally different. An example of an observational checklist for accomplishing this task is presented in the nearby Diversity Forum feature.

Even when culturally diverse students have been identified as gifted, programming often has not been sensitive to their needs. As Plummer (1995) notes, few programs have the resources (i.e., personnel, materials) available to tap the interests and strengths of these students. Often, the general education teacher needs such supports to address these students' educational needs in inclusive settings. The twofold challenge for teachers is (1) to respect racial, ethnic, and cultural differences of students from diverse backgrounds and (2) to integrate diverse cultural topics into the curriculum (Plummer, 1995).

FURTHER READING

For more information on students with disabilities who are gifted and/or talented, read the article "Inclusive Education for Gifted Students with Disabilities," by C. Yewchuk and J. Lupart, in *International Handbook of Giftedness and Talent* (2nd edition), edited by K. A. Heller et al., 2000 (pp. 659–672).

CONSIDER THIS

How can teachers take into consideration multicultural issues when identifying children who are gifted?

Observational Checklist for Identifying Strengths of Culturally Diverse Children

1. Ability to express feeling and emotions

2. Ability to improvise with commonplace materials and objects

3. Articulateness in role-playing, sociodrama, and storytelling

4. Enjoyment of and ability in visual arts, such as drawing, painting, and sculpture

5. Enjoyment of and ability in creative movement, dance, drama, etc.

6. Enjoyment of and ability in music and rhythm

7. Use of expressive speech

8. Fluency and flexibility in figural media

9. Enjoyment of and skills in group or team activities

10. Responsiveness to the concrete

11. Responsiveness to the kinesthetic

12. Expressiveness of gestures, body language, etc., and ability to interpret body language

13. Humour

14. Richness of imagery in informal language

15. Originality of ideas in problem solving

16. Problem-centredness or persistence in problem solving

17. Emotional responsiveness

18. Quickness of warmup

From "Identifying and Capitalizing on the Strengths of Culturally Different Children," by E. P. Torrance. In *The Handbook of School Psychology*, edited by C. R. Reynolds and J. B. Gulkin, 1982, pp. 451–500. New York: Wiley. Copyright 1982 by John Wiley & Sons. Reprinted by permission.

Strategies for Curriculum and Instruction for Students Who Are Gifted

The literature on providing effective services for students with exceptional abilities consistently stresses the need for **differentiated programming**. This means that learning opportunities provided to these students must differ according to a student's needs and abilities. Differentiation includes the content of what students learn, the processes used in learning situations, and the final products that students develop. Furthermore, as Lopez and MacKenzie (1993) note, "Difference lies in the depth, scope, pace, and self-directedness of the expectations" (p. 288).

VanTassel-Baska (1989) notes some of the mistaken beliefs that some educators have about educating students with exceptional abilities:

▷ A "differentiated" curriculum for the gifted means "anything that is different from what is provided for all learners." *Fact:* A "differentiated" curriculum implies a coherently planned scope and sequence of instruction that matches the needs of students and that typically does differ from the regular education curriculum.

▷ All experiences provided for learners who are gifted must be creative and focused on process. *Fact:* Core content areas are important areas of instructional focus.

▷ One curriculum package will provide what is needed for the entire gifted population. *Fact:* Students need a variety of materials, resources, and courses.

▷ **Acceleration**, moving through the curriculum at a more rapid pace, can be harmful because it pushes children socially and leaves gaps in their knowledge. *Fact:* This approach to meeting the needs of students with exceptional abilities is the intervention technique best supported by research. (pp. 13–14)

FURTHER READING

For further information and suggestions, read the document *The Journey: A Handbook for Parents and Children Who Are Gifted and Talented* (2004) from Alberta Learning (available at: www.learning.gov.ab.ca/k_12 specialneeds/resource.asp)

CROSS-REFERENCE

Review Chapters 3–9, and compare curriculum and instruction modifications suggested for students with other special needs.

Many professionals in the field of gifted education argue that the preferred setting for students who are gifted is not general education; they recommend differentiated programs delivered in separate classes for the greater part, if not all, of the school day. However, students who are gifted are more likely to spend nearly all day in general education classrooms, possibly receiving some differentiated opportunities in a pullout program.

Realities of the General Education Classroom

In general education settings, students who are gifted or talented are sometimes subject to conditions that indeed hinder the possibility for having their individual needs met. In the United States, the U.S. Department of Education (1993) has noted the following concerns related to educating students who are gifted in general education settings:

▶ Elementary level
  ▶ The general education curriculum does not challenge students who are gifted.
  ▶ Most students who are academically talented have already mastered up to one half of the required curriculum offered to them in elementary school.
  ▶ Classroom teachers do little to accommodate the different learning needs of children who are gifted.
  ▶ Most specialized programs are available for only a few hours a week.
  ▶ Students talented in the arts are offered few challenging opportunities.

▶ Secondary level
  ▶ Appropriate opportunities in junior high schools are scattered and unco-ordinated.
  ▶ High school schedules do not meet the needs of talented students (i.e., pacing of coverage of content).
  ▶ The university preparatory curriculum in the United States generally does not require hard work from able students.
  ▶ Small-town and rural schools often have limited resources and are unable to offer advanced classes and special learning opportunities.
  ▶ Specialized schools, magnet schools, and intensive summer programs serve only a fraction of the secondary students who might benefit from them.
  ▶ Dual enrolment in secondary school and university is uncommon.

CONSIDER THIS

Do you think many, or all, of these concerns about educating gifted students would also apply to Canadian schools?

Other more specific practices that can be problematic for students who are gifted include the following:

▶ When involved in group activities, students who are gifted may end up doing all of the work (Clinkenbeard, 1991).
▶ They are often subjected to more stringent grading criteria (Clinkenbeard, 1991).
▶ When they finish assignments early, they are given more of the same type of work or assigned more of the same types of tasks at the outset (Shaner, 1991).
▶ They are overused as co-teachers to help students who need more assistance.
▶ Vocabulary use in the average classroom is inappropriate for advanced learners (Clark, 1996).
▶ Advanced levels of critical thinking are not typically incorporated into lessons (Clark, 1996).
▶ Instructional materials in general education classrooms are frequently limited in range and complexity (Clark, 1996).

Unfortunately, most general education teachers are not provided with the necessary understanding, skills, and resources to deal appropriately with this population. This situation is exacerbated by the fact that teachers have to deal with a wide range of abilities and needs in their classrooms. The composition of the general education classroom in many of today's public schools requires an array of accommodative knowledge and skills.

In addition, some teachers feel uncomfortable working with students who have exceptional abilities. Figure 10.2 highlights this situation by way of a personal experience. Shaner (1991) remarks that a teacher working with a student who is gifted can be "intimidated by him or her, paralyzed with a fear of not being able to keep up, or threatened by the student's challenges to authority" (pp. 14–15). Teachers are also concerned about being asked questions they are unprepared to answer or challenged on points they may not know well. These are reasonable fears; however, they can be minimized by using these opportunities as a way of increasing everyone's knowledge and by understanding how to address the needs of students who are gifted within the general classroom setting.

Differentiated programming for students with exceptional abilities, wherever it occurs, must address individual needs and interests in the context of preparing the students for a world characterized by change and complexity. Reis (1989) suggests that we reassess how we look at gifted education and move away from the content-based nature of most current curricula to an orientation based on a realistic view of future education.

Continuum of Placement Options

A variety of ways exist for providing educational programs to students who are gifted and/or talented. The value of a particular option reflects the extent to which it meets an individual's needs. A continuum of potential settings for providing programs to students who are gifted is shown in Figure 10.3. As Clark (2002) points out, all of the options have some advantages; none address the needs of all students with exceptional abilities. For this reason, she feels that school systems should provide a range of programmatic alternatives.

FIGURE 10.2

A Personal Experience

From *Exceptional Children in Focus* (p. 216), by J. R. Patton, J. Blackburn, and K. Fad, 1996, Columbus, OH: Merrill. Used by permission.

Not long ago, I was invited to go on a "reef walk" with a class of gifted third- and fourth-graders. It was a very educational experience.

While we were wading in shallow water, we came upon a familiar marine organism commonly called a feather duster (tube worm). Forgetting that these students had vocabularies well advanced of their nongifted age peers, I was ready to say something like, "Look how that thing hangs on the rock."

Before I could get my highly descriptive statement out, Eddie, who always amazes us with his comments, offered the following: "Notice how securely anchored the organism is to the stationary coral?"

All I could reply was "Yes. I did."

FIGURE 10.3

Placement Options for
Gifted Students

From *Growing Up Gifted* (3rd ed.,
p. 256) by B. Clark, 2002, Upper
Saddle River, NJ: Merrill/Prentice
Hall. Copyright 2002 by Pearson
Education. Reprinted by
permission.

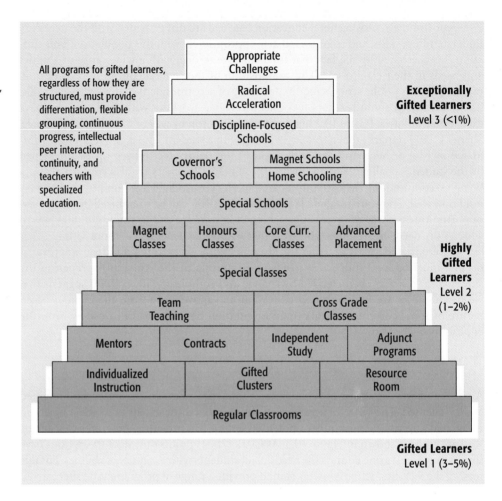

All programs for gifted learners, regardless of how they are structured, must provide differentiation, flexible grouping, continuous progress, intellectual peer interaction, continuity, and teachers with specialized education.

Appropriate Challenges

Radical Acceleration

Discipline-Focused Schools

Governor's Schools — Magnet Schools — Home Schooling

Exceptionally Gifted Learners
Level 3 (<1%)

Special Schools

Magnet Classes — Honours Classes — Core Curr. Classes — Advanced Placement

Special Classes

Highly Gifted Learners
Level 2 (1–2%)

Team Teaching — Cross Grade Classes

Mentors — Contracts — Independent Study — Adjunct Programs

Individualized Instruction — Gifted Clusters — Resource Room

Regular Classrooms

Gifted Learners
Level 1 (3–5%)

FURTHER READING

For more information on programs for students who are gifted and/or talented in Canada, read J. A. Leroux's article "A Study of Education for High Ability Students in Canada: Policy, Programs, and Student Needs," in *International Handbook of Giftedness and Talent* (2nd edition), edited by K. A. Heller et al., 2000 (pp. 695–702).

Students who are gifted who are in general education classrooms for the entire instructional day can have their needs met through a variety of special provisions such as **enrichment**, acceleration, or special grouping and clustering. The challenge for teachers is to co-ordinate these provisions with those required for other students in the classroom.

In some schools, students who have been identified as gifted are pulled out for a specified period of time each day to attend a special class. When they are in the general education setting, it may be possible for them to participate in an individualized program of study, apart from the regular curriculum.

Students who are gifted may also participate in various adjunct programs such as mentorships, internships, special tutorials, independent study, and resource rooms—many of which will occur outside the regular classroom. For students at the secondary level, spending time in special programming for part of the day, in addition to attending heterogeneous classes, is another possibility.

These programmatic options affect the role and responsibilities of the general education teacher. In some situations, the general education teacher will be the primary source of instruction for these students. In others, the general education teacher may serve as a manager, coordinating the services provided by others. However, it is probable that most teachers will be responsible for providing some level of instruction to students who are gifted.

Approaches to Programming

Three general practices are used in designing programs for students who have exceptional abilities: acceleration, enrichment, and special grouping. All three have merit and can be used in general education settings.

Acceleration refers to practices that introduce content, concepts, and educational experiences to students who are gifted sooner than for other students. According to Coleman and Cross (2001) accelerations can be thought of as a way "in which the learner completes a course of study in less time than ordinarily expected" (p. 298). This approach presents students who are gifted with more advanced materials appropriate to their ability and interests. There are many types of accelerative practices, as reflected in the array of options provided in the nearby Inclusion Strategies feature.

All of the accelerative options described by Southern and Jones (1991) have relevance for students who are gifted in general education classrooms. The techniques that have the most direct application in the general education classroom are **continuous progress**, **self-paced instruction**, **subject-matter acceleration**, **combined classes**, **curriculum compacting**, and **curriculum telescoping**. If these practices are to be used, teachers must plan and implement instructional activities.

Other accelerative practices have a more indirect impact on ongoing activities in the general education classroom. Nevertheless, teachers should be aware of them. They include early entrance to school, grade skipping, mentorships, extracurricular programs, concurrent enrolment, advanced placement, and credit by examination.

According to Gallagher and Gallagher (1994), the most common acceleration practices are (1) primary level—early admittance to school, ungraded primary, (2) upper elementary—ungraded classes, grade skipping, (3) junior high school—three years in two, senior high classes for credit, and (4) high school—extra load (early graduation), advanced placement (AP). Interestingly, some professionals (Davis, 1996) advocate separate advanced placement classes for students who are gifted because their needs differ from those of nongifted students enrolled in AP classes. Matthews (1993), from the University of Toronto, has argued that advanced programming needs to be done on a subject-specific basis since students who are gifted are likely to be advanced in specific areas.

Enrichment refers to techniques that provide topics, skill development, materials, or experiences that extend the depth of coverage beyond the typical curriculum. Coleman and Cross (2001) explain enrichment in the following way: "In its broadest interpretation, enrichment encompasses a number of modifications in standard educational practices. In its narrowest interpretation, enrichment means providing interesting and stimulating tributaries to the mainstream of school" (p. 298).

This practice is commonly used in general education classes to address the needs of students who move through content quickly. Many teachers' manuals and guides provide ideas on how to deliver enriching activities to students who finish their work quickly. Comprehensive lesson plans should include a section on "early finishers," which will often include students who are gifted, so that enriching activities are available for those who complete assignments before the rest of the class.

As Southern and Jones (1991) note, some enrichment activities ultimately involve acceleration. For instance, whenever topics of an advanced nature are introduced, a form of acceleration is actually being employed. There is, however, a distinction between materials or activities that are accelerated and possess a dimension of difficulty or conceptual complexity and materials or activities that provide variety but do not require advanced skills or understanding.

Special grouping refers to the practice whereby students who are gifted of similar ability levels or interests are grouped together for at least part of the instructional day. One

FURTHER READING

For more information on schoolwide enrichment, read Chapter 11 in the *Handbook of Gifted Education,* edited by N. Colangelo and G. A. Davis, published in 1997 by Allyn & Bacon.

Range and Types of Accelerative Options

1. Early entrance to kindergarten or Grade 1
The student is admitted to school prior to the age specified by the district for normal entry to first grade.

2. Grade skipping
The student is moved ahead of normal grade placement. This may be done during an academic year (placing a Grade 3 student directly into Grade 4), or at year end (promoting a Grade 3 student to Grade 5).

3. Continuous
The student is given material deemed appropriate for current achievement progress as the student becomes ready.

4. Self-paced instruction
The student is presented with materials that allow him or her to proceed at a self-selected pace. Responsibility for selection of pacing is the student's.

5. Subject matter acceleration
The student is placed for a part of a day with students at more advanced grade levels for one or more subjects without being assigned to a higher grade (e.g., a Grade 5 student going to Grade 6 for science instruction).

6. Combined classes
The student is placed in classes where two or more grade levels are combined (e.g., Grades 3 and 4 split rooms). The arrangement can be used to allow younger children to interact with older ones academically and socially.

7. Curriculum compacting
The student is given reduced amounts of introductory activities, drill review, and so on. The time saved may be used to move faster through the curriculum.

8. Telescoping curriculum
The student spends less time than normal in a course of study (e.g., completing a one-year course in one semester, or finishing junior high school in two years rather than three).

9. Mentorships
The student is exposed to a mentor who provides advanced training and experiences in a content area.

10. Extracurricular programs
The student is enrolled in course work or summer programs that confer advanced instruction and/or credit for study (e.g., fast-paced language or math courses offered by universities).

11. Concurrent enrolment
The student is taking a course at one level and receiving credit for successful completion of a parallel course at a higher level (e.g., taking algebra at the junior high level and receiving credit for high school algebra as well as junior high math credits upon successful completion).

12. Advanced placement
The student takes a course in high school that prepares him or her for taking an examination that can confer [university] credit for satisfactory performances.

13. Credit by examination
The student receives credit (at high school or [university] level) upon successful completion of an examination.

14. Correspondence
The student takes high school or college courses by mail (or, more recently, courses through video and audio presentations).

15. Early entrance into junior high, high school, or [university]
The student is admitted with full standing to an advanced level of instruction (at least one year early).

commonly cited technique is the use of cluster grouping. This practice allows for inter-action with peers who share a similar enthusiasm, bring different perspectives to topics, and stimulate the cognitive and creative thinking of others in the group.

Classroom Accommodations for Students Who Are Gifted

This section highlights techniques for addressing the needs of students with exceptional abilities. Teachers who will be working closely with these students are encouraged to consult resources that thoroughly discuss teaching students who are gifted in general education settings—see Maker (1993), Parke (1989), Smutny, Walker, and Meckstroth (1997), or Winebrenner (1992).

First and foremost, teachers should strive to create classroom settings that foster conditions in which students who are gifted feel comfortable and are able to realize their potential. They need a comprehensive long-term plan of education and must enjoy learning experiences that reflect this plan (Kitano, 1993).

Although special opportunities for enrichment, acceleration, and the use of higher-level skills are particularly beneficial to students who are gifted, these opportunities can also be extended to other students when appropriate (Roberts, Ingram, & Harris, 1992). Many students in general education settings will find practices such as integrated programming (combining different subject matter) to be exciting, motivating, and meaningful.

CONSIDER THIS

How can special opportunities for children who are gifted and/or talented benefit other students, including those with other special needs?

Management Considerations

It is essential to organize and systematically manage the classroom environment. Teachers must create a psychosocial climate that is open to a "variety of ideas, materials, problems, people, viewpoints, and resources" (Schiever, 1993, p. 209). The learning environment should be safe, accepting, and supportive. It is also useful to design instructional activities that allow for extensive social interactions among all students in the class.

Teachers must create a psychological classroom climate that is conducive to a variety of ideas and viewpoints.

Grouping students who are gifted is useful and can be done in a variety of ways—for example, co-operative cluster grouping on the basis of similar abilities or interests, dyads, or seminar-type formats. Students who are gifted should be afforded an opportunity to spend time with other students who are gifted, just as competitive tennis players must play opponents with similar or more advanced ability in order to maintain their skills.

Even though the merits of co-operative learning in classroom settings have been established, heterogeneous co-operative learning arrangements involving students who are gifted must be managed carefully. Teachers must guarantee that most of the work does not always fall on students who are gifted in such arrangements. Co-operative learning arrangements should be encouraged but continually monitored to ensure effectiveness and fairness.

Teachers should develop comprehensive record-keeping systems that monitor the progress of all students, including students who are gifted who may be taking part in a mix of enrichment and accelerated activities. A differentiated report card may be useful for conveying to parents more information about the performance of a student who is gifted. An example of such a report is shown in Figure 10.4. Qualitative information about student performance can be communicated through this document.

The following are some specific suggestions for dealing with students who are gifted:

- Get to know students who are gifted early in the school year through interviews, portfolios of previous work, child-created portfolios, and dynamic assessment (test-teach-retest) (Smutny et al., 1997).
- Enlist parents as colleagues early in the school year by soliciting information and materials (Smutny et al., 1997).
- Require students who are gifted to follow classroom rules and procedures while allowing them to explore and pursue their curiosity when appropriate (Feldhusen, 1993a and b).
- Include students who are gifted in the development of class procedures that emerge during the course of a school year (e.g., introduction of animals in the room).
- Explain the logic and rationale for certain rules and procedures.
- Use cluster seating arrangements rather than strict rows (Feldhusen, 1993a).
- Identify a portion of the room where special events and activities take place and where stimulating materials are kept.
- Develop lesson plan formats that include instructional ideas for students who are gifted.
- Consult teacher guides of textbook series for ideas for enrichment activities.
- Let students who are working in independent arrangements plan their own learning activities (Feldhusen, 1993a).
- Use contracts with students who are involved in elaborate independent study projects to maximize communication between teacher and students (Rosselli, 1993).
- Involve students in their own record keeping, thus assisting the teacher and developing responsibility.
- Use periodic progress reports, daily logs, and teacher conferences to monitor and evaluate students who are in independent study arrangements (Conroy, 1993), as described in Figure 10.4.

Curricular and Instructional Considerations

Many professionals interested in gifted education promote the use of differentiated programming. Keeping this in mind, general education teachers should develop instructional lessons that consider a range of abilities and interests. For students who are gifted, instructional activities should be qualitatively different from those assigned to the class in general—or completely different if certain accelerative options are being used.

Differentiated–Integrated Curriculum Report

Student: ___
Teacher: ___
Semester/Year: ___

CONTENT

DISCIPLINES

Area of Study	Broad-Based Theme	Language Arts Enrichment/Acceleration				Math/Science Enrichment		Social Science	Arts	Individual Extension Activities
		Reading	Written Expression	Oral Expression	Spelling	Math	Science	Social Studies/Social Issues	Music/Visual Arts/Performance Arts	

PROCESSES

Basic Skills

Research Skills
- Reading for general information
- Creating hypothesis
- Taking notes
- Making an outline
- Reading for supportive evidence
- Writing the thesis
- Using various sources
- Writing bibliography
- Making appendices

- Brainstorm
- Observe
- Classify
- Interpret
- Analyze
- Evaluate
- Judge

Productive Thinking/Critical Thinking Skills
- Compare
- Categorize
- Synthesize
- Exhibit fluency
- Display flexibility
- Demonstrate originality
- Problem solve

- Elaborate
- Hypothesize
- Exhibit awareness
- Appreciate
- Create
- Redesign
- Prove

PRODUCTS

a variety of ways to communicate and express selves ◄ the opportunity to share information with an audience

☐ Proposed } in-depth study of
☐ Completed } student's choice:

FIGURE 10.4

Differentiated–Integrated Curriculum Report

Adapted from Sandra N. Kaplan by Joy Kataoka, revised 1990. Copyright © ASSETS 1986.

Guiding Questions   When designing instructional activities for the entire class, teachers can use the following series of questions offered by Kitano (1993) to guide planning for students who are gifted:

▶ Do the activities include provisions for several ability levels?
▶ Do the activities include ways to accommodate a variety of interest areas?
▶ Does the design of activities encourage development of sophisticated products?
▶ Do the activities provide for the integration of thinking processes with concept development?
▶ Are the concepts consistent with the comprehensive curriculum plan? (p. 280)

Selecting Programming Ideas   An accelerative technique that can be used effectively with students who are gifted in general education classes is **curriculum compacting**, which allows students to cover assigned material in ways that are faster or different. As Renzulli, Reis, and Smith (1981) point out, this process has three phases: the assessment of what students know and the skills they possess, identification of ways of covering the curriculum, and suggestions for enrichment and accelerative options. Renzulli et al. have developed a form, presented in Figure 10.5, to assist teachers in compacting curriculum.

FIGURE 10.5

Curriculum Compacting Form

From *The Revolving Door Identification Model* (p. 79), by J. Renzulli, S. Reis, and L. Smith, 1981, Mansfield Center, CT: Creative Learning Press. Reprinted with permission from Creative Learning Press, copyright © 1981.

Individual Educational Programming Guide
The Compactor

Name _____ Age ____ Teacher(s) _____ Individual conference dates and persons participating in planning of IEP

School _____ Grade ____ Parent(s) _____

Curriculum areas to be considered for compacting. Provide a brief description of basic material to be covered during this marking period and the assessment information or evidence that suggests the need for compacting.	*Procedures for compacting basic material.* Describe activities that will be used to guarantee proficiency in basic curricular areas.	*Acceleration and/or enrichment activities.* Describe activities that will be used to provide advanced-level learning experiences in each of the regular curricula.

APPROPRIATE CONTENT FOR REGULAR STUDENTS

1. Discuss qualities of drama that make drama a unique genre of literature.
2. Discuss terms used in discussion of drama, such as *aside, soliloquy, prologue, epilogue, dramatic irony,* and *foreshadowing.*
3. Discuss overview of Elizabethan time period, political system, and the role of arts in the society.
4. Distinguish between Shakespeare's time period and setting of the play, giving brief explanation of Verona's social and political characteristics.
5. Discuss structure of Shakespeare's plays, using terms such as *act, scene,* and *line count.*
6. Discuss Shakespeare's language and such terms as *puns* and *asides.*
7. Discuss main plot, characterization, conflict, and ending of the play.

POSSIBLE ASSIGNMENTS:

a. Write an "updated" scene from Romeo and Juliet, stressing the same relationships, but making the scene's setting, names, language more contemporary.
b. Act out the original or rewritten scenes with emphasis on staging considerations.

ROMEO AND JULIET

APPROPRIATE CONTENT FOR GIFTED STUDENTS

1. Arrange students in small group to read play at rate appropriate to level of understanding.
2. Provide reference material dealing with Elizabethan time period, political and social characteristics, English theatre, and time period information about Verona and play's setting.
3. Provide reference material on critical analysis of *Romeo and Juliet.*
4. Encourage awareness of concepts found in play, such as decision making, personal identity, interpretation of the law.
5. Complete a Taba Teaching Strategy (Application of Generalization or Resolution of Conflict), stressing concepts as areas for individual research.
6. Facilitate student research and projects on conceptual subject matter from play.

POSSIBLE ACTIVITIES:

a. Visit and interview local agency for counselling youth or counselling for suicide prevention.
b. Become involved in local drama group.
c. Write an original play dealing with similar or related concepts found in *Romeo and Juliet.*

FIGURE 10.6

Adapting Curricular Content for Teaching Romeo and Juliet

From "Becoming Content with Content," by R. Shanley. In *Critical Issues in Gifted Education: Vol. 1. Defensible Programs for the Gifted,* edited by C. J. Maker, 1993, pp. 43–89. Austin, TX: Pro-Ed. Used by permission.

Many viable ways exist to address the needs of students who are gifted within the context of a general education lesson. An example of such practice is provided here:

> Enrichment: Literature. Figure 10.6 illustrates how the play *Romeo and Juliet* can be taught, keeping in mind the needs of the regular regular and students who are gifted. This example developed by Shanley (1993) shows how the content of the play and the activities used by the teacher can be adapted for students who are gifted.

The following are more specific suggestions related to areas such as questioning strategies and product differentiation:

◗ Balance coverage of basic disciplines and the arts (Feldhusen, 1993a).
◗ Consult teacher/instructor guides of textbook series for ideas for enrichment activities.
◗ Incorporate internet-based activities into lesson.
◗ Acquire an array of different learning-related materials for use with students who are gifted—these can include textbooks, magazines, artifacts, software, CD-ROM disks, and other media.
◗ Include time for independent study (Pugh, 1999).
◗ Teach research skills (data-gathering and investigative techniques) to students who are gifted to develop their independent study abilities (Reis & Schack, 1993).
◗ Use integrated themes for interrelating ideas within and across domains of inquiry (VanTassel-Baska, 1998). This type of curricular orientation can be used for all students in the general education setting, with special activities designed for students who are gifted. An example of an integrated unit on the topic of change is provided in Figure 10.7.

Goals for Curricula of Gifted Children

▶ Include more elaborate, complex, and in-depth study of major ideas, problems, and themes—those that integrate knowledge with and across systems of thought.

▶ Allow for the development and application of productive thinking skills that enable students to reconceptualize existing knowledge or generate new knowledge.

▶ Enable students to explore con-stantly changing knowledge and information, and to develop the attitude that knowledge is worth pursuing in an open world.

▶ Encourage exposure to, selection of, and use of appropriate and special-ized resources.

▶ Promote self-initiated and self-directed learning and growth.

▶ Provide for the development of self-understanding and the understanding of one's relationship to persons, soci-etal institutions, nature, and culture.

▶ Evaluate students with stress placed on their ability to perform at a level of excellence that demonstrates cre-ativity and higher-level thinking skills.

From *Diverse Populations of Gifted Children* (pp. 15–16) by S. Cline and D. Schwartz, 1999, Columbus, OH: Merrill.

▶ Include higher-order thinking skills in lessons (Johnson, 2001; Winocur & Mauer, 1997)—for example include questions that are open-ended and of varying conceptual levels in class discussions.

▶ Allocate time for students to have contact with adults who can provide special experi-ences and information to students who are gifted (e.g., mentors).

▶ Avoid assigning regular class work missed when students who are gifted spend time in special programs.

▶ Manage classroom discussions so that all students have an equal opportunity to con-tribute, feel comfortable doing so, and understand the nature of the discussion.

▶ Use standard textbooks and materials carefully, as students who are gifted will typically be able to move through them rapidly and may find them boring.

▶ Make sure students who are gifted have access to the latest developments in microcom-puters, including simulation software, interactive technologies, CD-ROM databases, and telecommunications (internet access). See the nearby Technology Today for some web-sites that contain curriculum-appropriate suggestions for students and teachers.

▶ Provide a range of options for demonstrating student mastery of curricular/instructional objectives—for instance, consider a range of options for final product development—see Figure 10.8 for a list of examples.

Career Development Students who are gifted and talented need to learn about possible career choices that await them. They may need to do so at an earlier time than other stu-dents because they may participate in accelerated programs that necessitate early deci-sions about career direction. Students should learn about various career options, the dynamics of different disciplines, and the training required to work in a given discipline.

Teachers can select different ways to address the career needs of students. One way is to ensure that students who are gifted have access to mentor programs, spending time with adults who are engaged in professional activities that interest them. Another method is to integrate the study of careers into the existing curriculum by discussing various

DISCIPLINES

CONTENTS

Area of Study	Terminal Objective Broad-Based Issue/Problem/Theme	Language Arts Enrichment/Acceleration — Reading	Written Expression	Oral Expression	Spelling	Math Enrichment — Math	Science	Social Science — Social Studies/Social Issues	Arts — Music/Visual Arts/Performance Arts
Geological Evolution Civil Rights	Change	Research to locate answers in various sources; Teacher-made handouts specific to area of study/issue; Poetry and/or short stories related to issues; Literature; Jr. great books	Reports; Essays; Poetry cinquains acrostics narrative poems; Short stories; Creation legends; Personal reaction papers	Oral presentation of each procedure outlined under written expression; Discussions; Inquiry discussions	Functional spelling; Dictionary skills; New vocabulary words; Word search; Crossword puzzles	Graphing reading designing; Problem solving; Logic	Geology (elements of change in geology); Metamorphosis; Archaeology; Astronomy beliefs seasons/tides	Historical and contemporary issues that have influenced change in our society; Civil rights	Redesigned lyrics; Team skits; 3-D posters; Illustrations; Improvisation; Role-playing/role reversals simulations
Evolution of Humanity's Beliefs Mythology → Scientific Fact → Literature		Research to gain/locate information on individual topics; Mythology; Literature (poetry on topic)	Note taking; Outlining; Referencing; Writing/editing; Final draft of integrated paper	Oral reports; Oral discussions; Demonstration of scientific project	Functional spelling; Dictionary/thesaurus skills; New vocabulary words; Word search	Graphs; Charts; Diagrams; Time lines where applicable	Research on scientific facts; Process diagram; Working model; Demonstration	How humanity's beliefs/ideas and knowledge evolved; Progress or dissension?; Compare/contrast with contemporary issues	Process diagram; Illustrations; 3-D diagram; Simulations
Hawaiiana		Research to locate information from various sources; Teacher-made handouts specific to discussion topics; Legends of old Hawaii	Legends; Creation myth; Migration letter; Evolution of plant life, birds, insects; Lava poetry; Reports on selected topics; Script for skit	Daily oral discussions; Oral presentations; Skits	Functional spelling; Dictionary/thesaurus skills; New vocabulary words; Vocabulary board; Word search	Averaging age of islands; Graphing; Problem solving; Logic	Geology and geography; Volcanism; Continental drift; Revegetation after eruption; How plants/animals got to Hawaii; Evolution of plant life, birds, insects	Study of ancient Hawaiian civilization and factors that influenced change:; *Migration:* reasons for beginning a new society; *Social Issues:* compare and contrast problems in ancient Hawaii to contemporary Hawaiian/world issues	Skit; Vocabulary board; Illustrations; Role-playing/role reversals simulations; Creative dramatics

FIGURE 10.7

A Differentiated–Integrated Curriculum

LITERARY
- Literary magazine (prose or poetry)
- Newspaper for school or class
- Class reporter for school newspaper
- Collections of local folklore (*Foxfire*)
- Book reviews of childrens' books for children, by children
- Storytelling
- Puppeteers
- Student editorials on a series of topics
- Kids' page in a city newspaper
- Series of books or stories
- Classbook or yearbook
- Calendar book
- Greeting cards (including original poetry)
- Original play and production
- Poetry readings
- Study of foreign languages
- Organizer of story hour in local or school library
- Comic book or comic book series
- Organization of debate society
- Monologue, sound track, or script

MATHEMATICAL
- Contributor of math puzzles, quizzes, games for children's sections in newspapers, magazines
- Editor/founder of computer magazine or newsletter
- Math consultant for school
- Editor of math magazine, newsletter
- Organizer of metrics conversion movement
- Original computer programming
- Programming book
- Graphics (original use of) films

MEDIA
- Children's television show
- Children's radio show
- Children's reviews (books, movie) on local news shows
- Photo exhibit (talking)
- Pictorial tour
- Photo essay
- Designing advertisement (literary magazine)
- Slide/tape show on self-selected topic

ARTISTIC
- Displays, exhibits
- Greeting cards
- Sculpture
- Illustrated books
- Animation
- Cartooning

MUSICAL, DANCE
- Books on life of famous composer
- Original music, lyrics
- Electronic music (original)
- Musical instrument construction
- Historical investigation of folk songs
- Movement—history of dance, costumes

HISTORICAL AND SOCIAL SCIENCES
- Roving historian series in newspaper
- "Remember when" column in newspaper
- Establishment of historical society
- Establishment of an oral history tape library
- Published collection of local folklore and historical highlight stories
- Published history (written, taped, pictorial)
- Historical walking tour of a city
- Film on historical topic
- Historical monologue
- Historical play based on theme
- Historical board game
- Presentation of historical research topic (World War II, etc.)
- Slide/tape presentation of historical research
- Starting your own business
- Investigation of local elections
- Electronic light board explaining historical battle, etc.
- Talking time line of a decade (specific time period)
- Tour of local historical homes
- Investigate a vacant lot
- Create a "hall" of local historical figures
- Archaeological dig
- Anthropological study (comparison of/within groups)

SCIENTIFIC
- Science journal
- Daily meteorologist posting weather conditions
- Science column in newspaper
- Science "slot" in kids television show
- Organizer at a natural museum
- Science consultant for school
- "Science Wizard" (experimenters)
- Science fair
- Establishment of a nature walk
- Animal behaviour study
- Any prolonged experimentation involving manipulation of variables
- Microscopic study involving slides
- Classification guide to natural habitats
- Acid rain study
- Future study of natural conditions
- Book on pond life
- Aquarium study/study of different ecosystems
- Science article submitted to national magazines
- Plan a trip to national parks (travelogue)
- Working model of a heart
- Working model of a solar home
- Working model of a windmill

FIGURE 10.8

Outlet Vehicles for Differentiated Student Products

From "Differentiating Products for the Gifted and Talented: The Encouragement of Independent Learning," by S. M. Reis and G. D. Schack. In *Critical Issues in Gifted Education: Vol. 3. Programs for the Gifted in Regular Classrooms,* edited by C. J. Maker, 1993, pp. 161–186. Austin, TX: Pro-Ed. Used by permission.

Websites That Offer Curriculum, Strategies, and Interventions

▶ www.kn.pacbell.com/wired/bluewebn
(lesson plans and teaching resources)

▶ www.education-world.com
(curriculum ideas)

▶ www.yahooligans.com
(child-safe search engine, links, discussion groups)

▶ rtec.org
(links to six regional technology consortia to support improved teaching)

▶ www.nyu.edu/projects/mstep/menu.html
(lesson plans, activities, and information for math and science teachers)

▶ www.planemath.com/
(InfoUse with NASA provides student activities in math and aeronautics)

▶ mathforum.org
(database of math lesson plans by topic and grade level)

▶ www.enc.org
(variety of math and science lessons for Grades 4 to 12)

From *Quick Guide to the Internet for Special Education* (2000 edition) by M. Male and D. Gotthoffer, 2000, Boston: Allyn and Bacon.

careers when appropriate and by requiring students to engage in some activities associated with different careers. Students can become acquainted with a number of different careers while covering traditional subject areas.

Career counselling and guidance are also recommended. As Hardman, Drew, Egan, and Wolf (1993) point out, because of their multiple exceptional abilities and wide range of interests, some students who are gifted have a difficult time making career choices or narrowing down mentorship possibilities. These students should spend some time with counsellors or teachers who can help them make these choices and other important post-secondary decisions.

Social-Emotional Considerations

Students who are gifted have the same physiological and psychological needs as their peers. They may also be dealing with perplexing concepts that are well ahead of the concerns of their peers. For instance, a girl in Grade 4 who was gifted asked her teacher questions related to abortion—a topic with which she was already dealing conceptually. In addition, students who are gifted may be dealing with some issues that are different from their nongifted peers, such as stress, hypersensitivity, control, perfectionism, underachievement/lack of motivation, coping mechanisms, introversion, peer relationships, need for empathy, self-understanding, and self-acceptance (Smutny et al., 1997).

Perhaps the most important recommendation is for teachers to develop relationships with students that make them feel comfortable discussing their concerns and questions. Teachers can become important resources to students who are gifted, not only for advice, but also for information. Regularly scheduled individual time with a teacher can have important paybacks for the student and the teacher.

Teachers may also find it beneficial to schedule weekly room meetings (Feldhusen, 1993b) or class councils (Kataoka, 1987) to identify and address social, procedural, or learning-related problems that arise in the classroom. The group discussion includes articulation of a problem, brainstorming and discussion of possible solutions, selection of a plan of action, and implementation, evaluation, and reintroduction of the problem if the plan of action is not effective.

TEACHING TIP

Arrange a career day for students, at which community members discuss various careers with students.

Personal Spotlight

Gifted Students Kaegan and Conal Shepherd

Kaegan and Conal, two brothers, have both been identified as gifted and are in inclusive settings. As with many gifted students, they feel the need to be with children at their developmental or ability level, which is unlikely to be their chronological age because of developmental differences.

Their mother, Lesley, states, "Scheduling appropriate groupings and pacing for gifted students in ability clusters rather than totally age-based inclusion is often essential to provide them with opportunities for learning and social support."

"It's lonely being gifted in a regular class," says 11-year-old Kaegan. "It's hard when teachers think I should fit in with my own age group. Kids my age aren't interested in the things I like. They don't read the same books or talk about stuff that interests me. I want to know about chemistry and marine biology. I work on those subjects at home, but I wish I could work on them now with someone else." Lesley notes that both her children feel lonely in the regular classroom and are subject to bullying for being different.

Conal, 15 years of age, finds his interests often lead him to a different outlook than that of his classmates. He says, "To fit in socially I find I have to politely fake an interest in things I feel remote from: popular TV shows, sports, clothes." This circumstance often makes it hard for him to take part in discussion when topics are chosen to fit the interests of most students his age. He really enjoys multi-age elective classes where he can be with students who share similar approaches despite their different ages.

Conal comments that he feels teachers misunderstand the concept of being gifted. "Most of the time I can't explain how or why I do things. My brain is always working in the background, like a bunch of windows open on a computer. I see different answers, different ways to do things. Being gifted doesn't mean I always answer questions the way my teachers expect or want," he notes. "Sometimes, I know material way beyond what is being taught and that gets in the way of answering questions about the lesson."

Kaegan agrees with his brother. "I can't explain what being gifted means. It doesn't mean I get all good marks. It means I think differently from other kids, but they don't really understand that. Everyone always expects me to know the answer and I don't like that. Like other gifted kids, I worry about things more. I can put myself in someone else's shoes and that gives me nightmares a lot of times. It upsets me when the teacher is angry at another student or when we talk about wars or poverty. The other kids think I'm weird, but they like it when I help them."

When Kaegan and Conal are asked what teachers should do to accommodate them, they express strong opinions. "Give me credit for what I already know and let me use the extra time to work on my own projects. Don't always make me do more when I show you I can already do the normal assignment. If I repeat things too many times, I start to change them around, embellish them so I don't get bored. I end up getting the information mixed up if there are too many repetitions. Usually repeating something once is enough," says Conal. Kaegan adds, "I need quiet time to work and concentrate because I like really getting into things. If I am reading a book, the teacher has to touch me on the shoulder to bring me back because I concentrate so hard I block out sounds. I don't like it when we change subjects before I am finished. It breaks my concentration and I hate having to start all over again some other time. If I know we only have a little time, I just don't bother to start on stuff. I like teachers who let me work at my own speed. I like long projects that don't get broken up into small parts. I hate repeating things. I wish there was a fullness gauge on my back that showed teachers how much I know, so they wouldn't keep testing me on the same stuff."

Kaegan and Conal, like many gifted students, know how they can learn best. They just need our support in letting them do it.

The following are specific suggestions for dealing with the social-emotional needs of students who are gifted:

▸ Know when to refer students to professionals trained to deal with certain types of emotional problems.
▸ Create a classroom atmosphere that encourages students to take academic risks and allows them to make mistakes without fear of ridicule or harsh negative critique.

Methods that are effective with gifted students are also useful for nongifted students.

▷ Provide time on a weekly basis, if at all possible, for individual sessions with students so that they can share their interests, ongoing events in their lives, or concerns.

▷ Encourage the involvement of volunteers (e.g., parents, college practicum students) to assist in addressing the needs of students who are gifted (Feldhusen, 1993a).

▷ Provide opinions for developing differentiated products as outcomes of various projects or lessons—see Figure 10.9 for a list of examples.

▷ Have students consider intended audiences when selecting potential final products of their endeavours.

▷ Maintain regular, ongoing communication with the families of students who are gifted, notifying them of the goals, activities, products, and expectations you have for their children.

▷ Require, and teach if necessary, appropriate social skills (e.g., appropriate interactions) to students who display problems in these areas.

▷ Work with parents on the personal development of students.

▷ Use different types of activities (e.g., social issues) to develop self-understanding and decision-making and problem-solving skills. Rosselli (1993) recommends the use of bibliotherapy (literature that focuses on children with disabilities).

▷ Teach students who are gifted how to deal with their "uniqueness."

▷ Recognize that students who are gifted may experience higher levels of social pressure and anxiety—for example, peer pressure not to achieve at a high level or lofty expectations originating internally or from others (Del Prete, 1996).

FURTHER READING

For more information on social-emotional considerations, read Chapter 30 in the *Handbook of Gifted Education,* edited by N. Colangelo and G. A. Davis, published in 1997 by Allyn & Bacon.

Enhancing Inclusive Classrooms for Students Who Are Gifted

Addressing the needs of students with exceptional abilities in the context of the general education classroom is a monumental challenge. Current realities and probable trends in programming for students who are gifted suggest that general education will continue

CROSS-REFERENCE

Review Chapters 3–9 and 11 to determine if methods of enhancing an inclusive classroom for students with other special needs will be effective with students who are gifted and/or talented.

TEACHING TIP

Assigning students who are gifted and/or talented to be peer tutors can both enhance their acceptance in the classroom and give them opportunities for leadership. However, do so in moderation.

FURTHER READING

Find out more about nurturing giftedness in females in S. M. Reis's article "External Barriers Experienced by Gifted and Talented Girls," in volume 24, issue 4 of *Gifted Child Today*, 2001 (pp. 33–34).

CONSIDER THIS

What kind of supports would be ideal to help general education teachers meet the needs of gifted and/or talented students in their classes?

to be the typical setting in which they receive instruction. Thus it is important that we do all that we can to enrich the educational experiences of this population in these settings. To do so requires (1) creating classrooms where students who are gifted feel wanted and supported, in addition to having their instructional needs met by appropriate programming, and (2) providing the necessary supports to general education teachers to achieve desired outcomes for this group of students.

Promoting a Sense of Community and Social Acceptance

The climate of any classroom is determined by the interaction between the teacher and the students in the class; in particular, the teacher plays a leading role in establishing the parameters by which a classroom operates and the foundation for classroom dynamics. The degree to which a classroom becomes a community in which students care for one another and strive to improve the daily experience for everyone will depend on each class's unique dynamics. When a healthy and nurturing classroom context is established, students who are gifted can be important members of the classroom community. In such an environment, their abilities are recognized as assets to the class rather than something to be jealous of, envied, or despised.

In order to promote acceptance of students who are gifted, teachers should strive to dispel prevailing stereotypes. Teachers should discuss the uniqueness of these students in terms of the diversity of the classroom, implying that everyone is different. The notion that we all have strengths and weaknesses is also useful. It is particularly important to support students who are gifted who come from underserved groups, such as students with disabilities, those who are economically disadvantaged, and those from different racial or ethnic groups. Special attention should also be given to the needs of females who are gifted. Some suggestions for nurturing giftedness in females are discussed in Reiss' (2001) article (see Further Reading Citation).

Instructionally, many of the strategies suggested for students who are gifted can also be used successfully with typically achieving students (Del Prete, 1996). By doing this, teachers can accommodate the needs of students who are gifted without drawing undue attention to the special programming they are receiving.

In order to be a successful general education teacher of students who are gifted, a wide range of competencies are needed. Maker (1993) highlighted the following competencies as important in teaching students who are gifted: commitment, belief that people learn differently, high expectations, organization, enthusiasm, willingness to talk less/listen more, facilitative abilities, creativity, and the ability to juggle.

Supports for the General Education Teacher

The responsibility to deliver a quality education to students who are gifted in general education settings rests on the shoulders of the instructional staff, especially general education teachers. As discussed earlier in this book, for an inclusion model to work successfully, these features must be in place:

- Classroom teachers need to be well trained in dealing with the many and varied needs of students who are gifted.
- Teachers need to be provided with resource personnel (specialists who assist the general education teacher by helping in the classroom or providing classroom teachers with strategies and materials).
- Teachers need adequate planning time. (Goree, 1996, p. 22)

Using school-based supports such as teacher assistance teams (Chalfant & Van Dusen Pysh, 1993) can also assist with addressing the needs of students who are gifted. When staffed properly, these teams become a rich resource of experience and ideas for dealing with a myriad of student needs. Parents also play an important, and often indirect, role in the school-based programs of their children. As Riley (1999) suggests, it is worthwhile to develop parents into good "dance partners" (i.e., to create and maintain positive relationships) in this process.

If appropriate training and supports are provided to general education teachers, we will do a great service to students with exceptional abilities. It is only when these conditions are met that teachers will be able to "stimulate the imagination, awaken the desire to learn, and imbue the students with a sense of curiosity and an urge to reach beyond themselves" (Mirman, 1991, p. 59).

Summary

- Definitions of giftedness and services to students who are gifted vary across Canada.
- Professionals do not agree on the best way to provide educational programs for children who are gifted.
- Children with exceptional abilities continue to be an underidentified, underserved, and often inappropriately served group.
- Controversy and confusion characterize the delivery of services to students who are gifted.
- There are many misconceptions about students who are gifted.
- The understanding of giftedness has changed over time.
- Remarkable potential to achieve is a key component of many definitions of giftedness.
- The concept of multiple intelligences suggests that there are different kinds of intelligence.
- The generally accepted prevalence rate of giftedness is 2 percent in the schools.
- Students who are gifted demonstrate a wide range of aptitudes, abilities, and skills.
- Identification of students who are gifted is a complex and multifaceted process.
- Students who are gifted with diverse cultural backgrounds and with disabilities are underidentified.
- Differentiated programming is necessary to meet the needs of students who are gifted.

- Enrichment, acceleration, and grouping are ways to address the educational programs of students who are gifted.
- Many general educators are not provided with the necessary understanding, skills, and resources to deal effectively with students who are gifted.
- There are numerous ways to accelerate programs for students who are gifted.
- Special methods used for students who are gifted are often very effective for other students.
- Students who are gifted should be encouraged to develop career interests early in their educational programs.
- Teachers need to address the social-emotional needs of students who are gifted.
- Teachers can do a great deal to promote a sense of community and social acceptance in their classrooms.
- General classroom teachers need to have a variety of supports in order to effectively meet the needs of students who are gifted.
- Comprehensive gifted programs must be committed to identify and serve underrepresented groups of students who are gifted. These include students who are female, culturally and ethnically different, economically disadvantaged, or disabled.

Resources

Winebrenner, Susan. (1998). *Excellence in educating gifted and talented learners*, 3rd ed. Denver, CO: Love Publishing Co.

This resource provides techniques and strategies to motivate and challenge gifted students in your class.

VanTassel-Baska, Joyce. (1992). *Planning effective curriculum for gifted learners.* (Available through the Council for Exceptional Children)

This resource focuses on curriculum for gifted students and provides a variety of checklists, forms, differentiated activities, and practical ideas for planning curriculum K–12. Sample units provide practical applications for all students, including disadvantaged and learning disabled populations.

British Columbia Ministry of Education, Special Programs Branch. (1996). *Gifted education: A resource guide for teachers.* Victoria: Author.

This very practical teacher's resource guide is a good starting point for understanding and working with gifted students.

 **eblinks**

Gifted Canada
www3.telus.net/giftedcanada/
Gifted Canada provides a variety of resources, information, and related links in the area of giftedness and lists provincial and territorial chapters. It covers organizations, research, and teaching strategies, useful for teachers and parents. There is an excellent collection of teaching resources on a teaching resource and manuals page.

The Association for the Gifted (TAG)
www.cectag.org
The U.S.-based association is a division of the Council for Exceptional Children. Its website provides a number of publications that are relevant for teachers of gifted students.

National Association of Gifted Children (NAGC)
www.nagc.org/
The U.S.-based association's Web site provides excellent resources relevant to all teachers of gifted students. Look especially for NAGC publications for teachers: these are useful, practical, and very affordable even with exchange.

Teaching Students Who Are at Risk

With Contributions from Sharon R. Morgan

After reading this chapter, you should be able to

- define students who are considered to be at risk
- describe the different types of children who are considered at risk for developing learning and behaviour problems
- discuss general considerations for teaching at-risk students
- describe specific methods for teaching at-risk students effectively

Kayla is a 9-year-old girl with blond hair and blue eyes. She is currently in Grade 3, having spent two years in kindergarten. Mr. Tate, her teacher, does not know how to help her. He referred Kayla for special education. Assessment revealed that she has average intelligence. Kayla is shy and very insecure.

Kayla has significant problems in reading and math. Although she seems sharp at times, she is achieving below even her own expected level. Her eyes fill with tears of frustration as she sits at her desk and struggles with her work.

Kayla frequently cries if Mr. Tate leaves the classroom; she is very dependent on her teacher. She should have a cluster of good friends, but she is a social outcast. Even though on rare occasions a few of the other girls in the classroom will include her, she is typically teased, ridiculed, and harassed by her peers. She has been unable to establish and maintain meaningful relationships with either her classmates or with adults. Kayla's attempts to win friends are usually couched in a variety of undesirable behaviours, yet she craves attention and friendship. She just does not demonstrate the appropriate social skills requisite of her age.

Kayla lives with her mother and one younger brother in a small apartment. Her mother has been divorced twice and works as a waitress at a local restaurant. Her mother's income barely covers rent, utilities, groceries, and other daily expenses. Occasionally, when Kayla's mother gets the chance to work extra hours at the restaurant, she will do so, leaving Kayla in charge of her brother. Although Kayla's mother appears interested in Kayla's schoolwork, she has been unable to get to a teacher's meeting with Mr. Tate, even though several have been scheduled. Kayla's mother's interest in helping her daughter with her homework is limited by the fact that Kayla's mother did not complete school and does not have a great command of the content that Kayla is studying.

Mr. Tate recognizes that Kayla could benefit from some assistance, particularly in reading and in social/affective areas.

Questions to Consider

1. What types of interventions does Kayla need? What services would you recommend?

2. Should Kayla be considered for special education support?

3. What can teachers do with Kayla and students like her to help prevent failure?

Issues to Consider before Referring Students from Culturally Diverse Backgrounds for Special Education Programs

▶ *Stage of language development:* At what stage of language proficiency, oral and written, is the student in L1 (student's first language) and L2 (student's second language)? What impact have past educational experiences had on language development? Will the environment facilitate further development?

▶ *Language skills:* What are the particular strengths and weaknesses of the student in oral and written L1 and L2 skills? What curriculum materials and instructional expertise are available to meet the student's needs? What skills are the parents able to work on at home?

▶ *Disability/at-risk status:* What impact does the student's specific disability or at-risk circumstances have on the acquisition of language skills in L1 and L2 and on other academic skills? Does the teacher have an adequate knowledge base to provide effective services? Does the school have access to community supports?

▶ *Age:* What impact does the student's age have on the ability to acquire L1 and L2 and to achieve in content areas? Is there a discrepancy between a child's age and

emotional maturity? Is the curriculum developmentally appropriate?

▶ *Needs of the student:* What are the short-term and long-term needs of the student in academic, vocational, and community life? What are the needs of the student in relation to other students in the environment?

▶ *Amount of integration:* How much time will be spent in L1 and L2 environments? Will the student be able to interact with students who have various levels of ability?

▶ *Personal qualities:* How might the student's personality, learning style, and interests influence the acquisition of L1 and L2, achievement in content areas, and social-emotional growth? How might personal qualities of the student's peers and teacher influence learning?

From *Assessment and Instruction of Culturally and Linguistically Diverse Students with or at Risk of Learning Problems* (pp. 221–222), by V. Gonzalez, R. Brusca-Vega, and T. Yawkey, 1997, Boston: Allyn & Bacon. Used by permission.

Students Who Grow Up in Poverty

Poverty is a social condition associated with many different kinds of problems. It has been related to crime, physical abuse, learning problems, behaviour problems, and emotional problems. Davis (1993) notes that poverty is the number one factor that places children at risk of academic failure. In 1995 Statistics Canada reported an increase in the percentage of children living in low-income families: the prevalence rose to 21 percent in 1995 from the 1989 rate of 15.3 percent. Statistics Canada notes that over the last 20 years fewer elderly people are represented in the low-income category and more lone-parent families headed by women are in this category. Thus, in 1995 one in five Canadian children was in a low-income family.

Poverty is associated with different kinds of exceptionalities (Smith & Luckasson, 1992), including intellectual disabilities (Beirne-Smith, Ittenbach, & Patton, 2002), learning disabilities (Smith, Dowdy, Polloway, & Blalock, 1997; Young & Gerber, 1998), and various health problems. Poverty is also associated with poor prenatal care, poor parenting, hunger, limited health care, single-parent households, and poor housing conditions.

> **CROSS-REFERENCE**
>
> Review Chapters 4 and 7 to read more about how poverty relates to incidence of intellectual disabilities and learning disabilities.

Hunger   Although many people in this country have a difficult time believing it, thousands of children go to bed hungry every night. Hunger leads to malnutrition, which in turn can result in damage to a developing neurological system. Children who are hungry have a difficult time concentrating on schoolwork and frequently display behaviour problems in the classroom. Although free school breakfast programs have been instituted over the past years as a result of nutrition budgets from ministries of education, hunger among schoolchildren remains a significant problem. Now that education budgets have

CONSIDER THIS

What kinds of actions can our society take to reduce poverty? What are some barriers to doing these things?

been cut, many of the nutrition programs have been decreased. Frequently, the local home and school association has worked in the school to provide this essential service. This parent-run organization is prominent in many Canadian schools.

School Personnel and Poverty   Unfortunately, there is not a great deal teachers and other school personnel can do to alleviate the poverty experienced by students. However, teachers can reduce the impact of poverty on achievement and behaviour in some ways:

1. Recognize the impact that poverty can have on students.
2. Make all students in the classroom feel important.
3. Avoid placing students in situations in which limited family finances become obvious to other students.
4. Co-ordinate with school social workers or other school personnel who can work with family members to secure social services.
5. Realize that students may not have supplies and other equipment required for certain class activities. Contingency funds or other means to help pay for these items should be available.

Students Who Are Homeless

The growing number of homeless people in society represents a tragedy. The problems of homeless people have only recently become commonly known. Whereas "the homeless" historically were aging adults, often with mental illness or alcohol abuse, today as many as 25 percent of all homeless persons are children (Davis, 1993).

Poverty is directly associated with homelessness, so the problems of poverty affect this group of children. The added impact of not having a home greatly compounds problems of poverty. Children and youth who are homeless are usually very embarrassed by the fact that they do not have a place to live. Although some are lucky enough to stay in a shelter, many live on the streets or in cars with their parents.

Of course, school personnel can do little to find homes for these children. Probably the best advice is to avoid putting students in situations in which their homelessness will result in embarrassment. For example, going around the room after Christmas and having everyone tell what gifts they received would be very uncomfortable for students who do not even have a home to go to after school. Also, if you insist on a home visit, families may avoid interaction with you to escape an embarrassing situation.

In order to work with parents who are homeless, teachers and other school personnel should consider the following:

TEACHING TIP

For students who are homeless, reduce the amount of homework and do not lower the students' grade if the work lacks neatness.

1. Arrange to meet parents at their place of work or at school.
2. Offer to assist family members in securing services from available social service agencies.
3. Do not require excessive school supplies that many families cannot afford.
4. Do not expect homework of the same quality as that of children who have homes.

Students in Single-Parent Homes

Of the 1 137 510 lone-parent families in Canada in 1996, 83 percent were headed by mothers. In these situations, the absence of a father generally has a more negative impact on boys than on girls. The academic achievement of both boys and girls has been shown to be affected, with lower achievement correlating with limited presence of the father.

Although not nearly as prevalent as single-parent homes headed by mothers, the number of single-parent homes headed by fathers has increased significantly over the past decade. The effects of growing up in a single-parent home headed by a father varies a great deal from child to child. Some study findings indicate that single-parent fathers are more likely to use other adults in their support networks than single-parent mothers, and children seem to fare better with a large adult support network than with a limited one (Santrock & Warshak, 1979).

Role of Schools with Children in Single-Parent Families   Children who find themselves in single-parent families, due to divorce, death, illness, or incarceration, require a great deal of support. For many of these children, the school may be their most stable environment. School personnel must develop supports to prevent negative outcomes, such as school failure, manifestation of emotional problems, or the development of behaviour problems. An interview conducted with children residing in single-parent homes resulted in the following conclusions on the positive role schools can play:

1. Schools are a place of security and safety for students from single-parent homes.
2. Students who lose parents due to death are often treated differently by school personnel than when the loss is from divorce. Unfortunately, the child's needs are similar in both situations.
3. Teachers are the most important people in the school for children who are in single-parent homes because of their tremendous influence on self-esteem.
4. Students want to be considered just as they were before they were from a single-parent home.
5. Trust with peers and teachers is the most important factor for students from single-parent homes.
6. School personnel often seem oblivious to the new financial situation of families with only one parent.
7. Keeping a log or diary is considered an excellent method to explore feelings and create opportunities for meaningful discussions. (Lewis, 1992)

There are many things schools should and should not do when dealing with students who are from single-parent homes (Wanat, 1992). Figure 11.2 summarizes some of these "do's" and "don'ts."

More than 14 percent of all children live with a single parent, usually a mother.

FIGURE 11.2

Some Do's and Don'ts When Working with Children with Single Parents

Adapted from "Meeting the Needs of Single-Parent Children: School and Parent Views Differ," by C. L. Wanat, 1992, *NAASP Bulletin, 76,* pp. 43–48. Used by permission.

Some DOs

▹ Collect information about students' families.
▹ Analyze information about students' families to determine specific needs.
▹ Create programs and practices that address areas of need unique to particular schools.
▹ Include curricular areas that help students achieve success, such as study skills.
▹ Provide nonacademic programs such as child care and family counselling.
▹ Involve parents in determining appropriate roles for school and family.
▹ Take the initiative early in the year to establish a communication link with parents.
▹ Enlist the support of both parents, when possible.
▹ Provide a stable, consistent environment for children during the school day.

Some DON'Ts

▹ Don't treat single parents differently than other parents.
▹ Don't call attention to the fact that a child lives with only one parent.
▹ Limit activities such as "father/son" night or other events that highlight the differences in a single-parent home.
▹ Don't have "room mothers," have "room parents."
▹ Don't overlook the limitations of single-parent homes in areas such as helping with projects, helping with homework, and so forth.

For children whose parents are divorced, schools must consider the involvement of the noncustodial parent. Unfortunately, many schools do not even include spaces for information on forms for students' noncustodial parents (Austin, 1992). In order to ensure that noncustodial parents are afforded their rights regarding their children, and to actively solicit their involvement, school personnel should

1. establish policies that encourage the involvement of noncustodial parents;
2. maintain records of information about the noncustodial parent;
3. distribute information about school activities to noncustodial parents;
4. insist that noncustodial parents be involved in teacher conferences;
5. structure parent conferences to facilitate the development of a shared relationship between the custodial and noncustodial parent;
6. conduct surveys to determine the level of involvement desired by noncustodial parents. (Austin, 1992)

TEACHING TIP

Involve the school counsellor and other support personnel when providing information on death and dying; invite these persons into the class when a student is experiencing a death in the family or of a friend.

Students Who Experience Significant Losses

Although the continued absence of one or both parents through separation or divorce is considered a loss, the loss created by the death of a parent can result in significantly more problems for children. Unlike children living in the early twentieth century, when extended families often lived together and children observed death close at hand, often in the home environment with grandparents, children of today are generally insulated from death. Therefore, when death does occur, especially that of a significant person in a child's life, the result can be devastating, often resulting in major problems in school.

Death of a Parent   When a child's parent dies, external events impinge on the child's personality in three main ways (Felner, Ginter, Boike, & Cowan, 1981; Moriarty, 1967; Tennant, Bebbington, & Hurry, 1980):

1. The child must deal with the reality of the death itself.
2. The child must adapt to the resulting changes in the family.
3. The child must contend with the perpetual absence of the lost parent.

Children respond in many different ways to a parent's death. Some responses are guilt, regression, denial, bodily distress, hostile reactions to the deceased, eating disorders, enuresis (incontinence), sleep disturbances, withdrawal, anxiety, panic, learning difficulties, and aggression (Anthony, 1972; Elizer & Kauffman, 1983; Van Eerdewegh, Bieri, Parrilla, & Clayton, 1982). It is also not unusual for sibling rivalry to become very intense and disruptive. Often, extreme family turmoil results from the death of a parent, especially when the parent who dies was the controlling person in the family (Van Eerdewegh et al., 1982).

Death of a Sibling   A sibling plays an important and significant part in family dynamics, so the death of a sibling can initiate a psychological crisis for a child. Sometimes the grief of the parents renders them unable to maintain a healthy parental relationship with the remaining child or children, significantly changing a child's life situation.

When experiencing the death of a sibling, children frequently fear that they themselves will die. When an older sibling dies, the younger child may revert to childish behaviours in hopes of not getting older, thereby averting dying. Older children often react with extreme fear and anxiety if they are ignored by parents during the grieving period. Often these children become preoccupied with the horrifying question about their own future: "Will it happen to me tomorrow, or next week, or next year?" (McKeever, 1983). Children often react with severe depression when a sibling dies (McKeever, 1983).

For the most part, the best advice for teachers is to be aware of how the student who experiences loss is doing when in school. Equally important is knowing when to contact the school counsellor, if he or she is not already involved in some ongoing work with the student. Some of the issues that may arise require intervention that is outside the training and expertise of most teachers. Therefore, it is valuable to know about other school-based and outside school resources.

Students Who Are Abused and Neglected

Growing up in an abusive or neglectful family places children at significant risk of problems. Child abuse and neglect occurs in families from every socioeconomic status, race, religion, and ethnic background in society. Family members, acquaintances, or strangers may be the source of the abuse. Although there is no single cause, there are many factors that add to the likelihood of abuse and neglect. These include poverty, large family size, low maternal involvement with children, low maternal self-esteem, low father involvement, and a stepfather in the household (Brown, Cohen, Johnson, & Salzinger, 1998).

Children can be abused in several different ways that place them at risk of problems in school. There are two major types of abuse: (1) **emotional abuse** and (2) **physical abuse**, which includes sexual abuse. Emotional abuse involves unreasonable demands placed on children by parents, siblings, peers, or teachers that cannot possibly be met.

CONSIDER THIS

Think about how being abused would affect you at this point in your life. Then consider these feelings from the perspective of a young child and how they would affect a child's school activities.

Although difficult to identify, several characteristics may be exhibited by children who are being emotionally abused. These include the following:

- Absence of a positive self-image
- Behavioural extremes
- Depression
- Psychosomatic complaints
- Attempted suicide
- Impulsive, defiant, and antisocial behaviour
- Age-inappropriate behaviours
- Inappropriate habits and tics
- Enuresis
- Inhibited intellectual or emotional development
- Difficulty in establishing and maintaining peer relationships
- Extreme fear, vigilance
- Sleep and eating disorders
- Self-destructive tendencies
- Rigidly compulsive behaviours (Gargiulo, 1990, p. 22)

FURTHER READING

For more information on long-term effects of abuse, read the article "The Long-Term Sequelae of Children and Adolescent Abuse: A Longitudinal Community Study," by R. B. Silverman, H. Z. Reinherz, and R. M. Giaconia, published in 1996 in volume 20 of *Child Abuse & Neglect* (pp. 709–723).

Physical abuse is more easily identified than emotional abuse and includes beating, strangulation, burns to the body, and other forms of physical brutalization. It is defined as "any physical injury that has been caused by other than accidental means, including any injury which appears to be at variance with the explanation of the injury" (*At Risk Youth in Crisis*, 1991, p. 9). In 1996, 3500 cases of physical or sexual abuse were investigated in Toronto. There are no national statistics for child abuse in Canada as it is under provincial/territorial jurisdiction. However, the rate of child abuse in the United States is staggering. Prevent Child Abuse America reported that over 3 million children were referred for child protective service agencies in the United States in 1997. More than 1 million children were confirmed as victims of abuse. The number of child abuse cases increased 41 percent between 1988 and 1997. Statistics indicate that the prevalence of child abuse is 1 out of every 1000 U.S. children.

Children who are physically abused are two to three times more likely than nonabused children to experience failing grades and to become discipline problems. They have difficulty with peer relationships, show physically aggressive behaviours, and are frequent substance abusers (Emery, 1989). Studies also show that children who suffer from physical abuse are likely to exhibit social skill deficits, including shyness, inhibited social interactions, and limited problem-solving skills. Deficits in cognitive functioning are also found in greater numbers in students who are abused than in their nonabused peers (Weston, Ludolph, Misle, Ruffins, & Block, 1990).

Sexual abuse is another form of physical abuse that puts children at risk for school failure. Children may be sexually abused by their own families as well as by strangers. Sexual abuse can include actual physical activities, such as touching a child's genital areas, attempted and completed sexual intercourse, and the use of children in pornography. Exposing children to sexual acts by adults with the intention of shocking or arousing them is another form of sexual abuse (Jones, 1982; Williamson, Borduin, & Howe, 1991). Children who are sexually abused are not only at risk of developing problems during their school years, but will typically manifest problems throughout their adulthood (Silverman, Reinherz, & Giaconia, 1996).

School personnel should be aware of typical physical and behavioural symptoms of sexual abuse:

- Physical injuries to the genital area
- Sexually transmitted diseases
- Difficulty in urinating

- Discharges from the penis or vagina
- Pregnancy
- Aggressive behaviour toward adults, especially a child's own parents
- Sexual self-consciousness
- Sexual promiscuity and acting out
- Inability to establish appropriate relationships with peers
- Running away, stealing, and abusing substances
- Using the school as a sanctuary, coming early, and not wanting to go home

Neglect refers to situations where a child is exposed to a substantial risk of harm. Neglect is much more difficult to recognize, as no visible physical signs of neglect are evident—unless, of course, physical harm does occur. Signs of neglect are reflected through behaviours. Examples of neglect could include placing a child in an unsupervised situation that could result in bodily injury, failing to seek and obtain proper medical care for a child, or failing to provide adequate food, clothing, or shelter. As mentioned earlier, it is this last element that casts fear into the minds of parents who are homeless.

The first thing that school personnel should be prepared to do when dealing with children who might be abused is to report any incident to the appropriate agencies (Pearson, 1996). School personnel have a moral and legal obligation to report suspected child abuse. If you suspect a student is being abused, you should follow your school district's procedures for reporting the problem. If you are uncertain about those procedures, contact your principal. School personnel need to understand their responsibility in reporting suspected abuse and know the specific procedures to follow when making such a report.

CROSS-REFERENCE

Review Chapter 6 for more information on emotional and behavioural disorders, and consider the impact of child abuse on emotional and behavioural functioning.

Students Who Abuse Substances

Substance abuse among children and adolescents results in major problems and places students significantly more at risk for school failure (Vaughn & Long, 1999). Students who are abusing substances have a much more difficult time succeeding in school than their peers. While most people consider substance abuse to relate to the improper use of alcohol and drugs, it can also refer to the use of tobacco, as many health issues are related to tobacco.

Although there were indicators that drug use among youth was declining (*The Condition of Education*, 1990), more recent data suggest that substance abuse among children and adolescents is once again on the increase (Teen drug use is on the rise again, 1996). A survey of students in junior high and high schools revealed that drug use was higher in all categories, including alcohol, cocaine, marijuana, hallucinogens, and inhalants. Twenty-eight percent of eighth-graders surveyed indicated that they had used marijuana at least once—almost double the number reporting use in 1991. More than 48 percent of all high school seniors in the class of 1995 reported that they had tried some type of illegal drug (Teen drug use, 1996). Nagel et al. (1996) report that boys have a tendency to use illegal drugs slightly more than girls, but that girls use more over-the-counter drugs inappropriately than boys do.

While no factors are always associated with drug use in children, some appear to increase the likelihood of such use. Parental factors, such as (1) drug use by parents, (2) parents' attitudes about drug use, (3) family management styles, and (4) parent–child communication patterns, have an impact on children's drug use (Young, Kersten, & Werch, 1996). Additional cross-pressures such as the perception of friends' approval or disapproval of drug use, peer pressure to use drugs, and the assessment of individual risk also play a role (Robin & Johnson, 1996).

Although a great deal of attention has been paid to the impact of marijuana, cocaine, and alcohol abuse on children and youth, only recently has attention been focused on

FURTHER READING

For more information on current drug use among children, read the article "Students' Self-Reported Substance Use by Grade Level and Gender" by L. Nagel, D. McDougall, and C. Granby, published in 1996 in volume 26 of the *Journal of Drug Education* (pp. 49–56).

inhalants. Inhalant use increased for every grade level from 1991 to 1995 (*The Condition of Education*, 1998). One of the problems with inhalants is the wide number of readily available ones that can be used by students. Examples include cleaning solvents, gasoline, room deodorizers, glue, perfume, wax, and spray paint.

School personnel must be alert to the symptoms of substance abuse, whether the substance is alcohol, marijuana, inhalants, or something else. The following characteristics might indicate possible substance abuse:

- inability to concentrate
- chronic absenteeism
- poor grades or neglect of homework
- poor scores on standardized tests not related to IQ or learning disabilities
- unco-operative and quarrelsome behaviour
- sudden behaviour changes
- shy and withdrawn behaviour
- compulsive behaviours
- chronic health problems
- signs of neglect and abuse
- low self-esteem
- anger, anxiety, and depression
- poor coping skills
- unreasonable fears
- difficulty adjusting to changes

Once a student is identified as having a substance abuse problem and the student has been referred to the appropriate agency, a supportive classroom environment must be provided. This includes a structured program to build self-esteem and create opportunities for students to be successful. Research has shown that substance-abusing adolescents do not respond positively to lecturing. Rather, successes appear to be related to the development of self-esteem and interventions that are supportive. School personnel involved with students who are substance abusers should consider establishing connections with Alcoholics Anonymous and Narcotics Anonymous to help provide support (Vaughn & Long, 1999).

Students Who Become Pregnant

There are many unfortunate outcomes from teenage pregnancies, and one of the most significant is the increased risk that young girls, and boys, who find themselves involved in a pregnancy will drop out of school (Trad, 1999). In an era of extensive sex education and fear of HIV/AIDS, the continued high levels of teenage pregnancy are surprising. Despite all of the information available for adolescents about sex and sexually transmitted diseases (STDs), it appears that many adolescents continue to engage in unprotected sexual activity (Weinbender & Rossignol, 1996).

School personnel should deal with teenage pregnancy issues before pregnancy occurs. Sex education, information about HIV/AIDS, and the consequences of unprotected sex should be a curricular focus. Unfortunately, sex education and practices such as distributing free condoms are very controversial, and many schools refuse to enter the fray of such emotion-laden issues.

In addition to having a pregnancy prevention program, school personnel can do the following to intervene in teenage pregnancy situations:

1. Provide counselling for girls who become pregnant.
2. Develop programs that encourage girls who are pregnant to remain in school.
3. Provide parenting classes for all students.

Teen empowerment can help at-risk students overcome the dangers of drugs and gangs.

4. Do not discriminate against girls who become pregnant, or boys who are married.
5. Consider establishing a school-based child care program for girls who have babies and wish to remain in school.
6. Work with families of girls who are pregnant to ensure that family support is present.

Students Who Are Gay, Lesbian, Bisexual, or Transgendered

One of the most vulnerable and overlooked groups who might be at risk comprises those students whose sexual identity differs from those around them. Currently referred to in general as GLBT youth, this group includes students who are gay, lesbian, bisexual, or transgendered. Statistics point to the fact that these students have experienced some uncomfortable situations when at school. A study conducted by the Gay, Lesbian, and Straight Education Network (GLSEN) (1999) in the United States found that GLBT youth had experienced the following:

- 61 percent were verbally harassed.
- 47 percent were sexually harassed.
- 28 percent were physically harassed (shoved, hit).
- 18 percent were physically assaulted (beaten, punched, kicked).

The home environment for this population may also be an unsafe environment. This is especially true in cases where parents have a difficult time accepting a child who "comes out" or tells family members about this difference. Many GLBT youth experience physical violence at home.

Youth who are GLBT come to school feeling that very few, if any, school-based staff understand their situation. To a great extent, they are correct. Most school personnel do lack understanding of their needs and the daily dynamics of their lives at school. Most of the time, this lack of understanding is unintentional; sometimes it is not. This group of students in general is prone to being absent more frequently than their classmates and to dropping out of school more often as a result of their discomfort and lack of safety at school.

On a personal level, GLBT youth are at greater risk for depression and attempting suicide. They often feel alienated and isolated. Substance abuse is greater with this group. Furthermore, these students find themselves homeless more often than their straight peers, as they are sometimes thrown out of their homes by parents. It should be noted that some GLBT students report very positive and productive school experiences.

A number of actions can be taken to improve the climate of acceptance for GLBT youth. Some district and school level suggestions include the following:

▶ Include sexual orientation in all anti-harassment and anti-discrimination policies.
▶ Educate all school-based personnel regarding GLBT issues.
▶ Commit resources to this issue.
▶ Have diversity days that include GLBT youth.
▶ Establish a clear anti-slur policy.
▶ Develop and disseminate positive images and resources.

Teachers, as mentioned earlier, play a key role. The following suggestions can be helpful to teachers and students who are GLBT:

▶ Recognize your own attitudes about this topic.
▶ Refer GLBT youth who are experiencing personal problems to personnel who are more comfortable with this issue, if you are not.
▶ Recognize your obligations to act on the behalf of GLBT youth when their rights are violated or policies are disregarded (e.g., harassment).
▶ Create and maintain a safe classroom environment.
▶ Let students know if you are a "safe" person with whom they can consult if they need to do so.
▶ Create and maintain a classroom environment where diversity is respected and different points of view are welcomed.
▶ Use language in the classroom that is sexual orientation neutral.
▶ Include GLBT topics in the curriculum if at all possible.

Students Who Are Delinquents

Students who get into trouble with legal authorities are frequently labelled juvenile delinquents. Morrison (1997) defines *delinquency* as "behavior that violates the rules and regulations of the society" (p. 189). **Juvenile delinquency** often results in school failure; students who take part in illegal activities often do not focus on school activities. Juvenile delinquency must be considered in light of other factors related to at-risk students, though the relationship of these factors may be difficult to discern. Juvenile delinquency is highly correlated with substance abuse and may be found in higher rates among poor children than among children who are raised in adequate income environments. It is also more prevalent in single-parent homes (Morgan, 1994b).

Juvenile delinquency is frequently related to gang activity. Gangs currently represent a major problem for adolescents, especially in large urban areas. Morgan (1994b) cites numerous studies showing that adolescents raised in single-parent homes or homes that sustain a great deal of conflict often join gangs and exhibit other delinquent behaviours. Again, although no single factor leads children to delinquent behaviours, certain factors can indicate high risk. Delinquent behaviours often disrupt school success. School personnel need to work with legal and social service agencies to reduce delinquency and academic failure.

Strategies for Curriculum and Instruction for Students Who Are at Risk

As educators, we want to promote **resilience** in students who are at risk or vulnerable. Resilience can be defined as:

> a dynamic process encompassing positive adaptation within the context of significant adversity. Implicit within this notion are two critical conditions: (1) exposure to significant threat or severe adversity; and (2) the achievement of positive adaptation despite major assaults on the developmental process. (Luthar, Cicchetti, & Becker, 2000, p. 543)

In other words, we want to promote "good outcomes in spite of serious threats to adaptation or development" (Masten, 2001, p. 228).

There are four primary approaches to dealing with students who are at risk of failure in schools: compensatory education, prevention programs, intervention programs, and transition programs. Figure 11.3 depicts these approaches. Compensatory education programs "are designed to compensate or make up for existing or past risk factors and their effects in students' lives" (Morrison, 1997, p. 192). Reading recovery, a program currently gaining popularity in Canada, has been shown to effectively improve the reading skills of at-risk students (Dorn & Allen, 1995; Ross, Smith, Casey, & Slavin, 1995).

Prevention programs focus on developing appropriate skills and behaviours that lead to success and, if used, are incompatible with other undesirable behaviours. Prevention programs focus on keeping certain negative factors from having an impact on students. Drug prevention programs, antismoking educational efforts, and sex education programs are examples of efforts designed to keep students from developing problem behaviours. Intervention programs focus on eliminating risk factors. They include teaching teenagers how to be good parents and helping at-risk preschool children (Sexton et al., 1996). Finally, transition programs are designed to help students see the relationship

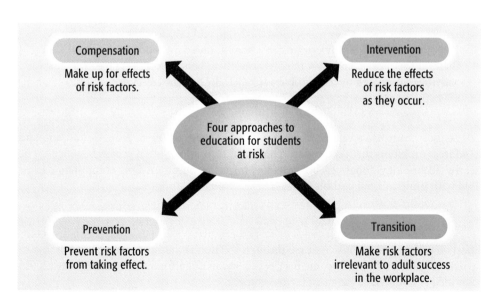

FIGURE 11.3

Four Approaches to Education for Students at Risk

From *Teaching in America* (p. 193), by G. S. Morrison, 1997, Boston: Allyn & Bacon. Used by permission.

Using Technology with Multicultural and Bilingual Students Who May Be at Risk– Microcomputers

As computerized language translators begin to develop, there may be a significant impact for special education students with a primary language other than English. Imagine if the student could use a computer to write an assignment in his or her primary language, check the spelling and punctuation, then press a button to translate the work into English and transmit it to the teacher. Or perhaps the student wrote the assignment in a dialect, and then the computer was able to translate it into the standard form of that language. Such technology is possible.

One successful use of the microcomputer has been for the students to write their journals and for the teacher to respond via computer (Goldman & Rueda, 1988). Multicultural and bilingual special education students were successful in developing their writing skills and their interaction skills with their teacher.

George Earl (1984) created a Spanish-to-English as well as an English-to-Spanish computerized version of the word game "hangman." Hangman is one of the many instructional games used by special education teachers to help improve language skills. Although the program had some difficulty (Zemke, 1985) with dialects (it translates standard Spanish), it demonstrates how technology can be applied to the learning needs of children who are multicultural and bilingual.

Computers have contributed to improved education for migrant children. A nationwide computerized transcript service, the Migrant Student Record Transfer System (MSRTS) in Little Rock, Arkansas, serves as a centralized location for transcripts and health records. A special education component contains information on the existence of a disability, assessment results, related services provided, and IEPs.

From *Introduction to Special Education* (3rd ed.) (p. 71), by D. D. Smith and R. Luckasson, 1998, Boston: Allyn & Bacon. Used by permission.

between what they learn in school and how it will be used in the real world. School-to-work programs, which help students move from school to work, are effective transition programs (Morrison, 1997).

After-school programs, along with involvement with various school-sponsored extracurricular activities, provide schools with an opportunity to implement many strategies that are effective with at risk students. Many students who are at risk for problems face extreme challenges in the afternoon hours following school.

> School-age children and teens who are unsupervised during the hours after school are far more likely to use alcohol, drugs, and tobacco, engage in criminal and other high-risk behaviours, receive poor grades, and drop out of school than those children who have the opportunity to benefit from constructive activities supervised by responsible adults. (U.S. Department of Education, 1998, p. 5)

After-school programs combine prevention, intervention, and compensatory programs.

Schools must use a variety of programs to prevent problems from developing and to address problems that do develop. The use of technology often proves beneficial. The nearby Technology Today feature provides information about how computers can be used with multicultural and bilingual groups, two at-risk populations.

Characteristics of Effective Programs

Effective programs are those that see through the myths that have evolved in relation to at-risk students and have become barriers to successful efforts. Barr and Parrett (2001) identified seven myths that must be overcome.

1. At-risk youth need slow learning. *They need to be academically challenged like all students.*
2. At-risk youth should be retained during the early grades until they are ready to move forward. *Research has shown that this can have disastrous effects.*

3. At-risk youth can be educated with the same expenditures as other students. *Additional programming that might be needed will require additional funds.*
4. Classroom teachers can adequately address the needs of at-risk youth. *Classroom teachers can contribute, but addressing the needs of at-risk students requires a team effort.*
5. Some students can't learn. *Reaffirmation of this overriding education theme is often needed.*
6. The most effective way to improve instruction for at-risk youth is to reduce classroom size. *This is a desirable but not necessary element.*
7. Students who are having learning difficulties need special education. *A tendency to refer to special education must be balanced with the idea of addressing the needs of at-risks students within the general education classroom with necessary assistance and supports.*

Table 11.1 provides a list of factors, culled from research over the last 25 years, that have been found to be essential to school programs where at-risk students are learning effectively.

The movement to include students with exceptionalities in general education classrooms provides an opportunity to meet the needs of at-risk students. In an inclusive classroom, students should be educated based on their needs rather than on their clinical labels. In fact, inclusion, rather than separate programming, is supported by the lack of evidence that different teaching techniques are required by students in different exceptionality groups. Techniques developed for a specific population often benefit everyone. By removing labels from students and providing programs based on individual needs, students who are at risk can benefit from the strategies and activities supplied for students with various exceptionalities (Wang, Reynolds, & Walberg, 1994–1995).

FURTHER READING

For more information on resilience, read the article "Ordinary Magic: Resilience Processes in Development," by A. Masten, published in 2001 in volume 56 of the *American Psychologist* (pp. 227–238).

TABLE 11.1   **Essential Components of Effective Programs**

Positive School Climate
Choice, commitment, and voluntary participation
Small, safe, supportive learning environment
Shared vision, co-operative governance, and local autonomy
Flexible organization
Community partnerships and co-ordination of services

Customized Curriculum and Instructional Program
Caring, demanding, and well-prepared teachers
Comprehensive and continuing programs
Challenging and relevant curricula
High academic standards and continuing assessment of student progress
Individualized instruction: personal, diverse, accelerated, and flexible
Successful transitions

Personal, Social, and Emotional Growth
Promoting personal growth and responsibility
Developing personal resiliency
Developing emotional maturity through service
Promoting emotional growth
Promoting social growth

From *Hope Fulfilled for at-Risk and Violent Youth: K–12 Programs That Work* (p. 73) by R. D. Barr and W. H. Parrett, 2001, Boston: Allyn and Bacon. Copyright 2001 by Allyn and Bacon. Reprinted by permission.

Mentor programs provide opportunities for at risk students to meet with adults in the community and develop positive personal relationships.

CROSS-REFERENCE

Review some of the teaching strategies included in Chapters 3–10, and determine whether any of these methods would be effective with children who are at risk.

Specific Strategies for Students at Risk

In addition to the general principles cited earlier, specific programs can prove effective with these students. These include an emphasis on teaching every child to read, **accelerated schools**, **alternative schools**, one-on-one tutoring, extended day programs, co-operative learning activities, **magnet schools**, teen parent programs, vocational-technical programs, mentoring, and school-to-work programs (Barr & Parrett, 1995). Table 11.2 provides a brief description of each of these approaches.

One program described in Table 11.2 has been used effectively in many schools: a **mentor program** (Slicker & Palmer, 1993). Elementary, middle, and high schools design such programs to provide students with a positive personal relationship with an adult—something that many children and youth lack (Barr & Parrett, 2001). A mentor can be any person of any background who is committed to serve as a support person for a child or youth.

Mentor programs range in scope from national programs such as Big Brothers/Big Sisters to programs developed by and for specific schools, such as a program wherein adults employed in the community have lunch with students (Friedman & Scaduto, 1995). Programs large and small proved effective for many children. It is important to ensure that a positive match is made between the mentor and the child. Other features of successful mentor programs are listed in the nearby Inclusion Strategies feature.

The population of at-risk children and youth is incredibly diverse. Many different professionals need to get involved in developing and implementing programs for this group of students. Nevertheless, teachers will continue to play a major role in the lives of students who are at risk. Teachers and students will spend a considerable amount of time together during the week; therefore, the importance of the teacher–student relationship is critical.

TABLE 11.2	Strategies for Teaching Students at Risk

Strategy	Description
Reading Emphasis	▶ Recognizes the importance of reading ▶ Emphasizes teaching reading early to each child
Accelerated schools	▶ Utilize the same approaches used with gifted and talented children ▶ Use an extended school day with emphasis on language and problem solving ▶ Stress acceleration rather than remediation
Alternative schools	▶ Have a separate focus that may meet the needs of at-risk students better than regular schools ▶ Example: Montessori schools, back-to-basics schools, nongraded schools, and open schools
One-on-one tutoring	▶ Provides concentrated time for direct instruction ▶ Uses volunteers from the community, peers, or older students as tutors ▶ Example: Reading Recovery, a one-on-one program (using a certified teacher) showing major success
Extended School Day	▶ Provides after-school programs as an opportunity for extra tutoring time ▶ Is staffed with regular teachers or volunteers
Co-operative Learning	▶ Provides opportunities for learning from other students in small groups ▶ Shown by research to be a very successful model for at-risk students
Magnet schools	▶ Focus on specific areas, such as the arts or international studies ▶ Give students an opportunity to focus on their strengths and interests
Teen Parent Programs	▶ Provide opportunities for students to learn parenting techniques ▶ Help students with young children stay in school
Vocational-Technical Programs	▶ Enable students to develop skills that are specific to jobs ▶ Help with transition from school to postschool environments ▶ Enable students who do poorly in academic areas to perform well in other areas
Mentoring	▶ Provides role models for students ▶ Creates opportunities for tutoring and social skills development
School-to-Work Programs	▶ Give students the opportunity to begin work early ▶ Provide training for students in real jobs

Components of Effective Mentoring Programs for At-Risk Students

▶ *Program compatibility:* The program should be compatible with the policies and goals of the organization. In a program for students in a community group, for example, program organizers should work closely with school personnel to ensure that the mentoring they provide complements the student's education.

▶ *Administrative commitment:* The program must be supported from the top as well as on a grassroots level. In a school-based program, all school and district administrators, teachers, and staff must provide input and assistance. For a sponsoring business, the president or chief executive officer must view the program as important and worthy of the time and attention of the employees.

▶ *Proactive:* Ideally the programs should be proactive; that is, not a quick-fix reaction to a crisis. Successful mentoring programs for youth work because they are well thought out, they have specific goals and objectives, and they exist within a larger realm of programs and policies that function together.

▶ *Participant oriented:* The program should be based on the goals and needs of the participants. These goals will determine the program's focus, recruitment, and training. For example, if the primary aim of a mentoring program is career awareness, students should be matched with successful businesspeople in the youth's area of interest. Activities and workshops should be job related.

▶ *Pilot program:* The first step should be a pilot program of 6 to 12 months, with 10 to 40 participants, in order to work out any problems before expanding to a larger audience. Trying to start out with a large-scale plan that

includes more than this number can prove unwieldy and disastrous. In the words of Oregon's guide to mentorship programs, "Think big but start small."

▶ *Orientation:* An orientation should be provided for prospective participants. It will help determine interest and enthusiasm, as well as give prospective mentors and students an idea of what to expect. In addition, it will provide them with opportunities to help design the program.

▶ *Selection and matching:* Mentors and their proteges should be carefully selected and matched. Questionnaires are helpful in determining needs, areas of interest, and strengths.

▶ *Training:* Training must be provided for all participants, including support people, throughout the program. Assuming that because a person is knowledgeable, caring, and enthusiastic he or she will make a good mentor is a mistake. Training must be geared to the specific problems experienced by at-risk youth as well as different styles of communication.

▶ *Monitoring progress:* The program should be periodically monitored for progress and results to resolve emerging conflicts and problems.

▶ *Evaluation and revision:* The program should be evaluated with respect to how well goals and objectives are achieved. This can be done using questionnaires, interviews, etc.

From *Mentoring Programs for At-Risk Youth* (pp. 5–6), by National Dropout Prevention Center, 1990, Clemson, SC: Clemson University.

Personal Spotlight

Inclusion Teacher Ling-shu Kao

Ling-shu Kao completed Grades 1–11 in Taipei, Taiwan, and came to Canada at the age of 17. She took Grade 12 at a private boarding school in Montebello, Quebec, then attended Centennial and Vanier colleges in Montreal before completing a bachelor of education degree in elementary teaching at McGill University. She has taught for three years as a Chinese Language teacher at the Montreal Metropolitan Chinese School and has also tutored students with special needs. She is currently leading a second-year professional seminar for teachers in training at McGill University; she is also working with the McGill Student Teaching Office, where she supervises second-year students in their field experience focused on working with children with individual differences.

Ling-shu feels strongly that she has something to share with her teachers in training. As a new teacher, she felt unprepared to deal with students with special needs. She has learned from those experiences. Although she is committed to inclusion, she believes there are both positives and negatives to an inclusive approach.

"I feel that different adaptations and strategies used for 'inclusion' are actually just good teaching—they are beneficial to everyone, not just students with special needs! For me, a big plus about inclusion is that everyone learns to accept individual differences. Not just exceptionalities, but race and cultural differences—multiculturalism is a part of inclusion too, and if no one is treated as an outsider, outcast, or 'freak,' but as a part of the community, that is so important."

For Ling-shu the negative side of the inclusive approach focuses on teachers' views and concerns.

"Teachers may be scared about working with students with exceptionalities because they feel they do not have sufficient knowledge or skills to do it. And if teachers aren't given the supports and resources they need to include the students, they may feel overwhelmed and angry at the system and even take it out on the student. I have seen and heard of this happening. If a teacher gets burnt out, everyone suffers! But I know that, with the right resources and a willingness to learn, it can work."

Asked to say why she is committed to inclusion when she sees the difficulties so clearly, Ling-shu replies: "The most influential individual with exceptionalities in my life so far is my [second cousin], Ming. She is two years older than I am, and she has Down's syndrome. Even though her mother, my cousin, and my family are close, I have seen [Ming] only twice in my life, and I remember that I was a little bit scared of her because she was different. So how can she be influential? You have to understand how important cultural diversity is in approach to people with exceptionalities. Chinese people are very private. We do not talk to outsiders about anything 'shameful' in the family—even to relatives. Having an individual with exceptional needs at home is such a taboo in Taiwan. People with special needs are sent to special education schools or institutions, and they are usually hidden from the public and even family members. My cousin also saw her daughter's exceptionality as a taboo and burden, and she was ashamed of her—she never brought Ming to family gatherings. Since Grade 1, Ming was sent to a special education school, where she stayed until the end of high school, completely segregated. Then Ming stayed with her grandmother, who had Alzheimer's and took care of her until her death just a few years ago. Now, Ming cleans and helps her mother around the home without complaints, while her brothers and sister offer no help. Only now, when Ming is at home with her mom and working with her cheerfully has her mom really gotten to know her and come to realize that Ming is not a burden, but a blessing! Only now, after 28 years does my cousin appreciate her daughter as a person and a member of the family.

"Ming has overcome many obstacles, and most important of all, she singlehandedly changed her own mother's attitude toward her. Ming is not only a person with special needs, but also an extraordinary individual. She managed against the odds, but when I hear stories like those of Tina and Hannah (see Chapter 7's Personal Spotlight) and think what might have been for Ming if the society were more accepting, I feel sad and determined to work toward that acceptance for all students with exceptionalities."

Summary

- Students who are at risk may not be eligible for special education programs.
- At-risk students include those who are in danger of developing significant learning and behaviour problems.
- Poverty is a leading cause of academic failure.
- Poverty among children is increasing in this country.
- Poverty is associated with homelessness, poor health care, hunger, and single-parent households.
- Hunger is a major problem in our country.
- Students in single-parent homes face major problems in school.
- About 14.5 percent of all children live in single-parent homes.
- Schools must take into consideration the rights of the noncustodial parent.

- The death of a parent, sibling, or friend can have a major impact on a child and school success.
- National statistics on child abuse in Canada are not available, but there are high prevalence rates in major urban centres.
- Child abuse is a major problem in this country and causes children to experience much emotional trauma.
- School personnel are required by law to report suspected child abuse.
- Drug use among students is on the increase.
- Teenage pregnancy continues to be a problem, despite the fear of HIV/AIDS and the presence of sex education programs.
- Numerous programs and interventions have proved effective in working with at-risk students.

Resources

Levin, Diane E. (1994). *Teaching young children in violent times: Building a peaceful classroom environment.* Gabriola, BC: New Society Publishers.

    Levin promotes ways of fostering a peaceful environment in the classroom, especially through teaching conflict resolution and acceptance of diversity.

Sprick, R., Sprick, M., and Garrison, M. (1993). *Interventions: Collaborative planning for students at risk.* Longmont, CO: Sopris.

    Interventions is a comprehensive resource designed to assist education professionals as they plan and imple-

ment strategies to meet the needs of at-risk students. It includes information on how to manage physically dangerous and severely disruptive behaviour, provide academic assistance and mentoring, and intervene in other ways to help students at risk.

Vaughn, Sharon, et al. (1996). *Teaching mainstreamed, diverse, and at-risk students in the general education classroom.* Needham Heights, MA: Allyn & Bacon.

    This textbook resource provides more background information and many practical suggestions for teaching students at risk.

Weblinks

Canadian Centre on Substance Abuse

www.ccsa.ca/

As part of the Centre's work to minimize the harm associated with the use of alcohol, tobacco, and other drugs, this site provides information and resources on a variety of issues related to at-risk youth, including prevention and education.

Substance Abuse Prevention Tool Kit

www.region.halton.on.ca/health/programs/ substanceabuse/default.htm

This Halton Region of Ontario website is dedicated to the prevention of substance abuse. It provides information on a variety of areas relating to substance abuse including definitions and information about different types of drugs, as well as tips for parents and teens.

The Internet Public Library on Substance Abuse
www.ipl.org
As an internet library, this site provides a catalogue of websites that pertain to teen substance abuse, including information, clubs, and support groups.

National Clearinghouse on Child Abuse and Neglect Information
http://nccanch.acf.hhs.gov/
This website provides online information about the prevention of child abuse and neglect and outlines how educators can help both prevent and treat the problem. It lists the different levels of prevention, the individuals at risk, the ways to evaluate risk, and how to work together with the community for prevention. A lot of information and some related resources are offered, but the funding information is not relevant because this site is American based; no equivalent Canadian site was found.

12 Classroom Organization and Management

After reading this chapter, you should be able to

- identify the key components of classroom management
- describe the roles of students, teachers, peers, and family members in promoting a positive classroom climate
- describe ways to increase desirable behaviours, decrease undesirable classroom behaviours, and maintain behaviours over time
- identify self-regulatory approaches and procedures
- identify possible strategies to enhance classroom and personal organization

This year has been particularly challenging for Laurie Sturby. Laurie has been teaching Grade 5 for ten years, but she cannot recall any year in which her students' needs were more diverse and the tasks of managing the classroom and motivating her students were more challenging.

While many of her students present unique needs, 11-year-old Sam clearly stands out as the most difficult student in the class. Sam is too frequently out of his seat and often yells out to other students across the room. He has great difficulty staying on task during instructional periods and at times spreads a contagion of misbehaviour in the classroom.

During large-group language arts lessons, Sam is inattentive and frequently unco-operative. Laurie is beginning to believe that his high level of inattentive behaviour may make it virtually impossible for him to progress and achieve in the general education classroom, although, at the same time, Laurie does not see him as a candidate for a special class or other pullout program. Further, his inattentive behaviour is gradually resulting in his falling far behind academically. Although it is only November, Laurie seriously wonders whether this will be a productive year for Sam.

Sam currently receives no special education supports or services. However, Laurie has referred Sam to the student support team, and they are pondering suggestions that may be effective within Laurie's classroom as well as considering a request for a more comprehensive assessment that may elucidate instructional and/or curricular alternatives.

Questions to Consider

1. What recommendations would you give Laurie for focusing on Sam's behaviour and its consequences?

2. Which procedures can Laurie use to significantly increase Sam's attention to task behaviours?

3. How can Sam's peers be involved in a comprehensive behaviour management program?

4. How can co-operative teaching facilitate successful intervention in the inclusive classroom?

Introduction

A teacher's ability to manage his or her classroom effectively and efficiently can greatly enhance the quality of the educational experience for all students. Well-organized and well-managed classrooms allow more time for productive instruction for all students, including those with special needs.

The overriding theme of this chapter relates to the notion of creating a classroom community. As noted by Kohn (1996), we should strive to "make the classroom a community where students feel valued and respected, where care and trust have taken the place of restrictions and threats" (p. ix). The absence of heavy-handed adult-directed management systems is characteristic of classrooms where students are valued and solid relationships between teachers and students are established (Bender, 2003). When attention is given to preventive action rather than reactive intervention, classrooms run smoothly and without notice.

This chapter presents a model for thinking about the major dimensions of *classroom management,* a discussion of these dimensions, and specific suggested pedagogical practices for creating an effective learning environment. Sound organizational and management tactics promote learning for all students and are particularly relevant to the successful inclusion of students with special learning needs. When management/organization tactics are devised by general and special educators working collaboratively, the likelihood of establishing an effective learning setting is further enhanced.

Basic Concepts about Classroom Management and Organization

The importance of good classroom management and organization techniques has been affirmed numerous times by professionals in the field of education. Although much attention is given to curricular and instructional aspects of students' educational programs, organizational and management dimensions are typically underemphasized, despite their importance as prerequisites to instruction. This area is consistently identified as most problematic by first-year teachers. Further, the smooth functioning of the general education classroom often represents a challenge for teachers as classrooms become more diverse. Evertson, Emmer, and Worsham (2003) accurately articulate the relationship between the diversity found in today's schools and the need for well-run classrooms.

> Students entering [North American] schools come with such widely diverse backgrounds, capabilities, interests, and skills that meeting their needs and finding appropriate learning activities requires a great deal of care and skill. Because one of the first and most basic tasks for the teacher is to develop a smoothly running classroom community where students are highly involved in worthwhile activities that support learning, establishing an effective management system is a first priority. (p. ix)

We feel that this particular topic is too important to be overlooked, as attention to the elements described within this chapter can benefit a wide range of students with exceptionalities in the general education classroom. Although reading about classroom management cannot take the place of practice and experience, this chapter offers a variety of management strategies to assist both new and experienced educators.

Most definitions describe **classroom management** as a systematic designing of the classroom environment to create conditions in which effective teaching and learning can occur. This chapter broadly defines the concept as all activities that support the efficient operations of the classroom and that help establish optimal conditions for learning (i.e., creating an effective learning environment). Noting Kohn's objections to the use of the term "management," because of its origins from business and overtones of directing and controlling, we will still use the term. However, our conceptualization of management and organization is not incompatible with Kohn's overall desire to empower students.

Model of Classroom Management

Every classroom environment involves a number of elements that have a profound impact on the effectiveness of instruction and learning (Doyle, 1986). Six of these are described briefly here:

1. *Multidimensionality* refers to the wide variety of activities that occur in a classroom within the course of an instructional day.
2. *Simultaneity* refers to the fact that many different events occur at the same time.
3. *Immediacy* refers to the rapid pace at which events occur in classrooms.
4. *Unpredictability* refers to the reality that some events occur unexpectedly and cannot consistently be anticipated, but require attention nonetheless.
5. *Publicness* refers to the fact that classroom events are witnessed by a significant number of students who are very likely to take note of how teachers deal with these ongoing events.
6. *History* refers to the reality that, over the course of the school year, various events (experiences, routines, and rules) will shape the evolving dynamics of classroom behaviour.

Considering these elements reaffirms the complexity of teaching large numbers of students who have diverse learning needs in our schools today. To address these classroom dynamics, teachers need to identify ways to organize and manage their classrooms to maximize the potential opportunities for learning. Figure 12.1 depicts a model of classroom organization and management that highlights the multifaceted dimensions of this topic. This particular model of organization and management evolved from one designed by Polloway, Patton, and Serna (2001), reflecting an adaptation of what they identify as "precursors to teaching."

The effective and efficient management of a classroom is based on numerous considerations. To create a positive, supportive, and nurturing environment conducive to learning, teachers must pay attention to psychosocial, procedural, physical, behavioural, instructional, and organizational variables that have a critical impact on learning and behaviour. Teachers need to consider much of the content of the dimensional model (see Figure 12.1), discussed in this chapter, *before* the beginning of the school year to prevent classroom-related issues from developing. Prevention is more effective than behavioural interventions that might be needed after issues have become significant problems.

TEACHING TIP

Teachers need to have a comprehensive behaviour management plan that not only includes consequences for actions by students (reactive elements) but more importantly, focuses on rules, procedures, and overall classroom organization (proactive elements).

Guiding Principles

Ten overarching principles guide the development and implementation of appropriate classroom organization and management procedures:

1. All students must be valued.
2. Meaningful relationships between teachers and students need to be developed and cultivated (Bender, 2003).
3. Successful management derives from a positive classroom climate.
4. Good classroom organization and management must be planned ahead of time.
5. Affording students choices contributes to effective classroom dynamics.
6. Teachers and students in effective classrooms are considerate of individual differences, including cultural and familial differences.

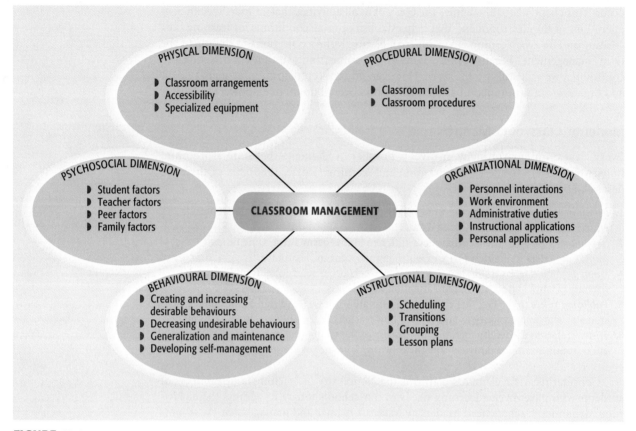

FIGURE 12.1

Dimensions of Classroom
Organization and
Management

7. Proactive management is preferable to reactive approaches.
8. Consistency is the key to establishing an effective management program.
9. Two characteristics identified in classic classroom research enhance a teacher's ability to manage classrooms effectively (Kounin, 1970):
    ▶ *With-it-ness:* Overall awareness of what is happening in the classroom.
    ▶ *Overlap:* The ability to deal with more than one event simultaneously.
10. Although sound classroom management practices are useful in working with all students, the recommendations provided in this chapter are particularly helpful for students who have special needs and require individualized consideration. Without question, these students struggle to learn in environments that are not well organized and effectively managed.

Components of Effective Classroom Organization and Management

This section of the chapter discusses the major elements and subcomponents of classroom management highlighted in the multidimensional model in Figure 12.1.

Psychosocial Dimension

This dimension refers to the psychological and social dynamics of the classroom. Its primary focus is on **classroom climate**, the classroom atmosphere in which students must function.

The dynamics of a class-room are determined by many different student factors.

The dynamics of classrooms are influenced by certain *student factors.* Their attitudes about school and their relationships with teachers and other authority figures, as well as their classmates, can have a remarkable impact on how they behave and react to organizational and management demands. Other factors that shape student attitudes include the nature of previous educational experiences, how they feel about themselves, and their own expectations concerning their scholastic futures (i.e., potential for success or failure). Teachers need to be mindful that all these factors are subject to cultural and familial variations.

The psychological atmosphere of any classroom depends in great part on certain *teacher factors,* including disposition, competencies and skills, and behaviours. A teacher's attitudes toward students with exceptionalities can dramatically affect the quality of education that a student will receive during the time he or she is in that teacher's classroom. Personal philosophies about education, management and discipline, and curriculum weigh heavily as well. The type of expectations a teacher holds for students can significantly influence learning outcomes.

One particular set of skills that has bearing on the psychological aspects of the classroom is teacher communication skills. Evertson and colleagues (2003) note that the ability to communicate clearly and effectively with students influences the nature of ongoing dynamics in the classroom. They stress that to become an effective communicator, teachers need to display three related skills: constructive assertiveness (e.g., describing concerns clearly); empathic responding (e.g., listening to the student's perspective); and problem solving (e.g., ability to reach mutually satisfactory resolutions to problems).

Peers are also key players in forming the psychological and social atmosphere of a classroom, especially among middle- and high school students. Teachers must understand peer values, pressures, and needs and use this knowledge to benefit students with exceptionalities. Valuable co-operative learning opportunities can evolve based on successful peer involvement strategies. As Kohn (1996) remarked, "Communities are built upon a foundation of cooperating throughout the day, with students continually being invited to work, play, and reflect with someone else" (p. 113).

The final component involves a variety of *family-related factors.* Three major issues, all of which have cultural implications, include family attitudes toward education, level of family support and involvement in the student's education, and amount of pressure placed on a child by the family. Extremes can be problematic—for example, a family that burdens a student (e.g., a gifted child) with overwhelming pressure to succeed can cause as many difficulties as one that takes limited interest in a child's education.

Efforts should be undertaken to establish relationships with parents and guardians. At the very least, a letter (with correct grammar, punctuation, and spelling) should be sent to each family, describing the nature of the classroom management system, and asking for feedback. This is particularly important if no other means exists for conveying this information, such as some type of orientation. A benefit of developing a relationship with parents is that the teacher can determine a family's status on the dimensions mentioned in the previous paragraph.

The following recommendations should help create a positive, nurturing environment that contributes to positive outcomes for all students:

- Let students know that you are sensitive to their needs and concerns.
- Convey enthusiasm about learning and the school experience.
- Create a supportive, safe environment in which students who are different can learn without fear of being ridiculed or threatened.
- Teach students what fairness is and model this by treating all students with fairness.
- Acknowledge all students in some personal way each day to affirm that they are valued within the room.
- Create a learning environment that is built on success and minimizes failure experiences common to the learning histories of students with disabilities.
- Understand the family and cultural contexts from which students come.
- Establish that each student in the classroom has rights (e.g., not to be interrupted when working or responding to a teacher inquiry) and that you expect everyone to respect those rights.
- Instill in students the understanding that they are responsible for their own behaviour through the choices they make.
- Convey to students that every student's thoughts and ideas are important.
- Encourage risk taking and nurture all students (i.e., gifted, average, and disabled) to take on scholastic challenges.

Procedural Dimension

As noted in Figure 12.1, the procedural dimension refers to the rules and procedures that are part of the operating program of a classroom. The guidelines discussed here provide direction to school staff and students as to what is expected of all. The teacher must identify all rules, procedures, and regulations before the school year begins and should plan to *teach* them to students during the first days of the school year.

Equally important is preparation for dealing with violations of rules. Immediate and consistent consequences are needed. Various disciplinary techniques can be implemented to ensure that inappropriate behaviour is handled effectively. (These will be covered in a subsequent section of the chapter.)

Students with exceptional needs will benefit from being taught systematically the administrative and social rules operative in a classroom (social skills). The suggestions provided in this section focus on classroom rules and in-class procedures.

Most individuals respond best when they know what is expected of them. *Classroom rules* provide a general sense of what is expected of students. The rules that are chosen should be essential to classroom functioning and help create a positive learning environment (Christenson, Ysseldyke, & Thurlow, 1989; Smith & Rivera, 1995). Reasonable

CONSIDER THIS

Why are classroom rules such an important component of classroom management? Describe the likely climate of classrooms with effective rules and those without effective rules.

classroom rules, presented appropriately, will be particularly beneficial to students with exceptionalities who are in general education settings because this process assists in clarifying expectations. Some specific suggestions related to classroom rules are presented in Table 12.1.

An area of classroom management that may be overlooked is the development of logical *classroom procedures*. Classroom procedures refer to the specific way in which various classroom activities will be performed or the way certain situations will be handled. For example, depending on age, procedures may need to be established for using the pencil sharpener, using the rest room, and entering and leaving the classroom. Evertson and colleagues have identified five general areas in which specific procedures should be developed:

- Room use: teacher's desk, student desks, storage, drinking fountains, sink, pencil sharpener, centres, computer stations, board.
- Individual work and teacher-led activities: attention during presentations, participation, talk among students, obtaining help, when work has been completed.
- Transitions into and out of the room: beginning of the day, leaving the room, returning to the room, ending the day.
- Procedures during teacher-led, small-group instruction: getting the class ready, student movement, expected behaviour in the group, expected behaviour of the students out of group, materials and supplies.
- General procedures: distributing materials, classroom helpers, interruptions or delays, rest rooms, library usage, office visits, cafeteria, playground, fire and disaster drills. (pp. 38–39)

Again, clearly defined procedures are of particular importance especially for some students with exceptionalities who may have difficulty attending to details or following instructions. This is one area where adequate consideration of these classroom/school activities can prevent many behaviour-related problems from developing.

Failing to address procedural issues in the classroom can cause distress for teachers if not attended to at the beginning of the school year. Teachers are often surprised by the

TABLE 12.1 Recommendations for Classroom Rules

Develop no more than seven rules for the classroom.

Consider involving the students in rule development.

Keep the rules brief, and state them clearly.

State the rules in a positive way—avoid statements that are worded in a negative way, such as "not allowed."

Teach the rules through modelling and practice, and verify that all have been learned.

Post the rules in a location that all students can see.

Discuss exceptions in advance so that students understand them.

Discuss specific consequences if rules are violated.

Review the rules on a regular basis and when new students join the class.

Use reminders of rules as a preventive measure for times when possible disruptions are anticipated.

Use positive reinforcement to encourage rule compliance.

complexity and detail associated with many seemingly trivial areas. The procedures for these areas combine to form the mosaic of one's management system. Here are some suggestions:

▶ Identify all situations for which a procedure will be needed.
▶ Develop the procedures collaboratively with the students.
▶ Explain (describe and demonstrate) each procedure thoroughly.
▶ *Teach* each procedure through modelling, guided practice, independent practice, and feedback, allowing every student to have an opportunity to practise the procedure and demonstrate learning on an appropriate level.
▶ Introduce classroom procedures during the first week of school, scheduling priority procedures for the first day and covering others on subsequent days.
▶ Avoid introducing too many procedures at once.
▶ Incorporate any school regulation of importance and relevance into classroom procedures instruction (e.g., hall passes).

Physical Dimension

The physical dimension includes the aspects of the physical environment that teachers can manipulate to enhance the conditions for learning. For students with certain disabilities, some features of the physical setting may need to be especially arranged to ensure that individual needs are met.

Classroom arrangements refer to physical facets of the classroom, including classroom layout (i.e., geography of the room), arrangement of desks, storage, wall space, and signage. Teachers are encouraged to consider carefully where to seat students who have problems with controlling their behaviours, those who experience attention deficit, and students with sensory impairments. Table 12.2 provides recommendations on seating arrangement. The judicious use of seating arrangements can minimize problems as well as create better learning opportunities for students. Carbone (2001) provides a host of suggestions for arranging the physical dimensions of a general education classroom for addressing the needs of students with AD/HD.

Other suggestions for classroom arrangement are listed here:

▶ Consider establishing areas of the classroom for certain types of activities (e.g., discovery or inquiry learning, independent reading).

TABLE 12.2	Seating Arrangements

Seat students with behaviour problems first so that they are in close proximity to the teacher for as much of the time as possible.

After more self-control is demonstrated, more distant seating arrangements are possible and desirable.

Locate students for whom visual distractions can interfere with attention to tasks (e.g., learning and attentional problems, hearing impairments, behaviour problems) so that these distractions are minimized.

Establish clear lines of vision (a) for students so that they can attend to instruction and (b) for the teacher so that students can be monitored throughout the class period (Rosenberg et al., 1991).

Ensure that students with sensory impairments are seated so that they can maximize their residual vision and hearing.

Consider alternative arrangements of desks (e.g., table clusters) as options to traditional rows.

- Clearly establish which areas of the classroom, such as the teacher's desk, are off limits—this recommendation is also a procedural one.
- Begin the year with a more structured environment, moving to more flexibility after rules and procedures have been established.
- Notify students with visual impairments of changes made to the physical environment.
- Arrange furniture so that the teachers and students can move easily around the classroom.
- Direct students' attention to the information to be learned from bulletin boards, if they are used for instructional purposes.
- Establish patterns that students can use in moving around the class which minimize disruption.
- Secure materials and equipment that are potentially harmful, if used without proper supervision, such as certain art supplies, chemicals, and science equipment.
- Avoid creating open spaces that have no clear purpose, as they often can become staging areas for problem behaviours (Rosenberg et al., 1991).
- Provide labels and signs for areas of the room to assist younger or more delayed students in better understanding what and where things are.

The concept of **accessibility**, of course, extends beyond physical accessibility, touching on overall program accessibility for students with exceptionalities. Students who are identified as disabled, as well as students qualifying as having substantial limitations in a major life function such as walking or learning, are able to benefit from needed accommodations.

Students with disabilities must be able to utilize the classroom like other students and the room must be free of potential hazards. Most of the time, making a classroom physically accessible is neither difficult nor costly. Specific suggestions for creating an accessible classroom include the following:

- Ensure that the classroom is accessible to students who use wheelchairs, braces, crutches, or other forms of mobility assistance—this involves doorways, space to move within the classroom, floor coverings, learning centres, microcomputers, chalkboards or dry-erase boards, bookshelves, sinks, tables, desks, and any other areas or physical objects that students use.
- Guarantee that the classroom is free of hazards (e.g., low-hanging mobiles or plants) that could injure students who have a visual impairment.
- Label storage areas and other parts of the classroom for students with visual impairments by using raised lettering or Braille.
- Pay special attention to signs identifying hazards by providing nonverbal cautions for non-readers.

CROSS-REFERENCE

Review Chapter 9 on students with low-incidence disabilities and Chapter 8 on those with sensory impairments, and consider the implications of equipment needed by these groups of students.

Some students with disabilities require the use of *specialized equipment,* such as wheelchairs, hearing aids and other types of amplification systems, communication devices, adaptive desks and trays, prone standers (i.e., stand-up desks), and medical equipment. This equipment allows programmatic accessibility and, in many instances, access to the general education curriculum. These types of assistive devices were introduced earlier in the book so that teachers may understand how the equipment works, how it should be used, and what adaptations will need to be made to the classroom environment to accommodate the student using it. The other students in the classroom should be introduced to the special equipment as well. Instructional lessons on specific pieces of equipment will not only be helpful in creating an inclusive environment, but may also provide a basis for curricular tie-ins in areas including health and science. Suggestions include the following:

- Identify the special equipment that will be used in the classroom prior to the arrival of the student who needs it.

> Learn how special equipment and devices work and how to identify problems or malfunctions.
> Find out how long students need to use time-specified equipment or devices.
> Structure learning activities in which the student with a disability (perhaps paired with a peer) demonstrates appropriate usage of the specialized equipment.

Behavioural Dimension

The ability to manage inappropriate behaviours that may disrupt the learning environment is an important component of classroom management. Yet, this ability is only a part of a comprehensive behaviour management program. To be most effective, such a plan should also include techniques for developing new behaviours or increasing desirable behaviours within the students' repertoire. Moreover, a sound program must ensure that behaviours learned or changed will be maintained over time and generalized (e.g., demonstrated in different contexts). It must also teach self-control and self-regulatory mechanisms.

Recently more attention is being given to behaviour that goes beyond the typical emphasis on external behavioural tactics. Bender (2003) promotes the concept of "relational discipline."

> Relational discipline focuses squarely on the relationship between the teacher and the student, and various tactics and strategies are implemented within that broader context. It is this relationship, rather than the specific disciplinary tactics that are used, that forms the basis for appropriate classroom behaviour and that eventually develops into self-discipline. (p. 3)

TEACHING TIP

Students should be involved in selecting positive reinforcers to make sure that they are indeed attractive to the student.

Related to the notion that relationship is important, Bender points out that "behavioural interventions practices" (i.e., disciplinary tactics) must be understood from a developmental perspective. Differential techniques must be considered in terms of age-related needs and predominant influences operative at a given age. Figure 12.2 illustrates these points. Bender notes that few disciplinary systems have, to any reasonable extent, built upon the influence of peer groups with older students.

Currently an Ontario based program for secondary students to develop healthy relationship skills is being taken national. Table 12.3 highlights the Guiding Principles of The Fourth R Project.

Given the importance of the behavioural dimension, most general educators will probably work regularly with special educators to develop effective programs for students with disabilities and for other students with behavioural problems. To provide a flavour of the areas for possible emphasis, Etscheidt and Bartlett (1999) identified the following sample factors:

> *Skill Training:* Could the student be involved in social skill instruction? Does the student need counselling?

FIGURE 12.2

Relational Discipline

From *Relational Discipline: Strategies for In-Your-Face Kids* (p. 35) by W. N. Bender, 2003, Boston: Allyn and Bacon. Copyright 2003 by Pearson Education. Reprinted by permission.

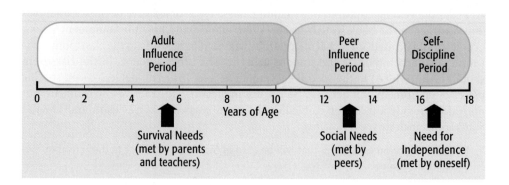

TABLE 12.3	The Fourth R: Promoting Positive Youth Relationships

Guiding Principles of The Fourth R

▶ Relationship skills are just as important for students to learn as reading, writing, and arithmetic. If students do not feel safe and connected to their schools, other learning can be impeded.

▶ Relationship skills can be taught like athletic skills, through skill development and practice.

▶ Education following the principles of harm reduction and health promotion is effective for reducing teen risk behaviour.

▶ The harm reduction approach assumes that most teens are likely to engage in some risk behaviours, or find themselves in unsafe situations. Practice using life skills can help them prevent or deal with these situations.

▶ Prevention of high-risk teen behaviours can be approached through holistic strategies involving healthy, non-violent teen relationships at the core.

▶ Our relationship-based, health-promotion approach goes beyond harm reduction in attempting to develop healthy relationship skills.

The Fourth R is supported in part by grants from the U.S. National Institute of Alcohol Addiction & Abuse (NIAAA), The Ontario Mental Health Foundation, The National Crime Prevention Centre's Community Mobilization Program (Canadian Department of Justice), The Canadian Institutes of Health, and a donation from the Royal Lepage Shelter Foundation.

The Fourth R Project Team: David A. Wolfe, Ph.D.; Peter Jaffe, Ph.D.; Claire Crooks, Ph.D.; Ray Hughes, M.Ed.

Reprinted with permission from: The Fourth R Project, in partnership with the Centre for Research on Violence Against Women & Children, The University of Western Ontario; The Thames Valley District School Board and the CAMH Centre for Prevention.

▶ *Behaviour Management Plan:* Does the student need a behaviour management plan that describes a reinforcement system, supportive signals, and corrective options?
▶ *Self-Management:* Could the student use self-monitoring of target behaviours?
▶ *Peer Support:* Could peers help monitor and/or redirect behaviour? Could peers take notes, help prepare for exams, etc.?
▶ *Class-Wide Systems:* Could the teacher implement an interdependent group contingency for the class? Could a "Circle of Friends" be initiated? (p. 171)

Because research confirms the effectiveness of behavioural techniques for promoting learning in students with exceptionalities (see Lloyd, Forness, & Kavale, 1998), such interventions should clearly be key components of a teacher's repertoire. Today, professionals in the area of behaviour have been stressing the need to implement positive behavioural interventions and supports. This emphasis has been accompanied by a de-emphasis on the use of more negative and punitive tactics.

Not all facets of behaviour management can be covered in sufficient detail in this chapter. However, the following sections provide recommendations that should guide practice in increasing desirable behaviours, decreasing undesirable behaviours, promoting generalization and maintenance, and enhancing self-management.

Creating and Increasing Desirable Behaviours The acquisition of desired new behaviours, whether academic, personal, behavioural, social, or vocational, is a classroom goal. A new desired behaviour can be affirmed with a **reinforcer**, any event that rewards, and thus strengthens and increases the frequency of the behaviour it follows. **Positive reinforcement** presents a desirable consequence for performance of an appropriate behaviour. Positive reinforcers can take different forms; however, what serves as reinforcement for one individual may not hold true for another. Reinforcers can consist

CONSIDER THIS

Some people say that contracts, as well as other forms of positive reinforcement, amount to little more than bribery. Do you agree or disagree, and why?

Personal Spotlight

National Co-ordinator of The Fourth R Project Ray Hughes

Ray Hughes is the national education co-ordinator for the Fourth R Project. Ray is also a teacher. He started teaching in 1979 in a rural high school in Ontario, where he taught physical education, health, science, and math. At that time, physical education and health classes were typically segregated, so he taught mostly boys. In 1985, Ray became the first male teacher to head a girl's physical education department. He discovered that the girls were very interested in violence-prevention education. When Ray returned to university for post-graduate studies, he decided to focus on violence prevention in schools.

Ray became involved with developing policies and procedures for safe schools at a board level. After amalgamation, the division he worked in had 190 schools and 80 000 students. Ray spent six years developing programs in violence prevention for K–12 schools in this large school division.

Ray provides regular professional development to superintendents, school administrators, teachers, parents, and students on violence prevention and safe schools initiatives. He has developed and implemented school-based programs related to substance abuse, domestic violence, gender equity, dating violence, human sexuality, interpersonal violence, conflict resolution, and anti-bullying. He has been the lead writer for many resource documents related to school-based violence-prevention programs and has successfully implemented a proactive response to violence in schools, called the Interpersonal Development Program. Ray is a regular presenter at conferences throughout Ontario and Canada. He was recently named as one of four members of the Ontario Safe Schools Action Team.

Ray believes that new teachers don't graduate from education programs with a good understanding of violence prevention. He has developed an elective course in safe schools for education students at the University of Western Ontario. Currently, he is developing a course in violence prevention as part of the additional qualifying courses for administrators in Ontario.

For more information about The Fourth R and Ray Hughes, go to the website at www.thefourthr.ca.

of praise, physical contact, tangible items, activities, or privileges. The use of reinforcement is the most socially acceptable and instructionally sound tactic for increasing desired behaviours. The goal of most behavioural regimens is to internalize the nature of reinforcement (i.e., self-reinforcement).

Three basic principles must be followed for positive reinforcement to be most effective. It must be meaningful to the student, contingent upon the proper performance of a desired behaviour, and presented immediately. In other words, for positive reinforcement to work, students must find the reinforcement desirable in some fashion, understand that it is being given as a result of the behaviour demonstrated, and receive it soon after they do what was asked. It must also happen more frequently than correction, so that the student feels encouraged to attempt the rewarding behaviour. Principles for the use of positive reinforcement are presented in Table 12.4. Generally, attention to the systematic nature of the reinforcement program should parallel the severity of a student's intellectual, learning, or behavioural problem. All too often, teachers do not pay close enough attention to the principles that we have noted, and, as a result, do not implement techniques with any power. Another potential problem is that some powerful positive behavioural interventions cannot be implemented because of such factors as cost or complexity (Bender, 2003).

The first illustrative application of the principle of positive reinforcement is **contingency contracting**, a concept introduced by Homme (1969). With this method, the teacher develops contracts with students that state (1) what behaviours (e.g., academic work, social behaviours) students are to complete or perform and (2) what consequences (e.g., reinforcement) the instructor will provide. These contracts are presented as binding

TABLE 12.4	Implementing Positive Reinforcement Techniques

Determine what reinforcements will work for particular students:

1. Ask the child by using direct formal or informal questioning or by administering an interest inventory or reinforcement survey.

2. Ask those knowledgeable about the student (e.g., parents, friends, or past teachers).

3. Observe the student in the natural environment as well as in a structured observation (e.g., arranging reinforcement alternatives from which the student may select).

Select meaningful reinforcers that are easy and practical to deliver in classroom settings (Idol, 1993).

"Catch" students behaving appropriately, and provide them with the subsequent appropriate reinforcement (referred to as the differential reinforcement of behaviour incompatible with problem behaviour). Begin this technique early so that students experience the effects of positive reinforcement.

Use the Premack (1959) principle ("Grandma's law": "yes, you can have dessert, as soon as you finish your vegetables") regularly.

Use reinforcement techniques as the student makes gradual progress in developing a desired behaviour that requires the mastery of numerous sub-steps (reinforce each successive approximation). This concept is called shaping.

Demonstrate to a student that certain behaviours will result in positive outcomes by reinforcing nearby peers, and/or by prompting.

agreements between student and teacher. To be most effective, contracts should (1) initially reward imperfect approximations of the target behaviour, (2) provide frequent reinforcement, (3) reward accomplishment rather than obedience, and (4) be fair, clear, and positive. Figure 12.3 shows an example of a contract for a secondary school student.

Group contingencies, which are set up for groups of students rather than individuals, provide excellent alternatives for managing behaviour and actively including students with exceptionalities in the general education classroom. There are three types:

1. *Dependent contingencies:* All group members share in the reinforcement if one individual achieves a goal (i.e., the "hero" strategy).
2. *Interdependent contingencies:* All group members are reinforced if all collectively (or all individually) achieve the stated goal.
3. *Independent contingencies:* Individuals within the group are reinforced for individual achievement toward a goal.

Whereas independent contingencies are commonly used, the other two forms are less widely seen in the classroom. The dependent strategy is sometimes referred to as a "hero approach" because it singles out one student's performance for attention. Although it can be abused, such an approach may be particularly attractive for a student who responds well to peer attention. A student with special needs may feel more meaningfully included in class when his or her talents are recognized in this way.

Others may feel reinforced and accepted as part of a group when interdependent contingencies are employed. The most common use of an interdependent strategy is the "good behaviour game." Because it is most often used as a behavioural reduction intervention, it is discussed later in the chapter.

The benefits of group-oriented contingencies (or peer-mediated strategies, as they are often called) include the involvement of peers, the ability of teachers to enhance

FIGURE 12.3

Sample Contract between
Student and Teacher

From *Behaviour Management:
Applications for Teachers and
Parents* (p. 189) by T. Zirpoli and
G. Melloy, 1993, Columbus, OH:
Merrill. Used by permission.

Contract

_____ will demonstrate the following appropriate behaviours
(Student's name)

in the classroom:

1. Come to school on time.
2. Come to school with homework completed.
3. Complete all assigned work in school without prompting.
4. Ask for help when necessary by raising hand and getting teacher's attention.

_____ will provide the following reinforcement:
(Teacher's name)

1. Ten tokens for the completion of each of the above four objectives. Tokens for the first two objectives will be provided at the beginning of class after all homework assignments have been checked. Tokens for objectives 3 and 4 will be provided at the end of the school day.
2. Tokens may be exchanged for activities on the Classroom Reinforcement Menu at noon on Fridays.

_____   _____
Student's signature   Teacher's signature

_____
Date

motivation, and increased efficiency for the teacher. In some instances, students will raise questions of fairness concerning group contingency programs. Those who typically behave appropriately may feel that they are being penalized for the actions of others if reinforcement occurs only when the whole group evidences a desired behaviour. You can assure them that, ultimately, they and everyone else will benefit from group success with particular guidelines or goals. Two resources—one for young students (*Practical Ideas That Really Work with Students Who Are Disruptive, Defiant, and Difficult: Preschool Through Grade 4* [McConnell, Ryser, & Patton, 2002a]) and the other for older students (*Practical Ideas That Really Work with Students Who Are Disruptive, Defiant, and Difficult: Grades 5–12* [McConnell, Ryser, & Patton, 2002b])—include many practical ideas for using individual and group contingencies.

Decreasing Undesirable Behaviours   Every teacher will face situations involving undesirable behaviours that require behaviour reduction techniques. Teachers can select from a range of techniques; however, it is best to begin with the least intrusive interventions (Smith & Rivera, 1995) and more neutrally oriented ones. A recommended sequence of reduction strategies is depicted in Figure 12.4. As teachers consider reductive strategies, they are cautioned to keep records, develop plans of action, and follow school and division guidelines.

The use of *natural* and *logical consequences* can help children and adolescents learn to be more responsible for their behaviours (West, 1986, 1994). These principles are particularly important for students with exceptionalities who often have difficulty seeing the link between their behaviour and the resulting consequences.

With **natural consequences**, the situation itself provides the contingencies for a particular behaviour. For example, if a student forgets to return a permission slip to

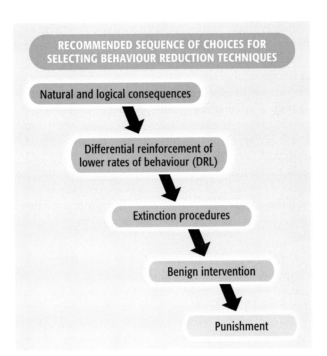

FIGURE 12.4

Recommended Sequence of Selected Behaviour Reduction Techniques

attend an off-campus event, the natural consequence is that the student is not allowed to go and must remain at school. Thus, rather than intervening in a given situation, the teacher allows the situation to teach the students. Natural consequences can be an effective means to teach common sense and responsibility (West, 1994).

In **logical consequences**, there is a logical connection between inappropriate behaviour and the consequences that follow. If a student forgets lunch money, a logical consequence might be that money must be borrowed from someone else. The uncomfortable consequence is the hassle or embarrassment of requesting financial assistance. These tactics can help students recognize that their own behaviour has created the discomfort and not something the teacher has done to them. When using this approach, teachers should clarify to students that they are responsible for their own choices of behaviour. Logical consequences relate the disciplinary response directly to the inappropriate behaviour.

As noted earlier in the chapter, an important, recently developed approach to behavioural reduction is through the use of positive behavioural supports. As Horner (2000) notes, "Positive behaviour support involves the assessment and reengineering of environments so people with problem behaviours experience reductions in (these behaviours) and increased social [and] personal quality in their lives.... It is an approach that blends values about the rights of people with disabilities with the practical science about how learning and behaviour change occur" (p. 181).

The essential element of positive behaviour support is the emphasis on fixing environments rather than focusing just on changing the behaviour of individuals. Thus, the key element is to design schools and curricula to prevent problem behaviours from occurring and thus make them "irrelevant, inefficient, and ineffective" (Horner, 2000, p. 182). As discussed in Chapter 6, the basis for effective positive behaviour support programs is the use of functional behaviour assessment which identifies classroom events that serve to predict the occurrence of problem behaviours and function to maintain positive behaviours (Horner, 2000). Thus, the reader is encouraged to consider the remaining behavioural reduction strategies discussed in this chapter in light of the need to balance

CONSIDER THIS

What are some advantages of using a DRL approach when working on a complex behaviour, rather than simply reinforcing the student only after a targeted behaviour has completely disappeared?

the focus on the individual with the more significant focus on designing a curriculum and operating a classroom in ways in which behavioural disturbances are minimized and students with exceptionalities are more accepted members of the classroom.

The next option on the continuum is the use of *differential reinforcement of lower (DRL) rates of behaviour*. This technique uses positive reinforcement strategies as a behaviour reduction tool. A teacher using this procedure provides appropriate reinforcement to students for displaying lower rates of a certain behaviour that has been targeted for reduction. It is important to remember that the goal should be to decrease the frequency or duration of the unwanted behaviour.

An example of this technique used with groups of students is the "good behaviour game" (originally developed by Barrish, Saunders, & Wolf, 1969), in which student teams receive reinforcement if the number of occurrences of inappropriate behaviours remains under a preset criterion. Tankersley (1995) provides a good overview of the use of the good behaviour game:

> First, teachers should define target behaviours that they would like to see improved and determine when these behaviours are most problematic in their classrooms. Criteria for winning must be set and reinforcers established; the students should be taught the rules for playing. Next, the classroom is divided into teams and team names are written on the chalkboard. If any student breaks a rule when the game is in effect, the teacher makes a mark by the name of the team of which the disruptive student is a member. At the end of the time in which the game is played, any team that has fewer marks than the pre-established criterion wins. Members of the winning team(s) receive reinforcers daily. In addition, teams that meet weekly criterion receive reinforcers at the end of the week. (p. 20)

A modification of this game that de-emphasized competition would have all students playing the game on the same team, and working to reach a frequency goal to win the game.

Here are additional considerations:

- Understand that undesirable behaviours will still occur and must be tolerated until target levels are reached.
- Reduce the criterion level after students have demonstrated stability at the present level.
- Avoid making too great a jump between respective criterion levels to ensure that students are able to meet the new demands.

Tankersley (1995, p. 23) stresses the value of this strategy in noting that it "can be very effective in changing students' behaviours, can lead to improved levels of academic skills..., can reduce the teacher's burden of incorporating several individual contingency systems for managing behaviour,... [makes] use of natural supports available in the classroom, [and] can help promote generalization" (p. 26).

The next reduction option involves **extinction** procedures. In this technique, the teacher withholds reinforcement for a behaviour. Over time, such action, in combination with the positive reinforcement of related desirable behaviours, should extinguish the inappropriate behaviour. One example is for the teacher to cease responding to student misbehaviour. For some situations, it will be necessary to involve a student's peers in the extinction process to eliminate a behaviour because the peers' actions are controlling the relevant reinforcers. The following are additional suggestions:

- Analyze what is reinforcing the undesirable behaviour, and isolate the reinforcer(s) before initiating this procedure.
- Understand that the extinction technique is desirable because it does not involve punishment, but it will take time to be effective.
- Do not use this technique with behaviours that require immediate intervention (e.g., fighting).

TEACHING TIP

When attempting to reduce an inappropriate behaviour by ignoring it, teachers must remember to positively reinforce alternate desired behaviours.

TEACHING TIP

Being physically close to students who often display behaviour problems is a powerful method of reducing inappropriate behaviours. It is sometimes referred to as proximity management.

◗ Recognize that the withholding of reinforcement (1) is likely to induce an increase ("spiking" effect) in the occurrence of the undesirable behaviour, as students intensify their efforts to receive the reinforcement they are used to getting, and (2) may produce an initial aggressive response.

◗ Provide reinforcement to students who demonstrate appropriate incompatible behaviours (e.g., taking turns versus interrupting).

The fourth option is the use of techniques that border on being punishment but are so unobtrusive that they can be considered *benign tactics*. These suggestions are consistent with a concept developed by Cummings (1983) called the "law of least intervention" and that of Evertson and colleagues (2003) called "minor interventions." The main idea is to eliminate disruptive behaviours quickly with a minimum of disruption to the classroom or instructional routine. The following suggestions can be organized into physical, gestural, visual, and verbal prompts:

◗ Position yourself physically near students who are likely to create problems (proximity).

◗ Redirect behaviour in unobtrusive ways (i.e., not embarrassing to an individual student) that are directed to the whole class or through the use of humour.

◗ Touch a student's shoulder gently to convey your awareness that the student is behaving in some inappropriate (albeit previously identified) way.

◗ Use subtle and not-so-subtle gestures to stop undesirable behaviours (e.g., pointing, head shaking, finger spelling).

◗ Establish eye contact and maintain it for a while with a student who is behaving inappropriately. This results in no disruption to the instructional routine.

◗ Stop talking for a noticeable length of time to redirect student attention.

◗ Call on students who are not attending, but ask them questions that they can answer successfully.

◗ Give the student a choice.

◗ Use an "I-Message."

◗ Minimize "dead" time.

◗ Avoid sarcasm and confrontation.

Positioning yourself by a student who is disruptive can be a powerful management technique.

The last option in this reduction hierarchy and the one that is most intrusive is the use of **punishment**. It is the least preferable option because it involves the presentation of something unpleasant or the removal of something pleasant as a consequence of the performance of an undesirable behaviour. This option should be considered only as a last resort. However, in situations in which a more immediate cessation of undesirable behaviours is required, punishment may be necessary. Because of their potency, punishment strategies should be weighed carefully; they can interfere with the learning process if not used sparingly and appropriately. Given that all teachers are likely to use punishment at some point, the key is to ensure that it is used appropriately.

Three punishment techniques are commonly used in classrooms: **reprimands**, **time out**, and **response cost**. For these forms of punishment to work, it is critical that they be applied immediately after the occurrence of the undesirable behaviour and that the students understand why they are being applied.

A reprimand represents a type of punishment in which an unpleasant condition (verbal reprimand from the teacher) is presented to the student. The following are some specific suggestions:

◗ Do not let this type of interchange dominate your interactions with students.

◗ Look at the student and talk in a composed way.

◗ Do not verbally reprimand a student from across the room. Get close to the student, maintain a degree of privacy, and minimize embarrassment.

◗ Let the student know exactly why you are concerned.

◗ Convey to the student that it is the behaviour that is the problem and not him or her.

TEACHING TIP

To ensure proper compliance, teachers must always be aware of division or school policies and practices when using time out for reducing student behaviour.

With time out a student is removed from a situation in which he or she typically receives positive reinforcement, thus being prevented from enjoying something pleasurable. Different ways are available to remove a student from a reinforcing setting: (1) students are allowed to observe the situation from which they have been removed (contingent observation); (2) students are excluded from the ongoing proceedings entirely (exclusion time out); and (3) students are secluded in a separate room (seclusion time out). The first two versions are most likely to be considered for use in general education classrooms. The following suggestions are extremely important if time out is to succeed.

▶ Confirm that the ongoing situation from which a student is going to be removed is indeed reinforcing; if not, this technique will not serve as a punisher and rather may be a form of positive reinforcement.
▶ Ensure that the time-out area is devoid of reinforcing elements. If it is not a neutral setting, this procedure will fail.
▶ Do not keep students in time out for long periods of time (i.e., more than 10 minutes) or use it frequently (e.g., daily), as students will miss significant amounts of instructional time.
▶ As a rule of thumb with younger children, never allow time-out periods to extend beyond 1 minute for every year of the child's age (up to a maximum of 10 minutes).
▶ Use a timer to ensure accuracy in the length of time out.
▶ Incorporate this procedure as one of the classroom procedures explained and taught at the beginning of the school year.
▶ Consider using a time-out system in which students are given one warning before being removed.
▶ Signal to the student when it is appropriate to return.
▶ Do not use this technique with certain sensitive students.
▶ Keep records on frequency, reason for using, and amount of time placed when using seclusion time-out procedures.

Response cost involves the loss of something the student values, such as privileges or points. It is a system in which a penalty or fine is levied for occurrences of inappropriate behaviour. The following are some specific suggestions:

▶ Explain clearly to students how the system works and how much one will be fined for a given offence.
▶ Make sure all penalties are presented in a non-personal manner.
▶ Confirm that privileges that are lost are indeed reinforcing to students.
▶ Make sure that all privileges are not lost quickly, resulting in a situation in which a student may have little or no incentive to behave appropriately.
▶ Tie this procedure in with positive reinforcement at all times.

CONSIDER THIS

Why is it so important to teach students to manage their own behaviours without external guidance from teachers? How can self-management assist students with disabilities in their inclusion in the community?

Generalization and Maintenance   After behaviours have been established at acceptable levels, the next stages involve transferring what has been learned to new contexts and maintaining established levels of performance. Teachers often succeed in teaching students certain behaviours but fail to help them apply the skills to new situations or to retain them over time. Teaching appropriate behaviours and then hoping that students will be able to use various skills at some later time is detrimental to many students with exceptionalities because a core difficulty they experience is performing independently in the classroom.

Teachers need to program for generalization—the wider application of a behaviour skill—by giving students opportunities to use new skills in different settings, with different people, and at different times. Students often need help in identifying the cues that should trigger the performance of an acquired behaviour, action, or skill.

Students also need to practise what they have learned previously, in order to maintain their skills. Instructional planning should allow time for students to determine how well they have retained what they have learned. This time usually can be provided during seatwork activities or other arrangements.

Suggestions for generalization and maintenance include the following:

- Create opportunities for students to practise in different situations what they have learned.
- Work with other teachers to provide additional opportunities.
- Place students in situations that simulate those that they will encounter in the near and distant future, both within school and in other areas of life.
- Show students how these skills or behaviours will be useful to them in the future.
- Prompt students to use recently acquired skills in a variety of contexts.
- Maintain previously taught skills by providing ongoing practice or review.

As noted previously, the use of positive behaviour supports has become more popular in working with students with exceptionalities, particularly because of its effectiveness and its emphasis on the environment rather than the individual. A key to behavioural generalization and maintenance, therefore, is to focus beyond the student and ensure that the learning environment is designed in such a way that students can use their newly acquired skills effectively to become accepted and active members of the classroom while enhancing their learning opportunities. In addition, key elements of generalization and maintenance relate to self-management strategies, which become essential in work with adolescents.

Self-Management   Ultimately, we want all students to be able to manage their own behaviours without external direction because this ability is a requirement of functioning independently in life. Special attention needs to be given to those who do not display independent behavioural control and thus must develop *student-regulated strategies*—interventions that, though initially taught by the teacher, are intended to be implemented independently by the student. Bender (2003) refers to this end state as the "self-discipline" phase.

The concept is an outgrowth of cognitive behaviour modification, a type of educational intervention for students with disabilities in use since the 1980s, and stresses active thinking about behaviour. Shapiro, DuPaul, and Bradley-Klug (1998) provide a good overview of self-management. They state:

> It is helpful to conceptualize self-management interventions as existing on a continuum. At one end, the intervention is completely controlled by the teacher...; this individual provides feedback regarding whether the student's behaviour met the desired criteria and administers the appropriate consequences for the behaviour. At the other end, the student engages in evaluating his or her own behaviour against the criteria for performance, without benefit of teacher... input. The student also self-administers the appropriate consequences. In working with students with behaviour problems, the objective should be to move a student as far toward the self-management side of the continuum as possible. Although some of these students may not be capable of reaching levels of independent self-management, most are certainly capable of approximating this goal. (p. 545)

Fiore, Becker, and Nerro (1993) state the rationale for such interventions: "Cognitive-behavioural [intervention] is... intuitively appealing because it combines behavioural techniques with cognitive strategies designed to directly address core problems of impulse control, higher order problem solving, and self-regulation" (p. 166). Whereas

CONSIDER THIS

Do you engage in any self-monitoring techniques? If so, how do you use them, and how effective are they?

traditional behavioural interventions most often stress the importance of teacher monitoring of student behaviour, extrinsic reinforcement, and teacher-directed learning, cognitive interventions instead focus on teaching students to monitor their own behaviour, to engage in self-reinforcement, and to direct their own learning in strategic fashion (Dowdy, Patton, Smith, & Polloway, 1997).

Such approaches have become particularly popular with students with learning and attentional difficulties because they offer the promise of

- increasing focus on selective attention.
- modifying impulsive responding.
- providing verbal mediators to assist in academic and social problem-solving situations.
- teaching effective self-instructional statements to enable students to "talk through" tasks and problems.
- providing strategies that may lead to improvement in peer relations. (Rooney, 1993)

While using self-management strategies with students with exceptionalities in inclusive settings has been far more limited than studies of using them in pull-out programs, the moderate to strong positive outcomes reported in research are encouraging (McDougall, 1998).

Student-regulated strategies form the essence of self-management. Although variations exist in how these are defined and described, the components listed in Figure 12.5 represent the central aspects of self-management.

Two components with particular utility for general education teachers are self-monitoring and self-instruction. **Self-monitoring**, a technique in which students observe and record their own behaviour, has been commonly employed with students with learning problems. Lloyd, Landrum, and Hallahan (1991) note that self-monitoring was initially seen as an assessment technique, but as individuals observed their own behaviour, the process also resulted in a change in behaviour. Self-monitoring of behaviour, such as attention, is a relatively simple technique that has been validated with children who have learning disabilities, mental retardation, multiple disabilities, attention deficits, and behaviour disorders; it has also been profitable for nondisabled students

FIGURE 12.5

Components of Self-Management

From *Guide to Attention Deficits in the Classroom* (p. 162) by C. A. Dowdy, J. R. Patton, E. A. Polloway, and T. E. C. Smith, 1998, Austin, TX: Pro-Ed. Used by permission.

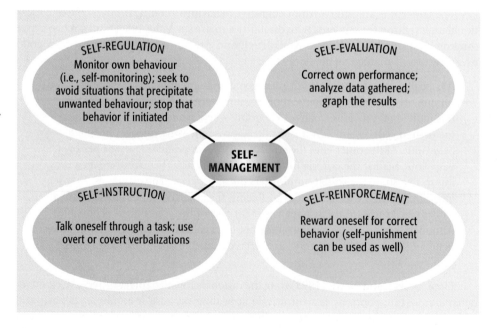

(McDougall, 1998; Lloyd et al., 1991; Prater, Joy, Chilman, Temple, & Miller, 1991). Increased attention, beneficial to academic achievement, has been reported as a result.

A common mechanism for self-monitoring was developed by Hallahan, Lloyd, and Stoller (1982). It involves using a tape-recorded tone, which sounds at random intervals (e.g., every 45 seconds), and a self-recording sheet. Each time the tone sounds, children ask themselves whether they are paying attention and then mark the *yes* or the *no* box on the tally sheet. While students are often not accurate in their recording, positive changes in behaviour have nevertheless been observed in many research studies. While self-monitoring procedures may prove problematic for one teacher to implement alone, a collaborative approach within a co-operative teaching arrangement offers much promise.

Teachers should consider ways to creatively use self-monitoring in their classrooms as an adjunct to other ongoing management strategies. McDougall (1998) offered this unique suggestion:

> Practitioners... could train students to use tactile cues to mediate self-management in much the same manner that students use visually cued, audio-cued, or covert self-monitoring. Tactile cues such as those produced by vibrating pagers might be a functional option for (a) students who have difficulty responding to visual and auditory cues, (b) students with multiple, profound, or sensory disabilities, (c) situations in which audio or visual cues might distract other students, and (d) students who wish to maintain privacy when self-monitoring. (p. 317)

Self-instruction represents another useful intervention. Pfiffner and Barkley (1991) describe components of a self-instruction program as follows:

> Self-instructions include defining and understanding the task or problem, planning a general strategy to approach the problem, focusing attention on the task, selecting an answer or solution, and evaluating performance. In the case of successful performance, self-reinforcement (usually in the form of a positive self-statement, such as "I really did a good job") is provided. In the case of an unsuccessful performance, a coping statement is made (e.g., "Next time I'll do better if I slow down") and errors are corrected. At first, an adult trainer typically models the self-instructions while performing a task. The child then performs the same task while the trainer provides the self-instructions. Next, the child performs the task while self-instructing aloud. These overt verbalizations are then faded to covert self-instructions. (p. 525)

Clear, simple self-instruction strategies form an appropriate beginning for interventions with students with learning or attentional difficulties in the general education classroom. Such approaches are likely to enhance success. Pfiffner and Barkley (1991) recommend the STAR program, in which "children learn to *Stop, Think* ahead about what they have to do, *Act* or do the requested task while talking to themselves about the task, and *Review* their results" (p. 529).

Detailed and systematic procedures have been developed for implementing self-management strategies. Some basic recommendations follow:

- Allocate sufficient instructional time to teach self-management to students who need it.
- Establish a sequence of activities that move by degrees from teacher direction to student direction and self-control.
- Include objectives relevant to improved behaviour and enhanced learning (e.g., increased attention yields reading achievement gains).
- Provide strategies and assistive materials (e.g., self-recording forms) for students to use.

CROSS-REFERENCE

Review Chapter 4 on learning disabilities; consider how self-monitoring and self-instructional techniques could be used with students with learning disabilities.

▶ Model how effective self-managers operate. Point out actual applications of the elements of self-management (as highlighted in Figure 12.5), and give students opportunities to practise these techniques with your guidance.
▶ Provide for the maintenance of learned strategies and for generalization to other settings in and out of school.

This section has outlined management strategies to use with a variety of students. Table 12.5 highlights strategies especially helpful to older students.

Instructional Dimension

All of the dimensions discussed in this chapter relate to the broad concern for instructional outcomes. However, certain aspects of instruction are closely related to sound organizational and management practices, such as scheduling, transitions, grouping, lesson planning, and technology and can have a significant impact on quality of instruction.

Scheduling involves the general temporal arrangement of events for both (1) the entire day (i.e., master schedule) and (2) a specific class period. This section focuses on the latter. The importance of a carefully planned schedule cannot be overemphasized. This is particularly true in classrooms that include students with exceptionalities.

The thoughtful scheduling of a class period can contribute greatly to the amount of time that students can spend actively engaged in learning. It can also add to the quality of what is learned. For instance, a science lesson might include the following components:

▶ Transitional activities (into the classroom)
▶ Attention-getting and motivating techniques
▶ Data-gathering techniques
▶ Data-processing techniques
▶ Closure activities
▶ Transitional activities (to the next class period)

All components support the instructional goal for the day. Reminders or cues from the teacher can augment such a system. The following are some specific suggestions:

▶ Provide time reminders (visual and audible) for students during the class period so that they know how much time is available.
▶ Plan for transitions (see next section).
▶ Require students to complete one activity or task before moving on to the next.

TABLE 12.5	Considerations for Working with Adolescents

Anticipate the likely consequences of any intervention strategy being considered.

Emphasize self-management strategies.

Stress the application of natural and logical consequences.

Use group-oriented contingencies to involve peers in a comprehensive plan for change.

Select only age-appropriate reinforcers.

Avoid response cost procedures that are likely to result in confrontation.

Collaborate with other professionals and parents in designing effective programs.

Select strategies that will not exacerbate problem situations.

▶ Vary the nature of class activities to keep students engaged and to create a stimulating instructional tempo and pace.
▶ Minimize noninstructional time when students are not academically engaged.

Scheduling involves planning for class period *transitions*. Efficient transitions can minimize disruptions, maximize the amount of time allocated to instructional tasks, and maintain desired conditions of learning. Structured approaches to transitions will be particularly helpful to students with exceptionalities. Several ways to ease transitions follow:

▶ Model appropriate transitions between activities (Rosenberg et al., 1991).
▶ Let students practise appropriate transition skills.
▶ Use specific cues (e.g., blink lights, a buzzer, teacher signal) to signal students that it is time to change instructional routine.

Several other examples of strategies for transitions are listed in Table 12.6.

Grouping refers to how students are organized for instructional purposes. The need to place students into smaller group arrangements depends on the nature of the curricular area or the goal of a specific lesson. For students with exceptionalities, the main concern within a group setting is attention to individual needs. Using innovative grouping arrangements and providing different co-operative learning opportunities allow for

---

TABLE 12.6 — Potential Transition Problems and Suggested Solutions

Transition Problem	Suggested Solution
Students talk loudly at the beginning of the day. The teacher is interrupted while checking attendance, and the start of content activities is delayed.	Establish a beginning-of-day routine, and clearly state your expectations for student behaviour at the beginning of the day.
Students talk too much during transitions, especially after a seatwork assignment has been given but before they have begun working on it. Many students do not start their seatwork activity for several minutes.	Be sure students know what the assignment is; post it where they can easily see it. Work as a whole class on the first several seatwork exercises so that all students begin the lesson successfully and at the same time. Watch what students do during the transition, and urge them along when needed.
Students who go for supplemental instruction stop work early and leave the room noisily while rest of the class is working. When these students return to the room, they disturb others as they come in and take their seats. They interrupt others by asking for directions for assignments.	Have a designated signal that tells these students when they are to get ready to leave, such as a special time on the clock. Have them practise leaving and returning to the room quietly. Reward appropriate behaviour. Leave special instructions for what they are to do, when they return, in a folder, on the chalkboard, or on a special sheet at their desks. Or for younger students, establish a special place and activity (e.g., the reading rug) for returning students to wait until you can give them personal attention.
During the late afternoon activity students quit working well before the end; they then begin playing around and leave the room in a mess.	Establish an end-of-day routine so that students continue their work until the teacher gives a signal to begin preparations to leave; then instruct students to help straighten up the room.
Whenever the teacher attempts to move the students from one activity into another, a number of students don't make the transition, but continue working on the preceding activity. This delays the start of the next activity or results in confusion.	Give students a few minutes' notice before an activity is scheduled to end. At the end of the activity students should put all the materials from it away and get out any needed materials for the next activity. Monitor the transition to make sure that all students complete it; do not start the next activity until students are ready.

From *Classroom Management for Elementary Teachers* (2nd ed., pp. 127–128) by C. M. Evertson, E. T. Emmer, B. J. Clements, J. P. Sanford, and M. E. Worsham, 1989, Englewood Cliffs, NJ: Prentice-Hall. Used by permission.

variety in the instructional routine for students with exceptionalities. Some specific suggestions follow:

▶ Give careful consideration to the makeup of groups.
▶ Make sure that group composition is not constant. Vary membership as a function of having different reasons for grouping students.
▶ Use different grouping arrangements that are based on interest or for research purposes (Wood, 1996).
▶ Use co-operative learning arrangements on a regular basis, as this approach, if structured properly, facilitates successful learning and socialization.
▶ Determine the size of groups based on ability levels: the lower the ability, the smaller the size of the group (Rosenberg et al., 1991).
▶ Use mixed-ability groups when cooperative learning strategies are implemented to promote the active involvement of all students.

Lesson plans help teachers prepare for instruction. Many teachers start out writing very detailed lesson plans and eventually move to less comprehensive formats. However, some teachers continue to use detailed plans throughout their teaching careers, as they find the detail helpful in providing effective instruction. Detailed planning is frequently needed for lessons that must be modified to be appropriate for gifted students or students with disabilities. Typical components include objectives, anticipatory set, materials, guided practice, independent practice, closure, options for early finishers, specific accommodations, and evaluation. Suggestions for developing lesson plans follow:

▶ Create interest in and clarify the purpose of lessons. This concern is particularly important for students with exceptionalities.
▶ Consider the importance of direct instruction to help students acquire an initial grasp of new material.
▶ Assign independent practice, some of which can be accomplished in class and some of which should be done as homework.
▶ Plan activities for students who finish early. Such planning might be particularly useful for gifted students.
▶ Anticipate problems that might arise during the course of the lesson, and identify techniques for dealing with them.

The application of *technology* to curriculum and instruction is widespread today. From a management perspective, teachers must consider a number of variables when deciding to use technology. While more software choices are available commercially these days, the selection of software that is appropriate for students and that relates to instructional objectives requires effort and knowledge. Some suggestions follow:

▶ Consider accessibility needs of students with disabilities.
▶ Obtain necessary input and output devices for students who require such hardware.
▶ Determine whether websites are considerate of students with disabilities.
▶ Make sure that websites are appropriate for usage.
▶ Consider the use of internet filters.
▶ Design lessons that utilize computers in ways that are engaging.
▶ Teach students do's and don'ts of using email and the internet (e.g., giving out private information).

Lesson planning helps teachers prepare for instruction and aids in managing classrooms.

Organizational Dimension

The increased diversity in today's general education classrooms has created numerous new challenges for the teacher. Some have likened the current classroom to a "one-room schoolhouse," in which the classroom teacher must respond to the unique needs of many students. This section acknowledges how time management in the areas of personnel interactions, the work environment, administrative duties, instructional applications, and personal applications can promote success.

In the typical education classroom, teachers regularly interact with special education teachers, other classroom teachers, professional support staff (e.g., speech-language pathologists, psychologists), paraeducators or educational assistants, student-teachers, volunteers, and peer tutors. To enhance *personnel interactions,* teachers should consider these recommendations:

▶ Establish good initial working relationships with support personnel.
▶ Clarify the supports professional personnel are providing to students in your class.
▶ Clarify the roles of these persons and the classroom teachers as collaborators for instructional and behavioural interventions.
▶ Establish the roles and responsibilities of educational assistants, volunteers, and student teachers.
▶ Determine the level of expertise of educational assistants, and discuss with them specific activities that they can perform and supports they can provide to students.
▶ Delegate non-instructional (and, as appropriate, instructional) duties to educational assistants when these assistants are available.
▶ In cases in which an educational assistant accompanies a child with a disability in the general education classroom, develop a comprehensive plan with the special education teacher for involving this assistant appropriately.

The **work environment** refers to the immediate work area used by teachers—usually the desk and files. Teachers must consider how to utilize work areas and how to organize them. For instance, a teacher's desk may be designated as off-limits to all students or may be used for storage only or as a work area. Suggestions for establishing a work environment are listed here:

▶ Keep the teacher's desk organized and free of stacks of papers.
▶ Organize files so that documents and information can be retrieved easily and quickly.
▶ Use colour-coded systems for filing, if possible.

Along with instructional duties, teaching includes numerous *administrative duties.* Two of the most time-demanding activities are participating in meetings and handling paperwork, including various forms of correspondence. The presence of students with exceptionalities will increase such demands. The following are some strategies for handling paperwork:

▶ Prepare form letters for all necessary events (e.g., permissions, notifications, status reports, memo formats, reimbursement requests).
▶ Prepare master copies of various forms that are used regularly (e.g., certificates and awards, record sheets, phone conversation sheets).
▶ Keep notes of all school-related phone conversations with parents, teachers, support staff, administrators, or any other person.
▶ Handle most paperwork only once.
▶ Make the most of meetings—request an agenda and ask that meetings be time-limited and be scheduled at times that are convenient.

Some additional *instructional applications* of time-management techniques are provided here, focusing on materials and technology that can make the job of teaching easier. The most attractive piece of equipment available to teachers is the computer. With the appropriate software, teachers can greatly reduce the amount of time spent on test generation, graphic organizers, IEP development, and so on. The following are some specific suggestions:

TEACHING TIP

Teachers must develop their own time-management strategies; however, adopting strategies that are effective for other teachers may or may not be effective for you.

▸ Use self-correcting materials with students to reduce the amount of time required to correct student work.
▸ Use grade-book programs for recording student scores and determining grades.
▸ Use computers to generate a variety of instructionally related materials (tests, graphic organizers, puzzles).
▸ Give students computer-generated calendars that include important dates.

Since it is impossible to completely divorce the management of one's personal time from management of professional time, it is worthwhile considering various time-management tactics that have a more *personal application* but can affect one's efficiency and effectiveness in the classroom as well. Some basic recommendations are provided here:

▸ Use a daily to-do list.
▸ Break down major tasks into smaller pieces and work on them.
▸ Avoid getting overcommitted.
▸ Work during work time. This might mean avoiding situations at school in which long social conversations will cut into on-task time.
▸ Avoid dealing with trivial activities if important ones must be addressed.
▸ Use idle time (e.g., waiting in lines) well. Always be prepared for these situations by having reading material or other portable work available.

The efficient management of one's professional and personal time can pay off in making day-to-day demands less overwhelming. Thus, the efforts to become a better time manager are certainly worthwhile.

Summary

▸ Classroom management includes all teacher-directed activities that support the efficient operations of the classroom and establish optimal conditions for learning.
▸ The key elements of the classroom environment that have a significant effect on instruction and learning include multidimensionality, simultaneity, immediacy, unpredictability, publicness, and history, while the key principles of successful management are careful planning, proactive strategies, consistency, awareness, and overlapping.
▸ Classroom rules provide a general sense of what is expected of students.
▸ Rules chosen should be essential for classroom functioning and for the development of a positive learning environment.
▸ Classroom procedures should include the specific ways in which certain activities or situations will be performed.
▸ Effective physical management includes classroom arrangement, accessibility, seating, and the use of specialized equipment.

▸ Desirable behaviours are increased through the use of positive reinforcement.
▸ Undesirable behaviours can be reduced through a variety of reduction strategies.
▸ Hierarchy of options would include (from least to most restrictive) natural and logical consequences, differential reinforcement, extinction, benign tactics, reprimands, response costs, and time out.
▸ Successful educational programs help students develop self-management strategies.
▸ Instructional management includes careful attention to scheduling, transitions, grouping, and lesson plans.
▸ Successful teachers are organized and engage in the careful management of time. Technology can assist teachers in time management.
▸ Teachers need to take the student's culture into consideration when dealing with management issues.

Resources

Emmer, E. T., Evertson, C., Worsham, M. E. (2003). *Classroom management for middle and high school teachers* (7th ed.). Boston: Allyn and Bacon.

Written for the prospective or new teacher, this text is ready to be applied in a classroom setting. This resource includes examples, checklists, case studies, and group activities.

Everston, C., Emmer, E. T., & Worsham, M. E. (2003). *Classroom management for elementary teachers* (6th ed.). Boston: Allyn and Bacon.

This text helps teachers plan, implement, and develop basic classroom management tasks in order to develop a smoothly running classroom that encourages learning. The authors address the planning decisions teachers must make, with particular attention paid to the growth of diverse and inclusive classrooms.

Kauffman, J. M., Mostert, M. P., Trent, S. C., & Pullen, P. L. (2006). *Managing classroom behaviour* (4th ed.). Boston: Allyn & Bacon.

This case-based text applies behaviour management principles to classroom teaching, with an emphasis on analyzing behaviour management as an instructional problem.

Jones, V. F., & Jones, L. S. (2004). *Comprehensive classroom management: Creating positive learning environments for all students* (7th ed.). Boston: Allyn and Bacon

This text presents practical methods for creating a positive learning environment, working with behavioural problems, and dealing with a range of challenges in the kindergarten to Grade 12 classroom.

Weblinks

The Canadian Education Association (CEA)
www.cea-ace.ca/abo.cfm
The Canadian Education Association is a bilingual, federally incorporated nonprofit organization with charitable tax status, actively linking students, parents, educators, researchers, writers, business, government, school administrators—and everyone who values education as a fundamental pillar of our society.

Classroom Management
http://home.cc.umanitoba.ca/~fboutin/
The Web-Based Interactive Teacher Development section at this website was developed to assist student teachers and beginning teachers to enhance their abilities and confidence in dealing with problems related to classroom management. Experienced teachers may also find these teacher development activities useful to validate their actions.

13 Teaching Students with Special Needs in Elementary Schools

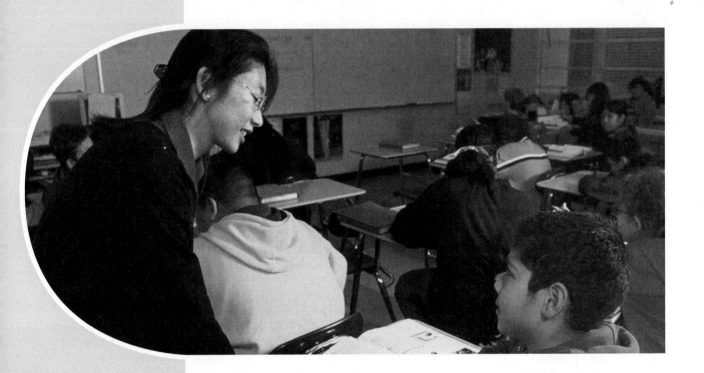

After reading this chapter, you should be able to

- describe the impact of the inclusion movement on the placement of elementary students with exceptionalities.
- define the concept of comprehensive curriculum for students at the elementary level
- identify curricular content considerations for academic, social skills, and transitional instruction
- identify appropriate instructional adaptations and/or accommodations for students with exceptionalities in elementary schools

J̲ulie Bennington was told by one of her university professors that elementary classrooms were becoming increasingly similar to the old "one-room school houses," encompassing a diversity of learning needs that had never been greater. Julie was excited by this challenge and, in her first year of teaching, often reflected on this comment.

Julie is teaching a class of Grade 3 students in a self-contained arrangement. She has full responsibility for 25 eager students for all subjects except art, music, and physical education. She has found their diversity to be both exciting and somewhat overwhelming.

Naturally, one of her greatest concerns has been in the area of language arts. After doing some informal evaluation and after reading the records of her students, she realized during the second week of the academic year that the ability levels of her students ranged greatly; two students were virtual nonreaders, whereas five pupils were significantly above grade level.

It has become apparent to Julie that these students do not all learn in the same way, but she continues to struggle to find approaches that will meet the needs of her diverse classroom. She is fortunate to be working two hours a day during her language arts block with Alisa Rinaldi, a special education teacher who is certified in learning disabilities.

Questions to Consider

1. How can Julie and Alisa develop effective co-operative teaching strategies that will take advantage of their own talents and meet the needs of their students?

2. How can they resolve the ongoing questions about the effectiveness of holistic versus decoding approaches for beginning reading instruction for those with learning difficulties?

3. What adaptations in the curriculum can be made to more effectively meet the needs of students with special needs in this classroom?

Introduction

As the opening vignette illustrates, elementary school presents both unique challenges and unique opportunities for young students with exceptionalities and other special needs to be included in general education. Although the learning needs of the students are frequently quite diverse and challenging, the degree of curricular differentiation (i.e., the need for alternative curricular focuses) tends to be more limited than it is at the secondary level. In elementary school, the necessity for similarity of educational content for all students is at its greatest. Thus, in terms of curricular content there is an excellent opportunity for students with special needs to prosper in general education with the support of special education professionals.

CONSIDER THIS

Inclusive classrooms are more common at the elementary than secondary level. Why do you think this is the case?

Elementary school also offers an important beginning point for students with exceptionalities to profit from positive interactions with their typically achieving peers. Preparation for successful lives beyond the school setting requires the ability to learn, live, and work with a diversity of individuals. Thus, inclusion offers benefits both to students who are exceptional and to their peers. There is clearly no better time for school interaction to take place than in early childhood and throughout the primary and elementary grades.

The advent of the inclusion movement has increased the likelihood that many students with exceptionalities will receive a significant portion, or all, of their instruction in the general education classroom. Thus, beginning at the elementary level, careful attention must be given to these students' educational needs.

This chapter provides an overview of curricular and instructional accommodations and/or adaptations for elementary-age students with special needs in inclusive settings. The initial section outlines core curriculum considerations. The discussion that follows emphasizes instructional accommodations and/or adaptations that provide the means for achieving curricular goals.

General Curricular Considerations

Curriculum has been defined in varied ways. For example, Armstrong (1990) refers to it as a "master plan for selecting content and organizing learning experiences for the purpose of changing and developing learners' behaviours and insights" (p. 4). For all students, any consideration of curriculum should include an outcomes orientation; our working definition of curriculum thus embraces the preparation of students for life after school.

Although curriculum design often is preordained in some general education programs, it is nevertheless important to consider the concept of *comprehensive curriculum*. The concept takes into account the reality that students are enrolled in school on a time-limited basis. Educators must consider what will happen to their students in the future and take into account the environments that students will need to adapt to in order to function successfully. Then curriculum design can be influenced by a focus on these **subsequent environments** (e.g., high school, college, community) (Polloway, Patton, Smith, & Roderique, 1992). The degree to which this subsequent environments attitude permeates general education will significantly affect the ultimate success of students with exceptionalities taught in such settings.

An elementary-level comprehensive curriculum has the following characteristics:

- Responsive to the needs of the individual at the current time
- Reflective of the need to balance maximum interaction with peers against critical curricular needs

▶ Derived from a realistic appraisal of potential long-term outcomes for individual students

▶ Consistent with relevant forthcoming transitional needs (e.g., transition from elementary to high school) (adapted from Polloway, Patton, Epstein, & Smith, 1989)

As mentioned before, the curricular needs of the vast majority of students at the elementary level, both those with and without special needs, are quite consistent. Thus, with appropriate adaptation in instruction and with collaborative arrangements, most students' needs can be met to a significant extent in the general education classroom.

Curricular Content

Academic Instruction

Elementary students in general, and certainly most students with exceptionalities, primarily need sound instruction in reading, writing, and mathematics to maximize their academic achievement. These needs can typically be met by a developmental approach to instruction, supplemented as needed by a remedial focus for students who experience difficulty. In the sections that follow, an overview of principles and practices is provided.

Reading Instruction   Reading problems are a foremost concern for all elementary teachers working in inclusive classrooms. Young students with special needs commonly experience difficulties in both the decoding processes inherent in word recognition as well as in reading comprehension. In a general sense, educators have responded to the need for quality instruction by selecting one (or a combination) of the three common approaches in elementary-level reading and language arts programs: (1) **basal series**, (2) **direct instruction**, and (3) **whole language**.

Basal Series   Basal series, or graded class-reading texts, are the most typical means of teaching reading—and, for that matter, other curricular domains including spelling and math—in the elementary school. Most reading basals are intended to meet developmental needs in reading. However, there is a multiplicity of programs, and it would be impossible to typify the focus of all basal series. Although basals are routinely criticized, Polloway, Miller, and Smith (2003) indicate that such series have both advantages and disadvantages. They note that on the positive side, basals contain inherent structure and sequence, a controlled vocabulary, a wide variety of teaching activities, and materials that provide preparation for the teacher. Weaknesses, on the other hand, include inappropriate pacing for an individual child, a common concern for certain skills to the exclusion of others, and encouragement of group instructional orientation.

Direct Instruction   Direct instruction (i.e., the directive teaching of reading skills) has often been associated with a remedial perspective, although it clearly has played a significant preventive role as well. Often it has been tied to a focus on basic skills, which has typically constituted the core of most elementary special education curricula. In the area of reading, direct instruction programs are often associated with an emphasis on skills-based decoding (i.e., phonetic analysis).

Basic skills programs typically are built on the development of phonological awareness (i.e., a sensitivity to the sounds inherent in our language system) and subsequently phonetic analysis instruction. Research on beginning reading emphasizes the critical importance of children developing sound-symbol correspondences as a basis for subsequent reading success (Center for Future of Teaching and Learning, 1996; Mather, Bos, & Babur, 2001; National Reading Panel, 2000; Pressley & Rankin, 1994; Shaywitz & Shaywitz, 1997).

CONSIDER THIS

Although general educators can rarely offer a truly "comprehensive curriculum," collaborative efforts with special educators can effect a more broad-based program. How does this work?

CONSIDER THIS

Basal programs vary significantly in terms of emphasis. How does this affect students with special needs?

FURTHER READING

The principles of direct instruction are based on the classic work in the mid-1960s by Carl Bereiter and Siegfried Engelmann with at-risk children. See *Teaching Disadvantaged Children in the Preschool,* published in 1966 by Prentice-Hall.

Basic skills programs typically have a long-term orientation based on the assumption that such skills ultimately will increase students' academic achievement and enable all to reach at least a minimal level of functional literacy. Not all basic skills programs are equally effective; those that incorporate effective instructional practice have most often empirically demonstrated substantial gains in achievement (e.g., Kavale & Forness, 1999). The characteristic features of successful direct instruction include high levels of academic engaged time, signals for attention, ongoing feedback to learners, group-based instruction, fast pacing, and error-free learning.

Whole Language Whole language approaches at the primary and elementary levels dramatically increased in popularity in the 1990s. Emphasizing meaning in the beginning of the reading process, they embrace a more holistic view of learning than direct instruction, which tends to be oriented to specific skills acquisition. Whole language programs attempt to break down barriers within the language arts between reading, writing, and speaking, as well as barriers between reading and other curricular areas, by stressing an integrated approach to learning.

Polloway, Patton, and Serna (2001) provide a series of examples of whole language:

> ... orally sharing stories by the teacher; sustained silent reading; silent reading time segments in which students write responses to what they are reading and share this with other students or with the teacher in individual conferences; language experience activities in which children write stories in a group or individually to be used for future reading experiences; time set aside for large group writing instruction followed by students' writing, revising, editing, and sharing their own writing; and finally reading and writing activities that involve a content area theme such as science or social studies. (p. 241)

Whole language programs rely on literature as the main source of content for reading opportunities. The use of literature (e.g., novels, stories, magazine articles) has the following advantages: it is authentic and varied; it is current, since it reaches the market quickly; it provides a basis for meeting diverse student needs and interests; and it offers alternative views on topics and issues as well as opportunities to study them in depth. In addition, with the broad spectrum of choices in literature, students can be given more opportunity to select their own reading material (Mandlebaum, Lightbourne, & Varden-Brock, 1994).

Though holistic programs remain popular, questions arose in the late 1990s about their use, particularly with students who are at risk or have identified exceptionalities. Mastropieri and Scruggs (1997) pointed to the issue of validation:

> In part, experimental research is lacking because of the position taken by many advocates of whole language that traditional, quantitative research, including quantitative measures of reading achievement, is not valid. However, qualitative research to date has failed to demonstrate the superiority of whole language methods in facilitating reading comprehension of students with learning disabilities over direct, skill-based teaching.... Until more empirical evidence... becomes available, teachers should be advised to proceed with caution. Nevertheless, some aspects of whole language, such as students making choices about their reading, having time for private reading, and taking ownership for their own learning, appear positive. (pp. 208–209)

The emphasis on meaning inherent in holistic approaches takes on greater emphasis as students move through the elementary grades. Comprehension thus becomes "arguably, the most important academic skill learned in school" (Mastropieri & Scruggs, 1997, p. 197).

Reading Perspectives These reading methods can each enhance the inclusion of students with exceptionalities in general academic programs. However, teachers must review progress on a regular basis and make adaptations as needed, because it is unlikely that a single program can meet all of a student's needs. Mather (1992) presents an excellent review of issues surrounding both whole language and the decoding emphasis of direct instruction programs. Her review of the literature argues persuasively that students who are not good readers need specific skill instruction to achieve satisfactory progress. The challenge for classroom teachers is to balance the needs of able readers (for whom explicit instruction in phonics may prove unnecessary and for whom meaning-based instruction is clearly most appropriate) with the needs of students who require more systematic instruction to unlock the alphabetic relationships within our written language.

Inclusion presents a complex challenge in the area of curriculum design. Teachers who rigidly adhere to one position in the controversy about reading instruction may inadvertently neglect the learning needs of individual children who experience difficulties in school. Outstanding teachers draw eclectically from a variety of approaches to design reading programs (Pressley & Rankin, 1994).

Writing Elementary-age children with special needs commonly experience problems with writing, especially with written expression. It is essential that they be given ample opportunities to write and that appropriate attention be given to handwriting and spelling (see Polloway, Miller, & Smith, 2003, for a discussion of writing instruction).

In a recent research review, Vaughn, Gersten, and Chard (2000) summarized findings in research with students in third through ninth grades. They concluded that best practices in expressive writing instruction included the following:

- *Explicit teaching of the critical steps in the writing process.* This was often supported by a "think sheet," prompt card, or mnemonic. However, the teacher invariably modelled how to use these steps by writing several samples.
- *Explicit teaching of the conventions of a writing genre.* These "text structures" provided a guide for undertaking the writing task at hand, whether it was a persuasive essay, a personal narrative, or an essay comparing and contrasting two phenomena.
- *Guided feedback.* Teachers or peers provided frequent feedback to students on the quality of their work, elements missing from their work, and the strengths of their work. (p. 103)

A key concern is to provide sufficient opportunities to write that are seen as meaningful tasks (e.g., writing for an authentic audience, or treating a topic that is important or interesting to the student).

Mathematics Mathematics represents another challenging academic area for students with exceptionalities. Development of both computational skills and problem-solving abilities forms the foundation of successful math instruction and learning.

Computation In the area of computation, teachers should focus first on the students' conceptual understanding of a particular skill and then on the achievement of automaticity with the skill. Cawley's (1984) interactive unit and Miller, Mercer, and Dillon's (1992) concrete/semiconcrete/abstract systems afford excellent options to the teacher (see Figure 13.1). The interactive unit gives teachers 16 options for teaching math skills, based on four teacher input variables and four student output variables. The resulting 4×4 matrix provides a variety of instructional approaches that can be customized to assist learners who experience difficulties. The interactive unit also reflects a logical process that begins with the important emphasis on the concrete instructional activities (manipulate/manipulate) to build mathematical concepts, moves to a semiconcrete focus (display/identify) to enhance concept development, and arrives at the abstract

CONSIDER THIS

The emphasis on meaning and the integration of the language arts make whole language approaches particularly attractive for use with students with special needs. Why do you think this is effective?

FURTHER READING

For a summary of the most effective instructional strategies, read the National Reading Panel's report "Teaching Children To Read" (2000), available at www.nationalreadingpanel.org/Publications/summary.htm.

	Group A: Geometry (8 students)	Group B: Fractions (10 students)	Group C: Addition (5 students)
15 minutes	**Manipulate/Manipulate*** *Input:* Teacher walks the perimeter of a geometric shape. *Output:* Learner does the same.	**Display/Write** *Input:* Write the fraction that names the shaded part. *Output:* Learner writes $\frac{1}{2}$	**Write/Write** *Input:* $$\begin{array}{r} 3 \\ +2 \\ \hline \end{array}$$ Write the answer. *Output:* Learner writes 5
15 minutes	**Display/Identify** *Input:* From the choices, mark the shape that is the same as the first shape. *Output:* Learner marks	**Manipulate/Say*** *Input:* Teacher removes portion of shape and asks learner to name the part. *Output:* Learner says, "One fourth"	**Display/Write** *Input:* Write the number there is in all. *Output:* Learner writes 5
15 minutes	**Write/Identify** *Input:* Circle Mark the shape that shows the word. *Output:* Learner marks Circle	**Write/Write** *Input:* one half Write this word statement as a numeral. *Output:* Learner writes $\frac{1}{2}$	**Say/Say*** *Input:* Teacher says, "I am going to say some addition items. Six plus six. Tell me the answer." *Output:* Learner says, "Twelve"

FIGURE 13.1

Interactive Unit Model

*Teacher present in group

From *Developmental Teaching of Mathematics for the Learning Disabled* (p. 246), by J. F. Cawley (Ed.), 1984, Austin, TX: Pro-Ed. Copyright 1984 by Pro-Ed, Inc. Reprinted by permission.

(say/say, write/write) which focuses on achieving automaticity (automatic responses to math facts). These emphases offer two proven benefits in the general education classroom: they have been used successfully with students with exceptionalities, and they offer alternative teaching strategies for all learners—a particularly significant advantage, given that math is the most common area of failure in schools.

Problem Solving   Problem solving can be particularly difficult for students with exceptionalities and thus warrants special attention. For learners with special needs, and for many other students as well, instruction in specific problem solving strategies can greatly enhance math understanding. A given strategy's steps should be taught and followed systematically so that students learn to reason through problems and understand problem-solving processes. One such example is the SOLVE-IT strategy (see Figure 13.2). The use of learning strategies and their value for students with and without exceptionalities are discussed further in Chapter 14.

The potential benefits of including students with special needs in general education classrooms to study core academic areas (i.e., basic skills) also extend to other academic areas. Subjects such as science, social studies, health and family life, and the arts offer excellent opportunities for social integration, while effective instructional strategies can lead to academic achievement. These subjects also lend themselves well to integrated curricular approaches (discussed later in the chapter). **Co-operative teaching** presents an excellent instructional alternative in these areas because it combines the expertise and resources of the classroom teacher with the special talents of the special education teacher, rather than requiring them each to develop separate curricula in these areas.

Social Skills Instruction

Virtually all students identified as having an intellectual disability or an emotional and behavioural disorder, and many with learning disabilities, need instruction in the area of **social skills** (Cullinan & Epstein, 1985). The challenge for classroom teachers will be to find ways to incorporate this focus in their classes. Seeking assistance from a special education teacher, a counsellor, or a school psychologist is a good idea. The development of social skills should not be neglected, since performance in the social domain is often predictive of success or failure in inclusive settings. Gresham (1984) notes that students with exceptionalities interact infrequently and, to a large extent, negatively with their peers because many lack the social skills that would enable them to gain acceptance by their peers. This observation remains valid.

Polloway et al. (2001) identified four approaches to educating students about appropriate social behaviour: direct social skills training, behavioural change, affective

FURTHER READING

John Cawley's research in mathematics over the past 30 years has been very influential in the development of effective programs for students with disabilities. See his recent article "Connecting Math and Science for All Students" in volume 34, issue 4 of *Teaching Exceptional Children*, 2002 (pp. 14–19).

FIGURE 13.2

Problem-Solving Strategy for Mathematics

S	SAY	the problem to yourself (repeat).
O	OMIT	any unnecessary information from the problem.
L	LISTEN	for key vocabulary indicators.
V	VOCABULARY	Change vocabulary to math concepts.
E	EQUATION	Translate problem into a math equation.
I	INDICATE	the answer.
T	TRANSLATE	the answer back into the context of the word problem.

From *Strategies for Teaching Learners with Special Needs* (6th ed.) (p. 183), by E. A. Polloway and J. R. Patton, 1997, Columbus, OH: Merrill. Reprinted by permission.

education, and cognitive interventions. *Direct social skills training* focuses on attaining skills that help students overcome situations in classrooms and elsewhere that prevent assimilation. A *behavioural change* strategy typically targets a behaviour that needs modification and creates a reinforcement system that will lead to a behaviour change. Steps in such programs typically include (1) selecting the target behaviour, (2) collecting baseline data, (3) identifying reinforcers, (4) implementing a procedure for reinforcing appropriate behaviours, and (5) evaluating the intervention (see Chapter 6). *Affective education* typically emphasizes self-control and the relationship between self and others in the environment. The emotional, rather than only the behavioural, aspects of social adjustment figure prominently in this approach. Finally, *cognitive interventions* have proved fruitful (Kavale & Forness, 1999) in effecting behavioural change and social skills acquisition; they involve teaching students to monitor their own behaviour, engage in self-instruction, and design and implement their own reinforcement programs. All four programs offer significant promise for social adjustment programming in the future. However, teachers should carefully evaluate their success and adapt programs accordingly.

FURTHER READING

The social skills program developed by Sargent is in the book *Social Skills for School and Community* by L. R. Sargent, published in 1991 by CEC-MR.

Korinek and Polloway (1993) note two key considerations related to social skills instruction for students who have difficulties in this area. First, priority should be given to skills most needed for immediate interactions in the classroom, thus enhancing the likelihood of a student's successful inclusion. Teachers can begin by teaching behaviours that will "naturally elicit desired responses from peers and adults" (Nelson, 1988, p. 21), such as sharing, smiling, asking for help, attending, taking turns, following directions, and solving problems (McConnell, 1987). These skills will promote social acceptance and can be applied across many settings.

A second consideration involves selecting a social adjustment program that promotes both social skills and *social competence.* Whereas social skills facilitate individual interpersonal interactions, **social competence** involves the broader ability to use skills at the right times and places, showing social perception, cognition, and judgment of how to act in different situations (Sargent, 1991). A focus limited to specific skill training may make it difficult for the child to maintain the specific social skills or transfer them to various settings. Table 13.1 outlines a typical sequence within a social skills curriculum.

The increasing placement of students with more severe disabilities in inclusive classes has significant implications for the social environment; there is little reason to believe that the social skills of these students will develop just because they are physically located in such classes. McEnvoy, Shores, Wehby, Johnson, and Fox's (1990) review of the literature on inclusion reveals that the more that teachers provide specific instruction, physical prompts, modelling, and praise directed to the acquisition and maintenance of social skills, the more successfully students learn social interaction skills.

Transitional Needs

In addition to the academic and social components of the curriculum, career education and transition form an important emphasis. For all elementary students, career awareness and a focus on facilitating movement between levels of schooling (i.e., vertical transitions) are curricular essentials.

Transition from Preschool to Primary School Research on students moving from preschool programs into school settings has identified variables that predict success in school. Four such variables include academic readiness skills, social skills, responsiveness to instructional style, and responsiveness to the structure of the school environment (Polloway et al., 1992). Analyzing the new school environment can help a teacher determine the skills a student will need to make this crucial adjustment.

TABLE 13.1	Sample Social Skills Curriculum Sequence

Session I

Listening

Meeting people—introducing self, introducing others

Beginning a conversation

Listening during a conversation

Ending a conversation

Joining an ongoing activity

Session II

Asking questions appropriately

Asking favours appropriately

Seeking help from peers and adults

Following directions

Session III

Sharing

Interpreting body language

Playing a game successfully

Session IV

Suggesting an activity to others

Working co-operatively

Offering help

Session V

Saying thank you

Giving and accepting a compliment

Rewarding self

Session VI

Apologizing

Understanding the impact your behaviour has on others

Understanding others' behaviour

From *Managing Attention Disorders in Children: A Guide for Practitioners* (pp. 342–343), by S. Goldstein and M. Goldstein, 1990, New York: John Wiley. Used by permission.

Academic readiness skills have traditionally been cited as good predictors of success at the primary school level. Examples include the ability to recognize numbers and letters, grasp a writing utensil, count to 10, and write letters and numbers. Yet a clear delineation between academic readiness and academic skills is not warranted. Rather, to use reading as an example, it is much more productive to consider readiness as inclusive of examples of early reading skills, or what has been termed emergent literacy. Programming in this area should focus on academic activities that advance the processes of learning to read, write, or calculate.

Social skills consistent with the developmental attributes of other five- and six-year-olds are clearly important to success in the elementary school. It is particularly critical that students be able to function in a group. Thus, introducing small group instructional activities in preschool programs prepares students to function in future school situations.

Developing responsiveness to a new instructional style is another challenge for the young child. Providing instructional experiences that the student can generalize to the new school setting will be helpful, since the instructional arrangement in the preschool program may vary significantly from that of the school program; some learning activities in the preschool class should approximate those of kindergarten. For example, a child entering an immersion program should have basic terms and phrases in the future language of instruction introduced in preschool.

Responsiveness to the daily learning environment is a fourth concern. Changes may include new transportation arrangements, extended instructional time, increased expectations of individual independence, and increased class size resulting in a reduction in individual attention. Teachers may set up opportunities for the preschoolers to visit kindergarten classes to familiarize them with the future environment.

TEACHING TIP

Teachers should accept responsibility to prepare students for their next school-life challenge or transition (e.g., preschool to elementary school, elementary school to secondary school).

	Consumer Economics	Occupational Knowledge	Health	Community Resources	Government and Law
Reading	Look for ads in the newspaper for toys.	Read books from library on various occupations.	Read the school lunch menu.	Find television listing in the *TV Guide*.	Read road signs and understand what they mean.
Writing	Write prices of items to be purchased.	Write the specific tasks involved in performing one of the classroom jobs.	Keep a diary of food you eat in each food group each day.	Complete an application to play on a Little League team.	Write a letter to the mayor inviting him/her to visit your school.
Speaking, Writing, Viewing	Listen to bank official talk about savings accounts.	Call newspaper in town to inquire about delivering papers in your neighbourhood.	View a film on brushing teeth.	Practise the use of the 911 emergency number.	Discuss park playground improvements with the mayor.
Problem Solving	Decide if you have enough coins to make a purchase from a vending machine.	Decide which job in the classroom you do best.	Role-play what you should do if you have a stomach ache.	Role-play the times you would use the 911 emergency number.	Find the city hall on the map. Decide whether you will walk or drive to it.
Interpersonal Relations	Ask for help finding items in a grocery store.	Ask a student in the class to assist you with a classroom job.	Ask the school nurse how to take care of mosquito bites.	Call the movie theatre and ask the show times of a movie.	Role-play being lost and asking a police officer for help.
Computation	Compute the cost of a box of cereal with a discount coupon.	Calculate how much you would make on a paper route at $3 per hour for 5 hours per week.	Compute the price of one tube of toothpaste if they are on sale at 3 for $1.	Compute the complete cost of going to the movie (admission, food, transportation).	Compute tax on a candy bar.

TABLE 13.2   Life Skills in the Elementary School Curriculum

From "Curricular Considerations: A Life Skills Orientation," by J. R. Patton, M. E. Cronin, E. A. Polloway, D. R. Hutchison, and G. A. Robinson. In *Best Practices in Mild Mental Retardation*, edited by G. A. Robinson, J. R. Patton, E. A. Polloway, and L. Sargent, 1989, p. 31. Reston, VA: CEC-MR. Used by permission.

Elementary Curricular Considerations   **Career education** in general, and **life skills** education in particular, have become major emphases among secondary school teachers, especially those who work with students who have exceptionalities. Yet life skills concepts should also be incorporated into elementary and middle school programs (Patton & Cronin, 1993; Patton & Dunn, 1998). Table 13.2 provides a matrix of topics that may be incorporated into an elementary-level life skills curriculum. Even programs for young children should be designed to encourage positive long-term outcomes for all students.

Concepts and topics related to life skills should be integrated into existing subject areas, thus broadening the curriculum without creating a "new subject." This can be done in three ways. The first approach, *augmentation*, uses career education–oriented materials to supplement the existing curriculum. The second approach *infuses* relevant career education topics into the lessons laid out in the existing curriculum. A third approach employs an *integrated curriculum*, similar to the unit approach traditionally used in many education programs. An integrated curriculum addresses a topic by drawing together content related to it from various academic areas, enabling students to apply academic skills across these areas. Life skills related to the broad topic can be woven into the curriculum. Using a matrix format (see Table 13.3), reading, math, and language skills, as well as career topics and life skills, can be tied together. This curriculum can also help primary- and elementary-age students understand that different academic subjects have important interrelationships.

Transition to Middle School   Students with exceptionalities in the elementary school need to be prepared for movement to junior high school. In order to make this a successful vertical transition, students need an organized approach to their work, time management and study skills, note-taking strategies, homework strategies, and the ability to use lockers. Robinson, Braxdale, and Colson (1988) observed that the new behaviour demands faced by students in junior high school fall into three categories: academic skills, self-management and study skills, and social-adaptive skills. Problems in any of these three areas may cause difficulties for students.

A variety of instructional strategies may assist in the transition process: having junior high school faculty visit elementary classes to discuss programs and expectations, viewing videotaped junior high school classes, and taking field trips to the junior high school to get a sense of the physical layout, the changing of classes, and environmental and pedagogical factors (Jaquish & Stella, 1986). Co-operative planning and follow-up between both general and special education teachers at the two school levels will smooth the transition.

Community-Based Instruction   In developing life skills and facilitating transition, community-based instruction can benefit all students but is particularly effective for students with exceptionalities, as it addresses common problems in applying academic learning to life outside the classroom. Field trips to stores to make purchases, to observe work patterns, and to learn about advertising and marketing techniques can be supplemented by bringing community members into the classroom to speak about careers or demonstrate life skills. Curriculum guides can assist teachers in integrating community resources into instructional programming.

Science class offers an excellent opportunity for social integration of students with special needs.

TABLE 13.3	Integrated Curriculum		

| Science Subtopics | Related Subject/Skill Areas | | |
	Science Activities	Math	Social Studies
Introductory lesson	Attraction of ants Collection Observation Research ant anatomy	Measurement of distance travelled as a function of time	Relationship of population demographics for ants and humans
Ant farms	Individual set-ups Daily observation Development of collection procedures	Linear measurement Frequency counts	Roles in the community Relationship to human situations
Food preferences chart	Research and predict Construct apparatus for determining preference Design data collection procedures Collect/record data Experiment with food substance positions	Frequency counts Graphs of daily results	Discussion of human food preferences Cultural differences
Ant races	Conduct races with and without food Data collection Predictive activities	Temporal measurement Averages	History of racing Sports and competition
Closing	Analyze information	Tabulate data	

From Kataoka, J. C., & Patton, J. R. (1989). Integrated curriculum. *Science and Children, 16*, 52–58. Reprinted with permission from NSTA Publications, copyright 1989, from *Science and Children*, National Science Teachers Association, 1840 Wilson Boulevard, Arlington, VA 22201-3000.

Diversity Considerations

Considerations of linguistic and cultural diversity must inform all aspects of curriculum design. In the past, multicultural education was frequently presented as special units or as "heritage days" that celebrated different cultures. Winzer and Mazurek (1998) from Alberta note that this approach still prevails in many elementary schools. They criticize what they see as a "tourist curriculum," deeming it neither effective nor sufficient, and call for an infusion approach to multicultural education.

Infusion, another approach, requires that the multicultural perspective is "infused" into all aspects of the curriculum on a day-to-day basis. It spans the perspectives, histories, traditions, and contributions of all groups, calling for culturally appropriate and relevant curriculum materials. McGill University's Ratna Ghosh, an international leader in the area of multicultural education, makes the point that multicultural education should neither showcase different cultures nor ignore the differences (Ghosh, 1996). She writes eloquently about the need to include all cultures, including that of the dominant group, in the multiculturalism in the schools: "multicultural education is not only for

Related Subject/Skill Areas			
Arts	**Computer Application**	**Life Skills**	**Language Arts**
Drawings of ant anatomy Ant mobiles Creative exploration	Graphic drawings of ants	Picnic planning Food storage and protection	Oral sharing of observations
Diagram of farm Diorama Ant models Role-playing of ant behaviour	Spreadsheets for calculations Graphing Database storing observations	Relate to engineers, architects, sociologists, geographers	Library skills Creative writing Spelling Research involving note taking, outlining, and reading Vocabulary development Oral reports
Design data collection forms Role-play ant eating behaviour		Graphic designer Food services Researchers	
Film making Rewrite lyrics to "The Ants Go Marching In" based on activities	Graphic animation	Athletics Coaches	
Finalize visual aids	Printout	Guest speakers	Presentation

minority groups... whiteness cannot remain invisible and outside the framework of multiculturalism" (p. 2).

The regular classroom teacher may recognize the need to have a multicultural curriculum, but may be at a loss about how to realize this goal. Gollnick and Chinn (1994) suggest a starting point when they state, "If students seldom see representations of themselves, their families, or their communities, it becomes difficult to believe that the academic content has any meaning or usefulness for them" (p. 300). Teachers need to incorporate material that is relevant to the cultures of students in the classroom.

In Canada, there will never be prepackaged relevant curricula due to the enormous diversity across the country. In Northern Quebec, a classroom will have a large proportion of First Nations peoples; in Vancouver, a significant number of students are of Asian heritage; in many rural areas across Canada, students of European and East European descent may predominate, although, in this instance, diversity will be less apparent— families may have been here for three or more generations. Therefore, the responsibility almost always remains with individual teachers to adapt their curricula to reflect the diversity in their classrooms.

Elementary Teacher, Special Needs Tutor Marla Bellin

Marla Bellin received her professional teaching certificate from the University of British Columbia, Vancouver, in 1992. She taught three years in Chilliwack, B.C.: one year team-teaching Grade 1 and French as a second language to kindergarten through Grade 3 classes and two years teaching her own Grade 3 class. She then chose to go overseas and taught for three years at the American School of Bucharest in Romania. Subsequently, she returned to Canada to obtain a master's degree in integrated education from McGill University; at the same time, she worked as a special needs tutor with a variety of children integrated into the regular schools.

In her eight years of teaching primary grades, Marla has worked with gifted students; a number of students with severe reading disabilities, behaviour problems, and attention-deficit disorder; a young girl diagnosed with Asperger syndrome; many students having general difficulties learning; and some children needing enrichment.

Marla is known for her creative approach to teaching basic skills. "She always works to find a fun way to teach some of the most boring materials! She finds a way to make a game out of so many things and then the kids really learn. We call her the game queen!" says one colleague.

"I have always taught in integrated classrooms, assuming this was the norm. In my second year I utilized a school's pull-out program for intensive teaching of reading for two students because I felt I did not have the knowledge or time to properly teach the skills they required. I found that the resource program interrupted the flow of my lessons and stigmatized the students. To change this, I sought high-interest and engaging systematic phonics programs to implement *in* my class for the benefit of *all* students. I continue to integrate the programs I learned into my daily language lessons. They now take less time to explain, and they have proven useful for decoding and spelling for all my students. Having children understand that not everyone learns in the same way or at the same pace and teaching them tolerance of and patience with others are lifelong lessons that they gain in inclusive environments.

"One year I set up a special spelling individualized program for my students with spelling problems. After all my planning I discovered my most needy student struggling with a very challenging list made for the most advanced students. Out of frustration at seeing him fail, and trying to send a message that this was not the appropriate work for him (and looking upon this as a waste of all my individualizing effort!), I took his paper and threw it in the garbage. After school I received a phone call from his mother. I learned that he was doing this harder list to try to impress me! I know the personal apology I gave him the following day did not erase the bad feelings that both he and I felt. Since then, I take the extra time needed to find out the reason behind students' actions before explaining my perspective to the student.

"Teachers' frustration, oftentimes not justified, only does harm. Being a good role model by taking the time to use polite communication to immediately clarify problems has been my most treasured lesson. Our children deserve it!"

Instructional Adaptations and/or Accommodations

In general, students with exceptionalities profit directly from the same types of teaching strategies that benefit all students. However, in particular, certain research-validated interventions are associated with successful learning outcomes for students with learning disabilities and other special needs. Vaughn et al. (2000) identified three instructional features that stand out as producing the most significant impact on learning:

- Control of task difficulty (i.e., sequencing examples and problems to maintain high levels of student success).
- Teaching students in small interactive groups of six or fewer students.
- Directed response questioning (i.e., involves the use of procedures... that promote "thinking aloud" about text being read, mathematical problems to be solved, or about the process of composing a written essay or story). (p. 101)

Vaughn et al. (2000) further noted that *all students* benefit when best practices for students with learning disabilities, such as these, are used.

The reflection of these basic principles in the adaptations and/or accommodations made to instructional programs in the general education classroom form the keys to successful inclusion (see Figure 13.3, in which multilevel instruction is identified as one of several effective inclusive practices). As the traditional adage goes, special education is not necessarily special, it is just *good teaching*. "Good teaching" often means making appropriate adaptations and/or accommodations. Assuming the curricular content is appropriate for individual students who have exceptionalities, the challenge is to adapt it to facilitate learning.

In inclusive programs, instruction must be adapted to ensure that all students learn successfully. As Fuchs, Fuchs, Hamlett, Phillips, and Karns (1995) note:

> General education's capacity to incorporate meaningful adaptation has become a critical issue during the past decade, as the rhetoric of the regular education initiative and the inclusive schools movement has increased pressure to provide educational programs to students with disabilities in general education classrooms. (p. 440)

Thus, a key component of successful inclusion is the treatment acceptability of specific interventions to accommodate the needs of students with exceptionalities. The term *treatment acceptability* has been used in a variety of ways. Polloway, Bursuck, Jayanthi, Epstein, and Nelson (1996) use the term in a broad sense to refer to the likelihood that certain specific classroom interventions will be acceptable to the general education teacher. Thus it may include, for example, the helpfulness, desirability, feasibility, and fairness of the intervention, as well as how other students will perceive it in a particular setting. As Witt and Elliott (1985) note, the "attractiveness" of an intervention is important: if the treatment is not deemed acceptable, it is unlikely to be implemented.

FIGURE 13.3

Effective Inclusive Practices

Adapted from "National Survey Identifies Inclusive Educational Practices," Appalachian Educational Laboratory, 1995, *The Link, 14*(1), Spring/Summer 1995, p. 8.

The following practices have been identified by the National Center on Educational Restructuring and Inclusion as supporting inclusive education:

- **Multilevel instruction** allows for different kinds of learning within the same curriculum. Here the focus is on key concepts to be taught, alternatives in presentation methods, acceptance of varying types of student activities and multiple outcomes, different ways in which students can express their learning, and diverse evaluation procedures.
- **Co-operative learning** involves heterogeneous groupings of students, allowing for students with a wide variety of skills and traits to work together. Models of co-operative learning differ in the amount of emphasis given to the process of the group's work and to the assessment of outcomes for individual members as well as for the team as a whole.
- **Activity-based learning** emphasizes learning in natural settings, the production of actual work products, and performance assessment. It moves learning from being solely classroom-based to preparing students to learn in community settings.
- **Mastery learning** specifies what a student needs to learn and then provides sufficient practice opportunities to gain mastery.
- **Technology** is often mentioned as being a support for students and teachers. Uses include record keeping, assistive devices such as reading machines and braille-to-print typewriters, and drill and instructional programs.
- **Peer support and tutoring programs** have multiple advantages. Placing students in instructional roles enhances the teaching resources of the school. It recognizes that some students learn by teaching others.

FURTHER READING

For more information on effective instructional adaptations, read Scott et al.'s article "Implementing Instructional Adaptations for Students with Disabilities in Inclusive Classrooms: A Literature Review" in volume 19 of *Remedial and Special Education*, 1998 (pp. 106–119).

FURTHER READING

J. J. Hoover provides a useful model for curriculum adaptation in the article "Curriculum Adaptation: A Five-Step Process for Classroom Implementation," published in 1990 in volume 25 of *Academic Therapy* (pp. 407–416).

In a review of research on adaptations, Scott, Vitale, and Masten (1998) summarized the types of adaptations that have been researched for their effectiveness. They use the qualifier *typical* to refer to specific examples that are routine, minor, or applicable to an entire class, and *substantial* to refer to those that are tailored to the needs of individual students. Their categories (as adapted) are as follows:

- *Adapting instruction:* typical (concrete classroom demonstrations, monitoring classroom understanding); substantial (adjusting the pace to individual learners, giving immediate individual feedback, using multiple modalities)
- *Adapting assignments:* typical (providing models); substantial (breaking tasks into small steps, shortening assignments, lowering difficulty levels)
- *Teaching learning skills:* typical (study skills, note-taking techniques); substantial (learning strategies, test-taking skills)
- *Altering instructional materials:* substantial (using alternative materials, taping textbooks, using supplementary aids)
- *Modifying curriculum:* substantial (lowering difficulty of course content)
- *Varying instructional grouping:* substantial (using peer tutoring, using co-operative groups)
- *Enhancing behaviour:* typical (praise, offering encouragement); substantial (using behavioural contracts, using token economies, frequent parental contact)
- *Facilitating progress monitoring:* typical (read tests orally; give extended test-taking time; give frequent, short quizzes; provide study guides); substantial (retaking tests, obtaining direct daily measures of academic progress, modifying grading criteria) (p. 107)

Finally, technology can assist teachers in adapting the curriculum, providing additional supports for the student, and increasing instructional effectiveness. The nearby Technology Today feature provides specific examples.

Specific adaptations and/or accommodations for students with exceptionalities in elementary classes are discussed next. They vary in nature and in terms of treatment acceptability. The authors do not intend to suggest that all suggestions will be appropriate

TrackStar

TrackStar (http://trackstar.hprtec.org) is an online resource that helps teachers and students organize and annotate websites (more specifically, the addresses or URLs to the websites) for lessons, presentations, assignments, or instructional resources. TrackStar allows users to organize favourite websites into tracks under a specific topic and make them accessible to anyone with internet access.

Tracks are created by teachers or students and are stored on servers. All the tracks (approximately 63 000) are organized and catalogued by grade level. Users can select from tracks created for early childhood, primary grades (K–2), intermediate grades (3–4), middle school (5–9), high school (9–12),

college/adult, or all grades. Likewise, users can select tracks organized by keyword (i.e., special education), by author, or by themes and standards. If you are interested in the most popular tracks, users have access to the month's "Track-A-Day," a list of all "Top Tracks," and tracks by subject or category. For the user uncertain of how to begin locating a track, TrackStar has a "How to Find a Track" tutorial.

Developed to help teachers and parents address some of the challenges the

World Wide Web offers, TrackStar features a variety of tools. These tools attempt to eliminate these internet hurdles and allow teachers to focus on instruction, access resources that will enhance classroom activities, and hopefully further individualize the general curriculum. More important, TrackStar saves time. For the novice or experienced user, TrackStar offers an environment where a learning community has already organized relevant information in a format that can be immediately shared with others.

Adapted from "Technology for Organizing and Presenting Digital Information" (pp. 306–310) by S. J. Smith & S. B. Smith, 2002, *Intervention in School and Clinic, 37.*

or desirable in a given situation. Teachers should determine how far to go in making specific adaptations. Many of the suggested adaptations will prove beneficial to all students, not only those with special needs.

Enhancing Content Learning through Listening

Many children will not listen carefully just because they are told to do so. Rather, they often need oral presentations provided in ways that promote successful listening. Students who struggle with selective attention (i.e., focus) or sustained attention (i.e., attention maintained over a period of time) respond more easily to speaking that supports the listener. Wallace, Cohen, and Polloway (1987) note that listeners attend more when:

- content is [emphasized] through repetition, vocal emphasis, and cueing;
- the message is meaningful, logical, and well organized;
- messages are given in short units;
- the speaker can be clearly heard and understood;
- the speaker allows for listener participation in the form of clarification, feedback, or responding;
- the speaker has focused attention by stating how the message will be of importance to the listener;
- reinforcement for attending is given in the form of participation, praise, or increased ability to perform;
- oral presentations are accompanied by visual aids that emphasize important points;
- the listener knows there will be an opportunity to reflect upon and integrate the message before having to formulate a response. (p. 75)

Adapting Oral Presentations

In order to facilitate learning, teachers must consider effective vehicles for the presentation of content. Adaptations and/or accommodations in this area typically prove beneficial to all students. Some specific considerations follow:

- When mastery of prior content is uncertain, use concrete concepts before teaching abstractions (e.g., teach the concept of human rights by discussing specific rights that the students are entitled to).
- Relate information to students' prior experiences.
- Provide students with an overview before beginning.
- Reduce the number of concepts introduced at a given time.
- Encourage children to detect errors in messages and report what they could not understand.
- Monitor and adapt presentation language to make sure that students understand you. Adjust vocabulary level and complexity of sentence structures accordingly. Avoid puns, idiomatic speech, and metaphors unless clear explanations are provided.
- Review lessons before additional content is introduced.
- Lessen distractions, such as visual and auditory ones, within the environment.
- Adjust pace as needed.
- Keep oral directions short and direct, and supplement them with written directions as needed.
- Provide repetition, review, and additional examples.
- Provide further guided practice by requiring more responses, lengthening practice sessions, or scheduling extra sessions.
- Clarify directions for follow-up activities so that tasks can be completed successfully. (Adapted from Chalmers, 1991; Cheney, 1989; Dowdy, 1990; McDevitt, 1990.)

Facilitating Note Taking   Learning from classroom presentations is obviously critical to academic achievement. For students in the primary grades, instruction is generally not delivered through lengthy oral presentation. However, as lecturing begins to become more common in the upper elementary grades and in junior high school, students will need to develop note-taking skills. The teaching of note taking may be undertaken by special education teachers; how content is presented by the teacher is an important factor to focus on. The following pointers are adapted from Beirne-Smith (1989a; 1989b); they overlap somewhat with ideas for listening and adapting presentations discussed earlier.

1. Organize your lecture.
2. Use key words and phrases, such as "first," or "the main theme."
3. Summarize ideas.
4. Repeat important statements to emphasize the importance of the statement.
5. Pause occasionally to allow students time to fill in blank spaces or catch up to the previous statement.
6. Provide advance organizers (e.g., topic outlines, partially completed notes) to assist the student in organizing and recording information.
7. Write important points on the board.
8. Simplify overhead transparencies. Too much information is confusing and less likely to be recorded.
9. Encourage students to record all visually presented material exactly as displayed and to leave space between main sections for questions about the material.
10. Use humour or anecdotes to illustrate important points.
11. Model note-taking skills (e.g., with the overhead projector).

Adapting Reading Tasks

In many instances, instructional tasks, assignments, or materials may be relevant and appropriate for students with exceptionalities, but may present problematic reading demands. Teachers should consider options for adapting the task or the materials. The following suggestions address problems that may arise in processing reading content:

▶ Clearly establish a given assignment's purpose and importance.
▶ Highlight key words, phrases (e.g., colour-coding text) and concepts (e.g., providing outlines and study guides).
▶ Encourage periodic feedback from students to check their understanding.
▶ Preview reading material with students to assist them in establishing purpose, activating prior knowledge, budgeting time, and focusing attention.
▶ Create vocabulary lists, and teach these words to ensure that students can use them rather than simply recognize them.
▶ Provide page numbers where specific answers can be found in a reading comprehension or content assignment.
▶ Use brief individual conferences with students to verify their comprehension.
▶ Locate lower-level content material on the same topic to adapt tasks for students with reading difficulties.
▶ Tape a reading of a text, or have it read orally to a student. Consider using peers, volunteers, and paraprofessionals in this process.
▶ Rewrite material (or solicit volunteers to do so) to simplify its reading level, or provide chapter outlines or summaries.
▶ Utilize advance organizers and visual aids (e.g., charts, graphs) to provide an orientation to reading tasks or to supplement them.
▶ Demonstrate how new content relates to content previously learned.
▶ Encourage students to facilitate their comprehension by raising questions about a text's content.

▶ Teach students to consider K-W-L as a technique to focus attention. "K" represents prior knowledge, "W" what the student wants to know, and "L" what has been learned as a result.

▶ Teach the use of active comprehension strategies in which students periodically pause to ask themselves questions about what they have read.

▶ Use reciprocal teaching. Have students take turns leading discussions that raise questions about the content read, summarize the most important information, clarify concepts that are unclear, and predict what will occur next. (Adapted from Chalmers, 1991; Cheney, 1989; Dowdy, 1990; Gartland, 1994; Hoover, 1990; Reynolds & Salend, 1990; Schumm & Strickler, 1991.)

Another key element to successful reading is the strategies acquired by students to promote independence. Students need to develop approaches that enable them to engage in the following:

▶ *Comprehension Monitoring* (i.e., teaching students to monitor their comprehension and use "repair strategies" when they begin to lose understanding of the text).

▶ *Text Structuring* (i.e., providing students with ways to ask themselves questions about what they read). (Vaughn et al., 2000, p. 104)

Enhancing Written Responses

The adaptations noted here may assist students who may have difficulty with responding in written form. These suggestions relate not to the presentation of material but rather to the responses implicit in the task or assignment. The suggestions will enhance the ability of children to meet the written language demands of the inclusive classroom.

▶ Avoid assigning excessive amounts of written classwork and homework.

▶ When appropriate, allow children to select the most comfortable method of writing, whether it be cursive, manuscript, or typing.

▶ Change the response mode to oral when appropriate.

▶ Set realistic, mutually agreed upon expectations for neatness.

▶ Allow children to circle or underline responses.

▶ Let students tape-record answers instead of giving them in writing.

▶ Fasten materials to the desk to alleviate co-ordination problems.

▶ Provide the student with a copy of lecture notes produced by the teacher or a peer.

▶ Reduce amounts of board copying or text copying; provide the written information itself or an outline of the main content.

▶ Allow sufficient space for answering problems.

▶ Allow group-written responses (via projects or reports) (see the section on involving peers later in the chapter). (Adapted from Chalmers, 1991; Cheney, 1989; Dowdy, 1990.)

In addition to enhancing written responses, teachers should work to improve students' writing ability. Provide sufficient opportunities to write relative to meaningful tasks (e.g., for an authentic audience, or on a topic important or interesting to the student). Graham (1992, p. 137) suggests the following ideas for providing frequent and meaningful writing opportunities:

▶ Assist students in thinking about what they will write.

▶ Ask students to establish goals for what they hope to achieve.

▶ Arrange the writing environment so that the teacher is not the sole audience for students' writing.

▶ Provide opportunities for students to work on the same project across days or even weeks.

▶ Incorporate writing as part of a larger, interesting activity.

CROSS-REFERENCE

Ultimately, students will need to learn to adapt reading tasks themselves, through the use of learning strategies, in order to become independent learners. See Chapter 14 for how this plays out at the secondary level.

FURTHER READING

The key consideration for all students is the provision of frequent opportunities to write. The work of Donald Graves has been particularly influential in encouraging teachers to increase chances for true writing. See Graves, Tuyay, and Green's recent article, "What I've Learned from Teachers of Writing" in volume 82, issue 2 of *Language Arts*, 2004 (pp. 88–94).

Portfolios also represent a positive approach to enhancing writing development. Portfolios involve students in the evaluation of their own writing samples by selecting samples to be kept and by comparing changes in their writing over time.

Promoting Following Instructions and Completing Assignments

Another key area is enhancing children's ability to follow instructions and complete work assignments. The following suggestions are adapted from *CEC Today* (1997, p. 15):

- Get the student's attention before giving directions.
- Use alerting cues.
- Give one direction at a time.
- Quietly repeat the directions to the student after they have been given to the entire class.
- Check for understanding by having the student repeat the directions.
- Break up tasks into workable and obtainable steps, and include due dates.
- Provide examples and specific steps to accomplish the task.
- List or post requirements necessary to complete each assignment.
- Check assignments frequently.
- Arrange for the student to have a study buddy.

Involving Peers

FURTHER READING

For more information on co-operative learning, see R.E. Slavin's article, "Cooperative Learning in Middle and Secondary Schools" in volume 69, issue 4 of *The Clearing House*, 1996 (pp. 200–204).

Co-operative Learning   Co-operative learning has been promoted as a means of facilitating the inclusion of students with exceptionalities in general education classrooms. It is categorized by classroom techniques that involve students in group learning activities, in which recognition and reinforcement are based on group, rather than individual, performance. Heterogeneous small groups work together to achieve a group goal, and an individual student's success directly affects the success of other students (Slavin, 1987).

A variety of formats can be used to implement co-operative learning. These include peer tutoring, group projects, the jigsaw technique, and student-team achievement divisions.

Peer Tutoring   Peer teaching, or **peer tutoring**, is a relatively easy-to-manage system of co-operative learning. It can benefit both the student being tutored and the tutor. Specific activities that lend themselves to peer tutoring include reviewing task directions, doing drill and practice, recording material dictated by a peer, modelling acceptable or appropriate responses, and providing pretest practice (such as in spelling).

One effective tutoring program is *classwide peer tutoring* (CWPT). As summarized by Seeley (1995), this system involves the following arrangements:

- Classes are divided into two teams, which engage in competitions of 1–2 weeks' duration.
- Students work in pairs, both tutoring and being tutored on the same material in a given instructional session.
- Partners reverse roles after 15 minutes.
- Typical subjects tutored include math, spelling, vocabulary, science, and social studies.
- The teacher breaks down the curriculum into manageable subunits.
- Students accumulate points for their team by giving correct answers and by using correct procedures, and they receive partial credit for corrected answers.
- Individual scores on master tests are then added to the team's total.

CWPT is a promising approach to use in inclusive settings. It has been positively evaluated in terms of enhancing content learning, promoting diversity and integration, and freeing teachers to prepare for other instructional activities (King-Sears & Bradley, 1995; Simmons, Fuchs, Hodge, & Mathes, 1994).

Another example of a successful peer tutoring approach is Peer Assisted Learning Strategies (PALS), described by Mathes and Torgesen (1998). In PALS, beginning readers are assisted in learning through paired instruction in which each member of the pair takes turns serving as a coach and a reader. The first coach is the reader who is at a higher achievement level who listens to, comments on, and reinforces the other student before the roles are reversed. These researchers found that the use of this approach enhanced students' reading by promoting careful attention to saying and hearing sounds, sounding out words, and reading stories. They recommended using the approach three times a week for approximately 16 weeks with each session lasting 35 minutes. The PALS program complements general education instruction by enhancing the academic engaged time of each student.

Co-operative Projects   *Group projects* allow students to pool their knowledge and skills to complete an assignment. The task is assigned to the entire group, and the goal is to develop a single product reflecting the contributions of all members. For example, in art, creating a collage is a good example of a group project. In social studies, a report on one of the provinces or territories might involve making individual students responsible for particular tasks: drawing a map, sketching an outline of province/territory history, collecting photos of scenic attractions, and developing a display of products from that province/territory. The benefits of groups are enhanced when they include high, average, and low achievers.

The Jigsaw Technique   The jigsaw format involves giving all students in a group individual tasks to be completed before the group can reach its goal. Each individual studies a portion of the material and then shares it with other members of the team. For example, Salend (1990) discussed an assignment related to the life of Dr. Martin Luther King, Jr., in which each student was given a segment of his life to research. The students then had to teach others in their group the information from the segment they had mastered.

Student-Team Achievement Divisions   The concept of student-team achievement divisions (STAD) involves assigning students to diversely constituted teams (typically four to a group), which then meet together to review specific teacher-generated lessons. This technique typically focuses on learning objectives that relate to one correct answer (e.g., facts). The teams work together toward content mastery, comparing answers, discussing differences, and questioning one another. Subsequently all students take individual quizzes, without assisting one another. The combined scores of the group determine how well the team succeeds. As Slavin (1987) notes, STAD embraces three concepts central to successful team learning methods: team rewards, individual accountability, and equal opportunities for success. Team rewards derive from content learning by members, who are then assessed by team scores produced by pooled individual scores. Individual accountability is essential because all must learn the content for the team to be successful. Equal opportunities for success come by focusing on degree of individual improvement.

Co-operative learning strategies offer much promise as inclusive practices. The various approaches can be used successfully with low, average, and high achievers to promote academic and social skills and to enhance independence. Co-operative learning also can enhance the social adjustment of students with special needs and help create natural support networks of which typically achieving peers are a part. However, co-operative learning strategies should be used only for part of the curriculum, not exclusively.

Adapting the Temporal Environment

Time is a critical element in the implementation of classroom adaptations. For many students with exceptionalities, adapting deadlines and other time constraints can help promote success. When handled properly, these adaptations need not impinge on the integrity of the assignments nor place undue burdens on the classroom teacher. Some suggestions follow:

▶ Develop schedules that balance routines (to establish predictability) with novelty (to sustain excitement).
▶ Review class schedules with students to reinforce routines.
▶ Provide each student with a copy of the schedule.
▶ Increase the amount of time allowed to complete assignments or tests.
▶ Contract with students concerning time allotment, and tie reinforcement to a reasonable schedule of completion.
▶ Consider reducing the amount of work or the length of tests rather than allow more time for completion (e.g., complete every other math problem).
▶ Allow extra practice time for students who understand content but need additional time to achieve mastery.
▶ Adjust homework assignments (e.g., the number of math problems, total length of a reading assignment) to produce equity in engaged time.
▶ Teach time-management skills (use of time lines and checklists, and prioritization of time and assignments).
▶ Space short work periods with breaks or changes of task (thus using the Premack principle for scheduling: making desirable events contingent on completion of less desirable events). (Adapted from Chalmers, 1991; Dowdy, 1990; Guernsey, 1989; Polloway et al., 2001)

Adapting the Classroom Arrangement

CROSS-REFERENCE

See also the discussion on classroom arrangement in Chapter 12.

Changes in the classroom arrangement can also help in accommodating students with special needs. Some specific examples are listed here:

▶ Establish a climate that fosters positive social interactions between students.
▶ Balance structure, organization, and regimentation with opportunities for freedom and exploration.
▶ Use study carrels.
▶ Locate student seats and learning activities in areas free from distractions.
▶ Allow students to select their own seats based on where it is best for them to work and study.
▶ Help students keep their work spaces free of unnecessary materials.
▶ Arrange materials in the class based on frequency of use.
▶ Provide opportunities for approved movement within the class.
▶ Establish high- and low-frequency areas for class work (thus using the Premack principle—allow students to move to "fun" areas contingent on work completion in more academically rigorous areas).
▶ Set aside space for group work, individual seatwork, and free-time activities. (Adapted from Cheney, 1989; Dowdy, 1990; Guernsey, 1989; Hoover, 1990; Minner & Prater, 1989; Polloway et al., 2001)

Enhancing Motivation

For many students with special needs, school activities may appear irrelevant or uninteresting. Given the failure often experienced by students with exceptionalities—as well as the boredom experienced by students who are gifted—motivational problems can seriously undermine the learning process. Although this typically becomes more problematic at the secondary level, young students must be taught in a way that prevents subsequent motivational problems. Attention to both the motivational qualities of the material and the characteristics of the student can enhance motivation. The following

Teachers should avoid assigning excessive amounts of written classroom and homework to some students with special needs.

suggestions, which are particularly apt for students with special needs, can help spark motivation:

▶ Have students set personal goals and graph their progress.
▶ Use contingency contracts in which a certain amount of work at a specified degree of accuracy earns the student a desired activity or privilege.
▶ Allow students to choose where to work, what tools to use, and what to do first, as long as their work is being completed.
▶ Make drill-and-practice exercises into a game.
▶ Provide immediate feedback (e.g., through teacher monitoring or self-correcting materials) on the correctness of work.
▶ Give extra credit for bonus work.
▶ For certain students with special needs, camouflage instructional materials at a lower instructional level (using folders, covers).
▶ Use high-status materials for instructional activities (magazines, catalogues, newspapers, chequebooks, drivers' manuals).
▶ Allow students to earn points or tokens to exchange for a valued activity or privilege.
▶ Provide experiences that ensure success, and offer positive feedback when students are successful. (Adapted from Cheney, 1989, p. 29.)

Developing Effective Homework Programs

Homework has always been an essential element of education, but recently its use by teachers in elementary education has increased. Research on the effectiveness of homework as an instructional tool suggests that it leads to increased school achievement for students in general, with particular benefits in the area of habit formation for elementary students (Cooper, 1989; Walberg, 1991). But without question, students with exceptionalities experience significant problems in this area because of difficulties in attention, independence, organization, and motivation (Epstein, Polloway, Foley, & Patton, 1993; Gajria & Salend, 1995).

FIGURE 13.4

Homework Communication Problems Noted by Elementary Teachers

Note: Items were ranked by general education teachers from *most* to *least* serious.

From "Homework Communication Problems: Perspectives of General Education Teachers" by M. H. Epstein, E. A. Polloway, G. H. Buck, W. D. Bursuck, L. M. Wissinger, F. Whitehouse, and M. Jayanthi, 1997. In *Learning Disabilities Research and Practice, 12,* pp. 221–227. Used by permission.

1. Do not know enough about the abilities of students with disabilities who are mainstreamed in their classes.
2. Do not know how to use special education support services or teachers to assist students with disabilities about homework.
3. Lack knowledge about the adaptations that can be made to homework.
4. Are not clear about their responsibility to communicate with special education teachers about the homework of students with disabilities.
5. Are not aware of their responsibility to communicate with parents of students with disabilities about homework.

CONSIDER THIS

The importance of homework adaptations to the successful inclusion of students with special needs has been confirmed in numerous recent research studies. How important do you think it is?

CROSS-REFERENCE

Parental involvement in home-work is discussed at length in Chapter 15.

Homework for students with exceptionalities presents several dilemmas for general education teachers. Epstein et al. (1996) recognized that communication concerning homework is often negatively affected by the inadequate knowledge base of general education teachers. Figure 13.4 presents typical problems (ordered from most to least serious by teachers) in this area.

Epstein et al. (1993) suggest the following homework interventions:

▶ Assess possible problem areas as a basis for designing individualized programming.
▶ Provide assistance in study and organizational skills.
▶ Increase the relevance of the assignment by relating it to student interests and life skills.
▶ Assign homework that can be completed on an independent basis.
▶ Provide sufficient initial guidance when assignments are made.
▶ Control the time that assignments may take so that successful completion is realistic.
▶ Provide feedback to students on specific assignments.

Finally, Polloway, Epstein, Bursuck, Jayanthi, and Cumblad (1994) asked teachers to rate specific strategies that were most helpful to students with exceptionalities. Table 13.4 summarizes these responses; each column reflects teachers' ratings from most to least helpful.

Developing Responsive Grading Practices

The assignment of grades is an integral aspect of education. Grading serves multiple purposes in contemporary education (Salend & Duhaney, 2002). For example, grading can be used to indicate progress, effort, and to provide feedback to students and their families (Salend & Duhaney, 2002). Thus, grading practices have been subject to frequent evaluation and review, generating a number of problematic issues.

Grading received little attention prior to the increased inclusion of students with exceptionalities in general education. A series of research papers has addressed various aspects of grading. In a study of school district policies, Polloway, Epstein, Bursuck, Roderique, McConeghy, and Jayanthi (1994) reported that over 60 percent of districts with grading policies had one related to students with exceptionalities; most common was the inclusion of stated adaptations and/or accommodations within the IEP. In one study, Bursuck, Polloway, Plante, Epstein, Jayanthi, and McConeghy (1996) found that approximately 40 percent of general educators shared responsibilities for grading with special education teachers. Thus, there is some evidence that the trend toward collabo-ration may be having an impact on this important area.

TABLE 13.4	Teachers' Ratings of Helpfulness of Homework Adaptations and Practices			
		Consequences		
Types of Homework	Teacher-Directed Activities	Failure to Complete	Complete Assignments	Adaptations
Practice of skills already taught	Communicate clear consequences about successfully completing homework.	Assist students in completing the assignment.	Give praise for completion.	Provide additional teacher assistance.
Preparation for tests	Begin assignment in class, and check for understanding.	Make adaptations in assignment.	Provide corrective feedback in class.	Check more frequently with student about assignments and expectations.
Unfinished class work	Communicate clear expectations about the quality of homework completion.	Talk to them about why the assignment was not completed.	Give rewards for completion.	Allow alternative response formats (e.g., oral or other than written).
Make-up work due to absences	Use a homework assignment sheet or notebook.	Require corrections and resubmission.	Monitor students by charting performance.	Adjust length of assignment.
Enrichment activities	Communicate clear consequences about failure to complete homework.	Call students' parents.	Record performance in grade book.	Provide a peer tutor for assistance.
Preparation for future class work	Give assignments that are completed entirely at school.	Keep students in at recess to complete the assignment.	Call students' parents.	Provide auxiliary learning aids (e.g., calculator, computer).
	Begin assignment in class without checking for understanding	Keep students after school to complete the assignment.		Assign work that student can do independently.
		Lower their grade.		Provide a study group.
		Put students' names on board.		Provide extra credit opportunities.
				Adjust (i.e., lower) evaluation standards.
				Adjust due dates.
				Give fewer assignments.

Note: Arranged from most helpful to least helpful.

From "A National Survey of Homework Practices of General Education Teachers" (p. 504) by E. A. Polloway, M. H. Epstein, W. Bursuck, M. Jayanthi, and C. Cumblad, *Journal of Learning Disabilities, 27.* Used by permission.

This collaboration is timely because existing grading systems make success challenging for students with exceptionalities. Prior studies on grading patterns have documented generally poor grades for students with exceptionalities in general education (e.g., Donahue & Zigmond, 1990; Valdes, Williamson, & Wagner, 1990; Zigmond, Levin, & Laurie, 1985). Further, although general education teachers reported that written comments and checklists are most helpful with these individuals, the most common systems in use at the elementary level are letter grades (Bursuck et al., 1996).

In Bursuck et al.'s study (1996), elementary general education teachers indicated that adaptations allowing for separate grades for process and product and grades indexed against student improvement were particularly helpful, whereas passing students "no matter what" or basing grades on effort alone was not. Figure 13.5 presents their ranking of grading adaptations.

FURTHER READING

For a discussion of effective grading practices and policies for meeting individual student needs, read Salend and Duhaney's article "Grading Students in Inclusive Settings," in volume 34 of *Teaching Exceptional Children,* 2002 (pp. 8–15).

CROSS-REFERENCE

Grading issues become more problematic at the secondary level; see Chapter 14 for more information.

A related issue is the feasibility of specific adaptations in general education. Bursuck et al. (1996) assessed this question by determining whether teachers actually use these same adaptations with students *without* exceptionalities. As can be seen in Figure 13.5, three of the four adaptations deemed most helpful for students with exceptionalities (i.e., grading on improvement, adjusting grades, giving separate grades for process and product) were used by 50 percent or more of the teachers (regardless of grade level) with typically achieving students. On the other hand, basing grades on less content and passing students no matter what are frowned upon.

Questions of fairness also influence the discussion on grading (e.g., Are adaptations in grading made only for students with exceptionalities really fair to other students?) Bursuck et al. (1996) report that only 25 percent of general education teachers thought such adaptations were fair. Those who believed they were fair noted that students should "not be punished" for an inherent problem such as a disability, that adaptations for effort are appropriate because the students are "fighting uphill battles," and that adaptations allow students to "be successful like other kids."

Those teachers who thought adaptations were unfair indicated that other students experience significant learning problems even though they have not been formally identified, that some students have extenuating circumstances (e.g., divorce, illness) that necessitate adaptations, and that all students are unique and deserve individual consideration (i.e., both students with and without exceptionalities may need specific adaptations). Such attitudes seem to indicate jointly developed adaptations. Finally, a significant minority of general educators believe that classes have standards to uphold; thus all students need to meet those standards without adaptations (Bursuck et al., 1996; Polloway et al., 1996).

One additional perspective on fairness is provided by Bursuck, Munk, and Olsen (1999) who reported that a majority of all students without exceptionalities felt that no adaptations were fair; while some were perceived as relatively more fair, the researchers concluded that equity was the greatest concern of these students.

Polloway et al. (2001) suggest these overall considerations about grading:

▸ Plan for special and general education teachers to meet regularly to discuss student progress.
▸ Emphasize the acquisition of new skills as a basis for grades assigned, thus providing a perspective on the student's relative gains.
▸ Investigate alternatives for evaluating content that has been learned (e.g., oral examinations for poor readers in a science class).
▸ Engage in co-operative grading agreements (e.g., grades for language arts might reflect performance both in the classroom and in the resource room).

FIGURE 13.5

Elementary Teachers' Ratings of Helpfulness of Grading Adaptations for Students with Exceptionalities

Note: Items ranked from most helpful to least helpful by general education teachers. Numbers in parentheses refer to general education rankings of adaptations from *most likely to least likely* to be used with typically achieving students.

Adapted from "Report Card Grading Practices and Adaptations," by W. Bursuck, E. A. Polloway, L. Plante, M. H. Epstein, M. Jayanthi, and J. McConeghy, 1996, *Exceptional Children, 62,* pp. 301–318.

1. Grades are based on the amount of improvement an individual makes. (#1)
2. Separate grades are given for process (e.g., effort) and product (e.g., tests). (#3)
3. Grades are based on meeting IEP objectives. (#9)
4. Grades are adjusted according to student ability. (#2)
5. Grading weights are adjusted (e.g., efforts on projects count more than tests). (#4)
6. Grades are based on meeting the requirements of academic or behavioural contracts. (#5)
7. Grades are based on less content than the rest of the class. (#7)
8. Students are passed if they make an effort to pass. (#6)
9. Grades are based on a modified grading scale (e.g., from 93 – 100 = A, 90 – 100 = A). (#8)
10. Students are passed no matter what. (#10)

▶ Use narrative reports as a key portion of, or adjunct to, the report card. These reports can include comments on specific objectives within the student's IEP.

▶ Develop personalized grading plans for students (see Munk and Bursuck, 2001).

The nearby Inclusion Strategies feature on grading provides additional perspectives.

Effective Grading Practices

Grading is a critical element of successful inclusion. Salend and Duhaney (2002) provided a series of recommendations, which include the following:

▶ **Communicating Expectations and Grading Guidelines.** Student performance is enhanced when teachers clearly communicate their expectations to students and families and share their grading guidelines and criteria with them.

▶ **Informing Students and Families Regarding Grading Progress on a Regular Basis.** Providing students and their families with ongoing information concerning current performance and grades helps all involved parties understand the grading guidelines. Ongoing sharing of students' grading progress facilitates the modifications of instructional programs so that students and families are not surprised by the grades received at the end of the grading period. It also prompts students to examine their effort, motivation, and attitudes and their impact on their performance and grades.

▶ **Using a Range of Assignments That Address Students' Varied Learning Needs, Strengths, and Styles.** Rather than assigning grades based solely on test performance or a limited number of assignments, many teachers determine students' grades by weighing a variety of student assignments (e.g., tests, homework, projects, extra credit, class participation, attendance, behaviour, and other factors).

▶ **Employing Classroom-Based Assessment Alternatives to Traditional Testing.** Whereas grades are frequently determined by students' performance on tests, they also can be based on classroom-based assessment techniques, such as performance assessment, portfolio assessment, and curriculum-based measurement. By using performance assessment, teachers grade students on authentic products (e.g., creating and making things, solving problems, responding to stimulations) that demonstrate their skills, problem-solving abilities, knowledge, and understanding of the learning standards. Similarly, student portfolios and curriculum-based measurements that are linked to the learning standards serve as tools for grading students and guiding the teaching and learning process.

▶ **Providing Feedback on Assignments and Grading Students After They Have Learned Something Rather Than While They Are Learning It.** Before grading students on an assignment or a test, teachers should provide a range of appropriate learning activities and give non-graded assignments that help students practice and develop their skills. As students work on these assignments, teachers should give them feedback and additional instructional experiences to improve their learning of the material, which is then assessed when they have completed the learning cycle.

▶ **Avoiding Competition and Promoting Collaboration.** While grading on a curve results in a consistent grade distribution, it hinders the teaching and learning process by promoting competition among students. Therefore, educators minimize competition by grading students in reference to specific learning criteria and refraining from posting grades. Teachers also promote collaboration among students by structuring learning and assessments activities so that students work together and are graded co-operatively.

▶ **Designing Valid Tests and Providing Students with Appropriate Testing Accommodations.** Teachers enhance the value of their tests and promote student performance by developing valid tests and providing students with appropriate testing accommodations. In designing valid tests, teachers select the content of the test so that it relates to the learning standards, the manner in which the content was taught, and the amount of class time devoted to the topics on the test. Teachers also carefully examine the format and readability of their tests, and provide students with the testing accommodations outlined on their IEPs.

▶ **Teaching Test-Taking to Students.** Instruction in test-taking skills helps students perform at their optimal levels by reducing testing anxiety and assisting them in feeling comfortable with the format of the test.

Adapted from "Grading Students in Inclusive Settings" (pp. 13–14) by S. Salend & L. M. G. Duhaney, 2002, *Teaching Exceptional Children, 34*(3).

Summary

▶ The curriculum for elementary students with exceptionalities should meet their current and long-term needs, facilitate their interactions with typically achieving peers, and facilitate their transition into junior high school.

▶ Reading instruction should reflect emphases on both decoding skills and whole language to provide a comprehensive, balanced program.

▶ Math instruction should provide students with concrete and abstract learning opportunities and should stress the development of problem-solving skills.

▶ Teachers should select programs and strategies that focus on the social skills most needed by students in their classrooms.

▶ Life skills instruction should be a part of the elementary curriculum through the use of augmentation, infusion, or an integrated curriculum.

▶ Instructional adaptations should be evaluated against their "treatment acceptability"—that is, their feasibility, desirability, helpfulness, and fairness.

▶ Listening is a skill that requires conscious effort on the part of students and planned intervention strategies on the part of teachers.

▶ Reading tasks can be adapted through a variety of instructional strategies such as clarifying intent, highlighting content, modifying difficulty level, and using visual aids.

▶ Written responses can be facilitated through modification of the response requirement.

▶ Co-operative learning affords teachers a unique opportunity to involve students with disabilities in classroom activities, but should not be used exclusively.

▶ Adaptations to class schedules or classroom arrangements should be considered in order to enhance the learning of students with exceptionalities.

▶ Motivation to learn cannot be taken for granted, and educational programs should be designed to reflect its importance.

▶ Homework creates significant challenges for students with special needs; these should be addressed by using intervention strategies.

▶ Classroom grading practices should be flexible enough to facilitate inclusion.

Resources

Teaching Exceptional Children

All articles provide practical hands-on suggestions for use in the elementary or secondary classroom. The practical magazine for teachers is available through Council for Exceptional Children at **www.cec.sped.org/**.

Deschenes, Cathy, Ebeling, David, and Sprague, Jeffery. (1994). *Adapting curriculum & instruction in inclusive classrooms: A teacher's desk reference*. Bloomington, IN: Center for School and Community Integration, Institute for the Study of Developmental Disabilities.

This practical listing of ways to adapt curriculum to have a successful inclusive classroom is an extremely useful resource. See also the Staff Development Kit.

Weblinks

Classroom Resources

http://classroomresources.com
Classroom Resources is an excellent Canadian website that offers a variety of classroom resources with Canadian content and representation of Canadian student diversity. It is a must visit for all teachers to see (and download) the latest Canadian Content flyer which reviews in detail different books and classroom resources and states their uses in curriculum design. This material will help teachers to include students from all backgrounds in their daily curricula.

School Psychology Resource

www.bcpl.net/~sandyste/school_psych.html
As a website for school psychologists, educators, and parents, this resource covers different exceptionalities, special education procedures (e.g., sample IEPs), and information on all topics relevant to psychology in the schools such as violence, child abuse, suicide, and parent collaboration. Although American based, it has excellent information and materials relevant to Canadian teachers.

The Education Planet—The Education Web Guide

http://educationplanet.com

This search engine covers all education-relevant sites. If you want to find specifically Canadian material, you can limit searches to Canadian sources. The highly interesting and rewarding resource provides access to lesson plans, videos, manuals, curriculum materials, and much more!

Teachers.net

http://teachers.net

As a huge U.S. website, Teachers.net covers a variety of topics of interest to teachers, including curriculum sugges-tions, resources, and chat rooms with different education issues. It has subject-specific listings of chatboards where ideas, such as teaching secondary school math in innovative ways, are shared. Many resources are available through this website for elementary and secondary teachers.

Canadian.Teachers.net

http://canadian.teachers.net/

This uniquely Canadian offshoot of Teachers.net provides a specifically Canadian forum with chat rooms, job postings, catalogues, information, professional development with guest speakers, and listings of related sites.

14 Teaching Students with Special Needs in Secondary Schools

After reading this chapter, you should be able to

- define the concept of a comprehensive curriculum and discuss curricular alternatives for students with exceptionalities
- discuss ways to determine the curricular needs of secondary school students
- discuss the transition planning process for students with exceptionalities
- identify and describe the key elements of effective instruction
- discuss the roles of general education and special education teachers in ensuring successful secondary school programs for students with special needs
- identify accommodations and/or adaptations that can facilitate learning for secondary school students
- identify and give examples of study skills and learning strategies that can enhance school performance for adolescent learners
- define transition and describe how school personnel should implement transition planning and services

Stephanie Hughes went through university loving the study of literature. She majored in English and selected as many courses as she could that focused on literature. Her particular interest was twentieth-century Canadian literature, and she completed an honours paper on Robertson Davies. After graduation, she chose to pursue her dream to teach high school English.

For the past three years, Stephanie has been teaching Grades 9 and 10 English. Because of the trend toward inclusion, her class roll often includes a number of students with special needs, particularly students with learning disabilities. The diversity of her class has led her to question how she can best instill her love of literature in these students while addressing their individual learning needs. She is greatly concerned about the low reading levels of some of the students (several at about Grade 3 or 4) and their lack of motivation for study in areas that they find neither inherently interesting nor relevant to their future.

Questions to Consider

1. How can co-operative learning be used to facilitate instruction in this secondary school classroom?

2. What accommodations, adaptations, and/or modifications will assist the students with special needs in learning important content and in being appropriately evaluated and graded?

3. How can Stephanie make the curricular content more relevant to the future lives of these students when they finish high school?

Introduction

CONSIDER THIS

Do special education support staff need different skills at the secondary level than they need in elementary schools? If so, what are some of the differences?

Important differences exist between elementary and secondary settings in terms of organizational structure, curricula, and learner variables. These differences create special challenges for successful inclusion. Certainly one concern is the gap found between the demands of the classroom setting and the ability of many students with exceptionalities. Academically, this gap widens; many students with exceptionalities exhibit limited basic skills and therefore experience difficulty in performing higher-level cognitive tasks. These basic skills include gaining information from textbooks, memorizing large amounts of information, paraphrasing, discriminating important information from the less important, taking notes, writing themes, proofreading papers, and taking tests successfully (Schumaker & Deshler, 1988).

A second concern is that teachers are often trained primarily as content specialists, yet are expected to present complex material in such a way that a diverse group of students can master the information (Masters, Mori, & Mori, 1999). Secondary teachers are more likely to focus on teaching the content than on individualizing instruction to meet the unique needs of each student. Further, because there may be reluctance to change grading systems or make other accommodations, it may become difficult for students with exceptionalities to experience success in general education settings.

A third challenge is the general nature of adolescence. Adolescence is a difficult and trying time for all young people. For students with exceptionalities, the developmental period is even more challenging. Problems such as a lack of motivation associated with adolescence are exacerbated by the presence of a disability (Masters et al., 1999).

Perhaps, given these concerns, it is not surprising to find that secondary teachers have been less positive overall toward efforts at inclusion (Scruggs & Mastropieri, 1996). However, regardless of the difficulties associated with placing adolescents with special needs in general education programs, more students with exceptionalities are going to depend on classroom teachers to help develop and provide appropriate educational programs. Therefore, classroom teachers in secondary schools must be prepared to offer specialized instruction and modified curricula to facilitate success for students with exceptionalities.

Secondary School Curricula

More curricular differentiation has been advocated at the secondary level to accommodate the individual needs and interests of the wide variety of students attending high school. At the same time, most high schools have a general curriculum that all students must complete. This curriculum, typically prescribed by the provincial education ministry, includes science, math, social studies, English, and French. Often, provinces and local education boards add to the required general curriculum such areas as education on sexuality, drug education, and third languages.

Although the specific curricula offered in different secondary schools vary, they generally follow provincial guidelines. Individual schools, however, do offer unique curricular options that appeal to particular students. The curricular focus that students choose should be an important consideration, because the decision could have long-term implications after the students exit school.

Special Education Curriculum in Secondary Schools

The curriculum for students with exceptionalities is the most critical programming consideration in secondary schools. Even if students have excellent teachers, if the curriculum is inappropriate to meet their needs, then the teaching may be ineffective. The high school curriculum for students with exceptionalities must be comprehensive—that is, it must

- be responsive to the needs of individual students;
- facilitate maximum integration with typically achieving peers;
- facilitate socialization;
- focus on the students' transition to post-secondary settings.

In 1979, Alley and Deshler identified five curricular approaches commonly used with secondary special education students: (1) basic skills remediation, (2) tutorial approach, (3) learning strategies model, (4) functional curriculum, and (5) work-study model. A more recent model includes these focuses:

- Basic skills (i.e., remediation of academic deficits)
- Social skills (i.e., stress on social adjustment)
- Tutorial (i.e., receiving support within the regular curriculum)
- Learning strategies (i.e., teaching students to be independent learners)
- Vocational (i.e., job training)
- Life skills (i.e., independent living training)

Each model has a different emphasis. Basic skills and social skills models endeavour to train students to develop the ability to successfully function in the general education classroom. Tutorial and learning strategies models present short-term and long-term solutions, respectively, to provide students with support to retain them in general education. Vocational and life skills programs focus on preparing the student for successful community living and adult adjustment. (See Polloway & Patton, 1997, for a detailed discussion.)

Determining Curricular Needs of Students

As noted in Chapter 13, the adoption of a curriculum for any student should be based on an appraisal of desired long-term outcomes and an assessment of current needs. At the elementary level, consideration of the future demands of middle and high school suggests a primary focus on the development and refinement of basic academic and social skills, as well as a beginning emphasis on career awareness and life skills.

Polloway and Patton (1997) suggest that elementary students also be taught specific skills that will facilitate success in high school, such as self-management, study skills, note taking, and homework skills. Still other nonacademic abilities, such as resisting peer pressure, negotiating, accepting negative feedback, and asking questions, should be addressed in the elementary curriculum to facilitate the success of students in secondary settings (Hazel, Schumaker, Shelon, & Sherman, 1982). Although some schools in the process of restructuring are providing learning opportunities in these areas, many schools continue to focus on academics.

Regardless of the seemingly "common" areas that should be included in an elementary curriculum, curricular variation is common. The result is that students arrive in secondary settings with a wide range of academic preparation and varying, often limited, degrees of exposure to transitional subjects such as life skills, career awareness, study

FURTHER READING

For more information on secondary special education models, read "Comprehensive Curriculum for Students with Mild Handicaps," by E. A. Polloway, J. R. Patton, M. H. Epstein, & T. E. C. Smith, 1989, *Focus on Exceptional Children, 21,* pp. 1–12.

skills, and self-management. Curricular considerations and decisions are critically important since high school represents a final chance for public education personnel to prepare students for their postschool futures. Data on school exit patterns and follow-up studies of students with exceptionalities have, for the most part, suggested that schools need to improve programs that prepare students with exceptionalities for life after high school. As many as 50 percent of students with learning disabilities will drop out of high school. Bender (1998) thinks that the true number of students with learning disabilities who do not finish high school is even higher.

Several studies have shown that adults with exceptionalities are likely to be employed part-time, underemployed, or unemployed to a significantly greater degree than their typically achieving peers (Edgar, 1988; Edgar & Polloway, 1994). Therefore, regardless of the efforts made in secondary schools to meet the individual needs of students with exceptionalities, many of these students seem unprepared to achieve success as young adults.

Students themselves are aware that they are not being adequately prepared for post–high school demands. In comparing the transitional needs of high school students with learning disabilities to those of their typically achieving peers, Dowdy, Carter, and Smith (1990) found that, although both groups expressed an interest in help with career decisions, significant differences were noted in their thoughts about the future. For example, students with learning disabilities were far more concerned with learning how to find a job, how to keep a job, and how to live independently. As a group, students with exceptionalities expressed greater insecurity about their futures than did students without exceptionalities.

In order to ensure that students have the optimum chance at success after schooling concludes, transition planning is essential. Transitions represent ongoing challenges that can be identified as horizontal (from a more segregated to a more integrated society) and vertical (across the lifespan) (see Figure 14.1). Of primary concern here is the transition to adulthood from school, which is in itself a multifaceted process (see Figure 14.2 for a model).

One helpful way for the schools to view this process is through the **future-based assessment** and intervention model (see Figure 14.3). In the first step of the model, parents and student have a conference with school personnel to identify the student's interests and goals in terms of post-secondary training, employment, and independent living. During this step, all parties involved in the planning identify the desired future for the student. The appropriateness of these goals is tested in the second step of the model, through administration of a comprehensive assessment battery. In this process, information on the student's future in areas such as academic potential, vocational potential and interests, and social skills is collected. In step 3, the original team is reconvened to consider the impact of the assessment data on the goals developed during step 1. Goals might be revised at this time to more accurately reflect the student's ability levels.

In step 4, the skills needed to succeed in the designated goals are identified. These skills are then compared to the current skill levels of the student, and the discrepancies are identified (step 5). After this analysis, in step 6, curricular choices are made: these provide the training and education necessary to facilitate the student's success in each area. For students with exceptionalities, these goals should be delineated in the IEP and also reflected in individual transition plans (ITPs). See Figure 14.4 for an example of the relationship between IEP and ITP goals.

The final step reflects the constant need for monitoring to affirm that the curricular choices are appropriate. This ongoing review and analysis allows teachers, parents, and the students themselves to know what progress is being made toward future goals. If progress is insufficient, or more rapid than anticipated, the goals may need to be adjusted.

Although students with exceptionalities have IEPs that detail specific goals, objectives, and services, the programs must be related to a particular curricular model. As previously noted, without an appropriate curriculum, educational programs necessarily

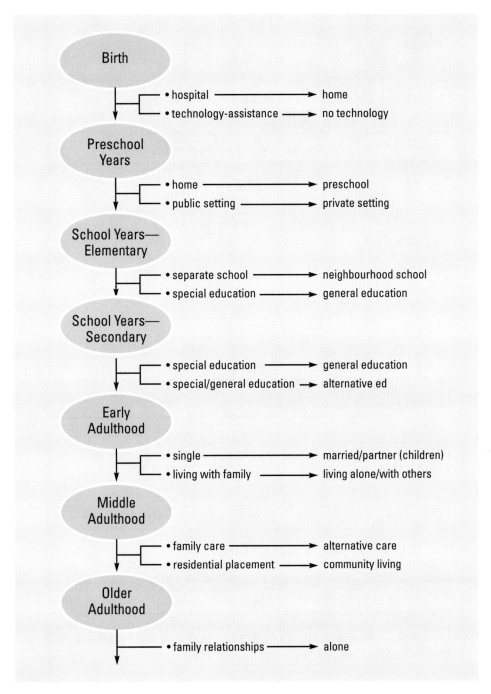

FIGURE 14.1

Vertical and Horizontal Transitions

From *Transition from School to Adult Life for Students with Special Needs: Basic Concepts and Recommended Practices* (p. 14), by J. R. Patton, 1995, Austin, TX: Pro-Ed. Copyright 1995 by Pro-Ed. Reprinted by permission.

become unfocused. Figure 14.5 summarizes factors related to making curricular decisions for students with exceptionalities.

Programs for Students in Secondary Schools

Most secondary students with exceptionalities are currently included in general education classrooms for at least a portion of each school day. Therefore, the responsibility for

FIGURE 14.2

Elements of the Transition Process

From *Transition from School to Adult Life for Students with Special Needs: Basic Concepts and Recommended Practices* (p. 10), by J. R. Patton, 1995, Austin, TX: Pro-Ed. Copyright 1995 by Pro-Ed. Reprinted by permission.

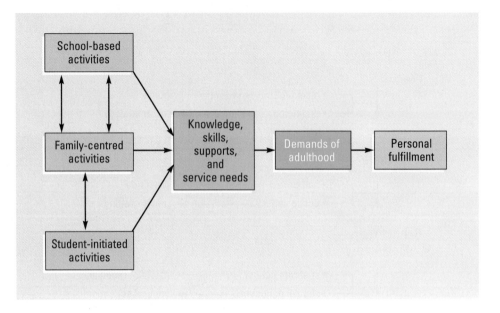

FIGURE 14.3

Future-Based Assessment and Intervention Model

From "Future-Based Assessment and Intervention for Students with Mental Retardation," by T. E. C. Smith and C. A. Dowdy, 1992, *Education and Training in Mental Retardation, 27*, p. 258. Used by permission.

STEP 1

Student/parent interview: Identify interests and goals for post-secondary training, employment, and independent living.

STEP 2

Conduct comprehensive assessment including academic, vocational, and independent living skills.

STEP 3

Interdisciplinary team meeting: Analyze assessment data and refine future goals.

STEP 4

Determine the characteristics/skills necessary for individuals to be successful in future vocational, academic, and independent living situations.

STEP 5

Identify discrepancies between the characteristics/skills of the student and the skills necessary for success in designated future academic, employment, and independent living situations.

STEP 6

Develop and implement intervention plans (IEPs and Transition plans) to address discrepancies identified in step 5.

STEP 7

Ongoing analysis of student characteristics and future vocational, academic, and social situations to determine if adjustments regarding future needs are to be made (must be done on an annual basis).

I. **Transition (ITP) Goals**	II. **Instructional (IEP) Annual Goals**
ITP activities or objectives	
A. Demonstrating self-advocacy about learning support needs	A. Demonstrate self-advocacy about learning support needs
	Objective 1: The student will identify own learning strengths.
	Objective 2: The student will identify own learning needs and related supports.
	Objective 3: The student will discuss necessary learning supports with high school counsellor.
B. Researching specific university offerings	B. Research five universities' academic and special support offerings
C. Selecting a major	C. Select a major for the freshman year in university
	Objective 1: The student will participate in career/vocational and academic assessment.
	Objective 2: The student will review findings of all assessment results with teacher or counsellor.
	Objective 3: The student will explore five occupational directions that emerge from the assessment, in library and on computer.
	Objective 4: The student will select one occupational area that seems most promising and match that area to major areas at the selected university.

FIGURE 14.4

Relationship between ITP Goals and IEP Goals and Objectives

Adapted from "Transition and Students with Learning Disabilities: Creating Sound Futures," by G. Blalock and J. Patton, 1996, *Journal of Learning Disabilities, 29*, p. 12. Copyright © 1996 by PRO-ED, Inc. Reprinted with permission.

these students becomes a joint effort between general education classroom teachers and special education personnel (Walther-Thomas et al., 2000). Unfortunately, many of these students do not experience success in the general classroom setting. They frequently fail classes, become frustrated and act out, and may even drop out of school because they are not prepared to meet the demands placed on them by secondary teachers. There are numerous reasons why many students with exceptionalities fail in secondary classes:

- Lack of communication between special education personnel and classroom teachers
- Discrepancies between the expectations of classroom teachers and the abilities of students
- Students' lack of understanding about the demands of the classroom
- Classroom teachers' lack of understanding and knowledge about students with exceptionalities
- Special education personnel's lack of knowledge in working with classroom teachers

Regardless of the reasons why some students with exceptionalities do not achieve success in general education settings, the fact remains that the majority will be taught in inclusive settings. Therefore, educators, both classroom teachers and special education personnel, must work together to increase the chances that these students will be successful.

Roles of Personnel

As noted, the responsibility for educating students with exceptionalities in public schools is shared by general classroom teachers and special education personnel. Therefore, educators must improve their skills at working together to help students with various learning and behaviour problems.

CONSIDER THIS

The roles of general educators and special educators must change for effective inclusion to occur. What are some likely barriers to these changes, and how can they be overcome?

FIGURE 14.5

Factors Related to Curricular Decisions

From "Comprehensive Curriculum for Students with Mild Handicaps," by E. A. Polloway, J. R. Patton, M. H. Epstein, and T. E. C. Smith, 1989, *Focus on Exceptional Children, 21*(8), p. 8. Used by permission.

1. Student variables
   - Cognitive-intellectual level
   - Academic skills preparedness
   - Academic achievement as determined by tests
   - Academic achievement as determined by class grades
   - Grade placement
   - Motivation and responsibility
   - Social interactions with peers and adults
   - Behavioural self-control

2. Family variables
   - Short- and long-term parental expectations
   - Degree of support provided (e.g., financial, emotional, academic)
   - Parental values toward education
   - Cultural influence (e.g., language, values)

3. General education variables
   - Teacher and nondisabled student acceptance of diversity (classroom climate)
   - Administrative support for integrated education
   - Availability of curricular variance
   - Accommodative capacity of the classroom
   - Flexibility of daily class schedules and units earned toward graduation
   - Options for vocational programs

4. Special education variables
   - Size of caseload
   - Availability of paraprofessionals or tutors in the classroom
   - Access to curricular materials
   - Focus of teacher's training
   - Consultative and materials support available
   - Related services available to students

General education teachers are primarily responsible for students with special needs in their classrooms.

General Education Teachers

The primary role of general classroom teachers is to assume the responsibility for students with exceptionalities in particular classes or subject areas. Most classroom teachers present information using one general technique, but they will probably have to expand their instructional activities when dealing with students with exceptionalities. Various accommodations, adaptations, and/or modifications in instructional techniques and materials will be discussed later in the chapter.

Classroom teachers have general responsibilities for *all* of the students in their classes. These include managing the classroom environment, providing instruction at an appropriate level and pace, using an appropriate curriculum, evaluating student success, and modifying instruction as appropriate. For students with exceptionalities, general classroom teachers have the added responsibility of participating on an interdisciplinary team (Masters et al., 1999).

In addition, teachers should ensure that all students have an opportunity to answer questions and a good chance at achieving at least moderate success in classroom activities. This is not a call for teachers to "give" students with exceptionalities passing grades, only a request that students with exceptionalities receive an equal chance at being successful.

Classroom teachers should also do all they can to work effectively with special education professionals. Open communication and dialogue between classroom teachers and special education personnel is crucial if inclusion is to be successful. Communication among all individuals providing services to students with exceptionalities is the most important factor related to the success of inclusion (Walther-Thomas et al., 2000).

When working with students who have exceptionalities, classroom teachers must realize that no single method always works; teachers have to individualize their efforts, constantly evaluating the effectiveness of their teaching efforts. Christenson, Ysseldyke, and Thurlow (1989) describe some of them:

1. *Classroom management:* Research has demonstrated that classes in which teachers have effective behaviour management procedures in place have more time for student involvement and instruction. The key is to be proactive in setting up a well-thought-out routine and a few clearly stated classroom rules and procedures. Classroom rules should always be stated in positive terms. Teachers cannot assume that students will know how to act if the rule only tells them how *not* to act. For example, instead of posting a rule that students may not sit on the tops of desks, state that students should sit on their chairs, with feet on the floor.

2. *Positive school environment:* Students learn more effectively in a classroom in which a humanistic focus combines with an academic orientation (Samuels, 1986). When planning each day's activities, teachers should build in tasks or adaptations and/or accommodations that will offer each student a measure of success. All students need to be successful from time to time to maintain their attention and motivation. Using co-operative learning activities, such as those described in Chapter 13, is another way to develop a positive atmosphere.

    Teachers should always set high goals for students and make students feel that the teacher is confident that they can achieve the goals. Students need to believe that their teachers care about them and will support them in their efforts.

3. *Appropriate instructional match:* The degree of instructional match can be determined by a discrepancy analysis comparing the characteristics of the student and the demands of the task. Analyzing the students' capabilities is often difficult because of the hidden nature of many mild cognitive disabilities.

    It is important for teachers to know the unique characteristics of their students, especially those with exceptionalities or who are at risk of developing behaviour problems or emotional problems. Achievement levels of students are frequently only the tip of the iceberg when it comes to functioning successfully in class. Less obvious characteristics, such as inattention, distractibility, slow work rate, and difficulty processing multiple directions, can be the major culprits preventing successful learning. Accommodations, adaptations, and/or modifications must address these specific characteristics (see Table 14.1).

4. *Clear teaching goals and expectations:* Effective teachers have a carefully developed master plan that includes teaching goals for each lesson. These goals are important for the teachers, to focus their instruction, but teachers should also communicate these goals to the students frequently and explicitly. Students have a tendency to perform better when they know the specific goals of the instruction. It is better for teachers to say, "Today you are going to learn the steps of the scientific method" than to say "Today we are going to study the scientific method." Teachers should set high expectations, monitor achievement continuously, and give frequent, task-specific feedback.

5. *Quality of instruction:* One of the primary roles for all teachers is to provide quality instruction. In order to do this, teachers need to explain lessons clearly, use modelling and demonstration techniques, and monitor whether the concepts are understood by students (Rosenshine & Stevens, 1986). The following outline of steps used in an effective lesson has been adapted from the work of Deshler, Schumaker, Lenz, and Ellis (1984):

- Review the previous lesson.
- Use an advance organizer or graphic organizer to introduce the lesson.
- Obtain student attention and commitment to learn.
- Provide direct instruction (include modelling, demonstration, examples, manipulatives).

FURTHER READING

For more information on specific techniques to use with students with exceptionalities in general education classrooms, read *Teaching Adolescents with Learning Disabilities,* by D. Deshler, E. Ellis, and K. Lenz, published in 1996 by Love Publishing.

TEACHING TIP

Perform self-monitoring (or monitor teachers you may be observing) to determine the amount of time spent in teaching. What are some ways to increase the amount of teaching?

TABLE 14.1	Examples of Accommodations and Modifications
Characteristic	**Accommodations and Modifications**
Difficulty Completing Assignments	▸ List or post (and say) all steps necessary to complete each assignment. ▸ Break the assignment into manageable sections with specific due dates. ▸ Make frequent checks for work/assignment completion. ▸ Arrange for the student to have a "study buddy," with phone number, in each subject area.
DifficultY with Tasks that require memory	▸ Combine seeing, saying, writing, and doing; student may need to subvocalize to remember. ▸ Teach memory techniques as a study strategy (e.g., mnemonics, visualization, oral rehearsal, numerous repetitions).
Difficulty with Test Taking	▸ Allow extra time for testing; teach test-taking skills and strategies; allow student to be tested orally. ▸ Use clear, readable, and uncluttered test forms. Use test format that the student is most comfortable with. Allow ample space for student response. Consider having lined answer spaces for essay and short-answer tests.
Confusion from non-verbal Cues (Misreads body language, etc.)	▸ Directly teach (tell the student) what nonverbal cues mean. Model them, and have student practise reading cues in a safe setting.
Confusion from written Material (Difficulty finding main idea from a paragraph; attributes greater importance to minor details)	▸ Provide student with copy of reading material with main ideas underlined or highlighted. ▸ Provide an outline of important points from reading material. ▸ Teach outlining, main idea versus details, concepts. ▸ Provide tape of text.
Confusion from spoken Material, lectures, and audio-visual Material (Difficulty finding main idea, attributes greater importance to minor details)	▸ Provide student with a copy of presentation notes. ▸ Allow peers to share carbon-copy notes from presentation (have student compare own notes with copy of peer's notes). ▸ Provide framed outlines of presentations (introducing visual and auditory cues to important information). ▸ Encourage use of tape recorder. ▸ Teach and emphasize key words (the following . . . , the most important . . . , etc.)

▸ Use a variety of tasks, activities, and questions to maintain interest and generate student response.

▸ Provide guided practice (monitor boardwork, simple worksheets, small group games with teacher).

▸ Provide independent practice for generalization (homework, workbooks, regular textbooks, computer, games).

▸ Ask students to evaluate learning/use informal tests (rapid-fire questioning, brief written assessment).

▸ Close with a summary and transition to next lesson. Provide student feedback as appropriate. Document observations: student and self-evaluation. (Table 14.2 shows a list of these steps with questions that can be used by teachers for self-evaluation following a lesson.)

6. *Instructional support for individual students:* Instruction is made more effective when teachers monitor students' work frequently and adjust or adapt instruction to meet individual needs of students. Some students require more guided practice, more drill, and more practice to reach automaticity.

When students are moved too quickly through the curriculum, they often do not

TABLE 14.2	Steps in an Effective Lesson and Corresponding Evaluation Questions

Steps	Questions
1. Reviews previous lesson	Was my transition smooth and meaningful?
2. Uses advanced organizer to introduce new lesson	Were my objectives clear? Did I have the right number of objectives?
3. Obtains student attention and commitment to learn	Was my motivational or attention-getting technique effective? Did I make the lesson relevant to the student?
4. Provides direct instruction (includes modelling, demonstration, manipulatives)	Was my subject matter background okay? Did I use overhead, chalkboard, graphics, models, etc.? Was there a balance between student and teacher talk?
5. Uses a variety of tasks, activities, and questions to maintain interest and generate student responses	Were my questions effective? Did my class ask questions? Did I wait for replies to my questions? Did I involve all students?
6. Provides guided practice (boardwork, simple worksheets, small group games with teacher)	Did I transform students from "passive listeners" to "active participants"? Was teacher activity balanced with student activity? Did I provide timely feedback?
7. Provides independent practice for generalization (workbooks, textbooks, computer, games)	Did I include appropriate homework? Did I use materials that require generalization?
8. Asks students to evaluate learning, uses informal tests (rapid-fire questioning, brief written assessment)	If I didn't know something, did I promise to look it up? Did I ask them what they had learned, to teach self-evaluation? Was my assessment directly related to my objective?
9. Closes with summary and transition to next lesson	Did I have a smooth closing and transition to the next activity?
10. Provides student feedback as appropriate	Did I identify students who needed an individual behaviour change plan?
11. Documents observations: students and self	Was my behaviour management technique effective? Was learning effective and fun?

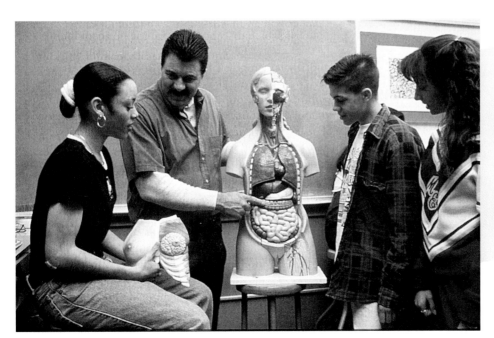

Effective teachers use a master plan for lessons, including specific teaching goals.

obtain sufficient practice to maintain and then generalize instruction. Waiting until evaluation time may result in several days of wasted instruction. By providing ongoing monitoring and instructional support, teachers can prevent students from sitting in classes without realizing success.

7. *Efficient use of time:* One of the most important roles of classroom teachers is to maximize instructional time with students. The amount of time teachers allocate to instruction, the amount of time students actually spend engaged in academic tasks, and the amount of time students spend in active academic responding are critical in determining a student's opportunity to learn. For students with exceptionalities, efficient use of time is even more important.

   Although the amount of time allotted for instruction is important, the quality of instruction is also critical. Simply having students spend large amounts of time in academic activities does not guarantee learning. An example is having students complete worksheets when they may not understand the concepts or have already learned the concepts. Teachers must consider allocation of time and the quality of activities designated for each time period.

8. *Substantive student interaction:* Teachers need to facilitate student interaction. Research has shown that the opportunity to engage in active academic responses is positively correlated with academic achievement (Reid, 1986). Effective teachers give cues and prompts that can increase students' correct responses and thus increase the amount of positive feedback they receive. It is important for all students to have an opportunity to actively participate. Many students with exceptionalities have slow processing abilities and oral language difficulties; therefore, teachers may need to develop strategies to facilitate their interactions. Peer tutoring, choral responding, and co-operative learning offer alternative opportunities for active responding that may benefit students with problems.

9. *Monitoring of student understanding and progress:* Active and frequent monitoring is the key to keeping the total instructional cycle effective (Good & Brophy, 1987). Although teachers plan instruction for groups of students, frequent monitoring of individuals and adapting the instruction help maintain the match between the individual and the instruction. Effective monitoring should require students to demonstrate the learned skill, not simply state that they have no questions. The first items of a practice set should be checked by the teacher. Students should also be asked to explain what they are doing to ensure that an efficient strategy has been selected.

   If teachers wait until a grade-reporting period to evaluate a student's progress, significant amounts of instructional time may be lost. Therefore, constant ongoing monitoring is an important task for teachers with students who have exceptionalities.

10. *Evaluation of student performance:* Direct assessment of student knowledge is essential for determining whether instructional goals and objectives have been reached. Effective assessment requires frequent evaluation designed to measure exactly what has been taught. Feedback should be explicit regarding the inaccuracy or accuracy of the response, and it should be directly related to the task being completed by the student. For example, "You have really learned the steps in the scientific method" is preferable to "You have really worked hard on this." Through frequent testing, teachers can make better, data-based decisions to determine future goals.

TEACHING TIP

Evaluation of student performance must be continual in order to provide teachers with feedback to determine the effectiveness of the instructional program and thereby necessary changes.

When teaching content courses, such as history and science, teachers should treat students with exceptionalities as they treat all other students, remembering that the students with special needs would not be placed in the general classroom setting if an interdisciplinary team had not determined that they could benefit from instruction in that environment.

Within the classroom, teachers can do several things that will facilitate the success of students with exceptionalities. They can modify the environment, alter the task presentation, vary the student requirements, and make the grading procedures more flexible (Finson & Ormsbee, 1998; Salend, 1998). They must remember that students with excep-

Personal Spotlight

Secondary Teacher Akapelwa Mweemba

Akapelwa Mweemba has been teaching math and science at the junior and senior high levels for more than a decade. He has been involved in a pilot project preparing the Science 10 documents for the Manitoba Department of Education. In 1996 he received the Prime Minister's Award for Excellence in Science Education.

Akapelwa is noted for use of peer tutoring in his inclusive classes. "A great part of my success lies in the use of peer tutoring as a viable and effective teaching strategy. New material is generally taught in conventional ways. Following this, to reinforce the new material learned, the class breaks into groups and peer tutoring ensues. Students who have a firm grasp of the concepts tutor those who are having difficulty. Through this strategy, I have found that the students' abilities to verbally communicate their knowledge improve. The bonus to this method is reversal of roles: the student today will become the tutor tomorrow. It provides every student with a chance to succeed at different points in the course."

Akapelwa speaks at length about the advantages of the peer-tutoring method in his classroom, listing efficiency, structure, a student-centred nature, and, perhaps most important of all, the development of a family atmosphere whereby students help each other. He has made inclusion work in his class but observes that there are hurdles to accomplishing this. "One of the greatest problems associated with inclusion in the secondary class lies in the fact that the pace may be somewhat compromised. The class may tend to move at the pace of the 'slowest' learner for any given unit. In a fast-paced, finish-the-curriculum-at-all-costs type agenda, the slower learners may not benefit. However, this is *not* an insurmountable obstacle. The challenge would be to create an environment where success for all learners is guaranteed. Success is defined in *personal* terms through what individuals can accomplish with their abilities."

Akapelwa did not always use peer tutoring, initially believing in a more traditional approach to instruction. However, being attuned to problem solving and analytical by nature led him to adopt the practice. "I had been in Westpark School a couple of years when it became evident that a number of students' math skills were below level. To help I tried conducting tutoring after school. Very often this meant repeating previous classes. As I thought about this dilemma, it became clear I needed to change the way I conducted my classes. One student in particular functioned at Grade 5 level in math when she was in Grade 7. After working with Patti for a long time and watching her in class, I realized she often sought the help of a particular student who connected with her. I realized, then, that if I could utilize peers in a more organized fashion, I would maximize my efforts and results. This was the birth of the peer-tutoring program. Subsequently, Patti even stated that math was fun! Earlier on in my training I bought into the philosophy that 'anybody can learn anything... provided conditions are right.' It has become my mission to provide those conditions to the best of my abilities."

tionalities, as well as students without exceptionalities, have different learning styles and needs and therefore may require some alteration of instruction.

Collaborative Role of the Special Education Teacher

The special education teacher plays an important role in the successful inclusion of students with exceptionalities in secondary schools. In addition to collaborating with general educators, the special education teacher must prepare students for the challenges that occur daily in the general education environment and equip them for future challenges in independent living and employment. Above all, special education teachers play a major support role for general classroom teachers. They should communicate regularly with classroom teachers and provide assistance through consultation or through direct instruction (Masters et al., 1999).

FURTHER READING

For more information on collaborative activities of special educators, read Sharon Cramer's book, *Collaboration: A Success Strategy for Special Educators*, published by Allyn & Bacon in 1997.

The specific roles of the special education teacher include counselling students for the personal crises that may occur daily and preparing students for content classes, high school exams, post-secondary training, independent living, and, ultimately, employment (Smith, Finn, & Dowdy, 1993). Special education teachers and general teachers often collaborate in performing these roles.

Counselling for Daily Crises Adolescence is a difficult time of change for all children; for children with exceptionalities, the period is even more challenging. In our society, students are constantly trying to grasp the subtle changes in roles for males and females. They experience more exposure to drugs and alcohol, and pregnancy and HIV/AIDS are common issues. The increased tension, frustration, and depression can lead to suicide, the second leading cause of death among adolescents (Smith et al., 1993; Spirito, Hart, Overholser, & Halverson, 1990), or a variety of behaviour and emotional problems. Special education teachers need to collaborate with general educators to help students deal with these problems.

CROSS-REFERENCE

Review materials in Chapters 3 through 11, and reflect on how different exceptionalities have an impact on preparation for high school content courses.

Preparing for High School Content Classes The special education teacher should be aware of factors such as classroom teacher expectations, teaching styles, and the demands of the learning environment (Welch & Link, 1991). One way special education teachers can help students deal with the "general education world" is to teach them how to self-advocate. In order to do this, students need to understand their specific learning problems. Therefore, special education teachers may need to have a discussion with their students about the nature of specific disabilities.

Deshler, Ellis, and Lenz (1996) suggest that the primary role of special education teachers should be to teach their students effective strategies for generalization to compensate for their learning deficits and therefore increase the likelihood of success in general education classes. They suggest teaching numerous strategies for memorizing, test taking, listening, note taking, proofreading, time management, and organization. Specific techniques for these will be discussed later in the chapter. If students with learning problems know how to use these kinds of strategies, they will have a better chance of achieving success in general classrooms.

When working with students with exceptionalities in general education classrooms, the role of the special educator expands. It includes informing the general educator as to the unique abilities and challenges presented by each student, providing ongoing support and **collaboration** for the student and teacher, and doing frequent monitoring to ensure that the arrangement is satisfactory for both the student and the teacher.

Preparing for High School Exams The requirements regarding final high school credit exams vary across Canada. These exams are monitored by the appropriate ministry of education and are aimed at maintaining a province- or territory-wide standard of performance.

Special education teachers, in conjunction with classroom teachers, have two roles regarding high school exams. On the one hand, they are obligated to help the student prepare for the exam if the student is required to take the exam. On the other hand, they may choose to focus on convincing the student and parents that time could more appropriately be spent on developing living skills rather than on preparing for exams. Information on testing is discussed later in the chapter.

Preparing for Post-secondary Training Students with exceptionalities absolutely should aim for post-secondary education if they have the ability and motivation. This is one component of a transition program for students. Post-secondary education does not have to mean attending a university. A community college, vocational-technical school, trade school, or some other form of post-secondary education and training are other possibilities. Teachers, both general and special education, need to inform students about future employment trends and help them select realistic careers with employment potential. A variety of reports regarding the importance of education in the future for students with and without exceptionalities have concluded the following:

1. Higher levels of academic achievement will be required, and very few jobs will be appropriate for individuals deficient in reading, writing, and math.
2. There will be an increase in service industry jobs and a decrease in manufacturing jobs.
3. More than half of new jobs created in the 1990s required education beyond high school, and more than a third were filled by university graduates.
4. Technology will play an increasing role for all individuals.

Preparing for Independent Living Independent living is a realistic goal for the vast majority of individuals with exceptionalities; however, to live successfully in today's complex, automated world, direct instruction in certain independent living skills may be required. This type of instruction is also important in a student's transition program. The following areas may be problematic for persons with exceptionalities:

▶ Sexuality
▶ Managing personal finances
▶ Developing and maintaining social networks
▶ Maintaining a home
▶ Managing food
▶ Employment
▶ Transportation
▶ Self-confidence and self-esteem
▶ Organization
▶ Time management

Special education teachers must help students with exceptionalities achieve competence in these areas. Several curricular guides are available to structure appropriate intervention. Two excellent resources are the Life-Centered Career Education program (Brolin, 1989) and Cronin and Patton's (1993) life skills program. The former presents a comprehensive curriculum for teaching life skills, whereas the latter is a guide for program development. Cronin and Patton (1993) present particularly useful models and strategies for infusing life skills into the regular curriculum. In addition, creative teachers can use community resources, gathering real materials from banks, restaurants, the local court house, and so forth, for developing their own program.

Preparing for Employment One important goal of education is the employment of graduates at their maximum vocational potential. Teachers need to help students prepare for employment by teaching them the necessary skills for vocational success.

Inclusive vocational and technical programs present a unique opportunity to offer students both a functional curriculum as well as integration with typically achieving peers. These programs can provide appropriate entry into work-study programs, business apprenticeships, and technical and trade school programs.

Teachers must be sure that students with exceptionalities can communicate their strengths and limitations to persons in post-secondary and future employment settings. Self-advocacy skills will empower individuals to seek employment and independent living opportunities on their own. Woodman (1995) suggests the following tips for teachers to enhance self-advocacy, empowerment, and competence in students with exceptionalities:

1. Help students understand their disabilities—not only their weaknesses, but more important, their strengths.

FURTHER READING

For more information on the inclusion of life skills into the curriculum, read *Life Skills Instruction for All Students with Special Needs* by M. E. Cronin and J. R. Patton, published in 1993 by Pro-Ed. Also see their recent article, "Curricular Implications of Transition: Life Skills Instruction as an Integral Part of Transition Education" in volume 18, issue 5 of *Remedial and Special Education*, 1997 (pp. 294–306).

TEACHING TIP

For students with exceptionalities planning to attend university, consult the National Educational Association of Disabled Students for information. Phone 1 (613) 526-8008; website: www.neads.ca.

CONSIDER THIS

In what ways can self-advocacy and self-determination affect young adults with exceptionalities? Should schools help teach self-advocacy skills to adolescents with exceptionalities? Why or why not?

FURTHER READING

See Field, Hoffman, and Spezia's book *Self-Determination Strategies for Adolescents in Transition* (pp. 29–31), published in 1998, for suggestions on assisting in the development of students' self-determination skills.

2. Encourage students to develop their strengths into compensatory strategies.
3. Teach students to capitalize on effective study techniques and individualized learning strategies. Model the use of aids such as highlighters, index cards, tape recorders, and spell-checkers.
4. Aid students in developing verbal abilities into a strength.
5. Encourage the development of social skills and self-esteem.
6. Teach students to ask for assistance when it is needed and to know that getting help is not a weakness.
7. Teach [university]-bound students to be aware of the range of services in [university] and to use the support services provided.
8. Instruct students on time-management skills and how to use a calendar to manage their lives.
9. Mentor these students, and give them the gift of confidence; teach them to value themselves and their abilities. (p. 43)

Methods to Facilitate Students' Success in General Education Classes

TEACHING TIP

For students with intellectual disabilities, consult the local branch of the Canadian Association for Community Living about transition issues; contact information can be found on their website: www.cacl.ca.

Students with exceptionalities traditionally have been placed in general education classrooms for instruction when they were determined to have the requisite academic ability necessary for success. With the advent of the inclusion movement, however, students with exceptionalities are often placed in such classes for other reasons. For most of these students, there is no need to dilute the curriculum; however, teachers will probably need to make accommodations and/or adaptations and students will need to use special learning strategies in order to achieve success.

Accommodations and/or Adaptations

In most instances, general education teachers are responsible for making accommodations and/or adaptations to help students with exceptionalities achieve in the secondary school. This process is hampered by the fact that typically only one fourth to one half of secondary teachers have either taken a class or participated in in-service training in this area (e.g., Bursuck et al., 1996; Struyk et al., 1996; Struyk et al., 1995). Thus, although some studies (Jayanthi et al., 1994; Polloway et al., 1994; Ysseldyke, Thurlow, Wotruba, & Nania, 1990) have indicated that teachers are frequently willing to make adaptations and would find them helpful, many do not have the necessary training (Scott, Vitale, & Masten, 1998). This problem needs to be addressed.

Recall from Chapter 2 that the term *accommodation* will be used in this text to refer to the "specialized support and services that are provided to enable students with diverse needs to achieve learning expectations. This may include technological equipment, support staff, and informal supports" (Saskatchewan Learning, 2000, p. 145). The term *adaptation* will be used to refer to the "adjustments to curriculum content, instructional practices, materials or technology, assessment strategies, and the learning environment made in accordance with the strengths, needs, and interests of the learner" (Saskatchewan Learning, 2000, p. 145). Finally, the term *modification* will be used to refer to changes in policy that will support students with exceptionalities in their learning (e.g., altering school curriculum or attendance policy). Adaptations are usually simple actions that make success for individual students much more likely. For example, allowing visually impaired students to read using Braille is universally accepted. Altering teaching methods or materials for students with other problems is a conceptually similar process. Ysseldyke et al. (1990) found that "altering instruction so that the student can experience success, modifying the curriculum in a number of ways, adjusting the lesson pace to meet a student's individual rate of mastery, and informing students frequently of their instructional needs were viewed as equally desirable by elementary and secondary teachers" (p. 6).

Accommodations and/or adaptations should be designed to offer the *least* amount of alteration of the regular programming that will still allow the student to benefit from instruction. This approach provides the students with exceptionalities with a realistic sense of their abilities and limitations. If too many accommodations and/or adaptations are made, some students may be set up for failure in a university or other academically demanding environment. Students with too many accommodations and/or adaptations may also begin to feel that they bring very little to the class; this assessment can further damage an already fragile self-concept. Accommodations and/or adaptations used in settings or classes designed to prepare an individual for a future job or post-secondary training program should reflect real conditions present in these future environments.

Many different adaptations can be used effectively with students with exceptionalities. These include altering the way information is presented (e.g., taped books, overhead projectors), the materials used (e.g., advance organizers, story guides), and the physical environment (e.g., seating arrangement).

Teachers can take other actions to accommodate a student's learning difficulties, such as using vocabulary guides, cued text, advance organizers, and a structured overview (Leverett & Diefendorf, 1992). Often, a great deal of a student's grade may be determined by the quality of work on assignments; yet sometimes students with exceptionalities may not understand an assignment or may lack the ability or time to complete it. Therefore, teachers may need to make some adaptations in the area of assignments. Chalmers (1991) suggests the following:

1. *Preteach vocabulary, and preview major concepts:* Students must have the vocabulary necessary to complete an assignment. If they do not know a particular word, they may not know how to find its definition, causing them to possibly fail the assignment. Similarly, students need to understand the major concepts required to complete the assignment.
2. *State a purpose for reading:* Students need to know *why* they have to do things. Helping them understand the context of the assignment may aid in motivating them.
3. *Provide repetition of instruction:* Choral responding, group work, and hands-on activities are examples of providing students with exceptionalities with the opportunities necessary for learning. One instance of instruction may simply not be sufficient to ensure learning.
4. *Provide clear directions and examples:* "I didn't understand" is a common response from students when they fail. For many students, this response may simply be an effort to evade negative consequences. For many students with exceptionalities, however, the statement may reflect a true misunderstanding of the assignment. Therefore, teachers need to make every effort to explain all assignments in such a way that they are understandable to all students.
5. *Make time adjustments:* Teachers should individualize the time requirements associated with assignments. Some students may be capable of performing the work successfully, only to become frustrated with time restraints. Teachers should make adjustments for students who simply need more time or who may become overwhelmed by the volume of work required in a particular time period.
6. *Provide feedback:* All individuals need feedback; they need to know how they are doing. For students with exceptionalities and a history of failure, the feedback, especially positive feedback, is even more critical. Teachers should provide feedback for every assignment as soon as possible after the assignment is completed.
7. *Have students keep an assignment notebook:* Often, students with exceptionalities are disorganized; they may need some organization imposed upon them externally. Requiring

CROSS-REFERENCE

Review Chapters 3 through 11 to determine specific accommodations and/or adaptations suggested for students with different exceptionalities.

CONSIDER THIS

Should teachers who refuse to make accommodations and/or adaptations for students with different learning needs in their classes be required to do so? What are the consequences for students included in classrooms where teachers refuse to make accommodations and/or adaptations?

students to keep an assignment notebook is an example. The assignment notebook not only negates the excuse "I did not have my assignment" or "I lost my assignment," but it also helps some students maintain a semblance of order in their assignments and facilitates their completion of all required work.

8. *Provide an alternate assignment:* Provide opportunities for students to complete an assignment differently. For example, if a student has difficulty with oral language, the teacher could accept a written book report rather than an oral one. Videotaped, tape-recorded, and oral presentations can be used in conjunction with written presentations.

9. *Allow manipulatives:* Cue cards, charts, and number lines are examples of manipulatives that can help some students comprehend information. Some students prefer to learn visually, whereas others prefer the auditory mode. Manipulatives can facilitate the learning of all students.

10. *Highlight textbooks:* Highlight the important facts in textbooks. These books can be passed on to other students with similar reading problems next year. Highlighting material enables students to focus on the important content.

TEACHING TIP

These accommodations and/or adaptations are helpful for all students, including those without exceptionalities who do not need specialized instruction. Many accommodations and/or adaptations simply reflect good teaching.

Another important adaptation that teachers can make is the alteration of materials. Deshler, Ellis, and Lenz (1996) describe a way to reduce the content in textbooks. Often, students are capable of reading and understanding, but it takes them significantly longer to read than their peers. Therefore, teachers may wish to reduce the amount of content without altering the nature of the content. When selecting materials, teachers should consider cultural diversity issues. The nearby Diversity Forum feature provides guidelines.

Teachers also have control over how they implement the school curriculum (Carnine, 1991; Simmons, Fuchs, & Fuchs, 1991). They can alter the speed of presentation of the materials, develop ways to inform students that certain information is important, and quickly cover information that is required, but that has limited importance to students. The only limitation in modifying the curriculum is the teacher's creativity. The nearby Inclusion Strategies feature presents creative curricular adaptations. It suggests ways in which students with varied levels of exceptionalities can be successfully included.

In addition to significant curricular adaptations, teachers can make numerous simple adjustments to teach specific information to students:

- Repeat important information several times.
- Write important facts on the board.
- Repeat the same information about a particular topic over several days.
- Distribute handouts that contain only the most important information about a particular topic.

Figure 14.6 provides a checklist teachers can use for further ideas, documentation, and evaluation of options implemented for accommodating learning needs.

Homework, Grading, and Testing

Homework, grading, and testing stand out as important considerations in students' success within secondary school classrooms. They have become more significant in light of trends toward an increase in academic standards and accountability in general education classrooms. This section explores these problem areas, focusing on adaptations to facilitate student success.

Homework   Problems in **homework** often become more pronounced at the secondary level. Roderique et al. (1994) report that for school districts with a homework policy, the average amount of homework assigned at the high school level was over 1 hour and 40 minutes per daily assignment, and the frequency was 4.28 nights per week. Struyk et al. (1995) report that 70 percent of the teachers assigned homework two to four times per

Diversity Forum

Checklist for Evaluating Materials Relative to Cultural Diversity Issues

☑ Are the perspectives and contributions of people from diverse cultural and linguistic groups—both men and women, as well as people with exceptionalities—included in the curriculum?

☑ Are there activities in the curriculum that will assist students in analyzing the various forms of the mass media for ethnocentrism, sexism, "handicapism," and stereotyping?

☑ Are men and women, diverse cultural/racial groups, and people with varying abilities shown in both active and passive roles?

☑ Are men and women, diverse cultural/racial groups, and people with exceptionalities shown in positions of power (i.e., the materials do not rely on the mainstream culture's character to achieve goals)?

☑ Do the materials identify strengths possessed by so-called "underachieving" diverse populations? Do they diminish the attention given to deficits, to reinforce positive behaviours that are desired and valued?

☑ Are members of diverse racial/cultural groups, men and women, and people with exceptionalities shown engaged in a broad range of social and professional activities?

☑ Are members of a particular culture or group depicted as having a range of physical features (e.g., hair colour, hair texture, variations in facial characteristics and body build)?

☑ Do the materials represent historical events from the perspectives of the various groups involved or solely from the male, middle-class, and/or Western European perspective?

☑ Are the materials free of ethnocentric or sexist language patterns that may make implications about persons or groups based solely on their culture, race, gender, or exceptionality?

☑ Will students from different ethnic and cultural backgrounds find the materials personally meaningful to their life experiences?

☑ Are a wide variety of culturally different examples, situations, scenarios, and anecdotes used throughout the curriculum design to illustrate major intellectual concepts and principles?

☑ Are culturally diverse content, examples, and experiences comparable in kind, significance, magnitude, and function to those selected from mainstream culture?

From "Toward Defining Programs and Services for Culturally and Linguistically Diverse Learners in Special Education," by S. B. Garcia and D. H. Malkin, 1993, *Teaching Exceptional Children, 26*, p. 35. Used by permission.

---

week; 11 percent assigned it five times per week. The time period needed to complete the homework varied from less than 30 minutes to 1.5 hours per day; 43 percent of the teachers assigned at least 30 minutes of homework per night. Given that students typically have 4 to 6 teachers, assignments represent a significant hurdle for junior and high school students with exceptionalities. While the amount of homework assigned provides a challenge, the unique difficulties of students with exceptionalities are underscored by the types of problems they are likely to have. Figure 14.7 lists the highest-rated homework problems of adolescents. Yet each problem carries implicit potential remedies.

Given that students with special needs experience problems with homework, a number of strategies can be pursued. For example, Struyk et al. (1995) found that, with regard to the helpfulness of specific *types of homework*, teachers rated preparation for tests and practice of skills already taught as moderately helpful, whereas enrichment activities and preparation for future class work were seen as least helpful. They rated in-class structures such as checking the level of the students' understanding when beginning an in-class assignment and using a homework assignment sheet or notebook as the most helpful *procedures*. Finally, teachers also rated the helpfulness of specific *adaptations* for students with exceptionalities. Their responses are summarized in Figure 14.8.

FURTHER READING

For more information on homework and students with exceptionalities, read "Improving Homework Completion and Academic Performance: Lessons From Special Education," by T. Bryan and K. Burstein, published in 2004 in volume 43 of *Theory into Practice* (pp. 213–219).

Curricular Adaptations: "Real Live Plants"

In a high school biology class, the goal for the class was to learn and understand various aspects of plant characteristics and growth. To ensure that all students had experiences in observing and learning about plants, the teacher and inclusion facilitator planned a visit to a nursery and a project involving growing a variety of plants in the classroom. In addition to the textbook, the team collected a variety of books on plants, such as books with pictures of plants in various stages of development, simple how-to gardening pamphlets, books containing stories about plants, videotapes of plant growth using time-lapse photography, and textbooks containing elementary- to university-level material about plants. Many of the students were responsible for the learning objectives of knowing and understanding types of plants, technical terminology of plant parts, and technical plant life processes such as the photosynthesis process....

During the unit, however, students had varying specific objectives while engaging in group activities with their classmates. For instance, Tammy was unable to read or comprehend the technical words and growth processes of plants. But she still could participate with her classmates... by concentrating her studies on learning objectives that included labelling the parts of the plants in everyday language such as the root, stem, and leaves. She also learned along with her peers how to put seeds, cuttings, roots, and young plants into the dirt and was responsible for their care.... The teacher asked Tammy questions about plants in everyday language and practical procedures for growing plants during class discussions. In a similar way he asked other students questions about technical terminology and growth processes.

All the students not only learned about plants, but also worked co-operatively together and contributed to the class by growing and nurturing a number of different plants in the classroom for everyone to observe and study.... That is, everyone benefited—Tammy learned practical everyday plant parts and how to grow plants, along with picking up a few of the technical words and aspects of the technical growth process by listening to and observing her classmates, while other classmates related the technical terminology, concepts, and ideas they were learning in the biology class to real live plants.

Adapted from "Learning Together in Inclusive Classrooms: What about the Curriculum?" by W. Stainback, S. Stainback, and G. Stefanich, 1996, *Teaching Exceptional Children, 28*, p. 17.

Collaboration among general and special education teachers and parents will encourage successful completion of homework. Teachers should attend to communication problems that can evolve regarding homework. Struyk et al. (1996) cite communication problems as experienced by parents, special education teachers, and general education teachers. Parents' highest-ranked problems were frequency of communication, early initiation of communication, and follow-through. Similar concerns were voiced by special education teachers (i.e., early initiation, frequency, follow-through). Finally, general education teachers cited the following challenges to regular communication: the competing demands of record keeping and paperwork, difficulty in coordinating schedules to set up time to talk with parents, and the large number of students with exceptionalities in their classes.

Certain policies and procedures can increase students' success with homework. The following ideas have proved effective for general education teachers:

▷ Schedule after-school sessions at which students can get extra help on their homework.
▷ Provide peer tutoring programs that concentrate on homework.
▷ Provide sufficient study hall time during school hours for students to complete their homework.
▷ Use community volunteers to assist students in completing homework. (Epstein et al., 1996)

Students can also get help with their homework through the internet. Secondary teachers need to become familiar with this new source of support and make this information available to students. The nearby Technology Today feature describes homework help available on the internet.

CONSIDER THIS

Should school policies on homework be altered to increase the likelihood of success for students with exceptionalities, or should these students be required to follow a rigid policy set for all students? Why or why not?

Student _____ Teacher _____ Date(s) _____

[Circle accommodations attempted; mark successful accommodations with plus (+), unsuccessful with minus (−)]

Classroom	Preferential seating (specify): _____			
Design	Group size:	___ 1–1 w/teacher	___ 1–1 w/peer	___ Small group	___ Large group
constructive	Need for movement:	___ Little	___ Average	___ High	
learning	Distraction management:	___ Carrels	___ Headsets	___ Seating	___ Other
environment.	Noise:	___ None	___ Quiet	___ Moderate	
	Lighting:	___ Dim	___ Average	___ Bright	
	Temperature:	___ Warm	___ Average	___ Cool	
	Other (specify): _____			

Schedule	Peak time:	___ Early morning	___ Late morning	___ Midday	___ Afternoon
Arrange	Lesson length:	___ 5–10 min.	___ 15–20 min.	___ 25–30 min.	___ 30+ min.
productive	Variation needed:	___ Little	___ Some	___ Average	___ Much
learning	Extra time needed:	___ Little	___ Some	___ Average	___ Much
schedule.	Other (specify): _____			

Lessons
Use best stimulus/response format.

Stimulus Format			*Response Format*		
Visual:	___ Observe	___ Read	Choose:	___ Point	___ Mark
Auditory:	___ Oral	___ Discuss	Tell:	___ Restate	___ Explain
Touch:	___ Hold	___ Feel	Write:	___ Short answer	___ Essay
Model:	___ Coach	___ Demonstrate	Word process:	___ Some	___ All
Multisensory:	___ Combination		Show:	___ Demonstrate	___ Make
Other (specify): _____					

Materials	___ Vary stimulus/response	___ Vary directions	___ Vary sequence
Make	___ Highlight essential content	___ Use partial content	___ Add steps
constructive	___ Expand practice	___ Add self-checking	___ Add Supplements
material	___ Segment	___ State key concepts in margins	(see below)
adjustments.	Other (specify): _____		

Supplements
Provide supplementary aids to facilitate learning.

Instructional Strategies	*Materials*	*Assignments*	*Human Resources*
___ Advance organizers	___ Adaptive/assistive	___ Adapted testing	___ Co-teacher
___ Charted progress	devise	___ Advance assignment	___ Co-operative group
___ Checklist of steps	___ Audiotapes of text	___ Alternate	___ Instructional coach
___ Computer activities	___ Calculator	assignments	___ Interpreter
___ Evaluation checklists	___ Captioned films	___ Extended time	___ Peer advocate
___ Graphic organizers	___ Coded text	___ Extra practice	___ Peer notetaker
___ Modelling	___ Computer programs	___ Outlined tasks	___ Peer prompter
___ Mnemonic guides	___ Games for practice	___ Partial outlines	___ Peer tutor
___ Multisensory	___ Highlighted text	___ Question guides	___ Personal attendant
techniques	___ Key term definitions	___ Reference access	___ Study buddy
___ Organization charts	___ Large print texts	___ Scripted practice	___ Volunteer tutor
___ Repeated readings	___ Manipulatives	___ Segmented tasks	
___ Scripted	___ Math number	___ Shortened	
demonstrations	charts	assignments	*Management Strategies*
___ Self-questioning	___ Multiple text	___ Simplified directions	___ Charted performance
___ Strategy posters	___ Parallel text	___ Simplified tasks	___ Checklists
___ Verbal rehearsal	___ Simplified text	___ Structured notes	___ Contracts
___ Video modelling	___ Summaries	___ Study guides	___ Extra reinforcement
___ Visual imagery	___ Video enactments	___ Timed practice	___ Other
___ Other	___ Other	___ Other	
_____	_____	_____	_____
_____	_____	_____	_____

FIGURE 14.6   Checklist of Options for Accommodating Learning Needs

From Choate, J. S. (2002). *Successful inclusive teaching: Proven ways to detect and correct special needs* (3rd ed.). Boston, Allyn and Bacon, p. 38.

FIGURE 14.7

Homework Problems of Adolescents with Behavioural Disorders

Note: These are the highest rated problems noted by special educators.

From "A Comparison of Homework Problems of Secondary School Students with Behavior Disorders and Nondisabled Peers," by J. Soderlund, W. Bursuck, E. A. Polloway, and R. A. Foley, 1995, *Journal of Emotional and Behavioral Disorders, 3,* p. 152. Used by permission.

1. Easily distracted by noises or activities of others.
2. Responds poorly when told by parent to correct homework.
3. Procrastinates, puts off doing homework.
4. Fails to complete homework.
5. Whines or complains about homework.
6. Easily frustrated by homework assignment.
7. Must be reminded to sit down and start homework.
8. Fails to bring home assignment and necessary materials.
9. Daydreams or plays with objects during homework session.
10. Refuses to do homework assignment.
11. Takes unusually long time to do homework.
12. Produces messy or sloppy homework.
13. Hurries through homework and makes careless mistakes.

Grading   The challenges of inclusion of adolescents with exceptionalities are perhaps most clearly reflected in the area of grading. The extant research in this area has not shown positive results. For example, Zigmond and her associates (Donahue & Zigmond, 1990; Zigmond, Levin, & Laurie, 1985) report that approximately 60 percent to 75 percent of high school students with learning disabilities received passing grades in their general education classes, but they consistently received below-average grade-point averages (GPAs) (i.e., an overall GPA of 0.99 on a 4.0 scale, or D work). These patterns seem to reflect a persistent lack of academic success for students with exceptionalities who were also found to receive lower grades than their peers in general education (Munk & Bursuck, 2001). Similarly, Valdes, Williamson, and Wagner (1990) report that 60.2 percent of high school students with exceptionalities had averages of C+ or lower, with a subset of 35.4 percent receiving averages below the C− level. Furthermore, these researchers note that more than one third of students enrolled in graded general education classes had at least one failing grade.

In researching classroom report card practices, Struyk et al. (1995) found that, in determining grades, teachers weighed tests and quizzes highest, and in-class work and homework second highest. Teachers reported that checklists indicating level of competence and skills, supplemented by written comments, were the most helpful apparatus for reporting grades for students with exceptionalities.

CONSIDER THIS

If alternative grading requirements are used with students with exceptionalities, should these students be eligible for the honour roll and honours programs? Why or why not?

FIGURE 14.8

Homework Adaptations for Adolescents with Exceptionalities

Note: Items are ranked from most helpful to least helpful.

From "Homework, Grading, and Testing Practices Used by Teachers with Students with and without Disabilities," by L. R. Struyk, M. H. Epstein, W. Bursuck, E. A. Polloway, J. McConeghy, and K. B. Cole, 1995, *The Clearing House, 69,* p. 52. Used by permission.

1. Provide additional teacher assistance.
2. Check more frequently with student about assignments and expectations.
3. Provide a peer tutor for assistance.
4. Allow alternative response formats (e.g., oral or other than written).
5. Provide auxiliary learning aids (e.g., calculator, computer).
6. Adjust length of assignment.
7. Assign work that student can do independently.
8. Provide a study group.
9. Provide extra credit opportunities.
10. Evaluate based on effort, not on performance.
11. Adjust (i.e., lower) evaluation standards.
12. Adjust due dates.
13. Give fewer assignments.

Homework Help on the Internet

Sometimes the questions that students have are not always going to arise during school hours. Wouldn't it be nice for students to have help available during evening hours when many are *doing* their homework? The internet to the rescue! There are dozens of bulletin boards, chat rooms, and forums that give students the opportunity to ask for help with any number of school-related homework problems. Many of these services have *real teachers online* to answer student homework questions. Commercial service providers often recruit teachers to become online electronic tutors. Teachers are usually reimbursed for their time with free online time with the service provider. Because these tutors are real professionals, adults can worry less about the students who just want easy answers. Online tutors will work through your students' questions, offering tips and explaining procedures—

not just doling out answers. Below are listed a few of the places where homework help may be found.

▶ America Online: Academic Assistance Center. Search word—"homework." Live chat with real teachers between 5:00 p.m. and 1:00 a.m. every day [EST]. In addition to this service, AOL provides a teacher paging service. Search word—"teacher pager." Type in your grade level, your questions, and click send. Email answers are guaranteed within 48 hours.

Homework help is also available for university students if your work is research based. Once in the AAC, enter "research."

▶ Any Internet Source: Teacher paging on the internet or with any CSP. Enter this address: homework24@aol.com.

▶ Compuserve: See the Student's Forum. Search word—"go stufo."

▶ GEnie: Access the Computer Assisted Learning Center. Homework questions are posted by subject. Real-time chat is available Mondays and Wednesdays, 9:00 p.m.–10:00 p.m. [EST] and Tuesdays and Thursdays, 10:00 p.m.–11:00 p.m. [EST].

▶ Prodigy: Access the Education Bulletin Board or Homework Helper. Helper is a premium service, and an extra charge is assigned for services rendered.

▶ For homework help specific to Canada: visit **www.altavista. canada.com** then type in "homework help" and the subject name.

Adapted from *Quick Guide for the Internet for Educators* (pp. 33–34), by J. D. Rivard, 1997. Published by Allyn and Bacon, Boston, MA. Copyright © 1997 by Pearson Education. Reprinted by permission of the publisher.

Teachers' responses for grading adaptations for students with exceptionalities are summarized in Figure 14.9. This list provides a basis for designing grading practices that help adolescents with exceptionalities succeed in school. In addition, teachers should carefully evaluate the fairness of their grading patterns for students with special needs.

Testing   The inclusion movement has raised concerns regarding how students with special needs will be assessed. Simple adaptations can make the difference between taking a test successfully or poorly. For example, reading a test to a student who is a very poor

1. Separate grades are given for process (e.g., effort) and product (e.g., tests).
2. Grades are based on the amount of improvement an individual makes.
3. Grading weights are adjusted (e.g., effort or projects count more than tests).
4. Grades are based on meeting the requirements of academic or behavioural contracts.
5. Grades are based on meeting IEP objectives.
6. Grades are adjusted according to student ability.
7. Grades are based on a modified grading scale (e.g., change 93–100 = A to 90–100 = A).
8. Grades are based on less content than required for the rest of the class.
9. Students are passed if they make an effort to pass.
10. Students are passed no matter what.

FIGURE 14.9

Grading Adaptations for Adolescents with Exceptionalities

Note: Items are ranked from most to least helpful.

From "Homework, Grading, and Testing Practices Used by Teachers with Students with and without Disabilities," by L. R. Struyk, M. H. Epstein, W. Bursuck, E. A. Polloway, J. McConeghy, and K. B. Cole, 1995. Reprinted with permission of the Helen Dwight Reid Educational Foundation. Published by Heldref Publications, 1319 Eighteenth St., NW, Washington, DC 20036-1802. Copyright © 1995.

CROSS-REFERENCE

Review Chapters 3 through 11, and determine specific testing adaptations that might be necessary with students with different types of exceptionalities.

reader gives the student a chance to display knowledge or skills. If such students have to read the questions themselves, test results will reflect students' poor reading skills and fail to assess knowledge of a particular content area. Teachers can address this situation in the following ways:

- Have another student read the test to the student.
- Have the special education teacher or aide read the test to the student.
- Give the student additional time to complete the test.
- Reword the test to include only words that are within the student's reading vocabulary.

A full consideration of adaptations in **testing**, however, extends beyond the consideration of reading ability. Smith et al. (1993) list ways in which teachers can make tests more accessible to students: generous spacing between items on the pages, adequate space allowed for responses, generous margins, readability of text, appropriate test length, logical organization, and clear instructions. The following examples are techniques to adapt measurement instruments:

- Using information about performance outside of school in making evaluations
- Administering frequent short quizzes throughout the course, rather than a few long tests
- Dividing tests or tasks into smaller, simpler sections or steps
- Developing practice items or pretest trials using the same response format as the test (teaching students how to respond), which may help reduce a student's fear of evaluation
- Considering the appropriateness of the instrument or procedure in terms of age or maturity
- Giving open-book tests
- Reducing the number of test items or removing items that require more abstract reasoning or have high levels of difficulty
- Using different levels of questions for different students (i.e., test items for low-functioning children should be at a more concrete level)
- Having a student develop a product or packet of materials that show knowledge and understanding of the content of a unit
- Providing alternative projects or assignments
- Having peers administer tests
- Allowing students to make up tests
- Videotaping a student performing a task and then playing it back to him or her to show skills learned and areas needing improvement
- Videotaping a model performing a task correctly, then videotaping the student completing the task, finally allowing the student to watch his or her performance on videotape to compare it to the performance of the model
- Using a panel of students to evaluate one another on task performance
- Allowing students to type answers
- Allowing students to use a computer during testing
- Allowing small groups to work together on a task to be evaluated (such as a project or test)
- Using short written or verbal measures on a daily or weekly basis to provide more feedback on student progress
- Increasing the amount of time allowed to complete the test, to compensate for slower reading, writing, or comprehension
- Altering the presentation (written, oral, visual) of tests or tasks to be evaluated
- Altering the types of responses to match a student's strengths (written, oral, short answer, or simple marking)
- Having a student review the course or unit content verbally so that he or she is not limited to test item recall
- Limiting the number of formal tests by using checklists to observe and record learning
- Assessing participation in discussions as an indicator of mastery of content
- Giving extra credit for correction of mistakes

Testing adaptations raise questions of treatment acceptability. Relative to this concern, Struyk et al. (1995) report that adaptations commonly used for students *without* exceptionalities include extending the time students have for completing the test (92 percent), giving feedback to individual students during the test (94 percent), and allowing students to take open-book or open-notes tests (96 percent). These techniques should be considered as the initial adaptation options for students with exceptionalities, since they already are commonly in use. General education teachers' preferences in testing adaptations for adolescent students with exceptionalities are summarized in Figure 14.10. A survey of middle school students' opinions found that the preferred adaptations were open-note or open-book tests, practice questions for study, and multiple choice instead of essay. Their least preferred adaptations were having the teacher read the test, tests with fewer questions, and tests covering less material (Nelson, Jayanthi, Epstein, & Bursuck, 2000).

For students to perform successfully on tests, they will need to learn individual test-taking and organizational strategies, which are often difficult for students with exceptionalities (Scruggs & Mastropieri, 1988). Such strategies are typically subsumed within the area of study skills, discussed in the next section.

CROSS-REFERENCE

Refer to Chapter 13 for information on treatment acceptability.

Study Skills and Learning Strategies

Teachers' accommodations and/or adaptations are insufficient to guarantee that students with special needs will be successful. Students must develop their own skills and strategies to help them overcome, or compensate for, a disability. Understanding how to use study skills will greatly enhance their chances for being successful in future academic, vocational, or social activities. Classroom teachers can help students by helping them acquire a repertoire of study skills.

1. Give extended time to finish tests.
2. Give extra help preparing for tests.
3. Simplify wording of test questions.
4. Give individual help with directions during tests.
5. Give practice questions as a study guide.
6. Use black and white copies (rather than ditto).
7. Read test questions to students.
8. Allow use of learning aids during tests (e.g., calculators).
9. Highlight key words in questions.
10. Use tests with enlarged print.
11. Give the actual test as a study guide.
12. Give feedback to individual students during test.
13. Change question type (e.g., essay to multiple choice).
14. Give open-book/note tests.
15. Allow students to answer fewer questions.
16. Teach students test-taking skills.
17. Allow oral instead of written answers (e.g., tape recorders).
18. Test on less content than rest of the class.
19. Provide extra space on tests for answering.
20. Allow word processors.
21. Allow answers in outline format.
22. Give tests to small groups.
23. Give take-home tests.

FIGURE 14.10

Testing Adaptations for Adolescents with Exceptionalities

Note: Items are ranked from most to least helpful.

From "Homework, Grading, and Testing Practices Used by Teachers with Students with and without Disabilities," by L. R. Struyk, M. H. Epstein, W. Bursuck, E. A. Polloway, J. McConeghy, and K. B. Cole, 1995, *The Clearing House, 69*, p. 54. Used by permission.

Study skills can be defined as the tools that students can use to assist them with their learning. They include listening, note taking, reading rate, test taking, remembering information, managing time, managing behaviour, motivation, and goal setting (Hoover & Patton, 1995).

Many students have an innate ability in these areas. For example, some students are good readers, adept at comprehension and able to read quickly; other students find it easy to memorize facts. These students may not need instruction in study skills. For other students, however, study skills represent an "invisible curriculum" that must be taught directly if they are to be successful.

For example, the study skill of listening is critical in most educational settings because teachers provide so much information verbally. If students are not able to attend to auditory information, they will miss a great deal of content. Table 14.3 summarizes key study skills and their significance for learning.

There are many ways to teach study skills. For example, in the area of reading comprehension, teachers might teach students to underline facts that are important, pay attention to margin notes, and use SQ3R (i.e., Survey-Question-Read-Recite-Review) (see the later discussion on Multipass). With this technique, students can focus their attention by asking themselves questions and trying to answer them during the reading process. In order to teach organizational skills relative to assignments, class materials, and time management, teachers can use logs and charts, colour coding of materials, and guided notes.

Closely related to study skills are *learning strategies*—ways to use active learning to acquire and use new information and solve problems ("learning to learn"). Teachers should be alert to ways to teach content and ways to learn and use the content. Reading comprehension, error monitoring in writing, problem solving in math, and test preparation are also important skills that can be developed and strengthened through strategy training. A comprehensive source on numerous strategies for learning (and their use) is

TABLE 14.3   Study Skills and Their Significance for Learning

Study Skill	Significance for Learning
Reading rate	Rates vary with type and length of reading materials; students need to adjust rate to content.
Listening	Ability to listen is critical in most educational tasks and throughout life.
Note taking/outlining	Ability to take notes and develop outlines is critical in content courses and essential for future study.
Report writing	Written reports are frequently required in content courses.
Oral presentations	Some teachers require extensive oral reporting.
Graphic aids	Visual aids can help students who have reading deficits understand complex material.
Test taking	Students must be able to do well on tests if they are to succeed in content courses.
Reference material/dictionary usage	Using reference materials makes learners more independent.
Time management	Ability to manage and allocate time is critical for success in secondary settings.
Self-management of behaviour	Self-management assists students in assuming responsibility and leads to independence.

Adapted from *Teaching Students with Learning Problems to Use Study Skills: A Teacher's Guide* (p. 7), by J. J. Hoover and J. R. Patton, 1995, Austin, TX: Pro-Ed.

Students with special needs often require instruction in study skills.

provided by Masters et al. (1999). Teachers may have to instruct students how to use a given learning strategy. Alley and Deshler (1979) described an eight-step procedure for teaching strategies to students. While this model has been modified from time to time, the general approach still remains effective. The following steps are included in the approach (Masters et al., 1999):

1. Testing the student's current level of functioning
2. Describing the steps of the strategy and providing a rationale for each step
3. Modelling the strategy so the student can observe all of the processes involved
4. Verbally rehearsing the steps of the strategy to criterion
5. Practising controlled materials written at the student's reading ability level
6. Practising content materials from the student's grade placement level
7. Giving positive and corrective feedback
8. Giving the post test (p. 119)

A comprehensive source on numerous strategies for learning (and their use) is provided by Deshler, Ellis, and Lenz (1996). Several sample strategies are discussed in the following paragraphs.

The **COPS** strategy (Schumaker et al., 1981) is an error-monitoring strategy for writing. The acronym stands for four tasks:

Capitalization

Overall appearance (e.g., neatness, appropriate margins)

Punctuation

Spelling

With this strategy, students review their initial drafts of papers, giving specific attention to these four types of errors. The strategy has proved effective for use with students with learning problems at the upper elementary, junior high, and secondary school levels (Shannon & Polloway, 1993).

CONSIDER THIS

What would it be like if all students were provided with instructional strategies that made them more effective learners? How would this affect the number and types of children needing special education?

Multipass (Schumaker, Deshler, Alley, & Denton, 1982) is a reading comprehension and study strategy originally derived from SQ3R. The term *multipass* refers to the fact that students are taught to make three passes through content reading material. In the *survey* pass, the student reviews, among other things, the title, bold headings, and the summary or conclusion. The *size-up* pass directs students to review the comprehension questions at the end of the chapter. The *sort-out* pass allows students to organize the information in the chapter in a way that helps them form responses to the comprehension questions.

Efforts to validate the use of specific strategies within inclusive classrooms continue. An exciting aspect of instruction in strategies is its potential to benefit students with and without exceptionalities (Fisher, Schumaker, & Deshler, 1995).

Summary

- Important differences exist between elementary and secondary settings in terms of organizational structure, curriculum, and learner characteristics.
- From a curricular perspective, integrating students with exceptionalities into general classes is more challenging at the secondary level than at the elementary level.
- The period of adolescence adds to the problems experienced by students with exceptionalities.
- Curricular options for students at the secondary level with particular relevance for students with exceptionalities include basic skills, social skills, tutoring, learning strategies, vocational skills, and life skills.
- Future-based assessment offers one method for developing programs for adolescents with exceptionalities.
- Classroom teachers and special education teachers must collaborate to ensure effective secondary school programs.

- Special education teachers must help prepare students for academic content classes.
- Transition to the secondary level is a major endeavour for students with exceptionalities.
- Accommodations, adaptations, and/or modifications are changes that teachers can make to facilitate the success of students with exceptionalities.
- Specific challenges for successful inclusion occur in the areas of homework, grading, and testing.
- Study skills are skills that students with exceptionalities can use to help them achieve success in general and special education classes.
- Learning strategies enable students to achieve independence as they "learn how to learn."

Resources

Emmer, E. T., Everston, C. M., Clements, B. S., & Worsham, M. E. (1999). *Classroom management for secondary teachers*, 5th ed. Toronto: Allyn & Bacon.

This small book that deals specifically with management issues at the high school level is an invaluable tool for all secondary teachers.

Fisher, D. B., Sax, C., and Pumpian, I. (1999). *Inclusive high schools: learning from contemporary classrooms.* Baltimore, MD: Brookes Publishing Company.

Since so many inclusive resources focus on the elementary level, this book makes a particularly important contribution. It provides a framework for developing inclusive high schools, illustrated by detailed accounts of high schools that have struggled, strategized, and ultimately achieved success in including all students.

eblinks

Classroom Resources

http://classroomresources.com

This excellent Canadian website offers a variety of classroom resources with Canadian content and representation of Canadian student diversity. It is a must visit for all teachers to see (and download) the latest Canadian Content flyer which reviews in detail different books and classroom resources and states their uses in curriculum design. Such support will help teachers to include students from all backgrounds in their daily curricula.

School Psychology Resource

www.bcpl.net/~sandyste/school_psych.html

This website for school psychologists, educators, and parents covers different exceptionalities, special education procedures (e.g., sample IEPs), and information on all topics relevant to psychology in the schools such as violence, child abuse, suicide, and parent collaboration. Although American based, it has excellent information and materials relevant to Canadian teachers.

The Education Planet—The Education Web Guide

http://educationplanet.com

A highly interesting and rewarding resource, this search engine covers all education-relevant sites, providing access to lesson plans, videos, manuals, curriculum materials, and much more. If you want to find specifically Canadian material, you can limit searches to Canadian sources.

Teachers.net

http://teachers.net

As a huge U.S. website, Teachers.net covers a variety of topics of interest to teachers, providing curriculum suggestions, resources, and chat rooms about different education issues. It also has subject-specific listings of chatboards where ideas are posted and shared. Many resources are available through this website for elementary and secondary teachers.

Canadian.Teachers.net

http://canadian.teachers.net/

Derived from Teachers.net, this site provides a specifically Canadian forum with chat rooms, job postings, catalogues, information, professional development with guest speakers, and listings of related sites.

15 Working with Families of Students with Exceptionalities

After reading this chapter, you should be able to

- identify changes in the Canadian family structure that have implications for the public schools of the first decade of the new millennium
- discuss the particular challenges experienced by parents of individuals with exceptionalities
- discuss effective ways to involve the family in education programs
- list principles of effective communication with parents
- delineate support roles that parents and family members can play

A s advocates for all children, teachers are frequently confronted with difficult family situations in which their assistance is requested and needed. Place yourself in the position of Jody Rinaldi, a primary school educator, who was approached by Josh and Sally Williams with the following concern.

"One month ago, Josh and I were told by our family doctor that our four-year-old daughter, Susie, is not developing as she should be. Her language is deficient and her learning is slow. This problem happened because of an accident. Our doctor suggested that Susie may eventually be identified as having an intellectual disability. Needless to say, this information came to us as a total shock. Since we heard it, we have gone over and over how this could have happened, why this happened, and what we should do about it.

"We haven't really adjusted to the news that our doctor gave us, and I guess we both would admit that our concerns and our disappointments have been a real problem for us. Our biggest worry now is, what lies ahead?

"Some of my 'friends' have said that in the past, a child like our Susie might have been sent away for institutional care. Certainly, we would never consider that, but still we don't know what we can do. Naturally, we would be very grateful for any assistance or information that can help us deal with our concerns and, most important, can help Susie. Thank you very much."

Questions to Consider

1. Analyze Josh and Sally's current and potential feelings, and discuss their possible reactions upon learning that their child has a disability.

2. What advice, recommendations, and assistance would you provide for these two concerned parents?

3. What would you convey to them about the advantages and challenges of inclusive school programs for their daughter?

389

Introduction

Since the 1980s, there has been a significant change in the provision of educational services to students with exceptionalities: the increased involvement of parents and family. In the past, schools frequently did not encourage parents to participate in the education of their children. As a result, parents were often left out of the decision-making process leading to interventions. Often, they were not even informed of the programs that the school was implementing for their children. Some school personnel did make significant efforts to include parents in the education of their children; others did little or nothing to promote this. Given the numerous concerns that parents may have and the value of parental involvement in the schools, the move to encourage parental involvement is welcome.

Legislation and parental advocacy have established the current high level of parental involvement in the education of students with exceptionalities. Virtually all school personnel now acknowledge the merit of having parents actively participate in the educational process, including identification, referral, assessment, program planning, and program implementation. Comprehensive programs of family involvement begin when children are young and continue until transition into adulthood. The natural challenge of preparation ultimately for adulthood is aptly stated by the parent of a high school senior:

> I feel my job isn't done. Tell that to a 17-year-old boy who thinks he's adult. I want him to fly—with a parachute. Some of this 'chute comes from school, some from home (Whitney-Thomas & Hanley-Maxwell, 1996, p. 75).

The challenge for educators is to consider diverse, effective ways to involve families in the education of children with exceptionalities. Table 15.1 describes six categories of **family support** principles and examples associated with each.

Some families will become more involved with the education of their child than others. School personnel need to encourage those parents who are active in their children's education to maintain their commitment while developing strategies to increase the active role of other parents.

Family participation can and should occur in many areas. These include assessment and IEP development, parent groups, observation of the student in the school setting, and communication with educators. Of these areas, participation in developing the IEP process occurs the most frequently.

Thus, some families have a very active role in their child's special educational program, whereas others have limited involvement. Schools meet the letter of the law by simply inviting parental participation. However, school personnel should develop strategies to facilitate it. Although some parents create challenges for the school because of their intense level of involvement, for the most part educational programs are greatly strengthened by parental support. This chapter provides perspectives on the family and identifies strategies for enhancing family involvement.

Families are playing a bigger part in special programs for their children. Some families are learning more about special education programs and particular types of disabilities through technology. The internet offers a wide variety of information about disabilities, educational programs, and how to provide supports for individuals at home. The nearby Technology Today feature provides information on families and technology access.

The Family

The viewpoint of what constitutes a **family** has changed dramatically in recent decades. Traditionally, a family has been described as a group of individuals who live together that

CROSS-REFERENCE

See Chapter 7 to review how family supports have been provided in the field of intellectual disabilities.

CONSIDER THIS

Not unexpectedly, the degree of parental participation in the IEP process is correlated with socio-economic level. Why do you think this is the case?

| TABLE 15.1 | Major Categories and Examples of Family Support Principles |

▶ Category/Characteristic	▶ Examples of Principles
1. Enhancing a sense of community Promoting the coming together of people around shared values and common needs in ways that create mutually beneficial interdependencies	▸ Interventions should focus on the building of interdependencies between members of the community and the family unit. ▸ Interventions should emphasize the common needs and supports of all people and base intervention actions on those commonalities.
2. Mobilizing resources and supports Building support systems that enhance the flow of resources in ways that assist families with parenting responsibilities	▸ Interventions should focus on building and strengthening informal support networks for families rather than depending solely on professionals' support systems. ▸ Resources and supports should be made available to families in ways that are flexible, individualized, and responsive to the needs of the entire family unit.
3. Shared responsibility and collaboration Sharing of ideas and skills by parents and professionals in ways that build and strengthen collaborative arrangements	▸ Interventions should employ partnerships between parents and professionals as a primary mechanism for supporting and strengthening family functioning. ▸ Resources and support mobilization interactions between families and service providers should be based on mutual respect and sharing of unbiased information.
4. Protecting family integrity Respecting the family's beliefs and values and protecting the family from intrusion upon its beliefs by outsiders	▸ Resources and supports should be provided to families in ways that encourage, develop, and maintain healthy, stable relationships among all family members. ▸ Interventions should be conducted in ways that accept, value, and protect a family's personal and cultural values and beliefs.
5. Strengthening family functioning Promoting the capabilities and competencies of families necessary to mobilize resources and perform parenting responsibilities in ways that have empowering consequences	▸ Interventions should build on family strengths rather than correct weaknesses or deficits as a primary way of supporting and strengthening family functioning. ▸ Resources and supports should be made available to families in ways that maximize the family's control over and decision-making power regarding services they receive.
6. Proactive human service practices Adoption of consumer-driven human service-delivery models and practices that support and strengthen family functioning	▸ Service-delivery programs should employ promotion rather than treatment approaches as the framework for strengthening family functioning. ▸ Resource and support mobilization should be cosumer-driven rather than service provider–driven or professionally prescribed.

From "Family-Oriented Early Intervention Policies and Practices: Family-Centered or Not?" by C. J. Dunst, C. Johanson, C. M. Trivette, and D. Hamby, 1991, *Exceptional Children, 58*, p. 117. Copyright 1991 by the Council for Exceptional Children. Reprinted by permission.

includes a mother, a father, and one or more children. However, this stereotypical picture has been challenged. The **nuclear family** with stay-at-home mother and wage earner father is no longer the typical family structure. Many, perhaps most, families do not resemble this model. Thus the "Leave It to Beaver" or "Ozzie and Harriet" family of the 1950s has given way to the diversity of today's family (Hanson & Carta, 1996).

Currently, numerous family constellations exist. For example, a large number of families are single-parent families, most frequently with father absent. In Canada in 1996, 14.5 percent of families were single-parent families, 83 percent of those female. Some single-parent families are headed by a father, and, in some cases, children live with one or more of their grandparents, without either mother or father present. Other families consist of a husband and wife without children. And, although not as common as they once were, some families constitute extended family units, with grandmother or grandfather living with the parents and child. Some children also live in foster homes, in which the foster parents fill all legal roles as birth parents would. Finally, regardless of individual opinions on this issue, school personnel must also be able to interact with families composed of parents living in gay or lesbian relationships.

FURTHER READING

For more information on the makeup of today's families, read "Addressing the Challenges of Families with Multiple Risks" by M. J. Hanson and J. J. Carta, published in 1996 in volume 62 of *Exceptional Children* (pp. 201–211).

The realities of the early twenty-first century pose further challenges to the family: the increase in both younger and older parents, the increase of families living below the poverty line, the realities of substance abuse, new considerations with regard to HIV/AIDs within the family, the permeation of violence throughout society, and the move away from residential care for children with serious support needs (see Agosta & Melda, 1996; Hanson & Carta, 1996; Lesar, Gerber, & Semmel, 1996; Simpson, 1996). There may never have been a time when family changes and challenges have more clearly called for understanding and support.

Although undergoing major changes in structure, the family remains the basic unit of our society. It is a dynamic, evolving social force. Despite the debate about the current role of families and their composition, the family remains the key ingredient in a child's life. Teachers must be sensitive to the background of the family—see the nearby Diversity Forum feature for a discussion of family values and effective strategies. In addition, it is critical that school personnel remember that students' parents, or grandparents when they are in the role of parents, should take part in educational programs regardless of the specific composition of the family. School personnel must put aside any personal feelings they may have about various lifestyles and work with students' families to develop and implement the best possible programs for the students. School personnel must include the family in all key decisions affecting children—both with special needs and those without (Wehmeyer et al., 1999).

Families and Children with Exceptionalities

The arrival of any child results in changes in family structure and dynamics. Obviously, a first child changes the lives of the mother and father, but subsequent births also affect the dynamics of the family unit, including finances, amount and quality of time parents can devote to specific children, relationship between the husband and wife, and future family goals. The birth of a child with an exceptionality exacerbates the challenges that such changes bring. For example, the almost immediate financial and emotional impact can create major problems for all family members, including parents and siblings.

When a child with an exceptionality becomes a member of the family, whether through birth, adoption, or later onset of the disability, the entire family must make adjustments. Critical problems that may face families of children with serious disabilities include the following:

FURTHER READING

For an extensive discussion of the historical role of families, read Chapter 1 in A. P. Turnbull and H. R. Turnbull's *Families, Professionals, and Exceptionality,* published by Merrill in 1997.

CONSIDER THIS

What are some problems faced by families following the birth of a child with an exceptionality (or the identification of a child with an exceptionality)?

Diversity Forum

Developing Strategies Sensitive to Diverse Cultures

Western Culture/Values	Family Culture/Values	Strategies for Working with Families
EFFICIENCY		
Value wise use of time; quality of task may be secondary	Efficient use of time not as important; OK to be late	Avoid scheduling parent–teacher conferences too closely together.
Direct approach; get right to the subject; solve problem	Indirect approach; discuss related issues; "talk story"	Avoid "quick fix"; respect quality of the interaction.
Tend to rush, fast paced	More slowly paced, need time to think	Slow pace of meetings with parents; allow "thinking time."
INDEPENDENCE		
Prefer to make own decisions	Interdependence, decisions are made as a family; natural family supports in place	Encourage extended family involvement; work with extended family members.
Individual right to privacy of feelings	Strong family ties; open sharing of personal feelings; actions of individual reflect on entire family	Respect sense of family; identify cultural attitudes or religious beliefs toward disabilities.
Parental responsibility for raising child	Extended family, shared responsibility of childrearing	Identify authority figures; respect deference to authority; allow parents time to take decision to others.
EQUITY		
Parents are equal partners in team	Perceive professionals as "above" family	Professionals need to be aware of and "read" parent perceptions; recognize parents as experts.
Prefer active parent involvement (e.g., input at meetings, work with child at home)	Accept teachers' opinion; teachers are experts	Decrease control of interaction; involve parents in planning, implementing, and monitoring programs.
Information sharing	Passive reception of information	Elicit wants, hopes, and concerns of parents; information sharing versus information giving and question asking; use parent suggestions when possible; provide timely feedback.
Democratic family decision making	Matriarchal or patriarchal family structures	Respect lines of authority

Adapted from "Parent and Professional Partnerships in Special Education: Multicultural Considerations," by T. W. Sileo, A. P. Sileo, and M. A. Prater, 1996, *Interventions in School and Clinic, 31,* p. 152. Reprinted with permission.

- Stressful medical treatment, surgery, or hospitalization that may occur repeatedly and for extended periods
- Heavy expenses and financial burdens beyond medical costs, incurred by needs such as special foods and equipment
- Frightening, energy-draining, often recurring crises, as when the child stops breathing or experiences a seizure
- Transportation problems
- Babysitting needs for the other children

FURTHER READING

For stories by, and about, families with children with exceptionalities, visit the Lanark County Chapter of the Ontario Association for Families of Children with Communication Disorders website at **www.oafccd.com**.

CROSS-REFERENCE

Review Chapters 3–11, which discuss specific disabilities that can affect children. Then reflect on how different types of problems can cause different reactions.

- Time away from jobs to get the child to consultation and treatment appointments
- Lack of affordable child care
- Continuous day-and-night demands on parents to provide routine but difficult caregiving tasks (for example, it may take an hour or more, five to six times during a 24-hour period, to feed a child with a severe cleft palate condition)
- Constant fatigue, lack of sleep, and little or no time to meet the needs of other family members
- Little or no opportunity for recreational or leisure activities
- Difficulty (and additional expense) of locating babysitters qualified to care for a child with an exceptionality
- Lack of respite care facilities
- Jealousy or feelings of rejection among brothers and sisters, who may feel the special child gets *all* the family's attention and resources
- Marital problems arising from finances, fatigue, differences about management of the child's disability, or feelings of rejection by husband or wife that he or she is being passed over in favour of the child (adapted from Allen, 1992, p. 321)

In addition to these problems, a primary difficulty is accepting and understanding the child and the disability. Understanding a diagnosis and its implications is critical to a family's acceptance of the child. Parents with a limited understanding of a diagnosis will probably have difficulty in developing realistic expectations of the child, possibly creating major problems between the child and other family members. For example, parents might not understand the nature of a learning disability and therefore accuse the child of being lazy and not trying. Parents who may overlook the potential of a child with an intellectual disability might develop low expectations that will limit the child's success. For example, parents of adolescents might not support a school work program for their son or daughter because they believe that adults with intellectual disabilities are not capable of holding a job.

Families who discover that a child has a disability may react in a variety of ways. Their responses have been compared to Elizabeth Kübler-Ross's stages of grief related to death and dying.

These responses may include the following (adapted from Smith, 1997):

- *Denial:* "This cannot be happening to me, to my child, to our family."
- *Anger:* An emotion that may be directed toward the medical personnel involved in providing the information about the child's problem or at a spouse because of the tendency to assign blame.
- *Grief:* An inexplicable loss that one does not know how to explain or deal with.
- *Fear:* People often fear the unknown more than they fear the known. Having the complete diagnosis and some knowledge of the child's future prospects can be easier than uncertainty.
- *Guilt:* Concern about whether the parents themselves have caused the problem.
- *Confusion:* As a result of not fully understanding what is happening and what will happen, confusion [may reveal] itself in sleeplessness, inability to make decisions, and mental overload.
- *Powerlessness:* [The feeling may relate to the parents' inability to] change the fact that their child has a disability, yet parents want to feel competent and capable of handling their own life situations.
- *Disappointment:* [The fact that] a child is not perfect may pose a threat to many parents' egos and a challenge to their value system.
- *Acceptance:* The child has needs to be met and has value as a member of the family. (pp. 2–3)

Although it cannot be assumed that all or even most parents experience these particular stages, many must deal with complicated emotions, often experienced as a "bombardment of feelings" that may recur over many years (Hilton, 1990). Sileo, Sileo,

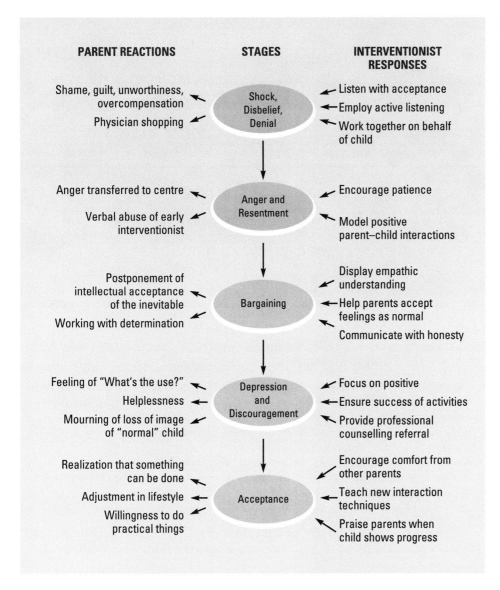

FIGURE 15.1

Parent Reactions and
Possible Interventions

Ruth E. Cook, Diane M. Klein,
Annette Tessier, *Adapting Early
Childhood Curricula for Children
in Inclusive Settings*, Sixth Edition,
© 2000, p. 24. Reprinted by
permission of Pearson Education,
Inc., Upper Saddle River, NJ.

and Prater (1996) refer to the "shattering of dreams" that underlies many of the feelings. School personnel, including teachers, school social workers, counsellors, and administrators, need to be aware of these dynamics and be prepared to deal with family members who are experiencing various feelings. For example, when parents say that they feel guilt after learning that their child has a disability, school personnel should listen with acceptance to the parents and help them understand the nature of the disability and the fact that they are not responsible for it. Figure 15.1 lists possible parental reactions and interventions that schools can use to help family members.

School personnel need to be aware of family members' acceptance level of children with exceptionalities and make appropriate efforts to support this acceptance. This effort begins with assisting parents in understanding the needs of their child; at the same time, the educator or administrator should listen to the parents in order to better understand the child from their perspective. Further, teachers must be sensitive to the fact that many parents do not see the school as a welcoming place for various reasons (e.g., problems the parents experienced as students themselves, negative responses communicated to

Many parents of students with special needs require assistance in accepting their child's problems.

CONSIDER THIS

As a teacher, how could you deal with families experiencing various reactions to a child with an exceptionality? What role, if any, should a teacher play in helping parents work through their reactions?

TEACHING TIP

Teachers need to be aware of the different reactions that parents may experience and know some specific strategies for dealing with these reactions.

FURTHER READING

For more information on fostering inclusive views, read S. J. Salend's article "Fostering Inclusive Views in Children: What Families Can Do," in volume 37, issue 1 of *Teaching Exceptional Children*, 2004 (pp. 64–69).

them as advocates for their child). Summarizing previous research on this issue, Wilson (1995) lists the following things that parents want (and need) from professionals:

▶ Parents want professionals to communicate without jargon. When technical terms are necessary, they would like to have them explained.
▶ When possible, they want conferences to be held so both parents can attend.
▶ They want to receive written materials that provide information to assist them in understanding their child's problem.
▶ They want to receive a copy of a written report about their child.
▶ Parents want specific advice on how to manage the specific behaviour problems of their children or how to teach them needed skills.
▶ Parents want information on their child's social as well as academic behaviour. (p. 31)

Finally, parents may struggle with the issue of inclusion itself. Educators remain divided on this issue, as do parents and parents' groups (see Hallahan & Kauffman, 1995, for further discussion).

Involvement of Fathers

Too often, when people hear that families are taking part in a child's education, they assume that the "family" is really the child's mother. This belief is unfortunate, because the involvement of the entire family is the goal. Often the individual who is left out of the planning is the father.

Hietsch (1986) describes a program that aims at encouraging fathers to get involved in the educational program of their child. The program focuses on Father's Day, when the fathers of children in the class are invited to participate in a specific activity. However, teachers need to be sensitive to single-parent (i.e., mother only) homes in arranging such events. The inclusion of a grandfather or an uncle may be a good alternative.

Involvement of Siblings

In addition to the adults in a family, siblings are also important in developing and implementing appropriate educational programs. Approximately 10 percent of the school population is identified as having a disability; therefore, the number of children with siblings identified with an exceptionality must be significant: a working estimate of 20 percent or more seems realistic. Although not all siblings experience adjustment problems, some doubtlessly will have significant difficulties responding to the disability. Nevertheless, these siblings also have a unique opportunity to learn about the diversity of individual needs.

Meyer (2001) summarized the literature and noted these areas of concern expressed by siblings:

- A lifelong and ever-changing need for information about the disability or illness.
- Feelings of isolation when siblings are excluded from information available to other family members, ignored by service providers, or denied access to peers who share their often ambivalent feelings about their siblings.
- Feelings of guilt about having caused the illness or disability, or being spared having the condition.
- Feelings of resentment when the child with special needs becomes the focus of the family's attention or when the child with special needs is indulged, overprotected, or permitted to engage in behaviours unacceptable by other family members.
- A perceived pressure to achieve in academics, sports, or behaviour.
- Increased caregiving demands, especially for older sisters.
- Concerns about their role in their sibling's future. (p. 30)

One way some schools are involving siblings of children with exceptionalities is through **sibling support groups** (Summers, Bridge, & Summers, 1991). In addition to disseminating basic information about disabilities, sibling support groups can also provide a forum in which children share experiences and support with other children who have siblings with exceptionalities. Similar to parent support groups, sibling support groups can help children cope with having a brother or sister with an exceptionality. Understanding that similar problems exist in other families and learning new ways to deal with them can be very helpful.

Building on his analysis of the challenges, concerns, and opportunities for siblings of a child with an exceptionality, Meyer (2001) provided a series of recommendations to alleviate concerns and to enhance opportunities; these are presented in Figure 15.2.

CONSIDER THIS

The recent emphasis on family (rather than parental) involvement reflects the importance of siblings and others in supporting the child. Is it a good idea to include siblings in the education of a brother or sister with an exceptionality? Why or why not?

FURTHER READING

For more information on sibling support groups, read L. L. Dyson's article "A Support Program For Siblings of Children with Disabilities," in volume 35, issue 1 of *Psychology in the Schools*, 1998 (pp. 57–65).

- Parents and service providers have an obligation to proactively provide brothers and sisters with helpful, age-appropriate information.

- Provide siblings with opportunities to meet other siblings of children with special needs. For most parents, "going it alone" without the benefit of knowing another parent in a similar situation is unthinkable. Yet, this happens routinely to brothers and sisters. Sibshops (workshops for siblings) and similar efforts offer siblings the same common-sense support that parents value.

- Encourage good communication with typically developing children. Good communication between parent and child is especially important in families where there is a child with special needs.

- Encourage parents to set aside special time to spend with the typically developing children. Children need to know from their parents' deeds and words that their parents care about them as individuals.

- Parents and service providers need to learn more about siblings' experiences. Sibling panels, books, newsletters, and videos are all excellent means of learning more about sibling issues.

FIGURE 15.2

Recommendations for Siblings

Adapted from "Meeting the Unique Concerns of Brothers and Sisters of Children with Special Needs" by D. Meyer, 2001, *Insight, 51*(4), p. 31.

Several additional suggestions can enhance the positive benefits of involving siblings:

1. Inform siblings of the nature and cause of the disability.
2. Allow siblings to attend conferences with school personnel.
3. Openly discuss the disability with all family members.

Parent Education

Many educators believe parents of children with exceptionalities benefit tremendously by attending parent education classes. One reason is that parents too frequently attribute normal and predictable misbehaviour to a child's disability rather than to the age and stage of a child. Seeing that all parents face similar challenges with their children can be both comforting and empowering to parents (West, 2002). Some helpful hints parents learn through parent education include the following (from West, 2002):

1. Never compare children.
2. Notice the improvements and accomplishments of each child in the family, and always reinforce the positive.
3. Hold family meetings that allow children a weekly opportunity to voice their concerns, accept chores, and plan enjoyable family nights and outings.
4. Learn to help children become responsible by the use of logical and natural consequences rather than using punishment or becoming permissive.
5. Spend special time alone with each child in the family. Be sure that no child feels lost or left out because others require more attention.
6. Plan family events that allow children to enjoy being together.
7. Reduce criticism and increase encouragement.
8. Be sensitive to the possibility that children functioning at a higher academic level in the family may be finding their place through perfectionism and a need to excel at all costs.
9. Invest time in your marriage. A strong marriage is important to your children's sense of well-being.
10. All families experience stress. The more stress is encountered, the more time they need together to share their feelings, plan ahead, solve problems mutually, and plan time to enrich relationships.

Family and School Collaboration

School personnel and families of students with problems need to collaborate in order to maximize educational efforts. All school personnel, classroom teachers, special education teachers, administrators, and support personnel need to be actively involved with families to improve the education of children with disabilities.

Need for Family and School Collaboration

Parents of children with exceptionalities and school personnel are partners in providing appropriate educational services. Parents actually should be seen as the "senior partners" because they are responsible for the children every day until they reach adulthood.

Family involvement can only enhance educational programs. Figure 15.3 outlines a comprehensive model of parent and family involvement. The nearby Inclusion Strategies feature presents ways to encourage a greater family role, with ideas for addressing multicultural considerations.

TEACHING TIP

Teachers and other school personnel must keep in mind that parents are not only equal partners in the education of their children, but are the senior partners and should be involved in all major decisions.

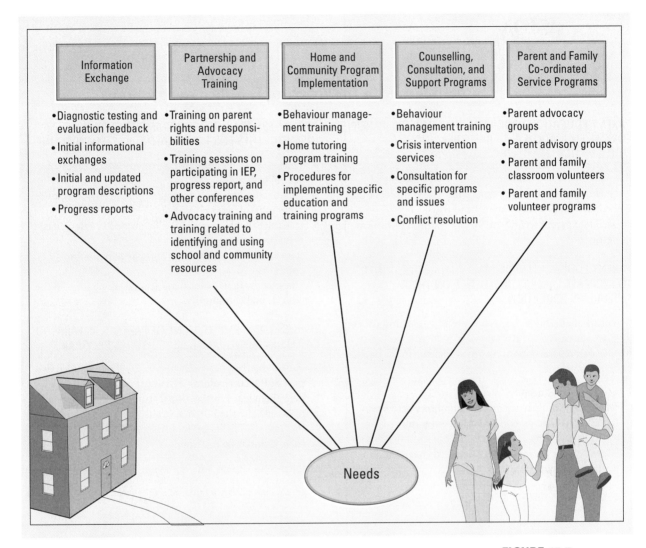

FIGURE 15.3

Model of Family
Involvement

Adapted from *Working with
Parents and Families of
Exceptional Children and Youth*
(p. 32), by R. L. Simpson, 1996,
Austin, TX: Pro-Ed. Used by
permission.

Legal Requirements for Collaboration

Although the important role of families in all aspects of child growth and development
has been acknowledged for a long time, public schools have historically excluded families from many decisions about the education of children (Krauss, 1990).

In Canada, parental rights for involvement in the assessment, programming
(IEP/IPP), and monitoring of children's school performance vary across the country.
William Smith of McGill University's Office of Research on Educational Policy has docu-
mented the legal rights of students with exceptionalities across Canada (Smith, 1994;
Smith & Foster, 1996). In his recent work examining parental rights for involvement, he
notes that, as of 1997, there was no legal requirement to include parents in assessment
or programming decisions in Alberta, Manitoba, Newfoundland, or Prince Edward
Island. In all other provinces and territories parents have the legal right to help make

Approaches to Facilitating Family Involvement

PARENT EDUCATION PROGRAMS THAT IMPROVE PARENTS' FORMAL EDUCATION (E.G., BASIC READING, MATHEMATICS, REASONING SKILLS)

▪ increase parents' self-esteem and self-confidence.
▪ facilitate positive interactions with school professionals.
▪ broaden employment opportunities.
▪ facilitate parent feelings of "being at home" in educational settings.

PARENT EDUCATION PROGRAMS THAT ARE DESIGNED TO INCREASE PARENTS' INFLUENCE ON THEIR CHILDREN'S EDUCATION

▪ ensure that schools are responsive to school and community values.
▪ give parents the opportunity to participate in the decision-making process.
▪ require that educators
  ▪ observe and participate in community activities.
  ▪ listen to parents' concerns to develop mutual understanding.
  ▪ encourage parents to define desired change and to develop an action plan.

AWARENESS TRAINING PROGRAMS THAT PROVIDE OPPORTUNITIES FOR ROLE-PLAYING AND SIMULATION

▪ increase parent confidence levels for interacting with school personnel.
▪ facilitate parents' understanding of and shared responsibility for children's education.
▪ teach new behaviours and skills needed to interact as team members.
▪ increase family interactions and participation in children's education.
▪ empower parents and extend leadership abilities in the educational community.

TRAINING AND EMPLOYMENT OF PARENTS AS PARAEDUCATORS IN BILINGUAL AND BICULTURAL PROGRAMS

▪ ensure that language and customs will be included as a part of the curriculum.
▪ help them learn instructional strategies that can be used to benefit their children at home.
▪ increase the likelihood that parents will choose to further their children's education.

Adapted from "Parent and Professional Partnerships in Special Education: Multicultural Considerations," by T. W. Sileo, A. P. Sileo, and M. A. Prater, 1996, *Interventions in School and Clinic, 31,* p. 148.

decisions (Smith & Foster, 1997). Furthermore, in New Brunswick and Saskatchewan parents are required to take part in assessment and programming, but not in the ongoing monitoring of the program; in all other provincial/territorial jurisdictions rights to involvement include the right to monitor the programming.

In summary, the legal rights pertaining to parental involvement vary across the country. In the majority of jurisdictions parents have the right to help make assessment and programming decisions. In all jurisdictions attempts are made to include parents wherever possible.

Specific Collaboration Activities

There are numerous ways parents and other family members can become involved with the education of a child with an exceptionality or one who is at risk for developing problems. The following suggestions focus on areas in which general education teachers can have a positive effect.

Personal Spotlight

Guidance Counsellor Ross Newhook

First an elementary teacher, Ross Newhook later earned his master of education degree in educational psychology and became a guidance counsellor. He is currently pursuing a doctorate in educational psychology.

As a guidance counsellor in Placentia, Newfoundland, Ross has many duties. He is responsible for an elementary and a secondary school with a total of 850 students. He completes all the assessments needed for identification for special services, consults with teachers in the prereferral stage to try to adapt the curriculum, provides students with personal and career counselling, and mediates between parents and teachers when difficulties arise. Following assessments, Ross reports to the parents about any identified exceptionality.

Although many teachers think that parents will be upset or angry at a diagnosis, Ross has found that this is not usually the case.

"When I tell parents that their son or daughter has an exceptionality, say a learning disability, it seldom comes as a shock. They are usually more relieved than anything. They have known for a while that things are not going well, and it is a relief to have it confirmed that their child is not lazy, that it is not their fault. And, of course, they are very relieved that now something will be done. Of course, some parents are angry and blame the school, the teachers, whoever—but for the most part that is not what happens."

When asked to provide advice to teachers on how to work with parents, Ross talks about the most common problems he sees between teachers and parents.

"Often when there is a problem between parents and teachers and I become involved, I find that it is not some big philosophical difference but really a personality conflict. They are different kinds of people and can't understand each other's perspective. Because the teacher is the professional, it is up to him or her to work through this and be able to communicate with the parent.

"So often teachers are angry because they feel the parent is telling them how to do their job, but you have to understand where the parent is coming from. The parent may have had a lot of previous problems with teachers and schools and is coming into the situation with certain negative expectations. To communicate with such parents, you need to meet with them in a non-threatening environment. Don't sit behind your desk. Try to be informal, not authoritarian. Be sure to keep at their level, don't be condescending, and don't use jargon or language they are not familiar with. Most importantly, listen, *really* listen to their frustrations—that is so important. Sometimes we, as educators, get so caught up in telling parents, talking at parents that we rarely listen to parents.

"Finally, make it clear you do not have all the answers. You can only do your best to work together to find what might help their child.

"You have to remember a difficult parent did not start out that way. They probably became difficult over time because of a number of experiences. If you can appreciate that and acknowledge those difficulties, you will have fewer problems with that parent."

Communicating with Parents

A critical element in any collaboration between school personnel and parents is communication. Many parents observe that simply too little communication flows between themselves and the school. Perhaps this is to be expected—approximately 50 percent of both general and special education teachers indicate that they have received no training in this area and consequently rate themselves as only moderately skilled (e.g., Buck et al., 1996; Epstein et al., 1996). This situation is particularly unfortunate, since problems between parents and school personnel often can be avoided by proper communication. School professionals should make a conscious effort to begin the year with a discussion of roles and responsibilities in terms of communication (Munk et al., 2001).

TEACHING TIP

When communicating with parents, avoid using educational jargon and acronyms because they might be meaningless to parents.

FURTHER READING

For more information on communicating with parents, read *Families, Professionals, and Exceptionality* by A. P. Turnbull and H. R. Turnbull, published by Merrill in 1997.

Wilson (1995) outlined the following principles of effective communication with the parents of students with exceptionalities:

- *Accept:* Show respect for the parents' knowledge and understanding, and convey a language of acceptance.
- *Listen:* Actively listen, and make an effort to confirm the perceptions of the speaker's intent and meaning.
- *Question:* Probe to solicit parents' perspectives. Often, questions will generate helpful illustrations.
- *Encourage:* Stress students' strengths along with weaknesses. Find positive aspects to share, and end meetings or conversations on an encouraging note.
- *Stay directed:* Keep the discussions focused on the emphases being discussed, and direct the parents to resources regarding concerns that lie beyond your scope.
- *Develop an alliance:* Stress that the parents and teachers share a common goal: to help the child. (pp. 31–32)

Effective communication must be regular and useful. Communicating with parents only once or twice per year, such as with IEP conferences, or communicating with parents regularly but with information that is not useful, will not facilitate meeting educational goals.

Communication between school personnel and parents can take many forms. It does not have to be formal written communication. Effective communication can be informal, for example, telephone calls, written notes, or newsletters. When communicating with parents, school personnel should be aware of how they convey messages. For example, they should never "talk down" to parents. They should also choose their words thoughtfully. Some words convey very negative meanings, whereas other words transmit the message effectively, yet are more positive. Table 15.2 lists words that should be avoided along with preferred alternatives. When communicating with parents, school personnel should also be aware of cultural and language differences. Taking these factors into consideration will enhance the quality of communication with family members.

Teachers must communicate regularly with parents to keep them informed about their child's progress and needs.

TABLE 15.2	Making Positive Word Choices
Avoid	*Use Instead*
Must	Should
Lazy	Can do more with effort
Culturally deprived	Culturally different, diverse
Troublemaker	Disturbs class
Unco-operative	Should learn to work with others
Below average	Works at his (her) own level
Truant	Absent without permission
Impertinent	Discourteous
Steals	Takes things without permission
Dirty	Has poor grooming habits
Disinterested	Complacent, not challenged
Stubborn	Insists on having his (her) own way
Wastes time	Could make better use of time
Sloppy	Could be neater
Mean	Has difficulty getting along with others
Time and time again	Usually, repeatedly
Poor grade or work	Works below his (her) usual standard

Adapted from *Parents and Teachers of Children with Exceptionalities: A Handbook for Collaboration* (2nd ed.) (p. 82), by T. M. Shea and A. M. Bauer, 1991, Boston: Allyn & Bacon. Used by permission.

The following discussion focuses on types of effective communication.

Informal Exchanges   Informal exchanges can take place without preparation. Teachers may see a parent in the community and stop and talk momentarily about the parent's child. Teachers should always be prepared to talk to parents about their children, regardless of the setting, but should avoid talking about confidential information in the presence of individuals who do not need to know about it. If the conversation becomes too involved, the teacher should request that it be continued later, in a more appropriate setting.

Parent Observations   Parents should be encouraged to visit the school to observe their child in the educational setting. Although the parents' presence could cause some disruption in the daily routine, school personnel need to keep in mind that parents have a critical stake in the success of the educational efforts. Therefore, parents should always feel welcome to observe the student in the educational setting. If the teacher feels that one time would be better than another, this information should be conveyed to the parent.

Telephone Calls   Many teachers use telephone calls a great deal and very effectively to communicate with parents. Parents feel that teachers are interested in their child if the teacher takes the time to call and discuss the child's progress with the parent. When using the telephone for communication purposes, teachers should remember to call when there is good news about the child as well as to report problems the child is experiencing. It makes parents feel very good to get a call from a teacher who says that the child is doing well and not having problems. Again, understanding the language and culture of the home is important when making telephone calls. Giving parents your home telephone number is an option that may prove reassuring to parents.

Written Notes   Written communication to parents is also an effective method of communicating about a child's progress. When using written communication, teachers should consider the literacy level of the parents and use words and phrases that will be readily understandable. They should also be aware of the primary language of the home. Written communications that are not understood can be very intimidating for parents. When using written communication, teachers should provide an opportunity for parents to respond, either in writing or through a telephone call. Increasingly, email offers opportunities for ongoing communication. However, as Patton, Jayanthi, and Polloway (2001) noted, "Although the use of new technologies [is] attractive in terms of their immediacy and efficiency, such use poses a dilemma, as a significant number of families may not have access to technology" (p. 228).

Home Visits   There is no better way to get an understanding of the family than by making a home visit. When possible, school personnel should consider making the extra effort required to arrange and make home visits. When visiting homes, school personnel need to follow certain procedures, including the following:

▶ Have specific information to deliver or obtain.
▶ If you desire to meet with parents alone, find out if it is possible to have the child elsewhere during the scheduled visit.
▶ Keep visits to an hour or less.
▶ Arrive at the scheduled time.
▶ Dress appropriately, but be sensitive to cultural variance (e.g., formal, professional dress may distance yourself from the family in some homes).
▶ Plan visits with another school system resource person.
▶ Be sure to do as much listening as talking.
▶ Leave on a positive note. (adapted from Westling & Koorland, 1988)

Although we list home visits as an option, we are also cognizant of the low "treatment acceptability" of this practice. General education teachers report that they consider home visits the least effective (and perhaps least desirable) alternative available to them in terms of home–school collaborations (Polloway et al., 1996). Among other possible concerns, home visits for a potentially large number of children may simply be unrealistic.

Other Forms of Communication   Another way for school personnel to convey helpful information to parents is to consider these options:

▶ Newsletters
▶ Parent or family support groups
▶ Open houses

School personnel should use every available means to communicate with parents. Both general and special education teachers have this responsibility. Teachers should never assume that other school personnel will take care of communicating with parents. Effective communication between school personnel and parents should involve many different people.

CONSIDER THIS

Some teachers think that daily written communication with parents is too much for them to do. When might this form of communication be necessary, and is it a legitimate responsibility for teachers?

TEACHING TIP

School personnel might support a parent newsletter that could go out to all school patrons, or at least a column or section in the school newsletter could be contributed by a parent.

Parent–Teacher Conferences

Parent–teacher conferences are another excellent method of communication. They can be formal, such as IEP meetings, or informal, arranged when parents call a teacher and request a meeting with one or more teachers about a particular problem. Most schools have twice yearly, or more regular parent–teacher meetings for all children. Regardless of the purpose or formality of the meeting, school personnel should focus attention on the topics at hand. They should send advance information home to parents and make the parents feel at ease about participating in the meeting.

When preparing to meet with parents to discuss children who are experiencing problems, school personnel need to anticipate the components of the discussion. They should gather information about the questions that parents may ask and know what questions to address to the parents. Figure 15.4 provides typical questions raised at such conferences. By anticipating the questions in advance, school personnel will be in a better position to have a successful meeting.

IEP Meetings   Parents should be involved in the development of students' individualized education programs for two reasons. First, most provincial/territorial jurisdictions require parental participation. The more important reason for involvement, however, is to gain the input of parents. In most regards, parents know more about their children than school personnel do. They have interacted with the child longer, and beyond the hours of a school day. Schools need to take advantage of this knowledge about the child when developing an IEP.

An example of how parents should be involved in the development of IEPs is described in the future-based assessment and intervention model (Smith & Dowdy, 1992) discussed in Chapter 14. In this model, school personnel, parents, and the student discuss likely "futures" for the student and the necessary interventions that will help the student achieve them. These agreed-upon goals then guide the development and implementation of educational programs for the student. Such a focus is critical to the joint development of individual transition plans, which are suggested for all students with disabilities by at least age 16.

School personnel must take steps to ensure parental involvement in their child's education program.

QUESTIONS PARENTS MAY ASK TEACHERS

- What is normal for a child this age?
- What is the most important subject or area for my child to learn?
- What can I work on at home?
- How can I manage her behaviour?
- Should I spank?
- When will my child be ready for community living?
- Should I plan on her learning to drive?
- Will you just listen to what my child did the other day and tell me what you think?
- What is a learning disability?
- My child has emotional problems; is it my fault?
- The doctor said my child will grow out of this. What do you think?
- Will physical therapy make a big difference in my child's control of his hands and arms?
- Have you become harder on our child? Her behaviour has changed at home.
- Can I call you at home if I have a question?
- What is the difference between delayed, retarded, and learning disabled?
- What kind of after-school activities can I get my child involved in?
- Can my child live on his own?
- What should I do about sexual activity?
- What's he going to be like in five years?
- Will she have a job?
- Who takes care of him when I can no longer care for him?
- What happens if she doesn't make her IEP goals?

QUESTIONS TEACHERS SHOULD ASK PARENTS

- What activities at home could you provide as a reward?
- What particular skill areas concern you most for inclusion on the IEP?
- What behaviour at home do you feel needs to improve?
- Would you be interested in coming to a parent group with other parents of my students?
- When is a good time to call at home?
- May I call you at work? What is the best time?
- Is there someone at home who can pick the child up during the day if necessary?
- Would you be interested in volunteering in our school?
- What is the most difficult problem you face in rearing your child?
- What are your expectations for your child?
- How can I help you the most?
- What is your home routine in the evenings? Is there a quiet place for your child to study?
- Can you or your spouse do some special activity with your child if he or she earns it at school?
- Can you spend some time tutoring your child in the evening?
- Would you like to have a conference with your child participating?
- When is the best time to meet?

FIGURE 15.4

Common Questions Asked by Parents and Teachers

Adapted from *The Special Educator's Handbook* (pp. 208–209), by D. L. Westling and M. A. Koorland, 1988, Boston: Allyn & Bacon. Used by permission.

In order to obtain increased parental involvement in IEP conferences, school personnel need to solicit parental input proactively. Simply inviting parents to attend is not sufficient. In facilitating exchanges between school personnel and parents, de Bettencourt (1987) suggests the following:

1. Hold conferences in a small location that is free from external distractions; hold phone calls and other interruptions so that parents feel you are truly interested in them and their child.
2. Hold conferences on time and maintain the schedule; do not let conferences start late or run late because many parents may be taking time off from work to attend.
3. Arrange the room so that parents and school personnel are comfortable and can look at one another without barriers, such as desks and tables, between them.
4. Present information clearly, concisely, and in a way that parents can understand; do not "talk down" to the parents.

Consider having a parent advocate assigned to attend the conference with the parents, to increase parental participation in the IEP conference. The advocate, a member of the school staff, can facilitate parental participation by introducing the parents to the other team members, verbally reinforcing parental participation, directing questions to the parents, and summarizing the discussion at the end of the conference.

Home-Based Intervention

Families can become involved with the education of a family member with an exceptionality through home-based intervention. For preschool children, home-based services are fairly common; however, parents less frequently provide instruction at home for older students. Still, many reports have noted that such instruction can be very beneficial to students with exceptionalities (e.g., Brown & Moore, 1992; Ehlers & Ruffin, 1990). Parents can be helpful in numerous ways.

Parents and other family members at home can further the student's educational program by providing reinforcement and direct instructional support, and supporting homework efforts.

Providing Reinforcement

Most students with exceptionalities experience lots of failure and frustration. Frequently, the more they attend school, the more they fail. This failure cycle becomes difficult to break, especially after it becomes established over several years. Reinforcing success can help break this cycle. Parents need to work with school personnel to provide positive reinforcement for all levels of success. If students are not capable of achieving full success in an area, then they need to be rewarded for their positive efforts in the appropriate direction.

Parents are in an excellent position to provide reinforcement. They spend more time with the child than school personnel do and are involved in all aspects of the child's life. As a result, parents can provide reinforcement in areas where a child most desires rewards, such as time with friends, money, toys, or trips. For many students, simply allowing them to have a friend over or to stay up late at night on a weekend may prove reinforcing. School personnel do not have this range of reinforcers available to them; therefore, parents should take advantage of their repertoire of rewards to reinforce the positive efforts of students.

CROSS-REFERENCE

A full description of the principles of reinforcement is presented in Chapter 6.

A special example of reinforcement in the home are *home–school contingencies*, which typically involve providing reinforcement contingencies in the home that is based on the documentation of learning or behavioural reports from school. The basic mechanism for home–school contingencies are written reports that highlight a student's behaviour relative to particular targets or objectives. Two popular forms are daily report cards and passports.

Daily report cards give feedback on schoolwork, homework, and behaviour. They range in complexity from forms calling for responses to simple rating scales to more precisely designed behavioural instruments with direct, daily behavioural measures. *Passports* typically take the form of notebooks, which students bring to each class and then take home daily. Individual teachers (or all of a student's teachers) and parents can make regular notations. Reinforcement is based both on carrying the passport and on meeting the specific target behaviours that are indicated on it (Walker & Shea, 1988).

Providing Direct Instructional Support

For many students with exceptionalities, direct involvement of family members in instruction can be critical to success. Unfortunately, many family members provide less direct instruction as the child gets older, assuming that the student is capable of doing the work alone. Too often, the reverse is true; students may need more assistance at home as they progress through the grades. Parents are generally with the child more than school personnel are; therefore, it is logical to involve them in selected instructional activities. Advocates for expanding the role of parents in educating their children adhere to the following assumptions:

- Parents are the first and most important teachers of their children.
- The home is the child's first schoolhouse.
- Children will learn more during the early years than at any other time in life.
- All parents want to be good parents and care about their child's development. (Ehlers & Ruffin, 1990, p. 1)

One effective intervention is a systematic home tutoring program. Thurston (1989) describes an effective program that includes four steps. In step 1, the parents and teachers discuss the area in which home tutoring would be most helpful. Many parents will feel more comfortable with helping their children "practise" skills than with teaching them new skills. Therefore, teachers should help identify topics in which practice would benefit the student. In step 2, family members implement home tutoring procedures: selecting the location for the tutoring, deciding on a time for tutoring, and so on. In step 3, the family member who provides the tutoring uses techniques for encouragement, reinforcement, and error correction. In step 4, family members complete the tutoring session and make a record of the student's accomplishments. Tutoring periods should be short, probably no more than 15 minutes, and should end with a record of the day's activities. A visual chart, on which the student can actually see progress, is often very reinforcing to the student (Thurston, 1989).

Providing Homework Support

In many ways, finishing this chapter with the topic of homework concludes this book with the area that may be most problematic for successful home–school collaboration. The problems of students with exceptionalities in this area are well documented (e.g., Epstein et al., 1993; Gajria & Salend, 1995) and outline the challenges faced by teachers and parents working together (Patton, 1994). For example, Jayanthi, Nelson, Sawyer, Bursuck, and

Epstein's (1994) report on issues of communication problems within the homework process reveals significant misunderstandings among general and special education teachers and parents regarding the development, implementation, and co-ordination of homework practices for students with exceptionalities in inclusive settings. Teachers and parents indicated concerns about failures to initiate communication (in terms of informing the other of a student's learning and behaviour characteristics as well as the delineation of roles and responsibilities) and to provide follow-up communications, especially early on, when problems first become evident. In addition, respondents identified several variables that they believed influence the severity of these problems (e.g., lack of time, student-to-teacher ratio, student interference, not knowing whom to contact). Munk et al.'s (2001) survey research on 348 parents confirmed this pattern of findings.

CROSS-REFERENCE

School-based aspects of homework are discussed in Chapters 13 and 14.

As Epstein et al. (1996) further reviewed these problem areas, they found that general education teachers reported the following key communication problems: lack of follow-through by parents, lateness of communication, the relative lack of importance placed on homework, parental defensiveness, and denial of problems. These concerns were generally consistent with the reports of special education teachers in a parallel study (Buck et al., 1996). However, these data are open to interpretation—they are survey responses by teachers *about* parents. Also, most of the general education teachers in the study had either primary responsibility for communication with parents of students with exceptionalities or shared this responsibility with special educators (Buck et al., 1996; Epstein et al., 1996).

The concerns raised in these two studies focus primarily on underinvolved parents. Teachers should also be sensitive to overinvolved parents and, when appropriate, encourage them to "not do for children what [they] can do for themselves."

Despite the numerous problems associated with homework, solutions can be found. Based on their study, Bursuck et al. (1999) found that special education teachers indicated the following recommendations:

- General educators and parents need to take an active and daily role in monitoring and communicating with students about homework.
- Schools should find ways to provide teachers with the time to engage in regular communication with parents and should provide students with increased opportunities to complete homework after school.
- Teachers need assistance in taking advantage of technological innovations (e.g., homework hotlines, computerized student progress records).
- Students need to be held responsible for keeping up with their homework.
- Special educators need to share with general educators more information about the needs of students with exceptionalities and appropriate instructional accommodations and/or adaptations.

Examples of strategies that general education teachers ranked most effective in resolving homework dilemmas are provided in Figure 15.5. Note that many of these strategies have validity for all students, not only those with special needs.

As Patton et al. (2001, p. 240) note, "Even conscientious parents who understand the significance of homework in their children's lives and the importance of their own role in supporting, nurturing, and helping their children have successful homework experiences sometimes simply fail at their daily responsibilities of checking the assignment book or asking 'What homework did you get today?' and 'Have you completed it?'" Thus, teachers should reflect an understanding in communication with parents that homework may be a lower priority for families when compared with other issues (e.g., school attendance, family illness) and respond accordingly by helping to address these other issues first.

Parents' Efforts to Communicate	Adopting Policies to Facilitate Communication
Parents should	*Schools should*
check with their child about homework daily.	provide release time for teachers to communicate with parents on a regular basis.
regularly attend parent–teacher conferences.	require frequent written communication from teachers to parents about homework (e.g., monthly progress reports).
sign their child's assignment book daily.	schedule conferences in the evenings for working parents.

General Education Teachers' Roles	Technologies to Enhance Communication
Teachers should	*Schools should*
require that students keep a daily assignment book.	establish telephone hotlines so that parents can call when questions or problems arise.
provide parents at the start of school with a list of suggestions on how parents can assist with homework.	regularly provide computerized student progress reports for parents.
remind students of due dates on a regular basis.	establish systems that enable teachers to place homework assignments on audiotapes so that parents can gain access by telephone or voice mail.

FIGURE 15.5

Effective Strategies
Relative to Homework

From "Strategies for Improving Home–School Communication Problems about Homework for Students with Disabilities," by M. H. Epstein, D. D. Munk, W. D. Bursuck, E. A. Polloway, and M. M. Jayanthi, 1999, *Journal of Special Education, 33,* pp. 166–176.

Final Thoughts

It is a safe assumption that establishing good working relationships with parents and families enhances the school experience of their children. Thus an important objective for the schools should be to achieve and maintain such relationships. Most professionals acknowledge the importance of parent and family involvement in the schooling of their children, and this importance can be especially critical for students with exceptionalities. However, programs that promote home–school collaboration must aim for more than students' classroom success. Often, parental involvement has been focused on their children's goals (i.e., student progress), with less attention given to parental outcomes (i.e., their particular needs). Teachers, parents, and other family members all should gain from co-operative relationships that truly flow in both directions and are concerned with success in both home and school settings. Both general and special education teachers need to help family members understand the importance of their involvement, give them suggestions on how to take part, and empower them with the skills and confidence they will need. Students with exceptionalities, and those at risk of developing problems, require assistance from all parties in order to maximize success. Family members are critical components of the educational team.

Summary

- The past two decades have seen a major change in provision of educational services to students with special needs: the active involvement of families.
- Encouraging parents to participate in school decisions may be difficult but is nevertheless essential.

- Schools need to take proactive steps to ensure the involvement of families of students with exceptionalities.
- Unlike families of the past, today's families vary considerably in their composition.

- Regardless of their own values, school personnel must involve all family members of a student with special needs, regardless of the type of family.
- Family members must make adjustments when a child with an exceptionality becomes a family member.
- Siblings of students with exceptionalities may also experience special problems and challenges.
- Families and schools must collaborate to ensure appropriate educational programs for students with exceptionalities.
- Most provincial/territorial policies require that schools involve families in educational decisions for students with exceptionalities.

- A critical component in any collaboration between school personnel and family members is effective communication.
- All types of communication between school and families are important.
- School personnel should encourage parents and other family members to participate during school conferences.
- Family members should be encouraged and taught how to become involved in the educational programs implemented in the school.
- A variety of strategies are available to facilitate successful home intervention programs (e.g., reinforcement, instruction, homework support).

Resources

Exceptional Parent

This monthly magazine on parenting a child with a disability or special health needs is an excellent resource, available through the website **www.eparent.com** or by order. An important resource to share with parents of children who have a disability, it will also inform the teacher about relevant organizations and different disabilities.

Alberta Education, Special Education Branch. (1998). *The parent advantage*. Edmonton: Author.

This informative booklet tells how a parent can help a student (kindergarten to Grade 9) be organized, learn to read, enjoy reading, read textbooks, memorize from

reading, write, spell, use technology, do math, prepare for tests, and complete projects. As a teacher, be sure to have the booklet on hand for parents to refer to—it will save you much time explaining to parents how they can help.

Canter, L., & Hausner, L. (1987). *Homework without tears: A parent's guide for motivating children to do homework and succeed in school.* Santa Monica, CA: Lee Canter & Associates.

The authors provide a very practical approach to handling homework issues which, for parents, are always a huge concern. If you, as the teacher, have this excellent resource on hand to refer parents to, it will make homework issues much easier to deal with.

Weblinks

Canadian Parents Online
www.canadianparents.com/
A wonderful resource for parents, Canadian Parents Online provides information on all aspects of parenting, with supports, resources, and questions/answers from lawyers, nutritionists, and physicians. It is also a resource for teachers to share with parents and to read for suggestions about schooling, homework, health, and behaviour.

Child and Family Canada
www.cfc-efc.ca/
The Child and Family Canada website provides information on all aspects of the family. There is some excellent information on parenting children with different special needs, as well as information on child abuse, family supports, and much more. The site is invaluable for teachers who have questions about family issues.

Parentbooks
www.parentbookstore.com/
Parentbooks, a Toronto-based bookstore, offers a huge selection of resources, including books, videos, and manuals in the area of parenting, families, and education. The store has numerous resources specifically for teachers and in the area of special needs.

National Parent Network on Disabilities (NPND)
www.npnd.org/
The U.S. association provides advocacy information for parents of individuals with disabilities. Although much material is specific to the United States, there is some extremely useful information on resources, related websites, different disabilities, planning for aging, and much more.

Mobility Resource
www.disabilityresource.com
The Mobility Resource site provides resources and other weblinks to parents and professionals working with children with disabilities. If you have any questions about a disability or its management, this site will direct you to a wealth of information.

Family Education Network
www.familyeducation.com
Although the material on this website is intended to be shared primarily with families/parents, it is also useful to the classroom teacher. There are suggestions for educational activities and resources, and tips on managing different special needs concerns.

Glossary

Accelerated schools Schools that provide optional programming for students considered at risk of failure.

Acceleration A form of programming for students who are classified as gifted and/or talented, where the students move through the curriculum at a more rapid pace than their chronological age peers.

Accessibility The ability of a person with an exceptionality to make use of a physical location or program.

Accommodations The specialized support and services provided to students with diverse needs to assist them in achieving learning expectations (e.g., technological equipment, support staff, etc.).

Acquired immune deficiency syndrome (AIDS) A disease transmitted by body-fluid contact that results in a depressed immune system.

Adaptation The changes made to instructional practices, materials or technology, assessment strategies, curriculum content, and the learning environment in order to meet the strengths, needs, and interests of individual students.

Adaptive behaviour A way of conduct that meets the standards of personal independence and social responsibility expected from that cultural and chronological age group.

Additions A speech production problem characterized by individuals inserting sounds into their speech.

Affective education Educational programs that focus on the emotional health of a child.

Allergens Substances that individuals are allergic to, such as dust, certain foods, or animal dander.

Alternative communication Any system of conveying ideas that is used in lieu of human speech.

Alternative schools Schools designed to provide alternative environments for students with behavioural and emotional disorders.

American sign language (ASL) A particular form of sign language used by many individuals with severe hearing impairments.

American Speech-Language-Hearing Association (ASHA) The major American professional organization for speech-language and hearing professionals.

Annual goals Goals for the year that are developed for each student served in special education and made a part of the student's individualized education program (IEP).

Antidepressants Medications for managing attention deficit/hyperactivity disorder.

Anxiety/withdrawal A form of emotional/behavioural disorder where children are very anxious and do not interact with their peers.

Articulation disorder The most common speech disorder, this problem centres around word and sound pronunciations.

Asperger syndrome First listed in 1994 in the fourth edition of the *Diagnostic and Statistical Manual of Mental Disorders* as one of five pervasive developmental disorders. There is significant impairment in social functioning, but otherwise no cognitive delay.

Assessment The process of collecting information about a particular student to determine eligibility for special services, and strengths and areas of need for programming purposes.

Assistive technology Devices that allow students, especially those with specific needs, to participate fully, or even partially, in ongoing classroom activities.

Asthma A disease that affects breathing that is due to narrowing of the small air passages in the lungs caused by irritation of the bronchial tubes by allergic reactions.

Astigmatism The distortion or blurring vision for objects at any distance due to the cornea curving more in one direction than the other.

At-risk students Students who are likely to develop learning or behaviour problems because of a variety of environmental factors.

Attention deficit/hyperactivity disorder (AD/HD) A problem associated with short attention problems and excessive motor movements.

Attention problems—immaturity A form of behaviour problems associated with attention deficits.

Auditory processing disorder A deficit in the processing of information specific to the auditory modality.

Augmentative communication Methods used to facilitate communication in individuals, including communication boards, computers, and sign language.

Autism A severe disorder that affects the language and behaviour of children, caused by neurological problems.

Basal series The type of reading programs traditionally used in most elementary schools in general education classrooms.

Behaviour management Systematic use of behavioural techniques, such as behaviour modification, to manage ways of conduct.

Behavioural approach An intervention model based on behaviourism that is often used with children with emotional problems.

Blind A category of disabilities characterized by severe visual impairment that usually results in an inability to read printed material.

Braille A system of writing for the visually impaired that uses characters made up of raised dots.

Canadian Association of Speech-Language Pathologists and Audiologists (CASLPA) The major Canadian professional organization for speech-language and hearing professionals.

Canadian Charter of Rights and Freedoms A part of Canada's *Constitution Act* that guarantees, among other rights, the rights of all individuals with exceptionalities.

Career education A curricular model that focuses on the future vocational opportunities for students.

Cerebral palsy A disorder affecting balance and voluntary muscles that is caused by brain damage.

Childhood cancer Any form of cancer that affects children; generally leukemia, bone cancer, or lymphoma.

Chronic health problem A physical condition that is persistent and results in school problems for the child.

Circle of friends A peer support network for an individual student fostered by the classroom teacher.

Classroom climate The nature of the learning environment, including teacher rules, expectations, discipline standards, and openness of the teacher.

Classroom management A combination of techniques used by teachers in classrooms to manage the environment, including behaviour modification.

Classroom organization Methods used by teachers to manage the learning environment through physical organization of the classroom, classroom rules, and use of other structure.

Clean intermittent bladder catheterization (CIC) A medical process where a tube is inserted into the catheter to allow for urinary waste to leave the body.

Cochlea The part of the inner ear containing fluid and nerve cells that processes information to the brain.

Cochlear implant A technological device inserted in the place of the cochlea that enables some individuals to hear sounds.

Cognitive deficiency A deficiency in the intelligence processes, including thinking, memory, and problem solving.

Cognitive-behavioural intervention Instructional strategies that use internal control methods, such as self-talk and self-monitoring, in ways that help students learn how to control their own behaviour.

Collaboration The process of interactions between teachers, special education teachers, and/or other professionals to provide instruction to an inclusive classroom.

Communication board An augmentative communication device that includes letters or symbols that enables a person to communicate either manually or through computer technology.

Community-based instruction (CBI) A model in which instruction is provided in a community setting where skills that are learned will actually be used.

Conduct disorder A type of behaviour problem that is characterized by negative and hostile behaviours, generally toward authority figures.

Conductive hearing loss A form of hearing impairment caused by problems with the outer or middle ear that impedes sound travelling to the inner ear.

Consultation The process where an instructional specialist provides suggestions for other educators to use in their inclusive classrooms.

Contingency contracting Developing behavioural contracts with students based on their completing specific tasks or meeting certain behavioural expectations in return for positive reinforcers.

Continuous progress A form of educational programming that allows students to move through a curriculum at their own pace.

Continuum of services A model that provides placement and programming options for students with exceptionalities along a continuum of least-to-most restrictiveness.

Co-operative learning An instructional and learning process that uses teams of children to teach each other and work together on various learning activities.

COPS An error-monitoring strategy for writing.

Creative A form of intelligence characterized by advanced divergent thinking skills and the development of original ideas and responses.

Criterion-referenced testing Tests that compare a child to a particular mastery level rather than to a normative group.

Curricular infusion The practice of infusing various enrichment activities into the general curriculum for students who are gifted and/or talented.

Curriculum A systematic grouping of content, coursework, extracurricular activities, and materials for students in an educational setting.

Curriculum compacting An approach used with gifted and/or talented students where less time is spent on general curriculum activities and more time on enrichment activities.

Curriculum telescoping An approach used with students who are achieving well academically that enables them to move through a curriculum at a more rapid pace than is typical.

Curriculum-based assessment A form of criterion-referenced assessment that uses the actual curriculum as the standard.

Cystic fibrosis A health disorder that is characterized by fluid and mucus buildup in the respiratory system, resulting in death.

Deaf A severe level of hearing impairment that generally results in the inability to use residual sound for communication purposes.

Developmental disability A disability that has a direct impact on a person's mental or physical development.

Developmental period The period of an individual's life, from birth to the eighteenth year, when most cognitive development occurs.

Developmentally appropriate A level of instruction that meets the developmental level of children being taught.

Diabetes A health condition where the pancreas does not produce sufficient levels of insulin to metabolize various substances, including glucose.

Diagnostic and Statistical Manual of Mental Disorders (DSM-IV-TR) The diagnostic manual used by medical and psychological professionals.

Diagnostic tests Tests and other evaluation methods that are designed to result in a diagnosis of a specific problem.

Differential rates of communicative behaviour Individuals are provided reinforcement as their inappropriate response rates are reduced.

Differential reinforcement of lower rates of behaviour (DRL) A model that provides reinforcement for behaviours that are moving the student in the desired direction.

Differentiated programs An instructional approach that requires various curricula or programs for different students in the same classroom.

Direct instruction A technique where the teacher instructs students on a particular topic.

Disability A condition that affects a person's functioning ability, either physical, mental, or both.

Distortions Speech production problems characterized by altering the sound(s) of letters and words.

Dual education system The education model that supports separate programs for students with exceptionalities and those in general education.

Duchenne dystrophy A very severe form of muscular dystrophy that results in fat replacing muscle tissue.

Dysarthria A disorder characterized by muscles that are weak, slowly moving, or do not move at all (e.g., muscles of the mouth, face, and respiratory system) as the result of a stroke or other brain injury.

Dyscalculia A disability in which a person has difficulty understanding math concepts and solving arithmetic problems.

Dysgraphia A disability in which a person finds it difficult to form letters or write within a defined space.

Dyslexia A specific learning disability in which a person typically experiences difficulties accurately and/or fluently recognizing, spelling, and decoding words.

Early infantile autism A term used early in the description of individuals with autism that is currently not used to describe these individuals.

Ecological assessment Evaluating individuals in the context of their environments and taking into consideration all environmental factors.

Educable mentally retarded (EMR) A term traditionally used to describe students with an intelligence quotient (IQ) in the 50–70 range.

Efficacy studies Research that investigates the efficacy, or effectiveness, of various programs for individuals with exceptionalities.

Emotional abuse A form of child abuse that centres around emotionally abusing a child, such as ridiculing the child in public or always making a child feel like a failure.

Emotional/behavioural disorder (EBD) The term used by many professionals to identify children with emotional and behavioural problems.

Enrichment A variety of methods that are used to facilitate appropriate education for students classified as gifted and/or talented enabling students to progress beyond the typical curriculum.

Epilepsy A disability that is caused by random, erratic electric impulses in the brain, which results in seizures.

Exceptionalities Special physical and/or intellectual needs that require special services for the students that have them.

Expressive language Language that is spoken, written, or communicated visually (e.g., sign language); language that is expressed in some way.

Extinction The removal of reinforcement from an individual that will result in a particular behaviour being terminated.

Facilitated communication A controversial method of dealing with children with autism in which an individual provides limited resistance to a child's arm, which then uses a communication board to communicate.

Family A unit of individuals who are related or who are together through legal means, providing support for each other.

Family support A model to provide services for individuals with exceptionalities by providing a wide array of supports for families.

Farsightedness (Hyperopia) The ability to clearly see objects at a distance, but difficulty clearly seeing objects up close.

Fetal alcohol spectrum disorder An umbrella term (not a diagnostic term) used to refer to the damage or range of disabilities caused by alcohol consumption during pregnancy.

Fetal alcohol syndrome A combination of physical and central nervous system abnormalities caused by maternal consumption of alcohol during pregnancy.

Fluctuating hearing loss Hearing loss that improves and/or gets worse over time (e.g., hearing loss due to otitis media).

Fluency The smoothness and rapidity in various skills, such as speech, oral language, reading, and other skills associated with thinking.

Form The rule systems of language: phonology, morphology, and syntax.

Full inclusion The movement or trend to fully include all students with exceptionalities, regardless of the severity, into all general education programs.

Functional behavioural assessment An analysis of the specific behaviours and behavioural patterns demonstrated by an individual within varied environmental contexts.

Future-based assessment An evaluation model that focuses on determining the likely future environments of individuals and proceeds to develop intervention programs around those future environments.

Gifted A term used to describe students who perform significantly above average in a variety of areas, including academic, social, motor, and leadership.

Gifted and/or talented (GT) A term frequently used to describe high-achieving students as well as students who excel in other areas, such as the arts.

Hard of hearing A disability category that refers to individuals who have a hearing loss but who can benefit from their residual hearing abilities.

Hearing-impairment A disability that affects an individual's sense of hearing. The term applies to any level of hearing loss, including being hard of hearing (residual hearing) or deaf.

Homework A form of individual practice that generally occurs in the home environment after school hours.

Human immunodeficiency virus (HIV) A major fatal disease that is currently impacting all areas of our society, including children in public schools.

Hyperkinetic disorders Another label to describe individuals who are hyperactive.

IEP Individualized education program. An IEP is required by most educational jurisdictions for every child receiving special education services. Other terms used to describe this type of program include individualized program plan (IPP) and personal program plan (PPP).

Inclusion A practice based on the belief that students with exceptionalities belong in general education settings, with support services provided in the general classroom by specialists.

Individuals with Disabilities Education Act (IDEA) U.S. legislation that requires states and local schools to provide an appropriate educational program for students with exceptionalities.

Infusion An approach to multicultural education in which the multicultural perspective is "infused" into all aspects of the curriculum day.

Inhalants A group of drugs and substances that can cause hallucinations and other reactions; examples include fingernail polish, paint thinner, and glue.

Integration A term that has been used to describe the placement of students with exceptionalities in general education classrooms, at least for a portion of each school day; otherwise known as mainstreaming.

Intellectual disability An impaired ability to learn which may cause difficulty in coping with the demands of daily life; usually present from birth.

Intelligence The term used to describe the cognitive capacity of an individual.

Intelligence quotient (IQ) A number used to express the apparent relative intelligence of a person determined by a standardized intelligence test.

Intelligence tests Tests that are designed to determine an individual's intelligence level, which is usually reported as an intelligence quotient (IQ).

Juvenile delinquency A legal term used to describe youth who have broken the law.

Language A formal method of communication used by people that uses signs and symbols to represent ideas and thoughts, and the rules that apply to standardize the system.

Language disabilities Any number of impairments that interfere with an individual's ability to communicate with others, such as voice disorders, expressive language skills, and receptive language abilities.

Language disorders Impairments of comprehension or use of language.

Learning disabilities (LD) The disability category that is characterized by students not achieving commensurate with their ability levels.

Least restrictive environment (LRE) The placement of students with exceptionalities alongside their typically achieving peers as much as possible.

Leukemia A form of cancer that attacks the blood cells, frequently found in children.

Levels of support The supports that are necessary to enable an individual with an exceptionality to function as independently as possible in the community.

Life skills A curricular orientation that emphasizes teaching abilities that will be required to function as an adult in a community setting.

Logical consequences Expected repercussions after a particular behaviour.

Low vision Students who have a visual impairment but who also have functional use of some residual vision; these students can read print.

Magnet schools Schools that offer an alternative curriculum to attract students.

Mainstreaming The term originally used to describe placing students with exceptionalities in general education classroom settings.

Meningocele A form of spina bifida where an outpouching occurs along the spinal cord, which has not been closed; there is no paralysis associated with this form of spina bifida.

Mental age A measure used in psychological testing that expresses a person's mental attainment in terms of the number of years it takes an average child to reach the same level.

Mental retardation The term preferred in the United States for a disability related to deficiencies in cognitive abilities that occurs before the age of 18 and is associated with deficits in adapted behaviour; this classification generally requires the individual to have an IQ score of about 70 or below.

Mentor program Program in schools where adults serve as mentors to children, especially children at risk of failure.

Mild mental retardation A level of mental retardation that usually includes those with an IQ range of about 50 to 70.

Mixed hearing loss A type of hearing loss occurring when both a conductive and sensorineural hearing loss are present.

Moderate mental retardation A level of mental retardation that usually includes those with an IQ range of about 35 to 50.

Modifications Changes in policy that will support students with exceptionalities in their learning.

Monocular A small telescope that enables a student to see print, pictures, diagrams, maps, and people.

Morphologic impairment An impairment in an individual's ability to use appropriate structure in oral language.

Morphology The rule system controlling the structure of words.

Motor excess A level of physical activity that is above expected levels for that age and cultural group.

Motor speech disorder Articulation disorders resulting from neurological damage such as stroke or head injury.

Multipass A reading and comprehension strategy whereby students make three passes through content reading material: a survey, size-up, and sort-out pass.

Multiple intelligences The theory that there are many different types of intelligences, rather than a single, general factor common in all individuals.

Multisensory impairments Disabilities of both the visual and auditory kind in the same person.

Muscular dystrophy A progressive disease that is characterized by a weakening of the muscles.

Myelomeningocele A form of spina bifida where part of the spinal cord is included in the outpouching, which usually results in lower trunk and limb paralysis.

Natural consequences The use of consequences typically found in a child's environment as a positive or negative consequence.

Nearsightedness (Myopia) The ability to clearly see objects up close but difficulty seeing objects at a distance.

Negative reinforcement The removal of an unpleasant consequence following a student's behaving or responding in the appropriate manner.

Nondiscriminatory assessment A method of evaluating students that prevents discrimination on the basis of differences (e.g., cultural differences, gender differences, etc.).

Normalization The process of attempting to make life as normal as possible for persons with exceptionalities.

Normalization movement A widely held belief that all individuals, regardless of any disability, should have as normal an education and living arrangement as possible; opposed to institutionalization.

Norm-referenced tests Evaluation procedures that are designed to enable the comparison of a child with a normative sample.

Nuclear family A reference to the modern family that is somewhat traditional in that there are two parents and children; however, both parents now generally work.

Omissions A speech production problem where individuals leave out sounds in their speech.

Ophthalmologist A medical doctor who specializes in the treatment of vision disorders and disorders of the eye.

Optometrist An individual who specializes in fitting eyeglasses to individuals with vision problems.

Orthomolecular therapy The use of dietary interventions to make an impact on learning and behavioural disorders; research does not support these interventions.

Orthopedic impairment The U.S. disability category that includes children with impairments caused by congenital anomaly (e.g., clubfoot, etc.), disease (e.g., bone tuberculosis, etc.), and other causes (e.g., cerebral palsy, amputations, etc.).

Other health impaired (OHI) The U.S. disability category that includes children with health problems that can result in eligibility for special education and related services.

Otitis media An inflammation of the area behind the ear drum or the middle ear typically associated with fluid buildup; the fluid may or may not be infected.

Paraeducator An individual who typically provides support to the classroom teacher. Other terms used to describe this individual may include paraprofessional, teacher aide, or teacher assistant.

Pediatric cancer Any form of cancer that occurs in children.

Peer tutoring An instructional technique that uses children to teach other children a variety of skills.

Peer-mediated instruction Adaptations in instruction provided by peers, such as reading a section of a textbook orally to a student with a reading disability.

Pharmacological intervention The use of drugs to combat behaviour or attention problems.

Phonation The process of putting speech sounds together to form words and sentences.

Phonemic awareness An understanding that words are composed of sound segments.

Phonologic impairment An impairment in an individual's ability to follow the rules that govern the formation of words and sentences from sounds.

Phonology The rule system that governs the individual and combined sounds of a language.

Physical abuse The treatment of children in inappropriate physical ways that are illegal and can lead to disabilities and even death.

Physical disabilities A variety of impairments related to health problems, such as spina bifida, cerebral palsy, and polio.

Placement The physical environment in which a student is being educated.

Portfolio assessment A method of evaluating children that considers their work, in addition to their performance on tests.

Positive reinforcement Affirmative, pleasant consequences that are given to an individual in recognition of an appropriate behaviour or response.

Prader-Willi syndrome A rare syndrome, caused by a problem with the fifteenth chromosome, which leaves an individual with mild intellectual disabilities and an obsession with eating.

Pragmatics The relationships among language, perception, and cognition; system controlling language function.

Prenatal Occuring prior to the birth of a child, during the approximately nine months of gestation.

Prereferral interventions A series of processes that should be attempted by general education teachers for students who are experiencing problems, prior to referring them for special education services.

Preventive discipline A method of behaviour management where emphasis is placed on preventing behaviour problems rather than reacting to them.

Procedural management The component of classroom management that deals with classroom procedures, such as rules, expectations, and daily routines.

Procedural safeguards Rights of children with exceptionalities and their parents regarding the provision of a free, appropriate public education.

Processing problems The primary problems experienced by students classified as having a learning disability, including thinking, memory, and organization.

Profound mental retardation The lowest level of functioning in the traditional classification system for individuals with intellectual disabilities, representing an IQ range below 20.

Program Refers to a child's educational program.

Psychodynamic approach An intervention model for students with serious emotional disturbance that focuses on psycho-analytical methods.

Psychosocial management An intervention model for students with serious emotional disturbance that focuses on the psychosocial elements.

Psychostimulants The most commonly prescribed medications for attention deficit/hyperactivity disorder.

Psychotic behaviour Ways of conduct indicative of a serious mental illness, such as schizophrenia.

Punishment The application of something that is unpleasant to a child after an inappropriate behaviour: the least-desired behaviour management method available.

Pure tone audiometry One of the methods used to evaluate hearing loss and hearing capabilities of individuals.

Receptive language Language that is received and decoded or interpreted.

Referral process The process of identifying and referring a child for special education services.

Reinforcement The process of providing consequences, positive or negative, following a particular behaviour or response.

Relative isolation The phase prior to the 1970s during which students with exceptionalities were served either outside the public schools or in isolated settings within them.

Remediation The offering of special aid or attention to learners who are struggling in a certain area.

Reprimand A statement to a student indicating that a certain behaviour(s) is inappropriate.

Residential programs The way in which many children with intellectual disabilities and/or sensory deficits were taught prior to the normalization movement.

Residual hearing Amount of hearing remaining after hearing loss; generally relates to a profound hearing loss.

Resilience The ability to thrive despite risk.

Resonance Tone of voice that is affected by air coming out of the nose—either too much air or not enough—resulting in hypernasality or hyponasality.

Resource room A special education classroom where students go from the general education classroom for brief periods during the day for specific help in problem areas.

Response cost A behaviour management technique where rewards or reinforcers are taken away from students who do not exhibit appropriate behaviours.

Restructuring The process of making major changes in public school programs, including site-based management and co-teaching activities.

School team The group of individuals, including classroom teachers, who develop an individualized education plan (IEP) for a child.

Self-contained classroom A special education environment where students are segregated from their typically achieving peers for most or all of the school day.

Self-evaluation A method that students can use to assess their own behaviours or work.

Self-injurious behaviours Behaviours exhibited by an individual that result in harm to that person, such as head banging.

Self-instruction Various techniques that students can use to teach themselves materials.

Self-management A cognitive strategy that helps individuals with attention or behaviour problems to manage their own problems.

Self-monitoring A cognitive strategy where students keep track of and record information about their own behaviours.

Self-paced instruction In this model for serving students who are classified as gifted and/or talented, students move through a curriculum at their own pace.

Self-recording A strategy that is used by an individual with a problem to help reduce inappropriate behaviours.

Self-regulation The ability to appropriately adapt one's behaviour to the environment or situation.

Self-reinforcement A cognitive strategy where students affirm themselves for appropriate behaviours.

Semantics The system within a language that governs content, intent, and meanings of spoken and written language.

Sensorineural hearing loss A type of hearing loss that affects the inner ear or cochlea.

Sensory impairment A disability affecting either the visual or auditory abilities of an individual.

Sequential phonics program Intervention program that follows a specified sequence of normal phonics development.

Severe mental retardation A level of intellectual disability pertaining to an IQ range of approximately 20 to 35.

Sibling support groups Groups developed for the siblings of individuals with exceptionalities to provide ongoing supports.

Snellen chart The chart used by schools and others to screen individuals for visual problems.

Social competence The ability to use social skills properly in appropriate contexts.

Social skills Any number of skills that facilitate an individual's successful participation in a group.

Socialized aggression A form of behavioural disorder affecting children whose inappropriate behaviours are acceptable in a group setting.

Sociological intervention An intervention model for children with emotional problems based on working with the entire family.

SOLVE-IT A learning strategy that helps students organize their responses to questions before giving an answer.

Specialized instruction Any educational activity that is not typical and that is generally utilized for children with particular needs.

Speech The vocal production of language that is the easiest, fastest, and most efficient means of communicating.

Speech disabilities Any number of disorders affecting an individual's ability to communicate orally.

Speech disorders These include impairments of voice, articulation, and fluency.

Speech-language pathologist The professional who works with students who experience speech and/or language problems.

Spina bifida A physical disability that results in the spinal column not closing properly, leaving an exposed spinal cord.

Splinter skills Skills that an individual with a severe disability, such as autism, possess that are beyond explanation.

Strategy A skill that is taught to students to give them the ability to deal with instructional content and social situations on their own.

Stuttering A disorder of speech fluency that results in a person's expressive language being difficult to understand due to breaks and repetitions in speech.

Subject matter acceleration In this system of providing accommodations for students classified as gifted and/or talented, students move through a particular subject area at an increased rate.

Subsequent environments attitude Educators with this attitude consider what will happen to their students in future and how they will need to adapt; they then design curriculum with a focus on these subsequent environments.

Substance abuse The practice of using illegal or inappropriate substances, such as alcohol, cocaine, or inhalants.

Substitutions A speech production problem characterized by the practice of substituting one sound for another.

Supported education The model of teaching used when students with exceptionalities are included in general education classes, with the supports necessary for them to achieve success.

Survey tests Tests that are used to determine general skill levels of students; results from these tests suggest if additional testing is necessary.

Syntax Various rules of grammar that relate to the endings of words and the order of words in sentences.

Talented The second component to the category of gifted and/or talented that includes children who excel in various arts and nonacademic areas.

Teacher-mediated content Modifications in instruction made by the teacher, such as modifying a homework assignment, that enable students with exceptionalities to be successful in inclusive settings.

Team teaching The utilization of more than one professional or paraprofessional who actually co-teach classes of students or lessons.

Testing The component of the assessment process where specific questions are asked an individual and a response is recorded.

Time out A behaviour management technique where the student is isolated from receiving reinforcement.

Tinted glasses Glasses with certain colour tints that have been used with persons with learning disabilities to correct reading problems; research data do not support their use.

Tourette syndrome A disorder that results in behaviour tics and inappropriate vocalizations, such as shouting cuss words.

Trainable mentally retarded (TMR) A term frequently used in schools to identify students with IQ ranges of 30 to 50.

Transactional approach An approach that encourages professionals to understand that a child's difficulties, especially if caused by attention deficit/hyperactivity disorder, will have an impact on the home and family, which will then have an impact on the child.

Transition The process of moving students from one setting to another, such as preschool programs to kindergarten, elementary school to junior high school, and high school to work.

Traumatic brain injury (TBI) A disability category that results from an injury to the brain, causing a student to have significant problems in school.

Tremor A mild form of cerebral palsy that causes trembling.

Tutorial model Educational approach where students with exceptionalities receive extra instructional opportunities either from teachers or peer tutors.

Validity The evidence collected to support appropriate inferences, uses, and consequences that result from an assessment.

Verbal apraxia A disorder of the nervous system, not due to muscular weakness or paralysis, affecting a person's ability to sequence and say sounds, syllables, and words.

Vestibular dysfunction medication A controversial therapy for treating dyslexia.

Vision therapy A controversial way to treat individuals with learning disabilities. It is based on the theory that the disabilities are caused by visual defects.

Voice disorders A speech production disorder that typically affects the pitch, loudness, and/or quality of the sounds being produced.

Vulnerable A term used to refer to children who are experiencing an episode of poor developmental outcomes.

Whole language A language arts curricular approach that focuses on teaching language arts as a whole, including written skills, reading, and oral language skills.

Whole language method Development in areas such as phonics is thought to occur naturally within a wider language context; the teacher teaches specific needed skills through mini-lessons.

References

Abbott, M. W., Walton, C., & Greenwood, C. R. (2002). Phonemic awareness in kindergarten and first grade. *Teaching Exceptional Children, 34*(4), 20–26.

Agnew, C. M., Nystul, B., & Conner, L. A. (1998). Seizure disorders: An alternative explanation for students' inattention. *Professional School Counselor, 2*, 54–59.

Agosta, J., & Melda, K. (1996). Supporting families who provide care at home for children with disabilities. *Exceptional Children, 62*, 271–282.

Alberta Learning. (2004). *Special education definitions 2004/2005*. Edmonton, AB: Alberta Learning.

Alberto, P. A., & Troutman, A. C. (1995). *Applied behavior analysis for teachers* (4th ed.). Englewood Cliffs, NJ: Merrill.

ALDs at a glance. 1996. *The Hearing Journal, 49*, 21.

Algozzine, B. (2001). Effects of interventions to promote self determination for individuals with disabilities. *Review of Educational Research, 71*, 219–277.

Algozzine, R., Serna, L., & Patton, J. R. (2001). *Childhood behavior disorders: Applied research and educational practices* (2nd ed.). Austin, TX: Pro Ed.

Allen, K. E. (1992). *The exceptional child: Mainstreaming in early childhood education* (2nd ed.). Albany, NY: Delmar.

Alley, G. R., & Deshler, D. D. (1979). *Teaching the learning disabled adolescent: Strategies and methods*. Denver, CO: Love Publishing.

Allsopp, D. H., Santos, K. E., & Linn, R. (2000). Collaborating to teach pro-social skills. *Intervention in School and Clinic, 33*, 142–147.

American Academy of Ophthalmology. (1984). Policy statement. *Learning disabilities, dyslexia, and vision*. San Francisco: Author.

American Academy of Pediatrics. (1988). *Learning disabilities and children: What parents need to know*. Elk Grove Village, IL: Author.

American Association on Mental Retardation. (1992). *Mental retardation: Definition, classification, and systems of supports* (9th ed.). Washington, DC: Author.

American Association on Mental Retardation. (2002). *Mental retardation: Definition, classification, and systems of supports* (10th ed.). Washington, DC: Author.

American Psychiatric Association. (2000). *Diagnostic and statistical manual of mental disorders (DSM-IV-TR)* (4th ed. rev.). Washington, DC: Author.

American Speech-Language-Hearing Association. (1982). Definitions: Communicative disorders and variations, *ASHA, 24*, 949–950.

American Speech-Language-Hearing Association. (1995, March). Position statement: Facilitated communication. *ASHA, 37* (Suppl. 14), 22.

American Speech-Language-Hearing Association. (1999). *Terminology pertinent to fluency and fluency disorders: Guidelines, 41*, 29–36.

American Speech-Language-Hearing Association. (2002). *Communication facts: Incidence and prevalence of communication disorders and hearing loss in children—2002 edition.*

Accessed on June 29, 2002 at http://professional.asha.org/resources/factsheets/children. cfm. Rockville, MD: Author.

American Speech-Language-Hearing Association. (2004c). *Introduction to Augmentative and Alternative Communication*. Retrieved August 2004, from ASHA website: http://www.asha.org/public/speech/disorders/Augmentative-and-Alternative.htm.

American Speech-Language Hearing Association. (2004d). *Types of hearing loss*. Retrieved August 2004, from ASHA website: http://www.asha.org.

American Speech-Language Hearing Association. (2004e). Technical report: Cochlear implants. *ASHA Supplement, 24*, in press.

American Speech-Language Hearing Association. (2004f). *Traumatic brain injury*. Retrieved December 2004, from ASHA website: http://www.asha.org.

American Speech-Language-Hearing Association Ad Hoc Committee on Service Delivery in Schools. (1993). Definitions of communication disorders and variations. *ASHA, 35* (Suppl. 10), 40–41.

Amerson, M. J. (1999). Helping children with visual and motor impairments make the most of their visual abilities. *Review, 31*, 17–20.

Anderson, J. A., Kutash, K., & Duchnowski, A. J. (2001). A comparison of the academic progress of students with ED and students with LD. *Journal of Emotional and Behavioral Disorders, 9*, 106–115.

Anthony, S. (1972). *The discovery of death in childhood and after*. New York: Basic Books.

Appalachian Educational Laboratory. (1995) National survey identifies inclusive educational practices. *The Link, 14*(1), 8. Available at: http://www.ael.org/page.htm?&pv=x&pd=1&index=138

Armstrong, D. G. (1990). *Developing and documenting the curriculum*. Boston: Allyn and Bacon.

At-risk youth in crisis: A handbook for collaboration between schools and social services. (1991). Albany, OR: Linn-Benton Education Service Digest.

Austin, J. F. (1992). Involving noncustodial parents in their student's education. *NASSP Bulletin, 76*, 49–54.

Autism Society of America. (2000a). *What is autism?* Retrieved December 2004, from Autism Society of America website: http://www.autism-society.org.

Autism Society of America (2000b). *Advocate, 33*, 3.

Babkie, A. M., & Provost, M. C. (2002). Select, write, and use metacognition strategies in the classroom. *Intervention, 37*, 172–175.

Baker, S. B., & Rogosky-Grassi, M. A. (1993). Access to school. In F. L. Rowlley-Kelly & D. H. Reigel (Eds.), *Teaching the students with spina bifida* (pp. 31–70). Baltimore, MD: Brookes.

Baren, M. (2000). *Hyperactivity and attention disorders in children: A guide for parents*. San Ramon, CA: Health Information Network.

Barkley, R. A. (1997). *Defiant children: A clinician's manual for assessment and parent training*. New York: Guildord Press.

Barkley, R. A. (1998). *Attention-deficit/hyperactivity disorder: A handbook for diagnosis and treatment* (2nd ed.). New York: Guilford Press.

Barkley, R. A. (1999–2000). *ADHD in children and adolescents.* Fairhope, AL: Institute for Continuing Education.

Barr, R. D., & Parrett, W. H. (1995). *Hope at last for at-risk youth.* Boston: Allyn and Bacon.

Barr, R. D., & Parrett, W. H. (2001). *Hope fulfilled for at-risk and violent youth: K–12 programs that work* (2nd ed.). Boston: Allyn and Bacon.

Barraga, N. C., & Erin, J. N. (1992). *Visual handicaps and learning* (3rd ed.). Austin, TX: Pro-Ed.

Barrish, H. H., Saunders, M., & Wolf, M. M. (1969). Good-behavior game: Effects of individual contingencies for group consequences on disruptive behavior in a classroom. *Journal of Applied Behavior Analysis, 2,* 119–124.

Bau, A. M. (1999). Providing culturally competent services to visually impaired persons. *Journal of Visual Impairment & Blindness, 93,* 291–297.

Bauwens, J., & Hourcade, J. J. (1995). *Cooperative teaching: Rebuilding the schoolhouse for all students.* Austin, TX: Pro-Ed.

Beale, I. L., & Tippett, L. J. (1992). Remediation of psychological process deficits in learning disabilities. In N. N. Singh & I. L. Beale (Eds.), *Learning disabilities: Nature, theory, & treatment* (pp. 526–568). New York: Springer-Verlag.

Beirne-Smith, M. (1989a). A systematic approach for teaching notetaking skills to students with mild learning handicaps. *Academic Therapy, 24,* 425–437.

Beirne-Smith, M. (1989b). Teaching note-taking skills. *Academic Therapy, 24,* 452–458.

Beirne-Smith, M., Ittenbach, R. F., & Patton, J. R. (2002). *Mental retardation* (6th ed.). Upper Saddle River, NJ: Prentice-Hall/ Merrill.

Beirne-Smith, M., Patton, J. R., & Ittenbach, R. (1994). *Mental retardation* (4th ed.). Columbus, OH: Merrill.

Bender, W. N. (1994). Social-emotional development: The task and the challenge. *Learning Disability Quarterly, 17,* 250–253.

Bender, W. N. (1998). *Learning disabilities: Characteristics, identification, and teaching strategies* (3rd ed.). Scarborough, ON: Allyn and Bacon.

Bender, W. N. (2001). *Learning disabilities: Characteristics, identification, and teaching strategies* (4th ed.). Boston: Allyn and Bacon.

Bender, W. N. (2003). *Relational discipline: Strategies for in-your-face kids.* Boston: Allyn and Bacon.

Benner, G. J., Nelson, J. R., & Epstein, M. H. (2002). The language skills of children with emotional and behavioral disorders: A review of the literature. *Journal of Emotional and Behavioral Disorders, 10*(1), 43–59.

Bereiter, C., & Engelmann, S. (1966). *Teaching disadvantaged children in the preschool.* Upper Saddle River, NJ: Prentice-Hall.

Bergland, M., & Hoffbauer, D. (1996). New opportunities for students with traumatic brain injury: Transition to postsecondary education. *Teaching Exceptional Children, 28,* 54–57.

Berry, V. S. (1995). Communication strategies for fully inclusive classrooms. In B. Rittenhouse & J. Dancer (Eds.), *The full inclusion of persons with disabilities in American society* (pp. 57–65). Levin, New Zealand: National Training Resource Centre.

Biederman, J., Faraone, S. V., Mick, E., Spencer, T., Wilens, T., Kiely, K. I., Guite, J., Ablone, J. S., Reed, E., & Warbufton, R. (1995). High risk for attention-deficit/hyperactivity disorder of parents with childhood onset of the disorder: A pilot study. *American Journal of Psychiatry, 152,* 431–435.

Bigge, J. L. (1991). *Teaching individuals with physical and multiple disabilities* (3rd ed.). New York: Macmillan.

Biklen, D. (1990). Communication unbound: Autism and praxis. *Harvard Educational Review, 60*(3), 291–314.

Biklen, D., Morton, M. W., Gold, D., Berrigan, C., & Swaminathan, S. (1992). Facilitated communication: Implications for individuals with autism. *Topics in Language Disorders, 2,* 23.

Blackman, J. A. (1990). *Medical aspects of developmental disabilities in children birth to three* (2nd ed.). Rockville, MD: Aspen.

Blalock, G., & Patton, J. (1996). Transition and students with learning disabilities: Creating sound futures. *Journal of Learning Disabilities, 29,* 7–16.

Blenk, K. (1995). *Making school inclusion work: A guide to everyday practices.* Cambridge, MA: Brookline Books.

Bowman, B. T. (1994). The challenge of diversity. *Phi Delta Kappan, 76,* 218–224.

Brackett, D. (1990). Communication management of the mainstreamed hearing-impaired student. In M. Ross (Ed.), *Hearing-impaired children in the mainstream* (pp. 119–130). Parkton, MD: York Press.

Breeding, M., Stone, C., & Riley, K. (n.d.). *LINC: Language in the classroom.* Unpublished manuscript. Abilene, TX: Abilene Independent School District.

British Columbia Ministry of Education. (August 2002). *Special education services: A manual of policies, procedures, and guidelines.* Retrieved December 2004, from B.C. Ministry of Education website: http://www.bced.gov.bc.ca.

British Columbia Ministry of Education, Special Education Branch. (1995). *Special education services: A manual of policies, procedures and guidelines.* Victoria: Author.

Brody, J., & Good, T. (1986). Teacher behavior and student achievement. In M. C. Wittrock (Ed.), *Handbook of research on teaching* (pp. 328–375). New York: Macmillan.

Brolin, D. E. (1989). *Life-centered career education.* Reston, VA: CEC.

Browder, D., & Snell, M. E. (1988). Assessment of individuals with severe disabilities. In M. E. Snell (Ed.), *Severe disabilities.* Columbus, OH: Merrill.

Brown, D. L., & Moore, L. (1992). The Bama bookworm program: Motivating remedial readers to read at home with their parents. *Teaching Exceptional Children, 24,* 17–20.

Brown, J., Cohen, P., Johnson, J. G., & Salzinger, S. (1998). A longitudinal analysis of risk factors for child maltreatment: Findings of a 17-year prospective study of officially recorded and self-reported child abuse and neglect. *Child Abuse & Neglect, 22,* 1065–1078.

Bruck, M. (1982). Language impaired children's performance in an additive bilingual education program. *Applied Psycholinguistics, 3,* 45–60.

Bryan, T., Bay, M., Lopez-Reyna, N., & Donahue, M. (1991). Characteristics of students with learning disabilities: A summary of the extent data base and its implications for educational programs. In. J. W. Lloyd, N. N. Singh, & A. C. Repp (Eds.), *The regular education initiative: Alternative perspectives* (pp. 121–131). Sycamore, IL: Sycamore.

Bryan, T., & Burstein, K. (2004). Improving homework completion and academic performance: Lessons from special education. *Theory into Practice, 43,* 213–219.

Bryant, D. P., Patton, J. R., & Vaughn, S. (2000). *Step-by-step guide: For including students with disabilities in state and district-wide assessments.* Austin, TX: Pro-Ed.

Buck, G. H., Bursuck, W. D., Polloway, E. A., Nelson, J., Jayanthi, M., & Whitehouse, F. A. (1996). Homework-related communication problems: Perspectives of special educators. *Journal of Emotional and Behavioral Disorders, 4,* 105–113.

Bullock, L. (1992). *Exceptionalities in children and youth.* Boston: Allyn and Bacon.

Burnley, G. D. (1993). A team approach for identification for an attention deficit hyperactivity disorder child. *The School Counselor, 40,* 228–230.

Burns, B. J., Hoagwood, K., & Maultsby, L. T. (1999). Improving outcomes for children and adolescents with serious emotional and behavioral disorders: Current and future directions. In M. H. Epstein, K. Kutash, & A. Duchnowski (Eds.), *Outcomes for children and youth with behavioral and emotional disorders in their families: Programs and evaluation of best practices* (pp. 685–707). Austin, TX: Pro-Ed.

Bursuck, W., Munk, D., & Olson, M. (1999). The fairness of report card grading adaptations: What do students with and without disabilities think? *Remedial and Special Education, 20,* 84–92, 105.

Bursuck, W. D., Polloway, E. A., Plante, L., Epstein, M. H., Jayanthi, M., & McConeghy, J. (1996). Report card grading and adaptations: A national survey of classroom practices. *Exceptional Children, 62,* 301–318.

Busch, T. W., Pederson, K., Espin, C. A., & Weissenburger, J. W. (2001). Teaching students with learning disabilities: Perceptions of a first-year teacher. *The Journal of Special Education, 35*(2), 92–99.

Bussing, R., Zima, B., Perwien, A. R., Belin, T. R., & Widawski, M. (1998). Children in special education programs: Attention deficit hyperactivity disorder, use of services, and unmet needs. *American Journal of Public Health 88*(6), 880–886.

Byrne, J. M., Bawden, H. N., DeWolfe, N. A., & Beattie, T. L. (1998). Clinical assessment of psychopharmacological treatment of preschoolers with ADHD. *Journal of Clinical & Experimental Neuropsychology, 20*(5), 613–627.

Canadian Association for Community Living. (2005). *Some definitions.* Retrieved April 2005 from CACL website: http://www.cacl.ca/english/aboutus/definitions.html

Canadian Association for Community Living. (2005). *Adult learning, training and employment.* Retrieved April 2005 from Canadian Association for Community Living website: http://www.cacl.ca/english/priorityresouces/altemployment/index.html.

Canadian Association of the Deaf (CAD). (2002). *Definition of deaf.* Retrieved August 2004, from CAD website: http://www.cad.ca.

Canadian Association of Speech-Language Pathologists and Audiologists (CASLPA). (2004). *Fact sheet: SLP's and AUD's—who we are and what do we do?* Retrieved August 2004, from CASLPA website: http://www.caslpa.ca.

Canadian National Institute for the Blind. (1999). *National Consultation on the crisis in vision loss.* Toronto: Author.

Candler, A. C., & Hildreth, B. L. (1990). Characteristics of language disorders in learning disabled students. *Academic Therapy, 25*(3), 333–343.

Carbone, E. (2001). Arranging the classroom with an eye (and ear) to students with ADHD. *Teaching Exceptional Children, 34,* 72–81.

Carey, S. T. (1987). Reading comprehension in first and second languages of immersion and francophone students. *Canadian Journal of Exceptional Children, 3,* 103–108.

Carnine, D. (1991). Curricular interventions for teaching higher order thinking to all students: Introduction to special series. *Journal of Learning Disabilities, 24,* 261–269.

Carpenter, S. L., & McKee-Higgins, E. (1996). Behavior management in inclusive classrooms. *Remedial and Special Education, 17,* 195–203.

Carr, E. G., Dozier, C. L., & Patel, M. R. (2002). Treatment of automatic resistance to extinction. *Research in Developmental Disabilities, 23,* 61–78.

Cassidy, V. M., & Stanton, J. E. (1959). An investigation of factors involved in the education placement of mentally retarded children: A study of differences between children in regular and special classes in Ohio. Columbus, OH: Ohio State University. (ERIC Document Reproduction Service No. ED 002752).

Cawley, J. (1984). *Developmental teaching of mathematics for the learning disabled.* Austin, TX: Pro-Ed.

Cawley, J., & Foley, J. F. (2001). Enhancing the quality of math for students with learning disabilities. *Learning Disabilities: A Multidisciplinary Journal, 11,* 47–59.

Cawley, J. F., & Foley, T. E. (2002). Connecting math and science for all students. *Teaching Exceptional Children, 34*(4), 14–19.

Center for Future of Teaching and Learning. (1996). *Overview of reading research.* Washington DC: Author.

Centers for Disease Control. (1988). *AIDS surveillance report.* Atlanta, GA: Author.

Chalfant, J. C., & Van Dusen Pysh, R. L. (1993). Teacher assistance teams: Implications for the gifted. In C. J. Maker (Ed.), *Critical issues in gifted education: Vol 3. Programs for the gifted in regular classrooms* (pp. 32–48). Austin, TX: Pro-Ed.

Chalmers, L. (1991). Classroom modifications for the mainstreamed student with mild handicaps. *Intervention in School and Clinic, 27*(1), 40–42, 51.

Chase, P. A., Hall, J. W., & Werkhaven, J. A. (1996). Sensorineural hearing loss in children: Etiology and pathology. In F. N. Martin & J. G. Clark (Eds.), *Hearing care for children* (pp. 73–88). Boston: Allyn and Bacon.

Cheney, C. O. (1989). The systematic adaptation of instructional materials and techniques for problem learners. *Academic Therapy, 25,* 25–30.

Choate, J. S. (2002). *Successful inclusive teaching: Proven ways to detect and correct special needs* (3rd ed.) Boston: Allyn and Bacon, p. 38.

Christenson, S. L., Ysseldyke, J. E., & Thurlow, M. L. (1989). Critical instructional factors for students with mild handicaps: An integrative review. *Remedial and Special Education, 10*(5), 21–31.

Clark, B. (1996). The need for a range of program options for gifted and talented students. In W. Stainback & S. Stainback (Eds.), *Contoversial issues confronting special education: Divergent perspectives* (2nd ed., pp. 57–68). Boston: Allyn and Bacon.

Clark, B. (2002). *Growing up gifted: Developing the potential of children at home and at school* (6th ed.). Upper Saddle River, NJ: Merrill/Prentice-Hall.

Clark, J. G., & Jaindl, M. (1996). Conductive hearing loss in children: Etiology and pathology. In F. N. Martin & J. G. Clark (Eds.), *Hearing care for children* (pp. 45–72). Boston: Allyn and Bacon.

Clary, D. L., & Edwards, S. (1992). Spoken language. In E. A. Polloway, J. R. Patton, J. S. Payne, & R. A. Payne (Eds.), *Strategies for teaching learners with special needs* (4th ed., pp. 185–285). Columbus, OH: Merrill.

Clinkenbeard, P. R. (1991). Unfair expectations: A pilot study of middle school students' comparisons of gifted and regular classes. *Journal for the Education of the Gifted, 15,* 56–63.

Cochran, P. S., & Bull, G. L. (1993). Computers and individuals with speech and language disorders. In J. D. Kindsey (Ed.), *Computers and exceptional individuals* (pp. 211–242). Austin, TX: Pro-Ed.

Colangelo, N., & Davis, G. A. (Eds.). (2003). *Handbook of gifted education* (3rd ed.). Boston: Allyn and Bacon.

Coleman, L. J., & Cross, T. L. (2001). *Being gifted in school: An introduction to developing, guidance, and teaching.* Austin, TX: Pro-Ed.

The Condition of Education. (1990). Washington, DC: Office of Educational Research and Improvement.

Conroy, J. (1993). Classroom management: An expected view. In C. J. Maker (Ed.), *Critical issues in gifted education: Vol. 3. Programs for the gifted in regular classrooms* (pp. 227–257). Austin, TX: Pro-Ed.

Conte, R. (1991). Attention disorders. In B. Y. L. Wong (Ed.), *Learning about learning disabilities* (pp. 55–101). New York: Academic Press.

Cook, R. E., Tessier, A., & Klein, M. D. (1992). *Adapting early childhood curricula for children with special needs.* New York: Merrill.

Cooper, H. (1989). *Homework.* White Plains, NY: Longman.

Corn, A. L., Hatlen, P., Huebner, K. M., Ryan, F., & Siller, M. A. (1995). *The national agenda for the education of children and youths with visual impairments, including those with multiple disabilities.* New York: American Foundation for the Blind.

Cosden, M. A. (1990). Expanding the role of special education. *Teaching Exceptional Children, 22,* 4–6.

Council for Children with Behavioral Disorders. (October 2000). Draft position paper on terminology and definition of emotional or behavioral disorders. Reston, VA: Author. (A Division of the Council for Exceptional Children, 1920 Association Drive, Reston, VA. p. 2).

Council for Exceptional Children. (1997). Effective accommodations for students with exceptionalities. *CEC Today, 4*(3), 1, 9, 15.

Council for Exceptional Children. (1999). The hidden problem among students with exceptionalities—depression. *CEC Today, 5*(5), 1, 5, 15.

Craig, S., Hull, K., Haggart, A. G., & Crowder, E. (2001). Storytelling addressing the literacy needs of diverse learners. *Teaching Exceptional Children, 33*(5), 46–51.

Cramer, S. (1997). *Collaboration: A success strategy for special educators.* Boston: Allyn and Bacon.

Crawford, H. (1998). Classroom acoustics: Creating favorable environments for learning. *ADVANCE for Speech-Language Pathologists and Audiologists, 36,* 25–27.

Crews, W. D., Bonaventura, S., Hay, C. L., Steele, W. K., & Rowe, F. B. (1993). Gilles de la Tourette disorder among individuals with severe or profound mental retardation. *Mental Retardation, 31,* 25–28.

Cronin, J. F. (1993). Four misconceptions about authentic learning. *Educational Leadership, 50*(7), 78–80.

Cronin, M. E., & Patton, J. R. (1993). *Life skills instruction for all students with special needs.* Austin, TX: Pro-Ed.

Cullinan, D., & Epstein, M. (1985). Teacher related adjustment problems. *Remedial and Special Education, 6,* 5–11.

Cummings, C. (1983). *Managing to teach.* Edmonds, WA: Teaching Inc.

Cummings, Maddux, and Casey. (2000). Individualized transition planning for students with learning disabilities. *The Career Development Quarterly, 49*(1), 60–72.

Cunningham, A. E., & Stanovich, K. E. (1997). Early reading acquisition and its relationship to reading ability ten years later. *Developmental Psychology, 33,* 934–945.

Dagenais, P. A., Critz-Crosby, P., Fletcher, S. G., & McCutcheon, M. J. (1994). Comparing abilities of children with profound hearing impairments to learn consonants using electropalatography or traditional aural–oral techniques. *Journal of Speech and Hearing Research, 37,* 687–699.

D'Angiulli, A., & Siegel, L. S. (2003). Cognitive functioning as measured by the WISC-R: Do children with learning disabilities have distinctive patterns of performance? *Journal of Learning Disabilities, 36*(1), 48–58.

Davies, P. W. S., & Joughin, C. (1993). Using stable isotopes to assess reduced physical activity of individuals with Prader-Willi syndrome. *American Journal on Mental Retardation, 98,* 349–353.

Davis, G. A., & Rimm, S. B. (1998). *Education of the gifted and talented* (4th ed.). Boston: Allyn and Bacon.

Davis, J. (1996). Two different flight plans: Advanced placement and gifted programs—different and necessary. *Gifted Child Today, 19*(2), 32–36, 50.

Davis, W. E. (1993). *At-risk children and educational reform: Implications for educators and schools in the year 2000 and beyond.* Orono, ME: College of Education, University of Maine.

Davis, W. E. (1995). Students at risk: Common myths and misconceptions. *The Journal of At-Risk Issues, 2,* 5–10.

Deiner, P. L. (1993). *Resources for teaching children with diverse abilities: Birth through eight.* Fort Worth, TX: Harcourt Brace Jovanovich.

Del Prete, T. (1996). Asset or albatross? The education and socialization of gifted students. *Gifted Child Today, 19*(2), 24–25, 44–49.

DeLong, R. (1995). Medical and pharmacological treatment of learning disabilities. *Journal of Child Neurology, 10* (suppl. 1), 92–95.

Deno, S. L., Foegen, A., Robinson, S., & Espin, C. (1996). Commentary: Facing the realities of inclusion for students with mild disabilities. *Journal of Special Education, 30,* 345–357.

Deno, S. L., & Fuchs, L. S. (1987). Developing curriculum-based measurement systems for data-based special education problem-solving. *Focus on Exceptional Children, 19*(8), 1–16.

Deshler, D., Schumaker, J. B., Lenz, B. K., & Ellis, E. S. (1984). Academic and cognitive interventions for LD adolescents (Part II). *Journal of Learning Disabilities, 17*(3), 170–179.

Deshler, D. D., Ellis, E. S., & Lenz, B. K. (1996). *Teaching adolescents with learning disabilities: Strategies and methods* (2nd ed.). Denver: Love Publishing.

Deshler, D. D., & Lenz, B. K. (1989). The strategies instructional approach. *International Journal of Disability, Development and Education, 36*(3), 203–224.

Desrochers, J. (1999). Vision problems—How teachers can help. *Young Children, 54,* 36–38.

Diefendorf, A. O. (1996). Hearing loss and its effects. In F. N. Martin & J. G. Clark (Eds.), *Hearing care for children* (pp. 3–18). Boston: Allyn and Bacon.

Donahue, K., & Zigmond, N. (1990). Academic grades of ninth-grade urban learning disabled students and low-achieving peers. *Exceptionality, 1,* 17–27.

Dorn, L., & Allen, A. (1995). Helping low-achieving first-grade readers: A program combining reading recovery tutoring and small-group instruction. *Journal of School Research and Information, 13,* 16–24.

Douglas, V. L., Barr, R. G., Desilets, J., & Sherman, E. (1995). Do high doses of stimulants impair flexible thinking in attention-deficit hyperactivity disorder? *Journal of the American Academy of Child & Adolescent Psychiatry, 34*(7), 877–885.

Dowdy, C. (1990). *Modifications for regular classes.* Unpublished manuscript, Alabama Program for Exceptional Children.

Dowdy, C. A., Carter, J., & Smith, T. E. C. (1990). Differences in transitional needs of high school students with and without learning disabilities. *Journal of Learning Disabilities, 23*(6), 343–348.

Dowdy, C. A., Patton, J. R., Smith, T. E. C., & Polloway, E. A. (1997). *Attention-deficit/hyperactivity disorder: A practical guide for teachers.* Austin, TX: Pro-Ed.

Dowdy, C. A., Patton, J. R., Smith, T. E. C., & Polloway, E. A. (1998). *Attention deficit/hyperactivity disorders in the classroom.* Austin, TX: Pro-Ed.

Dowdy, C. A., & Smith, T. E. C. (1991). Future-based assessment and intervention. *Intervention in School and Clinic, 27*(2), 101–106.

Downing, J. A. (2002). Individualized behavior contracts. *Intervention, 37,* 164–172.

Doyle, W. (1986). Classroom organization and management. In M. C. Wittrock (Ed.), *Handbook of research and teaching* (3rd ed., pp. 392–431). New York: Macmillan.

Dunn, L. M. (1968). Special education for the mildly handicapped: Is much of it justifiable? *Exceptional Children, 35,* 5–22.

Dunst, C. J., Johanson, C., Trivette, C. M., & Hamby, D. (1991). Family-oriented early intervention policies and practices: Family-centered or not? *Exceptional Children, 58,* 115–126.

DuPaul, G. J., & Eckert, T. L. (1998). Academic interventions for students with attention-deficit/hyperactivity disorder: A review of the literature. *Reading and Writing Quarterly, 14*(1), 59–83.

Dworet, D. H. & Rathgeber, A. J. (1998). Confusion reigns: Definitions of behaviour exceptionalities in Canada. *Exceptionality Education Canada, 8*(1), 3–19.

Dworet, D. H. & Rathgeber, A. J. (1990). Provincial and territorial government responses to behaviorally disordered students in Canada in 1988. *Behavioral Disorders, 15,* 201–209.

Dyches, T. (1998). The effectiveness of switch training on communication of children with autism and severe disabilities. *Focus on Autism and Other Developmental Disabilities, 13,* 151–162.

Dyson, L. L. (1998). A support program for siblings of children with disabilities. *Psychology in the Schools, 35*(1), 57–65.

Easterbrooks, S. R. (1999). *Adapting regular classrooms for children who are deaf/hard of hearing.* Paper presented to the Council for Exceptional Children convention, Minneapolis, MN.

Eaves, R. C. (1992). Autism. In P. J. McLaughlin and P. Wehman (Eds.). *Developmental disabilities* (pp. 68–80). Boston: Andover Medical Publishers.

Edgar, E. (1988). Employment as an outcome for mildly handicapped students: Current status and future directions. *Focus on Exceptional Children, 21*(1), 1–8.

Edgar, E., & Polloway, E. A. (1994). Education for adolescents with disabilities: Curriculum and placement issues. *Journal of Special Education, 27,* 438–452.

Edwards, C. (1996). Educational management of children with hearing loss. In F. N. Martin & J. G. Clark (Eds.), *Hearing care for children* (pp. 303–315). Boston: Allyn and Bacon.

Egel, A. L. (1989). Finding the right educational program. In M. D. Powers (Ed.), *Children with autism: A parent's guide.* New York: Woodbine House.

Ehlers, V. L., & Ruffin, M. (1990). The Missouri project—Parents as teachers. *Focus on Exceptional Children, 23,* 1–14.

Elizer, E., & Kauffman, M. (1983). Factors influencing the severity of childhood bereavement reactions. *American Journal of Orthopsychiatry, 53,* 393–415.

Elksnin, L. K., Bryant, D. P., Gartland, D., King-Sears, M., Rosenberg, M. S., Scanlon, D., Strosnider, R., & Wilson, R. (2001). LD summit: Important issues for the field of learning disabilities. *Learning Disability Quarterly, 24,* 297–305.

Elksnin, L. K., & Elksnin, N. (1998). Teaching social skills to students with learning and behavioral problems. *Intervention in School and Clinic, 33,* 131–140.

Ellenwood, A. E., & Felt, D. (1989). Attention-deficit/hyperactivity disorder: Management and intervention approaches for the classroom teacher. *LD Forum, 15,* 15–17.

Emery, R. E. (1989). Family violence. *American Psychologist, 44,* 321–327.

Engelmann, S., & Carnine, D. (1982). *Theory of instruction.* New York: Irvington.

Epilepsy Foundation of America. (1992). *Seizure recognition and observation: A guide for allied health professionals.* Landover, MD: Author.

Epstein, M. H. (1999). The development and the validation of a scale to assess the emotional and behavioral strengths of children—adolescents. *Remedial and Special Education, 20,* 258–262.

Epstein, M. H., & Charma, J. (1998). *Behavioral and emotional rating scale: A strength-based approach to assessment.* Austin, TX: Pro-Ed.

Epstein, M. H., Munk, D. D., Bursuck, W. D., Polloway, E. A., & Jayanthi, M. M. (1999). Strategies for improving home-school communication problems about homework for students with disabilities: Perceptions of general educators. *Journal of Special Education, 33,* 166–176.

Epstein, M. H., Patton, J. R., Polloway, E. A., & Foley, R. (1992). Educational services for students with behavior disorders: A review of individualized education programs. *Teacher Education and Special Education, 15,* 41–48.

Epstein, M. H., Polloway, E. A., Buck, G. H., Bursuck, W. D., Wissinger, L. M., Whitehouse, F., & Jayanthi, M. (n.d.). Homework-related communication problems: Perspectives of general education teachers. Manuscript submitted for publication.

Epstein, M. H., Polloway, E. A., Bursuck, W., Jayanthi, M., & McConeghy, J. (1996). Recommendations for effective homework practices. Manuscript in preparation.

Epstein, M. H., Polloway, E. A., Foley, R. M., & Patton, J. R. (1993). Homework: A comparison of teachers' and parents' perceptions of the problems experienced by students identified as having behavioral disorders, learning disabilities, or no disabilities. *Remedial and Special Education, 14*(5), 40–50.

Erickson, J. G. (1992, April). *Communication disorders in multicultural populations.* Paper presented at the Texas Speech-Language-Hearing Association Annual Convention, San Antonio, TX.

Etscheidt, S. K., & Bartlett, L. (1999). The IDEA amendments: A four-step approach for determining supplementary aids and services. *Exceptional Children, 65,* 163–174.

Evertson, C., Emmer, E. T., & Worsham, M. E. (2000). *Classroom management for elementary teachers* (5th ed.). Boston: Allyn and Bacon.

Evertson, C. M., Emmer, E. T., Clements, B. J., Sanford, J. P., & Worsham, M. E. (1989). *Classroom management for elementary teachers* (2nd ed.). Englewood Cliffs, NJ: Prentice-Hall.

Evertson, C. M., Emmer, E. T., Clements, B. J., Sanford, J. P., & Worsham, M. E. (2003). *Classroom management for elementary teachers* (6th ed.). Englewood Cliffs, NJ: Prentice-Hall.

Favazza, P. C., Phillipsen, L., & Kumar, P. (2000). Measuring and promoting acceptance of young children with disabilities. *Exceptional Children, 66*, 491–508.

Federico, M. A., Herrold, W. G. Jr., & Venn, J. (1999). Helpful tips for successful inclusion. *Teaching Exceptional Children, 32*(1), 76-82.

Fedorowitz, C., Benezra, E., MacDonald, W., McElgunn, B., Wilson, A., & Kaplan, B. (2001). Neurological brains of learning disabilities: An update. *Learning Disabilities Association Multidisciplinary Journal, 11*, 1–74.

Feingold, B. F. (1975). *Why your child is hyperactive.* New York: Random House.

Feldhusen, H. J. (1993a). Individualized teaching of the gifted in regular classrooms. In C. J. Maker (Ed.), *Critical issues in gifted education: Vol. 3. Programs for the gifted in regular classrooms* (pp. 263–273). Austin, TX: Pro-Ed.

Feldhusen, H. J. (1993b). Synthesis of research on gifted youth. *Educational Leadership, 22*, 6–11.

Feldhusen, J. F. (1998). Programs for the gifted few or talent development for the many. *Phi Delta Kappan, 79*(10), 735–738.

Felner, R., Ginter, M., Boike, M., & Cowan, E. (1981). Parental death or divorce and the school adjustment of young children. *American Journal of Community Psychology, 9*, 181–191.

Fennick, E. (2001). Coteaching: An inclusive curriculum for transition. *Teaching Exceptional Children, 33*(6), 60-66.

Ferguson, D. L. (1995). The real challenge of inclusion: Confessions of a "rabid inclusionist." *Phi Delta Kappan, 77*, 281–287.

Ferri, B. A., Keefe, C. H., & Gregg, N. (2001). Teachers with learning disabilities: A view from both sides of the desk. *Journal of Learning Disabilities, 34*(1), 22–32.

Field, S., Hoffman, A., & Spezia, S. (1998). *Self determination strategies for adolescents in transition.* Austin, TX: Pro-Ed.

Finson, K. D., & Ormsbee, C. R. (1998). Rubrics and their use in inclusion science. *Intervention in School and Clinic, 34*, 79–88.

Fiore, T. A., Becker, E. A., & Nerro, R. C. (1993). Educational interventions for students with attention deficit disorder. *Exceptional Children, 60*, 163–173.

Fisher, J. B., Schumaker, J., & Deshler, D. D. (1995). Searching for validated inclusive practices: A review of the literature. *Focus on Exceptional Children, 28*, 1–20.

Fleming, J. L., & Monda-Amaya, L. E. (2001). Process variables critical for team effectiveness. *Remedial and Special Education, 22*, 158–171.

Flexer, C. (1999). *Facilitating hearing and listening in young children* (2nd ed.). San Diego, CA: Singular Publishing.

Flick, G. L. (1998). Managing AD/HD in the classroom minus medication. *Education Digest, 63*(9), 50–56.

Foley, R. M., & Kittleson, M. J. (1993). Special educators' knowledge of HIV transmission: Implications for teacher education programs. *Teacher Education and Special Education, 16*, 342–350.

Foorman, B. R., & Torgesen, J. (2001). Critical elements of classroom and small group instruction promoting reading success in all children. *Research and Practice, 16*, 203–212.

Forness, S. R. (1999). Stimulant medication revisited: Effective treatment of children with attention deficit disorder. *Journal of Emotional and Behavior Problems, 7*, 230–233.

Forness, S. R., & Kavale, K. A. (1988). Planning for the needs of children with serious emotional disturbance: The National Mental Health and Special Education Coalition. *Behavior Disorders, 13*, 127–133.

Foster-Johnson, L., & Dunlap, G. (1993). Using functional assessment to develop effective, individualized interventions for challenging behaviors. *Teaching Exceptional Children, 56*, 44–52.

Fowler, M. (1992). *C.H.A.D.D. educators manual: An in-depth look at attention deficit disorder for an educational perspective.* Fairfax, VA: CASET Associates, Ltd.

Fox, P., & Emerson, E. (2001). Socially valid outcomes of intervention for people with MR and challenging behavior: Views of different stakeholders. *Journal of Positive Behavior Interventions, 3*(3), 183–189.

Fraenkel, J. R., & Wallen, N. E. (2000). *How to design & evaluate research in education* (4th ed.). Toronto, ON: McGraw-Hill.

Frederico, M. A., Herrold, W. G., & Venn, J. (1999). Helpful tips for successful inclusion: A checklist for educators. *Teaching Exceptional Children, 32*, 76–82.

Freeze, R., Lutfiyya, Z. M., Van Walleghem, J., & Cozzual M. C. (2004). The roles of non-disabled peers in promoting the social competence of students with intellectual disabilities in inclusive classrooms. *Exceptionality Education Canada, 14*(1).

Friedman, D., & Scaduto, J. J. (1995). Let's do lunch. *Teaching Exceptional Children, 28*, 22–26.

Friend, M., Bursuck, W., & Hutchinson, N. (1998). *Including exceptional students: A practical guide for classroom teachers.* Scarborough, ON: Allyn and Bacon.

Friend, M. F., & Bursuck, W. D. (2002). *Including students with special needs: A practical guide for classroom teachers* (3rd ed.) Boston: Allyn and Bacon.

Fritzell, B. (1996). Voice disorders and occupations. *Logopedics, Phoniatrics, and Vocology, 21*, 7–12.

Fuchs, D., Fernstrom, P., Scott, S., Fuchs, L., & Vandermeer, L. (1994). Classroom ecological inventory. *Teaching Exceptional Children, 26*, 14–15.

Fuchs, D., & Fuchs, L. S. (1994–1995). Sometimes separate is better. *Educational Leadership, 52*, 22–24.

Fuchs, L. S., & Fuchs, D. (2001). Helping teachers formulate sound test accommodation decisions for students with learning disabilities. *Learning Disability Research and Practice, 16*(3), 174–181.

Fuchs, L. S., Fuchs, D., Hamlett, C. L., Phillips, N. B., & Karns, K. (1995). General educators' specialized adaptations for students with learning disabilities. *Exceptional Children, 61*, 440–459.

Fulk, B. M., & Montgomery-Grymes, D. J. (1994). Strategies to improve student motivation. *Intervention in School and Clinic, 30*(1), 28–33.

Gable, R. A., Arllen, N. L., & Hendrickson, J. M. (1994). Use of students with emotional/behavioural disorders as behavior change agents. *Education and Treatment of Children, 17*, 267–276.

Gajria, M., & Salend, S. J. (1995). Homework practices of students with and without learning disabilities: A comparison. In W. Bursuck (Ed.), *Homework: Issues and practices for students with learning disabilities* (pp. 97–106). Austin, TX: Pro-Ed.

Gallagher, J. J., & Gallagher, S. A. (1994). *Teaching the gifted child* (4th ed.). Boston: Allyn and Bacon.

Garcia, J. G., Krankowski, T. K., & Jones, L. L. (1998). Collaboration intervention for assisting students with acquired brain injury. *Professional School Counselor, 2,* 33–38.

Garcia, S. B., & Malkin, D. H. (1993). Toward defining programs and services for culturally and linguistically diverse learners in special education. *Teaching Exceptional Children, 26,* 35.

Gardner, H. (1983). *Frames of mind: The theory of multiple intelligences.* New York: Basic Books.

Gardner, H., & Hatch, T. (1989). Multiple intelligences go to school: Educational implications of the theory of multiple intelligences. *Educational Researcher, 18*(8), 4–9.

Gargiulo, R. M. (1990). Child abuse and neglect: An overview. In R. L. Goldman & R. M. Gargiulo (Eds.), *Children at risk* (pp. 1–35). Austin, TX: Pro-Ed.

Gartland, D. (1994). Content area reading: Lessons from the specialists. *LD Forum, 19*(3), 19–22.

Gay, Lesbian, and Straight Education Network. (1999). *GLSEN's national school climate survey.* Washington, DC: Author.

Gearheart, B. R., Weishahn, M. W., & Gearheart, C. J. (1996). *The exceptional student in the regular classroom* (6th ed.). Columbus, OH: Merrill.

Geneva Centre for Autism. (2004). *Fact sheet—autism.* Retrieved December 2004, from Geneva Centre website: http://www.autism.net.

Gersh, E. S. (1991). What is cerebral palsy? In E. Geralis (Ed.), *Children with cerebral palsy: A parents' guide.* New York: Woodbine House.

Gerstein, R., Brengleman, S., & Jimenez, R. (1994). Effective instruction for culturally and linguistically diverse students: A reconceptualization. *Focus on Exceptional Children, 27*(1), 1–6.

Gerstein, R., & Woodward, J. (1994). The language-minority student and special education: Issues, trends, and paradoxes. *Exceptional Children, 60*(4), 310–322.

Gersten, R., & Chard, D. (1999). Number sense: Rethinking arithmetic instruction for students with math disorders. *Journal of Special Education, 33,* 18–28.

Getch, Y. Q., & Neuhart-Pritchett, S. (1999). Children with asthma: Strategies for educators. *Teaching Exceptional Children, 31,* 30–36.

Gibb, G. S., & Dyches, T. T. (2000). *Guide to writing quality individualized educational programs.* Boston: Allyn and Bacon.

Ghosh, R. (1996). *Redefining multicultural education.* Toronto: Harcourt Brace Canada.

Giangreco, M. F., Edelman, S. W., Broer, S. M., & Doyle, M. B. (2001). Paraprofessional support of students with disabilities: Literature from the past decade. *Exceptional Children, 68,* 45–63.

Goldman, S., & Rueda, R. S. (1988). Developing writing skills in bilingual exceptional children. *Exceptional Children, 56*(2), 121–129.

Goldstein, S., & Goldstein, M. (1990). *Managing attention disorder in children: A guide for practitioners.* New York: John Wiley & Sons.

Gollnick, D. M., & Chinn, P. C. (1994). *Multicultural education in a pluralistic society* (4th ed.). New York: Macmillan College Publishing.

Gonzalez, V., Brusca-Vega, R., & Yawkey, T. (1997). *Assessment and instruction of culturally diverse students.* Boston: Allyn and Bacon.

Good, T. L., & Brophy, J. E. (1987). *Educational psychology* (3rd ed.). New York: Longman.

Goree, K. (1996). Making the most out of inclusive setting. *Gifted Child Today, 19*(2), 22–23, 43.

Gorman, J. C. (1999). Understanding children's hearts and minds. *Teaching Exceptional Children, 31,* 72–77.

Graham, S. (1992). Helping students with LD progress as writers. *Intervention in School and Clinic, 27,* 134–144.

Graham, S., & Harris, K. R. (1997). Whole language and process writing: Does one approach fit all? In I. W. Lloyd, E. J. Kameenui, & D. Chard (Eds.), *Issues in educating students with disabilities* (pp. 239–258). Mahwah, NJ: Erlbaum.

Graves, D., Tuyay, S., & Green, J. (2004). What I've learned from teachers of writing. *Language Arts, 82*(2), 88–94.

Greenbaum, P. E., Dedrick, R. F., Friedman, R. M., Kutash, K., Brown, E. C., Lardieri, S. P., & Pugh, A. M. (1998). National adolescent and child treatment study (NACTS): Outcomes for children with serious emotional behavioral disturbance. In M. H. Epstein, K. Kutash, & A. Duchnowski (Eds.), *Outcomes for children and youth with emotional and behavioral disorders and their families: Programs and evaluation of best practices* (pp. 21–54). Austin, TX: Pro-Ed.

Greer, J. V. (1991). At-risk students in the fast lanes: Let them through. *Exceptional Children, 57,* 390–391.

Gresham, F. M. (1984). Social skills and self-efficacy for exceptional children. *Exceptional Children, 51,* 253–261.

Griswold, D. E., Barnhill, G. P., & Myles, B. S. (2002). Asperger's syndrome and academic achievement. *Focus on Autism and Other Developmental Disabilities, 17,* 94–102.

Grosenick, J. K., George, N. L., George, M. P., & Lewis, T. J. (1991). Public school services for behaviorally disordered students: Program practices in the 1980s. *Behavioral Disorders, 16,* 87–96.

Grossman, H. J. (1983). *Classification in mental retardation.* Washington, DC: American Association on Mental Deficiency.

Guernsey, M. A. (1989). Classroom organization: A key to successful management. *Academic Therapy, 25,* 55–58.

Guilford, J. P. (1959). *Personality.* New York: McGraw-Hill.

Guterman, B. R. (1995). The validity of categorical learning disabilities services: The consumer's view. *Exceptional Children, 62,* 111–124.

Guyer, B. (2000). Reaching and teaching the adolescent. In B. D. Guyer (Ed.), *ADHD: Achieving success in school and in life.* Boston: Allyn and Bacon.

Hall, B. J., Oyer, H. J., & Haas, H. J. (2001). Speech, language, and hearing disorders: A guide for the teacher (3rd ed.). Boston: Allyn & Bacon.

Hallahan, D. P., & Kauffman, J. M. (1991). *Exceptional children: Introduction to special education* (5th ed.). Boston: Allyn and Bacon.

Hallahan, D. P., & Kauffman, J. M. (1995). *The illusion of full inclusion.* Austin, TX: Pro-Ed.

Hallahan, D. P., & Kauffman, J. M. (1997). *Exceptional learners: Introduction to special education* (7th ed.). Boston: Allyn and Bacon.

Hallahan, D. P., & Kauffman, J. M. (2000). *Exceptional children: Introduction to special education* (8th ed.). Boston: Allyn and Bacon.

Hallahan, D. P., & Kauffman, J. M. (2003). *Exceptional children: Introduction to special education* (9th ed.). Boston: Allyn and Bacon.

Hallahan, D. P., Kauffman, J. M., & Lloyd, J. W. (1996). *Introduction to learning disabilities.* Boston: Allyn and Bacon.

Hallahan, D. P., Kauffman, J. M., & Lloyd, J. W. (1999). *Introduction to learning disabilities* (2nd ed.). Boston: Allyn and Bacon.

Hallahan, D. P., Lloyd, J. W., & Stoller, L. (1982). *Improving attention with self-monitoring: A manual for teachers.* Charlottesville, VA: University of Virginia Press.

Halvorsen, A. T., & Neary, T. (2001). *Building inclusive schools: Tools and strategies for success.* Boston: Allyn and Bacon.

Hamaguchi, P. A. (2002). *It's time to listen: Metacognitive activities for improving auditory processing in the classroom* (2nd ed.) Austin, TX: Pro-Ed.

Hammill, D. (1990). On defining learning disabilities: An emerging consensus. *Journal of Learning Disabilities, 23*, 74–84.

Hammill, D. (1993). A brief look at the learning disabilities movement in the United States. *Journal of Learning Disabilities, 26*, 295–310.

Hammill, D. D., & Bryant, B. R. (1991). The role of standardized tests in planning academic instruction. In H. L. Swanson (Ed.), *Handbook on the assessment of learning disabilities* (p. 377). Austin, TX: Pro-Ed.

Hammill, D. D., & Larsen, S. C. (1974). The effectiveness of psycholinguistic training. *Exceptional Children, 41*, 5–14.

Hansen, C. R. (1992). What is Tourette syndrome? In T. Haerle (Ed.), *Children with Tourette syndrome: A parents' guide* (pp. 1–25). Rockville, MD: Woodbine House.

Hanson, M. J., & Carta, J. J. (1996). Addressing the challenges of families with multiple risks. *Exceptional Children, 62*, 201–212.

Hardman, M. L., Drew, C. J., Egan, M. W., & Wolf, B. (1993). *Human exceptionality: Society, school, and family* (4th ed.). Boston: Allyn and Bacon.

Harwell, J. M. (1989). *Learning disabilities handbook.* West Nyack, NY: Center for Applied Research in Education.

Hasselbring, T., & Goin, L. (1993). Integrated media and technology. In E. A. Polloway & J. R. Patton (Eds.), Strategies for teaching learners with special needs (5th ed., pp. 145–162). Columbus, OH: Macmillan.

Haynes, W. O., & Pindzola, R. H. (1998). *Diagnosis and evaluation in speech pathology* (5th ed). Engelwood Cliffs, NJ: Prentice Hall.

Hazel, J. S., Schumaker, J. B., Shelon, J., & Sherman, J. A. (1982). Application of a group training program in social skills to learning disabled and non-learning disabled youth. *Learning Disability Quarterly, 5*, 398–408.

Heath, N. L. (1995). Distortion and deficit: Self-perceived versus actual academic competence in depressed and non-depressed children with and without learning disabilities. *Learning Disabilities Research & Practice, 10*, 2–10.

Heath, N. L. (1996). The emotional domain: Self-concept and depression in children with learning disabilities. *Advances in Learning and Behavioral Disabilities, 10*, 47–75.

Heath, N. L., & MacLean-Heywood, D. (1999). Research highlights: A clinic school partnership program for including students with behavioral problems. In J. Andrews & J. Lupart (Eds.), *The inclusive classroom, instructor's manual.* Toronto: ITP Nelson.

Heath, N. L., & Wiener, J. (1996). Depression and nonacademic self-perceptions in children with and without learning disabilities. *Learning Disability Quarterly, 19*, 34–44.

Heaton, S., & O'Shea, D. J. (1995). Using mnemonics to make mnemonics. *Teaching Exceptional Children, 28*(1), 34–36.

Heflin, L. J., & Simpson, R. (1998). The interventions for children and youth with autism: Prudent choices in a world of extraordinary claims and promises: Part II. *Focus on Autism and Other Developmental Disabilities, 13*, 212–220.

Heiligenstein, E., Conyers, L. M., Berns, A. R., & Miller, M. A. (1998). Preliminary normative data on DSM-IV attention deficit hyperactivity disorder in college students. *Journal of American College Health, 46*(4), 185–188.

Heinrich, S. R. (1999). Visually impaired students can use the internet. *NASSP Bulletin, 83*, 26–29.

Heller, K. A., et al. (Eds.). (2000). *International handbook of giftedness and talent* (2nd ed). (pp. 695–702). Kidlington, Oxford: Elsevier Science.

Heller, K. W., Alberto, P. A., Forney, P. E., & Schwartzman, M. N. (1996). *Understanding physical, sensory, and health impairments.* Pacific Grove, CA: Brooks Publishing Co.

Herer, G., & Reilly, M. (1999). Pediatric audiology: Poised for the future. *ASHA, 13*, 24–30.

Heward, W. L. (2000). *Exceptional children: An introduction to special education* (6th ed.). Englewood Cliffs, NJ: Prentice-Hall.

Heward, W. L. (2003). *Exceptional children: An introduction to special education* (7th ed.). Upper Saddle, NJ: Merrill.

Hietsch, D. G. (1986). Father involvement: No moms allowed. *Teaching Exceptional Children, 18*, 258–260.

Hill, D. (1991). Tasting failure: Thoughts of an at-risk learner. *Phi Delta Kappan, 73*, 308–310.

Hiller, J. F. (1990). Setting up a classroom-based language instruction program: One clinician's experience. *Texas Journal of Audiology and Speech Pathology, 16*(2), 12–13.

Hilton, A. (1990). Parental reactions to having a disabled child. Paper presented at annual International Conference of the Council for Exceptional Children.

Hobbs, T., & Westling, D. L. (1998). Promoting successful inclusion. *Teaching Exceptional Children, 34*, 10–14.

Hoida, J. A., & McDougal, S. E. (1998). Fostering a positive school environment for students with cancer. *NASSP Bulletin, 82*, 59–72.

Holcomb, D., Lira, J., Kingery, P. M., Smith, D. W., Lane, D., & Goodway, J. (1998). Evaluation of jump into action: A program to reduce the risk of non–insulin-dependent diabetes mellitus in school children on the Texas–Mexico border. *Journal of School Health, 68*, 282–287.

Homme, L. (1969). *How to use contingency contracting in the classroom.* Champaign, IL: Research Press.

Hoover, J. J. (1990). Curriculum adaptations: A five-step process for classroom implementation. *Academic Therapy, 25*, 407–416.

Hoover, J. J., & Patton, J. R. (1995). *Teaching students with learning problems to use study skills: A teacher's guide.* Austin, TX: Pro-Ed.

Horner, R. H. (2000). Positive behavior supports. In M. L. Wehmeyer & J. R. Patton (Eds.), *Mental retardation in the 21st century* (pp. 181–196). Austin, TX: Pro-Ed.

Housego, B. E. J. (1990). Student teachers' feelings of preparedness to teach. *Canadian Journal of Education, 15*, 37–56.

Howell, R. W., Evans, C. T., & Gardiner, R. W. (1997). Medication in the classroom: A hard pill to swallow? *Teaching Exceptional Children, 29*, 58–61.

Hoy, C., & Gregg, N. (1994). *Assessment: The special educator's role.* Pacific Grove, CA: Brooks/Cole.

Huff, C. R. (1999). *Comparison of criminal behaviors of youth gangs and at-risk youth*. Washington, DC: Department of Justice National Institute of Justice.

Hughes, C., Copeland, S. R., Guth, C., Rung, L. L., Hwang, B., Kleeb, G., & Strong, M. (2001). General education students' perspectives on their involvement in a high school peer buddy program. *Education and Training in Mental Retardation and Developmental Disabilities, 36,* 343–355.

Hunt, P., Doering, K., & Hirose-Hatae, A. (2001). Across-program collaboration to support students with and without disabilities in general education classrooms. *Journal of the Association for Persons with Severe Handicaps, 26,* 240–256.

Hunt, P., Hirose-Hatae, A., & Doering, K. (2000). "Communication" is what I think everyone is talking about. *Remedial and Special Education, 21,* 305–317.

Huure, T. M., Komulainen, E. J., & Aro, H. M. (1999). Social support and self-esteem among adolescents with visual impairments. *Journal of Visual Impairment & Blindness, 93,* 326–337.

Hux, K., & Hackley, C. (1996). Mild traumatic brain injury. *Intervention in School and Clinic, 31,* 158–165.

Idol, L. (1983). *Special educator's consultation handbook*. Austin, TX: Pro-Ed.

Infusini, M. (1994). From the patient's point of view. *The Journal of Cognitive Rehabilitation, 12,* 4–5.

Inge, K. J. (1992). Cerebral palsy. In P. J. McLaughlin & P. Wehman (Eds.), *Developmental disabilities* (pp. 30–53). Boston: Andover Press.

International Dyslexia Association (IDA). (2002). What is dyslexia? Author (www.interdys.org).

Iskowitz, M. (1998). Psychosocial issues. *ADVANCE for Speech-Language Pathologists and Audiologists, 36,* 14–15.

Jaquish, C., & Stella, M. A. (1986). Helping special students move from elementary to secondary school. *Counterpoint, 7*(1), 1.

Jayanthi, M., Nelson, J. S., Sawyer, V., Bursuck, W. D., & Epstein, M. H. (1994). Homework-communication problems among parents, general education, and special education teachers: An exploratory study. *Remedial and Special Education, 16*(2), 102–116.

Jenkins, J., & O'Connor, R. (2001). *Early identification and intervention for young children with reading/learning disabilities*. Paper presented at the 2001 LD Summit: Building a Foundation for the Future. Available online from http://www.air.org/ldsummit.

Jenkins, J. R., & Heinen, A. (1989). Students' preferences for service delivery: Pull-out, in-class, or integrated models. *Exceptional Children, 55,* 516–523.

Jerger, J., & Musiek, F. (2000). Report of the consensus conference on the diagnosis of auditory processing disorders in school-aged children. *Journal of the American Academy of Audiology, 11*(9), 467–474.

Johnson, A. (2001). How to use thinking skills to differentiate curricula for gifted and highly creative students. *Gifted Child Today, 24*(4), 58–63.

Johnson, D. J. (1999). The language of instruction. *Learning Disabilities: A Multidisciplinary Journal 9*(2), 1–7.

Johnson, G., Johnson, R. L., & Jefferson-Aker, C. R. (2001). HIV/AIDS prevention: Effective instructional strategies for adolescents with mild mental retardation. *Teaching Exceptional Children, 33,* 28–32.

Johnson, L. J., Pugach, M. C., & Devlin, S. (1990). Professional collaboration. *Teaching Exceptional Children, 22,* 9–11.

Johnson, R. M. (1994). *The picture communication symbols combination book*. Solana Beach, CA: Mayer-Johnson.

Jones, J. G. (1982). Sexual abuse of children: Current concepts. *American Journal of Diseases of Children, 136,* 142–146.

Jones, V. F., & Jones, L. S. (1995). Comprehensive classroom management (4th ed.). Boston: Allyn and Bacon.

Jones, V. F., & Jones, L. S. (2001). *Comprehensive classroom management* (6th ed.). Boston: Allyn and Bacon.

Kaderavek, J. N., & Pakulski, L. A. (2002). Minimal hearing loss is not minimal. *Teaching Exceptional Children, 34,* 14–18.

Kamps, D. B., Leonard, B. R., Vernon, S., Dugan, E. P., Delquadri, J. C., Gershon, B., Wade, L., & Folk, L. (1992). Teaching social skills to students with autism to increase peer interactions in an integrated first-grade classroom. *Journal of Applied Behavior Analysis, 25,* 281–288.

Kaplan, P. S. (1996). *Pathways for exceptional children: School, home, and culture*. St. Paul, MN: West Publishing.

Kaplan, S.N. (1979). *Inservice training manual*. Los Angeles: National/State Leadership Training Institute on the Gifted and the Talented.

Kataoka, J. C. (1987). *An example of integrating literature*. Unpublished manuscript.

Kataoka, J. C., & Patton, J. R. (1989). Integrated curriculum. *Science and Children, 16,* 52–58.

Kauffman, J. M. (1997). *Characteristics of emotional and behavioral disorders of children and youths* (6th ed.). New York: Merrill/Macmillan.

Kauffman, J. M., Lloyd, J. W., Baker, J., & Riedel, T. M. (1995). Inclusion of all students with emotional or behavioral disorders? Let's think again. *Phi Delta Kappan,* 542–546.

Kauffman, J. M., & Wong, K. L. H. (1991). Effective teachers of students with behavioral disorders: Are generic teaching skills enough? *Behavioral Disorders, 16,* 225–237.

Kavale, K. A., (2001). *Discovering models in the identification of learning disabilities. Executive summary*. Washington, DC: LD Summit.

Kavale, K. A., & Forness, S. R. (1996). Treating social skill deficits in children with learning disabilities: A meta-analysis of the research. *Learning Disability Quarterly, 19*(1), 2–13.

Kavale, K. A., & Forness, S. R. (1999). The future of research and practice in behaviour disorders. *Journal of Behaviour Disorders, 24,* 305–318.

Kavale, K. A., & Forness, S. R. (2000). History, rhetoric, and reality: Analysis of the inclusion debate. *Remedial and Special Education, 21,* 279–296.

Kazdin, A. E. (1989). Developmental psychopathology: Current research issues and directions. *American Psychologist, 44,* 180–187.

Keller, W.D., & Tillery, K.L. (2002). Reliable differential diagnosis and effective management of auditory processing and attention deficit hyperactivity disorders. *Seminars in Hearing, 23*(4), 337–347.

Kerr, L., Delaney, B., Clarke, S., Dunlap, G., Childs, K. (2001). Improving the classroom behavior of students with emotional and behavioral disorders using individualized curricular modifications. *Journal of Emotional and Behavioral Disorders, 9,* 239–247.

Kerrin, R. G. (1996). Collaboration: Working with the speech-language pathologist. *Intervention in School and Clinic, 32*(1), 56–59.

Keyser-Marcus, L., Briel, L., Sherron-Targett, P., Yasuda, S., Johnson, S., & P. Wehman. (2002). Enhancing the schooling of students with traumatic brain injury. *Teaching Exceptional Children, 34,* 62–65.

King-Sears, M. E. (2001). Three steps for gaining access to the general education curriculum for learners with disabilities. *Intervention in School and Clinic, 37,* 67–76.

King-Sears, M. E., & Bradley, D. (1995). Classwide peer tutoring: Heterogeneous instruction in general education classrooms. *Preventing School Failure, 40,* 29–36.

Kirk, S. A. (1962). *Educating exceptional children.* Boston: Houghton Mifflin.

Kirk, S. A., Gallagher, J. J., & Anastasiow, A. (2000). *Educating exceptional children* (8th ed.). Boston: Houghton Mifflin.

Kirk, S. A., & Gallagher, J. J., & Anastasiow, N. J. (1993). *Educating exceptional children* (7th ed.). Boston: Houghton Mifflin.

Kirsten, I. (1981). *The Oakland picture dictionary.* Wauconda, IL: Don Johnston.

Kitano, M. K. (1993). Critique of Feldhusen's "individualized teaching of the gifted in regular classrooms." In C. J. Maker (Ed.), *Critical issues in gifted education: Vol. 3. Programs for the gifted in regular classrooms* (pp. 274–281). Austin, TX: Pro-Ed.

Klassen, R. (2002). A question of calibration: A review of the self-efficacy beliefs of students with learning disabilities. *Learning Disabilities Quarterly, 25,* 88–102.

Kluwin, T. N. (1996). Getting hearing and deaf students to write to each other through dialogue journals. *Teaching Exceptional Children, 28,* 50–53.

Knitzer, J., Steinberg, Z., & Fleisch, B. (1990). *At the schoolhouse door.* New York: Bank Street College of Education.

Koegel, L. K., Koegel, R. L., Hurley, C., & Frea, W. D. (1992). Improving social skills and disruptive behavior in children with autism through self-management. *Journal of Applied Behavior Analysis, 25,* 341–353.

Kohn, A. (1996). *Beyond discipline: From compliance to community.* Washington, DC: Association for Supervision and Curriculum Development.

Korinek, L., & Polloway, E. A. (1993). Social skills: Review and implications for instruction for students with mild mental retardation. In R. A. Gable & S. F. Warren (Eds.), *Advances in mental retardation and developmental disabilities* (Vol. 5, pp. 71–97). London: Jessica Kingsley.

Korinek, L., Walther-Thomas, C., McLaughlin, V. L., & Williams, B. T. (1999). Creating classroom communities and networks for student support. *Intervention in School and Clinic, 35*(1), 3–8.

Kounin, J. (1970). *Discipline and group management in classrooms.* New York: Holt, Rinehart & Winston.

Krauss, M. W. (1990). New precedent in family policy: Individualized family service plan. *Exceptional Children, 56,* 388–395.

Kübler-Ross, E. (1969). *On death and dying.* New York: Macmillan

Lahey, M. (1988). *Language disorders and language development.* New York: Macmillan.

Lambros, K. M., Ward, S. L., Bocian, K. M., MacMillan, D. L., & Gresham, F. M. (1998). Behavioral profiles of children at-risk for emotional and behavioral disorders: Implications for assessment and classification. *Focus on Exceptional Children, 30*(5), 1–16.

Landau, S., Milich, R., & Diener, M. B. (1998). Peer relations of children with attention-deficit hyperactivity disorders. *Reading and Writing Quarterly, 14*(1) 83–106.

Lang, G., & Berberich, C. (1995). *All children are special: Creating an inclusive classroom.* York, ME: Stenhouse Publishers.

Lang, L. (1998). Allergy linked to common ear infection. *ADVANCE for Speech-Language Pathologists and Audiologists, 36,* 8–9.

Lavoie, R. (Writer). (1989). *How difficult can this be? Understanding learning disabilities: The F.A.T. city workshop* [Video]. (Available from PBS Video, 1320 Braddock Place, Alexandria, VA 22314).

Learning Disabilities Association of Canada (LDAC). (1987). *LDAC definition of learning disabilities.* Ottawa, ON: Author.

Learning Disabilities Association of Canada (LDAC). (2002). *Official definition of learning disabilities.* Ottawa, ON: Author.

Leonard, L. (1994). Language disorders in preschool children. In G. H. Shames, E. H. Wiig, & W. A. Second (Eds.), *Human communications disorders: An introduction* (4th ed., p. 179). New York: Macmillan.

Lerner, J. W. (1993). *Learning disabilities: Theories, diagnosis, and teaching strategies.* Boston: Houghton Mifflin.

Lerner, J. W. (2000). *Learning disabilities: Theories, diagnosis, and teaching strategies* (4th ed.) Boston: Houghton Mifflin.

Leroux, J. A. (2000). A study of education for high ability students in Canada: Policy, programs and student needs. In K. A. Heller et al. (Eds.), *International handbook of giftedness and talent* (2nd ed) (pp. 695–702). Kidlington, Oxford: Elsevier Science.

Lesar, S., Gerber, M. M., & Semmel, M. (1996). HIV infection in children: Family stress, social support, and adaptations. *Exceptional Children, 62,* 224–236.

Leverett, R. G., & Diefendorf, A. O. (1992). Suggestions for frustrated teachers. *Teaching Exceptional Children, 24,* 30–35.

Lewis, J. K. (1992). Death and divorce—Helping students cope in single-parent families. *NAASP Bulletin, 76,* 49–54.

Lewis, R. B. (1993). *Special education technology: Classroom applications.* Pacific Grove, CA: Brooks Publishing Co.

Lewis, T. J., & Sugai, G. (1999). Effective behavior support: A systems approach to proactive school-wide management. *Focus on Exceptional Children, 31*(6), 1–24.

Lloyd, J. (1988). Academic instruction and cognitive techniques: The need for attack strategy training. *Exeptional Education Quarterly, 1,* 53–63.

Lloyd, J. W., Forness, S. R., & Kavale, K. A. (1998). Some methods are more effective than others. *Intervention in School and Clinic, 33,* 195–200.

Lloyd, J. W., Landrum, T., & Hallahan, D. P. (1991). Self-monitoring applications for classroom intervention. In G. Stoner, M. R. Shinn, & H. M. Walker (Eds.), *Interventions for achievement and behavior problems* (pp. 201–213). Washington, DC: NASP.

Loehr, J. (2002). *Read the picture stories for articulation* (2nd ed.). Austin, TX: Pro-Ed.

Lopez, R., & MacKenzie, J. (1993). A learning center approach to individualized instruction for gifted students. In C. J. Maker (Ed.), *Critical issues in gifted education: Vol. 3. Programs for the gifted in regular classrooms* (pp. 282–295). Austin, TX: Pro-Ed.

Lord, J. (1991). *Lives in transition: The process of personal empowerment.* Kitchener, ON: Center for Research and Education in Human Services.

Luckasson, R. (2002). *Mental retardation: Definition, classification and systems of supports.* Washington, DC: American Association on Mental Retardation.

Luckasson, R., Coulter, D., Polloway, E. A., Reiss, S., Schalock, R., Snell, M., Spitalnik, D., & Stark, J. (1992). *Mental retardation: Definition, classification and systems of supports*. Washington, DC: American Association of Mental Retardation.

Luckasson, R., Schalock, R., Snell, M., & Spitalnik, D. (1996). The 1992 AAMR definition and preschool children: Response from the committee on terminology and classification. *Mental Retardation, 34*, 247–253.

Luckner, J. (1994). Developing independent and responsible behaviors in students who are deaf or hard of hearing. *Teaching Exceptional Children, 26*, 13–17.

Luckner, J. (1999). An example of two coteaching classrooms. *American Annals of the Deaf, 44*, 24–34.

Luckner, J., & Denzin, D. (1998). In the mainstream: Adaptions for students who are deaf or hard of hearing. *Perspectives in Education and Deafness, 17*, 8–11.

Luthar, S. S., Cicchetti, D., & Becker, B. (2000). The construct of resilience: A critical evaluation and guidelines for future work. *Child Development, 71*(3), 543–562.

Lyon, G. R., Fletcher, J. M., Shaywitz, S. E., Shaywitz, B. A., Torgesen, J. K., Wood, F. B., Schulte, A., & Olson, R. (2001). Rethinking learning disabilities. In C. E. Finn, A. J. Rotherham, & C. R. Hokanson, Jr. (Eds.), *Rethinking special education for a new century* (pp. 259–287). Washington, DC: Thomas B. Fordham Foundation.

Maag, J. W., & Katsiyannis, A. (1998). Challenges facing successful transition for youths with E/BD. *Behavioral Disorders, 23*, 209–221.

MacDougall, J. Irreconcilable differences: The education of deaf children in Canada. (2004). *Education Canada, 44*(1).

MacMillan, D. L. (1989). Mild mental retardation: Emerging issues. In G. Robinson, J. R. Patton, E. A. Polloway, & L. R. Sargent (Eds.), *Best practices in mild mental retardation* (pp. 1–20). Reston, VA: CEC-MR.

MacMillan, D. L., Gresham, F. M., & Siperstein, G. N. (1993). Conceptual and psychometric concerns about the 1992 AAMR definition of mental retardation. *American Journal of Mental Retardation, 98*, 325–335.

MacMillan, D. L., & Siperstein, G. N. (2001). *Learning disabilities as operationally defined by schools*. Paper presented at the 2001 LD Summit: Building a Foundation for the Future. Washington, DC.

Maheady, L., Harper, G. F., & Mallette, B. (2001). Peer-mediated instruction and interventions and students with mild disabilities. *Remedial and Special Education, 22*, 4–14.

Maker, C. J. (1993). Gifted students in the regular education classroom: What practices are defensible and feasible? In C. J. Maker (Ed.), *Critical issues in gifted education: Vol. 3. Programs for the gifted in regular classrooms* (pp. 413–436). Austin, TX: Pro-Ed.

Male, M. & Gotthoffer, D. (2000). *Quick guide to the internet for special education, 2000 edition*. Boston: Allyn and Bacon.

Malott, R. W., Whaley, D. L., & Malott, M. E. (1997). *Elementary principles of behavior* (3rd ed.). Upper Saddle River, NJ: Prentice-Hall.

Mandlebaum, L. H., Lightbourne, L., & VardenBrock, J. (1994). Teaching with literature. *Intervention in School and Clinic, 29*, 134–150.

Mangold, S. S., & Roessing, L. J. (1982). Instructional needs of students with low vision. In S. S. Mangold (Ed.), *A teacher's guide to the special educational needs of blind and visually handicapped children*. New York: American Foundation for the Blind.

Marchant, J. M. (1992). Deaf-blind handicapping conditions. In P. J. McLaughlin & P. Wehman (Eds.), *Developmental disabilities* (pp. 113–123). Boston: Andover Press.

Marschark, M., Lang, H.G., & Albertini, J.A. (2002). Educating deaf students: From research to practice. London: Oxford University Press.

Martini, R., Heath, N. L., & Missiunia, C. (1999). A North American analysis of the relationship between learning disabilities and developmental coordination disorder. *International Journal of Special Education, 14*, 46–58.

Masten, A. S. (2001). Ordinary magic: Resilience processes in development. *American Psychologist, 56*(3), 227–238.

Masters, L. F., Mori, B. A., & Mori, A. A. (1999). *Teaching secondary students with mild learning and behavior problems*. Austin, TX: Pro-Ed.

Mastropieri, M. A., & Scruggs, T. E. (1993). *A practical guide for teaching science to students with special needs in inclusive settings*. Austin, TX: Pro-Ed.

Mastropieri, M. A., & Scruggs, T. E. (1997). Best practices in promoting reading comprehension in students with learning disabilities: 1976 to 1996. *Remedial and Special Education, 18*, 197–218.

Mastropieri, M. A., & Scruggs, T. E. (2001). Promoting inclusion in secondary classrooms. *Learning Disability Quarterly, 24*, 265–274.

Mather, N. (1992). Whole language reading instruction for students with learning disabilities: Caught in the crossfire. *Learning Disabilities Research and Practice, 7*, 87–95.

Mather, N., Bos, C., & Babur, N. (2001). Perceptions and knowledge of preservice and inservice teachers about early literacy instruction. *Journal of Learning Disabilities, 34*, 472–482.

Mathes, P., & Torgesen, J. (1998, November). *Early reading basics: Strategies for teaching reading to primary-grade students who are at risk for reading and learning disabilities*. Paper presented at the Annual Council for Learning Disabilities Conference, Albuquerque, NM.

Matthews, D. J. (1993). Linguistic giftedness in the context of domain-specific development. *Exceptionality Education Canada, 3*, 1–23.

Mayer, C., Akamatsu, C. T., & Stewart, D. (2002). A model for effective practice: Dialogic inquiry with students who are deaf. *Exceptional Children, 68*(4), 485–502.

McAnally, P. L., Rose, S., & Quigley, S. P. (1999). *Reading practices with deaf learners*. Austin, TX: Pro-Ed.

McCardle, P., Cooper, J., Houle, G. R., Karp, N., & Paul-Brown, D. (2001). Next steps in research and practice. *Learning Disabilities Research and Practice, 16*(4), 250–254.

McConaughy, S. H., & Wadsworth, M. E. (2000). Life history reports of young adults previously referred for mental health services. *Journal of Emotional and Behavioral Disorders, 8*, 202–215.

McConnell, J. (1987). Entrapment effects and generalization. *Teaching Exceptional Children, 17*, 267–273.

McConnell, J. (1999). Parents, adolescents, and career planning for visually impaired students. *Journal of Visual Impairment & Blindness, 93*, 498–515.

McConnell, K. (2001). Placement. In R. Algozzine, L. Serna, & J. R. Patton (Eds.), *Childhood behavior disorders: Applied research and educational practice* (pp. 309–330). Austin, TX: Pro-Ed.

McConnell, K., Ryser, G., & Patton, J. R. (2002a). *Practical ideas that really work for disruptive, defiant, and difficult students: Preschool through grade 4*. Austin, TX: Pro-Ed.

McConnell, K., Ryser, G., & Patton, J. R. (2002b). *Practical ideas that really work for disruptive, defiant, and difficult students: Grades 5 through 12.* Austin, TX: Pro-Ed.

McConnell, M. E., Hilvitz, P. B., & Cox, C. J. (1998). Functional assessment: A systematic process for assessment and intervention in general and special education classrooms. *Intervention in School and Clinic, 34,* 10–20.

McDevitt, T. M. (1990). Encouraging young children's listening. *Academic Therapy, 25,* 569–577.

McDonnell, J. J., Hardman, M. L., McDonnell, A. P., & Kiefer-O'Donnell, R. (1995). *An introduction to persons with severe disabilities.* Boston: Allyn and Bacon.

McDougall, D. (1998). Research on self-management techniques used by students with disabilities in general education settings: A descriptive review. *Remedial and Special Education, 19,* 310–320.

McEachlin, J. J., Smith, T., & Lovaas, O. I. (1993). Long-term outcome for children with autism who received early intensive behavioral treatment. *American Journal on Mental Retardation, 97,* 359–372.

McEnvoy, M. A., Shores, R. E., Wehby, J. H., Johnson, S. M., & Fox J. J. (1990). Special education teachers' implementation of procedures to promote social interaction among children in integrated settings. *Education and Training in Mental Retardation, 25,* 267–276.

McEvoy, A., & Welker, R. (2000). Antisocial behavior and academic failures and school climate: A critical review. *Journal of Emotional and Behavior Disorders, 8,* 24–33.

McGrail, L. (1998). Modifying regular classroom curricula for high ability students. *Gifted Child Today, 21,* 36–39.

McIntosh, R., Vaughn, S., Bennerson, B., (1995). FAST social skills with a SLAM. *Teaching Exceptional Children, 28,* 37–41.

McKamey, E. S. (1991). Storytelling for children with learning disabilities: A first-hand account. *Teaching Exceptional Children, 23,* 46–48.

McKeever, P. (1983). Siblings of chronically ill children: A literature review with implications for research and practice. *American Journal of Orthopsychiatry, 53,* 209–217.

McLaughlin, P. J. & Wehman, P. (1997). *Developmental Disabilities.* Boston: Andover Press.

McLaughlin-Cheng, E., (1998). The Asperger syndrome and autism: A literature review and meta-analysis. *Focus on Autism and Other Developmental Disabilities, 13,* 234–245.

McLesky, J., Henry, D., & Hedges, D. (1999). Inclusion: What progress is being made across disability categories? *Teaching Exceptional Children, 31,* 60–64.

McLoughlin, J. A., & Lewis, R. B. (2000). *Assessing special students* (5th ed.). Columbus, OH: Merrill.

McNeill, J. H., & Fowler, S. A. (1996). Using story reading to encourage children's conversations. *Teaching Exceptional Children, 28*(2), 43–47.

McPartland, J. M., & Slavin, R. E. (1990). *Policy perspectives increasing achievement of at-risk students at each grade level.* Washington, DC: U.S. Department of Education.

Mercer, C., Jordan, L., Alsop, D., & Mercer, A. (1996). Learning disabilities definitions and criteria used by the state education departments. *Learning Disability Quarterly, 19*(2), 217–232.

Mercer, C. D. (1997). *Students with learning disabilities* (5th ed.). New York: Merrill.

Meyer, D. (2001). Meeting the unique concerns of brothers and sisters of children with special needs. *Insight, 51,* 28–32.

Michaels, C. (1994). *Transition strategies for persons with learning disabilities.* San Diego: Singular.

Miller, R. (1996). *The developmentally appropriate inclusive classroom in early education.* Scarborough, ON: Delmar.

Miller, R. J. (1995). Preparing for adult life: Teaching students their rights and responsibilities. *CEC Today, 1*(7), 12.

Miller, S. P., Mercer, C. D., & Dillon, A. S. (1992). CSA: Acquiring and retaining math skills. *Intervention in School and Clinic, 28,* 105–110.

Minner, S., & Prater, G. (1989). Arranging the physical environment of special education classrooms. *Academic Therapy, 25,* 91–96.

Minnesota Department of Education. (2003). Introduction to auditory processing disorders. Retrieved August 2004, from http://education.state.mn.us/content/059872.pdf.

Mira, M. P., Tucker, B. F., & Tyler, J. S. (1992). *Traumatic brain injury in children and adolescents: A sourcebook for teachers and other school personnel.* Austin, TX: Pro-Ed.

Mirman, N. J. (1991). Reflections on educating the gifted child. *G/C/T, 14,* 57–60.

Moecker, D. L. (1992, November). Special education decision process: For Anglo and Hispanic students. Paper presented at the *Council for Exceptional Children* Topical Conference on Culturally and Linguistically Diverse Exceptional Children, Minneapolis.

Montague, M., McKinney, J. D., & Hocutt, L. (1994). Assessing students for attention deficit disorder. *Intervention in School and Clinic, 29*(4), 212–218.

Moore, J. A., & Teagle, H. F. B. (2002). An introduction to cochlear implant technology, activation, and programming. *Language, Speech, and Hearing Services in Schools, 33,* 153–161.

Moores, D. (2001). Educating the deaf: Psychology, principles, and practices (6th ed.). Columbus, OH: Merrill.

Morgan, S. R. (1994a). *At-risk youth in crises: A team approach in the schools* (2nd ed.). Austin, TX: Pro-Ed.

Morgan, S. (1994b). *Children in crisis: A team approach in the schools* (2nd ed.). Austin, TX: Pro-Ed.

Moriarty, D. (1967). *The loss of loved ones.* Springfield, IL: Charles C Thomas.

Morris, S. (2002). Promoting social skills among students with nonverbal learning disabilities. *Teaching Exceptional Children, 34,* 66–70.

Morrison, G. S. (1997). *Teaching in America.* Boston: Allyn and Bacon.

Morrison, G. M., & Cosden, M. A. (1997). Risk, resilience, and adjustment of individuals with learning disabilities. *Learning Disability Quarterly, 20,* 43–60.

Munk, D. D., & Bursuck, W. D. (2001). Preliminary findings on personalized grading plans for middle school students with learning disabilities. *Exceptional Children, 67,* 211–234.

Munk, D. D., Bursuck, W. D., Epstein, M. H., Jayanthi, M., Nelson, J., & Polloway, E. A. (2001). Homework communication problems: Perspectives of special and general education parents. *Reading and Writing Quarterly, 17,* 189–203.

Musselwhite, C. R. (1987). Augmentative communication. In E. T. McDonald (Ed.), *Treating cerebral palsy: For clinicians by clinicians* (pp. 209–238). Austin, TX: Pro-Ed.

Myles, B. S., & Simpson, R. L. (1998). Asperger syndrome: A guide for educators and parents. Austin, TX: Pro-Ed.

Nagel, L., McDougall, D., & Granby, C. (1996). Students' self-reported substance use by grade level and gender. *Journal of Drug Education, 26,* 49–56.

Naremore, R. C. (1980). Language disorders in children. In T. J. Hixon, L. D. Shriberg, & J. H. Saxman (Eds.), *Introduction to communication disorders* (pp. 111–132). Englewood Cliffs, NJ: Prentice-Hall.

National Dropout Prevention Center. (1990). *Mentoring programs for at-risk youth.* Clemson, SC: Clemson University.

National Heart, Lung, and Blood Institute. (1998). How asthma friendly is your school? *Journal of School Health, 68,* 167–168.

National Joint Committee on Learning Disabilities. (1993). A reaction to full inclusion: A reaffirmation of the rights of students with learning disabilities to a continuum of service. *Journal of Learning Disabilities, 26,* 96.

National Joint Committee on Learning Disabilities. (1988). Letter to NJCLD member organizations.

National Reading Panel. (2000). *Report of the National Reading Panel: Teaching children to read.* Washington, DC: National Institute of Child Health and Human Development.

National study on inclusion: Overview and summary report. (1995). *National Center on Educational Restructuring Inclusion, 2,* 1–8.

Nelson, J. S., Jayanthi, M., Epstein, M. H. & Bursuck, W. D. (2000). Using the nominal work technique for homework communication decisions. *Remedial & Special Education, 23*(6), 379–386.

Nelson, N. W. (1988). Curriculum-based language assessment and intervention. *Language, Speech and Hearing Services in School, 20,* 170–183.

Nessner, K. (1990, Winter). Children with disabilities. *Canadian Social Trends,* 18–20.

Nolan, E. E., Volpe, R. J., Gadow, K. D., & Sprafkin, J. (1999). Developmental, gender, and co-morbidity differences in clinically referred children with ADHD. *Journal of Emotional & Behavioral Disorders, 7*(1), 11–21.

Northern, J. L., & Downs, M. P. (2002). *Hearing in children* (5th ed.). Philadelphia, PA: Lippincott Williams & Wilkins.

Norwich, B. (1999). The connotation of special education labels for professionals in the field. *British Journal of Special Education, 26*(4), 179–183.

Nowacek, E. J., & McShane, E. (1993). Spoken language. In E. A. Polloway & J. R. Patton (Eds.), *Strategies for teaching learners with special needs* (5th ed., pp. 183–205). Columbus, OH: Merrill.

O'Brien, J., Forest, M., Snow, J. E., & Hasbury, D. (1989). *Action for inclusion: How to improve schools by welcoming children with special needs into regular classrooms.* Toronto, ON: Frontier College Press.

Olson, J. L., & Platt, J. M. (1996). *Teaching children and adolescents with special needs* (2nd ed). Englewood Cliffs, NJ: Merrill.

Orr, T. J., Myles, B. S., & Carlson, J. R. (1998). The impact of rhythmic entertainment on a person with autism. *Focus on Autism and Other Developmental Disabilities, 13,* 163–166.

O'Shaughnessy, T. E. & Swanson, H. L. (1998). Do immediate memory deficits in students with learning disabilities in reading reflect a developmental lag or deficit? *Learning Disability Quarterly, 21,* 123–148.

Owens, R. E. (1996). Language development: An introduction (4th ed.). Boston: Allyn & Bacon.

Palinscar, A., & Klenk, L. (1992). Fostering literacy learning in supportive contexts. *Journal of Learning Disabilities, 25,* 211–225.

Palmer, D. S., Fuller, K., Arora, T., & Nelson, M. (2001). Taking sides: Parent views on inclusion for their children with severe disabilities. *Exceptional Children, 67,* 467–484.

Pancheri, C., & Prater, M. A. (1999, March/April). What teachers and parents should know about Ritalin. *Teaching Exceptional Children,* 20–26.

Pandiani, J. A., Schacht, L. M., & Banks, S. M. (2001). After children's services: A longitudinal study of significant life events. *Journal of Emotional and Behavioral Disorders, 9,* 131–138.

Parke, B. N. (1989). *Gifted students in regular classrooms.* Boston: Allyn and Bacon.

Patton, J. R. (1994). Practical recommendations for using homework with students with learning disabilities. *Journal of Learning Disabilities, 27,* 570–578.

Patton, J. R. (1995). *Transition from school to adult life for students with special needs: Basic concepts and recommended practices* (p. 14). Austin, TX: Pro-Ed.

Patton, J. R., Blackburn, J., & Fad, K. (2001). *Focus on exceptional children* (8th ed.). Columbus, OH: Merrill.

Patton, J. R., & Cronin, M. E. (1993). *Life skills, instruction for all students with disabilities.* Austin, TX: Pro-Ed.

Patton, J. R., Cronin, M. E., Polloway, E. A., Hutchison, D. R., & Robinson, G. A. (1989). Curricular considerations: A life skills orientation. In G. A. Robinson, J. R. Patton, E. A. Polloway, & L. Sargent (Eds.), *Best practices in mild mental retardation* (p. 31). Reston, VA: CEC-MR.

Patton, J. R., & Dunn, C. R. (1998). *Transition from school to adult life for students with special needs: Basic concepts and recommended practices.* Austin, TX: Pro-Ed.

Patton, J. R., Jayanthi, M., & Polloway, E. A. (2001). Home-school collaboration about homework. *Reading and Writing Quarterly, 17,* 230–236.

Patton, J. R., Polloway, E. A., & Smith, T. E. C. (2000). Educating students with mild mental retardation. In M. L. Wehmeyer & J. R. Patton (Eds.), *Mental retardation in the 21st century.* Austin, TX: Pro-Ed.

Patton, J. R., Polloway, E. A., Smith, T. E. C., Edgar, E., Clark, G. M., & Lee, S. (1996). Individuals with mild mental retardation: Postsecondary outcomes and implications for educational policy. *Education and Training in Mental Retardation and Developmental Disabilities, 31,* 77–85.

Pearpoint, J., Forest, M., & O'Brien, J. (1996). MAPs, circles of friends, and PATH. In S. Stainback & W. Stainback (Eds.), *Inclusion: A guide for educators* (pp. 67–86). Baltimore, MD: Brookes.

Pearson, S. (1996). Child abuse among children with disabilities. *Teaching Exceptional Children, 29,* 34–38.

Peckham, V. C. (1993). Children with cancer in the classroom. *Teaching Exceptional Children, 26,* 31.

Perske, R. (1988). *Circles of friends: People with disabilities and their friends enrich the lives of one another.* Nashville, TN: Abingdon Press.

Pfiffner, L., & Barkley, R. (1991). Educational placement and classroom management. In R. Barkley (Ed.), *Attention deficit hyperactivity disorder: A handbook for diagnosis and treatment* (pp. 498–539). New York: Guilford.

Physicians' Desk Reference. (1994). Oravell, NJ: Medical Economics Company.

Physicians' Desk Reference. (1999). Oravell, NJ: Medical Economics Company.

Pierce, C. (1994). Importance of classroom climate for at-risk learners. *Journal of Educational Research, 88,* 37–44.

Plummer, D. L. (1995). Serving the needs of gifted children from a multicultural perspective. In J. L. Genshaft, M. Bireley, & C. L. Hollinger (Eds.), *Serving gifted and talented students: A resource for school personnel* (pp. 285–300). Austin, TX: Pro-Ed.

Pocock, A., Lambros, S., Karvonen, M., Test, D. W., Algozzine, B., Wood, W., & Martin, J. S. (2002). Successful strategies for promoting self-advocacy among students with learning disabilities: The LEAD Group. *Intervention in School and Clinic, 37*(4), 209–216.

Podemski, R. S., Marsh, G. E., Smith, T. E. C., & Price, B. J. (1995). *Comprehensive administration of special education.* Columbus, OH: Merrill.

Polloway, E. A. (1997). Developmental principles of the Luckasson et al. AAMR definition: A retrospective. *Education and Training in Mental Retardation and Developmental Disabilities, 32,* 174–178.

Polloway, E. A., Bursuck, W., Jayanthi, M., Epstein, M., & Nelson, J. (1996). Treatment acceptability: Determining appropriate interventions within inclusive classrooms. *Intervention in School and Clinic, 31,* 133–144.

Polloway, E. A., Epstein, M. H., & Bursuck, W. D. (2002). Homework for students with learning disabilities. *Reading and Writing Quarterly, 17,* 181–187.

Polloway, E. A., Epstein, M. H., Bursuck, W. D., Jayanthi, M., & Cumblad, C. (1994). Homework practices of general education teachers. *Journal of Learning Disabilities, 27,* 500–509.

Polloway, E. A., Epstein, M. H., Bursuck, W. D., Roderique, T. W., McConeghy, J., & Jayanthi, M. (1994). Classroom grading: A national survey of policies. *Remedial and Special Education, 15*(2), 162–170.

Polloway, E. A., & Jones-Wilson, L. (1992). Principles of assessment and instruction. In E. A. Polloway & T. E. C. Smith (Eds.), *Language instruction for students with disabilities* (pp. 87–120). Denver, CO: Love Publishing.

Polloway, E. A., Miller, L., & Smith, T. E. C. (2003). *Language instruction for students with disabilities* (3rd ed.). Denver: Love.

Polloway, E. A., & Patton, J. R. (1993). *Strategies for teaching learners with special needs* (5th ed.). Columbus, OH: Merrill/Macmillan.

Polloway, E. A., & Patton, J. R. (1997). *Strategies for teaching learners with special needs* (6th ed.). Columbus, OH: Merrill.

Polloway, E. A., Patton, J. R., Epstein, M. H., & Smith, T. E. C. (1989). Comprehensive curriculum: Program design for students with mild handicaps. *Focus on Exceptional Children, 21*(8), 1–12.

Polloway, E. A., Patton, J. R., & Serna, L. (2001). *Strategies for teaching learners with special needs* (7th ed.). Columbus, OH: Merrill.

Polloway, E. A., Patton, J. R., Smith, J. D., & Roderique, T. W. (1992). Issues in program design for elementary students with mild retardation: Emphasis on curriculum development. *Education and Training in Mental Retardation, 27,* 142–150.

Polloway, E. A., Patton, J. R., Smith, T. E. C., & Buck, G. H. (1997). Mental retardation and learning disabilities: Conceptual issues. *Journal of Learning Disabilities, 30,* 219–231.

Polloway, E. A., Smith, J. D., Chamberlain, J., Denning, C., & Smith, T. E. C. (1999). Levels of deficit vs. levels of support in mental retardation classification. *Education and Training in Mental Retardation and Development Disabilities, 34,* 48–59.

Polloway, E. A., Smith, J. D., Patton, J. R., & Smith, T. E. C. (1996). Historic changes in mental retardation and developmental disabilities. *Education and Training in Mental Retardation and Developmental Disabilities, 31,* 3–12.

Polloway, E. A., & Smith, T. E. C. (1992). *Language instruction for students with disabilities.* Denver, CO: Love Publishing.

Polloway, E. A., Smith, T. E. C., Patton, J. R., & Smith, J. D. (1996). Historical perspectives in mental retardation. *Education and Training in Mental Retardation and Developmental Disabilities, 31,* 3–12.

Prater, M. A. (1992). Increasing time-on-task in the classroom. *Intervention in School and Clinic, 28*(1), 22–27.

Prater, M. A., Joy, R., Chilman, B., Temple, J., & Miller, S. R. (1991). Self-monitoring of on-task behavior by adolescents with learning disabilities. *Learning Disability Quarterly, 14,* 164–177.

Pressley, M., & Rankin, J. (1994). More about whole language methods of reading instruction for students at risk for early reading failure. *Learning Disabilities Research & Practice, 9,* 157–168.

Prince Edward Island Education. (2001). *Minister's Directive No. MD 2001-08.* Retrieved April 2005, from Prince Edward Island Education website: http://www.gov.pe.ca/educ/index.php3?number=76715

Pugach, M. C., & Warger, C. L. (2001). Curriculum matters. *Remedial and Special Education, 22,* 194–196.

Pugh, K. R., Mencl, W. E., Jenner, A. R., Lee, J. R., Katz, L., Frost, S. J., Shaywitz, S. E., & Shaywitz, B. A. (2001). Neuroimaging studies of reading development and reading disability. *Learning Disabilities Research and Practice, 16*(4), 240–249.

Quay, H., & Peterson, D. (1987). *Revised behavior problem checklist.* Coral Gables, FL: University of Miami.

Quinn, M. M., Kavale, K. A., Mathur, S. R., Rutherford, R. B., Jr., & Forness, S. R. (1999). A meta-analysis of social skill interventions for students with emotional and behavioral disorders. *Journal of Emotional and Behavioral Disorders, 7,* 54–64.

Rankin-Erickson, J. L., & Pressley, M. (2000). A survey of instructional practices of special education teachers nominated as effective teachers of literacy. *Learning Disabilities Research and Practice, 15*(4), 206–225.

Raskind, M. H., Goldberg, R. J., Higgins, E. L., & Herman, K. L. (2002). Teaching life success to students with learning disabilities: Lessons learned from a 20-year study. *Intervention in Schools and Clinic, 37*(4), 201–208.

Raskind, W. W. (2001). Current understanding of the genetic basis of reading and spelling differences. *Learning Disabilities Quarterly, 24,* 141–157.

Ratner, V. L., & Harris, L. R. (1994). *Understanding language disabilities: The impact of language.* Eau Claire, WI: Thinking Publications.

Reeve, R. E. (1990). ADHD: Facts and fallacies. *Intervention in School and Clinic, 26,* 71–78.

Reid, E. R. (1986). Practicing effective instruction: The exemplary center for reading. *Exceptional Children, 52,* 510–519.

Reid, R. (1999). Attention deficit hyperactivity disorder: Effective methods for the classroom. *Focus on Exceptional Children, 32,* 1–19.

Reid, R., Maag, J. W., Vasa, S. F., & Wright, C. (1994). Who are the children with attention-deficit-hyperactivity disorder? A school-based study. *The Journal of Special Education, 28,* 117–137.

Reid, R., & Nelson, J. R. (2002). The utility, acceptability, and practicality of functional behavioral assessment for students with high-incidence problem behaviors. *Remedial and Special Education, 23,* 15–23.

Reis, S. M. (1989). Reflections on policy affecting the education of gifted and talented students. *American Psychologist, 44,* 399–408.

Reis, S. M. (2001). External barriers experienced by gifted and talented girls. *Gifted Children Today, 24,* 31–36.

Reis, S. M., & Schack, G. D. (1993). Differentiating products for the gifted and talented: The encouragement of independent learning. In C. J. Maker (Ed.), *Critical issues in gifted education: Vol. 3. Programs for the gifted in regular classrooms* (pp. 161–186). Austin, TX: Pro-Ed.

Renzulli, J. S. (1979). *What makes giftedness: A reexamination of the definition of the gifted and talented.* Ventura, CA: Ventura County Superintendent of Schools Office.

Renzulli, J. S., Reis, S. M., & Smith, L. M. (1981). *The revolving door identification model.* Wethersfield, CT: Creative Learning Press.

Reynolds, C. T., & Salend, S. J. (1990). Teacher-directed and student-mediated textbook comprehension strategies. *Academic Therapy, 25,* 417–427.

Rhodes, L., & Dudley-Marling, C. (1996). *Readers and writers with a difference.* Portsmouth, NH: Heinemann.

Richards, T. L. (2001). Functional magnetic resonance imaging and spectroscopic imaging of the brain: Application of fMRI and fMRS to reading disabilities and education. *Learning Disabilities Quarterly, 24*(3), 189–203.

Rieck, W. A., & Wadsworth, D. E. (1999). Foreign exchange: An inclusion strategy. *Intervention, 35,* 22–28.

Riley, T. (1999). The role of advocacy: Creating change for gifted children throughout the world. *Gifted Child Today, 22,* 44–47.

Rivard, J. D. (1997). *Quick guide for the internet for educators.* Boston: Allyn & Bacon.

Roach, V. (1995). Supporting inclusion: Beyond the rhetoric. *Phi Delta Kappan, 77,* 295–299.

Roberts, C., Ingram, C., & Harris, C. (1992). The effect of special versus regular classroom programming on higher cognitive processes of intermediate elementary aged gifted and average ability students. *Journal of the Education of the Gifted, 15,* 332–343.

Robertson, J., Alper, S., Schloss, P. J., & Wisniewski, L. (1992). Teaching self-catheterization skills to a child with myelomeningocele in a preschool setting. *Journal of Early Intervention, 16,* 20–30.

Robin, S. S., & Johnson, E. O. (1996). Attitude and peer cross pressure: Adolescent drug and alcohol use. *Journal of Drug Education, 26,* 69–99.

Robinson, C. S., Manchetti, B. M., & Torgesen, J. K. (2002). Toward a two-factor theory of one type of mathematics disability. *Learning Disabilities Research and Practice, 17,* 81–89.

Robinson, S. M., Braxdale, C. T., & Colson, S. E. (1988). Preparing dysfunctional learners to enter junior high school: A transitional curriculum. *Focus on Exceptional Children, 18*(4), 1–12.

Rock, E. E., Rosenberg, M. S., & Carran, D. T. (1995). Variables affecting the reintegation rate of students with serious emotional disturbance. *Exceptional Children, 6,* 254–268.

Roderique, T. W., Polloway, E. A., Cumblad, C., Epstein, M. H., & Bursuck, W. (1994). Homework: A study of policies in the United States. *Journal of Learning Disabilities, 22,* 417–427.

Roeher Institute of Canada. (1996). *Disability, community and society: Exploring the links.* North York, ON: Author.

Rooney, K. (1993). *Attention deficit hyperactivity disorder: A videotape program.* Richmond, VA: State Department of Education.

Rooney, K. J. (1991). Controversial therapies: A review and critique. *Intervention in School and Clinic, 26*(3), 134–142.

Roseberry-McKibbin, C., & Brice, A. (2002). Choice of language instruction: One or two? *Teaching Exceptional Children, 33,* 10–16.

Rosenberg, M. S., O'Shea, L., & O'Shea, D. J. (1991). *Student teacher to master teacher: A handbook for preservice and beginning teachers of students with mild and moderate handicaps.* New York: Macmillan.

Rosenberg, M. S., Wilson, R., Maheady, L., & Sindelar, P. (1992). *Educating students with behavior disorders.* Boston: Allyn and Bacon.

Rosenshine, B., & Stevens, R. (1986). Teaching functions. In M. Wittrock (Ed.), *Handbook of research on teaching* (3rd ed., pp. 376–391). New York: Macmillan.

Ross, S. M., Smith, L. J., Casey, J., & Slavin, R. E. (1995). Increasing the academic success of disadvantaged children: An examination of alternative early intervention programs. *American Educational Research Journal, 32,* 773–800.

Rosselli, H. (1993). Process differentiation for gifted learners in the regular classroom: Teaching to everyone's needs. In C. J. Maker (Ed.), *Critical issues in gifted education: Vol. 3. Programs for the gifted in regular classrooms* (pp. 139–155). Austin, TX: Pro-Ed.

Ruble, L. A., & Dalrymple, M. J. (2002). COMPASS: A parent–teacher collaboration model for students with autism. *Focus on Autism and Other Developmental Disabilities, 17,* 76–83.

Ryan, A. G., & Price, L. (1992). Adults with LD in the 1990s. *Intervention in School and Clinic, 28*(1), 6–20.

Rylance, B. J. (1998). Predictors of post-high school employment for youth identified as severely emotionally disturbed. *The Journal of Special Education, 32,* 184–192.

Sabatino, D. A. (1987). Preventive discipline as a practice in special education. *Teaching Exceptional Children, 19,* 8–11.

Sacks, S., Wolffe, B. A., & Tierney, F. (1998). Lifestyles of students with visual impairments: Preliminary studies of social networks. *Exceptional Children, 64,* 63–78.

Safford, P. L., & Safford, E. J. (1998). Visions of the special class. *Remedial and Special Education, 19,* 229–238.

Safran, J. S. (2002). A practical guide to research on Asperger's syndrome. *Intervention in School and Clinic, 37,* 283–293.

Salend, S., & Duhaney, L. G. (1999). The impact of inclusion on students with and without disabilities and their education. *Remedial and Special Education, 20,* 114–126.

Salend, S. J. (1990). *Effective mainstreaming.* New York: Macmillan.

Salend, S. J. (1994). *Effective mainstreaming: Creating inclusive classrooms* (2nd ed.). Columbus, OH: Merrill/Prentice-Hall.

Salend, S. J. (1998). *Effective mainstreaming: Creating inclusive classrooms.* Upper Saddle River, NJ: Merrill.

Salend, S. J. (1999). Facilitating friendships among diverse students. *Intervention in School and Clinic, 35,* 9–15.

Salend, S. J. (2000). Parental perceptions of inclusive placement. *Remedial and Special Education, 21,* 121–128.

Salend, S. J. (2004). Fostering inclusive values in children: What families can do. *Teaching Exceptional Children 37*(1), 64–69.

Salend, S. J., & Duhaney, L. M. G. (2002). Grading students in inclusive settings. *Teaching Exceptional Children, 34*(3), 8–15.

Salvia, J., & Yssledyke, J. E. (2004). *Assessment in special and inclusive education* (9th ed.). Houghton Mifflin.

Samuels, S. J. (1986). Why children fail to learn and what to do about it. *Exceptional Children, 53*, 7–16.

Sander, E. K. (1972). When are speech sounds learned? *Journal of Speech and Hearing Disorders, 37*, 62.

Santrock, J. W., & Warshak, R. A. (1979). Father custody and social development in boys and girls. *Journal of Social Issues, 35*, 112–125.

Sargent, L. R. (1991). *Social skills for school and community.* Reston, VA: CEC-MR.

Sargent, L. R. (1998). *Social skills for school and community: Systematic instruction for children and youth with cognitive delays.* Virginia: CEC publication.

Saskatchewan Institute on Prevention of Handicaps. (2004). Fetal alcohol spectrum disorder characteristic of FAS. Retrieved April 2005 from Saskatchewan Prevention Institute website: http://www.preventioninstitute.sk.ca/fascharacteristics.php

Saskatchewan Learning. (2000). Directions for diversity: Enhancing supports to children and youth with diverse needs. Regina, SK: Author.

Saskatchewan Learning. (2001). *Strengthening supports: Minister's response to the Special Education Review Committee.* Retrieved April 2005 from Saskatchewan Learning website: http://www.sasked.gov.sk.ca/

Saskatchewan Learning. (2004). Planning for students with fetal alcohol syndrome disorder: A guide for educators. Regina, SK: Author.

Savage, R. C. (1988). Introduction to educational issues for students who have suffered traumatic brain injury. In R. C. Savage & G. F. Wolcott (Eds.), *An educator's manual: What educators need to know about students with traumatic brain injury.* Southborough, MA: National Head Injury Foundation.

Scanlon, D., & Melland, D. F. (2002). Academic and participant profiles of school-age drop-outs with and without disabilities. *Exceptional Children, 68*, 239–258.

Schaffner, C. B., & Buswell, B. E. (1996). Ten critical elements for creating inclusive and effective school communities. In S. Stainback & W. Stainback (Eds.), *Inclusion: A guide for educators* (pp. 49–65). Baltimore, MD: Brookes.

Schalock, R. L., Stark, J. A., Snell, M. E., Coulter, D. L., Polloway, E. A., Luckasson, R., Reiss, S., & Spitalnik, D. M. (1994). Changing conceptualizations of and definition of mental retardation: Implications for the field. *Mental Retardation, 32*, 181–193.

Schaughency, E. A., & Rothlind, J. (1991). Assessment and classification of attention deficit hyperactivity disorders. *School Psychology Review, 20*(2), 197–202.

Scheuerman, B., Jacobs, W. R., McCall, C., & Knies, W. (1994). The personal spelling dictionary: An adoptive approach to reducing the spelling hurdle in written language. *Intervention in School and Clinic, 29*(5), 292–299.

Scheuerman, B., & Webber, J. (2002). *Autism: Teaching does make a difference.* Belmont, CA: Wadsworth.

Schiever, S. W. (1993). Differentiating the learning environment for gifted students. In C. J. Maker (Ed.), *Critical issues in gifted education: Vol. 3. Programs for the gifted in regular classrooms* (pp. 201–214). Austin, TX: Pro-Ed.

Schleichkorn, J. (1993). *Coping with cerebral palsy: Answers to questions parents often ask* (2nd ed.). Austin: TX: Pro-Ed.

Schumaker, J. B., & Deshler, D. D. (1988). Implementing the regular education initiative in secondary schools: A different ball game. *Journal of Learning Disabilities, 21*(1), 36–42.

Schumaker, J. B., Deshler, D. D., Alley, G. R., & Denton, D. H. (1982). Multipass: A learning strategy for improving comprehension. *Learning Disability Quarterly, 5*, 295–304.

Schumaker, J. B., Deshler, D. D., Nolan, S., Clark, F. L., Alley, G. R., & Warren, M. M. (1981). *Error monitoring strategy: A learning strategy for improving academic performance of LD adolescents.* (Research Report No. 32). Lawrence, KS: University of Kansas IRLD.

Schumm, J. S., & Strickler, K. (1991). Guidelines for adapting content area textbooks: Keeping teachers and students content. *Intervention in School and Clinic, 27*, 79–84.

Schwartz, S. E., & Karge, B. D. (1996). *Human diversity: A guide for understanding* (2nd ed.). New York: McGraw-Hill.

Schwean, V. L., Parkinson, M., Francis, G., & Lee, F. (1993). Educating the AD/HD child: Debunking the myths. *Canadian Journal of School Psychology, 9*(1), 37–52.

Schwean, V. L., Saklofske, D. H., Shatz, E., & Falk, L. K. (1996). Achieving supportive integration for children with behavioral disorders in Canada: Multiple paths to realization. *Canadian Journal of Special Education, 11*, 33–50.

Scott, A. (1997). Education and acceptance. *ADVANCE for Speech-Language Pathologists and Audiologists, 36*, 10–12.

Scott, B. J., Vitale, M. R., & Masten, W. G. (1998). Implementing instructional adaptations for students with disabilities in inclusive classrooms: A literature review. *Remedial and Special Education, 19*, 106–119.

Scott, T. M., & Nelson, M. C. (1998). Confusion and failure in facilitating generalized social responding in the school setting: Sometimes 2+2=5. *Behavioral Disorders, 23*, 264–275.

Scruggs, T. E., & Mastropieri, M.A. (1987). *Effective instruction for special education.* Boston: Little Brown.

Scruggs, T. E. & Mastropieri, M. A. (1994). Successful mainstreaming in elementary science classes: A qualitative study of three reputational cases. *American Educational Research Journal, 31*, 785–811.

Scruggs, T. E., & Mastropieri, M. A. (1996). Teacher perceptions of mainstreaming/inclusion, 1958–1995: A research synthesis. *Exceptional Children, 63*, 59–74.

Searcy, S., & Meadows, N. B. (1994). The impact of social structures on friendship development for children with behavior disorders. *Education and Treatment of Children, 17*, 255–268.

Seeley, K. (1995). Classwide peer tutoring. Unpublished manuscript, Lynchburg College (VA).

Seery, M. E., Davis, P. M., & Johnson, L. J. (2000). Seeing eye to eye: Are parents and professionals in agreement about the benefits of preschool inclusion? *Remedial and Special Education, 21*, 368–378.

Semrud-Clikeman, M., Biederman, J., Sprich-Buckminster, S., Lehman, B.K., Farone, S., & Norman, D. (1992). Comorbidity between ADDH and learning disabilities: A review and report in a clinically referred sample. *Journal of American Academy of Child and Adolescent Psychiatry, 31*, 439–448.

Sexton, D., Snyder, P., Wolfe, B., Lobman, M., Stricklin, S., & Akers, P. (1996). Early intervention inservice training strategies: Perceptions and suggestions from the field. *Exceptional Children, 62*, 485–496.

Shames, G. H., & Wiig, E. H. (1990). *Human communication disorders* (3rd ed.). New York: MacMillan.

Shaner, M. Y. (1991). Talented teachers for talented students. *G/C/T, 22,* 14–15.

Shanker, A. (1994–1995). Educating students in special programs. *Educational Leadership, 52,* 43–47.

Shanley, R. (1993). Becoming content with content. In C. J. Maker (Ed.), *Critical issues in gifted education: Vol. 1. Defensible programs for the gifted.* (pp. 43–89). Austin, TX: Pro-Ed.

Shannon, T., & Polloway, E. A. (1993). Promoting error monitoring in middle school students with learning disabilities. *Intervention in School and Clinic, 28,* 160–164.

Shapiro, E. S., DuPaul, G. J., & Bradley-Klug, K. L. (1998). Self-management as a strategy to improve the classroom behavior of adolescents with ADHD. *Journal of Learning Disabilities, 31,* 545–555.

Shaywitz, S., & Shaywitz, B. (1997, November). *The science of reading: Implications for children and adults with learning disabilities.* Paper presented at the 13th Annual Harvard University Institute on Learning Disorders, Cambridge, MA.

Shea, T. M., & Bauer, A. M. (1991). *Parents and teachers of children with exceptionalities: A handbook for collaboration.* Boston: Allyn and Bacon.

Shimon, D. A. (1992). *Coping with hearing loss and hearing aids.* San Diego: Singular Publishing.

Siegel, B., & Zimnitzky, B. (1998). Assessing "alternative" therapies for communication disorders in children with autism spectrum disorders: Facilitated communication and auditory integration training. *Journal of Speech-Language Pathology and Audiology, 22*(2), 61–73.

Siegel, L. (1989). IQ is irrelevant to the definition of learning disabilities. *Journal of Learning Disabilities, 22*(8), 469–486.

Siegel, L. S. (1999). Issues in the definition and diagnosis of learning disabilities: A perspective on Guckenberger v. Boston University. *Journal of Learning Disabilities, 32*(4), 304–319.

Sileo, T. W., Sileo, A. P., & Prater, M. A. (1996). Parent and professional partnerships in special education: Multicultural considerations. *Intervention in School & Clinic, 31,* 145–153.

Silver, L. B. (1995). Controversial therapies. *Journal of Child Neurology, 10* (suppl. 1), 96–100.

Silverman, A. B., Reinherz, H. Z., & Giaconia, R. M. (1996). The long-term sequelae of child and adolescent abuse: A longitudinal community study. *Child Abuse and Neglect, 20,* 709–723.

Silverthorn, K. H., & Hornak, J. E. (1993). Beneficial effects of exercise on aerobic capacity and body composition in adults with Prader-Willi syndrome. *American Journal on Mental Retardation, 97,* 654–658.

Simmons, D., Fuchs, D., Hodge, J., & Mathes, P. (1994). Importance of instructional complexity and role reciprocity to classwide peer tutoring. *Learning Disabilities Research and Practice, 9,* 203–212.

Simmons, D. C., Fuchs, D., & Fuchs, L. S. (1991). Instructional and curricular requisites of mainstreamed students with learning disabilities. *Journal of Learning Disabilities, 24,* 354–359.

Simpson, R. (1996). *Working with parents and families of exceptional children and youth* (3rd ed.). Austin, TX: Pro-Ed.

Simpson, R. (2001). ABA and students with autism spectrum disorders. *Focus on Autism and Developmental Disabilities, 16,* 68–71.

Sitlingon, P. L., & Frank. A. C. (1998). *Follow-up studies: A practical handbook.* Austin, TX: Pro-Ed.

Sladeczek, I. E., & Heath, N. L. (1997). Consultation in Canada. *Canadian Journal of School Psychology, 1,* 1–15.

Slavin, R. E. (1987). *What research says to the teacher on cooperative learning: Student teams* (2nd ed.). Washington, DC: National Education Association.

Slavin, R.E. (1996). Cooperative learning in middle and secondary schools. *The Clearing House, 69*(4), 200–204.

Sleeter, C. E. & Grant, C. A. (1994). Making choices for multicultural education: Five approaches to race, class, and gender (2nd ed.). New York: Merrill.

Slicker, E. K., & Palmer, D. J. (1993). Mentoring at-risk high school students: Evaluation of a school-based program. *The School Counselor, 40,* 327–334.

Smith, C. R. (1994). *Learning disabilities: The interaction of learner, task, and setting* (3rd ed.). Boston: Allyn and Bacon.

Smith, C. R. (1998). From gibberish to phoneme awareness: Effective decoding instruction. *Teaching Exceptional Children, 30,* 20–25.

Smith, D. D., & Luckasson, R. (1992). *Introduction to special education: Teaching in an age of challenge.* Boston: Allyn and Bacon.

Smith, D. D., & Luckasson, R. (1995/1998). *Introduction to special education: Teaching in an age of challenge.* Boston: Allyn and Bacon.

Smith, D. D., & Rivera, D. P. (1995). Discipline in special and regular education. *Focus on Exceptional Children, 27*(5), 1–14.

Smith, G., & Smith, D. (1989). Schoolwide study skills program: The key to mainstreaming. *Teaching Exceptional Children, 21,* 20–23.

Smith, J. D. (1994). The revised AAMR definition of mental retardation: The MRDD position. *Education and Training in Mental Retardation and Developmental Disabilities, 29,* 179–183.

Smith, J. D. (1995). Inclusive school environments and students with disabilities in South Carolina: The issues, the status, the needs. *Occasional Papers, 1,* 1–5.

Smith, J. W., & Smith, S. B. (2002). Technology for organizing and presenting digital information. *Intervention in School and Clinic, 37,* 306–310.

Smith, P. M. (1997). You are not alone: For parents when they learn that their child has a disability. *NICHY News Digest, 2,* 2–5.

Smith, T. E. C. (1990). *Introduction to education* (2nd ed.). St. Paul, MN: West Publishing.

Smith, T. E. C. (2001). Section 504, the ADA, and public schools: What educators need to know. *Remedial and Special Education, 21,* 335–343.

Smith, T. E. C., & Dowdy, C. A. (1992). Future-based assessment and intervention and mental retardation. *Education and Training in Mental Retardation, 27,* 23–31.

Smith, T. E. C., Dowdy, C. A., Polloway, E. A., & Blalock, G. (1997). *Children and adults with learning disabilities.* Boston: Allyn and Bacon.

Smith, T. E. C., Finn, D. M., & Dowdy, C. A. (1993). *Teaching students with mild disabilities.* Ft. Worth, TX: Harcourt Brace Jovanovich.

Smith, T. E. C., & Hendricks, M. D. (1995). *Prader-Willi syndrome: Practical considerations for educators.* Little Rock: Ozark Learning.

Smith, T. E. C., & Hilton, A. (1994). Program design for students with mental retardation. *Education and training in mental retardation and developmental disabilities, 29,* 3–8.

Smith, T. E. C., Price, B. J., & Marsh, G. E. (1986). *Mildly handicapped children and adults.* St. Paul, MN: West Publishing.

Smith, T. E. C., & Puccini, I. K. (1996). Secondary programming issues. *Education and Training in Mental Retardation and Developmental Disabilities, 31,* 320–327.

Smith, W. J., & Foster, W. F. (1996). *Equal educational opportunity for students with disabilities*. Montreal, PQ: McGill University, Office of Research on Educational Policy.

Smith, W. J., & Foster, W. F. (1997). *Equal educational opportunity for students with disabilities in Canada: 1996 legislative update*. Montreal, QC: Office of Research on Educational Policy, McGill.

Smutny, J. F., Walker, S. Y., & Meckstroth, E. A. (1997). *Teaching young gifted children in the regular classroom: Identifying, nurturing, and challenging ages 4–9*. Minneapolis, MN: Free Spirit.

Snell, M., & Drake, G. P. (1994). Replacing cascades with supported education. *Journal of Special Education, 27*, 393–409.

Soderlund, J., Bursuck, W., Polloway, E. A., & Foley, R. A. (1995). A comparison of homework problems of secondary school students with behavior disorders and nondisabled peers. *Journal of Emotional and Behavioral Disorders, 3*, 152.

Southern, W. T., & Jones, E. D. (1991). Academic acceleration: Background and issues. In W. T. Southern & E. D. Jones (Eds.), *Academic acceleration of gifted children* (pp. 1–17). New York: Teachers College Press.

Spirito, A., Hart, K. I., Overholser, J., & Halverson, J. (1990). Social skills and depression in adolescent suicide attempters. *Adolescence, 25*, 543–552.

Stainback, S., Stainback, W., East, K., & Sapon-Shevin, M. (1994). A commentary on inclusion and the development of a positive self-identity by people with disabilities. *Exceptional Children, 60*, 486–490.

Stainback, W., & Stainback, S. (1984). A rationale for the merger of special and regular education. *Exceptional Children, 51*, 102–111.

Stainback, W., & Stainback, S. (1987). Integration versus cooperation: A commentary, *Exceptional Children, 54*, 74–97.

Stainback, W., Stainback, S., & Bunch, G. (1989). A rationale for the merger of regular and special education. In S. Stainback et al. (Eds.), *Educating all students in the mainstream of regular education* (pp. 15–26). Baltimore, MD, England: Paul H. Brookes Publishing.

Stainback, W., Stainback, S., & Stefanich, G., (1996). Learning together in inclusive classrooms: What about the curriculum? *Teaching Exceptional Children, 28*, 17.

Stainback, W. C., Stainback, S., & Wehman, P. (1997). Toward full inclusion into general education. In P. Wehman (Ed.), *Exceptional individuals in school, community, and work* (pp. 531–557). Austin, TX: Pro-Ed.

Stanovich, P. J., & Jordan, A. (1998). Canadian teachers' and principals' beliefs about inclusive education as predictors of effective teaching in heterogeneous classrooms. *The Elementary School Journal, 98*(3), 221–238.

Stanovich, P. J., & Jordan, A. (2002). Preparing general educators to teach in inclusive classrooms: Some food for thought. *The Teacher Educator, 37*(3), 173–185.

Stephien, S., & Gallagher, S. (1993). Problem-based learning: As authentic as it gets. *Educational Leadership, 50*(7), 25–28.

Stewart, D. A., & Kluwin, T. N. (2001). *Teaching deaf and hard of hearing students*. Boston: Allyn and Bacon.

Struyk, L. R., Cole, K. B., Epstein, M. H., Bursuck, W. D., & Polloway, E. A. (1996). Homework communication: Problems involving high school teachers and parents of students with disabilities. Manuscript submitted for publication.

Struyk, L. R., Epstein, M. H., Bursuck, W., Polloway, E. A., McConeghy, J., & Cole, K. B. (1995). Homework, grading, and testing practices used by teachers with students with and without disabilities. *The Clearing House, 69*, 50–55.

Summers, M., Bridge, J., & Summers, C. R. (1991). Sibling support groups. *Teaching Exceptional Children, 23*, 20–25.

Tankersley, M. (1995). A group-oriented management program: A review of research on the good behavior game and implications for teachers. *Preventing School Failure, 40*, 19–28.

Tavzel, C. S., & Staff of LinguiSystems. (1987). *Blooming recipes*. East Moline, IL: LinguiSystems.

Taylor, R. L. (2000). *Assessment of individuals with mental retardation*. San Diego: Singular.

Teen drug use is on the rise again. (1996). *Executive Educator, 18*, 7–8.

Templeton, R. A. (1995). ADHD: A teacher's guide. *The Oregon Conference Monograph, 7*, 2–11.

Tennant, C., Bebbington, P. R., & Hurry, J. (1980). Parental death in childhood and risk of adult depressive disorders: A review. *Psychological Medicine, 10*, 289–299.

Thomas, P. J., & Carmack, F. F. (1993). Language: The foundation of learning. In J. S. Choate (Ed.), *Successful mainstreaming: Proven ways to detect and correct special needs* (pp. 148–173). Boston: Allyn and Bacon.

Thurston, L. P. (1989). Helping parents tutor their children: A success story. *Academic Therapy, 24*, 579–587.

Tirosh, E., & Canby, J. (1993). Autism with hyperlexia: A distinct syndrome? *American Journal on Mental Retardation, 98*, 84–92.

Toliver-Weddington, G., & Erickson, J. G. (1992). Suggestions for using standardized tests with minority children. In J. G. Erickson (Ed.), *Communication disorders in multicultural populations* (1992, April). Paper presented at Texas Speech-Language-Hearing Association Annual Convention, San Antonio, TX.

Torrance, E. P. (1982). Identifying and capitalizing on the strengths of culturally different children. In C. R. Reynolds & J. B. Gulkin (Eds.), *The handbook of school psychology* (pp. 451–500). New York: Wiley.

Torres, I., & Corn, A. L. (1990). *When you have a visually handicapped child in your classroom: Suggestions for teachers*. New York: American Foundation for the Blind.

Trad, P. V. (1999). Assessing the patterns that prevent teenage pregnancy. *Adolescence, 34*, 221–238.

Trites, R. (1981). Primary French immersion: Disabilities, and prediction of success. *Review and Evaluation, 2*.

Turnbull, A. P., & Turnbull, H. R. (1997). *Families, professionals, and exceptionality: A special partnership*. Columbus, OH: Merrill.

Turnbull, H. R., Pereira, L., & Blue-Banning, M. (2000). Teachers as friendship facilitators. *Teaching Exceptional Children, 32*, 66–70.

Tver, D. F., & Tver, B. M. (1991). *Encyclopedia of mental and physical handicaps*. Austin, TX: Pro-Ed.

U.S. Department of Education. (1993). *15th annual report to Congress on the implementation of IDEA*. Washington, DC: Author.

U.S. Department of Education. (1995). *17th annual report to Congress on the implementation of IDEA*. Washington, DC: Author.

U.S. Department of Education. (1998). *Safe and smart: Making the after-school hours work for kids*. Washington, DC: Author.

U.S. Department of Education. (2002). *23rd annual report to Congress on the implementation of the Individuals with Disabilities Education Act.* Washington, DC: Author.

U.S. Office of Education (USOE). (1977). Assistance to states for education of handicapped children: Procedures for evaluating specific learning disabilities. *Federal Register, 42,* 65082–65085.

Valdes, K. A., Williamson, C. L., & Wagner, M. M. (1990). *The national longitudinal transition study of special education students* (Vol. 1). Menlo Park, CA: SRI International.

Van Eerdewegh, M. M., Bieri, M. D., Parrilla, R. H., & Clayton, P. J. (1982). The bereaved child. *British Journal of Psychiatry, 140,* 23–29.

Van Laarhoven, T., Coutinho, M., Van Laarhoven-Myers, T., & Repp, A. C. (1999). Assessment of the student instructional setting, and curriculum to support successful integration. In M. J. Coutinho & A. C. Repp (Eds.), *Inclusion: The integration of students with disabilities.* Belmont, CA: Wadsworth Publishing.

Van Riper, C., & Emerick, L. (1984). *Speech correction: An introduction to speech pathology and audiology* (7th ed.). Englewood Cliffs, NJ: Prentice-Hall.

VanTassel-Baska, J. (1989). Appropriate curriculum for gifted learners. *Educational Leadership, 47,* 13–15.

VanTassel-Baska, J. (1998). *Gifted and talented learners.* Denver: Love.

VanTassel-Baska, J., Patton, J., & Prillaman, D. (1989). Disadvantaged gifted learners at-risk for educational attention. *Focus on Exceptional Children, 22*(3), 1–16.

Vaughn, C., & Long, W. (1999). Surrender to win: How adolescent drug and alcohol users change their lives. *Adolescence, 34,* 9–22.

Vaughn, S., Gersten, R., & Chard, D. J. (2000). The underlying message in learning disabilities intervention research: Findings from research synthesis. *Exceptional Children, 67,* 99–114.

Vaughn, S., & Kingner, J. (1999). Teaching reading comprehensive skills to students with learning disabilities in general education classrooms. *Learning Disabilities, 9,* 6–11.

Vaughn, S., & Schumm, J. S. (1994). Middle school teachers' planning for students with learning disabilities. *Remedial and Special Education, 15*(3), 152–161.

Vellutino, F. R., Scanlon, D. M., & Lyon, G. R. (2000). Differentiating between difficult-to-remediate and readily remediated poor readers: More evidence against the IQ-achievement discrepancy definition of reading disability. *Journal of Learning Disabilities, 33*(3), 223–238.

Voltz, D., Brazil, N., & Ford, A. (2001). What matters most in inclusive education. *Intervention in School and Clinic, 37,* 23–30.

Wadsworth, D. E., & Knight, D. (1999). Preparing the classroom for students with speech, physical, and health needs. *Intervention in School and Clinic, 34,* 170–175.

Walberg, H. J. (1991). Does homework help? *School Community Journal, 1*(1), 13–15.

Walker, B. (1993, January). *Multicultural issues in education: An introduction.* Paper presented at Cypress–Fairbanks Independent School District In-Service, Cypress, TX.

Walker, J. E., & Shea, T. M. (1995). *Behavior management* (6th ed.). Columbus, OH: Merrill.

Wallace, G., Cohen, S., & Polloway, E. A. (1987). *Language arts: Teaching exceptional children.* Austin, TX: Pro-Ed.

Wallace, G., Larsen, S. C., & Elksnin, L. K. (1992). *Educational assessment of learning problems.* Boston: Allyn and Bacon.

Walker, J. E., & Shea, T. M. (1995). *Behavior management: A practical approach for educators* (6th ed.). Columbus, OH: Merrill.

Walther-Thomas, C., Korinek, L., McLaughlin, V. L., & Williams, B. T. (2000). *Collaboration for inclusive education.* Boston: Allyn and Bacon.

Wanat, C. L. (1992). Meeting the needs of single-parent children: School and parent views differ. *NASSP Bulletin, 76,* 43–48.

Wang, M. C., & Birch, J. W. (1984). Effective special education in regular classes. *Exceptional Children, 52,* 36–49.

Wang, M. C., Reynolds, M. C., & Walberg, H. J. (1994–1995). Serving students at the margins. *Educational Leadership, 52,* 12–17.

Warren, D. (1994). *Blindness in children.* Cambridge, MA: Cambridge University Press.

Waterman, B. B. (1994). Assessing children for the presence of a disability. *NICHY News Digest, 4*(1), Washington, DC: U.S. Government Printing Office.

Wayland, L. A., & Sladeczek, I. E. (1999). Work in progress: Conjoint behavioral consultation with children who are socially withdrawn. *Canadian Journal of School Psychology, 14,* 45–50.

Wayman, K., Lynch, E., & Hanson, M. (1990). Home-based early childhood services: Cultural sensitivity in a family systems approach. *Topics in Early Childhood Special Education, 10*(4), 65–66.

Webber, J. (1997). Responsible inclusion: Key components for success. In P. Zionts (Ed.), *Effective inclusion of students with behavior and learning problems.* Austin, TX: Pro-Ed.

Webber, J., & Scheuermann, B. (1991). Accentuate the positive… Eliminate the negative! *Teaching Exceptional Children, 24,* 14–17.

Weber, K. (1994). *Special education in Canadian schools.* Thornhill, ON: Highland Press.

Weber, K., & Bennett, S. (1999). *Special education in Ontario schools.* Don Mills, ON: Highland Press.

Wehby, J. H., Symons, F. J., Canale, J. A., & Go, F. J. (1998). Teaching practices in classrooms for students with emotional and behavioral disorders: Discrepancies between recommendations and observations. *Behavioral Disorders, 24,* 51–56.

Wehman, P. (Ed.). (1997). *Exceptional individuals in school, community, and work.* Austin, TX: Pro-Ed.

Wehman, P., & Parent, W. (1997). Severe mental retardation. In P. Wehman (Ed.), *Exceptional individuals in school, community, and work* (pp. 170–171). Austin: Pro-Ed.

Wehmeyer, M. (1993). Self-determination as an educational outcome. *Impact, 6*(4), 16–17, 26.

Wehmeyer, M. (1994). Perceptions of self-determination and psychological empowerment of adolescents with mental retardation. *Education and Training in Mental Retardation and Developmental Disabilities, 29,* 9–21.

Wehmeyer, M. L., Lattin, D., & Agram, M. (2001). Achieving access to the general education curriculum for students with mental retardation: A curriculum decision-making model. *Education and Training in Mental Retardation and Developmental Disabilities, 36,* 327–342.

Wehmeyer, M. L., Morningstar, M., & Husted, D. (1999). *Family involvement in transition planning and implementation.* Austin, TX: Pro-Ed.

Weinbender, M. L. M., & Rossignol, A. M. (1996). Lifestyle and risk of premature sexual activity in a high school population of Seventh-Day Adventists: Valuegenesis 1989. *Adolescence, 31,* 265–275.

Weisel, A., Tur-Kaspa, H. (2002). Effects of labels and personal contact on teachers' attitudes toward students with special needs. *Exceptionality, 10*(1), 1–10.

Welch, M., & Link, D. P. (1991). The instructional priority system: A method for assessing the educational environment. *Intervention in the School and Clinic, 27*(2), 91–96.

West, G. K. (1986). *Parenting without guilt.* Springfield, IL: Thomas.

West, G. K. (1994, Nov. 10). Discipline that works: Part 1. *The News and Daily Advance.*

West, G. K. (2002). Parent education programs and benefits for parents of children with disabilities. Unpublished manuscript, Lynchburg College in Lynchburg, VA.

Westling, D. L., & Koorland, M. A. (1988). *The special educator's handbook.* Boston: Allyn and Bacon.

Weston, D., Ludolph, P., Misle, B., Ruffins, S., & Block, J. (1990). Physical and sexual abuse in adolescent girls with borderline personality disorder. *American Journal of Orthopsychiatry, 60,* 55–66.

Weyandt, L. L. (2001). *An ADHD primer.* Boston: Allyn and Bacon.

Whitney-Thomas J., & Hanley-Maxwell, C. (1996). Packing the parachute: Parents' experiences as their children prepare to leave high school. *Exceptional Children, 63*(1), 75–87.

Wicks-Nelson, R., & Israel, A. C. (1991). *Behavior disorders of childhood.* Englewood Cliffs, NJ: Prentice-Hall.

Wiener, J., & Harris, P. J. (1993). Social relations in subgroups of children with learning disabilities. *Enfance, 47*(3), 295-316.

Wiener, J., Harris, P. J., & Shirer, C. (1990). Achievement and social-behavioral correlates of peer status in LD children. *Learning Disability Quarterly, 13,* 114–127.

Wiener J., & Siegel, L. (1992). A Canadian perspective on learning disabilities. *Journal of Learning Disabilities, 25,* 340–350.

Wiig, E. H. (1986). Language disabilities in school-age children and youth. In G. H. Shames & E. H. Wiig (Eds.), *Human communication disorders* (2nd ed., pp. 331–383). Columbus, OH: Merrill.

Wiig, E. H., & Semel, E. (1984). *Language assessment and intervention for the learning disabled* (2nd ed.). Columbus, OH: Merrill.

Williamson, J. M., Borduin, C. M., & Howe, B. A. (1991). The ecology of adolescent maltreatment: A multilevel examination of adolescent physical abuse, sexual abuse, and neglect. *Journal of Consulting and Clinical Psychology, 59,* 449–457.

Willms, J. D. (Ed.). (2002). *Vulnerable children: Findings from Canada's national longitudinal survey of children and youth.* Edmonton, AB: University of Alberta Press.

Wilson, C. L. (1995). Parents and teachers: Can we talk? *LD Forum, 20*(2), 31–33.

Winebrenner, S. (1992). *Teaching gifted kids in the regular classroom.* Minneapolis, MN: Free Spirit Publishing.

Winocur, S. L., & Mauer, P. A. (1997). Critical thinking and gifted students: Using IMPACT to improve teaching and learning. In N. Colangelo and G. A. Davis (Eds.), *Handbook of gifted education* (2nd ed., pp. 308–317). Boston: Allyn and Bacon.

Winzer, M. (1999). *Children with exceptionalities in Canadian classrooms* (5th ed.). Scarborough, ON: Prentice-Hall Canada.

Winzer, M. A., & Mazurek, K. (1998). *Special education in multicultural contexts.* Upper Saddle River, NJ: Prentice-Hall.

Witt, J. C., & Elliott, S. N. (1985). Acceptability of classroom management strategies. In T. R. Kratochwill (Ed.), *Advances in school psychology* (Vol. 4, pp. 251–288). Hillsdale, NJ: Erlbaum.

Wolfe, P. S. (1997). Deaf-blindness. In P. Wehman (Ed.), *Exceptional individuals* (pp. 357–381). Austin, TX: Pro-Ed.

Wolfensberger, W. (1972). Voluntary citizen advocacy in the human services. *Canada's Mental Health, 20*(2), 14–18.

Wong, B. (1996). *The ABCs of learning disabilities.* San Diego, CA: Academic Press.

Wong, B. L. (1998). *Learning about learning disabilities* (2nd ed.). Toronto, ON: Academic Press.

Wong, B. Y. L. (1991). The relevance of metacognition to learning disabilities. In B. Y. L. Wong (Ed.), *Learning about learning disabilities* (pp. 231–258). New York: Academic Press.

Wood, D. K., & Frank, A. R. (2000). Using memory-enhancing strategies to learn multiplication facts. *Teaching Exceptional Children, 32,* 78–82.

Wood, J. W. (1984). *Adapting instruction for the mainstream.* Columbus, OH: Merrill.

Wood, J. W. (1996). *Adapting instruction for mainstreamed and at-risk students* (3rd ed.). New York: Merrill.

Woodrich, D. L. (1994). *What every parent wants to know: Attention deficit hyperactivity disorder.* Baltimore, MD: Brookes.

Woronov, T. (1996). Assistive technology for literacy produces impressive results for the disabled. In E. Miller & R. Tovey (Eds.), *Inclusion and special education* (pp. 9–11). Cambridge, MA: Harvard Educational Letter.

Wright, J. V. (1995). Multicultural issues and attention deficit disorders. *Learning Disabilities Research and Practice, 10*(3), 153–159.

Yehle, A. K., & Wambold, C. (1998). An ADHD success story: Strategies for teachers and students. *Teaching Exceptional Children, 30*(6), 8–13.

Yewchuk, C., & Lupart, J. (2000). Inclusive education for gifted students with disabilities. In K. A. Heller et al. (Eds.), *International handbook of giftedness and talent* (2nd ed). (pp. 659–672). Kidlington, Oxford: Elsevier Science.

Ylvisaker, T., Szekeres, N., Hartwick, R., & Tworek, L. L. (1994). Collaboration in preparation for personal injury suits after TBI. *Topics in Language Disorders, 15,* 1–20.

Young, G., & Gerber, P. J. (1998). Learning disabilities and poverty: Moving towards a new understanding of learning disabilities as a public health and economic-risk issue. *Learning Disabilities, 9,* 1–6.

Young, M. E., Kersten, L., & Werch, T. (1996). Evaluation of patient-child drug education program. *Journal of Drug Education, 26,* 57–68.

Ysseldyke, J. E., & Olsen, K. (1999). Putting alternative assessments into practice: What to measure and possible sources of data. *Exceptional Children, 65,* 175–185.

Ysseldyke, J. E., Thurlow, M. L., Wotruba, J. W., & Nania, P. A. (1990). Instructional arrangements: Perceptions from general education. *Teaching Exceptional Children, 22,* 4–8.

Zabel, R. H., & Zabel, M. K. (1996). *Classroom management in context.* Boston: Houghton Mifflin.

Zhang, D. (2001). Self-determination and inclusion: Are students with mild mental retardation more self-determined in regular classrooms? *Education and Training in Mental Retardation and Developmental Disabilities, 36*(4), 357–362.

Zigmond, N., Levin, E., & Laurie, T. (1985). Managing the mainstream: An analysis for teacher attitudes and student performance in mainstream high school programs. *Journal of Learning Disabilities, 18,* 535–541.

Zirpoli, T., & Melloy, G. (1993). Behavior management: Applications for teachers and parents. Columbus, OH: Merrill.

Name Index

Subject Index